Law for Accountancy Students

Law for Accountancy Students

Sixth Edition

RICHARD CARD   LLB, LLM, FRSA
Professor of Law at De Montfort University

JENNIFER JAMES   LLB, BCL
Senior Lecturer in Law at the University of Reading

Butterworths
London, Edinburgh, Dublin
1997

United Kingdom	Butterworths a Division of Reed Elsevier (UK) Ltd, Halsbury House, 35 Chancery Lane, LONDON WC2A 1EL and 4 Hill Street, EDINBURGH EH2 3JZ
Australia	Butterworths, SYDNEY, MELBOURNE, BRISBANE, ADELAIDE, PERTH, CANBERRA and HOBART
Canada	Butterworths Canada Ltd, TORONTO and VANCOUVER
Ireland	Butterworth (Ireland) Ltd, DUBLIN
Malaysia	Malayan Law Journal Sdn Bhd, KUALA LUMPUR
New Zealand	Butterworths of New Zealand Ltd, WELLINGTON and AUCKLAND
Singapore	Reed Elsevier (Singapore) Pte Ltd, SINGAPORE
South Africa	Butterworths Publishers (Pty) Ltd, DURBAN
USA	Michie, Charlottesville, VIRGINIA

A CIP Catalogue record for this book is available from the British Library.

ISBN 0 406 89107 9

Printed and bound in Great Britain by Mackays of Chatham plc, Chatham, Kent

Preface

We were prompted to write this book by the belief that there was a need for a comprehensive textbook for accountancy students studying foundation or similar courses in law, particularly one which treated the subject-matter in some depth. The response to the first five editions has confirmed our belief.

We have had in mind the syllabuses for the Graduate Conversion Courses or Foundation Courses of the Institute of Chartered Accountants in England and Wales, the Chartered Association of Certified Accountants and the Chartered Institute of Management Accountants, as well as those for comparable courses in accountancy degree schemes. Despite its title, this book should also prove useful for those following similar courses in law for other types of qualification.

This book is divided into four parts. Part II, which deals with the Law of Contract, is the most substantial since this branch of the law appears, universally, to be the most significant part of the syllabuses mentioned above. Part I outlines the English Legal System. Part III is concerned with the Law of Torts, and Part IV with Commercial Law. We have made extensive changes to Part IV to reflect the altering needs of our readers. In particular, we have expanded the material on the elements of Company Law and we have deleted the chapter on Employment Law. The extent to which a student will have to study in detail particular chapters in Parts III and IV will depend on the particular syllabus which is being followed.

In addition to these changes in coverage, we have made significant changes to the text throughout the book in order to reflect the flood of case law in the areas covered since the last edition.

Our thanks go to those of our colleagues and students who assisted in many ways with the preparation of this edition, and also to the publishers, for compiling the tables of cases and statutes and the index.

We have tried to summarise and explain the law as it was on 1 March 1997, although by amendments made in proof we have been able to incorporate a few important changes in the law made in the period up to the end of May 1997.

Richard Card
Jennifer James

June 1997

Contents

Contents

Contents

Table of Statutes

References in this Table to *Statutes* are to Halsbury's Statutes of England (Fourth Edition) showing the volume and page at which the annotated text of an Act may be found.

Table of Cases

Table of cases

Table of cases

Table of cases

l

Table of cases

Decisions of the European Court of Justice are listed below numerically. These
decisions are also included in the preceding alphabetical list.

Part I

Outline of the
English Legal System

Chapter 1

Introduction

Classification of the Law

1.1 It must be stressed at the beginning that this book is concerned with aspects of *English* law. The laws and legal systems of Scotland and, to a lesser extent, Northern Ireland are distinct from those of England and Wales, and while Scots and Northern Irish law may coincide with English law in certain fields it cannot be assumed that this is always the case.

It is usual to divide English law into categories. These categories are not laid down by any statute but have been devised as aids to exposition. They are by no means hard and fast.

One set of facts may involve more than one category of law. If A, an accountant, gives financial advice to a client which he intends should be passed on to a third party (T) and that advice was carelessly prepared, with the result that the client and T lose money, various categories of law are in issue. A is liable to the client for breach of contract because he has broken an implied term of his contract with his client that he will exercise reasonable care and skill in giving financial advice[1]. Additionally, he may incur liability in tort to T[2] and he may even incur criminal liability if he was not authorised to give financial advice. Likewise, if B, an accountant, buys a computer from C, a retailer, and is injured when it explodes in his face as a result of being carelessly manufactured by D, an employee of E Computers plc, C will be liable for breach of an implied term of his contract with B that the computer is of satisfactory quality[3], D may be liable in tort to B[2] and E Computers plc may be vicariously liable to B for any tort committed by D[4]. These examples illustrate classification of law by reference to the subject matter of the dispute.

Law may also be classified by reference to the source of a particular rule.

1 Para 8.37, below.
2 As to whether there would be liability in tort, see Chaps 18 and 19, below.
3 Para 8.24, below.
4 Para 17.15, below.

Classification by reference to the subject matter of a dispute
1.2   When using this method of classification, a major distinction can be drawn between civil and criminal law. It is criminal law which occupies most of the attention of non-lawyers, but lawyers are frequently more concerned with non-criminal, ie civil, law. Civil law can be sub-divided into categories, for example, contract and tort. These categories of civil law are no less important than criminal law.

1.3   It is surprisingly difficult in theory, though not in practice, to distinguish between civil and criminal law. Criminal cases, which are called prosecutions, are normally initiated by the state[1], but they may be brought by a private citizen, although this is rare. If a prosecution is successful the accused, or defendant, is liable to punishment. This affords no direct benefit to the victim of the crime since he does not receive fines payable or the fruits of a criminal's labours in prison. The victims of some crimes, such as an attempted theft or blackmail, may have suffered no loss from the commission of the crime anyway. Some crimes can be committed without there being a victim, for example, homosexual offences involving consenting adults and offences involving obscene publications. Although punishment does not compensate victims, it is now possible for the criminal courts to order the criminal to make reparation directly to his victim. The victim of a criminal offence cannot prevent a prosecution nor order its discontinuance, however much he may wish to avoid a criminal trial.

In contrast, civil actions are brought by an individual (the plaintiff) who is seeking to obtain compensation for the loss he has suffered or to establish his legal rights. If damages are awarded as the result of a successful civil action, they are payable to the plaintiff and are generally assessed on the basis that they should compensate him and not on the basis of punishing the defendant. In certain restricted circumstances the courts may award exemplary damages over and above what is necessary to compensate the plaintiff for the specific purpose of punishing the defendant, but in such cases all the damages are payable to the plaintiff and not merely the compensatory element. A victim is not required to commence a civil action, and a plaintiff can discontinue it at any time before judgment.

The rules of evidence and procedure are also substantially different for civil and criminal cases. Perhaps the most important distinction relates to the standard of proof required. In civil cases the relevant party (generally the plaintiff) must prove his case 'on a balance of probabilities', ie the facts necessary for his case to succeed must be established to the satisfaction of the judge (or jury, on the rare occasion when one is used at a civil trial[2]) as more probable than not to have occurred. In a criminal case the burden of proof borne by the prosecution is to prove the case 'beyond reasonable doubt', ie the magistrates or jury should have no serious doubt as to the guilt of the accused.

Facts which disclose a criminal offence may also form the basis of a civil action but the victim cannot have both claims adjudicated by the same court even in those rare cases when a court has jurisdiction to hear both civil and criminal actions[3]. It is necessary to bring a separate civil action as well as any prosecution which the state may initiate.

1   Most prosecutions are initiated by the police and thereafter conducted by the Crown
Prosecution Service, whose head is the Director of Public Prosecutions.
2   Judges sit without juries in all but a tiny handful of civil cases; defamation which we discuss
in paras 20.29–20.35, below, is the principal exception.
3   The court structure is discussed in Chap 3.

Contract
1.4   A contract is an agreement which is binding in law if certain requirements
are complied with. We make a contract when we buy a computer, purchase a
railway ticket, employ a trainee accountant or order some computer software
to be devised. All contracts, whatever their subject matter and however large
or small the sums of money involved, are subject to the same basic rules. Once
the existence of a valid contract has been established, an inexcusable failure to
perform the contractual obligations, or defective performance of those
obligations, constitutes a breach of contract for which an action can be brought.
The usual, but not only, remedy for breach of contract is an action for damages.
Oral agreements which comply with the legal requirements for the formation
of a legally binding contract are no less binding, except in certain recognised
cases, than a contract made in writing. The principal disadvantages of oral
contracts are the difficulty of proving that they have been made and what their
terms are.

Tort
1.5   There is no universally accepted definition of a tort, perhaps because
English law does not have a law of tort but a law of torts. These different torts
share many characteristics but can also vary dramatically from each other.
Perhaps we can best explain what is meant by the law of tort if we say that the
law imposes certain duties on all of us, for example, not to injure other people,
physically, financially or by lowering their reputation. If X injures Y, X will be
liable in tort provided that he owed Y a legal duty not to injure him, that the
injury suffered by Y was a type which the law recognises and that the injury
was caused by X's failure to comply with his duty. The usual remedy for the
victim of a tort is to seek damages, but other remedies are available.

The most frequently encountered tort is negligence and its most common
manifestation is in road accidents and accidents at work. Other torts seek to
prevent us defaming other people or being a nuisance to our neighbours.

Restitution
1.6   The law of contract and the law of tort are two categories of the civil law
of obligations. The law of restitution is a third category. In some circumstances,
a person who has been unjustly enriched at the expense of another may be
compelled by law to make restitution. For instance, if A pays money to B
under certain mistakes of fact, B may be ordered to return it. This category of
law falls outside the law of contract because the obligation to restore does not
arise from any agreement between the person under the obligation and the
person to whom the obligation is owed. It also falls outside the definition of a
tort because A is not claiming damages; nor, indeed, can it meaningfully be
said that B has broken any legal duty in merely receiving the money.

Property
1.7 The law of property is an amalgam of:

a. special rules relating purely to property; and
b. special applications of general legal rules. For example, there are rules of contract which apply specifically to property and which form a gloss on general contractual principles.

There are basically two types of property known to the law: 'personal property' and 'real property'. 'Personal property' (otherwise known as chattels personal or pure personalty) means movable things, such as cars, jewellery and books, and the various types of intangible things (other than interests in land) which can be owned, such as copyrights, patents, trade marks and shares in a company. 'Real property' refers to immovable things, such as land and buildings, and freehold interests in land. For historical reasons, leasehold interests in land have a hybrid classification and are classed as chattels real or real personalty.

The rules relating specifically to land were much modified by statute in 1925 and are generally outside the scope of this book.

Some other categories of civil law
1.8 There are many other generally accepted categories of civil law. Examples are:

a. *Commercial law* This is concerned with agency, sale of goods, negotiable instruments and other matters relating to business transactions.

b. *Employment law* This involves special and general rules of contract but also embraces statutory rights and obligations between employer and employee. It includes such topics as health and safety at work (which is also covered by the law of tort) and unfair dismissal.

c. *Company law* Companies are legal persons and are subject to special rules both common law and statutory, partly because they are artificial legal persons and partly because of the need to regulate their dealings with shareholders, employees and creditors.

d. *Constitutional law* This is a slightly different category of law in that it is that branch of the law which regulates the principal organs of government and their impact on the individual citizen, as opposed to providing rules which regulate the relationship between one member of society and another.

These categories are merely illustrations of the diversity of civil law; other categories are revenue law and family law. New categories arise when an area of life develops a sufficiently large and distinct body of legal rules; a relatively recent arrival has been environmental law.

Classification by reference to the source of the legal rule

1.9 It is also possible to classify law by reference to its source. Common law and legislation are sources of law.

Common law and legislation

1.10 Common law means judge-made law. It is contained in the decisions or judgments made by the English judiciary over many centuries. Legislation comprises Acts of Parliament, subordinate legislation (examples of which are byelaws and statutory instruments deriving their authority from Acts of Parliament) and the legislation of the European Community. Legislation can change the common law, but judges cannot change or ignore legislation, although their interpretation of it may occasionally stultify or modify the wishes of Parliament[1]. Some categories of law, the law of contract and the law of tort, for example, are almost entirely based on judicial decisions, and such legislation as amends them is narrow in its scope, whereas employment law and company law, for example, largely have a statutory basis. Sometimes, Acts of Parliament seek merely to clarify and codify existing law. In other cases, Acts of Parliament may create a body of rights and duties where none existed before, as has occurred, for example, in relation to much of employment law and of company law.

1 Chap 4.

Common law and equity

1.11 The common law can be further subdivided into common law and equity. If both are branches of the common law and therefore both judge-made law, wherein lies the difference between them? The difference between them is that of their origins. Prior to the Judicature Acts of 1873–1875 there were two systems of courts in England, the common law courts and the Court of Chancery.

1.12 The common law courts had evolved from the centralised system for the administration of justice developed by a powerful monarchy between the eleventh and thirteenth centuries, which had gradually ousted the jurisdiction of the local courts. Therefore, common law is that body of law developed by the common law courts, such as the Court of Exchequer (whose judges were called Barons), the Court of Common Pleas and the Court of King's Bench, prior to the fusion of the administration of justice in 1875, and modifications and extensions effected since 1875. The common law is not static but subject to constant affirmation, revision and development by modern judges.

It is generally accepted that it was only the administration of the law, and not the law itself, which was fused in 1875 and thus it is still possible to speak of common law and equity as distinct bodies of law. Since 1875 a case involving both common law and equitable principles can be heard in one court which can, where necessary, apply both sets of rules. Prior to 1875 the unfortunate litigant might have had to bring two actions, one to establish his common law rights and another before the Court of Chancery to establish his equitable rights. An even more unfortunate party might have succeeded at common law, but have had the efficacy of the common law court's judgment nullified in equitable proceedings.

1.13   Equity is that body of law developed in the Court of Chancery prior to 1875 and its subsequent amendments and developments. The Court of Chancery developed later than the common law courts because of defects in those courts and in the law which they administered. The common law courts had entangled themselves in an extremely rigid procedure which made it difficult to initiate actions and severely limited the development of the common law, and the remedies available in the common law courts for the successful litigant were inadequate. Thus, the habit arose in the fourteenth and fifteenth centuries of petitioning the King to remedy injustice. After a while, the King delegated the task of determining these petitions to his Chancellor. Initially, the Chancellor decided cases in the name of the King, but in 1474 he began to do so in his own name, and this marked the beginning of the Court of Chancery presided over by the Lord Chancellor. Until 1529, the Lord Chancellor was an ecclesiastic whose decisions were supposedly guided by conscience, but thereafter he was a lawyer. The procedure in the Court of Chancery was originally less rigid than that of the common law courts; and the basis of decisions was supposed to be the merits of each action and what was just between the parties, with little reference to previous cases. Subsequently, both procedure and substantive law became more rigid; the notion of creating a remedy to fit the particular case before the court disappeared and the Court of Chancery became as much influenced by previous cases as the common law courts. By the nineteenth century the Court of Chancery had a well deserved reputation for tardiness. This was partly due to the fact that until 1813 all cases were heard by the Lord Chancellor, and partly to the innate conservatism and caution of some Lord Chancellors.

The rules of equity developed by the Court of Chancery were concerned either with entirely new rights totally unknown to the common law or with remedies (such as rectification and specific performance[1]) designed to counter the inefficacy or injustice of the common law. Equity did not amend the common law but enabled a litigant who had failed to establish a claim at common law, or been disappointed by the remedies available there, to seek an equitable remedy which made good the defects of the common law in a particular case. For example, if the parties to a contract agree to vary their agreement, the common law provides that the variation cannot take effect unless it is supported by consideration, whereas equity may prevent one of the parties enforcing the unvaried agreement, for a time at least[2].

1   For rectification see para 13.21, below; for specific performance see paras 12.27–12.29, below.
2   Paras 6.17–6.21, below.

1.14   Even modern courts, which administer both common law and equity, will tend to consider the common law first and then see if it is affected by equity. This process is reversed where a case is concerned with a body of rules developed almost entirely by equity, for example, the law of trusts. If there is a conflict between the rules of the common law and those of equity, the rules of equity prevail[1]. It cannot be emphasised too much that the remedies developed by equity cannot be demanded as of right (unlike common law remedies) but, reflecting the origins of equity in conscience, are discretionary and may or may not be awarded by the court. A litigant who has acted unfairly or inequitably may find that the court will decline to award an equitable remedy and that he must be content with common law remedies. If, for example, a purchaser delays completing the purchase of a house, the vendor has a right to the common law remedy of damages for breach of the contract of sale but no right to have the completion enforced by an order for the equitable remedy of specific performance of the contract (although he may be awarded it at the court's discretion).

1   Judicature Act 1873, s 25, re-enacted in the Supreme Court Act 1981, s 49.

Elements of Civil Evidence

1.15   When a civil case comes to court[1] the judge (or the jury, on the rare occasion when one is used) is required first to decide any disputed questions of fact and then to apply the law to those and any agreed facts. The rules of law determine what facts are relevant to a particular issue: the rules of evidence determine which party is required to prove (or disprove) those facts, and to what standard, and also what material can be tendered in evidence.

1   Most legal claims are, in practice, settled out of court.

The burden and standard of proof

The burden of proof
1.16   The burden of proof is the requirement placed upon a party to proceedings to prove, to the requisite standard, an issue arising in those proceedings. Failure by such a party to adduce sufficient evidence on an issue results in it being lost. For example, a party bringing an action for breach of contract must prove the existence of the contract and breach by the defendant. Failure to prove the existence of the contract is fatal to the plaintiff's case for then there can be no issue of breach.

In civil cases the burden of proof generally rests upon the party making a claim: he is alleging that he has a cause of action so he must prove all the facts necessary in law to establish that cause of action. Similarly, a party defending an action bears the burden of proving any defence on which he proposes to rely. It must be stressed that this is a general rule and there are exceptions in most areas of civil litigation. Generally, the allocation of the burden of proof on a particular issue is well established by previous cases.

1.17   A party who prima facie bears the burden of proof on an issue may be able to rely upon a rebuttable presumption of law (an assumption which must be drawn on his behalf, in the absence of evidence to the contrary, by the judge) to satisfy the burden of proof cast upon him. For an illustration of such a presumption of law and its operation see paras 18.48 to 18.50, below, in which the maxim res ipsa loquitur is discussed.

The standard of proof
1.18   A party bearing a burden of proof on an issue in a civil case will be required to prove that issue on 'a balance of probabilities'. He is not required

to produce absolute proof, nor prove the issue beyond reasonable doubt; instead, he must convince the court that it is more probable than not that the facts which he is asserting are true. The balance of probabilities is a remarkably flexible standard. In some cases, eg when a party to a civil action alleges fraud or some other criminal offence on the part of his opponent, the court, while still holding that the standard of proof is the balance of probabilities, will in practice require more convincing than is usual before it will hold that the burden of proof is satisfied[1].

Any single piece of cogent evidence (perhaps the testimony of a single witness or even that of the plaintiff himself) can be sufficient to satisfy the burden of proof cast upon a party. One good witness may convince a judge and the case be won despite a plethora of witnesses supporting the opposing case, if they are less than convincing. Of course, the more credible the evidence that can be gathered by a party the more likely the balance of probabilities will be held to have tipped in his favour.

1   See, for example, *Hornal v Neuberger Products Ltd* [1957] 1 QB 247, [1956] 3 All ER 970, CA.

Admissibility of evidence

1.19   Material will be considered by a court only if it is both relevant to an issue before the court and admissible as evidence.

Provided that material is admissible as evidence, it can be oral, documentary or 'real'. Real evidence consists of material objects, other than certain documents, open to inspection by the court. Printouts from breath/alcohol testing machines[1], an automatic radar trace of a ship's course[2] and even a dog, which was the subject of the action in that it was alleged to be dangerous[3], have been produced in court. The dog was kept on a chain.

1   *Castle v Cross* [1985] 1 All ER 87, [1984] 1 WLR 1372.
2   *The Statue of Liberty, Sapporo Maru M/S (Owners) v Steam Tanker Statue of Liberty (Owners)*, [1968] 2 All ER 195, [1968] 1 WLR 739.
3   *Line v Taylor* (1862) 3 F & F 731.

1.20   Essentially anyone is a competent witness (ie can give evidence) in a civil case and can be asked by either party to the action questions on any relevant issue and be compelled (ie required) to answer them, provided that the answers are admissible as evidence.

A competent and compellable witness may be permitted to refuse to answer questions about matters which are the subject of a privilege. For example, communications between a lawyer and his client are privileged, with the result that a lawyer cannot reveal information about his client or his affairs without the client's permission[1]. This privilege is accepted because it is thought to encourage honesty between lawyer and client, and thereby to improve the quality of justice. Communications between an accountant and a client are not similarly privileged[2].

The principal case where material will not be admitted as evidence in a civil case is when it constitutes an opinion.

1   This privilege will not operate in some criminal litigation.

2 Professional practice would require an accountant to decline to release information about a client unless required to do so by a court; see, for example, *R v Crown Court at Guildford, ex p DPP* [1996] 4 All ER 961, DC.

Opinion

1.21 A non-expert witness must state facts and not give his opinion on or draw inferences from those facts. However, it is frequently impossible to distinguish absolutely between fact and opinion and a witness is allowed to give his opinion in so far as it constitutes a means of conveying relevant facts. Even if a non-expert witness is allowed to combine his opinion with his factual evidence, he is not allowed to draw conclusions on the basis of his opinion because it is for the court to decide the significance of evidence, and not the witness. Thus, a non-expert witness is entitled to say that a vehicle seemed to be travelling very fast, giving reasons for this view, but could not say that the driver was driving negligently; negligence is the issue of law on which the court must adjudicate.

1.22 *Expert witnesses* A witness who is an expert on a particular area can state facts and give his opinion on those facts, provided that the issue about which the opinion is being given requires expert analysis[1]. A witness is an expert if the judge rules him to be qualified in the relevant area either because he holds formal qualifications or by appropriate experience.

It must be stressed that merely because a witness is an expert he cannot give his opinions on anything and everything. Expert opinion evidence is admitted only when the issue falls within the area of expertise of the witness (accountants are experts but not on medical matters) and the judge needs assistance in drawing inferences from the facts before the court. In *Alchemy (International) Ltd v Tattersalls Ltd*[2], the judge permitted several experts to testify as to what was, in their opinion, the appropriate procedure to follow in the event of a disputed bid at an auction. Having ruled that this was a case where an auctioneer could not be negligent if he followed sound commercial practice, ie a practice regarded as appropriate by a body of competent professionals, the judge considered the expert opinion evidence on what was sound commercial practice. On the facts he found no negligence on the part of the defendant auctioneers.

An expert witness should give independent testimony and not tailor his evidence simply to meet the needs of the party calling him[3].

A party wishing to call an expert witness should seek leave to do so from the court. The court can order advance disclosure of an expert's report to the opposing party[4].

1 Areas calling for expert analysis are constantly expanding; recent cases have allowed expert evidence in voice identification, DNA testing and the abilities of tracker dogs.
2 [1985] 2 EGLR 17.
3 *Whitehouse v Jordan* [1981] 1 All ER 267, [1981] 1 WLR 246, HL.
4 See the Rules of the Supreme Court, Order 38. For a summary of the duties of an expert witness see *National Justice Cia Naviera SA v Prudential Assurance Co Ltd, The Ikarian Reefer* [1993] 2 Lloyd's Rep 68.

Hearsay

1.23 A statement, made otherwise than by a person while giving oral evidence in the proceedings, which is tendered as evidence of the fact stated is hearsay evidence. Thus, the evidence of a witness as to what X, who is not a witness, said to him is hearsay, and so is evidence of what the witness said out of court to X. However, not all out- of-court statements are hearsay; if a statement is produced merely to prove the fact that it was made, as opposed to the truth of what was stated in it, it is not hearsay evidence. For example, if it was an issue in proceedings whether X had died at or after a particular time, a witness could testify that he heard X (who is patently not a witness) call for medical aid after the time in issue to prove that he could speak after that time (so that he must then have been alive).

At common law, hearsay evidence was inadmissible in civil cases. However, the position has been changed by statute. The general position is now governed by the Civil Evidence Act 1995.

1.24   *Civil Evidence Act 1995, s 1*   This section provides that in civil proceedings to which the rules of evidence apply (in law or by agreement of the parties) a statement shall not be excluded on the ground that it is hearsay. Hence, subject to certain safeguards in later sections, hearsay evidence is now admitted in civil cases. Where a statement is, but for this section, inadmissible as hearsay and for some other reason it remains inadmissible.

A statement is defined as 'any representation of fact or opinion however made'[1]. Thus, s 1 applies to statements made orally or in writing or in some other form and it allows the admission of out-of-court statements made by the witness currently testifying or some other person.

Section 1 does not limit its application to 'first-hand' hearsay, that is an out-of-court statement made by X, heard by Y, which Y is proposing to give in evidence, but can apply to any out-of-court statement no matter how remote the relationship between the maker of the statement and the witness. Thus, if A were to give an out-of-court opinion, based on observations made by B, which he dictates to C who writes it down and then shows it to D who relates its contents to E, E could testify as to the contents of A's opinion in court. Obviously in cases of multiple hearsay the chances of error are magnified and the Act addresses this in later sections to which we now turn.

1 Section 13.

1.25   *Safeguards applicable to s 1*   Section 1 does not give a party to a civil action an unfettered right to introduce hearsay evidence in proceedings. In particular, a statement is not admissible at all if the maker of it (not the witness but the person whose words it is sought to admit) would not have been a competent witness. In addition a number of sections provide specific safeguards.

a.   Section 2 of the Act provides that a party proposing to adduce hearsay evidence must give notice to that effect and provide further details if requested to do so by the other party to the action. Failure to give notice (or provide further details if requested) does not affect the admissibility of the evidence but may affect the weight that is given to it.

b.   Section 4 of the Act provides that in estimating the degree of weight which is given to the statement the court 'shall have regard to any circumstances from which any inference can reasonably be drawn as to the reliability or otherwise of the evidence.' Section 4(2) lists a number of factors to which the court should have regard in assessing weight but does not restrict the court to these factors. Factors listed include whether it would have been reasonable and practicable to call the maker of the statement, whether the statement was contemporaneous with events narrated in it and whether the statement involved multiple hearsay. Thus, in cases of multiple hearsay, a court may well give little credence to evidence which is many steps removed from the maker of the statement since each transmission of a statement increases the scope for inaccuracy to arise.

c.   Section 5 of the Act allows the credibility of the maker of the statement to be impeached and also allows the admission of inconsistent statements made by the maker of the statement. With the leave of the court the maker of the statement, if available, may be called as a witness. Thus, if it was suggested that a party was seeking to call X to testify as to an out-of-court statement made by Y because Y might have proved to be a less than convincing witness who would have broken down under cross-examination, the court might allow, at the request of the other party, Y to be called as a witness.

1.26   *Civil Evidence Act 1995, s 9*   This section, which complements s 1, permits the admission of certain documents[1] in evidence. While documents admissible under this section would also be admissible under s 1 the advantage of using s9 is that the safeguards outlined in para 1.25, above, do not apply, although a court may direct that s 9 shall not apply having regard to the circumstances of the case. Thus, if there was doubt as to the authenticity of the document or as to whether it was genuinely contemporaneous with the information it purported to record, a court might reject it wholly or in part.

1   A document is defined in s 13 as 'anything in which information of any description is recorded'. Consequently, it includes tapes, computer disks and CDs as well as paper records.

1.27   Section 9 can be used to admit a document when it forms part of the records of a business or public authority[1].

Both records and business are defined in very general terms. Section 9(4) defines a record as 'a record in whatever form'. A business is defined as including any activity carried on over a period of time whether for profit or not.

1   A document forms part of such a record if it is certified as such by an officer of the business or authority.

Chapter 2

Persons and Property

2.1 In this chapter we consider who is subject to English law, the nature of property and the use of property as security.

Persons

2.2 Not every person or dispute is subject to English law. The English courts will not waste their time in hearing actions relating to parties against whom they could not enforce their judgments[1]. The absence of a person from this country does not necessarily mean that the judgment of an English court is unenforceable. Even if its judgment is enforceable, an English court may only hear an action if it has the capacity (ie jurisdiction) to do so. Such capacity may be conferred by statute or by the common law.

English law applies not only to individual human beings but also to companies, partnerships, clubs, trade unions, local authorities and other entities. Human beings are natural legal persons; companies, local authorities and other incorporated bodies are artificial legal persons. The other bodies mentioned above can be described generally as unincorporated associations, which do not have a separate and distinct personality from their members.

The Queen exercises the office of Sovereign or head of state under the British constitution. In her private capacity, the Sovereign is a natural legal person; in her official capacity she is a corporation sole, an artificial legal person, with the result that the official property of the Sovereign passes on the death of the holder of that office to the successor as if he was the same person.

1 *Richard West & Partners (Inverness) Ltd v Dick* [1969] 2 Ch 424, [1969] 1 All ER 943, CA.

Natural legal persons[1]
2.3 Human beings are, of course, potentially the subjects of any rule of English law and can sue and be sued if and when necessary. However, some legal

persons who apparently fall within the jurisdiction of the English courts may be immune from process. The most obvious immunity is that granted to the Sovereign (in her private capacity, as well as her official one). The Sovereign is immune from both the criminal and the civil jurisdictions of the English courts. Foreign Sovereigns and Heads of State are likewise immune[2]. Foreign diplomats have a slightly more limited immunity since they are not subject to the criminal jurisdiction of the English courts, nor to the civil jurisdiction except in certain types of case, for example, actions relating to land in the United Kingdom which they own in a personal capacity[3].

Legal personality begins at birth and ends at death. Consequently, if a child dies before birth because of injuries inflicted negligently by a doctor, an action cannot be brought in respect of its injuries[4]. Similarly, a deceased person's estate cannot sue for injuries inflicted upon his body after his death. On the other hand, legal proceedings initiated before death can continue afterwards (except an action for defamation) and an action can be initiated by a deceased person's estate in respect of the cause of the death, where appropriate.

1 The Interpretation Act 1978 provides that a statutory reference to 'he' should be taken as applying equally to 'she' and 'they' unless the context demands otherwise; para 4.28, below.
2 State Immunity Act 1978.
3 Diplomatic Privileges Act 1964. Foreign states are also exempt from the jurisdiction of the English courts, except in respect of their purely commercial activities: State Immunity Act 1978.
4 But see the Congenital Disabilities (Civil Liability) Act 1976; para 17.7, below.

2.4 Particular rules may be inapplicable to natural legal persons; for example, corporation tax is only payable by companies. Alternatively, a particular legal rule may be inappropriate for all but particular people; for example, only employers can be subject to the statutory provision requiring them to give their employees written particulars of their terms of employment. Of course, anyone can become an employer and thus be subject to that statutory provision, but there is one category of natural legal persons who are subject to special provisions: minors.

Some of the most important limitations applicable to minors (ie persons under 18) are that:

a. a person under the age of 10 cannot be convicted of a crime and criminal liability is restricted for those under 14;
b. minors have limited contractual capacity[1]; and
c. minors cannot hold a legal estate in land.

1 Chap 16.

Artificial legal persons

2.5 Companies are associations of people who have amalgamated their ideas or resources to pursue some common lawful purpose. Companies may be formed for any lawful purpose which their progenitors or promoters choose.

It is extremely rare (as well as difficult and expensive) to form a company other than under the Companies Act 1985 (companies so formed are called registered companies) although it can be done by Private Act of Parliament or by Royal Charter. The Companies Act 1985 permits the formation of private companies and public companies. Only public companies can apply for listing on the Stock Exchange or the Alternative Investment Market (AIM). Company law usually applies equally to both types of registered company, but there are important differences between them. Both types of registered company are easy to form and the costs of formation are modest, although flotation of a public company on the Stock Exchange or AIM is expensive.

2.6 Companies are artificial legal persons and as such they are subject to all the rules that apply to natural legal persons unless inappropriate; for example, a company cannot commit bigamy (marrying while already married). Since companies are artificial legal persons, a statutory reference to a person prima facie includes a company. Even if a company is totally dominated by one shareholder, the company and that shareholder are distinct legal persons. This was first established in *Salomon v A Salomon & Co Ltd*[1], in which the validity of a secured debt contracted by the company in favour of Salomon was contested in the winding-up of the company. The House of Lords ruled that, even though the company was formed to take over Salomon's existing business, and even though he held 20,001 of the 20,007 shares which had been issued by the company, the company and Salomon were distinct legal beings: they could not be regarded as synonymous. Lord MacNaghten stated firmly: 'the company is at law a different person from the subscribers to the memorandum [ie the first shareholders]; and, though it may be that after incorporation the business is precisely the same as it was before . . ., the company is not the agent of the subscribers or trustee for them.'
In addition to being subject to those rules applicable to any person, natural or legal, companies are subject to a specific legal regime applicable only to them which we discuss in chapters 25 and 26.
Other associations of people may pursue some common purpose – trade unions, clubs and partnerships are examples. A company can be distinguished from other associations in that, since the company is itself a legal person, it is totally distinct from its shareholders (who are also called members) and employees.

1 [1897] AC 22, HL.

2.7 There are many consequences arising from the separate legal identities of a company and its members. For example:

a. a company can sue and be sued in its own name;
b. a company can make contracts on its own behalf, and its members cannot claim the benefit nor be subject to the burdens of such contracts[1];
c. a company can own property in its own right, and its members have no direct interest in the property of the company; and

d.   while the company is operational its debts are not the responsibility of its members. However, if an unlimited company is wound up, its members are personally liable for its debts. Because of this, the majority of companies are formed with limited liability. On the winding-up of a limited liability company its members are only liable to pay towards the discharge of the company's debts the nominal value of their shares in so far as this has not yet been paid (if the company is limited by shares) or a prearranged fixed sum (if the company is limited by guarantee).

In an average year, over 90,000 companies are formed with limited liability and 150 with unlimited liability.

1   This is merely the effect of the doctrine of privity, paras 6.24–6.34, below.

2.8   There are some circumstances in which a court will ignore the separate legal personality of a company and find its members responsible for the actions of the company. This is called lifting or piercing the veil; the veil being the veil of incorporation which usually hides the members from view. This disregard of corporate legal status may be required by statute or, in exceptional cases, be decreed by the courts[1].

1   See further para 25.8, below.

Contractual capacity
2.9   Natural legal persons, with the exception of minors, mental patients and drunkards[1], have the capacity to make any contract. A company is a legal person, but until 1989 the contractual capacity of companies was considerably restricted and even now the contractual capacity of a company is not co-extensive with that of natural persons[2].

1   Chap 16.
2   See further paras 25.29 and 25.30, below.

Unincorporated associations
2.10   It may come as no surprise to the reader to learn that any association which is not in corporate form is an unincorporated association. Unincorporated associations are many and varied. They may be large or small, transient or well-established, profit-making or charitable, open to all or with restricted membership. They all differ from companies, which are equally varied, in that (as already indicated) they do not possess a legal personality separate and distinct from their members. Many unincorporated associations, particularly partnerships, resemble companies in what they do, yet lack the advantages of separate legal personality.

Trade unions
2.11   A trade union is an organisation, consisting wholly or mainly of workers, whose principal purpose includes the regulation of relations between workers and employers. Trade unions cannot become bodies corporate and hence are

not legal persons, but many of the benefits of incorporation have been bestowed on them by statute. For example:

a.   a union can make contracts on its own behalf;
b.   a union's property is vested in trustees who hold it for the benefit of the trade union and the members of the union have no interest in it; and
c.   a union can sue or be sued in its own name, and judgment is enforceable against the union and its property and not against the property of the members.

Partnerships[1]
2.12   A partnership will usually be governed by the rules laid down in the Partnership Act 1890, but it is possible to create limited partnerships and they are governed by the Limited Partnerships Act 1907. The limited partnership, which is a partnership with some of the characteristics of a limited liability company, is not very popular in the United Kingdom, though much used in continental Europe.

Although a partnership and its partners are not separate legal entities, a partnership can usually sue and be sued in its own name.

1   Partnerships are discussed in detail in Chap 24.

2.13   Section 1 of the Partnership Act 1890 defines a partnership as 'the relation existing between two or more persons carrying on a business in common with a view to profit'. Because the partners and the partnership are not separate legal entities, unlike shareholders and the company in which they hold shares, there are important differences between being a partner and being a shareholder. For example:

a.   a partner is liable for the debts and liabilities of the partnership: a shareholder is not liable for the debts and liabilities of the company;
b.   a partner has a legal interest in the assets of the partnership: a shareholder does not have any legally recognised interest in the assets of the company;
c.   shares in a partnership are not transferable: shares in a company are; and
d.   the death of a partner technically terminates the partnership, although the remaining partners may agree to carry on the partnership: the death of a shareholder leaves the company unaffected.

It is unusual to find large businesses run as partnerships. While there are advantages for partnerships over companies in that there is less publicity for the affairs of a partnership, these benefits will probably be outweighed by the advantages enjoyed by a company, especially limited liability and tax-saving once profits reach a certain size.

The maximum number of partners permissible for a partnership is 20, unless the partnership is one of solicitors, specified categories of accountants, estate agents or certain other professional people.

2.14   A limited partnership is a partnership where one or more partners has only a limited liability for the debts of the partnership. Every limited partnership must have at least one general partner (ie with full liability for debts) and any limited partner who is active in the affairs of the partnership becomes a general partner. The limited partnership is only suitable for those who wish to invest money in a partnership but take no part in its running; their lack of popularity seems hardly surprising.

2.15 In making contracts, a partnership has to work through agents – usually the partners – but there is no restriction on its contractual capacity. In theory, a partnership can make any contract it wishes. Whether a contract entered into by a partner binds his fellow partners depends on the usual rules of agency[1], with the additional rule that any contract entered into by a partner which would be within the usual practice of the partnership will bind his fellow partners[2].

1 Chap 23.
2 Partnership Act 1890, s 5.

Clubs and societies
2.16 If a club or society is carried on with a view to gain it must register as a company if its membership exceeds 20[1]. In addition, many clubs and societies which are not required to be registered as companies have chosen to be so registered.

The internal management of a club or society which has not registered as a company is regulated by its rules (which have contractual force between its members). Such a club or society does not have a legal personality distinct from its members. Consequently, it will usually arrange to have its property held on trust for its benefit (so that such property is kept distinct from its members' property). However, where this does occur, all the members together can (subject to the rules of the club or society) call for the dissolution of the trust, in which case the property would be divided in accordance with the rules of the club or society. Legal actions can be brought by or against the committee as the agents of the club or society, although the committee as individuals do not generally owe any duty to the members[2]. In addition, it may be possible for a member to sue the club or society (rather than the committee), but this can be very difficult.

1 Companies Act 1985, s 716.
2 *Robertson v Ridley* [1989] 2 All ER 474, [1989] 1 WLR 872, CA.

2.17 The contractual capacity of a club or society which is not a company is technically that of a natural legal person but, since it can only make contracts through an agent, whether a particular contract binds a club or society and who is liable on it depend on its rules and the principles of the law of agency[1].

1 Chap 23.

The Crown
2.18 'The Crown' (ie the Sovereign's government and armed forces) has legal personality. It can, for example, hold property and make contracts. However, originally the Crown could not be made a party to court action and

hence could not be sued. Thus, prior to 1947, a person who had been knocked down by a tank, or who had been supplied with defective goods under a contract of sale with the Minister for Supply, had no redress against the army or government department, although Crown employees could be sued in their personal capacity. However, since 1947[1], the Crown may generally be sued in contract or tort. However, if it declines to meet an award of damages or refuses to comply with a court order, judgment cannot be enforced against it.

The Crown can still refuse to give evidence in a particular case if such evidence, if revealed, would be prejudicial to the interests of the state (public interest immunity). Members of the armed forces used generally not to be able to sue for injuries received while on duty, nor for injuries received while on premises (including ships or aircraft) being used by the armed forces. This restriction on Crown liability has been abolished, although the government of the day can revive it in time of national danger, great emergency or warlike operations outside the United Kingdom[2].

It must be emphasised that what has been said above does not apply to the liability of the Sovereign herself. As indicated in para 2.3, above, although the Sovereign is a legal person, she is immune from the jurisdiction of the courts in her private capacity and in her official capacity.

1   Crown Proceedings Act 1947.
2   Crown Proceedings (Armed Forces) Act 1987. See, also, *Mulcahy v Ministry of Defence* [1996] QB 732, [1996] 2 All ER 758, CA, para 18.6, below, for a discussion of the duties owed by the Crown to its servicemen-employees.

Property

2.19   As we said in para 1.7, above, property (assets) can be divided into real and personal property. Real property is land, buildings and freehold interests in land. Personal property is movable assets whether tangible, eg cars, jewellery or books, or intangible, eg debts, copyrights, trade marks, shares in a company or other choses in action[1]. Tangible personal property is otherwise known as 'goods' or 'chattels'. Leasehold interests in land constitute a unique legal hybrid in that they are classified as real personalty or chattels real.

1   Para 22.2, below.

Legal and equitable interests

2.20   Property, real or personal, can be the subject of one or more legal and equitable interests, which interests can exist simultaneously and may be held by different people. A legal interest is a right recognised by the law; an equitable interest is also a right recognised by law but one which originated in the Court of Chancery prior to it being subsumed within the reorganised court structure in 1873–1875[1]. Equitable interests were created by the Court of Chancery to recognise that, while legal title to property might be vested in X, conscience might require X, in his dealing with the property, to take into account Y.

An example of the separation of legal and equitable interests is afforded by the trust. The trust is a device whereby the trustees hold property, real or personal, to which they have the legal title, for the benefit of the beneficiaries who have an equitable interest in that property. In law, the trustees own the property and can do what they like with it, but equity requires them to use the property as specified by the trust and they are accountable to the beneficiaries for their dealings with the property.

1   Paras 1.11–1.14, above.

2.21   Legal interests are rights in rem (rights affecting the property itself) and can be enforced against anyone attempting to intermeddle with the property. In contrast, equitable interests are rights in personam (rights enforceable against certain persons who have the property, but not attached to the property itself). The distinction between rights in rem and rights in personam is relevant in relation to the purchaser for value without notice.

Purchasers for value
2.22   Legal rights and interests bind everyone, whether or not they know of the existence of such rights and interests. For example, if the owner of land has granted you a legal lease of it, your lease is binding on a subsequent purchaser of the land, even if he foolishly neglected to inquire whether the land was subject to a prior legal right or not.

In contrast, an equitable interest in property is vulnerable in that, while it binds persons who take subsequent equitable interests in that property, it does not bind bona fide purchasers of the legal estate for value without notice of it. Indeed, any successor of a bona fide purchaser for value without notice also takes free of an equitable interest, even if he knew of its existence.

'Bona fide' means that the person claiming to take free of an equitable interest must not have acted fraudulently or in bad faith. 'Purchaser for value' includes someone taking a mortgage or lease of land. 'Value' does not necessarily mean full value since any consideration in money, or even by way of money's worth[1] or by a promise of marriage, suffices.

1   'Money's worth' means non-monetary consideration, such as property or services.

Without notice
2.23   Perhaps the most important point to recognise is that, to escape being bound by a prior equitable interest, the purchaser of the legal estate must not have notice of the existence of the equitable interest.

Notice may be actual, constructive or imputed. Actual notice means what it suggests – that the purchaser in fact knew of the prior equitable interest, but this has been modified by statute in relation to interests in land. Certain equitable interests in land must be registered in the Land Charges Register if they are to bind a subsequent purchaser. Failure to register renders the equitable interest void[1] against a purchaser for money or money's worth of the legal estate, even if he had actual notice of its existence. Conversely, registration of an equitable interest in the Land Charges Register is actual notice to all the world of its existence and therefore registration of such an interest means that no one can be a purchaser for value without notice.

Constructive notice means that a purchaser who did not actually know of an equitable interest (being a non-registrable interest[2]) will be deemed to have notice of the interest if he ought to have known about it. If a purchaser could defeat equitable interests by declining to inquire whether any interest existed, non-registrable equitable interests would be sadly unprotected. Therefore, purchasers are required to show that they undertook reasonable inquiries and inspection in seeking out equitable interests. Failure to exercise due diligence means that the purchaser will be fixed with constructive notice of any equitable interests which diligence would have revealed.

Imputed notice merely means that the actual or constructive notice of an authorised agent of the purchaser is imputed to the purchaser.

1   Land Charges Act 1972, s 4.
2   By virtue of the Law of Property Act 1925, s 2 and the Settled Land Act 1925, ss 18, 72 and 75 some non-registrable equitable interests in land are 'overreached' when the land is purchased, whether by a purchaser without notice or not. Such interests are not destroyed but they are no longer attached to the land, but to the purchase money paid for the land, and the purchaser takes the land unencumbered.

Registration
2.24   It should be noted that in much of England and Wales a system of registration of title to land applies under which the distinction between legal and equitable interests is of much reduced significance. Under that system interests are categorised as registrable interests, minor interests (which also require registration) and overriding interests (which are binding although not entered on the register).

Security interests in property
2.25   When a person enters into a contract he may require some security to ensure that the other party performs his contractual duty or to provide him with a remedy if the other party fails to perform. Such security may be a personal right of action against a third party, ie a contract of guarantee[1], or it may be an interest enforceable against property, a 'real' right.

Security interests against property comprise:
a. pledges;
b. mortgages and charges; and
c. liens.

1   Paras 7.8–7.9, below.

Pledges
2.26   A pledge is a bailment of goods as security for a loan. Bailment is a transaction involving the transfer of possession of goods by one person (the bailor) to another (the bailee) on the condition, express or implied, that the bailee will either keep and deliver back the actual goods to the bailor or otherwise deal with the actual goods according to the bailor's instructions.

Land and choses in action cannot be pledged but may be the subject of a mortgage. Normally, a pledge involves the borrower of the money (the 'pledgor' or 'pawnor') transferring actual possession of the goods to the lender (the 'pledgee' or 'pawnee'). However, it may be impossible to transfer actual possession, in which case the transfer of constructive possession – eg the delivery of a key to the warehouse where the goods are stored – suffices, provided that the pledgee obtains full control over the goods.

The pledgee may sell the goods if the pledgor fails to pay at the stated date, or, if no date is fixed, after the pledgee has made a proper demand for payment and a reasonable time for payment has elapsed. Any surplus above the amount of the debt and the costs of the sale must be handed over to the pledgor. The pledgee, like any other bailee, is liable for any negligence in relation to the goods, proof of lack of negligence being on him. The pledgee must not use the goods. If the pledgor repays the loan at the stipulated date, or, if no date is fixed, whenever he pays or validly tenders payment, the pledgee must deliver back the goods.

2.27 Where an individual receives a loan not exceeding £15,000 by pledging goods, the agreement constitutes a regulated consumer credit agreement and is subject to the general provisions of the Consumer Credit Act 1974 and certain special provisions contained in it.

Mortgages
2.28 A mortgage is a transaction whereby a borrower of money (the 'mortgagor') uses property as security for the repayment of the loan to the lender (the 'mortgagee'). Mortgages of land fall outside the scope of this book, and we confine ourselves to mortgages of personal property. A mortgage of personal property can be contrasted with a pledge in this way: a pledgor transfers immediate possession to the pledgee but retains ownership of it; a mortgagor transfers, contingently, legal or equitable ownership of the property but retains possession of it.

2.29 *Mortgages of choses in action* Choses in action[1], examples of which are debts, copyrights and shares, can be the subject of a legal or equitable mortgage. A legal mortgage of a chose in action is effected by an assignment[2] of the chose to the mortgagee, with a proviso for re-assignment on due repayment of the loan. An equitable mortgage is normally effected by a deposit of the title documents to the chose. In an equitable mortgage, the mortgagor retains legal ownership and the mortgage merely operates as an agreement to create a legal mortgage. A mortgage of shares is normally an equitable mortgage (to avoid payment of stamp duty) effected by deposit with the mortgagee of the share certificate and an executed blank share transfer with a proviso for the return of the share certificate on due repayment. If the money is not repaid the mortgagee completes the blank transfer in his own name and is registered as the legal owner of the shares.

The mortgagee of a chose in action has power to sell it if the mortgagor fails to pay the amount due at the stipulated date, or after reasonable notice if no date is fixed[3]. The mortgagee also has a right in such a case to foreclose the mortgage (ie to acquire the chose in action absolutely, freed from the mortgagor's right to redeem). In addition, if the mortgage is by deed executed by the mortgagor, the mortgagee has power to sell if the mortgagor fails to pay an instalment of interest for two months after it falls due or breaks any other covenant on his part[4].

1   Para 22.2, below.
2   Chap 22.
3   *Deverges v Sandeman, Clark & Co* [1902] 1 Ch 579, CA.
4   Law of Property Act 1925, ss 101 and 103.

2.30   *Mortgage of goods*   A mortgage of goods may be effected orally, but it is more common to effect it by a document. Such a document must be in the form prescribed by the Bills of Sale Act (1878) Amendment Act 1882 and comply with the rules laid down by the Act[1]. Such a document is known as a conditional bill of sale. The grantor of a conditional bill of sale is entitled to redeem the goods subject to it on due repayment of the loan. A bill of sale cannot be made in respect of shares or other choses in action.

The grantee of the bill (the mortgagee) cannot take possession of the goods comprised in it except in certain specified circumstances. An example of such a circumstance is where the grantor (the mortgagor) fails to perform a covenant in it or becomes bankrupt. Should the mortgagee in one of these specified cases take possession, the mortgagor has a right to apply to the High Court within five days of the seizure for permission to redeem the goods. If the court is satisfied that by payment or otherwise the cause of seizure no longer exists, the court may make such order as it thinks just. It is implicit in the 1882 Act that after seizure the mortgagee has a power of sale.

1   These rules are highly complex and failure to comply with them may render the bill either completely or partially void.

2.31   The 1882 Act does not apply to mortgages by registered companies. These are governed by special provisions in the Companies Act 1985.

Liens
2.32   There are three types of lien:
a. possessory liens;
b. equitable liens; and
c. maritime liens (rights which attach to, and are enforceable against, a ship or its cargo in respect of the payment of seamen's wages, salvage, payment of compensation for negligent collision and the like).

Only the first two require any further discussion.

2.33   *Possessory lien*   A possessory lien is the right of a person in possession of goods belonging to another to retain them until his monetary claims against that other are satisfied.

Since a possessory lien is simply a right to retain goods until satisfaction of the relevant monetary claims, no claim can be made for storage or any other expense incurred in exercising the lien. Nor is there a right to sell the goods, except where this is provided by trade usage, contract or statute. Unless one of these exceptions applies, the lienor (the person with the lien) must apply to the courts for an order to sell. In comparison, a pledgee always has a right of sale if the goods pledged are not redeemed within a certain period. A possessory lien is obviously lost if the lienor loses possession of the goods.

It is also lost if the debt to which the lien relates is paid, or the valid tender of it is refused, or if the lienor takes a security in substitution for the lien.

A possessory lien can be distinguished from both other types of lien in that they do not depend on the possession of the thing subject to the lien. A possessory lien can also be distinguished from a mortgage in that it does not involve the contingent transfer of ownership to the lienor.

2.34 Possessory liens can be of two types: particular or general.

A *particular* lien is the right to retain particular goods in the lienor's possession until payment of a debt in respect of those goods has been made. At common law, people who are legally obliged to provide a service, eg common carriers[1], have a particular lien on the goods of those for whom the services are performed. In addition, in *Woodworth v Conroy*[2], the Court of Appeal held that accountants have a particular lien for unpaid fees over any books, files and papers delivered to them in the course of their professional work by clients, and also over any other document which comes into their possession while acting as their clients' agents in the course of their ordinary professional work. Architects and arbitrators have a similar lien. These common law rights of lien generally cannot arise until the carriage, work, etc contracted to be done has been completed.

A *general* lien is the right to retain goods in the lienor's possession until all his monetary claims against the person to whom the goods belong have been satisfied, irrespective of whether they relate to those goods. A general lien only arises by contract or by trade usage, as in the case of bankers, solicitors, and stockbrokers[3]. A general lien under trade usage can be restricted or excluded by an agreement to the contrary.

A right to exercise a possessory lien may not be enforceable in some circumstances. For example, by s 246(2) of the Insolvency Act 1986, a particular lien over books, papers and other records belonging to a company in administration or liquidation is unenforceable to the extent that its enforcement would deny possession of those things to the administrator or liquidator. Nor is a possessory lien over documents enforceable if statute requires them to be kept in a particular place[4]. Consequently, for example, an accountant cannot exercise a lien over a company's accounting records because statute[5] specifies that they are to be kept at its registered office (or at another place specified by its directors), and are to be at all times open for inspection by the company's officers[6].

1 A common carrier is a person who, by way of business, holds himself out as being ready for reward to transport goods or persons or both for anyone who requires him to do so.
2 [1976] QB 884, [1976] 1 All ER 107, CA.
3 *Brandao v Barnett* (1846) 12 Cl & Fin 787, HL (bankers); *Ex p Sterling* (1809) 16 Ves 258 (solicitors); *Re London and Globe Finance Corpn* [1902] 2 Ch 416 (stockbrokers).
4 In *Re Capital Fire Insurance Association* (1883) 24 Ch D 408, CA (solicitors' lien); *DTC (CNC) Ltd v Gary Sargeant & Co* [1996] 2 All ER 369, [1996] 1 WLR 797 (accountants' lien).
5 Companies Act 1985, ss 221 and 222.
6 *DTC (CNC) Ltd v Gary Sergeant & Co* [1996] 2 All ER 369, [1996] 1 WLR 797.

2.35 *Equitable lien* An equitable lien is the right to have a specific piece of property allocated to the payment of a specific liability. An example is the right of a partner on dissolution of the partnership by death, retirement or bankruptcy to have the firm's assets applied in satisfaction of the firm's liabilities. Another example is the right of a vendor of land who has not been paid to apply to the court for a sale of the property in satisfaction of his claim, which is particularly important where the unpaid vendor has conveyed the land to the purchaser.

Chapter 3

Administration of the Law

The Courts

3.1   The first thing to be noted in any discussion of the court system is that not every type of court exercises both a civil and a criminal jurisdiction. Moreover, within the sphere of either of these jurisdictions, the particular type of court which will try the case (or hear an appeal) will depend on a number of disparate factors. Overleaf is a chart which shows the outline of the court structure and the following paragraphs explain this, beginning at the bottom.

Magistrates' courts[1]

3.2   A magistrates' court is constituted by justices of the peace. The terms 'justice of the peace' and 'magistrate' are synonymous and henceforth to avoid confusion we shall use the word 'magistrate'.

Magistrates are appointed by the Lord Chancellor (or by the Chancellor of the Duchy of Lancaster) in the name of the Queen as magistrates for a particular area (normally a county). Each county is divided into a number of petty sessional divisions (ie magistrates' courts districts). There are about 30,000 magistrates; all but some 90 of them are 'lay' magistrates. Lay magistrates are unpaid but get an allowance for loss of earnings and for expenses. They are not required to possess any legal qualifications; for legal advice they rely on their clerk, but even though the clerk to the magistrates is legally qualified, an individual court may be served by an unadmitted assistant. In the inner London area, and in some other places, jurisdiction is exercised both by lay magistrates and by stipendiary (ie salaried) magistrates. To be appointed as a stipendiary magistrate, a person must for seven years have had a right of audience in relation to any class of case in the Supreme Court[2], or all proceedings in county courts or magistrates' courts. Currently, only barristers and solicitors can satisfy this requirement.

The Lord Chancellor can dismiss a magistrate without showing cause. Magistrates are put on the supplemental list at the age of 70, which is de facto

THE COURT STRUCTURE

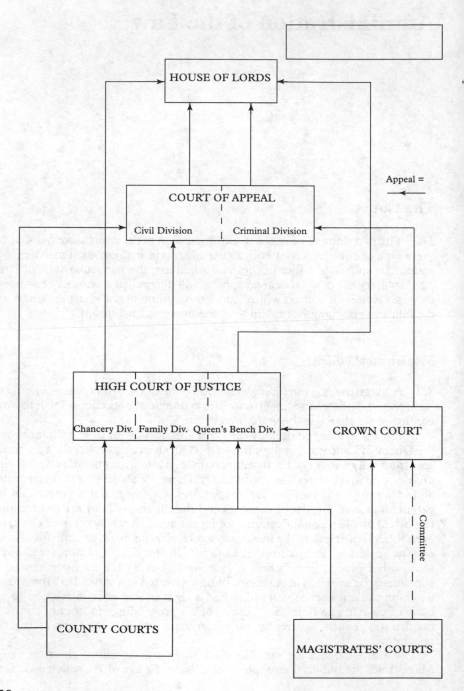

HOUSE OF LORDS

Appeal = ←

COURT OF APPEAL

Civil Division | Criminal Division

HIGH COURT OF JUSTICE

Chancery Div. Family Div. Queen's Bench Div.

CROWN COURT

Committee

COUNTY COURTS

MAGISTRATES' COURTS

retirement in that they cease to be entitled to exercise judicial functions. Magistrates may be put on the supplemental list before that age either at their own request or on the ground of 'age, infirmity or other like cause' or neglect of judicial duties.

Usually, a magistrates' court is composed of three lay magistrates, the maximum permitted number. The normal minimum number of lay magistrates who must comprise the bench is two. The most important exception is that one lay magistrate can conduct committal proceedings in his capacity of examining magistrate. Stipendiary magistrates sit alone and have all the powers of two lay magistrates in a magistrates' court. Some of the powers of a single lay magistrate may be exercised by the clerk to the magistrates.

There are 600 magistrates' courts in England and Wales. Magistrates' courts have jurisdiction in both criminal and civil matters. Their summary procedure is inexpensive and speedy but their jurisdiction only extends to matters of minor importance compared with that of the other courts of trial in the court system.

1   The principal statute governing the constitution and jurisdiction of magistrates' courts is the Magistrates' Courts Act 1980.
2   Para 3.14, below.

Criminal jurisdiction
3.3   There are two methods of trying persons accused of criminal offences. One is by judge and jury in the Crown Court after committal for trial on a written accusation of crime called an indictment; the other is summary trial by a magistrates' court without a jury. Over 95% of criminal cases are tried summarily. Magistrates' courts have two functions:

a.   That of a court of summary jurisdiction or petty sessions, which hears and determines cases, subject to appeal. Not only do magistrates' courts deal summarily with those minor offences which are defined in the statute creating them as summary offences (offences which are only triable in a magistrates' court) but they may also try offences which are 'triable either way' (either in a magistrates' court or on indictment in the Crown Court) with the consent of the accused. Magistrates cannot impose a sentence in excess of six months' imprisonment, except that they may impose consecutive sentences up to a total of 12 months if the accused has been convicted of more than one offence triable either way. In the case of an either way offence, they can commit an offender for sentence to the Crown Court if these powers are inadequate.
b.   That of examining magistrates by whom committal proceedings are held as a necessary preliminary, in almost all cases, to a trial by jury in the Crown Court. The function of examining magistrates is different from that when they sit to hear and determine a case. All they have to decide is whether on paper there is evidence from the prosecution upon which a reasonable jury properly directed could convict. It matters not that the magistrates themselves would not have convicted on the evidence before

them. The magistrates' function as examining magistrates can be carried out by a single justice, or in certain circumstances by a justices' clerk or a duly authorised member of his staff if the accused is legally represented and the legal representative does not claim that there is insufficient evidence to commit[1]. The system acts as a filter so that persons against whom there is no evidence upon which a reasonable jury could convict are spared the anxiety and expense of a trial. If the magistrates decide that there is no prima facie case against the accused, they decline to commit him for trial and discharge him.

1 Justices' Clerks Rules 1970, rr 3 and 4 and Sch 1.

3.4 A person convicted by a magistrates' court may appeal to the Crown Court against conviction, or against sentence, or against both, except that if he pleaded guilty he may appeal to the Crown Court against sentence only. An alternative avenue of appeal is to appeal to a divisional court of the Queen's Bench Division. This is open to the prosecution or the defence, or to any other party to a proceeding before a magistrates' court, if aggrieved with the determination of the magistrates as being wrong in law or in excess of jurisdiction. This type of appeal is solely concerned with questions of law or jurisdiction, but for practical reasons it is usually the preferable course to adopt when the appeal is founded on such questions alone.

Civil jurisdiction
3.5 This is very varied. It extends over the recovery of certain civil debts, such as income tax; the grant and renewal of licences; and 'family proceedings'.

'Family proceedings' are the most important aspect of the civil jurisdiction of magistrates' courts. They are dealt with by magistrates sitting as a 'family proceedings court'. Magistrates in these courts are drawn from special 'family proceedings panels'. Family proceedings heard by magistrates in a family proceedings court include proceedings for maintenance orders for the complainant spouse on proof that the defendant spouse has failed to provide reasonable maintenance for the complainant spouse or a child of the family. In such proceedings the magistrates may also make orders concerning the separation of the spouses. Family proceedings courts also have powers under a number of statutes to make orders as to whom a child should live with and as to the care or supervision of a child under 17. They may also make adoption orders.

When hearing family proceedings, a magistrates' court must include, so far as practicable, both a man and a woman. Unless the court otherwise directs, only the officers of the court, the parties to the case and their legal representatives, witnesses, and news reporters may attend. There are strict limitations on the particulars which may be published in a news report of family proceedings.

3.6 Appeals in civil proceedings in magistrates' courts generally lie to the Crown Court with a further (or alternative) appeal on a point of law to the Queen's Bench Division of the High Court by case stated, except that in family proceedings appeal is to the Family Division and there is no alternative of appeal to the Crown Court.

Youth courts
3.7 Generally, someone aged under 18 who is charged with a criminal offence must be tried in a youth court.

The bench in a youth court consists of magistrates from a special panel. The bench must consist of three magistrates, of whom at least one must be female and one male. There are restrictions similar to those which apply in a family proceedings court in relation to attendance and news reporting. Appeal from a youth court lies to the Crown Court with a further (or alternative) appeal by case stated on point of law to a divisional court of the Queen's Bench Division.

County courts
3.8 The jurisdiction of the county courts is exclusively civil. There are some 270 county courts in England and Wales, of which about 75 are trial centres providing facilities for the continuous hearing of cases lasting more than one day. Each trial centre takes in the more substantial cases from a number of satellite courts.

The full jurisdiction of the county courts is typically exercised by circuit judges. Circuit judges are appointed by the Queen on the recommendation of the Lord Chancellor to serve in the Crown Court[1] and in the county courts, and to carry out such other judicial functions as may be conferred on them. There are about 420 circuit judges. Generally, only circuit judges specifically assigned for the purpose sit in county courts. Those qualified to be a circuit judge are:

a. people who for ten years have had a right of audience in relation to all proceedings in the Crown Court or to all proceedings in county courts;
b. recorders; and
c. provided that they have held the appointment on a full-time basis for three years, district judges, stipendiary magistrates and certain other people exercising a judicial function[2].

Circuit judges retire at 72, or 70 if appointed on or after March 31 1995, although in either case the Lord Chancellor can extend a circuit judge's appointment by one year at a time until he is 75 if the Lord Chancellor thinks that this is in the public interest. A circuit judge can be dismissed by the Lord Chancellor on grounds of incapacity or misbehaviour[3]. Since the circuit judiciary was established in 1971, only one circuit judge has been dismissed, and that was after he had been convicted of smuggling.

To reduce delay in the administration of justice, the Lord Chancellor can appoint deputy circuit judges on a temporary basis. Deputy circuit judges can exercise the full jurisdiction of a county court judge, and so can two other types of judge, recorders and assistant recorders. Recorders and assistant recorders are part-time judges appointed by the Lord Chancellor. The duration of their appointment and the grounds on which they may be dismissed are similar to those for a circuit judge. The only people who can be appointed as a recorder or assistant recorder are those who for ten years have had rights of audience in relation to all proceedings in the Crown Court or all proceedings in county courts. There are over 750 recorders and 420 assistant recorders.

Currently, only barristers and solicitors can satisfy any of the requirements for appointment as a circuit judge, recorder or assistant recorder.

There are also some 230 district judges, appointed and removable by the Lord Chancellor. There are also a substantial number of part-time deputy district judges[4]. To be appointed as a district judge (or a deputy district judge, hereafter the term 'district judge' includes a deputy), a person must for seven years have had a right of audience in relation to any class of proceedings in the Supreme Court[5], or all proceedings in county courts or magistrates' courts. Currently, only barristers and solicitors can satisfy this requirement. District judges deal with the interlocutory work of the county courts and also have jurisdiction to try claims not exceeding £5,000 in value (although normally a claim for less than £3,000 will be referred to arbitration, as we show in para 3.13, below). In addition, by leave of a judge of the court and with the consent of the parties, a district judge may try any other action. A district judge has the full jurisdiction of a circuit judge in all undefended actions. An appeal lies from a district judge to a circuit judge.

1 Paras 3.21–3.23, below.
2 In practice, a person will not be appointed a circuit judge unless he is a recorder.
3 Courts Act 1971, ss 16 and 17; Judicial Pensions and Retirement Act 1993, s 26.
4 In practice, a person will not be appointed a district judge unless he is a deputy district judge.
5 Para 3.14, below.

Jurisdiction
3.9 Under the provisions of the County Courts Act 1984, county courts have jurisdiction over a wide range of civil matters. This jurisdiction includes:

a. Jurisdiction over actions in contract or tort, except defamation, or for money recoverable by statute. A county court has jurisdiction over defamation if the parties agree to accept its jurisdiction or if the High Court transfers the case to it.

    An action in contract or tort may be *commenced* in a county court or the High Court, save that a personal injury claim must be commenced in a county court unless the value of the action is £50,000 or more.

    An action of which the value is less than £25,000 must be *tried* in a county court unless:

    i.   where the action was commenced in a county court, the county court considers that it ought to be transferred to the High Court (and the High Court agrees), having regard to:

        a   the importance of the action and, in particular, whether it raises questions of importance to people who are not parties or questions of public importance;

    b   the complexity of the action;
    c   the financial substance of the action, including the value of a
        counterclaim; and
    d   whether a transfer will result in a speedier trial (although a transfer
        will not be ordered on this ground alone); or
  ii. the case commenced in the the High Court and the High Court, having
     regard to the above criteria, considers that it ought to try the action.

An action whose value is £50,000[1] or more must be *tried* in the High
Court unless:

  a. it is commenced in a county court and the county court, having regard
     to the above criteria, considers that the action ought not to be
     transferred to the High Court; or
  b. where it is commenced in the High Court, the High Court, having
     regard to the same criteria as above, considers that it ought to transfer
     the action to a county court for trial.

In other words, there is a rebuttable presumption that actions whose value
is less than £25,000 will be tried in a county court, and those whose value
is £50,000[1] or more in the High Court.

b. An equity jurisdiction, eg in cases of administration of estates, foreclosure
    of mortgages and specific performance of contracts for the sale of land,
    where the amount of the estate, the amount owing under the mortgage or
    purchase price, as the case may be, does not exceed £30,000.

1 £200,000 in respect of a case listed in the Business List at the Central London County
  Court: County Court Rules 1981, Order 48C. Cases in this list are more complex commercial
  cases transferred from county courts in the south east of England.

3.10 Types of county court jurisdiction under other statutes include:

a. (in designated courts) divorce, separation and annulment of marriage cases
    and proceedings ancillary to them (eg for financial provision);
b. (in designated courts) care, guardianship and adoption of children;
    contested cases can only be heard at designated family hearing centres;
c. (in designated courts) domestic violence;
d. bankruptcy;
e. proceedings under the Rent, Landlord and Tenant, Housing and Consumer
    Credit Acts; and
f. (in the Patents County Court sitting in the Central London County Court)
    proceedings relating to patents and registered designs.

3.11 The procedure in the county courts is simpler, speedier and less costly
than in the High Court. To discourage the conduct of minor litigation in the
High Court which could have been brought in a county court, the fact that a
party has commenced proceedings in the High Court on a matter falling within
the county courts' jurisdiction may be taken into account when the amount of
his costs (if he has succeeded in his action) is determined and may lead to a
lower award of costs than otherwise[1].

1 Supreme Court Act 1981, s 51.

3.12   Appeal from a county court judge lies to the Court of Appeal (subject to certain conditions), except in a few cases, such as bankruptcy, where appeals are heard by a single judge of the High Court.

Small claims[1]

3.13   A defended action[2] in the county court must be referred to arbitration if the sum claimed or amount involved is not in excess of £3,000 (or £1,000 in the case of a personal injury claim). If referral to arbitration occurs the hearing takes place before an arbitrator, generally in private, without the formalities associated with a trial. The arbitrator will usually be a district judge, but a party may apply for the appointment of any other suitable person. A referral to arbitration of a claim not in excess of the relevant limit may be rescinded by a district judge, on the application of a party, if the parties are agreed that the case should be tried in court, or if the case involves a difficult question of law or of fact or an allegation of fraud, or if it would otherwise be unreasonable for the claim to proceed to arbitration, having regard to its subject matter, the size of any counter-claim, the parties' circumstances or the interests of any party likely to be affected by the award.

   If the amount in dispute exceeds the relevant limit the matter can still be referred to arbitration if the parties agree to this or if one of the parties does not object to a district judge deciding the application for arbitration. If a party does object, a judge of the court can decide whether the case should be dealt with by arbitration.

   The award of the arbitrator is entered as a judgment in the court proceedings, and is binding as such. A judge of the court has power, on application, to set the award aside.

   The advantage of the arbitration procedure is that it is eminently suitable for the litigant in person in small claims cases, which are mainly 'consumer disputes', since it is even more informal and inexpensive than trial in the county court. The arbitration may take place round a table and the oath may not be administered. The arbitrator is responsible for helping the parties by putting questions to them, if necessary. Legal representation is discouraged by the fact that, contrary to the usual rule, a successful party cannot normally recover the costs of legal representation from his opponent. Formality is kept to the minimum necessary to protect the interests of each party.

1   County Courts Act 1984, s 64; County Court Rules 1981.
2   Actions for possession of land are excluded from the automatic referral to arbitration regime.

The High Court of Justice

3.14   The High Court is part of the Supreme Court of Judicature, the Crown Court and the Court of Appeal being the other two constituent parts. The High Court was established by the Judicature Acts 1873–1875, replacing the separate Courts of Chancery, Queen's Bench, Common Pleas, and Exchequer, and also the Courts of Admiralty, Probate, and Matrimonial Causes.

   For historical reasons, and to ensure the resolution of disputes by judges with the relevant expertise[1], the High Court consists of three divisions, each of which has a separate jurisdiction. Although High Court judges are assigned to a particular division according to their expertise, they are judges of the High Court and can exercise any jurisdiction appertaining to a High Court judge, irrespective of the division to which they have been assigned[2].

High Court judges are appointed by the Queen on the recommendation of the Lord Chancellor. Those qualified for appointment are persons who have for ten years had a right of audience in relation to all proceedings in the High Court (currently only barristers and some solicitors[3] can have this right) or who have been a circuit judge for at least two years[4]. To reduce delay, the Lord Chancellor can appoint deputy High Court judges on a temporary basis. Because of the shortage of High Court judges, a significant number of cases, mainly in the Queen's Bench Division, are heard by deputy High Court judges.

A High Court judge has greater security of tenure than a circuit judge since he is only removable on an address presented by both Houses of Parliament to the Queen, except that the Lord Chancellor may, with the concurrence of senior judges, declare vacant the office of a judge who is subject to permanent medical incapacity and is unable to tender his resignation[5]. No High Court judge has been removed in modern times. High Court judges appointed before 31 March 1995 must retire on attaining the age of 75. Those first appointed to judicial office on or after that date must retire on reaching 70[6]. Like any other retired judge, a retired High Court judge can be invited to sit as a judge on an ad hoc basis, in the courts in which he could have sat before retirement, up to the age of 75[6].

Some cases in the High Court are heard by one of eight official referees or an 'official referee recorder'. An official referee is a circuit judge specially assigned to official referee work. Official referee's business includes any Chancery or Queen's Bench cause or matter:

a.   which involves a prolonged examination of documents or accounts, or technical, scientific or local investigation, such as could more conveniently be conducted by an official referee; or

b.   for which trial by an official referee is desirable in the interests of one or more of the parties on grounds of expedition, economy or convenience or otherwise.

The majority of official referee cases come from the construction industry and concern architects, engineers, surveyors, contractors, house-builders, developers and others involved in that industry.

1   This latter reason was doubted by the Court of Appeal in *Barclays Bank plc v Bemister* [1989] 1 All ER 10, [1989] 1 WLR 128, on the ground that nowadays judges have acquired sufficient expertise before appointment to enable them to handle a wide range of High Court work across divisional boundaries.

2   See *Re Hastings (No 3)* [1959] Ch 368, [1959] 1 All ER 698; *Re Kray* [1965] Ch 736, [1965] 1 All ER 710; *Re L* [1968] P 119, [1968] 1 All ER 20, CA.

3   Para 3.58, below.

4   Supreme Court Act 1981, s 10.

5   Supreme Court Act 1981, s 11.

6   Ibid; Judicial Pensions and Retirement Act 1993, s 26.

Chancery Division
3.15   The Chancery Division consists of the Lord Chancellor, as its nominal head, although he never sits at first instance, a Vice-Chancellor, and, at present, 14 judges. The jurisdiction of the Chancery Division is exercised in London and seven provincial towns.

There are six masters of the Chancery Division. To be appointed as a Chancery master, a person must have had for seven years a right of audience in relation to any class of proceedings in the Supreme Court, or all proceedings in county courts or magistrates' courts. Currently, only barristers and solicitors can satisfy this requirement. Applications are made to the masters in chambers in the preliminary stages of litigation, and they make orders thereon in the name of the judge to whom they are assigned. Complicated accounts and inquiries are also referred to them. If a party is not satisfied with the master's ruling, he may adjourn the matter to a Chancery judge.

Masters of the Chancery Division are based at the Royal Courts of Justice in London. Elsewhere district judges at designated county courts which also operate as district registries of the High Court perform similar functions to those performed by a master of the Chancery Division.

3.16   The jurisdiction of the Chancery Division is entirely civil and can be split into original and appellate jurisdictions.

a. *Original jurisdiction*   By virtue of s 61 and Sch 1 of the Supreme Court Act 1981, jurisdiction over a number of matters is assigned to the Chancery Division. These include:
  i.   the administration of estates of deceased persons;
  ii.   the execution of trusts;
  iii. the redemption and foreclosure of mortgages;
  iv.   the rectification and cancellation of deeds;
  v.   partnership actions;
  vi.   bankruptcy;
  vii. the sale, exchange or partition of land, or the raising of charges on land;
  viii. all causes and matters under enactments relating to companies; and
  ix.   proceedings relating to patents and registered designs (which are heard by specialist judges in the Patents Court).
As can be seen, there is some concurrence between the Chancery Division's original jurisdiction and some of the heads of jurisdiction possessed by the county courts (save for the financial limits which apply, for example, to their equity jurisdiction).

b. *Appellate jurisdiction*   This is much more limited. Certain statutes empower a single judge to hear appeals of various kinds, eg income tax appeals from the Commissioners of Inland Revenue and bankruptcy appeals from a county court.

Queen's Bench Division
3.17   This division is the largest of the three divisions and has the most varied jurisdiction. Its head is the Lord Chief Justice. At present, 55 judges are assigned

to it. The original civil jurisdiction of this division is exercised in first-tier Crown Court centres[1], as well as in London.

There are nine masters of the Queen's Bench Division. The qualification for appointment is the same as for a Chancery master. Masters of the Queen's Bench Division supervise the Central Office of the Supreme Court in which official documents are issued and registered. Applications are made to a master in chambers in the preliminary stages of litigation in the Queen's Bench Division, appeal lying from his order to a judge. Masters of the Queen's Bench Division are based in London. Outside London, their functions are carried out by district judges at district registries.

1 Para 3.21, below.

3.18 The jurisdiction of the Queen's Bench Division can be divided into four heads, the first of which is the busiest:

a. *Original civil jurisdiction* The principal aspects of this are actions in contract and tort. Commercial matters are dealt with by six specialist judges in the Commercial Court which sits in London, and whose procedure is more flexible than the normal High Court procedure. Traditionally, cases in the Commercial Court were dealt with more speedily than elsewhere in the High Court. The success of the Commercial Court has meant that it has become inundated with work. Because of this, cases can take as long to get to trial as elsewhere, or even longer. To avoid the cost and inconvenience of advocates having to travel to London, commercial cases are also heard by specialist circuit judges in the Mercantile Courts which sit in Birmingham, Bristol, Leeds, Liverpool, Manchester and Newcastle and can hear any commercial dispute – other than one relating to land and certain company regulatory matters.

b. *Appellate civil jurisdiction* A single judge (or, if the High Court's decision is final, a divisional court) has jurisdiction to hear appeals from certain tribunals and certain other appeals. In addition, a single judge (or, if the court so directs, a divisional court) hears appeals by way of case stated on a miscellaneous collection of civil matters from magistrates' courts (excluding family proceedings), the Crown Court and certain other bodies. A divisional court consists of two or more judges, increasingly two, of whom one will normally be the Lord Chief Justice or a Lord Justice of Appeal (a member of the Court of Appeal). An appeal by case stated must be on the ground that the determination or decision is wrong in law or is in excess of jurisdiction. The case is not reheard, the judge or court merely hearing legal argument.

c. *Appellate criminal jurisdiction* A divisional court hears appeals in criminal matters by case stated from magistrates' courts and the Crown Court (in that court's appellate capacity)[1]. The appeal must be on the same ground, and is conducted in the same way, as in b. above.

d. *Supervisory jurisdiction* The most important aspects of this are the jurisdiction to issue the writ of habeas corpus and the jurisdiction on an application for judicial review to make 'prerogative orders' against magistrates' courts, county courts, the Crown Court (except in matters relating to trial on indictment)[1], tribunals and other decision-making bodies of a public nature, such as local authorities[2].

The prerogative orders are mandamus, prohibition and certiorari. An order of mandamus is used to compel the body to whom it is directed to carry out a definite public duty imposed on it by law. The order cannot be used to compel the body to exercise its discretion in a particular way, but it may be used to compel it to hear and determine a case, or to state a case for the opinion of the High Court[3]. An order of prohibition or certiorari will issue only in relation to an order or decision of a body which is under a public duty to 'act judicially' or 'act fairly' in making that decision, as opposed to purely administratively. This does not mean that prohibition and certiorari issue only to courts or tribunals, for many other bodies, such as local authorities, may sometimes be required to act judicially, and in other cases are required to act fairly. The order of prohibition is used to *prevent* such a body from acting in excess of jurisdiction or otherwise acting improperly. The order of certiorari covers much the same area but *after* such a body has done something and it is desired to review it and, if necessary, quash it on the ground of excess of jurisdiction, denial of natural justice, or error of law on the face of the record. Natural justice will be denied if a party is not given a chance to state his case, or if the case is heard by a person who is a judge in his own cause.

In addition, on an application for judicial review, the court may grant a declaration as to the legality of an administrative action or decision, and it may award damages in appropriate cases.

Applications for judicial review in civil cases are heard by a single judge, unless the court directs a hearing by a divisional court. Applications for judicial review in criminal cases are heard by a divisional court, as are applications for habeas corpus.

1   Supreme Court Act 1981, s 29(3); para 3.22, below.
2   In contrast, the supervisory jurisdiction does not extend to arbitrations in pursuance of an agreement out of court, which we discuss in paras 3.39–3.48, below: *Bremer Vulkan Schiffbau und Maschinenfabrik v South India Shipping Corpn Ltd* [1981] AC 909, [1981] 1 All ER 289, HL.
3   Magistrates' Courts Act 1980, s 111(6).

Family Division
3.19   The Family Division consists of the President of the Division and, at present, 16 judges. The jurisdiction of this division is entirely civil, and is exercised in London and at first-tier Crown Court centres. It can be divided into original and appellate jurisdictions:

a. *Original jurisdiction*   The division deals with all aspects of family law; the following are the most important examples:

i.   on transfer from a county court, proceedings for divorce, separation or annulment of marriage and ancillary relief (eg financial provision) connected therewith;

ii.   proceedings for the determination of title to property in dispute between spouses;

iii.   proceedings concerning the occupation of the matrimonial home and/or the exclusion of a violent spouse;

iv.   wardship of court, guardianship and adoption proceedings.

The Family Division has exclusive jurisdiction in wardship. Otherwise, it has concurrent jurisdiction with county courts and, in some cases, with magistrates' courts in relation to family proceedings.

b. *Appellate jurisdiction*   This is principally concerned with appeals from the decisions of magistrates' courts sitting as family proceedings courts[1]. Some such appeals, eg against the making of a maintenance order, must be heard by a divisional court composed of two or more judges, but others, for example, appeals against the making of a care order, will be heard by a single judge unless the court directs a hearing by a divisional court. Appeals of the second type are by case stated.

1   Para 3.5, above.

3.20   Appeals from the original jurisdiction of any division of the High Court lie to the Court of Appeal (Civil Division), as do appeals from the appellate jurisdiction of any division[1], save that appeals from the criminal appellate jurisdiction of a divisional court of the Queen's Bench Division go straight to the House of Lords.

1   But note the 'leap-frogging' exception mentioned at para 3.28, below.

The Crown Court
3.21   The jurisdiction and powers of the Crown Court are exercised by:

a.   any judge of the High Court;
b.   any circuit judge;
c.   any recorder[1]; and
d.   in some circumstances any judge of the High Court, circuit judge or recorder sitting with lay magistrates.

In this paragraph, references to circuit judges and recorders include deputy circuit judges and assistant recorders.

The Crown Court in England and Wales is divided into six circuits, in which there are a total of 90 court centres. The court centres in each circuit are divided into first-tier, second-tier and third-tier centres. The first- and second-tier centres are served by High Court and circuit judges and by recorders; the distinction between the two centres is that in the former sittings of the High Court are held for civil cases[2] as well as of the Crown Court for criminal cases. Like the second-tier centres, third-tier centres are limited to Crown Court work but they are only served by circuit judges and recorders with the result that a few very serious offences, such as murder, cannot be tried at them.

Lay magistrates cannot act as judges of the Crown Court by themselves but only with a High Court or circuit judge or with a recorder. They must form part of the Crown Court when it hears appeals from magistrates' courts and also when it is sentencing persons who have been committed for sentence by magistrates' courts, but the Lord Chancellor has power to dispense with this requirement. The number of magistrates so sitting must be not less than two nor more than four[3]. Rulings on questions of law are for the judge but decisions on other questions, eg sentence, are the product of all members of the court.

1   See para 3.8, above, in relation to these apppointments.
2   Paras 3.15–3.19, above.
3   Supreme Court Act 1981, s 74.

Criminal jurisdiction
3.22   The Crown Court has exclusive jurisdiction over all offences tried by jury on indictment, an appeal by a convicted person lying to the Court of Appeal.
The Crown Court also has jurisdiction:

a.   to deal with convicted persons committed for sentence by magistrates' courts because their sentencing powers are inadequate; and
b.   to hear appeals from magistrates' courts, including youth courts, against conviction or sentence. An appeal to the Crown Court against conviction takes the form of a full re-hearing of the case, ie the case is tried all over again, witnesses being called, etc. Where the Crown Court has given its decision on an appeal from a magistrates' court against conviction or sentence, either the prosecution or the defence, if dissatisfied with the determination of the Crown Court as being wrong in law or in excess of jurisdiction, may appeal to a divisional court of the Queen's Bench Division by way of case stated.

Juries are not used in the Crown Court when it deals with persons committed for sentence or with appeals.

Civil jurisdiction
3.23   The civil jurisdiction of the Crown Court is far less important. It is principally concerned with betting, gaming and liquor licensing appeals, but other appeals within its jurisdiction are appeals from various administrative decisions made by local authorities.

The Court of Appeal
3.24   The Court of Appeal is composed of the Master of the Rolls, the Lord Chief Justice, the President of the Family Division, the Vice-Chancellor and, at present, 35 Lords Justice of Appeal (which is the permitted maximum). Lords Justice are appointed by the Queen on the recommendation of the Prime Minister who acts on the advice of the Lord Chancellor. They must have been judges of the High Court or for ten years have had a right of audience in relation to all

proceedings in the High Court[1]. The tenure of office for Lords Justice is the same as for High Court judges[2]. Any High Court judge may be required to sit in the Court of Appeal if this is necessary[3]. The Court of Appeal is divided into a civil and a criminal division. The Master of the Rolls is the President of the Civil Division, and the Lord Chief Justice of the Criminal Division[4].

1 Supreme Court Act 1981, s 10. See para 3.14, above, in relation to this requirement.
2 Para 3.14, above.
3 Supreme Court Act 1981, s 9.
4 Ibid, s 3.

Court of Appeal (Civil Division)
3.25 This hears appeals from:

a. The decisions in civil matters of all three divisions of the High Court[1]. In some cases, leave to appeal is required from the Court of Appeal or the court appealed from. An example is an appeal from the determination of an appeal by a divisional court.
b. The decisions of a county court judge, save for a few exceptions (such as bankruptcy) where appeal lies to the High Court. In actions in contract or tort, and in certain other cases, the leave of the county court judge or of the Court of Appeal is required if the amount of the claim does not exceed a prescribed limit ($£5,000$ in the case of contract or tort[2]).
c. The decisions of the Restrictive Practices Court and, with the leave of the Court of Appeal or of the tribunal, from decisions of the Employment Appeal Tribunal and certain other tribunals[3].

Except in the case of certain appeals from tribunals and appeals from the Restrictive Practices Court (which are by case stated), the method of appeal is by way of re-hearing. This means that the court reviews the whole case from the shorthand notes of the trial and the judge's notes and in the light of the legal argument: it does not mean that the witnesses heard in the trial court are re-called, nor that fresh evidence will normally be admitted. Since the Court of Appeal does not have the advantage of seeing the trial witnesses and observing their demeanour, it does not normally upset direct findings of fact (as opposed to inferences from the facts).

Generally, a civil appeal must be heard by three members of the Court of Appeal. However, in certain cases, such as appeals from a county court, an appeal may be heard by two members. A single judge may, and normally does, determine an application for leave to appeal and deal with other matters arising incidentally. The division may be sitting simultaneously in as many as ten courts. While most appeals are on points of law, an appeal may be against a finding of fact or the exercise of a discretion by the trial judge or against the damages which have been awarded, except in the case of appeals by case stated.

1 In a few cases the High Court's decision on a procedural point is final, which means that it cannot be appealed to the Court of Appeal.
2 County Courts Act 1984, s 77; County Courts Appeals Order 1991.
3 Paras 3.34 and 3.36, below.

Court of Appeal (Criminal Division)
3.26   The Criminal Division hears appeals from persons convicted in the Crown Court on indictment. The convicted person may appeal against conviction or against sentence, unless the sentence is one fixed by law[1]. An appeal requires the leave of the Court of Appeal or a certificate from the trial judge that the case is fit for appeal[1].

In the case of an appeal against conviction, the court must allow the appeal if it thinks that the conviction was unsafe, otherwise it will dismiss the appeal[2]. On appeal against sentence, the court may reduce it or vary it, provided that in the result the appellant is not dealt with more severely than he was in the court below[3].

Although the prosecution has no right of appeal against an acquittal on indictment, the Attorney-General may refer to the Court of Appeal a point of law arising at a trial on indictment where the accused was acquitted[4]. The Court of Appeal's opinion does not affect the acquittal but provides authoritative guidance on the point for the future. Likewise, although the prosecution cannot appeal against a sentence imposed by the Crown Court, in certain cases the Attorney-General may refer such a sentence imposed by the Crown Court to the Court of Appeal with its leave if it appears to him to be unduly lenient[5]. On such a reference, the court may impose a more severe sentence.

This division normally sits in at least three, and on occasions as many as six, courts: one composed of the Lord Chief Justice and two judges of the Queen's Bench Division, and the others of a Lord Justice and two Queen's Bench judges. A circuit judge, especially approved for this purpose by the Lord Chancellor, may also sit as a judge of the Criminal Division in most cases[6]. Very occasionally, when it is necessary to resolve a conflict between Court of Appeal decisions, a five-judge court will hear the case. By way of exception to the general requirement that criminal appeals must be heard by three judges, a two-judge court may hear an appeal against sentence[7]. A single judge (other than an approved circuit judge[7]) may deal with applications for leave to appeal and perform certain other incidental functions.

1   Criminal Appeal Act 1968, ss 1, 9–11.
2   Ibid, s 2.
3   Ibid, s 11.
4   Criminal Justice Act 1972, s 36.
5   Criminal Justice Act 1988, s 36.
6   Supreme Court Act 1981, s 9.
7   Ibid, s 55.

The House of Lords
3.27   While the House of Lords has original jurisdiction over disputed claims to peerages and breaches of privilege, such as contempt of the House or wrongs committed within its precincts, this is of minor importance compared with its appellate jurisdiction. The House of Lords' appellate jurisdiction is discharged by its Appellate Committee. The Appellate Jurisdiction Act 1876 provides that at the hearing of an appeal there must be present at least three of the following – the Lord Chancellor, the Lords of Appeal in Ordinary and such peers who hold or have held high judicial office (for example, ex-Lord Chancellors).

Normally, five Lords of Appeal in Ordinary hear an appeal and by convention peers other than the above do not attend meetings of the Appellate Committee. Lords of Appeal in Ordinary (commonly called 'Law Lords', and not to be confused with Lords Justice of Appeal[1]) must have held high judicial office for two years or for 15 years have had rights of audience in relation to all proceedings in the Supreme Court[2]. Lords of Appeal are appointed by the Queen on the advice of the Prime Minister, who acts on the advice of the Lord Chancellor. They have the same security of tenure and retirement age as High Court judges[3]. At present there are 12 Lords of Appeal in Ordinary (which is the permitted maximum). Normally, one or two of the Lords of Appeal are appointed from Scotland. Unless the Lord Chancellor is sitting, the proceedings of the Appellate Committee are presided over by one or other of two senior Lords of Appeal nominated for this purpose by him. The House of Lords has both a civil and a criminal appellate jurisdiction.

1 Para 3.24, above.
2 Appellate Jurisdiction Act 1876, s 6.
3 Para 3.14, above.

Civil appellate jurisdiction

3.28 The House of Lords hears:

a. Appeals from the Court of Appeal (Civil Division), provided that leave has been granted by that Court or by the House.
b. 'Leap-frog' appeals from the High Court. To save cost and delay, the Administration of Justice Act 1969 provides that in most civil cases appeal may be made direct from the High Court to the House of Lords. This procedure may only be used where:
   i.   the parties agree to it;
   ii. the High Court judge grants a certificate to sanction it (which he may do only if he is satisfied that a point of law is involved which is of general public importance and which either relates to a matter of construction of an Act – or of a statutory instrument – or else is one in respect of which he considers that he is 'bound' by a decision of the Court of Appeal or of the House of Lords); and
   iii. the House of Lords gives leave to appeal.
The 'leap-frog' procedure is used in comparatively few cases.

The House of Lords will not generally interfere with findings of fact on which the trial judge and appellate court are agreed, unless it can be shown that both courts were clearly wrong[1].

1 *Hicks v Chief Constable of the South Yorkshire Police* [1992] 2 All ER 65, HL.

Criminal appellate jurisdiction
3.29 The House of Lords can hear an appeal by either the prosecution or the accused from the determination of an appeal by the Court of Appeal

(Criminal Division) or by a divisional court of the Queen's Bench Division provided:

a.   the court below (ie the Court of Appeal or divisional court) has certified that a point of law of general public importance is involved and that court or the House of Lords is satisfied that the point of law is one which ought to be considered by the House; and
b.   either the court or the House of Lords has granted leave to appeal[1].

As can be seen, an appeal to the House of Lords on a question of fact is not possible in a criminal case.

1   Criminal Appeal Act 1968, s 33.

The Court of Justice of the European Communities (European Court)

3.30   The European Court operates under the Treaties establishing the European Communities. The court consists of 15 judges and is assisted by nine Advocates-General, a type of official unknown to English law. The duty of an Advocate-General is, with complete impartiality and independence, to make reasoned submissions in open court on cases brought before the court in order to assist it in the performance of its functions. The Court sits in plenary session, ie as a 'court' (generally consisting of 11 judges), unless the decision has been made to hear the case in a 'chamber' of three or five judges.

Judges and Advocates-General are appointed for six-year periods by the governments of member states acting in agreement and are eligible for reappointment. They are chosen from those who fulfil the conditions required for the holding of the highest judicial office in their respective countries or who are jurisconsults (persons learned in the law) of recognised competence.

Before 1973 the House of Lords was the final court of appeal in all cases in this country, but the accession of the United Kingdom to membership of the European Community meant that the European Court became the ultimate court (ie its decisions are binding on the House of Lords and other United Kingdom courts[1]) *in matters within its jurisdiction*. Nevertheless, in the great majority of cases arising within the United Kingdom the House of Lords remains the ultimate court. The fundamental point that the treaties under which the European Court operates are concerned only with those matters which have a European element must be firmly grasped in order to understand the relationship of the European Court to the rest of our legal system[2].

1   *Litster v Forth Dry Dock and Engineering Co Ltd* [1990] 1 AC 546, [1989] 1 All ER 1134, HL.
2   See *H P Bulmer Ltd v J Bollinger SA* [1974] Ch 401, [1974] 2 All ER 1226, CA.

Jurisdiction
3.31   The jurisdiction of the European Court can be divided into the following principal categories:

a. Matters concerning the conduct of member states or of the institutions of the Community, such as:
   i. the hearing of complaints brought by member states or by the Commission of the European Community that a member state has failed to fulfil its obligations under the treaties;
   ii. the review of the legality of the regulations, directives and decisions of the Council (of Ministers) of the European Union and of the Commission;
   iii. the hearing of disputes between member states which relate to the subject matter of the Treaties, provided the states in question agree.

b. Matters of direct concern to litigants or prospective litigants in a member state which have been referred for a preliminary ruling by the European Court under art 177 of the European Economic Community Treaty by a court in a member state. The European Court may give a preliminary ruling on three matters:
   i. on the interpretation of the European Economic Community Treaty;
   ii. on the validity and interpretation of the regulations, directives, decisions and other acts of the institutions of the European Community or the European Central Bank;
   iii. on the interpretation of certain statutes of bodies established by an act of the Council.

The essence of a preliminary ruling is that it should precede the judgment of the referring court. Accordingly, once the domestic court has given judgment, it cannot make a reference under art 177[1].

Where a question of the type referred to in b. is raised before any court or tribunal of a member state, the court or tribunal *may*, if it considers that a decision on the question is necessary to enable it to give judgment, refer the matter to the European Court for a ruling. However, where any such question is raised in a case pending before a court or tribunal of a member state, against whose decisions there is no judicial remedy under national law, that court or tribunal *must* generally refer the matter to the European Court for a ruling. This provision refers to the House of Lords where an appeal lies to the House of Lords, despite the fact that its leave to appeal is required if the necessary leave has not been given by the court below[1]. On the other hand, it appears that, where there is no right of appeal at all from a lower court to a higher court in respect of the matter in issue, that court is the court of 'last resort'[1]. The obligation to refer just mentioned does not apply if the question raised is not relevant to the outcome of the proceedings, or if it has already been answered in a previous ruling of the European Court, or if the correct interpretation of the Community law is so obvious as to leave no reasonable doubt[2].

Where a matter is referred to the European Court for a preliminary ruling, only the request for interpretation or decision on validity is referred. The case itself is not transferred. Consequently, the court making the reference remains seised of it, although its procedure is suspended until the European Court has given its ruling on the reference[3]. The European Court will only give a ruling on a question material to the outcome of the proceedings from which the reference comes. It will not give an opinion on a question merely of a general or hypothetical nature[4].

In terms of the relationship between the European Court and English courts it is important to distinguish between the task of interpreting the treaties, regulations etc – to see what they mean – and the task of *applying* them to the case in hand. The English judges have the final say in applying the treaties, etc; only they are empowered to find the facts and give judgment for one side or the other. However, before they can apply the treaties etc, they have to see what they mean, and in this task of interpretation English judges are not the final authority; the European Court is[5].

The purpose of the preliminary rulings procedure is to ensure uniform interpretation of Community law throughout the Community, without which the Community could not function effectively.

c.   Appeals from the European Court of First Instance.

1   *Chiron Corpn v Murex Diagnostics Ltd (No 8)* [1995] All ER (EC) 88, CA.
2   *CILFIT Srl v Ministry of Health* [1982] ECR 3415, [1983] 1 CMLR 472, ECJ; *Magnavision NV SA v General Optical Council (No 2)* [1987] 2 CMLR 262, DC; *Zabala Erasun v Instituto Nacional de Empleo* [1995] All ER (EC) 758, ECJ.
3   *Zabala Erasun v Instituto Nacional de Empleo* [1995] All ER (EC) 758, ECJ.
4   *Société d'Importation Édouard Leclerc-Siplac v TFI Publicité SA* [1995] All ER (EC) 343, ECJ.
5   See *H P Bulmer Ltd v J Bollinger SA* [1974] Ch 401, [1974] 2 All ER 1226, CA.

European Court of First Instance

3.32   Because of the increasing workload of the European Court, and its increasing inability to deal expeditiously with it, the European Court of First Instance (the Court of First Instance) came into being in the autumn of 1989. The Court of First Instance has 15 judges. It normally sits in chambers of three or five judges.

The Court of First Instance's jurisdiction was designed to relieve the European Court of types of cases, many quite minor, which were taking up an inordinate amount of that court's time. The main areas of the Court of First Instance's jurisdiction are:

a.   over disputes between the Community institutions and their employees (or ex-employees);
b.   over actions for review by the court, and in some cases for compensation, brought against Community measures taken in implementation of competition rules applicable to undertakings.

Appeal on a point of law against decisions of the Court of First Instance may be made to the European Court on grounds of lack of jurisdiction, infringement of Community law by the Court of First Instance or breach of procedure before it. If the European Court allows the appeal, it may give final judgment or it may remit the case to the Court of First Instance, which will be bound by the European Court's decision on points of law.

Specialist Courts and Tribunals

The Judicial Committee of the Privy Council
3.33   The Judicial Committee of the Privy Council is the final court of appeal from the courts of some Commonwealth countries. It also entertains appeals against 'striking-off' from the disciplinary committees of the medical, dental and related professions, and certain other appeals. The Committee is normally composed of five Lords of Appeal, but other Privy Councillors who are holders or past holders of high judicial office in this country or a Commonwealth country may, and do occasionally, sit.

The Restrictive Practices Court
3.34   This court was established by the Restrictive Trade Practices Act 1956, and is now governed by the Restrictive Practices Court Act 1976. The Restrictive Practices Court deals with applications under the Restrictive Trade Practices Act 1976 for the validation of cartel agreements and other restrictive trade practices. The court consists of three High Court judges (of whom one is president of the court), one judge of the Court of Session in Scotland, one judge of the Supreme Court of Northern Ireland, and not more than ten lay members appointed by the Lord Chancellor. Cases are heard by a presiding judge and at least two other members, except that where only an issue of law is involved a case may be heard by a single member who is a judge.

The Court of Protection
3.35   This court, which is an 'office' of the Supreme Court, can assume jurisdiction over the management and administration of the property and affairs of a person who it is satisfied is incapable of managing his property or affairs by reason of mental disorder. Its jurisdiction is conferred by Part VII of the Mental Health Act 1983. Certain orders (eg those authorising proceedings for divorce or the making of a will on the patient's behalf) can only be made by the Lord Chancellor or one of the Chancery judges whom he has nominated to the court. Otherwise, the jurisdiction (including the assumption of responsibility) is, in practice, exercised by the master, deputy master and other officers of the court, subject to appeal to a judge.

The Employment Appeal Tribunal
3.36   This tribunal, established in 1975, is now governed by the Industrial Tribunals Act 1996. It consists of judges from the High Court and Court of Appeal (one of whom is president) nominated by the Lord Chancellor, at least one judge nominated from the Scots Court of Session, and lay members with specialised knowledge of industrial relations. The lay members may be removed by the Lord Chancellor, after consultation with the Secretary of State for Education and Employment, on specified grounds, eg incapacity or misbehaviour. The tribunal has a central office in London but can sit anywhere

in Great Britain, in any number of divisions. It is duly constituted when sitting with a judge and two (or, exceptionally, four) lay members; a judge and one member will suffice if the parties consent.

The tribunal's jurisdiction is entirely appellate. It can hear appeals on points of law from Industrial Tribunals under legislation relating to the following matters: unfair dismissal; redundancy payments; equal pay; sex discrimination; racial discrimination; disability discrimination; contracts of employment; trade unions; and employment protection. In addition, the tribunal can hear appeals on questions of law or fact concerning the certification of a trade union as independent. The tribunal's procedure is designed to be as speedy, informal and simple as possible.

Tribunals

3.37 A large number of different tribunals have been created to deal with particular matters arising under modern legislation, especially social welfare legislation. The function of most administrative tribunals is to enable individual citizens to challenge the administrative decisions of a government department. For example, the Special Commissioners of Income Tax hear appeals against the decisions of the Inland Revenue, and Social Security Appeals Tribunals against social security decisions. Some tribunals, however, adjudicate disputes between individuals; Industrial Tribunals are an example.

Tribunals are usually composed of a legally qualified chairman and lay members. Their hallmarks have traditionally been said to be speed, accessibility, informality, cheapness and freedom from technicality. For these reasons they have been compared favourably with courts. However, there has been concern recently that tribunal procedures can often no longer be described as speedy or free from technicality.

The nature and powers of tribunals vary but they have the common function of determining the facts of a case and deciding it according to law rather than the dictates of policy. In the case of some 'first instance' tribunals there is a right of appeal to an appellate tribunal or to a minister. In addition, there is generally a right of appeal to the High Court, on a question of law only, from the decision of an appellate tribunal or (if there is not such a tribunal) a 'first instance' tribunal. Whether or not there is the possibility of an appeal, a tribunal's decision may be challenged by applying to the High Court for judicial review (which we mentioned in para 3.18, above).

In addition, a number of 'domestic tribunals' have been established by private or professional associations to resolve disputes between their own members or to exercise disciplinary powers over them. The jurisdiction of these tribunals is sometimes derived from statute. In other cases it rests solely on contract, in that, by joining the association, a member contracts to accept the jurisdiction of its domestic tribunal.

Arbitration

3.38 Whether it is used as an alternative to proceedings in court or as part of such proceedings, arbitration is a method for the settlement of civil disputes, other than those affecting status (such as divorce and bankruptcy). Arbitration is generally more informal and private, and can be cheaper and quicker, than a trial in a court. However, where the main issues are questions of commercial law (as opposed to the facts or commercial practice), trial in the Commercial Court or a Mercantile Court[1] may be as cheap and quick, and certainly more appropriate.

A dispute may be referred to arbitration in three ways: by agreement out of court, by statute or by order of the court.

1 Para 3.18, above.

Reference by agreement out of court

3.39 Particularly in commercial matters, the parties to a dispute may prefer to go straight to arbitration rather than become involved in court proceedings. Hence, they may voluntarily agree before or after the dispute to refer it to arbitration. Many commercial contracts provide for such a reference, as do various codes of practice initiated by trade associations which are incorporated in their standard form contracts used by members.

A growing tendency for arbitration clauses to be inserted in standard form contracts made with consumers has caused concern in recent years since consumers have less choice than business organisations over the terms on which they contract and such a clause may be to their prejudice (as where a consumer's claim would otherwise have been dealt with much more cheaply under the 'small claims procedure' described in para 3.13, above, or, in a case involving a larger claim, where the consumer would have received legal aid for a court case). For this reason, an arbitration agreement which has not been individually negotiated is unfair for the purposes of the Unfair Terms in Consumer Contracts Regulations 1994, and therefore not enforceable against a consumer, so far as it relates to a pecuniary claim not exceeding £3,000[1].

1 The Regulations were extended in the way indicated by the Arbitration Act 1996, ss 89–91; paras 14.61–14.65, below.

3.40 If an arbitration agreement is in writing, as is usually the case, it, and the arbitration under it, is governed by the Arbitration Act 1996[1], provided that the seat (ie place) of arbitration is designated as being in England and Wales or Northern Ireland under the agreement or in accordance with it[2]. We set out below the position under that Act.

Normally, if a party to an arbitration agreement brings court proceedings in respect of a dispute covered by the agreement without referring it to arbitration, the court has jurisdiction to try the case. However, if such proceedings are instituted the other party to an arbitration agreement may apply to the court for an order staying the proceedings. On such an application, the court must stay the proceedings, unless satisfied that the arbitration agreement is null and void, inoperative or incapable of being performed, or (in the case of a 'domestic arbitration agreement' only) unless satisfied that there are other sufficient grounds for not requiring the parties to abide by the arbitration agreement[3]. A 'domestic arbitration agreement' is one under which the seat of arbitration is not designated or determined or is in the United Kingdom, and to which neither:

a.   an individual who is a national of, or habitually resident in, a foreign state, nor

b.   a corporation incorporated in, or centrally managed in, a foreign state,

is a party[4].

The normal position outlined above does not apply if the arbitration agreement contains a *'Scott v Avery'*[5] clause, which is an agreement to refer a dispute to arbitration as a condition precedent to an action in the courts. Since no right of action accrues until the arbitration has taken place, non-observance of the clause will afford a complete defence to a court action.

1   Arbitration Act 1996, s 5. 'Agreement in writing' is given an extended meaning by s 5. It includes, for example, an agreement made by exchange of communications in writing.
2   Arbitration Act 1996, ss 2 and 3.
3   Arbitration Act 1996, ss 9 and 86.
4   Arbitration Act 1996, s 85.
5   (1856) 5 HL Cas 811; para 15.4, below.

Appointment of arbitrators and umpires
3.41   The parties are free to agree on the number of persons whom they wish to act as arbitrators and whether there is to be a chairman or umpire. Subject to any agreement to the contrary, an agreement that there shall be two or any other even number of arbitrators requires the appointment of an additional arbitrator as chairman. If there is no agreement as to the number of arbitrators, a sole arbitrator will be appointed[1].

The parties are also free to agree on the procedure for appointing the arbitrator or arbitrators, including the chairman or umpire. They may, for example, provide that the appointment shall be made by the President of a relevant professional society. If there is no agreement as to the procedure for appointment, and the agreed number of arbitrators is one, that person must be appointed by the parties jointly. Where the agreed number is two, each party must appoint one arbitrator. The same is the case where the agreed number is three; the third arbitrator is then appointed as chairman by the two arbitrators so appointed. The like procedure applies where there are to be two arbitrators and an umpire. In any other case, the same rules apply as in the case of a failure of the appointment procedure (see below)[2]. Lawyers are appointed quite frequently as arbitrators, but in some cases a person with the relevant technical expertise, eg an accountant or surveyor, is appointed.

Where a party who is to make an appointment fails to do so within a specified time, the other party, if he has made his appointment, can then appoint his arbitrator as sole arbitrator if he gives the other party seven days' notice and that party still does not appoint his arbitrator[3].

If there is a failure in an agreed procedure for appointment, the situation is governed by any further agreed provision or, failing that, a party to the arbitration agreement can apply to the High Court or a county court, which may give directions as to what should happen or make any necessary appointments itself[1].

The parties can agree on the functions of a chairman or umpire. If they do not, the position is as follows:

a. in the case of a chairman, decisions, orders and awards are made by all or a majority of the arbitrators (including the chairman, whose view prevails if the views of the arbitrators are equally divided);
b. in the case of an umpire, decisions, orders and awards are made by the other arbitrators unless and until they cannot agree on a matter relating to the arbitration, in which case the umpire shall replace them and act as if he were the sole arbitrator[5].

A judge of the Commercial Court (or an official referee) may, if in all the circumstances he thinks fit, accept appointment as sole arbitrator or umpire by or by virtue of an arbitration agreement, provided that the Lord Chief Justice has informed him that the state of business in the High Court (or the state of official referee's business) permits him to be made available[6].

1 Arbitration Act 1996, s 15.
2 Ibid, s 16.
3 Ibid, s 17.
4 Ibid, s 18.
5 Ibid, ss 20 and 21.
6 Arbitration Act 1996, s 93. Official referees are described in para 3.14.

Conduct of the proceedings
3.42 In reaching a decision (called 'the award') arbitrators must do so in accordance with the law (eg English law) chosen by the parties or, if they agree, in accordance with non-legal considerations agreed by them or determined by the arbitrator(s). If the parties do not make a choice of the applicable law, the arbitrator(s) must decide which body of law is applicable under the rules of the conflict of laws[1].

1 Arbitration Act 1996, s 46.

3.43 The award may provide for the payment of money, direct costs to be paid[1], order the specific performance of a contract (other than one relating to land or an interest in land), order a party to do or not to do something, or order rectification of a document[1], unless the arbitration agreement is to the contrary.

The award is final and binding on the parties and persons claiming through them, unless the arbitration agreement otherwise provides[2], and there is no right of appeal to the courts except on a point of law. However, the High Court or a county court has power, on application by a party, to intervene where an award is challenged on the ground that there was no valid arbitration agreement, or that the arbitral tribunal was not properly constituted, or that a matter has been considered which was not submitted for arbitration in accordance with the arbitration agreement. In such a case, the court may confirm the award, vary it or set it aside. An appeal from its decision lies to the Court of Appeal, but only with the court's leave[3].

In addition, the High Court or a county court, on application by a party, has power to set aside an award, or declare it to be of no effect, or remit it for reconsideration, on the ground of a serious irregularity affecting the arbitral tribunal, the proceedings or the award. An appeal from the court's decision lies to the Court of Appeal, but only with the court's leave[4]. Lastly, the High Court or a county court has power to remove an arbitrator whose impartiality is doubtful, or who lacks the qualifications required by the arbitration agreement, or whose capability to conduct the proceedings is doubtful, or who has improperly conducted the proceedings[5]. Examples of misconduct for these purposes are the receipt by the arbitrator of evidence from one party in the absence of the other, and the failure by him to deal with some of the matters submitted or to put to the parties certain matters on which he relies. On the other hand, a mere error of law or fact is not misconduct for these purposes[6]. A decision about the removal of an arbitrator can be appealed to the Court of Appeal, but only with the court's leave[5].

1   Arbitration Act 1996, s 48.
2   Ibid, s 58.
3   Ibid, s 67.
4   Ibid, s 68.
5   Ibid, s 24.
6   *Blexen v G Percy Trentham Ltd* [1990] 2 EGLR 9, CA.

Enforcement of an award
3.44   An award may, by leave of the High Court or a county court, be enforced in the same manner as a judgment or order of that court[1]. Otherwise, the award is enforced by bringing a court action on the award as a contractual debt.

1   Arbitration Act 1996, s 66.

Resort to the courts on a point of law
3.45   There are two procedures whereby the courts may intervene in arbitration cases on a point of law:

a.   an appeal on a point of law after an award has been made; and
b.   an application for the determination of a preliminary point of law in the course of a reference.

3.46   Unless otherwise agreed by the parties, appeals lie to the High Court or a county court on any question of law[1] arising out of an award made in arbitral proceedings. Such appeal may be brought by any of the parties to the reference, but, unless all the other parties consent, the leave of the court must be obtained. Leave can only be granted if the court is satisfied:

a.   that the determination of the question of law could substantially affect the rights of one or more parties;

b.   that the question of law is one which the arbitrators were asked to determine;
c.   that the arbitrators' decision is obviously wrong or that the question is one of general public importance and the decision is at least open to serious doubt; and
d.   that it is just and proper in the circumstances for the court to determine the question, despite the parties' agreement to resolve the matter by arbitration[2].

An appeal against a decision to grant or refuse leave itself requires the court's leave[2]. Leave cannot be granted if the parties to the reference in question have effectively agreed to exclude the right of appeal.

The philosophy behind the requirement for leave is to avoid delay and expense in arbitrations arising out of commercial or shipping contracts by giving primacy to finality over questions concerning the correctness of awards. Consequently, it was not surprising that, in *Pioneer Shipping Ltd v BTP Tioxide Ltd, The Nema*[3], the House of Lords took a restrictive view concerning the exercise by judges of their discretion to grant leave. It held that, generally, leave to appeal should not be granted unless it is shown either that the arbitrator has misdirected himself in point of law or that the decision is such that no reasonable person could have reached it. Where the question of law concerns the construction of a contract or contractual clause in standard terms, leave should only be granted if the judge considers that a strong prima facie case has been made out that the arbitrator was wrong in his construction[4]. The test is even stricter where the question of law concerns the construction of a 'one-off' contract or contractual clause (ie one which is not of a standard term nature). Here, leave to appeal should not be granted unless it is apparent to the judge, on a mere perusal of the arbitrator's reasoned award without hearing argument from counsel, that the meaning ascribed to the clause by the arbitrator is obviously wrong. The guidelines laid down in *Pioneer Shipping Ltd v BTP Tioxide Ltd* by the House of Lords are not applicable in all cases. It has been held that they do not apply where complex questions of European Community law arise[5]. In such cases, the approach of the court to the granting of leave is less strict.

On the determination of an appeal the High Court may confirm, vary or set aside the award, or remit it for reconsideration in the light of its determination on the question of law which was the subject of the appeal[6]. In order that an appeal, if it takes place, may be effective, the court has power to order an arbitrator to give reasons for his decision[7]. An appeal to the Court of Appeal from the court's determination of an appeal is possible; but only if the court gives leave, which it cannot do unless it considers that the question of law is one of general public importance or is one which for some other special reason should be considered by the Court of Appeal[6].

A further appeal from the Court of Appeal to the House of Lords is only possible with the leave of that Court or of the House.

1   An appeal cannot be brought on a question of fact. It is normally obvious whether a question is one of fact or of law but it should be noted that a question concerning the construction or

frustration of a contract is a question of law: *Tsakiroglou & Co Ltd v Noblee Thorl GmbH* [1962] AC 93, [1961] 2 All ER 179, HL; *Pioneer Shipping Ltd v BTP Tioxide Ltd, The Nema* [1982] AC 724, [1981] 2 All ER 1030, HL.

2   Arbitration Act 1996, s 69. An appeal cannot be brought if any further recourse within the arbitral proceedings (eg a review) has not been exhausted: ibid, s 70. As to the parties' ability to exclude an appeal, see para 3.48, below.

3   [1982] AC 724, [1981] 2 All ER 1030, HL.

4   *Antaios Cia Naviera SA v Salen Rederierna AB, The Antaios* [1985] AC 191, [1984] 3 All ER 229, HL; *Ipswich Borough Council v Fisons plc* [1990] Ch 709, [1990] 1 All ER 730, CA.

5   *Bulk Oil (Zug) AG v Sun International Ltd* [1984] 1 All ER 386, [1984] 1 WLR 147, CA.

6   Arbitration Act 1996, s 69.

7   Arbitration Act 1996, s 70.

3.47   Unless otherwise agreed by the parties, the High Court may determine any question of law arising in the course of a reference to arbitration (a preliminary point of law) on the application of a party. However, unless all the other parties agree to the application, the court must not entertain it unless it has the permission of the arbitrators (including the umpire, if there is one) *and* it is satisfied that the determination of the question is likely substantially to reduce costs and that the application was made without delay[1]. Notwithstanding any agreement of the parties, the court is not bound to entertain the application. Instead, the court should only entertain it in exceptional circumstances; for example, where the preliminary point of law, if rightly decided, would determine the whole dispute[2]. Unless the court gives leave, no appeal lies from a decision of the court whether the conditions described above are met[1].

Subject to the same restrictions as apply to an appeal from the court's determination of an appeal on a point of law after an award, an appeal lies to the Court of Appeal from a decision on a preliminary point of law[1].

A further appeal from the Court of Appeal to the House of Lords is only possible with the leave of that Court or of the House.

1   Arbitration Act 1996, s 45.

2   *Babanaft International Co SA v Avant Petroleum Inc, The Oltenia* [1982] 3 All ER 244, [1982] 1 WLR 871, CA.

Exclusion agreements

3.48   At common law an agreement, whether contained in the arbitration agreement or made thereafter, which excludes the courts' power to give a final decision on a question of law is void on grounds of public policy and thus of no effect[1]. However, this rule has been severely curtailed by statute, since the parties to an arbitration agreement, by 'otherwise agreeing', can exclude the jurisdiction of the courts to determine a point of law after an award or to make a determination on a preliminary point of law. The parties' power to 'otherwise agree' is limited in the case of a domestic arbitration agreement[2] because an exclusion agreement is only effective if it was entered into after commencement of the relevant arbitral proceedings[3].

1   *Czarnikow v Roth, Schmidt & Co* [1922] 2 KB 478, CA.

2   Para 3.40, above.

3   Arbitration Act 1996, s 87.

Reference by statute
3.49 Numerous statutes provide for the reference of certain types of dispute to arbitration. In some cases, eg disputes involving building societies, the parties have an option to refer; in others reference is compulsory, eg disputes involving street works. The provisions of the Arbitration Act 1996 apply to statutory references, with minor exceptions, unless the particular statute otherwise provides[1].

1 Arbitration Act 1996, ss 94–98.

Reference by order of the court
3.50 The High Court may refer any case within its jurisdiction, or any particular issue in such a case, to be *tried* by an official referee[1], by a senior officer of the court, such as a master, or, where the issue is of a technical nature requiring specialist knowledge, by a special referee. A reference to such an arbitrator can be made even against the wishes of the parties and is particularly likely to be made if:

a. the prolonged examination of documents, or scientific or local examination, is required; or
b. the examination of accounts is involved.

The award of the arbitrator is entered as a judgment in the court proceedings, and is binding as such. In certain circumstances an appeal lies to the Court of Appeal (Civil Division).

In addition, the High Court has a similar power to refer to the same persons as above any question in a cause or matter before it for *inquiry and report*. The report may be adopted wholly or partially by the court, and if so adopted is as binding as a judgment to the same effect[2].

The power of a county court to refer a case to arbitration has been discussed in para 3.13, above. In addition, any questions in a case before a county court judge may be referred to a district judge or a referee for inquiry and report[3].

1 Para 3.14, above.
2 Supreme Court Act 1981, s 84; Rules of the Supreme Court, Ord 36.
3 County Courts Act 1984, s 65; County Court Rules 1981.

3.51 References to arbitration by the courts must be distinguished from references to arbitration by agreement or under a statutory provision because they operate in the context of court proceedings rather than as an alternative to them.

Alternative Dispute Resolution
3.52 Alternative dispute resolution (ADR) refers to any method of resolving an issue capable of resolution by litigation in the courts or by arbitration without resorting to that type of process.

Normally, the results of ADR are not binding, although the parties can agree otherwise. In the normal type of case, ADR is concerned with aiding the parties to reach a solution, as opposed to imposing one. It follows that ADR is only worth pursuing if the parties are likely to be voluntarily co-operative or there is a contractual obligation to pursue it.

ADR is a quicker and cheaper method than litigation in the courts or, even, arbitration. It is therefore of interest both to consumers and to businesses involved in commercial disputes. In addition to speeding up settlement, ADR has the advantage of making it possible to reach settlements reflecting commercial or personal interests as well as strict rights. It also has the advantage of focusing on the issues rather than on the combat involved in the courts or in arbitration. It is, therefore, less destructive of relationships between the parties.

These benefits have been recognised by legislation, in respect of matrimonial disputes, and by the Commercial Court which has issued a *Practice Direction*[1] encouraging judges in that court to consider adjourning appropriate cases to enable the parties to give thought to, and set in motion, ADR procedures.

1   [1996] 3 All ER 383, [1996] 1 WLR 1024.

3.53   A number of organisations offer ADR services, for example, the Centre for Dispute Resolution (CEDR), the City Disputes Panel, the Chartered Institute of Arbitrators, and Mediation UK. Lawyers are often involved in conducting the ADR process, but this is not essential.

Negotiation could be described as a form of ADR but the term is normally used to refer to mediation, to conciliation and to a formalised settlement conference.

Mediation

3.54   In mediation a neutral mediator helps the parties to reach a common position. It can be 'facilitative' or 'evaluative'. It is 'facilitative' if the mediator does not advise the parties of his own opinion of the merits of the dispute. It is 'evaluative' if he is expected to express his own opinion.

Mediation is particularly appropriate where the claim is small or not complex, or both. It is also appropriate where it is particularly important to reduce conflict and bitterness between the parties.

Mediation can take place in the context of the courts' organisation whereby a case before the courts is referred to mediation or some other form of ADR, as in the Commercial Court or (in a pilot project) in a county court.

Conciliation

3.55   This is similar to mediation but differs in that the conciliator moves from one party to the other, discussing the merits of each side's case and the risks in litigation. Sometimes, if the conciliation does not lead to a settlement, the conciliator's role may extend to advising the parties of his assessment of the likely result of a trial. Of course, this is not binding, but it often leads to a settlement.

Formalised settlement conference

3.56 At a formalised settlement conference, advocates present their client's best case to a panel composed of one executive decision-maker representing each party, often assisted by a neutral person to assist the panel in assessing representations. This method of ADR is sometimes called a 'mini-trial'.

The Legal Profession

Barristers

3.57 Barristers in private practice, of whom there are about 8,500, must work as sole practitioners, and not as members of a partnership or employees, although (with a very few exceptions) they do so in sets of chambers, sharing rent and other expenses. Their work comprises drafting legal documents and writing opinions on points of law, as well as appearing as advocates. A barrister in private practice may appear in any court or tribunal. Generally, barristers in private practice are not permitted to work directly for lay clients but must have their work channelled to them through solicitors. By way of exception, for example, a barrister in private practice may take instruction direct from a chartered accountant or chartered surveyor, but not from that person's firm as a whole, in relation to a range of work including advisory work and arbitrations but excluding advocacy in formal court proceedings. Most sets of chambers are in London in the Inns of Court (two-thirds of barristers in private practice are based in London) but there are also chambers in many other major cities.

A significant number of barristers are not in private practice but are employed in a legal capacity by commercial or industrial undertakings or by central or local government. The advocacy rights of employed barristers are more limited than those of barristers in private practice, being limited to those cases in which any solicitor can currently appear.

A barrister of more than ten years' standing may apply to be made a Queen's Counsel by the Queen on the Lord Chancellor's advice. The work of a member of the Bar who is made a Queen's Counsel is confined to the most important cases and chiefly involves advocacy[1].

Barristers are members of one of the four Inns of Court (Middle Temple, Inner Temple, Lincoln's Inn and Gray's Inn). The Bar as a profession is represented by the General Council of the Bar.

---

1 It is now possible for a solicitor to be made a Queen's Counsel, but such an appointment does not carry with it any rights additional to those already enjoyed as a solicitor. The first solicitor QCs were appointed in 1997.

Solicitors

3.58 There are some 60,000 solicitors. Unlike barristers in private practice, solicitors in private practice are normally members of a partnership or employed by a partnership. Solicitors act as legal advisers on commercial, family and personal matters; they handle the transfer of land and draft wills, and they prepare cases involving litigation. Just as in the case of barristers, a significant number of solicitors are employed by commercial or industrial undertakings or by central or local government. In addition, solicitors can act as advocates in various tribunals, magistrates' and county courts, and in the Crown Court when it is hearing appeals from, or sentencing persons committed for sentence by, magistrates' courts. Solicitors with additional training can be authorised to act as advocates in all proceedings in the Crown Court or in the High Court, or both, and appeals therefrom, according to their particular expertise. However, if they are not in private practice, they cannot appear on their own at a *trial* in either Court.

The Law Society is responsible for the solicitors' branch of the legal profession, the Council of that Society being the ultimate authority.

Legal executives

3.59   Legal executives are qualified legal assistants in solicitors' offices who, while working under the control and authority of a solicitor, possess a high degree of expertise in their chosen field. Their professional body is the Institute of Legal Executives which, like the other professional bodies, is responsible for admission to its numbers and holds examinations.

The Jury

3.60   The only courts mentioned above in which juries are found are the Crown Court and the High Court (12 jurors) and the county courts (eight jurors). The use of juries in civil cases is rare and the parties generally have no right to demand a jury; except that a jury must be ordered on the application of either party in cases of defamation, malicious prosecution and false imprisonment, or on the application of a party against whom fraud is charged, unless the case requires a prolonged examination of accounts or documents, or a scientific or local investigation which cannot conveniently be made with a jury[1]. The only civil cases where a jury is common are defamation cases. Provided the accused has pleaded not guilty, a jury is always empanelled in trials on indictment in the Crown Court.

1   Supreme Court Act 1981, s 69; see *Rothermere v Times Newspaper Ltd* [1973] 1 All ER 1013, [1973] 1 WLR 448, CA.

3.61   A person is eligible for jury service if he or she is between the ages of 18 and 70, is included on the electoral register for parliamentary and local government elections, and has been resident in the United Kingdom, the Channel Islands or the Isle of Man for five years since the age of 13. There are certain exceptions. Some persons are ineligible for jury service, including judges, barristers and solicitors, police officers, clergymen and the mentally ill. Certain ex-prisoners and certain other people who have received non-custodial sentences are disqualified and persons such as peers, people aged more than 65, soldiers and doctors are excusable as of right[1].

1 Juries Act 1974, ss 1 and 3, and Sch 1.

3.62 The division of labour between judge and jury is that the judge rules on law, the jury on fact. The judge directs the jury as to the law and they apply it to the facts. Their discussions are in secret, they choose their own foreman and they give no reasons for their decisions. Their verdict in a civil case can be overturned by the Court of Appeal but only if no reasonable jury properly directed could have reached it. In his summing up the judge may comment on the plausibility of the evidence and may give guidance as to what inferences may be drawn. Generally, the jury must reach a unanimous verdict, but a majority of ten (seven in the county courts) may be accepted after the jury have had a reasonable time in all the circumstances for deliberation; there is a minimum time of two hours in the Crown Court. In civil cases the parties can always consent to accept any majority verdict[1].

1 Juries Act 1974, s 17.

Chapter 4

Sources of English Law

4.1 The direct means by which law is made or comes into existence constitute legal sources, while a literary source is simply the written material in which a legal source is recorded.

Legislation and judicial precedent are the principal legal sources of English law and the only other source, custom, is now of very little relevance. The courts must consciously look to these sources to determine what the law is, and are bound to apply the rules which they create. The literary sources of legislation are the various publications of statutes and statutory instruments. The literary sources of precedent are law reports and, to a lesser extent, certain books of authority.

Legislation

4.2 Unlike many continental countries where, the law having been codified, most legal rules are derived from legislation, English law is predominantly derived from judicial precedent. Leaving aside certain areas which have been codified, such as the law relating to the sale of goods and to partnership (by the Sale of Goods Act 1893, which was re-enacted with later amendments in the Sale of Goods Act 1979, and by the Partnership Act 1890 respectively), the body of law concerning private rights is essentially derived from judicial precedent with relatively few alterations made by statute. Normally, the purpose of statutory alteration or revision of this area of the law is to revise a legal rule which has become inappropriate in changing social circumstances and which, because of the operation of the doctrine of judicial precedent, is incapable of adaptation by the courts.

The generation of law reform proposals has been greatly assisted since 1965 by the existence of the Law Commission, consisting of full-time Commissioners, assisted by a research staff. Under the Law Commissions Act 1965, it is the duty of the Law Commission to keep under review all the law with a view to its systematic development and reform, including in particular the codification of such law, the elimination of anomalies, the repeal of obsolete and unnecessary enactments, the reduction in the number of separate enactments, and generally the simplification and modernisation of the law. A large number of the 250 Law Commission reports and draft Bills have been implemented by Act of Parliament. A decline in recent years in the number which have resulted in legislation is a cause for concern.

Legislation plays a more important part in criminal law, mainly in defining most offences, and in the spheres of company law and employment law. Another notable example is legislation concerning the revenue, eg the Finance Acts which implement the budget proposals. The great majority of modern statutes can be put into the category of 'social legislation'. Such legislation is concerned essentially with regulating the day-to-day running of the social system rather than with creating criminal offences or rights and duties between individuals. In this area, in particular, much of the flesh is put on the bones of the relevant Act by delegated legislation[1].

1   Para 4.10, below.

4.3   Sometimes a statute is described as a consolidating or codifying statute. Where a branch of statute law has evolved piecemeal, a consolidating statute may be passed, for the purpose of clarification, containing substantially the existing law in a consolidated form. Three examples of modern consolidation Acts are the County Courts Act 1984, the Companies Act 1985 and the Trade Union and Labour Relations (Consolidation) Act 1992. A consolidation Act only consolidates statute law: a codifying Act may codify both case law and statute law, a notable example being the Sale of Goods Act 1893 (which has now been consolidated with subsequent amending statutes in the Sale of Goods Act 1979). However, the object of both consolidation and codification is to simplify and clarify the existing law rather than to effect substantial alterations to it.

4.4   There are essentially three types of legislation: Acts of Parliament; subordinate legislation, which mainly consists of delegated legislation made by government ministers, local authorities and other bodies under powers derived from Parliament; and the legislation of the European Community. Subject to an exception which we discuss in para 4.40, below, Parliament (which consists of the Queen, House of Lords and House of Commons) is sovereign, which means that it is not subject to any legal limits on its powers to create, alter and repeal English law. It also means that an Act of Parliament cannot be questioned in, or by, the courts: it has to be applied by them. In certain cases the validity of subordinate legislation and of most types of legislation of the European Community can be challenged[1].

1 Paras 4.13 and 4.41, below.

Acts of Parliament
4.5   While it is going through the parliamentary process, and before it receives the Royal Assent, an Act is known as a Bill. Most Bills originate from government departments, having been drafted by parliamentary draftsmen, and are introduced into either House of Parliament by a government minister.

However, although the opportunities are rather limited, a Bill may be introduced by an ordinary member of the House of Commons or House of Lords. So far we have concentrated on Public Bills, ie Bills which when enacted will be general in their application. In addition, Private Bills – Bills of a local or personal nature – may be presented by local authorities, public corporations, companies, members of either House or other individuals and are subject to a different parliamentary procedure. A third type of Bill is the Hybrid Bill. A Hybrid Bill is one which is introduced as a Public Bill but which affects the private interests of particular bodies or individuals. Part of the parliamentary procedure for a Hybrid Bill is similar to that for a Private Bill.

4.6   The 'official' copies of Acts of Parliament are printed by the Queen's Printer and published by the Stationery Office, which also publishes annual volumes of Public Acts. The Incorporated Council of Law Reporting publishes texts of Acts taken from the Queen's Printer's copies, as do certain commercial publishers who publish annual volumes of Acts of Parliament verbatim, as well as in unbound parts soon after the Act is passed; a leading series is *Halsbury's Statutes of England*.

Citation
4.7   Until 1963, statutes were cited by the date of the regnal year or years of the parliamentary session in which the Act was passed, the regnal year being assessed from the monarch's accession, together with a chapter number which denoted the order in which it received the royal assent. Thus, the Bills of Exchange Act 1882 is cited '45 and 46 Vict, c 61'. Acts passed after 1962 are cited by reference to the calendar year, not the regnal year, in which they were passed. Thus, the Misrepresentation Act 1967 is cited '1967, c 7'.
   Of course, the more usual way to cite an Act is by its short title.

Commencement and repeal
4.8   An Act of Parliament comes into operation on the date on which it receives the royal assent unless, as frequently occurs, some other date is specified in the Act or is to be appointed by a commencement order made either by Order in Council[1] or by a government minister by way of statutory instrument[2]. Sometimes, a commencement order is not made for a considerable time. An extreme example concerns the Easter Act 1928, which provides a fixed date for Easter but for which a commencement order has not yet been made.
   An Act of Parliament may be repealed expressly by a subsequent statute, or impliedly by being inconsistent with it (although there is a presumption against implied repeal)[3]. Unless the contrary intention appears, repeal does not:

a.   revive a previously repealed rule of law; or
b.   affect existing rights and liabilities, or legal proceedings, civil or criminal[4].

   No statute becomes obsolete through the passing of time, except for certain Acts, usually of an experimental or transitional nature, which are expressed to be operative only for a limited period.

One way of finding out whether a statute has been wholly or partly repealed or amended is to look it up in the *Chronological Table of the Statutes* published biennially by the Stationery Office. This covers the period from 1235 to the end of the year preceding publication. Other ways are to consult LEXIS, a computerised legal database, or to look at the index to *The Statutes in Force*, which is published annually by the Stationery Office.

1 Ie Orders made by a meeting of the Privy Council, normally four or five Cabinet ministers presided over by the Queen.
2 Interpretation Act 1978, s 4.
3 Para 4.26, below.
4 Interpretation Act 1978, ss 15 and 16.

Subordinate legislation

4.9 Various institutions, such as the Crown, ministers, public corporations and local authorities, have legislative powers. Such legislation is subordinate since it is made by bodies with limited powers and it is always subject to abrogation or amendment by Act of Parliament. Moreover, it may be required to be subject to parliamentary scrutiny. In addition, subordinate legislation may be held invalid in certain cases by the courts. In this respect, it may be contrasted with an Act of Parliament, which cannot be overridden by our courts, except to the extent that it is inconsistent with Community law which is directly applicable or of direct effect[1].

Subordinate legislation can be of two types: delegated legislation and autonomic legislation.

1 Para 4.40, below.

Delegated legislation

4.10 Delegated legislation comprises the great bulk of subordinate legislation. Delegated legislation is legislation made by some executive body under powers delegated to it by Act of Parliament. An Act of Parliament often gives powers to some bodies, such as the Queen in Council (in effect the government), a minister or a local authority or public corporation, to make regulations and prescribe for their breach. Delegated legislation includes sub-delegated legislation which may validly be made where it is authorised by an Act of Parliament, as where an Act provides that the Queen in Council may make regulations empowering a particular minister to make further regulations.

There is a vast amount of delegated legislation – the number of pieces made annually being numbered in thousands, whereas the number of Public and Private Acts of Parliament a year rarely exceeds 90. Examples of Acts giving very wide powers of delegated legislation are the European Communities Act 1972[1] and the Companies Act 1985.

Delegated legislation made by the central executive may be required to be made by Order in Council made by the Queen in Council; otherwise it takes the form of regulations, rules or orders made by a minister or government department. Generally, delegated legislation of these types must be made by statutory instrument (formerly Statutory Rules and Orders). Statutory instruments are printed by the Queen's Printer and are available in the same way as Acts of Parliament. They are cited by calendar year and number and by a short title. For instance, the County Court Rules 1981 are cited SI 1981/1687. A statutory instrument comes into effect when made unless, as is usual, it specifies a later date[2]. Unlike an Act of Parliament, it is a defence for a person charged with contravening a statutory instrument to prove that it had not been issued by the Stationery Office at the date of the alleged offence, unless it is proved that at that date reasonable steps had been taken to bring the purport of the instrument to the notice of the public, or of persons likely to be affected by it, or of the person charged[3].

1   Para 4.41, below.
2   *Johnson v Sargant & Sons* [1918] 1 KB 101.
3   Statutory Instruments Act 1946, s 3.

4.11   Parliamentary control over statutory instruments is secured to some extent by requirements of 'laying' and of publication. Often the enabling statute will require the instrument to be laid before Parliament, in which case it must be so laid before it comes into operation, and in addition an affirmative resolution by Parliament may be required to give it effect or it may be made subject to cancellation by a negative resolution of either House within 40 'sitting' days[1]. Closer parliamentary scrutiny of new statutory instruments is provided by the Joint Select Committee on Statutory Instruments, which is composed of members of both Houses and reports to Parliament. Its terms of reference include consideration of every statutory instrument laid or laid in draft before Parliament, with a view to seeing whether the special attention of Parliament should be drawn to the instrument on one of a number of grounds, eg that it is obscurely worded, or appears to impose charges on the subject or on the public revenue, or purports to have a retrospective effect unauthorised by the parent statute. The Select Committee is not concerned with the merits of delegated legislation.

1   Statutory Instruments Act 1946, ss 4 and 5, as clarified by the Laying of Documents before Parliament (Interpretation) Act 1948.

4.12   Another type of delegated legislation is the byelaw. Byelaws are made by local authorities, public corporations and certain other bodies authorised by statute. Although general in operation, they are restricted to the locality or undertaking to which they apply. They are not made by statutory instrument.

4.13   All forms of delegated legislation are invalid if they are ultra vires. Delegated legislation is ultra vires if it is in excess of the powers conferred by the enabling statute on the rule-making body (substantive ultra vires); or if it is made in breach of a mandatory part of the procedure concerning its making prescribed by that statute (procedural ultra vires); or, in the case of byelaws only, if it is patently unreasonable or excessively uncertain or repugnant to the general law (in which cases it is regarded as substantively ultra vires)[1].

If delegated legislation is partly ultra vires and partly not, because it purports (or its effect is) to deal with matters outside the delegated powers as well as matters within them, it may be valid and enforceable to the extent that it is not ultra vires. It will be valid to that extent if the ultra vires part can be severed. Severance is always possible if the ultra vires part can be removed simply by cutting out the relevant words. If this is not possible, severance may be effected by modifying the text so as to omit the ultra vires aspect of it, provided that this does not change the substantial purpose and effect of the provision as a whole[2].

1 *Nash v Finlay* (1901) 85 LT 682, DC; *Powell v May* [1946] KB 330, [1946] 1 All ER 444, DC; *Bugg v DPP* [1993] QB 473, [1993] 2 All ER 815, DC.
2 *DPP v Hutchinson* [1990] 2 AC 783, [1990] 2 All ER 836, HL; *Woolwich Equitable Building Society v IRC* [1991] 4 All ER 92, HL.

4.14 The principal advantages of delegated legislation are:

a. Parliament has insufficient time to deal with details. The availability of delegated legislation enables Parliament to limit itself to settling the general policy of a measure, leaving a minister to supply the detailed provisions in the form of regulations and orders.
b. Delegated legislation is eminently suitable in the case of provisions on technical matters which would be inappropriate for parliamentary discussion.
c. In some cases, the power to make delegated legislation enables a minister to deal speedily with urgent situations, such as an economic crisis or a strike in an essential industry.
d. The power to make delegated legislation is also useful in that, within the terms of the parent Act, it enables the application of an Act to be tailored to deal with contingencies which were not foreseen when the Act was passed.

4.15 On the other hand, delegated legislation is open to the following criticisms:

a. Parliament has neither the time nor the opportunity to supervise all delegated legislation effectively.
b. The detail which delegated legislation provides may be just as important as the general policy of the parent Act, yet Parliament cannot discuss its merits.

Autonomic legislation
4.16 Autonomic legislation is legislation made by the Queen by Order in Council, or by autonomous associations within the state, under powers which are not delegated by Parliament but which are recognised by the courts. Trade unions and professional associations, such as the Institute of Chartered Accountants for England and Wales and the other accountancy bodies, are examples of autonomous associations in this context. The legislation of such autonomous associations is directly binding only on their members, though negatively it binds everyone since interference with it is wrongful; it is invalid if ultra vires. Autonomic legislation made by the Queen in Council is made under the royal prerogative. There is no power under the prerogative to alter

the general law of the land[1] but there is a limited prerogative power to legislate for the colonies, the armed forces and the civil service. The prerogative comprises those independent powers left to the Crown by Parliament, and legislation by the Crown outside its prerogative powers will be held invalid by the courts if it is not delegated legislation.

1   *Proclamations' Case* (1611) 12 Co Rep 74.

Interpretation

4.17   Language being inherently capable of ambiguity and human affairs being capable of great diversity, the courts are often faced with the question whether a particular matter or piece of conduct falls within the wording of a particular legislative provision. The exposition which follows is concerned with the interpretation of Public Acts of Parliament but, essentially, the same rules apply to the interpretation of other Acts of Parliament and of subordinate legislation. In interpreting statutes, the courts are trying to discover Parliament's intentions from the words used. There are two, radically different, approaches to this task: the 'literal approach' and the 'purposive approach'. It is impossible to know in advance which approach the court will adopt in a particular case. We shall consider them in turn, and then deal with various rules of interpretation which apply whichever of the two approaches is adopted.

The two approaches to interpretation

The literal approach
4.18   The literal approach to statutory interpretation is otherwise known as the literal rule. The literal rule states that Parliament's intention must be found by interpreting the words used in their ordinary, literal and grammatical sense. If the words can be so interpreted a judge must give effect to that interpretation, unless the statute or the legal context in which the words are used compels him to give the words a special meaning, even though he considers that it produces an undesirable, inexpedient or unjust result or that Parliament cannot have intended it or that the situation is one which was not contemplated when the statute was enacted[1]. In *IRC v Hinchy*[2], the House of Lords had to interpret s 25(3) of the Income Tax Act 1952, which provided that a person who failed to deliver a correct income tax return should forfeit 'the sum of twenty pounds and treble the tax which he ought to be charged under this Act'. The House of Lords held that, in addition to the penalty of £20, a taxpayer who had declared only part of his Post Office interest was liable to pay treble the whole tax chargeable for the year, and not merely treble the tax on the undeclared income.

1   *Duport Steels Ltd v Sirs* [1980] 1 All ER 529, [1980] 1 WLR 142, HL; *Leedale (Inspector of Taxes) v Lewis* [1982] 3 All ER 808, [1982] 1 WLR 1319, HL; *Comdel Commodities Ltd v Siporex Trade SA (No 2)* [1991] 1 AC 148, [1990] 2 All ER 552, HL.
2   [1960] AC 748, [1960] 1 All ER 505, HL. The actual decision in this case would now be governed by the Finance Act 1960, s 44, which amended the wording of the provision in question.

4.19 It may happen that to interpret statutory words according to their ordinary, literal and grammatical sense in their context would give rise to manifest absurdity or to repugnance or inconsistency *with the rest of the statute*. In such a case, the so-called 'golden rule' permits a judge to modify the literal interpretation so as to avoid such a result. The classical exposition of the golden rule was given by Lord Wensleydale in *Grey v Pearson*[1]:

> 'in construing . . . statutes . . . the grammatical and ordinary sense of the words is to be adhered to, unless that would lead to some absurdity or some repugnance or inconsistency with the rest of the instrument, in which case the grammatical and ordinary sense of the words may be modified so as to avoid that absurdity or inconsistency, but no further.'

A modern example is provided by the House of Lords' decision in *McMonagle v Westminster City Council*[2]. M was charged with the offence of using premises as a 'sex encounter establishment' without a licence, contrary to the Local Government (Miscellaneous Provisions) Act 1982. The definition of such an establishment was 'premises at which performances which are *not* unlawful are given, which ... comprise the sexual stimulation of persons admitted to the premises ...'. M's defence was that it had not been proved that the performances in question were *not* unlawful and that, if they were unlawful, a licence was not required under the plain words of the Act. The House of Lords rejected this interpretation, as being absurd, and held that the words 'which are not unlawful' were mere surplusage which had been introduced by an incompetent draftsman solely to emphasise that a licence conferred no immunity from the ordinary criminal law. Thus, the prosecution did not have to prove that the performances were not unlawful and it was no defence that they were unlawful.

1   (1857) 6 HL Cas 61 at 106.
2   [1990] 2 AC 716, [1990] 1 All ER 993, HL.

Purposive approach
4.20 Under this approach to statutory interpretation, the words in a statute are interpreted not only in their ordinary, literal and grammatical sense but also with reference to their context and purpose. If the judge thinks that the interpretation of the words in their ordinary, literal and grammatical sense would produce a result contrary to the purpose of the statute as he understands it to be, the judge may construe them in any other way consistent with that purpose which the words are capable of bearing. This approach differs from the literal approach in that, while the court starts with a consideration of the ordinary, literal and grammatical meaning of the words, it can depart from that meaning not only in cases covered by the golden rule but also where that meaning would give rise to a result contrary to the purpose of the statute. In *Richard Thomas and Baldwins Ltd v Cummings*[1], for example, a provision in the Factories Act 1937, which required the fencing of dangerous parts of a machine while it was in motion, was held not to apply where a worker turned the machine by hand. The machine could not have been repaired while it was fenced, and the purpose of the statute was to protect workers operating machines with dangerous parts.

1   [1955] AC 321, [1955] 1 All ER 285, HL.

4.21   As part of the purposive approach, judges can imply or substitute words where the words are 'necessarily implied' by words already in the statute. For example, in *Federal Steam Navigation Co Ltd v Department of Trade and Industry*[1], where the Oil in Navigable Waters Act 1955 provided that, where oil was discharged from a British Ship in a prohibited area, 'the owner or master of the ship' committed an offence, it was held that, if the owner or master were separate people, both could be convicted, the words being construed as if they read 'the owner *and/or* master of the ship'. On the other hand, if a court is faced with a factual situation for which the statute has not provided, even the purposive approach does not permit the court to fill the gap. To do so would be to attribute to Parliament an intention which it never had. Like the literal approach, the purposive approach is limited to giving effects to the words of the statute. It does not extend to reading words into it to rectify an anomaly or absurdity, *unless clear reason is found within the body* of the Act itself[2]; a judge cannot attribute to Parliament an intention which Parliament never had. For a judge to do so was condemned by Lord Simonds in *Magor and St Mellons RDC v Newport Corpn*[3], as a 'naked usurpation of the legislative function under the thin disguise of interpretation'. His Lordship added that if a gap is disclosed the remedy lies in an amending Act.

1   [1974] 2 All ER 97, [1974] 1 WLR 505, HL.
2   *Stock v Frank Jones (Tipton) Ltd* [1978] 1 All ER 948, [1978] 1 WLR 231, HL.
3   [1952] AC 189 at 191, [1951] 2 All ER 839 at 841.

General rules of interpretation
4.22   Whichever of the two approaches to interpretation is adopted, the court will be assisted by various general rules of interpretation. Indeed, if the provision proves to be uncertain or ambiguous, one or more of these rules may be determinative of the court's interpretation.

Consideration of the whole enactment
4.23   Consideration of the whole enactment assists in resolving apparent ambiguities, inconsistencies or redundancies in a particular provision. A statute must be read as a whole. Every section must be read in the light of every other section[1], including its interpretation section (if any) normally found towards the end of a statute. The definitions in an interpretation section apply throughout the Act, unless a contrary intention, express or implied, appears in a particular context.

1   *Beswick v Beswick* [1968] AC 58, [1967] 2 All ER 1197, HL.

The mischief rule
4.24   The literal approach, in particular, breaks down in the case of an ambiguity. In such a case, a judge may apply the mischief rule, which is often called the rule in *Heydon's Case* since it was formulated there[1]. The rule is best paraphrased by the statement by Lord Halsbury in *Eastman Photographic Materials Co Ltd v Comptroller-General of Patents, Designs and Trade Marks*: 'We are to see what was the law before the Act was passed, and what was the

mischief or defect for which the law had not provided, what remedy Parliament appointed, and the reason for the remedy'[2].

An example of the application of the mischief rule is *Gorris v Scott*[3]. The plaintiff claimed in respect of the loss of his sheep which were washed overboard and drowned while the defendant was engaged in carrying them by sea. The loss was due to the fact that, in breach of the statutory duty to do so, no pens had been provided. The plaintiff based his claim on the fact that the loss had been caused by the breach of the statutory duty. However, it was held that the purpose of the relevant provision was not to prevent loss overboard but to minimise the spread of contagious diseases, and that therefore the claim did not fall within the 'mischief' of the Act.

1 (1584) 3 Co Rep 7a.
2 [1898] AC 571 at 573.
3 (1874) LR 9 Exch 125.

Other rules
4.25 The rule that the whole enactment must be considered is really part of the principle that words must be taken in their context. A word in itself does not have an absolute meaning: its meaning is relevant to its context (this statement is often described by the Latin tag *noscitur a sociis*). Another important example of this principle is the *ejusdem generis* (of the same class) rule. Enactments often list things which are so similar as to form a class to which a provision is to apply, following the list with some general words implying that some other similar things are intended to fall within the class. Whether something which is not specified in the list of things falls within the general words depends upon whether or not it is *ejusdem generis* as the specified things. In *Powell v Kempton Park Racecourse Co Ltd*[1], an Act prohibited the keeping of a 'house, office, room or other place' for betting with persons resorting thereto. The House of Lords held that Tattersall's Ring (an uncovered enclosure of a superior sort) at a racecourse was not *ejusdem generis* as the specified things, and was not therefore an 'other place' within the meaning of the Act, since the specific words 'house, office, room' created a *genus* (class) of indoor places. There cannot be a *genus* for the purposes of the present rule unless the 'other' thing is preceded by a list of at least two or more specific things which share the same common characteristics[2].

1 [1899] AC 143, HL. Also see *Brownsea Haven Properties Ltd v Poole Corpn* [1958] Ch 574, [1958] 1 All ER 205, CA.
2 *Quazi v Quazi* [1980] AC 744, [1979] 3 All ER 897, HL.

Presumptions
4.26 There are a number of presumptions as to the intentions of Parliament, which may be rebutted by express words or by necessary implications from the subject matter in the Act itself.

a. *An Act applies to the United Kingdom* There is a presumption that an Act applies to the whole of the United Kingdom but not elsewhere. Acts frequently reveal a contrary intention by containing a section restricting their operation to one or more of the four home countries, or, in the case of a local Act, to a particular locality. On the other hand, an extension of the application of an Act outside the United Kingdom is rarely provided for.

b. *Against retrospective effect of legislation* This presumption is not concerned with when a statute comes into operation but with whether it affects factual situations which arose before that date. Parliament is presumed not to have intended to alter the law applicable to past events and transactions in a manner which is unfair to those concerned in them, unless a contrary intention appears[1]. The presumption is particularly strong where the statute creates offences or tax obligations. The greater the degree of unfairness, the stronger will have to be the evidence that Parliament intended the legislation to have retrospective effect[1].

c. *Against alteration of the law* Parliament is presumed to know the common law and not to intend to change it, with the result that, unless the words of the statute unmistakably indicate that the common law is changed, they must be interpreted so as not to alter it[2]. As part of the presumption against alteration in the law there are certain more specific presumptions: against the restriction of individual liberty; against compulsory deprivation of property, at least without compensation; and that there should be no criminal liability without fault. The presumption against alteration of the law also applies in relation to statute law. In particular, a consolidating Act is presumed not to introduce a change in the law by a change of words[3].

d. *Against the Crown being bound* The Crown is not bound by a statute unless there can be gathered from it an intention that it should be bound[4]. The presumption also extends to employees of the Crown, in the course of their duties, and to Crown property. However, statutes frequently provide that they are to bind the Crown. Even if a statute does not expressly bind the Crown, a court may construe it as doing so by *necessary* implication.

Other presumptions made in construing a statute are those against implied repeal of earlier legislation by later, apparently inconsistent, legislation (the earlier only being impliedly repealed if reconciliation is logically impossible); against ousting the jurisdiction of the courts; and against inconsistency with European Community law or international law.

We deal with the presumption against inconsistency with European Community law in para 4.40, below.

A criticism of the present law is that there is no rule about which presumption should be applied where two of them conflict.

1 *L'Office Cherifien des Phosphates v Yamashita-Shinnihon Steamship Co Ltd* [1994] 1 AC 486, [1994] 1 All ER 20, HL.
2 *Leach v R* [1912] AC 305, HL.
3 *Beswick v Beswick* [1968] AC 58, [1967] 2 All ER 1197, HL.
4 *Tamlin v Hannaford* [1950] 1 KB 18, [1949] 2 All ER 327, CA; *Lord Advocate v Dumbarton District Council* [1990] 2 AC 580, [1990] 1 All ER 1, HL.

Aids to interpretation

Intrinsic aids
4.27 The rule that the whole enactment must be considered makes it of obvious importance to know what parts of an Act may be regarded as intrinsic aids to interpretation.

a. *Long title and short title*   These are part of the Act, but, in practice, the courts do not refer to the short title and only refer to the long title to resolve an ambiguity; in other words the long title is not allowed to restrict the clear meaning of a provision. In *Re Groos*[1], it was held that s 3 of the Wills Act 1861 applied to the will of an alien, even though the long title read: 'An Act to amend the law with respect to wills of personal estates made by British subjects'.

b. *A preamble* is part of the Act. It appears at the beginning and sets out the background and purpose of the enactment. Modern statutes very rarely contain a preamble and the best known examples appear in earlier statutes. The preamble can only be looked at for guidance if the body of the Act is not clear and unambiguous[2].

c. *Punctuation, marginal notes, and headings* to a section or group of sections are inserted into a Bill by the parliamentary draftsmen and can be altered any time up to royal assent. They are not debated by Parliament and are therefore not part of the Act. As a result, they may only be looked at to determine the purpose, as opposed to the scope, of the section[3], although it may be that headings have a wider use[4]. Even in their limited sphere of operation, punctuation and marginal notes in particular carry little weight and cannot oust a meaning indicated by some part of the Act itself.

d. *Schedules*, which are used, for instance, to list repeals and set out transitional or more detailed provisions, are part of the Act, but they cannot affect the interpretation of a word in the body of the Act unless it is ambiguous or uncertain[5].

1 [1904] P 269. Also see *R v Galvin* [1987] QB 862, [1987] 2 All ER 851, CA.
2 *Powell v Kempton Park Racecourse Co Ltd* [1899] AC 143 at 157.
3 *DPP v Schildkamp* [1971] AC 1, [1969] 3 All ER 1640, HL; *R v Kelt* [1977] 3 All ER 1099, [1977] 1 WLR 1365, CA.
4 *DPP v Schildkamp* [1971] AC 1 at 28, [1969] 3 All ER 1640.
5 *Ellerman Lines Ltd v Murray* [1931] AC 126, HL.

Extrinsic aids
4.28 While a court may look at the enactment as a whole it may not, unlike most continental courts, generally look at material outside the four walls of the Act to find Parliament's intention. It cannot, for instance, generally look at reports of the parliamentary debates or proceedings relating to the Bill which became the Act[1]. This may appear to fly in the face of common sense but it must be admitted that it might be difficult in some cases to determine a legislative intent from a two, or more, sided parliamentary debate, especially

where the Bill has been subject to amendment in Parliament. However, the following extrinsic aids (including parliamentary debates) can be looked at for limited purposes:

a. *Dictionaries* can be consulted to ascertain the ordinary and natural meaning, for the purposes of the literal rule, of words which have no particular legal meaning[2].

b. *Parliamentary debates*   In 1992, the majority of the House of Lords in *Pepper v Hart*[3] held that the courts can refer to reports of debates or proceedings in Parliament relating to the provision in question[4] as an aid to its interpretation *if it is ambiguous or obscure or if its literal meaning would lead to absurdity*. However, it held that, even in such cases, reference to parliamentary reports is *only* permissible if:
i.   it discloses the mischief aimed at or the legislative intention behind the ambiguous or obscure words;
ii.   the statements relied on were by a minister or other promoter of the Bill; and
iii.   those statements are clear.

In *Pepper v Hart* a public school operated a concessionary fees scheme for members of staff. The education of the children at a reduced rate was a taxable benefit under s 61(1) of the Finance Act 1976, which provided that an amount equal to the cash equivalent of the benefit was chargeable to tax. By s 63(1) the cash equivalent of the benefit was 'an amount equal to the cost of the benefit' and by s 63(2) the cost of the benefit was 'the amount of any expense incurred in or in connection with its provision'. Although the concessionary fees more than covered the marginal cost to the school of educating the employees' children, the employees were assessed to income tax on the basis that they were liable for a rateable proportion of the expenses in running the school, which proportion was roughly equal to the ordinary school fee. The employees appealed, claiming that since all the costs of running the school would have had to be incurred in any event the only expense incurred by the school 'in or in connection with' the education of their children was the small marginal cost to the school caused by the presence of their children, which was covered by the concessionary fees paid, and so the 'cash equivalent of the benefit' was nil.

The majority of the House of Lords held that s 63(2) was clearly ambiguous because the 'expense incurred in or in connection with' the provision of in-house benefits could be interpreted either as the marginal cost caused by the provision of the benefit or as a proportion of the total cost incurred in providing the service for all parents of pupils (the average cost). Allowing the employees' appeal, the majority of the House held that the requirements set out above were satisfied and that reference to a statement made by the Financial Secretary to the Treasury at the Committee stage of the Bill made it clear that Parliament had intended to assess the expense incurred in the provision of in-house benefits, particularly concessionary fees, on the basis of the marginal cost to the employer, and not on the average cost of the benefit. Most of the majority would have reached the contrary conclusion if they had had to interpret s 63 without reference to the parliamentary report.

There is authority at first instance that, where the purpose of the legislation is to introduce into English law the provisions of an international convention or of a European directive, the strict criteria for admissibility of parliamentary materials set out above do not apply, so that recourse to them can be made on a wider basis[5].

The admissibility of parliamentary materials is of obvious importance where a purposive approach is being taken to the interpretation of a statute.

c. *Reports of committees* containing proposals for legislation which have been presented to Parliament and resulted in the enactment in question can be looked at, for the purpose of the mischief rule, to discover the state of the pre-existing law and the mischief which the enactment was passed to remedy. An example is provided by the House of Lords' decision in *Black-Clawson International Ltd v Papierwerke Waldhof-Aschaffenburg AG*[6], where their Lordships, in order to interpret s 8 of the Foreign Judgments (Reciprocal Enforcement) Act 1933, referred to the report of a committee, which had resulted in the passing of the Act, to discover what the pre-existing law was understood to be and what its mischief was. Two of the five Lords of Appeal, Viscount Dilhorne and Lord Simon, went further and stated that it was permissible to look at such a report for a direct statement of what the resulting enactment meant. This minority statement went further than our courts have been prepared to go in the past. Lord Reid and Lord Wilberforce disagreed with it expressly in *Black-Clawson*, and subsequent House of Lords' decisions have indicated that it is not correct[7].

Government White Papers which have resulted in legislation may, like the reports of committees just mentioned, be referred to in order to ascertain the mischief which Parliament intended to remedy[8].

d. *Judicial precedent* The interpretation given by a court to a statutory provision or word may be binding in relation to *that* provision or word in *that* Act, in accordance with the principles of the doctrine of judicial precedent (paras 4.43–4.55, below). Moreover, a judicial interpretation of a particular provision in one Act will be a similarly binding precedent in a subsequent one if they both deal with the same subject matter, as where the latter is a consolidating Act.

e. *Interpretation Act 1978* The Act lays down various definitions which apply unless there is a contrary intention, express or implied, in a particular statute. For example, 'unless the contrary intention appears, (a) words importing the masculine gender shall include females; and (b) words in the singular shall include the plural and words in the plural shall include the singular'[9]. Again, 'person' includes any body of persons corporate or unincorporate[10].

1 *Assam Railways and Trading Co Ltd v IRC* [1935] AC 445, HL; *Davis v Johnson* [1979] AC 264, [1978] 1 All ER 1132, HL; *Hadmor Productions Ltd v Hamilton* [1983] 1 AC 191, [1982] 1 All ER 1042, HL.

2 *Re Ripon (Highfield) Housing Confirmation Order 1938* [1939] 2 KB 838, [1939] 3 All ER 548, CA.
3 [1993] AC 593, [1993] 1 All ER 42, HL. See also *R v Warwickshire County Council, ex p Johnson* [1993] AC 583, [1993] 1 All ER 299, HL.
4 But not other provisions: *Melluish (Inspector of Taxes) v BMI (No 3) Ltd* [1996] AC 454, [1995] 4 All ER 453, HL.
5 *Three Rivers District Council v Governor of the Bank of England (No 2)* [1996] 2 All ER 363. The statement was only an obiter dictum term defined and explained in paras 4.45 and 4.55, below.
6 [1975] AC 591, [1975] 1 All ER 810, HL. Also see *Davis v Johnson* [1979] AC 264, [1978] 1 All ER 1132, HL.
7 *R v Ayres* [1984] AC 447, [1984] 1 All ER 619, HL; *R v Allen* [1985] AC 1029, [1985] 2 All ER 641, HL. For views in support of the minority statement, see *R v Shivpuri* [1987] AC 1 at 21, [1986] 2 All ER 334 at 343; *Aswan Engineering Establishment Co v Lupdine Ltd* [1987] 1 All ER 135 at 146–147; *R v Gomez* [1993] 1 All ER 1 at 24.
8 *Black-Clawson International Ltd v Papierwerke Waldof-Aschaffenburg AG* [1975] AC 591 at 638; *A-G's Reference (No 1 of 1988)* [1989] 1 All ER 321 at 324.
9 Section 6.
10 Schedule 1.

Acts giving effect to international conventions

4.29 Increasingly, the purpose of an Act of Parliament is to put into domestic effect an international convention. In such a case recourse may be had to the terms of the convention if a provision of the Act is ambiguous or vague[1]. Sometimes, an Act actually incorporates the convention. In such a case there are no limits on recourse to the terms of the convention because they have been made provisions of the Act. Conventions are apt to be more loosely worded than Acts of Parliament, and in *James Buchanan & Co Ltd v Babco Forwarding and Shipping (UK) Ltd*[2] the House of Lords held that a court must interpret the English text of an incorporated convention in a broad and sensible manner, unconstrained by the technical rules of English law. Moreover, the majority of their Lordships held, if there is doubt about the true construction of the English text the court can look at an authorised text in a foreign language to resolve it. In the event of ambiguity or obscurity in the convention, the court can look at material in the public records of the international conference at which it was drafted provided that that material was intended to clear up the ambiguity or obscurity[3].

1 *Post Office v Estuary Radio Ltd* [1968] 2 QB 740, [1967] 3 All ER 663, CA.
2 [1978] AC 141, [1977] 3 All ER 1048, HL. Also see *Rothmans of Pall Mall (Overseas) Ltd v Saudi Arabian Airlines Corpn* [1981] QB 368, [1980] 3 All ER 359, CA.
3 *Fothergill v Monarch Airlines Ltd* [1981] AC 251, [1980] 2 All ER 696, HL.

Legislation of the European Community

4.30 This legislation is to be found in the treaties, including amending treaties, which established the three Communities, the European Economic Community (EEC), the European Coal and Steel Community (ECSC) and the European Atomic Energy Community (EURATOM) which now make up the European Union. It is also to be found in regulations, directives and decisions of its organs. It is largely concerned with economic matters, such as agriculture, free trade and fair competition, but it also deals with other matters, such as immigration, employment and other social matters.

Regulations, directives and decisions

4.31 Regulations have general application and are made by the Council of Ministers of the European Union (a political body composed normally of foreign ministers) or the Commission (a supranational body composed of the highest officials) under the treaties.

Directives can be issued or decisions made by the Council or the Commission. Directives are directed to member states, who are obliged to implement them although they have a choice as to the form and methods of implementation. Decisions are addressed either to a member state or to an individual or institution. They are a formal method of enunciating administrative decisions effecting the policy of the Community and are binding on the addressee.

Direct applicability and direct effect

4.32 In discussing the types of legislation of the Community, a fundamental point must be emphasised at the outset: regulations are '*directly applicable*' in the sense that they confer rights and duties on individuals and institutions which are enforceable in the courts of member states without being re-enacted by legislation in those states. This is provided by the treaties establishing the Community. However, although the treaties conclude the matter according to *Community law*, they do not in themselves give the concept of 'direct applicability' legal effect in the *law of the United Kingdom*. The reason is that treaty provisions do not become part of our law unless they have been incorporated into it by legislation. Such incorporation has been achieved by the European Communities Act 1972, s 2(1), which provides that those rights and duties which are, as a matter of Community law, 'directly applicable' or 'directly effective' are to have legal effect in the UK.

Section 2(4) of the Act goes on to provide that Acts of Parliament passed or to be passed shall have effect subject to the rules of Community law which are directly applicable or of direct effect. According to the decisions of the House of Lords in *R v Secretary of State for Transport, ex p Factortame Ltd*[1] and *R v Secretary of State for Transport, ex p Factortame Ltd (No 2)*[2], the effect of s 2(4) seems to be to imply into every piece of United Kingdom legislation a term that it takes effect subject to directly applicable or directly effective Community law and to require the United Kingdom courts to override a piece of United Kingdom legislation to the extent that it is inconsistent with Community law which is directly applicable or of direct effect.

It is inconceivable that a UK court would so act without first seeking a preliminary ruling from the European Court confirming the inconsistency[3]. Pending the preliminary ruling, a UK court may suspend the operation of the Act of Parliament by granting an interlocutory injunction[4]. Whether or not a court will grant an interlocutory injunction in such a case against a public authority seeking to enforce the Act of Parliament depends on the balance of convenience, whether damages would be an appropriate remedy, the importance

75

of upholding the law and the obligation of certain authorities to enforce the law, and whether the challenge to the Act is prima facie so firmly based as to justify so exceptional a course[5].

To the extent that directly applicable or directly effective Community law prevails over an Act of Parliament under United Kingdom law, the sovereignty of Parliament has been limited.

1   [1990] 2 AC 85, [1989] 2 All ER 692, HL.
2   [1991] 1 AC 603, [1991] 1 All ER 70, ECJ and HL.
3   Para 2.31, above.
4   *R v Secretary of State for Transport, ex p Factortame Ltd* [1990] 2 AC 85, [1989] 2 All ER 692, HL.
5   *R v Secretary of State for Transport, ex p Factortame Ltd (No 2)* [1991] 1 AC 603, [1991] 1 All ER 70, ECJ and HL.

4.33   No other form of Community legislation is expressly stated in the treaties establishing the Community to be directly applicable. It was once thought that these other forms could only take effect in member states if they were implemented by them. However, in 1963 it was established by the European Court of Justice that the provisions of treaties of the Community could directly confer rights or impose obligations on individuals without implementation in national law[1]. This concept of *direct effect* has subsequently been extended to directives[2] and decisions[3]. In *Van Duyn v Home Office*[4], for example, the European Court held that a directive was of binding effect so as to confer rights on the plaintiff against the United Kingdom government even though the UK had not implemented that directive.

In order to have direct effect, a treaty provision, directive or decision must be unconditional and sufficiently precise. Not surprisingly, it cannot be directly effective if details remain to be resolved by a member state before it can be implemented[5].

Where it exists, the direct effect of a directive is narrower than the direct applicability of a regulation or the direct effect of a treaty provision. The reason is that directives can only have 'vertical' direct effect (ie in favour of an individual against the state or an arm of the state) and not, unlike regulations and treaty provisions, 'horizontal' effect (ie as between individuals in the state or in favour of the state or an arm of the state against an individual). In other words, they can only confer rights on individuals, and not obligations on them. This was held by the European Court in *Marshall v Southampton and South West Hampshire Area Health Authority*[6], where a woman who had been dismissed by an area health authority on reaching the retirement age for women (60, as opposed to 65 for men), succeeded in her claim that this constituted sexual discrimination contrary to a directive. The directive had not been incorporated into English law by United Kingdom legislation but the European Court held that it was directly effective vis-à-vis the employer, the area health authority, because it was an arm of the state. The European Court has held that the concept of direct effect can be relied on against any organisation or body providing a public service, which is subject to the authority or control of the state and which has for that purpose special powers beyond those which result from the normal rules applicable to relations between individuals; these can all be regarded as an arm of the state. Accordingly, directives have been held directly effective against local or regional authorities, police authorities and nationalised industries, and the governors of a voluntarily aided school[7], as well as public authorities providing public health services.

Whether or not a directive is directly effective depends on an examination of the nature, general scheme and wording of its provisions to see whether they are capable of producing direct effects[3]. In practice, very few directives are likely to be regarded as having direct effect.

1 *Algemene Transport-en Expedite Onderneming Van Gend en Loos v Nederlande Administratie Der Belastingadministratie* [1963] ECR 1, ECJ.
2 *Van Duyn v Home Office* [1975] Ch 358, [1975] 3 All ER 190, ECJ.
3 *Grad v Finanzamt Traunstein* [1970] ECR 825, [1971] CMLR 1, ECJ.
4 [1975] Ch 358, [1975] 3 All ER 190, ECJ.
5 *Becker v Finanzamt Münster-Innenstadt* [1982] ECR 53, [1982] 1 CMLR 499, ECJ.
6 [1986] QB 401, [1986] 2 All ER 584, ECJ. In *Faccini Dori v Recreb Srl* [1994] ECR I-3325, [1995] All ER (EC) 1, ECJ. The European Court affirmed its view in *Marshall* that a directive cannot have horizontal effect.
7 See, respectively, *Fratelli Costanzo SpA v Comune di Milano* [1989] ECR 1839, [1990] 3 CMLR 239, ECJ; *Johnston v Chief Constable of the Royal Ulster Constabulary* [1987] QB 129, [1986] 3 All ER 135, ECJ; and *Foster v British Gas plc* [1991] 2 AC 306, [1991] 2 All ER 705, HL, where it was held that the British Gas Corporation, a public corporation (and not to be confused with the subsequent privatised public limited company), under the ultimate control of the state which could dictate its policies and retain its surplus revenue, was a body against whom a directive could be directly applicable; *National Union of Teachers v Governing Body of St Mary's C of E Aided Junior School* [1997] ICR 334, CA. Contrast *Doughty v Rolls-Royce plc* [1992] 1 CMLR 1045, CA, where a directive was held not to be directly effective against a commercial undertaking notwithstanding that all its shares were held by nominees of the government.

Unimplemented directives: any effect in English law?
4.34 A directive which has not been implemented into the law of a member state and is not of direct effect in the circumstances is not devoid of all effect under that law. It may have effect in two ways, according to the European Court of Justice. First, a national court can have regard to an unimplemented directive in interpreting national regulations. Second, the failure of a member state to implement a directive may give rise to a liability in damages.

4.35 As the Court held in *Marleasing SA v La Comercial Internacional de Alimentación SA*[1], national law, whenever passed, must be interpreted by a national court in such a way as to give effect to Community directives so far as possible. In this case, there was a dispute in a Spanish court between two Spanish companies. One sought to have the memorandum and articles of association of the other (company A) set aside on a ground prescribed by Spanish legislation. Company A argued in reply that its memorandum and articles were in accordance with a directive of the EC Commission, the First Company Law Directive. That directive had not been enacted into Spanish law. The European Court held that company A could not rely directly on the unenacted directive in an action with a private entity, but went on to state that the Spanish court was obliged to interpret the Spanish legislation 'in every way possible in the light of the text and aim of the directive to achieve the result envisaged by it'. This, the European Court held, required that in the particular case the Spanish court should ignore a specific provision of Spanish law which was inconsistent with the aim of the directive.

The ruling in *Marleasing* only requires a national court interpreting national law to do so *so far as possible* in such a way as to give effect to a directive which has not been implemented nationally. The words italicised led the European Court of Justice in *Criminal proceedings against Arcaro*[2] to hold that the ruling in *Marleasing* did not extend to permitting a national court to interpret a national law so as to impose on an individual an obligation laid down by a directive which has not been implemented in national law or, more especially, so as to impose or increase the criminal liability of persons who act in breach of a directive. In other words, a national court cannot eliminate national provisions contrary to a provision of a directive which has not been implemented nationally and substitute the terms of the directive. To do so would be to introduce direct effect between individuals under the guise of interpretation.

The correct approach of an English court to the interpretation of unimplemented directives has been stated in similar terms in our courts. It has been said that it is for an English court to construe an Act of Parliament so as to accord with a directive, if this can be done without distorting the meaning of the Act, whether the Act came after or before the directive[3]. This has been explained as consistent with the statement in *Marleasing* that a national court must construe a domestic law to accord with a relevant directive if it is possible to do so, which it will not be if the domestic law is not open to an interpretation consistent with the directive[4].

1   [1990] ECR I-4135, [1992] 1 CMLR 305, ECJ.
2   [1997] All ER (EC) 82, ECJ.
3   *Webb v EMO Air Cargo (UK) Ltd* [1992] 4 All ER 929 at 939–940; *Duke v GEC Reliance Ltd* [1988] AC 618, [1988] 1 All ER 626, HL.
4   *Webb v EMO Air Cargo (UK) Ltd*, ibid.

4.36   The European Court's decision in *Francovich v Italy*[1] indicates that a person may be able to claim from a member state in the courts of that state damages for loss suffered as a result of its failure to implement nationally a directive. In this case, the Italian government had failed to implement a directive requiring a national institution to be established to ensure that employees of insolvent employers received arrears of salary. Employees of companies which had become insolvent owing substantial arrears of salaries brought proceedings in an Italian court against the Italian Republic, seeking payments under the directive. The European Court held that the directive was not of direct effect because it was insufficiently precise, in that it did not specify which organ of state was to bear the liability. Consequently, the employees could not rely on it in an action in an Italian court. However, the European Court held that the employees could succeed in their claim against the Italian Republic for damages for loss resulting from its failure to implement the directive in breach of its obligation to do so under Community law. The court stated that three conditions must be fulfilled before such a claim could succeed:

a.   the objective of the directive must include the conferment of rights on individuals;

b.   the content of those rights must be ascertainable from the directive itself; and
c.   there must be a causal link between the state's failure to fulfil its obligations and the loss sustained by the individual.

1   [1991] ECR I-5357, [1993] 2 CMLR 66, ECJ.

4.37   *Francovich* concerned non-implementation of a directive. It left unclear the extent to which a member state might be liable for damages where it was otherwise in breach of its obligations under Community law. A relevant example, in the present context, would be where the state had tried to implement its obligations but had done so inadequately or erroneously. The issue was addressed by the European Court in the joined cases of *Brasserie du Pêcheur SA v Germany* and *R v Secretary of State for Transport, ex p Factortame Ltd (No 3)*[1]. In *Brasserie du Pêcheur* a French brewery, which had been forced to discontinue exports to Germany because its beer did not comply with a German purity law which was contrary to art 30 of the EC Treaty (a provision not directly effective), claimed damages against Germany. In *Factortame Ltd (No 3)* Spanish fishermen, who had suffered loss as a result of British legislation which had imposed strict conditions on eligibility to fish under the British flag in breach of non-directly effective articles in the Treaty, claimed damages against the United Kingdom. The cases were referred to the European Court under art 177 of the EEC Treaty for preliminary rulings.

The Court held that the principle of state liability established in *Francovich* applied to all acts or omissions in a state, whether legislative, executive or judicial, in breach of Community law, whether or not directly effective. This does not mean that a member state will always be liable if, for example, it fails to implement by legislation its obligations under Community law, or does so inadequately or erroneously. This is because the conditions for liability laid down in *Brasserie du Pêcheur* and *Factortame Ltd (No 3)* introduce an important restriction. The European Court held that, where a member state is faced with a situation involving legislative choices comparable to those made by Community institutions when they adopt Community measures (legislation), as it is in respect of legislating to implement Community law, the state will only be liable to individuals who have suffered loss for breach of the Community law if three conditions are met:

a.   the rule of law infringed must be intended to confer rights on the individuals;
b.   the breach must be sufficiently serious, in that the state or institution concerned has manifestly and gravely disregarded the limits on its discretion; and
c.   there must be a direct causal link between the breach of the state's obligation and the loss sustained by the injured individuals.

To some extent these conditions say no more than expressly said in *Francovich*, but the second condition (breach must be sufficiently serious) is an addition to what was said in *Francovich*. Given the explanation of 'sufficiently serious' given by the Court, a breach of Community law by a state facing a choice as to its actions would not be sufficiently serious unless, for example, it should have known that it was acting in breach of Community law.

Further consideration to the 'sufficiently serious' condition was given by the European Court in *R v HM Treasury, ex p British Telecommunications plc*[2], which concerned a claim for damages by BT for loss suffered as a result of the alleged improper implementation by the United Kingdom of a Council directive. The Court found that the UK's implementing legislation had incorrectly transposed the directive, but it held that the UK was not liable for BT's loss because the breach of Community law was not sufficiently serious. Its reason was that one of the factors to be taken into consideration in determining whether a manifest and grave disregard by a state or institution of the limits of its legislative discretion, and therefore whether there was a sufficiently serious breach, was the clarity and precision of the Community law breached. Here the article of the Treaty in question was imprecisely worded and the UK's interpretation made in good faith was one which the provision was reasonably capable of bearing, although it was not the interpretation given by the Court.

1   [1996] QB 404, [1996] All ER (EC) 301, ECJ.
2   [1996] QB 615, [1996] All ER (EC) 411, ECJ.

4.38   The conditions laid down in *Brasserie du Pêcheur* and *Factortame Ltd (No 3)* were laid down in the context of the situation where the member state has legislative choices comparable to those made by Community institutions when they adopt measures. It has now been established that they also apply where the state has no legislative choices (as where it is obliged to legislate along certain lines by a set date) and has considerably reduced discretion, or even no discretion. In this type of case, the condition of a sufficiently serious breach is much more easily established. The mere infringement may in itself be enough to establish it, regardless, for example, of intentional fault or negligence[1].

1   *R v Ministry of Agriculture, Fisheries and Food, ex p Hedley Lomas (Ireland) Ltd* [1996] All ER (EC) 493, ECJ; *Dillenkofer v Germany* [1996] All ER (EC) 917, ECJ.

4.39   The operation of the rule of state liability established in *Francovich* and developed in later cases has yet to be worked out. A plaintiff can only succeed in a civil action before an English court if he can establish that it falls within a cause of action in English law. To recover damages, the plaintiff must establish a tort such as misfeasance in public office (which requires the public body maliciously or, at least, knowingly to exceed its powers) or negligence or breach of statutory duty (both of which are hedged with restrictive rules which may make them inapplicable).

Supremacy of European Community law
4.40   In Community law, where there is a conflict between binding Community law and a national law of a member state, Community law takes precedence over that national law, whether the latter was enacted before or after the Community law in question[1].

The position under United Kingdom law, which is the law that an English court must apply English law, is more complicated.

Where a provision in an Act of Parliament is followed by an inconsistent directly applicable or directly effective provision[2] of Community law, the latter has precedence[3]. The same is true if the inconsistent directly applicable or directly effective Community law provision preceded the provision in the Act if both were made before the European Communities Act 1972[2]. However, if the subsequent Act was made after the 1972 Act the position is as follows. If the Act of Parliament is unclear, an English court will seek to interpret it so as to be consistent with the directly applicable or directly effective Community law provision[3]. The reason is that, as already stated, a statute is presumed to be consistent with Community law. On the other hand, if the Act clearly conflicts with the prior Community law, then, unless the wording of the Act unambiguously compels the court to do otherwise, an Act of Parliament must be construed so as to be consistent with directly applicable or directly effective Community law, and if the Act is unintentionally inconsistent, precedence must be given to Community law[4].

1   *Costa v ENEL* [1964] ECR 585, ECJ.
2   As to these terms, see paras 4.32 and 4.33, above.
3   European Communities Act 1972, s 2.
4   *Macarthys Ltd v Smith* [1979] 3 All ER 325, [1979] 1 WLR 1189, CA.

Validity of legislation of European Community
4.41 Regulations, directives and decisions are subject to review by the European Court. They can be held invalid by it (but not by a court of a member state[1]) on the grounds of lack of competence, or infringement of any essential procedural requirement, or infringement of the treaties or of any rule of law concerning their application, or misuse of power[2]. Where the validity of a piece of Community legislation is referred to the European Court under art 177 of the European Economic Community Treaty, the referring court may adopt interim measures suspending the application of that law[3].

Directives and decisions are implemented in the UK by delegated legislation made under powers given by the European Communities Act 1972, s 2(2), which also governs the implementation in further detail of regulations made by the Council or Commission. Orders in Council and departmental regulations made under these powers can include any provision which might be made in an Act of Parliament[4]. This power to make delegated legislation is the widest given to the executive in modern times apart from times of war. The power must be exercised by way of statutory instrument and presumably such an instrument will be ultra vires if it is not related to the affairs of the Communities. There are a number of limits on this power of delegated legislation; for instance, it cannot be used to impose taxation.

1   *Foto-Frost v Hauptzollamt Lübeck-Ost* [1987] ECR 4199, [1988] 3 CMLR 57, ECJ.
2   EEC Treaty, art 173; Euratom Treaty, art 146. Also see ECSC Treaty, art 33.
3   *Atlanta Fruchthandelsgesellschaft mbH v Bundesant für Ernährung und Forswirtschaft* [1995] ECR I-3761, ECJ.
4   European Communities Act 1972, s 2(4). Also see Sch 2.

Interpretation of the legislation of the European Community
4.42   The drafting of the legislation of the Community is quite unlike that of English legislation but, like the legislation of other European countries, is drafted in terms of broad principle, leaving the courts to supply the detail by giving effect to the general intention of the legislature. As an essential aid to this process, the regulations, directives and decisions mentioned above are required to state the reasons on which they are based and to refer to any proposals or opinions which were required to be obtained pursuant to the Treaties. These are usually incorporated in a preamble.

The result of this difference in drafting is that the interpretation of the legislation of the Community, whether by the European Court or by an English court[1], is not based on a slavish interpretation of the words or the grammatical structure of the sentences but on the purpose or intent of the legislation[2]; in other words, a purposive approach is taken to the interpretation of such legislation.

1   *HP Bulmer Ltd v J Bollinger SA* [1974] Ch 401 at 425–426, [1974] 2 All ER 1226 at 1237–1238.
2   *HP Bulmer Ltd v J Bollinger SA*; *Van Duyn v Home Office* [1975] Ch 358, [1975] 3 All ER 190, ECJ; *Litster v Forth Dry Dock and Engineering Co Ltd* [1990] 1 AC 546, [1989] 1 All ER 1134, HL.

Judicial Precedent

4.43   This is the other important legal source and consists of the 'decisions' of courts made in the course of litigation. As will be seen, the 'decisions' of certain courts are more than just authoritative statements of the law since they can be binding (ie must be applied) in subsequent cases where the legally material facts are the same, whether or not the later court considers them to be correct or appropriate. Whether a particular statement of law made by a judge in one case is binding in a subsequent case depends partly on whether the statement formed the ratio decidendi (the reason for the decision) of the case or was merely an obiter dictum (something said by the way), and partly on the relative position of the two courts. Even if it is not binding, a judicial statement of the law has a persuasive effect in subsequent cases, the strength of its persuasiveness being a matter of degree, as we explain in para 4.55, below.

Ratio decidendi and obiter dictum
4.44   Only the ratio decidendi of a case can have binding effect. A judgment usually contains the following elements:

a.   A statement of the facts found with an indication, express or implied, of which of them are material facts. In reading the report of a judgment, great care must be taken to ascertain what facts were found to be material.
b.   Statements by the judge of the legal principles which apply to the legal issues raised by the material facts and which are the reason for his decision.

Normally these statements are only made after a review of existing precedents and general legal principles.

c. The actual judgment, decree or order delivered by the judge after application of b. to a., eg that the defendant is liable coupled with an award of damages.

Part c. is binding only on the parties to the case and is not a precedent for the future, nor is part a. in itself. It is part b. of this process which constitutes the ratio decidendi.

4.45 Sometimes the statements of the applicable principles made by the judge may be wider than the material facts necessitate. In such a case the ratio of the decision will be limited to that part of it which applies to the material facts and, to the extent that the statement is wider, it will be obiter dictum[1]. Apart from that just mentioned, there are two other types of obiter dictum.

First, a statement of legal principle is obiter if it relates to facts which were not found to exist in the case or, if found, were not material. Two famous cases provide good examples. In *Central London Property Trust Ltd v High Trees House Ltd*, which we discuss later in this book[2], Denning J's principal statement about promissory estoppel was obiter, since it applied to a set of facts which were not found to exist in the case. Similarly, in *Rondel v Worsley*[3], the House of Lords expressed opinions that a barrister who was negligent when acting other than in connection with litigation might be held liable in tort and that a solicitor, when acting as an advocate, might be immune from liability. Both statements were obiter since the case concerned the tortious liability of a barrister when acting as an advocate, so that these statements were not necessary to the court's decision.

Second, a statement of legal principle which relates to some or all of the material facts but is not the basis of the court's decision, eg because it is given in a dissenting judgment or because another material fact prevents the principle applying, is also obiter. A leading example is *Hedley Byrne & Co Ltd v Heller & Partners Ltd*[4]. The House of Lords expressed the opinion that the maker of a statement owes a duty of care, in certain circumstances, to persons who suffer loss in reliance on it. This opinion was obiter because, although it was based on material facts found to exist in the case, the actual decision – that there was no breach of such a duty – was based on another material fact, that the maker of the statement had made it subject to an effective disclaimer of responsibility.

1 *Cassidy v Ministry of Health* [1951] 2 KB 343, [1951] 1 All ER 574, CA.
2 Para 6.17, below.
3 [1969] 1 AC 191, [1967] 3 All ER 993, HL; para 18.34, below.
4 [1964] AC 465, [1963] 2 All ER 575, HL; para 18.14, below.

The hierarchy of the courts and judicial precedent
4.46 We saw in the previous chapter that the system of courts is a hierarchy. Essentially, one court is bound by the ratio decidendi of a case decided by another court if it is lower in the hierarchy than the latter and will not be

bound by it if it is higher. Magistrates' courts and county courts are bound by the rationes decidendi in cases decided by a High Court judge or the courts above such judges. A High Court judge is bound by the rationes decidendi of cases decided by the Court of Appeal and the House of Lords, and the Court of Appeal is bound by those of the House of Lords. This basic statement will be expanded by taking courts in turn, starting from the top of the hierarchy. For convenience, the word 'decision' will be used to indicate 'ratio decidendi'.

The Court of Justice of the European Communities

4.47   As we said in para 3.31 above, the European Court is now the ultimate court in the following matters:

a.   the interpretation of the European Economic Community Treaty;
b.   the validity and interpretation of the acts of the institutions of the European Community and of the European Central Bank; and
c.   the interpretation of the statutes of bodies established by an act of the Council of the European Union.

Consequently, in these limited areas of jurisdiction the decisions of the European Court bind all English courts. Indeed, s 3(1) of the European Communities Act 1972 provides that any question as to the meaning or effect of any of the treaties, or as to the validity, meaning or effect of any Community instrument, shall be treated as a question of law (and, if not referred to the European Court, be for determination in accordance with the principles laid down by, and any relevant decision of, the European Court or any court attached thereto).

The European Court does not observe a doctrine of binding precedent and does not regard itself as bound by its previous decisions[1], although it leans in favour of consistency with its previous decisions.

1   *Da Costa en Schaake NV v Nederlandse Belastingadministratie* [1963] ECR 31, [1963] CMLR 224, ECJ.

The House of Lords

4.48   A decision of the House of Lords binds all courts inferior to it. Until 1966, a decision of the House of Lords also bound that House; a principle which was finally established at the end of the nineteenth century. This meant that a legal principle might become unalterable by the House of Lords, in which case legislation was the only remedy if a change in the law was desired. In 1966, the House of Lords reversed this principle in an extra-judicial statement made by the Lord Chancellor (which has been regarded as having the force of law) declaring that it would not be bound by its own decisions where it appeared right to depart from them[1]. The declaration added that in this connection the House would bear in mind the danger of disturbing retrospectively the basis on which contracts, settlements of property and fiscal arrangements have been entered into and also the special need for certainty as to the criminal law. The declaration emphasised that it was not intended to apply elsewhere than in the House of Lords.

So far their Lordships have not made much use of their new-found freedom and have held that it is not enough that they should consider their previous decision was wrong; there must be an additional factor, such as a change of circumstances on which the decision was based or that it is productive of manifest injustice[2]. In addition, they have held that they should not embark upon a review of a previous decision of theirs unless they felt free, if necessary, to depart both from the reasoning and the decision in the previous case and, in addition, were satisfied that the review would be of relevance to the resolution of the dispute in the case before them[3]. One of the few cases in which the House of Lords has overruled one of its previous decisions is *Murphy v Brentwood District Council*[4] where it overruled its decision in *Anns v Merton London Borough Council*[5] that a local authority, exercising its statutory function of exercising control over building works, was under a common law duty to take reasonable care to ensure that the building complied with building regulations.

1   [1966] 3 All ER 77.
2   *Fitzleet Estates Ltd v Cherry* [1977] 3 All ER 996, [1977] 1 WLR 1345, HL.
3   *Food Corpn of India v Antclizo Shipping Corpn, The Antclizo* [1988] 2 All ER 513, [1988] 1 WLR 603, HL.
4   [1991] 1 AC 398, [1990] 2 All ER 908, HL; para 18.11, below.
5   [1978] AC 728, [1977] 2 All ER 492, HL.

The Court of Appeal

4.49   The Civil Division of the Court of Appeal is bound by the previous decisions of the House of Lords. It is also bound by the previous decisions of either division of the Court of Appeal[1]. This was settled by the Court of Appeal in *Young v Bristol Aeroplane Co Ltd*[2]. However, three exceptional circumstances were recognised where an earlier Court of Appeal decision is not binding on the Civil Division:

a.   Where two of its previous decisions conflict. The decision not followed will be deemed to be overruled[3].
b.   The court must refuse to follow a previous decision of its own which, although not expressly overruled, is inconsistent with a later House of Lords' decision.
c.   The court is not bound to follow its previous decision if that decision was given per incuriam (ie through lack of care). The usual ground on which a decision is regarded as having been given per incuriam is where some relevant statute or binding precedent, which would have affected the decision, was overlooked by the court in the previous case[4]. Only in very rare instances will a decision not strictly within this formulation be held to have been decided per incuriam, since such a decision must involve a manifest slip or error and it must be likely to cause serious inconvenience in the administration of justice or serious injustice or some equally serious consequence[5]. The court is not bound to follow another of its decisions (decision B) if, although not itself per incuriam, decision B was based solely on another Court of Appeal decision (decision A) which, unknown to the Court of Appeal when it made decision B, was per incuriam[6].

While the per incuriam doctrine is also open to the House of Lords as a basis for rejecting one of its own previous decisions, the refusal of the Court of Appeal to follow the House of Lords' decision in *Rookes v Barnard*[7], on the basis that it had been reached per incuriam because of two previous House of Lords' decisions, was rejected in strong terms by the House of Lords on appeal in *Cassell & Co Ltd v Broome*[8].

In addition to the exceptions mentioned in *Young v Bristol Aeroplane Co Ltd*, three other exceptions have been indicated by subsequent cases: a decision by a two-judge Court of Appeal hearing an interlocutory appeal does not bind a court of three[9]; a Court of Appeal decision subsequently disapproved by the Privy Council need not be followed by the Court of Appeal[10]; and, if a Court of Appeal decision goes to the House of Lords and the House decides the appeal on a different ground from that argued in the Court of Appeal, being of the opinion that the issue decided in the Court of Appeal did not arise, the Court of Appeal's decision is not binding on a subsequent Court of Appeal[11].

1 And those of its predecessors: the Court of Exchequer Chamber and the Court of Appeal in Chancery, but not by the decisions of the now defunct Court of Criminal Appeal.
2 [1944] KB 718, [1944] 2 All ER 293, CA. The rule in *Young v Bristol Aeroplane Co Ltd* was reaffirmed by the House of Lords in *Davis v Johnson* [1979] AC 264, [1978] 1 All ER 1132.
3 As happened in *Fisher v Ruislip-Northwood UDC and Middlesex County Council* [1945] KB 584, [1945] 2 All ER 458, CA.
4 See, for example, *Miliangos v George Frank (Textiles) Ltd* [1976] AC 443 at 477, [1975] 3 All ER 801; *Duke v Reliance Systems Ltd* [1988] QB 108, [1987] 2 All ER 858, CA (affirmed without adverting to this point: [1988] AC 618, [1988] 1 All ER 626, HL).
5 *Williams v Fawcett* [1986] QB 604, [1985] 1 All ER 787, CA; *Rickards v Rickards* [1990] Fam 194, [1989] 3 All ER 193, CA; *Re Probe Data Systems Ltd (No 3)* [1992] BCC 110, CA.
6 *Rakhit v Carty* [1990] 2 QB 315, [1990] 2 All ER 202, CA.
7 [1964] AC 1129, [1964] 1 All ER 367, HL.
8 [1972] AC 1027, [1972] 1 All ER 801, HL.
9 *Boys v Chaplin* [1968] 2 QB 1, [1968] 1 All ER 283, CA. A *final* decision of a two-judge Court of Appeal has the same binding effect as that of a court of three: *Langley v North West Water Authority* [1991] 3 All ER 610, [1991] 1 WLR 697, CA.
10 *Doughty v Turner Manufacturing Co Ltd* [1964] 1 QB 518, [1964] 1 All ER 98, CA; *Worcester Works Finance Ltd v Cooden Engineering Co Ltd* [1972] 1 QB 210, [1971] 3 All ER 708, CA.
11 *Al-Mehdawi v Secretary of State for the Home Department* [1990] 1 AC 876, sub nom *R v Secretary of State for the Home Department, ex p Al-Mehdawi* [1989] 1 All ER 777, CA; reversed on appeal on another point [1990] 1 AC 876, [1989] 3 All ER 843, HL.

4.50 The Criminal Division of the Court of Appeal is bound not only by the decisions of the House of Lords and Court of Appeal but also by those of its predecessor, the Court of Criminal Appeal[1]. However, in the case of decisions of the two last named courts there are exceptions:

a.   The three exceptions mentioned in *Young v Bristol Aeroplane Co Ltd*[2] and the other exceptions mentioned in the previous paragraph.

b.   The Criminal Division has power to overrule a previous decision of itself or the Court of Criminal Appeal, on the grounds that the law has been 'misapplied or misunderstood'[3], but only if this is necessary in the interests of the appellant[4].

1 *R v Hoskyn* (1977) 67 Cr App Rep 88 at 91.

2 *R v Taylor* [1950] 2 KB 368 at 371, [1950] 2 All ER 170; *R v Ewing* [1983] QB 1039 at 1047, [1983] 2 All ER 645.
3 *R v Taylor* [1950] 2 KB 368, [1950] 2 All ER 170, CA; *R v Newsome; R v Browne* [1970] 2 QB 711, [1970] 3 All ER 455, CA.
4 *R v Spencer; R v Smails* [1985] QB 771, [1985] 1 All ER 673, CA.

Divisional courts

4.51 Divisional courts are bound by decisions of the House of Lords and of the Court of Appeal, except, apparently, a Court of Appeal decision which is per incuriam, in that a relevant decision of the House of Lords was not cited[1]. A divisional court is bound by one of its own previous decisions unless the *Young v Bristol Aeroplane Co Ltd* principles apply[2] or, in criminal cases and cases where it is exercising the supervisory jurisdiction of the High Court[3], unless that previous decision was clearly wrong[4].

1 *R v Northumberland Compensation Appeal Tribunal, ex p Shaw* [1952] 1 KB 338, [1952] 1 All ER 122, CA.
2 *Huddersfield Police Authority v Watson* [1947] KB 842, [1947] 2 All ER 193, DC.
3 Para 3.18, above.
4 *R v Greater Manchester Coroner, ex p Tal* [1985] QB 67, [1984] 3 All ER 240, DC; *Hornigold v Chief Constable of Lancashire* [1985] Crim LR 792, DC; *Wakeley v Hyams* [1987] RTR 49, DC.

High Court judges

4.52 A High Court judge is bound by the decisions of the courts mentioned above (other than a divisional court exercising the supervisory jurisdiction of the High Court), but he is not bound by decisions of another High Court judge, although he will treat such a decision as strong persuasive authority and will only refuse to follow it if he is convinced that it is wrong, and with a clear statement of the reason for doing so[1]. Where a High Court judge is faced with two conflicting decisions of other High Court judges, he should normally treat the legal point at issue as settled by the second decision, provided the judge in that case had reached his decision after full consideration of the first decision. The only, rare, exception is where the third judge is convinced that the second judge was wrong in not following the first, as, for example, where a binding or persuasive precedent had not been cited in either of the first two cases[2].

Although, strictly, a High Court judge is not bound by a decision of a divisional court exercising the supervisory jurisdiction of the High Court, he will follow that decision unless he is convinced that it is wrong[3].

1 *Re Hillas-Drake, National Provincial Bank Ltd v Liddell* [1944] Ch 235, [1944] 1 All ER 375.
2 *Colchester Estates (Cardiff) v Carlton Industries plc* [1986] Ch 80, [1984] 2 All ER 601.
3 *R v Greater Manchester Coroner, ex p Tal* [1984] 3 All ER 240 at 248.

Other courts

4.53 County courts, magistrates' courts and other inferior tribunals are bound by the decisions of all courts mentioned in the previous paragraphs, and by those of High Court judges sitting alone. The decisions of one of these courts are not binding on another mainly because they are not reported.

Although it is part of the Supreme Court, a judge in the Crown Court is similarly bound, even – it seems – by a decision of a High Court judge sitting alone. A legal ruling by a judge in the Crown Court is never a binding precedent but is merely of persuasive authority.

Application of judicial precedents

4.54   The fact that a judicial precedent may be binding or merely persuasive in a subsequent case has already been touched on. It may also be noticed that a judicial precedent will become devoid of effect if it is overruled by a court competent to do so (normally, one higher in the hierarchy). As opposed to overruling by statute[1], judicial overruling operates retrospectively, which may have the effect of disturbing financial interests or vested rights generally. For this reason the courts are reluctant to overrule a previous decision unless they consider it is clearly wrong.

Where a precedent is binding on a court, that court must follow it unless that court can distinguish it on the facts. Suppose that the House of Lords has held that if facts A and B exist, principle X applies, and that a case is heard by a High Court judge at first instance where facts A and B exist as well as fact E, which did not exist in the House of Lords' case. The judge may distinguish the House of Lords' case on its material facts and consequently, since that decision will not be binding in relation to the case before him, decide to apply some other principle or to apply principle X by analogy. Since the facts are never identical in any two cases there is wide scope for 'distinguishing'. However, a court inferior to that which gave the previous decision will not normally distinguish it on strained grounds.

1   Para 4.8, above.

4.55   There are various types of persuasive precedents:

a.   Those decisions of courts inferior in the hierarchy of courts to a court which subsequently hears a similar case. Into this category one can also put decisions of the Judicial Committee of the Privy Council on appeals from Commonwealth states, which do not bind English courts or the Privy Council itself. However, the decisions of the Privy Council are particularly persuasive (since the Judicial Committee normally consists of Lords of Appeal in Ordinary), and, as we indicated in para 4.49, above, the Court of Appeal has held that if one of its previous decisions has been disapproved by the Privy Council it is at liberty to depart from it and apply the Privy Council decision[1].

b.   Where otherwise binding precedent is distinguishable; it will nevertheless have persuasive authority[2].

c.   Obiter dicta, the persuasiveness of which depends on the seniority of the court or prestige of the judge by whom the words were uttered and the relative position of that court and a subsequent court. One of the most significant examples is the 'neighbour principle' expounded by Lord Atkin in 1932 in *Donoghue v Stevenson*[3], which was much wider than the actual case required but has become the basis of the modern tort of negligence and has been applied in numerous cases since.

d.   Decisions of Irish, Scottish, Commonwealth and United States courts, which decisions are being referred to increasingly by our courts.

1   *Doughty v Turner Manufacturing Co Ltd* [1964] 1 QB 518, [1964] 1 All ER 98, CA; *Worcester Works Finance Ltd v Cooden Engineering Co Ltd* [1972] 1 QB 210, [1971] 3 All ER 708, CA; para 4.49, above.
2   Especially if it is a House of Lords' decision: *Re House Property and Investment Co Ltd* [1954] Ch 576, [1953] 2 All ER 1525.
3   [1932] AC 562, HL.

General comments
4.56   Essentially, judicial decisions are declaratory of the common law, merely applying existing law to new fact situations. However, where there is no relevant statute or judicial precedent on a particular point, as still happens occasionally, a judge has to decide the case in accordance with general principles and his decision becomes the original source of a new rule since he is making law rather than applying it.

4.57   The advantages of the system of judicial precedent are its precision and detail, and consequent certainty of application, and in these respects it is far superior to a code or statute which cannot hope to anticipate the innumerable factual situations which can arise in a given area of law. It is sometimes said that the system also has the advantage of flexibility in that outmoded or unsound decisions can be overruled or distinguished. Too much should not be made of this since overruling may be difficult, if not impossible, given the relationship of the courts in question. There is also the danger of illogical or over-subtle distinctions being drawn to avoid hardship in a particular case, but increasing the complexity of the law. Moreover, the vast mass of reported cases can make discovering the law an arduous task and cause a precedent to be overlooked.

Literary sources of judicial precedent
4.58   The most important of these are, of course, the law reports. A law report must be differentiated from a court record which simply contains the names of the parties, the pleadings, the main facts and the decision, decree or order of the court. Apart from containing most of these things, a law report also contains the judgment of the court, which includes the reasoning on which the result was based.

It may appear surprising that there is no official series of law reports. By no means all cases in the superior courts are reported: only those of legal interest. Law reports may be divided roughly into those published from the time of Henry VIII to 1865, and those published subsequently. Before Henry VIII's time there were the Year Books dating from the time of Edward I, which contained notes on the argument, exchanges between Bench and Bar and rulings on points of law in cases. The publication of law reports began in about 1535. They were usually published under the names of the reporter and, initially, were little more detailed than the Year Books but gradually developed until they came to resemble the modern law report. Altogether there were some hundreds of different series. Most, but not all, of them have been reprinted in a series known as the English Reports. These 'nominate reports', as they are sometimes called, vary a good deal in quality. However, the reports of Coke, often simply referred to as 'The Reports', Dyer, Plowden, Burroughs and certain others are regarded as particularly outstanding and authoritative. The name of the report or reporters is traditionally cited in abbreviated form in footnote references, eg Co Rep (Coke), Burr (Burroughs), B & Ald (Barnewell and Alderson) and Term Rep (Term Reports).

In 1865, the semi-official Law Reports commenced. One or more volumes is published annually under each of the following titles: 'Queen's Bench' (QB) (covering cases decided in the Queen's Bench Division or by the Court of Appeal on appeals therefrom or from a county court), 'Chancery' (Ch) (covering cases decided in the Chancery Division or by the Court of Appeal on appeal therefrom), 'Family' (Fam)[1] (covering cases decided in the Family Division or by the Court of Appeal on appeal therefrom or from a county court in family matters) and 'Appeal Cases' (AC) (covering decisions of the House of Lords and Privy Council). Since 1952, cases appearing in the Law Reports have appeared previously, soon after judgment has been given, in the Weekly Law Reports (WLR) published by the same organisation, the Incorporated Council of Law Reporting, as do some cases not subsequently published in the Law Reports. The difference between the two series is that the Law Reports contain a summary of the arguments of counsel.

Although the Law Reports superseded the nominate reports, there is quite a substantial number of commercially owned reports. The All England Reports (All ER), published weekly since 1936, are a general series of reports, while others, such as Butterworths Company Law Cases (BCLC) and the Industrial Cases Reports, published by the Incorporated Council of Law Reporting, are more specialised.

Cases decided by the European Court may be found in the Official Reports of the court and in the Common Market Law Reports (CMLR). Since 1996, they have also been reported in a separate volume of the All England Reports (All ER (EC)). European Court cases are occasionally reported in the other series of reports referred to in the previous two paragraphs.

1   Until 1972 the citation was 'P' since what is now the Family Division was known as the Probate, Divorce and Admiralty Division until its name, and jurisdiction, were changed.

4.59   A judgment can be cited to a court even though it has not been published in any series of law reports but is merely contained in a transcript. The transcripts of many recent judgments are now available on LEXIS, a computerised legal database. For reasons which are unconvincing, the House of Lords has held that transcripts of unreported judgments of the Court of Appeal (Civil Division) should not be cited on appeals to the House, except with its leave (which will only be given if counsel gives an assurance that the transcript contains a statement of a relevant principle of law whose substance is not to be found in any reported judgment of the Court of Appeal)[1]. Likewise, the Court of Appeal has directed that it will only give leave for transcripts of unreported cases to be cited if the transcript in question contains a relevant statement of legal principle not found in a reported case[2].

1   *Roberts Petroleum Ltd v Bernard Kenny Ltd* [1983] 2 AC 192, [1983] 1 All ER 564, HL.
2   *Practice Note* [1996] 3 All ER 382, CA.

4.60   Mention can be conveniently made at this stage of a secondary literary source, certain 'books of authority'. On the Continent the writings of legal authors form an important source of law. In England, in accordance with the traditional approach that the common law is to be found in judicial decisions, the works of writers are of no official effect, except for books of authority. These are books of some antiquity by authors of great eminence which are regarded as being persuasive authority on the common law as it was when they were written and on the present law if it is not shown to have changed. Generally, these do not contain reports of cases but state principles instead. Perhaps the best known books of authority are Coke's *Institutes*, written in the seventeenth century, and Blackstone's *Commentaries* of the eighteenth century. While the works of modern authors are not authoritative in the above sense, the courts are increasingly being referred to them for guidance on the correct interpretation of the law.

Custom

4.61   In Anglo-Saxon times, custom, in the sense of patterns of behaviour recognised and enforced by the courts, was the principal source of law. However, general customs, ie customs universally observed throughout the land, have either fallen into desuetude or become absorbed into judicial precedent or statute.

A process of absorption has also occurred in relation to the general customs of merchants, which were assimilated by our courts in the seventeenth and eighteenth centuries and developed into commercial law as we now know it.

On the other hand, local customs, ie customs operative in a particular locality or among a particular group of people in a particular locality, are even now occasionally recognised by the courts as establishing a local 'law' for the locality in question at variance with the general law of the land, although they must not be contrary to statute or to a fundamental principle of the common law.

Local customs are largely to be found in rights of way and common. Recognition of a local custom depends on a number of conditions being satisfied, the most important of which are that the alleged custom must:

a.   Have existed since 'time immemorial', which, theoretically, it will only do if it goes back to 1189 (for reasons of historical accident).
b.   Have been continuous. The custom must have been in existence continuously. This means that the right to exercise it must not have been interrupted; but the fact that the right has not actually been exercised for a period of time, even 100 years in one case[1], does not negative the existence of a local custom (although if the evidence of custom is dubious it will go far to negative any customary right).
c.   Not be unreasonable[2].
d.   Be certain; in other words the right claimed must be certain in nature and scope and prove to adhere to a defined locality or group of people.
e.   Be recognised as compulsory[3].

The first condition is not as strict as it may appear since the plaintiff can succeed in proving it if he can prove that the practice in question has existed in the locality for a substantial time: the oldest local inhabitant is often called as a witness in this context. If the plaintiff proves this, existence since 1189 will be presumed[4], provided, of course, that such a practice was possible in 1189. In *Simpson v Wells*[5], a person who was charged with obstructing a public footway with his refreshment stall pleaded that he did so by virtue of a custom existing at a 'statute sessions', a fair held for hiring servants. His defence failed because statute sessions were first introduced by a fourteenth-century statute, so that the custom could not have existed before then.

1 *New Windsor Corpn v Mellor* [1975] Ch 380, [1975] 3 All ER 44, CA.
2 *Wolstanton Ltd v Newcastle-under-Lyme Borough Council* [1940] AC 860, [1940] 3 All ER 101, HL.
3 Blackstone's *Commentaries*: 'a custom that all the inhabitants shall be rated towards the maintenance of a bridge will be good, but a custom that every man is to contribute thereto at his own pleasure is idle and absurd, and indeed not custom at all'.
4 *Mercer v Denne* [1905] 2 Ch 538 at 577.
5 (1872) LR 7 QB 214.

Part II

The Law of Contract

Chapter 5

Agreement

5.1 In this part of the book we adopt the following order. In this chapter, and in chapters 6 and 7, we outline those basic elements of the law of contract which relate to the existence of a valid contract. In the following five chapters (chapters 8 to 12) we deal with contractual obligations, with how they are discharged, and with the remedies available if they are broken. Sometimes, what would otherwise be a valid contract is invalidated or liable to be set aside because of mistake, misrepresentation, illegality, the incapacity of a party or certain other factors. We deal with these matters in chapters 13 to 16.

5.2 For there to be a contract (ie a binding agreement):

a. there must be an agreement;
b. the parties must have intended their agreement to be legally binding; and
c. the contract must be supported by consideration or be made by deed.

Except for the cases discussed in chapter 7, an oral contract is as binding or enforceable as a written one, but there are obvious advantages in reducing a contract into writing. Although it is usual to talk about enforcing a contract, it must not be forgotten that what is being enforced is a promise by one party to an agreement by the other party to it; a mere statement of present fact to which another person agrees cannot be enforced, even if it relates to the fact of the present intentions of the person making the statement (as where a company says 'it is our policy to ensure that any of our subsidiaries is always in a position to meet its liabilities in respect of a loan made to it')[1].

Another point which must be made at the outset is that contracts may be either bilateral or unilateral. A bilateral contract is one in which a party (A) promises to do something if the other party (B) promises to do something in return and B makes that counter-promise. In such a case, the mere exchange of promises normally renders them both enforceable. A unilateral contract, on the other hand, arises where A promises to do something in return for an *act* by B, rather than a counter-promise, as where A promises to pay B a reward if

95

he finds some lost property or where A promises to pay B £10 if he completes a sponsored walk, and B responds by doing the requested act. In such a case B is not bound to do anything at all; however, only if B does the act will A's promise become enforceable. A less obvious example of a unilateral contract, though one which is of great commercial importance, is the normal type of commission agreement entered into by estate agents, mortgage brokers and the like. According to the decision of the House of Lords in *Luxor (Eastbourne) Ltd v Cooper*[2], an estate agent instructed to find a purchaser is under no obligation to take any action at all; only when he complies with the client's instructions, however, does the client's promise of commission become enforceable.

We commence with the basic requirement of any contract: agreement between the parties.

1   *Kleinwort Benson Ltd v Malaysia Mining Corpn Bhd* [1989] 1 All ER 785, [1989] 1 WLR 379, CA.
2   [1941] AC 108, [1941] 1 All ER 33, HL.

Agreement

5.3   An 'agreement' is often said to require a meeting of the minds of the parties to it, but this is rather misleading. The reason is that the law tends to take an objective, rather than a subjective, approach to an agreement. It is concerned not so much with what is actually in the minds of the parties, but with what a reasonable person would infer, from their conduct and the circumstances, as being in their minds (ie did they agree and, if so, on what terms?). This approach is not surprising: when the question of whether or not there is agreement is raised it is not possible to look back into the actual minds of the parties.

The following quotation indicates the approach of the courts:

> 'In contracts you do not look into the actual intent in a man's mind. You look at what he said and did. A contract is formed when there is, to all outward appearances, a contract.' [1]

1   *Storer v Manchester City Council* [1974] 3 All ER 824 at 828.

5.4   The agreement involved in most contracts can be reduced to an offer by one party which has been accepted by the other. However, not all agreements can easily be so reduced. This is the case, for example, where two parties agree to terms suggested by a third person. It may also be the case where several parties agree independently with X that they will be bound by terms stipulated by him. In such an event the parties may have entered into a contract not merely with X but with each other. In *Clarke v Dunraven*[1] yachtsmen wrote to the secretary of a yacht club agreeing to be bound by certain rules during a yacht race. The House of Lords held that a contract containing those rules existed between the yachtsmen, with the result that a yachtsman whose yacht was damaged was able to recover damages in accordance with the rules. While there was an agreement between the yachtsmen to be bound by the rules, it cannot really be said that there was an offer and acceptance between them.

Despite exceptional cases such as these, it is the law that generally, for there to be an agreement, what has occurred must be capable of analysis into an offer by one party accepted by the other. Some judges have taken a more liberal approach. For example, in *Gibson v Manchester City Council*[2], Lord Denning MR said: 'To my mind it is a mistake to think that all contracts can be analysed into the form of offer and acceptance ... You should look at the correspondence as a whole and at the conduct of the parties ... and see therefore whether the parties have come to an agreement on everything that was material'. However, on appeal in that case, Lord Denning's approach was disapproved by the House of Lords. For example, Lord Diplock said: 'My Lords there may be certain types of contract, *though I think they are exceptional*, which do not fit easily into the normal analysis of a contract as constituted by offer and acceptance; but a contract alleged to have been made by an exchange of correspondence between the parties in which the successive communications other than the first are in reply to one another is not one of these... I venture to think that it was in departing from this conventional approach that the majority of the Court of Appeal was led into error'[3]. Lord Diplock's statement represents the weight of judicial opinion, although Lord Denning's approach is a more appropriate reflection of what happens in business than a strict 'offer and acceptance approach'.

Since the agreement in the vast majority of contracts is formed by an offer being made by one party which is accepted by the other, we must now consider what constitutes an offer, what constitutes an acceptance, whether an acceptance must be communicated to the offeror, and how an offer can be terminated.

1   [1897] AC 59, HL.
2   [1978] 2 All ER 583 at 586. Also see *New Zealand Shipping Co Ltd v A M Satterthwaite & Co Ltd, The Eurymedon* [1975] AC 154, [1974] 1 All ER 1015, PC, and *G Percy Trentham Ltd v Archital Luxfer Ltd* [1993] 1 Lloyd's Rep 25 at 29–30.
3   [1979] 1 All ER 972 at 974.

Offer

5.5   An offer is made where a person (the offeror) unequivocally expresses to another (the offeree) his willingness to make a binding agreement on the terms specified by him if they are accepted by the offeree.

An offer may be made to a specific person, to a group of people, or to the world at large[1]. An offer to a specific person cannot be accepted by anyone except that person[2].

The fact that an offer requires an expression of an unequivocal willingness to contract means that quotations of rates or prices are not offers[3]. It also means that inquiries and replies to inquiries are not offers, although sometimes they may resemble them. In *Harvey v Facey*[4], one party inquired as to the lowest acceptable price for certain land, and the other party telegraphed his lowest acceptable price. This was held not to be an offer but merely a reply to the inquiry. Likewise, in *Gibson v Manchester City Council*[5], where a letter had been sent saying that the council 'may be prepared to sell the house to you', it was held by the House of Lords that the letter did not constitute an offer to sell but merely an invitation to treat.

An offer must be distinguished from an 'invitation to treat' (ie an invitation to enter into negotiations which may lead to the making of an offer). In certain situations, what may appear to be an offer by X to Y will be regarded by a court merely as an invitation to treat, unless there is clear evidence that X was willing to be bound as soon as Y indicated his assent or satisfied a particular condition. Examples of these situations are given in the following paragraphs.

1 *Carlill v Carbolic Smoke Ball Co* [1893] 1 QB 256, CA.
2 *Cundy v Lindsay* (1878) 3 App Cas 459, HL.
3 *Scancarriers A/S v Aotearoa International Ltd* [1985] 2 Lloyd's Rep 419, PC.
4 [1893] AC 552, PC.
5 [1979] 1 All ER 972, [1979] 1 WLR 294, HL.

Invitation to treat
5.6   An invitation to treat is a starting point for contractual negotiations and precedes the making of an offer. In *Fisher v Bell*[1], a shopkeeper was charged with offering for sale a flick knife which was on display in his shop window[2]. A divisional court held that the display of goods in a shop window was not an offer to sell but an invitation to treat; it was for customers to make the offer. The rationale behind this decision is that a shop is a place for negotiation over the terms of a contract, including the price, and the shopkeeper invites customers to make him an offer which he can accept or reject as he pleases. This is an unrealistic view of how shops operate today. Circulars sent to potential customers are also invitations to treat for the supply of goods, and not offers[3].

Like the display of goods in shop windows, the display of goods on shelves in self-service shops is an invitation to treat. In *Pharmaceutical Society of Great Britain v Boots Cash Chemists (Southern) Ltd*[4], statute required certain drugs to be sold only under the supervision of a qualified pharmacist. A pharmacist was at the cash desk but, if the sale of drugs had been made before a customer reached it, the statute would have been infringed. The Court of Appeal had no hesitation in finding that the display of goods was only an invitation to treat, that the offer to buy was made by the customer at the cash desk, and that the contract was concluded when the offer was accepted there. Consequently, Boots were not in breach of the statute.

1 [1961] 1 QB 394, [1960] 3 All ER 731, DC.
2 Contrary to the Restriction of Offensive Weapons Act 1959. The Restriction of Offensive Weapons Act 1961 reverses the actual decision in the case.
3 *Grainger & Son v Gough* [1896] AC 325, HL.
4 [1953] 1 QB 401, [1953] 1 All ER 482, CA.

5.7   *Advertisements* Whether an advertisement is an offer or an invitation to treat depends on the intention with which it is made. Advertisements of rewards and the like are normally offers since the advertiser does not intend any further negotiation to take place. An example is provided by *Carlill v Carbolic Smoke Ball Co*[1], where the defendants advertised that they would pay £100 to anyone catching influenza after using their product in a specified manner. The Court of Appeal held that, since no further negotiations on the defendants' part were intended, the advertisement constituted an offer made to all the world which would ripen into a contract with anyone who came forward and fulfilled the conditions.

On the other hand, an advertisement of goods for sale is presumptively an invitation to treat, and not an offer[2], because otherwise the advertiser might find himself contractually obliged to supply the advertised goods to a greater number of people (those who had responded positively to the advertisement) than the number of specified goods which had been advertised.[3] Similarly, the advertising of an auction is not an offer; instead, those who bid at auction make an offer which the auctioneer is free to accept or reject, and an offer can be withdrawn at any time before the auctioneer accepts[4]. Because the advertisement of an auction is merely a declaration of an intention to hold the auction, potential buyers have no claim against the auctioneers if they fail to hold the auction[5]. Although these rules even apply where an auctioneer advertises an auction as 'without reserve' (ie that the bid of the highest bona fide bidder will be accepted and that the property will not be withdrawn if a reserve price is not reached), so that there is no contract *of sale* if the auctioneer refuses to accept the highest bid and withdraws the property, the auctioneer is liable in such circumstances for breach of a contract *that the sale would be without reserve*. This contract comes into existence as follows: by advertising the sale as without reserve the auctioneer makes an offer to this effect to whoever is the highest bona fide bidder, which is accepted by the person who makes the highest bona fide bid before the property is withdrawn[6].

1   [1893] 1 QB 256, CA.
2   *Partridge v Crittenden* [1968] 2 All ER 421, [1968] 1 WLR 1204, DC.
3   This reason would not apply if the advertiser was the manufacturer of the goods advertised, because he could make more. In *Partridge v Crittenden* [1968] 2 All ER 421 at 424, Lord Parker CJ suggested that an advertisement or circular for the sale of goods by a manufacturer could be interpreted as an offer.
4   *Payne v Cave* (1789) 3 Term Rep 148; Sale of Goods Act 1979, s 57(2).
5   *Harris v Nickerson* (1873) LR 8 QB 286.
6   *Warlow v Harrison* (1859) 1 E & E 309.

5.8 *Tenders* Normally, an announcement that the provision of goods or services (or the purchase of goods or services) is open to tender is not an offer but only an invitation to treat. Consequently, a person who submits a tender normally makes an offer, which may be accepted or rejected by the person seeking tenders[1]. In *Spencer v Harding*[2], for example, the defendant issued a circular offering by tender the stock in trade of X. This was held not to be an offer. Thus, the defendant was not required to sell the goods to the plaintiff who had submitted the highest tender.

A person seeking tenders who indicates that he will accept the highest or lowest tender, as the case may be, will be contractually bound to do so. The reason is that, in accompanying his request for tenders with such an indication, he thereby accompanies his invitation to treat with an offer of a unilateral contract to accept the highest or lowest tender, as the case may be. The highest or lowest tender, as the case may be, will constitute an acceptance of that offer, and the person seeking tenders will be contractually obliged to accept that tender[3].

Where an invitation to tender is made only to a small, selected group of persons, it will be held to be accompanied by an offer to consider all conforming tenders submitted by the stipulated deadline, which offer is accepted by so submitting such a tender. Consequently, in such a case, it will be a breach of contract (a contract to consider a conforming tender submitted in time) to fail to consider such a tender[4].

1   For acceptance of tenders, see para 5.13 below.
2   (1870) LR 5 CP 561.
3   *Harvela Investments Ltd v Royal Trust Co of Canada (CI) Ltd* [1986] AC 207, [1985] 2 All ER 966, HL.
4   *Blackpool and Fylde Aero Club Ltd v Blackpool Borough Council* [1990] 3 All ER 25, [1990] 1 WLR 1195, CA.

Acceptance

Requirements
5.9   To convert an offer into a contract the offeree must unequivocally and unconditionally accept the offer; if, for example, A offers to sell B a computer for £5,000, payable in advance, B does not accept the offer if he replies purporting to accept the offer but saying that he will pay the £5,000 on delivery[1]. In addition, the offeree is normally required to communicate his acceptance to the offeror.

1   *Hyde v Wrench* (1840) 3 Beav 334.

5.10   It should come as no surprise to anyone to learn that one cannot accept an offer of which one is ignorant. This is important in the case where B offers a reward for the performance of a particular action, eg finding his lost dog. If A, who is ignorant of the offer, finds the dog, his action cannot constitute an acceptance of the offer and he cannot claim the reward successfully[1]. However, if someone who knows of the offer performs the specified action, motivated partly by the offer and partly by other reasons, there is a valid acceptance[1].

A related point is that, if two offers which are identical in terms cross in the post, there can be no contract. The courts will not construe one offer as the offer and the other offer as the acceptance[2]. The practical basis for such a view would seem to be that neither party would know if he was bound, although if the terms of the offers were identical the parties would surely have no objection to being bound.

1   *Williams v Carwardine* (1833) 5 C & P 566.
2   *Tinn v Hoffmann & Co* (1873) 29 LT 271.

5.11   *Counter-offers distinguished*   As stated in para 5.9, above, for an acceptance there must be an unequivocal and unconditional agreement to the terms proposed in the offer. If an offeree who purports to accept the offer seeks to introduce an entirely new term in his acceptance, eg as to the amount of goods to be delivered or the time of payment, this is not an acceptance. Instead, it is a counter-offer which may or may not be accepted by the original offeror.

A counter-offer puts an end to the original offer, so that it cannot subsequently be accepted by the offeree. In *Hyde v Wrench*[1], for instance, the defendant offered to sell property to the plaintiff for £1,000. The plaintiff 'agreed' to buy the property for £950. This was rejected and the plaintiff then purported to accept the original offer of £1,000. The Master of the Rolls held that the plaintiff's purported acceptance for £950 was a counter-offer which destroyed the original offer, so that it was no longer capable of acceptance when the plaintiff purported to accept it.

A counter-offer must be distinguished from an inquiry or request for information by an offeree. Such an inquiry or request, even if answered negatively by the offeror, does not destroy the offer. An example is *Stevenson, Jaques & Co v McLean*[2]. The defendant offered to sell iron to the plaintiffs at 40 shillings a ton with immediate delivery. The plaintiffs asked the defendant by telegram if he would sell at the same price if delivery was staggered over two months. On receiving no reply, the plaintiffs accepted the original offer but the defendant failed to deliver and claimed the telegram was a counter-offer. The court rejected the defendant's claim and held that the telegram was a mere request for information, and not a counter-offer, so that the original offer could still be accepted.

A contract may arise during the course of long and complicated negotiations, during which one party offers to contract on certain terms (eg terms A, B and C contained in a document sent by him) and the other agrees to contract, but on different terms (eg terms A, B and D contained in a document sent by him), and so on. Even if it is expressed to be an acceptance, such a response will in law be a counter-offer and not an acceptance. If neither party expressly accepts the other's terms, what is the legal situation? The orthodox view is that if, after the communication of the last set of terms, the recipient does something which indicates a relevant agreement with the sender, for example delivering the goods which the sender has ordered, the recipient will be held to have accepted[3] the sender's counter-offer and thus contracted on the sender's terms[4]. Of course, this approach does not produce a contract at all if the last set of terms is not followed by anything on the recipient's part which can be described as acceptance. An alternative approach, taken by Lord Denning MR in *Butler Machine Tool Corpn (Enland) Ltd v Ex-Cell-O Ltd*[5], which does not yet represent the law, is that in such a case a 'compromise' contract can be constructed by the court on reasonable terms.

1   (1840) 3 Beav 334.
2   (1880) 5 QBD 346.
3   Acceptance can be by conduct; see para 5.12, below.
4   *British Road Services Ltd v Arthur v Crutchley Ltd* [1968] 1 All ER 811, CA; *Butler Machine Tool Co Ltd v Ex-Cell-O Corpn (England) Ltd* [1979] 1 All ER 965, [1979] 1 WLR 401, CA.
5   [1979] 1 All ER 965 at 968–969.

5.12   *Acceptance by conduct*   An acceptance may be express, as where the offeree accepts the offer by a written or oral statement intended to constitute an acceptance[1], or it may be manifested by the offeree's conduct. For instance, a cover note issued by an insurance company is an offer to insure which would be accepted by using a car in reliance on it[2]. A more complicated case of acceptance by conduct is that of *Brogden v Metropolitan Rly Co*[3], in which

Brogden was sued for failing to deliver coal. Brogden regularly supplied the company with coal and they decided to draw up a contract for such supply. A draft contract was submitted to Brogden with a blank space for the name of a mutually agreeable arbitrator, and this constituted an offer. Brogden filled in the name of the arbitrator, marked the draft 'approved', and returned it to the agent of the company (who put it in a drawer where it remained). Brogden's action was not an acceptance but a counter-offer[4], because the company had to consider whether to accept his choice of arbitrator. Nevertheless, the parties bought and sold coal in accordance with the terms of the draft contract. Subsequently, Brogden refused to supply more coal and claimed that there was no binding contract for its supply. The House of Lords inferred from the conduct of the parties, the buying and selling of coal on terms exactly the same as those in the draft contract, that a contract had been concluded on the terms contained in the final draft, which came into effect either with the first order of coal by the company on the terms of the draft (since this conduct could be said to have manifested the company's acceptance of Brogden's counter-offer) or, at least, when Brogden supplied the coal. The first explanation is easily the more acceptable. The House of Lords stressed that mere mental acquiescence by the parties that the contract should exist would not have sufficed.

1   See, eg *Wilson Smithett & Cape (Sugar) Ltd v Bangladesh Sugar and Food Industries Corpn* [1986] 1 Lloyd's Rep 378 (letter of intent to supply materials as per terms of offer held to constitute an acceptance, because it was found to have been intended to constitute an acceptance).
2   *Taylor v Allon* [1966] 1 QB 304, [1965] 1 All ER 557 at 559.
3   (1877) 2 App Cas 666, HL.
4   Para 5.11, above.

5.13   *Acceptance of tenders*   Tenders can be in two forms:

a.   Where people are invited to tender for the supply of specified goods or services over a given period, a contract for the supply of those goods or services is constituted when a person's tender (offer) is accepted.
b.   However, if people are invited to tender for the supply of such goods and services as may be required over a given period, a contract is not immediately concluded with the successful tenderer. Instead, his offer is treated as a standing offer and each time an order is placed this constitutes acceptance of the standing offer and there is a contract for the goods or services ordered. Because the person making the successful tender has no definite contract, he can revoke his offer before any particular order is placed, and the person who invited tenders need never place an order[1].

1   *Great Northern Rly Co v Witham* (1873) LR 9 CP 16.

Communication of acceptance
5.14   If an offer has been made and the offeree has decided to accept, there is normally no completed agreement until he (or his agent) has communicated his acceptance to the offeror (or his agent), by words or conduct which manifests his acceptance[1]. The reason for this is practical: if the offeror is not told that

his offer has been accepted he does not know whether he has made a contract or can make offers to others.

Communication of acceptance usually requires actual communication. Consequently, an oral acceptance which is drowned by a passing aeroplane or is inaudible because of interference on the telephone is not effectively communicated[2]. Telex messages (and presumably fax messages) sent during office hours are regarded as instantaneous communications and are subject to the same principles as oral acceptances; they take effect when printed on the offeror's telex (or fax) machine[3]. However, if an oral acceptance or one by telex or fax does not completely reach the offeror and the party accepting does not realise this, there may be a valid communication of acceptance. But this will only be the case where the offeror realises he has missed some of what the offeree is seeking to communicate and does not attempt to discover what he has missed[4].

1 Para 5.12, above.
2 *Entores Ltd v Miles Far East Corpn* [1955] 2 QB 327, [1955] 2 All ER 493, CA; *Brinkibon Ltd v Stahag Stahl und Stahlwarenhandel GmbH* [1983] 2 AC 34, [1982] 1 All ER 293, HL.
3 *Brinkinbon Ltd v Stahag Stahl und Stahlwarenhandel GmbH*. It was held that the legal position would be different where the communication was not instantaneous, as where the telex message is sent out of office hours, and that the time of acceptance in such a case would depend on the parties' intentions and sound business practice, and in some cases on a judgment as to where the risk should lie.
4 *Entores Ltd v Miles Far East Corpn* [1955] 2 QB 327 at 333.

5.15 *Dispensation from need for communication of acceptance* The offeror may by the terms of the offer expressly or impliedly dispense with the need to communicate acceptance. In particular, dispensation with the need for communication will normally be implied where the alleged contract is of the unilateral variety. An example is provided by *Carlill v Carbolic Smoke Ball Co*[1], where the advertisers of a product argued that a user of it, who claimed a reward which they had offered to anyone catching influenza after using the product, should have told them of her acceptance of their offer of a reward. The advertisers' claim was rejected, since it was clear they had not intended every purchaser of the product to write to them formally accepting the offer of a reward if illness was not avoided; consequently, they had impliedly dispensed with the need for communication of acceptance.

1 [1893] 1 QB 256, CA.

5.16 If the offeror does expressly or impliedly dispense with the need for communication of acceptance, the offeree's non-communication of acceptance does not enable the offeror successfully to deny that there is a contract enforceable against him[1]. In addition, there will be a contract enforceable against the offeree if he has unambiguously manifested his acceptance, as by driving a car in reliance on an offer of motor insurance[2]. On the other hand, an offeree is not bound simply because an offeror has framed his offer in such terms that a contract is presumed to exist unless non-acceptance is communicated. Contractual liability cannot be imposed on the offeree in this way; as against the offeree, silence is not assent. In *Felthouse v Bindley*[3], the plaintiff offered to buy X's horse and said that he would presume his offer to be accepted unless he heard to the contrary. X did not reply. It was held that no contract binding on X had been formed: the plaintiff was not entitled to presume acceptance unless he heard to the contrary.

1   This is certainly the case in a unilateral contract, as *Carlill v Carbolic Smoke Ball Co*, para 5.15, above, shows.
2   *Taylor v Allon* [1966] 1 QB 304, [1965] 1 All ER 557 at 559.
3   (1862) 11 CBNS 869.

5.17   While some offers dispense with the need for communication of acceptance, others require a particular form of acceptance to be employed (as where the offer states: 'acceptance must be made in writing and sent by first class post to our Liverpool branch'). If the offer states that the acceptance may *only* be made in the specified manner, an acceptance in any other way cannot be effective (unless the offeror waives the requirement)[1]. On the other hand, if the offer does not state that only the specified method may be used, an acceptance made in some other way (eg by telex to the Liverpool branch in the above example) can be effective as long as it is no less advantageous to the offeror than the prescribed method[2]; but if it is not, it is ineffective[3] (unless the offeror waives the specified mode).

1   *Compagnie de Commerce et Commission SARL v Parkinson Stove Co Ltd* [1953] 2 Lloyd's Rep 487, CA.
2   *Tinn v Hoffmann* (1873) 29 LT 271; *Yates Building Co Ltd v R J Pulleyn & Sons (York) Ltd* (1975) 119 Sol Jo 370, CA.
3   *Financings Ltd v Stimson* [1962] 3 All ER 386, [1962] 1 WLR 1184, CA.

5.18   *Postal acceptances*   There is another exception to the general rule that acceptance must be actually communicated to be effective. It is that a posted acceptance is effective when it is posted, and this is so even if that acceptance is delivered late or is never delivered. This was first established in *Adams v Lindsell*[1], where a letter of acceptance was posted the day that a postal offer to sell wool was received. The acceptance arrived two days later than expected and, after it had been posted but before it arrived, the offeror sold the wool to another. It was held that a contract had been formed as soon as the letter of acceptance had been posted. A letter is 'posted' when it is placed, correctly stamped, in an official letter box or into the hands of a Post Office employee or agent authorised to receive letters[2]; most postmen who deliver letters are not so authorised.

The offeror can exclude the special postal acceptance rule in his offer by specifying that acceptance must be *actually* communicated to him[3]. In addition, the postal acceptance rule will be disregarded, and the general rule requiring communication prevail, if it is not reasonable to accept by post[4] or if the special rule would give rise to 'manifest inconvenience or absurdity'[5]. For example, it would not be reasonable to accept by post an offer by telex to sell highly perishable goods.

The justification for the special rule for postal acceptances seems to be that the offeror, by expressly or impliedly (eg by making the offer by post) allowing an acceptance to be made by post, must stand the risk of failures of the postal system. However, if a postal acceptance is delayed in the post because of the negligence of the offeree, as where he wrongly addresses the letter, there seems no reason why the court should not decide the acceptance to have been effective at whatever time is least advantageous to the negligent offeree.

1   (1818) 1 B & Ald 681.
2   *Re London and Northern Bank, ex p Jones* [1900] 1 Ch 220.
3   For an example see *Holwell Securities Ltd v Hughes* [1974] 1 All ER 161, [1974] 1 WLR 155, CA.
4   *Henthorn v Fraser* [1892] 2 Ch 27, CA.
5   *Holwell Securities Ltd v Hughes* [1974] 1 All ER 161, [1974] 1 WLR 155, CA.

5.19   If an acceptance made by letter is effective when it is posted, then, logically, an attempt to withdraw the acceptance after the letter has been posted should be ineffective since the contract has been concluded. There are no English cases which support this view, although the principle stated is consistent with decisions in New Zealand and South Africa[1]. On the other hand, the Scottish case of *Countess of Dunmore v Alexander*[2] has been cited as authority for the view that, if a revocation of an acceptance is communicated before a postal acceptance arrives, the revocation is effective. However, the facts of this case are somewhat obscure and it is by no means certain that this is what the case decided.

1   *Wenkheim v Arndt* (1861–1902) 1 JR 73; *A to Z Bazaars (Pty) Ltd v Minister of Agriculture* 1974 (4) SA 392.
2   (1830) 9 Sh (Ct of Sess) 190.

Termination of offers

5.20   An offer may be terminated in several ways: by rejection (including a counter-offer[1]), by revocation, by lapse of time and by death.

1   Para 5.11, above.

Revocation
5.21   At any time until acceptance by the offeree, the offeror can withdraw his offer. The fact that the offeror has given the offeree time to make up his mind does not mean that the offeror is required to keep the offer open for that length of time. In *Routledge v Grant*[1], a reply to an offer was required within six weeks; it was held that nevertheless the offer could be withdrawn within that period.

There is an exception to the rule that the offer need not be kept open for a specified period. This is where there is a separate contract whereby the offeror contracts to keep the offer open for a given time. If there is such a contract the offer can be accepted at any time within the specified period. An example of such a contract is the granting of an option.

The revocation of an offer only becomes effective when it is communicated to the offeree. In *Byrne & Co v Van Tienhoven & Co*[2], the defendants in Cardiff wrote on 1 October to the plaintiffs in New York, offering to sell them goods.

The plaintiffs received the offer on 11 October and accepted it by telegram on the same day. Meanwhile, on 8 October the defendants had sent a letter to the plaintiffs revoking their offer; this letter reached the plaintiffs on 20 October. It was held that the revocation was ineffective because the plaintiffs' acceptance had taken effect on 11 October (acceptance by telegram being treated in the same way as acceptance by letter) and therefore the defendants' offer was no longer capable of being revoked when their letter of revocation reached the plaintiffs. Consequently, there was a contract between the plaintiffs and defendants for the sale of the goods. There is no parallel rule to that which treats a posted acceptance as an effective acceptance on posting in certain circumstances; a revocation must always be communicated.

This raises a question which has yet to be authoritatively determined: does communication by letter, telex or fax require that the revocation is actually read by the offeror[3] or does it occur when the letter is delivered, or the telex or fax is printed out, at his premises, regardless of whether it comes to the attention of the offeror[3] at that time? In the case of a business, the latter is probably the answer provided that the delivery or print-out is during normal business hours[4]. The answer in other cases is less certain.

Communication of revocation may be indirect, in that, if the offeree hears from a reliable source that the offer has been withdrawn and thereby knows beyond all question of the withdrawal, the courts will regard this as an effective revocation[5]. The problem inherent in this is that it is difficult to know what constitutes a reliable source.

1   (1828) 4 Bing 653.
2   (1880) 5 CPD 344.
3   Or his agent.
4   Suggested by the decision in another context in *The Brimnes* [1975] QB 929, [1974] 3 All ER 88, CA.
5   *Dickinson v Dodds* (1876) 2 Ch D 463, CA.

5.22   Special rules apply in the case of unilateral contracts, where A does something (eg returning lost property) in response to B's offer (promise) to do something (eg to pay a reward) if he does it. The general rule is that once the offeree has embarked on the performance of the stipulated act or acts necessary for acceptance, as where B has found lost property and is en route to return it in response to the offer of a reward, the offer cannot be withdrawn[1]. The reason is that, when the offer is made which will mature into a unilateral contract when accepted, there is alongside that principal offer a collateral offer to keep the principal offer open once performance in relation to it has begun, which is accepted by the offeree starting to perform the stipulated act or acts[2]. In *Errington v Errington and Woods*[3], a father purchased a house, partially by means of a mortgage, and allowed his daughter and her husband to live in it. The daughter and her husband paid the mortgage instalments in response to the father's offer that, if they did so, he would give them the house when it was paid for. The Court of Appeal held that this offer could not be revoked once the daughter and her husband had begun performance of the conduct specified in the offer. Of course, in the present type of case the offeror is not bound unless and until the offeree has fully performed the act or acts specified in the offer. This is subject to the important qualification that, if the offeror prevents performance of the necessary act or acts being completed, he cannot rely on the offeree's failure fully to perform as a defence to a breach of contract action by the offeree. The reason is that there is an implied obligation on the part of the offeror (which arises as soon as the offeree starts to perform) not to prevent performance by the offeree[2].

What we have just said will not apply if the terms of the offer, or its surrounding circumstances, indicate that it was not intended to become irrevocable before the offeree had completely performed the envisaged act. A good example is the kind of commission agreement commonly used by estate agents. Although this is a unilateral contract (as we explained in para 5.2, above) it is well settled that the client may revoke his instructions at any time, notwithstanding that the agent may have expended time and money in attempting to find a purchaser[4]. The courts take the view that a change of mind by a client is simply one of the business risks which an estate agent must bear, and his fees for successful negotiations should be at a level sufficient to cover other abortive work.

1   *Offord v Davies* (1862) 12 CBNS 748; *Errington v Errington and Woods* [1952] 1 KB 290, [1952] 1 All ER 149, CA; *Daulia Ltd v Four Millbank Nominees Ltd* [1978] Ch 231 at 239, [1978] 2 All ER 557.
2   *Daulia Ltd v Four Millbank Nominees Ltd* [1978] Ch 231 at 239, [1978] 2 All ER 557.
3   [1952] 1 KB 290, [1952] 1 All ER 149, CA.
4   *Luxor (Eastbourne) Ltd v Cooper* [1941] AC 108, [1941] 1 All ER 33, HL.

Lapse of time

5.23   Obviously, an offer which is to remain open for a set time lapses at the end of that time and cannot thereafter be accepted. If no time limit is expressly set for the offer, it will normally lapse after a reasonable period[1]. In *Ramsgate Victoria Hotel Co v Montefiore*[2], for example, it was held that an offer to buy shares, which was made in June, could not be accepted in November since the offer had lapsed by then. What is a reasonable period varies, depending on the facts of the case.

1   *Chemco Leasing SpA v Rediffusion plc* [1987] 1 FTLR 201, CA.
2   (1866) LR 1 Exch 109.

Death

5.24   Death after an offer has been accepted cannot affect the validity of a contract[1]. There are, however, cases where either the offeror or the offeree dies before the offer is accepted. If *the offeror* dies, the offer does not seem to terminate automatically (except where the offer is clearly of such a type that it must end on death, eg an offer to work for X). However, the offeree cannot accept the offer once he knows of the death of the offeror[2].

The effects of the death of *the offeree* have not been decided conclusively but uncontradicted dicta suggest that the offer lapses. In *Reynolds v Atherton*[3], it was suggested that an offer, being made to a living person, cannot survive his death and be accepted by someone else. This may be an illustration of the basic rule that an offer made to A cannot be accepted by B. On the other hand, if an offer is made to A or B there seems no reason why the death of B should prevent A accepting it.

1   But it may discharge the contract: see para 11.5, below.
2   *Bradbury v Morgan* (1862) 1 H & C 249; *Coulthart v Clementson* (1879) 5 QBD 42.
3   (1921) 125 LT 690; affd by the House of Lords who did not comment on this point.

Uncertain, inconclusive and conditional agreements

5.25   Here we are concerned with cases where, although there is an agreement, there may not be a legally binding contract because the agreement is uncertain in its terms, or is merely an agreement to agree in the future, or is subject to the operation of a condition.

Uncertainty

5.26   Where particular terms are vague or unclear, the courts will try to divine the intention of the parties and find a contract, but if such intention cannot be discovered the agreement is not a legally binding contract and cannot be enforced[1]. In *Bushwall Properties Ltd v Vortex Properties Ltd*[2], for instance, A agreed to buy from B $51\frac{1}{2}$ acres of land for £500,000. Under the terms of the agreement the price was to be paid in three instalments and on each payment a 'proportionate part' of the land was to be conveyed to A. The Court of Appeal held that the agreement was void for uncertainty because it did not provide the machinery for identifying the proportionate part to be conveyed in each phase, nor could a term (based on the parties' presumed intention) be implied as to how each proportionate part was to be identified. Other terms which have been held to be unclear include 'subject to war clause', since there was no universally accepted war clause[3], an agreement to 'purchase on hire purchase terms', since there was more than one form of hire purchase terms[1], and an agreement to continue to negotiate in good faith for an *unspecified* period, since a party would never know whether he was entitled to withdraw from the negotiations and the court could not be expected to decide whether a proper reason existed for him to do so[4].

On the other hand, a court can supply the details of an apparently vague term, so that the agreement is a valid contract, if the parties have provided the machinery to ascertain its precise nature, as where there is an agreement for the sale of land at 'market price' (in which case the court can fix that price after making an inquiry)[5], or if the details which the parties must have intended can be implied by reference to the practices of a particular trade to which they belong or by reference to their previous dealings. In *Hillas & Co Ltd v Arcos Ltd*[6], the parties had entered into an agreement for the sale and purchase of timber in 1930. The agreement contained an option to buy 100,000 standards of timber in 1931 but the size and quality of the timber were not specified. The House of Lords refused to find the agreement unenforceable, clarifying any uncertainties by reference to the previous dealings of the parties and usual practice in the timber trade. The judgment of the House is permeated by the view that the courts ought to strive to give effect to business arrangements and not zealously demand absolute certainty of all terms.

Another case where there can be a valid contract despite the apparent uncertainty of a term is where the parties have provided the machinery for one of them, or for a third party or third parties, to fix the precise nature of that term. This was recognised in *Sudbrook Trading Estate Ltd v Eggleton*[7], where the House of Lords dealt with the situation where the price of a piece of property was left to be decided by two valuers, one to be appointed by each party. It held that if the task of the valuers, expressly or impliedly, was to fix a fair and reasonable price and that method proved ineffective, either because a party refused to appoint a valuer or because the valuers failed to agree, a court could substitute its own machinery to ascertain the price, eg by appointing its own valuers. On the other hand, it held, if the price was to be fixed by a *named* valuer or valuers it could not be implied that the price was to be a fair and reasonable one because the implication was that the price was to be fixed by a specified means, the use of the named valuer or valuers. In such a case, it held, a court could not substitute its own machinery if for some reason the named valuer or valuers failed to fix the price, and there would not be an enforceable contract for the sale of the property.

There can be a valid contract for the sale of goods or the supply of a service, even though the price is not fixed, or left to be fixed in an agreed manner, and cannot be determined by a course of dealings between the parties. Statute provides that, in such a case, a reasonable price must be paid[8].

Where an apparently uncertain term can be determined in one of the above ways, the contract is complete on the agreement of the parties even though the precise nature of that term remains to be fixed[9].

If a transaction has been performed on both sides, it will be difficult for a party to submit successfully that there is no agreement or that there is not a legally binding contract on grounds of uncertainty or vagueness.[10]

1 *G Scammell and Nephew Ltd v Ouston* [1941] AC 251, [1941] 1 All ER 14, HL.
2 [1976] 2 All ER 283, [1976] 1 WLR 591, CA.
3 *Bishop and Baxter Ltd v Anglo-Eastern Trading and Industrial Co Ltd* [1944] KB 12, [1943] 2 All ER 598, CA.
4 *Walford v Miles* [1992] 2 AC 128, [1992] 1 All ER 453, HL. Such an agreement for a specified period is enforceable because the element of uncertainty is removed: ibid; *Pitt v PHH Asset Management Ltd* [1993] 4 All ER 961, [1994] 1 WLR 327, CA.
5 *Bushwall Properties Ltd v Vortex Properties Ltd* [1976] 2 All ER 283 at 289.
6 (1932) 147 LT 503, HL.
7 [1983] 1 AC 444, [1982] 3 All ER 1, HL.
8 Sale of Goods Act 1979, s 8; Supply of Goods and Services Act 1982, s 15.
9 *Sudbrook Trading Estate Ltd v Eggleton* [1983] 1 AC 444, [1982] 3 All ER 1, HL.
10 *G Percy Trentham Ltd v Archital Luxfer Ltd* [1993] 1 Lloyd's Rep 25 at 27.

5.27 Sometimes it may be possible to ignore uncertainty in an agreement. This can be done, for instance, where the uncertainty relates to what is a meaningless term. In *Nicolene Ltd v Simmonds*[1], the agreement contained a statement that 'the usual conditions of acceptance apply'. There were no usual conditions of acceptance, but the Court of Appeal said the phrase was meaningless and, since it did not relate to an important term or part of the contract, it could be ignored. A distinction must be drawn between meaningless phrases and phrases which denote that terms are still to be agreed. A phrase is unlikely to be considered meaningless, and thus capable of being ignored, if it concerns an important term of the contract.

1   [1953] 1 QB 543, [1953] 1 All ER 822, CA.

Agreement to agree

5.28   If the parties have agreed the vital terms of an agreement and agreed to be bound immediately, there is a concluded agreement despite the fact that further terms must be negotiated[1]. On the other hand, if a vital term of an agreement is open to further negotiation, or if the parties have not agreed to be bound immediately because further negotiation is necessary before a binding agreement can be concluded, there is no concluded agreement, but merely an agreement to agree. An example is where an agreement for the sale of goods leaves the price to be fixed by agreement between the parties. In *May and Butcher Ltd v R*[2], the price of surplus tentage which was being sold by a government department to the plaintiffs was such as 'shall be agreed upon from time to time between the government department and the purchasers'. The House of Lords found that, because a vital term was left open for future negotiation, the agreement was not a legally binding contract.

However, if the agreement expressly or impliedly provides a method for resolving the lack of agreement, there will be a valid contract. An example is provided by *Foley v Classique Coaches Ltd*[3], where the Court of Appeal held that an agreement containing the words 'price to be agreed by the parties' was a binding contract. The court felt able to distinguish *May and Butcher Ltd v R*[4] on two grounds. First, on the basis that the parties had acted on the agreement for three years and their implied belief that they had been contractually bound during that period must be given effect, and, second, because the contract provided that in the absence of agreement on price it was to be determined by arbitration. *Beer v Bowden*[5] provides another example. Premises were let for ten years (later extended to 14) at a fixed rent for the first five years, but at a rent 'to be agreed' thereafter. The Court of Appeal implied a term that in the absence of agreement a reasonable rent determined by the court should be paid.

1   *Pagnan SpA v Feed Products Ltd* [1987] 2 Lloyd's Rep 601, CA.
2   [1934] 2 KB 17n, HL.
3   [1934] 2 KB 1, CA.
4   [1934] 2 KB 17n, HL.
5   [1981] 1 All ER 1070, [1981] 1 WLR 522n, CA.

Operation of a condition

5.29   An agreement which appears to be a binding contract may never come into operation because it is subject to a condition precedent which is not satisfied[1]. An example is afforded by *Pym v Campbell*[2]. In this case an agreement to purchase a share in an invention was subject to the condition precedent that the invention be approved by X. X failed to approve and thus no binding contract to buy came into existence.

An agreement subject to a condition precedent is not necessarily devoid of all effect. It all depends on the interpretation which the court gives to it.

On its true construction, the effect of an agreement subject to a condition precedent may be that, although the agreement containing it is not binding before the condition is satisfied, neither party can withdraw until it is clear whether or not the condition will be satisfied[3].

Alternatively, or in addition, the effect of such an agreement may be that one party must do his best to fulfil the condition[4] or, at least, not obstruct its fulfilment[5]. For example, the phrase 'subject to survey' in an agreement for the sale of land has been construed as meaning that the purchaser must proceed with due diligence to obtain a surveyor's report and, having received it, consider it, and must act in good faith. If, in good faith, he is not satisfied with the report he is not obliged to proceed with the purchase, but in the meantime neither party can withdraw[6].

Lastly, a condition precedent may be construed as imposing no obligation on either party. This is prima facie[7] the construction which has been given to the condition precedent, 'subject to contract', which is usually inserted initially in an agreement to buy land which is for sale by private treaty. Unless there are very exceptional circumstances which oust the prima facie meaning of the phrase[7], such agreements are simply 'agreements to agree' and arc not binding, nor are the parties required to try to ensure that a contract is concluded[8]. Phrases similar to 'subject to contract' have the same effect, as do 'letters of intent' where one party indicates to another that he will probably conclude a contract with him[9].

1 For a different type of condition precedent, see para 10.12, below.
2 (1856) 6 E & B 370.
3 *Smith v Butler* [1900] 1 QB 694, CA. In *Smallman v Smallman* [1972] Fam 25, [1971] 3 All ER 717, CA, a buyer, who withdrew from an agreement to purchase which was subject to a condition precedent before it was clear whether the condition was satisfied, was unable to recover the deposit he had paid.
4 *Marten v Whale* [1917] 2 KB 480, CA.
5 *Mackay v Dick* (1881) 6 App Cas 251, HL.
6 *Ee v Kakar* (1979) 40 P & CR 223.
7 *Alpenstow Ltd v Regalian Properties plc* [1985] 2 All ER 545, [1985] 1 WLR 721.
8 *Winn v Bull* (1877) 7 Ch D 29.
9 See, for example, *British Steel Corpn v Cleveland Bridge and Engineering Co Ltd* [1984] 1 All ER 504.

5.30 An agreement may also be subject to the operation of a condition subsequent. In such cases an agreement will be a binding contract unless and until the condition occurs. If it does occur, either the contract will automatically cease to bind or one party will have the right to cancel it, depending on the construction of the condition. In *Head v Tattersall*[1], a contract for the sale of a horse was subject to the condition subsequent that, if the purchaser found within a given time that the horse did not meet its contractual description, the horse could be returned and the contract terminated. During that period, the purchaser found that the horse did not correspond with its description. It was held that he could return it, and recover the price, even though it had been injured in the meanwhile.

1 (1871) LR 7 Exch 7.

Payment for work done in anticipation of concluding a contract

5.31   Where, in anticipation of concluding a contract with the defendant, the plaintiff has commenced *at the defendant's request* to perform the work which would be required under the contract, but no contract is entered into, the defendant is liable to pay a reasonable sum for the work done pursuant to his request[1]. This is of obvious importance, for example, in the type of case where the defendant has given the plaintiff a 'letter of intent' to contract and asked him to start work immediately but never finally concluded a contract.

1   *William Lacey (Hounslow) Ltd v Davis* [1957] 2 All ER 712, [1957] 1 WLR 932; *British Steel Corpn v Cleveland Bridge and Engineering Co Ltd* [1984] 1 All ER 504; cf *Regalian Properties plc v London Dockland Development Corpn* [1995] 1 All ER 1005, [1995] 1 WLR 212.

Chapter 6

Consideration and Privity

6.1 An agreement which complies with the rules specified in the previous chapter will constitute a legally binding contract, provided it is supported by consideration and the parties intended to enter into a legally binding contract. Alternatively, it will constitute a legally binding contract if it is made by deed. If a legally binding contract has been formed, only those persons who are parties to the contract can sue or be sued on it. Even where a person has provided consideration, or a contract is expressly intended to confer a benefit or burden on him, he cannot sue or be sued if he is not a party to the contract: this is the doctrine of privity.

Intention to create legal relations
6.2 If an agreement is supported by consideration there is usually an intention to create legal relations, although the parties to an agreement rarely state this intention expressly. If the parties do not wish their agreement to be legally binding, they may expressly state this and the courts will give effect to their intention.

In the absence of an express indication of intention, the courts rely on two presumptions in deciding whether there was an intention to create legal relations, both of which can be rebutted:

a. parties to social, domestic and family arrangements do not intend to be legally bound[1]; and
b. parties to business and commercial agreements expect their agreements to be legally binding[2].

An example of the first type of arrangement is an agreement to give lifts to work, even if it is on an organised basis and involves payment to the car owners for their petrol[3]. While arrangements made within the family or household are presumed not to be intended to be legally binding, the nature of the agreement may clearly indicate that the parties intended a particular arrangement to be legally binding. In *Simpkins v Pays*[4], three members of the same household submitted a joint entry to a competition on the basis that they would share any winnings. This arrangement was held to be legally binding on the parties.

If there is a business arrangement it is extremely difficult to rebut the presumption that the arrangement is to be legally binding, other than by clear words. A case where clear words led to the presumption being rebutted is *Rose and Frank Co v J R Crompton & Bros Ltd*[5], in which the defendants appointed the plaintiffs their agents to sell their products in America under an agreement which contained an 'honour clause', ie a clause which said the agreement was merely recording the intention of the parties and was binding in honour only and not in law. The plaintiffs sued for alleged breach of contract. The Court of Appeal and the House of Lords held that the honour clause constituted a clearly expressed intention that the agreement was not to be legally binding and that effect had to be given to this intention.

Even where the presumption is rebutted by clear words, this does not prevent the subsequent conduct of the parties to the agreement constituting a legally binding contract. In *Rose and Frank Co v J R Crompton & Bros Ltd*, the parties to the agency agreement ordered and supplied goods for sale in America. It was held that these orders and acceptances gave rise to binding contracts, even though the agency agreement was not legally binding.

An important statutory exception to the presumption that business and commercial dealings are intended to be legally binding is contained in s 179 of the Trade Union and Labour Relations (Consolidation) Act 1992, which provides that collective agreements between employers and trade unions are presumed not to be legally enforceable unless they are made in writing and expressly state that the agreement is to be legally enforceable. However, if terms in a collective agreement are incorporated in an individual employee's contract of employment, they are presumed to be intended to be binding[6].

1 *Balfour v Balfour* [1919] 2 KB 571, CA.
2 *Edwards v Skyways Ltd* [1964] 1 All ER 494, [1964] 1 WLR 349.
3 *Coward v Motor Insurers' Bureau* [1963] 1 QB 259, [1962] 1 All ER 531, CA.
4 [1955] 3 All ER 10, [1955] 1 WLR 975.
5 [1925] AC 445, HL.
6 *Robertson v British Gas Corpn* [1983] ICR 351, [1983] IRLR 302, CA; *Marley v Forward Trust Group Ltd* [1986] ICR 891, [1986] IRLR 369, CA.

Consideration

6.3 Agreements not made by deed[1] must be supported by consideration if they are to be legally binding, and a person who wishes to enforce a contract must show that he himself provided consideration for the promise which he is seeking to enforce. It is in the requirement of consideration that English law recognises the idea that a contract is a bargain.

In order to provide consideration for a promise, the promisee (the person to whom the promise was made) must have made a promise or done an act:

a. in return for that promise; *and*

b.   at the express or implied request of the promisor (the person making that promise).

It follows from the requirement that the promisee's act or promise must have been requested by the promisor that a 'gratuitous' act or promise by a promisee is not consideration. This is shown by *Re Cory*[2]. The YMCA wished to build a hall. It needed £150,000 to do so. £85,000 had been promised or was available. However, the YMCA decided not to commit itself to going on with the project until it saw that its efforts to raise the whole sum were likely to succeed. C then promised a donation of 1,000 guineas (£1,050) for the purpose of building the hall. The YMCA subsequently entered into a building contract for the hall, which they alleged they were largely induced to do by C's promise. C then died and the question arose whether his promise to pay was legally binding, in which case his estate would be bound by it. It was held that C's promise was not legally binding; the YMCA had not provided any consideration for C's promise because C had not expressly or impliedly requested the YMCA to do (or promise to do) anything in return.

It also follows from the definition of consideration that a promise (not made by deed) to give property on condition that something occurs is not legally binding if the promisee is not expressly or impliedly requested by the promisor to do or promise anything in return. In *Dickinson v Abel*[3] A told B that he was willing to pay £100,000 for a farm which was vested in a bank as trustees. B had no proprietary interest in the farm but had previously passed on to the bank offers for the farm. B asked: 'What's in it for me?' and was told that he would be paid £10,000 if A bought the farm for £100,000 or less. A did not ask B to perform any specific services, but B telephoned the bank and told them that an offer of £100,000 was on its way and that he personally would accept it. The farm was sold to A for less than £100,000 and B was paid the £10,000. The question later arose as to whether the £10,000 was taxable, which it would be if paid under a contract. It was somewhat surprisingly found as a fact that A had not expressly or impliedly requested B to do anything. Consequently, it was held, what B had done was not consideration for A's promise and there was therefore no binding agreement (ie contract) between A and B but merely a conditional gift. While the finding on the facts is hard to accept, the important legal point is the judge's application of the law to those facts.

1   Para 7.4, below.
2   (1912) 29 TLR 18.
3   [1969] 1 All ER 484, [1969] 1 WLR 295.

6.4   In a number of cases, particularly in the nineteenth century[1], consideration has been defined as follows: that X provides consideration for Y's promise if he confers a benefit on Y, in return for which Y's promise is given, or if he incurs a detriment, in compensation for which Y's promise is given. Certainly if there is either a benefit or a detriment to the appropriate party that is good consideration, but this definition has been criticised and some cases cannot be explained in terms of benefit and detriment. A more modern view of consideration is that, if one party's action or forbearance, promised or actual, is the price for which the other's promise is bought[2] the former party has provided consideration for the latter's promise.

1   See, eg, *Currie v Misa* (1875) LR 10 Exch 153. For a more recent reference to this type of definition, see *Midland Bank Trust Co Ltd v Green* [1981] AC 513 at 531, [1981] 1 All ER 153; *Johnsey Estates Ltd v Lewis & Manley (Engineering) Ltd* (1987) 54 P & CR 296, CA.
2   *Dunlop Pneumatic Tyre Co Ltd v Selfridge & Co Ltd* [1915] AC 847 at 855.

Executed and executory consideration

6.5   In the case of a unilateral contract, ie where a person does something at the request of another, such as finding a lost dog, in return for the promise of a reward, the person doing the requested act thereby provides consideration for the other's promise. In a unilateral contract, consideration is only given by one party and only the other party is bound (hence the description 'unilateral contract'). The consideration provided in a unilateral contract is said to be 'executed' because it consists of the actual doing of something in response to a promise by the other party and at his request.

In the case of a bilateral contract, ie where a party to an agreement promises to do something in response to a promise by the other and at his request, as where X promises to pay for goods to be supplied by Y, a party provides consideration by giving his promise. Thus, in the above example, X provides consideration for Y's promise to supply the goods. In a bilateral contract, consideration is given by both parties and both parties are bound (hence the description 'bilateral contract'). The consideration here is said to be 'executory' because it consists of a promise by each party which need not be executed (ie the promise need not be carried out) in order for the promise of the other party, for which it is exchanged, to be binding. The concept of executory consideration illustrates the difficulty of the benefit or detriment theory of consideration. When no one has done anything and there are merely promises there is no benefit or detriment to anyone, but it is possible to say that the price of one party's promise was the promise made by the other party. Both executed and executory consideration are good consideration in law, unlike 'past consideration'.

Past consideration

6.6   'Past consideration' is said to have been given by a person when, only *after* he has done something, a promise (eg to reward him) is made in return by another person. 'Past consideration' is an inaccurate expression, since it is not consideration at all and a person who has given it cannot enforce another's promise made in return for it.

The fact that past consideration is not good consideration illustrates the idea that consideration is the price of a promise. In *Re McArdle*[1], work was done by X on a house which had been left to her and other members of her family. The other members then promised to reimburse the cost to her of the work but failed to keep their promise. X sued on the promise to pay but failed because she had provided no consideration for it, since her acts (doing the work on the house) which she alleged constituted consideration pre-dated the promise by the relatives.

It would be wrong to think that all actions which are not preceded by an express promise constitute past consideration. If an act is done by X at the request of Y in circumstances where X and Y must have understood that the act was to be remunerated (so that a prior promise of remuneration by Y can be *implied*), the act by X is good consideration[2]. An act done in response to a request accompanied by an implied promise of remuneration may be followed by an express promise to pay a particular sum or confer a particular benefit. If this is so, the promise quantifies the amount due to the party who performed the requested act[2]. If there is no subsequent promise, the amount due is determined on the basis of reasonable remuneration for the services provided or the things supplied. What transforms apparently past consideration into good consideration is the fact that the action is in response to a request which raises an implied promise of payment. The requested action is the price of the implied promise to pay. In *Re McArdle* there was no prior request or expectation of payment. However, there was in *Re Casey's Patents, Stewart v Casey*[3], where the plaintiffs wrote to Casey saying that 'in consideration of your [past] services as practical manager' they would give him a one-third share in certain patents. This promise was fulfilled but subsequently the plaintiffs sought to recover the patents, claiming that Casey had given no consideration for their promise. The Court of Appeal rejected this argument, saying that Casey's services as manager clearly raised an implication that they would be remunerated and thus Casey had provided consideration, the subsequent express promise merely fixing the amount of that remuneration.

1   [1951] Ch 669, [1951] 1 All ER 905, CA.
2   *Lampleigh v Brathwait* (1615) Hob 105; *Kennedy v Broun* (1863) 13 CBNS 677; *Re Casey's Patents, Stewart v Casey* [1892] 1 Ch 104, CA; *Pao On v LauYiu Long* [1980] AC 614, [1979] 3 All ER 65, PC.
3   [1892] 1 Ch 104, CA.

6.7   In determining whether a contract is supported by consideration, the courts have regard to two factors:

a.   consideration must have some value but need not be adequate; and
b.   consideration must be real and sufficient, ie what is alleged to be consideration must be an action or promise which the law recognises as capable of being consideration.

Adequacy
6.8   Provided that the alleged consideration has some economic value in the eyes of the law, the courts will not question its adequacy, even though one party is apparently making a very good bargain and the other is not. The reasoning behind this is not that the courts cannot value promises but that they should not interfere with bargains freely made. In *Mountford v Scott*[1], £1, paid for an option to purchase a house, was found to be good consideration. Money is always considered to have an economic value and the fact that the amount was small was irrelevant.

Although the courts will not question the adequacy of consideration, the fact that the consideration is clearly inadequate may indicate that the contract has been procured by fraudulent misrepresentation, undue influence or duress on the part of the party benefiting from the inadequacy, in which case the contract may be set aside if the rules described in chapter 14 are satisfied.

The next paragraph provides another illustration that the courts will not question the adequacy of consideration which has some value.

1   [1975] Ch 258, [1975] 1 All ER 198, CA.

Forbearance to sue

6.9   If a person who could sue another agrees not to pursue his claim, that constitutes good consideration for a promise by the other person. It might be thought that agreeing to abandon an invalid claim[1] cannot be good consideration. However, the abandonment of an invalid claim will be good consideration if the party abandoning it can show that the claim was reasonable in itself, that he genuinely believed the claim had some chance of success and intended to pursue it, and that he was not concealing from the other party facts which would constitute a defence to the claim[2]. The argument is that abandoning a doubtful claim saves the parties from the uncertainties of litigation and its attendant expense.

1   Eg in *Poteliakhoff v Teakle* [1938] 2 KB 816, [1938] 3 All ER 686, CA, creditor's promise not to sue on unenforceable gaming debts was not good consideration for a promise by the debtor because the creditor knew that the claim was invalid.
2   *Horton v Horton (No 2)* [1961] 1 QB 215, [1960] 3 All ER 649, CA; *Miles v New Zealand Alford Estate Co* (1886) 32 Ch D 266, CA; *Syros Shipping Co SA v Elaghill Trading Co, The Proodos C* [1981] 3 All ER 189.

Sufficiency

6.10   The law refuses to recognise certain types of action or promise as capable of constituting consideration, with the result that a person making such an action or promise cannot enforce another's promise given in return for it. Such an action or promise is said not to be sufficient consideration, which is rather confusing since in law it is not consideration at all.

Performance of an existing duty imposed by law

6.11   The law imposes obligations on all people, and it is necessary to discuss whether performing or promising to perform such an obligation can also be good consideration for a contractual promise of another. The basic position was stated in *Collins v Godefroy*[1], in which the plaintiff sued the defendant for payment of a sum which the latter had promised him if he would attend court to give evidence in a case involving the defendant. It was held that he could not succeed because he had provided no consideration since, having been subpoenaed to attend, he was obliged by law to do so. It is now clear[2] that the principle in *Collins v Godefroy* has been refined by the principle in *Williams v Roffey Bros & Nicholls (Contractors) Ltd*, referred to in para 6.13, below. The result is that, except where the existing duty is to pay money, if A makes a promise to B in return for B's promise to perform (or mere performance of) his existing duty, imposed by law, to do something, B will provide consideration for A's promise if, as a result of B's promise, A obtains a practical benefit (or avoids a 'disbenefit'). It must be emphasised that this refinement does not apply if B promises to pay (or pays) money which he is obliged by law to pay.

1   (1831) 1 B & Ad 950.
2   *Re Selectmove Ltd* [1995] 2 All ER 531 [1995] 1 WLR 474, CA.

6.12   The principle in *Collins v Godefroy* does not apply if the party seeking to show that he provided consideration promised to do, or did, more than was required by law, as where he has paid more than he was legally obliged to pay, because that is good consideration. Since consideration need not be adequate it does not matter that what is promised or done exceeds the legal requirements only slightly. This may be demonstrated by *Glasbrook Bros Ltd v Glamorgan County Council*[1], where the company requested greater protection for its mine during a strike than the police thought necessary and offered to pay for the increased police presence. The company later refused to pay, claiming that, since the police were under a legal duty to protect property, they had provided no consideration for the company's promise of payment. The House of Lords held that the company was obliged to pay because, while the police were required to guard the mine, they were free to choose the form of protection, and in this case they had provided more protection than they reasonably thought necessary at the request of the company.

1   [1925] AC 270, HL. Also see *Ward v Byham* [1956] 2 All ER 318, [1956] 1 WLR 496, CA.

Performance of an existing contractual duty owed to the other party
6.13   If a person is already under a contractual duty to do something, a mere promise to perform it (or mere performance of it) cannot be good consideration for another promise by the person to whom the contractual duty was already owed. In *Stilk v Myrick*[1], the crew of a ship were paid a lump sum for a voyage including all normal emergencies. During the voyage two of the crew deserted and the captain promised to pay the wages of the deserters to the rest of the crew if they would continue the voyage short-handed. Once returned to England, the extra wages were not paid and the seamen sued. Their claim failed, the court finding they had provided no consideration since they were required to cope with normal emergencies by their existing contracts. Desertion or death of fellow crew members was a normal emergency so they had done no more than they had contracted to do. But the court stressed that, if they had promised to do more than they were obliged to do by their existing contracts, they would have provided good consideration. For example, if they had promised to face exceptional hazards that would have been good consideration for their employer's promise[2].

In *Williams v Roffey Bros & Nicholls (Contractors) Ltd*[3] the Court of Appeal propounded a major limitation on the principle in *Stilk v Myrick*. It held that, where A makes a further promise to B in return for B's promise to perform (or performance of) his contractual obligations already owed to A, and as a result of B's promise (or performance) A obtains a practical benefit (or avoids a 'disbenefit'), B provides good consideration for A's further promise. The facts

119

of this case were that the plaintiff had been engaged by the defendants, who were main contractors in refurbishing a block of flats, to carry out carpentry work for £20,000 which turned out to be unprofitable for him. The main contract contained a time penalty clause and, fearful that the plaintiff would not complete the work on time, the defendants promised him an extra £10,300, payable at the rate of £575 per flat, if he would carry out the work on time. The plaintiff promised to do so, and completed the work in a number of flats but was not paid the extra amount promised. The Court of Appeal held that the plaintiff could recover the unpaid amount; the defendants' promise was binding, consideration having been given for it by the plaintiff, since his promise benefited the defendants (apparently by avoiding the penalty for delay and avoiding the trouble and expense of engaging other people to complete the carpentry work). The Court of Appeal added that, if the defendant's promise had been obtained by fraud or duress, the contract could have been set aside on that ground.

Since it is unlikely that A will make a further promise to B if he is not going to obtain some benefit from B's promise to perform (or performance of) his contractual obligations to A, the decision appeared to refine the principle in *Stilk v Myrick* almost out of existence. However, in the subsequent case of *Re Selectmove Ltd*[4], the Court of Appeal indicated a restrictive approach to its decision in *Williams v Roffey Bros*, saying that it did not apply where the existing obligation was one to pay money. It held that a promise to pay (or the payment of) money already due could not be good consideration. It emphasised that the existing obligation in *Williams v Roffey Bros* was to do work and supply materials and distinguished that case on that ground.

1   (1809) 2 Camp 317.
2   *Hartley v Ponsonby* (1857) 7 E & B 872.
3   [1991] 1 QB 1, [1990] 1 All ER 512, CA.
4   [1995] 2 All ER 531, [1995] 1 WLR 474, CA.

Performance of an existing contractual duty owed to a third party
6.14   If a party to a contract with X (the 'third party') is obliged by it to perform some action, a subsequent promise by him to perform that action (or his performance of it) can be good consideration for a promise by another person, whether or not there is any benefit to that person. The principle in *Stilk v Myrick*[1] has never applied to this situation. In *Scotson v Pegg*[2], for example, the plaintiffs had contracted to deliver coal to X, or wherever X ordered it to be delivered. X sold the coal to the defendant and told the plaintiffs to deliver it to him. The defendant then promised the plaintiffs that if they delivered the coal he would unload it at a given rate. The defendant failed to unload at this rate and, when sued, argued that the plaintiffs had not provided consideration for his promise by delivering the coal, because they were obliged to do so under their contract with X. The court held that the plaintiffs had provided consideration.

In two modern cases, *New Zealand Shipping Co Ltd v A M Satterthwaite & Co Ltd, The Eurymedon*[3] and *Pao On v Lau Yiu Long*[4], the Privy Council has affirmed that a promise to discharge, or the discharge of, a pre-existing contractual obligation to a third party can be valid consideration for another's promise. In the former case, consideration for the promise consisted of unloading a ship which the promisee was already bound to unload under a contract with a third party.

1   See para 6.13, above.
2   (1861) 6 H & N 295.
3   [1975] AC 154, [1974] 1 All ER 1015, PC.
4   [1980] AC 614, [1979] 3 All ER 65, PC.

Part payment of debts

6.15   *Position at common law*   If A is under a contractual obligation to pay B and B agrees to forego part of the debt, A's payment of the rest of the debt (ie his partial performance of his existing contractual obligation to B) is not consideration for B's promise and, according to the common law, B can subsequently recover the remainder of the debt. In *Foakes v Beer*[1], Mrs Beer was owed money under a judgment debt by Dr Foakes. She agreed to accept payment by instalments but the agreement did not refer to the question of interest, which is payable on a judgment debt. Dr Foakes paid the debt. Mrs Beer then sued for the interest. In reply Dr Foakes pleaded the agreement between them, in which Mrs Beer had agreed to bring no further action on the judgment. Mrs Beer contended successfully that there was no consideration for her promise and that, therefore, it was not binding. Dr Foakes' payment by instalments of the judgment debt could not be consideration for a promise by her to take no further action. He was merely paying less than what he was obliged to do. The House of Lords regretted that this decision had to be reached, but considered itself bound by previous cases.

There are exceptions to the rule that part payment of a debt is no consideration for a promise to remit the rest of the debt. In *Pinnel's Case*[2], for instance, it was said that, provided it was done at the creditor's request, early payment of part of a debt, or part payment at another place than that specified for payment, or payment in kind, even if the value of the goods is less than the debt, is good consideration for a promise by the creditor to forego the remainder of the debt. Thus, if A owes B £100 payable on 1 January 2001 at Reading and, at B's request, A pays £1 on 31 December (or pays £1 at Leicester on the correct day, or gives B a rose or a scarf on the correct day), then the debt is validly discharged. It used to be thought that a part payment by cheque was good consideration for a promise to remit a debt payable in cash. This has been rejected by the Court of Appeal who decided that nowadays there is no effective difference between cash and a cheque which is honoured[3].

1   (1884) 9 App Cas 605, HL.
2   (1602) 5 Co Rep 117a.
3   *D & C Builders Ltd v Rees* [1966] 2 QB 617, [1965] 3 All ER 837, CA.

6.16   There are two other somewhat anomalous areas where partial payment of a debt discharges it. First, where a debtor makes an arrangement with all his creditors that they will all be paid a given percentage of what they are owed, no creditor who has been paid it can recover more than that given percentage[1]. Second, when a third party pays part of a debt in full settlement, that is a valid discharge of the whole debt, and the creditor cannot recover the balance from the debtor[2]. The reason which has been given is that it would be a fraud on the third party if the creditor could do so[3].

Neither of these areas can satisfactorily be explained in terms of principle (ie consideration by the debtor for the creditor's promise) and are best explained as based on grounds of public policy.

1   *Good v Cheesman* (1831) 2 B & Ad 328.
2   *Welby v Drake* (1825) 1 C & P 557; *Hirachand Punamchand v Temple* [1911] 2 KB 330, CA.
3   *Hirachand Punamchand v Temple* [1911] 2 KB 330, CA.

6.17   *Position in equity: promissory estoppel*   Apart from these exceptions it appeared that a debtor who paid part of a debt, believing that the creditor had agreed to remit the remainder of the debt, had no defence if the creditor sought to recover the amount foregone. However, in 1947 Denning J (as he was then) called upon equity to aid the debtor. In *Central London Property Trust Ltd v High Trees House Ltd*[1], the plaintiffs let a block of flats to the defendants in 1937 for 99 years at a rent of £2,500 per year. The defendants intended to sub-let the flats but, because of the war, found they had many vacant flats and could not pay the rent out of profits. The plaintiffs agreed to accept a reduced rent of £1,250, which was paid quarterly from 1941 until September 1945, by which time all the flats were let. The plaintiffs demanded full rent from September 1945 and claimed the amount of rent underpaid during the previous quarters. The defendants had provided no consideration for the promise by the plaintiffs to remit the rent, but Denning J found that, while the common law could provide no defence in such a case, equity could. The judge, drawing on two little known cases decided in the nineteenth century, said that where one party gave a promise which he intended to be binding and to be acted on, and which was acted on, that promise could be raised as a defence by the promisee if the promisor sought to enforce his strict legal rights. In this case the plaintiffs had promised to reduce the rent; they intended their promise to be binding, they knew the defendants would act on it and the defendants did so act; therefore the rent underpaid in the past could not be demanded by the plaintiffs since this would be inequitable. However, the judge found that the promise was understood by the parties only to apply under the conditions prevailing at the time it was made, namely, when the flats were only partially let, and that when the flats became fully let, early in 1945, the promise to remit part of the rent ceased to bind the plaintiffs. The judge also suggested that a promise of this type might be terminated by notice. This case illustrates the equitable doctrine known as promissory estoppel[2], which applies to promises to remit debts (in whole or part) and also to promises not to enforce other contractual rights.

1   [1947] KB 130, [1956] 1 All ER 256n.
2   Estoppel (as opposed to promissory estoppel) is a legal doctrine whereby if a person misrepresents to another an existing fact and intends this misrepresentation to be acted on, and it is acted on by the other who suffers detriment in consequence, he cannot subsequently deny the truth of that fact. The doctrine was inapplicable in the *High Trees* case because the representation was as to the future and not as to an existing fact.

6.18   Under the doctrine of promissory estoppel a promise not to enforce a contractual right is given some effect, despite the absence of consideration for it, where it would be inequitable for the promisor simply to go back on his promise and enforce that right. There is authority that the doctrine can even apply where the promise is made before the contract is entered into, as where a person who is negotiating to lease property to another promises not to enforce a repairing covenant in the draft lease[1]. This goes beyond the previous authorities, which required or assumed that there must be an existing relationship between promisor and promisee when the promise was made, and its compatibility with certain other rules[2] of the law of contract is as yet unexplained.

1   *Brikom Investments Ltd v Carr* [1979] 2 All ER 753 at 758.
2   Such as the law relating to pre-contractual misrepresentations, Chap 14.

6.19   The precise scope of promissory estoppel is not entirely clear; indeed, in *Woodhouse A C Israel Cocoa Ltd SA v Nigerian Produce Marketing Co Ltd*[1], Lord Hailsham LC said that it may need to be reviewed and reduced to a coherent body of doctrine by the courts. Nevertheless, its requirements appear to be as follows:

a. *Unequivocal promise*   There must be an unequivocal promise[2] by one party that he will not, at least for the time being, enforce his strict contractual rights against the other. The promise may be either express or implied from conduct[3]. Silence and inaction cannot by themselves give rise to a promissory estoppel because they are by their nature equivocal, since there can be more than one reason why the party concerned is silent and inactive[4].

b. *Alteration of position*   The promisor must have intended that his promise should be acted on by the promisee, and the promisee must have acted on it in the sense of altering his position in reliance on the promise[5]. This requirement was satisfied in *Hughes v Metropolitan Rly Co*[6], where a tenant, who had been given six months' notice to repair the premises in accordance with a repairing covenant but who had been induced by the landlord's conduct soon afterwards to believe that the lease would not be forfeited for failure to repair, failed to repair in reliance on this belief. It is not so easy to discern an alteration of position in the *High Trees* case, but the requirement has been said to be satisfied by the fact that the lessees elected to pay a lower rent and to continue liable as lessees in reliance on the lessor's promise that a lesser rent would be accepted in satisfaction[7].
   The present requirement means that promissory estoppel cannot arise if the promisee does nothing, by action or inaction, in reliance on the promise but simply does what he was going to do anyway regardless of whether or not the promise was made[8]. This is illustrated by *Fontana NV v Mautner*[9]. T, the tenant of a flat which was not subject to the Rent Act, refused to leave when his tenancy expired, on the grounds that he had been a model tenant for many years and that a move would be disastrous for the health of his chronically ill wife. At a meeting with a representative of the landlord, T was assured by the representative that he could stay on in the flat as long as he wished, but he subsequently received a notice to quit. In proceedings for possession, Balcombe

J rejected T's claim that the assurance gave rise to a promissory estoppel, and made an order for possession. The judge held that this was not a case of promissory estoppel because T had done nothing, by action or inaction, in reliance on the assurance but had simply done what he was going to do *anyway* (and that was to sit tight for as long as he possibly could).

c. *Inequitable for promisor to resile*   It must be inequitable for the promisor to go back on his promise[10]. It will only be inequitable for the promisor to resile from his promise if the promisee can show that he has suffered 'detriment', ie some prejudicial effect on his interests. This is judged by looking at the promisee's position *at the moment when the promisor proposes to resile* and seeing whether it would be unjust to allow him to do so, having regard to what was promised, what the promisee has done (or refrained from doing) in reliance on the promise and the position in which he would be if the promisor was allowed immediately to resume his strict rights[11]. 'Detriment', then, is not judged by a comparison of the promisee's position before and after acting on the promise on the assumption that it will be honoured. Normally, the present requirement will be satisfied if the promisee has altered his position in reliance on the promise. However, this will not always be the case, as is shown by *The Post Chaser*[12], where the promisors resiled from their promise not to enforce their strict rights only two days after making it. It was held that this was not inequitable because, in this short period, the promisees had not suffered any prejudice, despite having relied on the promise.

The present requirement has another aspect; even if it can be said that the promisee has suffered 'detriment', it is not inequitable for the promisor to go back on his promise, and the promisee is therefore not protected by promissory estoppel, if the promise has been procured by improper pressure or fraud on the part of the promisee or an associate (or by other similar conduct which would render it unfair to the promisor to hold him to his promise). In *D & C Builders Ltd v Rees*[13], the plaintiffs were owed £482 by the defendant, who knew that they were in desperate need of money to stave off bankruptcy. The defendant's wife offered the plaintiffs £300 in settlement of the debt, saying in effect that if they refused they would get nothing. The plaintiffs accepted the £300 reluctantly in settlement of the debt but later sued successfully for the balance. Lord Denning MR refused to allow the defendant to rely on promissory estoppel; his wife's conduct had been improper and therefore it was not inequitable for the plaintiffs to go back on their promise and insist on their strict contractual right to payment of the balance.

1   [1972] 2 All ER 271 at 282, HL.
2   *Woodhouse AC Israel Cocoa Ltd SA v Nigerian Produce Marketing Co Ltd* [1972] AC 741, [1972] 2 All ER 271, HL; *China-Pacific SA v Food Corpn of India, The Winson* [1981] QB 403, [1980] 3 All ER 556, CA; revsd on other grounds [1982] AC 939, [1981] 3 All ER 688, HL; *Scandinavian Trading Tanker Co AB v Flota Petrolera Ecuatoriana, The Scaptrade* [1983] QB 529, [1983] 1 All ER 301, CA; affd [1983] 2 AC 694, [1983] 2 All ER 763, HL.
3   *Hughes v Metropolitan Rly Co* (1877) 2 App Cas 439, HL; *BP Exploration Co (Libya) Ltd v Hunt (No 2)* [1979] 1 WLR 783 at 810.
4   *Allied Marine Transport Ltd v Vale do Rio Doce Navegacao SA, The Leonidas D* [1985] 2 All ER 796, [1985] 1 WLR 925, CA.

5   *Hughes v Metropolitan Rly Co* (1877) 2 App Cas 439, HL; *Central London Property Trust Ltd v High Trees House Ltd* [1947] KB 130, [1956] 1 All ER 256n; *Tool Metal Manufacturing Co Ltd v Tungsten Electric Co Ltd* [1955] 2 All ER 657, [1955] 1 WLR 761, HL; *Ajayi v R T Briscoe (Nigeria) Ltd* [1964] 3 All ER 556, [1964] 1 WLR 1326, PC. Cf *Brikom Investments Ltd v Carr* [1979] 2 All ER 753 at 758–759.
6   (1877) 2 App Cas 439, HL.
7   Spencer Bower and Turner *Estoppel by Misrepresentation* (3rd edn) p 393.
8   *Fontana NV v Mautner* (1979) 254 Estates Gazette 199; *Scandinavian Trading Tanker Co AB v Flota Petrolera Ecuatoriana, The Scaptrade* [1983] QB 529, [1983] 1 All ER 301, CA; affd [1983] 2 AC 694, [1983] 2 All ER 763, HL.
9   (1979) 254 Estates Gazette 199.
10 *Birmingham and District Land Co v London and North Western Rly Co* (1888) 40 Ch D 268 at 286; *Tool Metal Manufacturing Co Ltd v Tungsten Electric Co Ltd* [1955] 2 All ER 657, [1955] 1 WLR 761, HL; *Ajayi v R T Briscoe (Nigeria) Ltd* [1964] 3 All ER 556, [1964] 1 WLR 1326, PC.
11 *Fontana NV v Mautner* (1979) 254 Estates Gazette 199; *Grundt v Great Boulder Pty Gold Mine Ltd* (1937) 59 CLR 641 at 674–675.
12 [1982] 1 All ER 19.
13 [1966] 2 QB 617, [1965] 3 All ER 837, CA.

6.20   *Effect of promissory estoppel*   Generally, promissory estoppel only suspends, and does not discharge (ie does not wholly extinguish), an obligation. Where promissory estoppel operates to suspend an obligation the promisor may, by giving reasonable notice to the promisee, revert to his strict contractual rights thereafter[1]. If a promise not to enforce a strict contractual right was clearly intended to be operative only for a certain period, as in the *High Trees* case, the promisor automatically reverts to that right on the expiry of the period, if he has not previously determined his promise by giving reasonable notice[2].

Where an obligation has been suspended, the effect of the promisor's reversion to the strict contractual position varies. If the obligation is to pay a lump sum or to perform some other act, such as to repair under a repairing covenant in a lease, the effect of a reversion is that after the period of reasonable notice the promisee must then perform his strict contractual obligation. An example is provided by *Hughes v Metropolitan Rly Co*[3], discussed above, where the House of Lords held that the six months' notice to repair which had been suspended ran from the time of the landlord's reversion to his strict contractual rights. This can be contrasted with the situation where the obligation in question is to make periodic payments (such as the payment of rent) or to make some other performance by instalments. In such a case, a reversion to the strict contractual position, after a promise to accept part payment (or part performance) in lieu or to waive it entirely, results in the promisee being liable to make future payments (or other performance) in full in respect of instalments due after the period of reasonable notice, but (unless the promise otherwise provides) does not render him liable to pay (or perform) what was due, and unpaid (or unperformed), during the currency of the estoppel[4].

Exceptionally, the effect of promissory estoppel may be to make a promise irrevocable, and thereby to discharge, and not just suspend, the promisee's obligations. A promise subject to promissory estoppel becomes irrevocable if the promisee cannot revert to his strict contractual position[5].

1   *Tool Metal Manufacturing Co Ltd v Tungsten Electric Co Ltd* [1955] 2 All ER 657, [1955] 1 WLR 761, HL; *Ajayi v R T Briscoe (Nigeria) Ltd* [1964] 3 All ER 556, [1964] 1 WLR 1326, PC. Cf *D & C Builders Ltd v Rees* [1966] 2 QB 617, [1965] 3 All ER 837 at 841; *Brikom Investments Ltd v Carr* [1979] QB 467, [1979] 2 All ER 753 at 758.
2   *Birmingham and District Land Co v London and North Western Rly Co* (1888) 40 Ch D 268 at 288.
3   (1877) 2 App Cas 439, HL.
4   *Central London Property Trust Ltd v High Trees House Ltd* [1947] KB 130, [1956] 1 All ER 256n; *Tungsten Electric Co Ltd v Tool Metal Manufacturing Co Ltd* (1950) 69 RPC 108, CA; *Tool Metal Manufacturing Co Ltd v Tungsten Electric Co Ltd* [1955] 2 All ER 657, [1955] 1 WLR 761, HL.
5   *Ajayi v R T Briscoe (Nigeria) Ltd* [1964] 3 All ER 556, [1964] 1 WLR 1326, PC.

6.21   *A shield, not a sword* Promissory estoppel only prevents the promisor from enforcing his strict rights (at least, without reasonable notice) despite the absence of consideration from the promisee for the promise; it cannot be used to found a cause of action. In *Combe v Combe*[1], an ex-husband promised, informally, to pay his divorced wife maintenance. In reliance on his promise she did not bring court proceedings for financial provision. He failed to pay and she sued him. She had provided no consideration for her ex-husband's promise because he had not requested her not to bring proceedings for financial provision. Consequently, she alleged that he was estopped from going back on his promise (so that it was binding on him) because she had relied on his promise. The Court of Appeal rejected her claim, saying that promissory estoppel was a shield and not a sword. This does not mean that promissory estoppel can only be relied on by a defendant; it can also be relied on by a plaintiff who has *an independent cause of action* to prevent a person setting up by way of defence a strict legal right which he has promised not to enforce.

1   [1951] 2 KB 215, [1951] 1 All ER 767, CA. See also *Argy Trading Development Co Ltd v Lapid Developments Ltd* [1977] 3 All ER 785, [1977] 1 WLR 444; *Syros Shipping Co SA v Elaghill Trading Co, The Proodos C* [1981] 3 All ER 189.

6.22   We return to promissory estoppel in paras 6.38 and 6.40, below.

Consideration must move from the promisee
6.23   It is not sufficient that there is consideration in the abstract; it is also necessary for a person who wishes to enforce a promise to show that he (or his agent on his behalf) has provided consideration. This bears a strong resemblance to the doctrine of privity of contract which states that a person who is not party to a contract cannot sue on it. In some early cases claims failed either on the basis that the party seeking to enforce the contract had provided no consideration or because he was not a party to the agreement[1]. But later cases have shown that consideration and privity are two separate requirements and not two facets of the same rule[2]. In many cases it is not necessary to decide on which basis a claim fails but if, as it seems, the rules are separate it is not sufficient to be a party to an agreement to enforce it; consideration must also be provided. We return to the requirement that consideration must move from the promisee in para 6.25, below.

1   *Price v Easton* (1833) 4 B & Ad 433.
2   Eg *Dunlop Pneumatic Tyre Co Ltd v Selfridge & Co Ltd* [1915] AC 847, HL.

Privity of Contract

6.24   It is a distinct rule of English law that only those persons who are parties to a contract may sue and be sued on that contract, subject to certain recognised exceptions. There are two consequences of the doctrine: a person not a party to a contract is not entitled to enforce the contract, even if it was intended to benefit him and he has provided consideration; and a contract cannot impose obligations on a stranger to it. Suggested reasons for the first consequence are:

a.   that mere donees should not be able to enforce a contract; and
b.   that the parties to the contract should not have their freedom to vary it restricted by the existence of third party rights.

There seems more justification for refusing to allow a contract to impose a burden on a third party than for denying the benefit of a contract to a third party whom the contract sought to benefit.

Benefits

Enforcement by the party intended to benefit
6.25   Prior to *Tweddle v Atkinson*[1], a benefit enforceable by a third person could be conferred on him if there was some family relationship between him and one of the contracting parties. However, in *Tweddle v Atkinson*, a contract between the plaintiff's father and X for the benefit of the plaintiff was regarded as unenforceable by the plaintiff because he was not a party to the contract and had not provided consideration.

It may be possible to confer a benefit which he can enforce on someone not really involved in a contract by making him a party to it, even if in name only. However, that party will only be able to enforce the promised benefit if he has provided consideration for the promise. This is subject to the following possible exception. Suppose that a contract is made in which A, on the one part, and B and C, on the other, are named as parties, and that in response to A's promise B promises 'on behalf of [himself] and C' to do something. Can B's promise, expressed as it is, constitute consideration on C's part, so that C can enforce A's promise? The answer 'yes' is persuasively provided in the Australian case of *Coulls v Bagot's Executor and Trustee Co Ltd*[2], where a contract for the right to quarry a mine made all royalties payable to the owner of the land, who had granted the right, and his wife, jointly. The High Court of Australia was not unanimous about the meaning of the contract but a majority was agreed that, if she was a party to the contract, the wife was entitled to the royalties after her husband's death, even though she had personally provided no consideration for it, because the promise to pay her and her husband was supported by consideration furnished by the husband expressly on behalf of himself and his wife. The basis of the wife's entitlement was that joint consideration had been provided by the husband and wife through the husband's promise expressed to be on behalf of both of them. The concept of joint consideration may be acceptable if there is a *genuine* joint consideration (ie where A looks to C to honour the promise if B does not). However, there cannot be a genuine joint consideration when, as in *Coulls*, it is clear that C is not able (legally or physically) to honour the promise made by B on his behalf, as where C does not own the subject matter which B has promised to sell to A. For this reason, it is submitted that *Coulls* goes further than is legitimate.

1   (1861) 1 B & S 393.
2   [1967] ALR 385.

6.26   The fact that, under the doctrine of privity, a third party to a contract is not entitled by virtue of the contract itself to enforce a benefit arising under it does not mean that a contract can never indirectly benefit him. For example, if it is foreseeable that negligent performance of a contract by a party to it will cause physical injury to a third party, that party may owe a duty of care to the third party and be liable to him in the tort of negligence if he is in breach of that duty. By way of another example, accountants, surveyors and other professional people may be held liable in tort to people who are not their clients if they cause them foreseeable economic loss in negligently carrying out a contract made with a client. However, it is exceptional for a person to be held liable in tort for negligently causing foreseeable economic loss. We discuss liability in tort in Part III; Chapter 18 is particularly relevant in the present context.

Exceptions and qualifications
6.27   There are certain established exceptions and qualifications to the doctrine of privity of contract:

a.   If an agent enters into an authorised contract with a third party on behalf of his principal, there is a contract between the principal and the third party[1].
b.   It is possible to assign rights under a contract[2].
c.   A third party can sue on a bill of exchange or cheque[3].
d.   Beneficiaries under certain types of contract of insurance have a statutory right to claim the benefit of the contract even if they are not parties to it. An example is where one spouse has made a life insurance contract which is expressed to be for the benefit of the other[4].

In certain circumstances, a third party to a contract can take the benefit of a clause in it excluding or restricting liability[5].

The requirements of land law have also necessitated some modifications of the strict rules of privity. For example, the benefits of covenants in leases are transferred to successors in title of the landlord and tenant, despite the absence of privity, if the covenants affect the land[6].

1   Chap 23.
2   Chap 22.
3   Bills of Exchange Act 1882, s 29.
4   Married Women's Property Act 1882, s 11.
5   Paras 10.39 and 10.40, below.
6   Law of Property Act 1925, ss 78, 141 and 142.

6.28   The above situations are exceptions or qualifications to the doctrine of privity. It may also be possible to outflank the rule. For example, if a collateral contract can be found, a person not a party to the principal contract can sue on the collateral contract instead. In *Shanklin Pier Ltd v Detel Products Ltd*[1], the plaintiffs employed contractors to paint their pier. They instructed the contractors to buy and use the defendants' paint, having been promised by the defendants that the paint would last for seven to ten years. The paint lasted for only three months. It was held that, while the plaintiffs could not sue on the contract of sale of the paint, to which they were not parties, they could sue on a collateral contract between them and the defendants which contained a promise by the defendants that the paint would last seven to ten years, for which promise the plaintiffs had provided consideration by requiring their contractors to use the defendants' paint. Similarly, in *Andrews v Hopkinson*[2], the plaintiff entered into a contract of hire purchase with a finance company for a car after the car dealer had misrepresented that she was a 'good little bus'. It was held that the dealer was liable under a collateral contract between himself and the plaintiff[3].

1   [1951] 2 KB 854, [1951] 2 All ER 471.
2   [1957] 1 QB 229, [1956] 3 All ER 422.
3   See now Consumer Credit Act 1974, ss 56 and 75, for a possible claim against the finance company in relation to the dealer's misrepresentation.

6.29   Another method of evasion of the privity doctrine is the use of a trust. The subject matter of a trust is normally tangible property, but when used in this context the subject matter of the trust is the right to sue on the promise given by one party to a contract to the other party that he will benefit a third party; a right to sue on a contract is an intangible piece of property. In equity, if a trust of a promise can be discovered, the courts will enforce an agreement for the benefit of the third party; he is regarded as a beneficiary and the party contracting for his benefit as a trustee. In *Lloyd's v Harper*[1], Lush LJ said that, 'when a contract is made with A for the benefit of B, A can sue on the contract for the benefit of B and recover all that B could have recovered if the contract had been made by B himself'. The case concerned a contract which guaranteed that the creditors of a Lloyd's underwriter would be paid. The contract was with Lloyd's, not the creditors, but the Court of Appeal held that Lloyd's could recover on behalf of the creditors, and not merely for their own loss. The decision in *Lloyd's v Harper* allowed the trustee-party to recover for the third party beneficiary (the creditors in that case); it did not give a right to sue to the third party beneficiary. However, it seems that if the third party beneficiary wishes to sue he can do so by joining as co-plaintiff the trustee-party[2]. If the trustee-party pursues a claim for the third party beneficiary any damages are payable to the third party beneficiary. If the trustee-party refuses to sue either alone or as co-plaintiff, there seems no reason why he should not be joined as co-defendant in an action by the third party beneficiary.

1   (1880) 16 Ch D 290, CA.
2   *Les Affréteurs Réunis SA v Leopold Walford (London) Ltd* [1919] AC 801, HL.

6.30   The difficulty with using the trust concept to defeat the doctrine of privity is that it is not certain when it will apply. Although no formal words are required, an intention to create a trust, not merely an intention to benefit a third party, must exist, and this is the principal reason why the application of the trust concept is uncertain. In modern times, the courts generally seem reluctant to impute such an intention, in the absence of clear words. For example, in *Re Schebsman*[1], decided in 1943, a contract between Schebsman and X Ltd, which provided that in certain circumstances his wife and daughter should be paid a lump sum, was held not to create a trust. The Court of Appeal was influenced by the fact that Schebsman and the company might have wished to vary the agreement, which would have been impossible had the contract created a trust. In *Green v Russell*[2], decided in 1959, a contract of insurance between Russell and an insurance company made certain sums payable if any of his employees died. Green, an employee, died; the Court of Appeal held that there was no trust in his favour of the sum due under the contract of insurance.

Beswick v Beswick[3], the most important modern case on privity of contract, does not discuss trusts and so this attempt to outflank privity seems to have been limited by the courts.

1   [1944] Ch 83, [1943] 2 All ER 768, CA.
2   [1959] 2 QB 226, [1959] 2 All ER 525, CA.
3   [1968] AC 58, [1967] 2 All ER 1197, HL.

Enforcement by a party to the contract
6.31   The party who was promised that the benefit would be conferred on the third party may be prepared to sue if the other party to the agreement does not carry out his contractual obligations. Damages, the usual remedy for failure to perform contractual obligations, are available, but, unless the contracting party is suing as agent or trustee for the third party, he cannot normally recover any damages on behalf of the third party in respect of his loss[1]. The reason is that, generally[2], a plaintiff can only recover damages for the loss which he has suffered[3]. If the contract was intended solely to benefit the third party, so that the contracting party has suffered no loss, only nominal damages (usually in the region of £2 to £20) will normally be recoverable by the contracting party[4].

This being so, it is preferable for the contracting party to seek the enforcement of the contract by means of the equitable remedy of specific performance. The advantages of this remedy are illustrated by *Beswick v Beswick*[5]. In this case, in consideration of Peter Beswick transferring his business to his nephew, the nephew agreed to pay his uncle a pension and, after his death, a weekly annuity to his widow. The nephew paid his uncle the pension but only one payment of the annuity was made. The widow, the administratrix of her husband's estate, successfully sued her nephew for specific performance of the contract to pay the annuity, although the House of Lords held that she would not have succeeded if she had sued merely as the intended recipient. Thus, if specific performance of a contract can be ordered, a party to a contract or his personal representative can ensure enforcement of the contract for the benefit of a third party. However, it would be wrong to think that specific performance will always be ordered in the present type of case. It is a discretionary remedy and is subject to a number of other limitations described in para 12.28, below.

1   If the contracting party sues for, and recovers, damages for the third party as agent or trustee, he will be obliged as trustee or agent to hand over the damages to the third party. Although there is no binding authority on this point, it seems that, in any other case where the contracting party can, and does, recover damages in respect of the third party's loss, the third party may recover any damages obtained by the contracting party in respect of it, either under the law of restitution (*Jackson v Horizon Holidays Ltd* [1975] 3 All ER 92 at 96, [1975] 1 WLR 1468) or on the basis that the contracting party holds the damages in trust for the third party (*Darlington Borough Council v Wiltshier Northern Ltd* [1995] 3 All ER 895 at 902-903 and 908, [1995] 1 WLR 68).
2   For the general rule, and some exceptions to it, see para 12.2, below.
3   If the contract is one to provide a contracting party with a benefit which others will also enjoy, such as a contract for a family holiday or a group coach trip, he is entitled to substantial damages for *his* loss (the family holiday or group coach trip) if the other party breaks the contract by failing to provide the benefit: *Jackson v Horizon Holidays Ltd* [1975] 3 All ER 92, [1975] 1 WLR 1468, CA, as explained in *Woodar Investment Development Ltd v Wimpey Construction (UK) Ltd* [1980] 1 All ER 571, [1980] 1 WLR 277, HL.
4   *Beswick v Beswick* [1968] AC 58, [1967] 2 All ER 1197, HL.
5   [1968] AC 58, [1967] 2 All ER 1197, HL.

Burdens
6.32   As we have already indicated, the general rule is that only a person who is a party to a contract can be subject to any obligations contained in it; consequently, a third party cannot generally be sued for contravening a provision in a contract made between others[1].

The principal exceptions or qualifications to this general rule can be summarised as follows:

a.   the burdens of a contract apply to a person on whose behalf the contract was made by an agent[2];
b.   the burdens of covenants in leases are transferred to the successors in title of the landlord and tenant, despite the absence of privity of contract, but in the case of leases created before 1 January 1996 only if the covenants affect the land;
c.   the burdens of negative covenants affecting the use of land (ie covenants *not* to do specified things on the land), inserted in a contract of sale of land, bind subsequent purchasers of the land, provided certain conditions are satisfied;
d.   where someone hands over goods to another for repair, cleaning, carriage, loading or the like, the transaction gives rise to what is called a 'bailment', the transferor being the 'bailor' and the recipient the 'bailee'. If the bailee sub-contracts the work to someone else, the terms of the contract between

the bailee and that person will bind the bailor (a third party to the contract, which involves a 'sub-bailment') if the bailee had the bailor's authority to make the sub-bailment and the bailor had expressly or impliedly authorised him to make the sub-bailment on the terms in question[3];

e.   in certain cases, a third party can be bound by a provision as to the resale price of goods contained in a contract between others;

f.   in certain cases, the rights of a person, by virtue of a contract to which he is party, to make use of a chattel are enforceable against a third party.

The last two items in this list merit further examination at this point.

1   For an authority, see *McGruther v Pitcher* [1904] 2 Ch 306, CA. The actual decision in this case would now be governed by the Resale Prices Act 1976, the relevant provisions of which are described in the next paragraph.

2   Chap 23.

3   *K H Enterprise (Cargo Owners) v Pioneer Container (Owners), The Pioneer Container* [1994] 2 AC 324, [1994] 2 All ER 250, PC; see, further, in respect of exemption clauses, para 10.42, below.

Restrictions on price

6.33   At common law, a contract of sale which fixed the resale price of goods could not, because of the doctrine of privity, bind a third party who could sell any goods he acquired for whatever price he desired.

The matter is now governed by statute. Under s 26 of the Resale Prices Act 1976, a supplier who sells goods under a contract which provides a maximum resale price can enforce that price against anyone not party to the contract who acquires the goods for resale with notice of that maximum resale price. Any attempt to fix a *minimum* price is void by virtue of s 9 of the Resale Prices Act 1976, unless the goods are exempt from the operation of the Act (in which case s 26 applies and a minimum resale price provision in a contract can be enforced by the supplier against a third party who acquires the goods for resale with notice of the provision).

Restrictions on the use of chattels

6.34   The issue with which we are concerned here can be exemplified as follows. Suppose that there is a contract between X and Y, whereby X grants Y the right to use a specific chattel for a specified period. What is the effect of that contract on Z, a third party, who purchases the chattel from X during the currency of the contract between X and Y?

If Y is in possession of the chattel, eg under a contract of hire, hire purchase or pledge, his possessory right is enforceable against Z, whether or not Z had notice of Y's rights under the contract. In other words, the enforceability of Y's possessory right is governed by the same rules as apply where a person has acquired legal ownership under a contract[1].

The legal position is more complicated where, under the contract, Y does not acquire any proprietary or possessory right but merely a right to have the use of the chattel. Examples of such a contract are a time charterparty and a voyage charterparty. Under either of these, the charterer does not obtain possession of the ship but merely the right to have the use of it, the possession and control over it remaining in the shipowner. Suppose that X, a shipowner, who has chartered a ship to Y under a time charterparty, sells (or mortgages) the ship to Z during the currency of the charterparty. If, but only if, when he 'acquires' the ship, Z actually knows of Y's contractual rights under the charterparty, Z will be liable in damages to Y under the tort of knowingly and unjustifiably interfering with contractual rights if he interferes with Y's contractual rights (eg by preventing him having any use of the ship) and thereby injures Y[2]. Alternatively, if Z 'acquires' the ship with actual knowledge of Y's contractual rights and interferes (or threatens to interfere) with them, Y can obtain an injunction restraining Z from doing so[3]. On the other hand, specific performance of the contract between X and Y cannot be ordered against Z[4].

In the case of a claim for damages in tort for knowing interference with contractual rights, the same principles apply to any other contract (ie other than a charterparty) whereby the owner of a chattel undertakes to use it to perform his contractual obligations. Moreover, an injunction can be granted against a third party in relation to such a contract under the principle just outlined[5].

1 Notice would be relevant if Y only has an equitable interest in the chattel, as in the rare case (see para 12.28) of a specifically enforceable agreement to sell a chattel.
2 *British Motor Trade Association v Salvadori* [1949] Ch 556, [1949] 1 All ER 208.
3 *De Mattos v Gibson* (1858) 4 De G & J 276; on appeal (1859) 4 De G & J 284; *Lord Strathcona SS Co Ltd v Dominion Coal Co* [1926] AC 108, PC; *Swiss Bank Corpn v Lloyds Bank Ltd* [1979] Ch 548, [1979] 2 All ER 853; revsd on different grounds [1982] AC 584, [1981] 2 All ER 449, HL. Cf *Port Line Ltd v Ben Line Steamers Ltd* [1958] 2 QB 146, [1958] 1 All ER 787.
4 *De Mattos v Gibson* (1859) 4 De G & J 284 at 297.
5 *Swiss Bank Corpn v Lloyds Bank Ltd* [1979] Ch 548, [1979] 2 All ER 853; revsd on different grounds [1982] AC 584, [1981] 2 All ER 449, HL; *Law Debenture Trust Corpn plc v Ural Caspian Oil Corpn Ltd* [1995] Ch 152, [1995] 1 All ER 157, CA.

Consideration: Discharge and Variation

6.35 We have seen that consideration is necessary for the formation of contracts which are not made by deed, and that a promise by the creditor to remit a debt is not binding at common law without the provision of consideration by the debtor[1]. We will now discuss whether consideration is necessary when the parties agree (otherwise than by deed) to discharge (ie end) or to vary their contract before it is completely performed.

The discharge of a contract by agreement may be either mutual or unilateral. It will be mutual, subject to the rules discussed later, where both parties still have contractual obligations to perform, ie there is executory consideration on both sides; it will be unilateral, subject to what we say in para 6.37, below, where one party still has contractual obligations to perform but the other party has completed his performance of the contract. Apart from the question of whether consideration is necessary to effect a binding discharge or variation, it is also necessary to consider whether the agreement which purports to discharge or vary the contract must be made in any particular form.

1 For two cases which are probable exceptions, see para 6.16, above.

Mutual discharge

6.36   An agreement to discharge a contract must be supported by consideration. However, if both parties still have contractual obligations to perform, an agreement to discharge the contract relieves both parties from further performance of it. In such a case, both parties have provided consideration, for each party promises not to require further performance of contractual obligations by the other party in return for being absolved himself from further performance.

Unilateral discharge

6.37   A unilateral discharge by agreement is only effective if the party to be absolved has provided separate consideration for the other's promise to absolve him. In other words, where one party has performed all his contractual obligations prior to the agreement, his promise to release the other party from further performance does not bind him unless that other party provides separate consideration. Unilateral discharge by agreement is also known as accord (agreement to discharge) and satisfaction (consideration for that agreement). In relation to whether simply performing (or promising to perform) the existing contractual obligation (in whole or part) in response to a promise of release can constitute the separate consideration, the reader is referred to paras 6.13 and 6.15, above, in particular.

Accord without satisfaction is ineffective to discharge a contract. Satisfaction usually consists of doing something in return for the promise to discharge, but the satisfaction which is offered may be a promise to do something. If so, it is necessary to decide whether the original contract is discharged from the moment of the accord or only when the promise, which is the alleged satisfaction, has been translated into action. It is a question of construction. If the accord can be construed to mean that the promise to do something was intended to be satisfaction, the original contract is discharged from the making of the accord. However, if, on its true construction, the accord means that *performance* of a promise to do something was intended to be satisfaction, the original contract can only be discharged when the promise is performed.

6.38   Promissory estoppel[1] could be available as a defence to a person who has been promised a release from further performance in circumstances where his obligation has not been discharged by accord and satisfaction because he has not provided consideration for the promise.

1   Paras 6.17–6.21, above.

Variation

6.39   If there is an agreement to vary a contract[1], the agreement must be supported by consideration. Consequently, if the variation of a contract benefits both parties (or could benefit one or other of them[2] depending on the outcome of a contingency) it will have contractual effect, but it will have no effect (because of lack of consideration) if it can only be of benefit to one party. Suppose that a contract between A and B requires A to deliver 100 tons of copper to B in Leicester on 1 June at a contract price of £x. If A and B agree that A should, instead, deliver 95 tons on 1 May the variation has contractual effect because it benefits both parties; in contrast, a variation whereby B agreed to accept the delivery of 95 tons in Leicester on 1 June at a contract price of £x would have no contractual effect because it could only be of benefit to A.

1 For the distinction between agreements to discharge and agreements to vary, see para 6.41, below.
2 As where the variation consists of the alteration of the currency of payment, whose exchange rate against the original currency of payment may go up or down by the time payment is due: *W J Alan & Co Ltd v El Nasr Export and Import Co* [1972] 2 QB 189, [1972] 2 All ER 127, CA.

6.40 Where a variation is not enforceable for lack of consideration, promissory estoppel may be available as a defence to the person promised a variation of his obigations.

Form
6.41 If a contract is *discharged* by an agreement supported by consideration from both parties, the agreement is binding whatever form it is in. For example, a contract by deed can be discharged by deed or in writing or orally[1].

Variations, on the other hand, are not so straightforward. If the contract which is alleged to have been varied had to be made in writing or evidenced in writing, eg a contract of guarantee (which must be evidenced in writing in order to be enforceable[2]), the variation must be in writing or evidenced in writing[3], as the case may be. In the case of such a contract, an oral variation is ineffective (unless it gives rise to a promissory estoppel) and the validity of the original contract is not affected[4]. However, what the parties choose to call a variation may be regarded by the courts as a discharge of the original contract and the substitution of a new one. If this is the case, the informal 'variation' is effective to discharge the original contract, though whether the new agreement is enforceable or not depends on whether it satisfies the rules for the creation of an enforceable contract[5].

1 *Berry v Berry* [1929] 2 KB 316.
2 Para 7.6, below.
3 *Goss v Lord Nugent* (1833) 5 B & Ad 58; *McCausland v Duncan Lawrie Ltd* [1996] 4 All ER 995, [1997] 1 WLR 38, CA.
4 *United Dominions Corpn (Jamaica) Ltd v Shoucair* [1969] 1 AC 340, [1968] 2 All ER 904, PC; *McCausland v Duncan Lawrie Ltd* [1996] 4 All ER 995, [1997] 1 WLR 38, CA.
5 So that, if the subject matter of the new contract was a guarantee, the contract would have to be evidenced in writing.

Chapter 7

Form

7.1 With the exception of the contracts mentioned hereafter, English law does not require an agreement to be in writing in order to be a valid and enforceable contract, but there are obvious advantages in reducing it into writing.

Contracts which must be Made by Deed

Leases for three years or more
7.2 Unless made by deed, these are void at law and cannot therefore confer a legal interest on the purported tenant[1]. However, such a lease not made by deed can take effect as a contract to grant a lease[2], which can be specifically enforced and will create the same rights as a lease between the parties for many purposes.

1 Law of Property Act 1925, ss 52 and 54. A lease for less than three years which does not take effect in possession or is not for the best rent reasonably obtainable must also be made by deed.
2 *Walsh v Lonsdale* (1882) 21 Ch D 9, CA.

Contracts in which there is no consideration
7.3 If there is no consideration for the promise made by one party to the other there cannot be a valid and enforceable contract unless the promise is made by deed[1]. A common example of a contract made by deed is a covenant for the gratuitous payment of a sum to a charity over a period of more than three years, whereby the charity is enabled to claim the income tax paid by the donor in addition to the covenanted sum.

1 *Rann v Hughes* (1778) 7 Term Rep 350n, HL.

7.4 A contract is not made by deed unless the instrument in which it is written:

a. makes it clear on its face that it is intended to be a deed by the person making it or, as the case may be, by the parties to it (either because it describes itself as such or because it expresses itself to be executed or signed as such); and
b. it is validly executed as a deed by that person or, as the case may be, by one or more of those parties[1].

An instrument is validly executed as a deed by an individual if it is signed by him in the presence of an attesting witness and delivered by him or by a person authorised to effect delivery on his behalf[2]. A deed is regarded as delivered as soon as there are acts which show that the person making it intends unconditionally to be bound by it: physical delivery of it to the other party is no longer required and a deed may be delivered even though it remains in the custody of its maker[3].

There are special statutory provisions governing the execution of a deed by a company[4].

A contract made by deed is known as a contract by specialty: all other contracts, whether written or not, are known as simple contracts.

1   Law of Property (Miscellaneous Provisions) Act 1989, s 1(2).
2   Ibid, s 1(3). An individual can also direct another to sign a deed on his behalf provided the signing is in his presence and there are two attesting witnesses: ibid.
3   *Vincent v Premo Enterprises (Voucher Sales) Ltd* [1969] 2 QB 609, [1969] 2 All ER 941, CA.
4   Companies Act 1985, s 36A (substituted by the Companies Act 1989, s 130).

Contracts which must be in Writing

7.5   Some contracts such as those below are invalid or unenforceable unless they are in writing:

a. *Bills of exchange and promissory notes*[1].
b. *Regulated agreements under the Consumer Credit Act 1974* Regulated consumer credit agreements and regulated consumer hire agreements which are not executed in writing in the manner required by the Act of 1974 are enforceable against the debtor or hirer only on an order of the court[2].
c. *Contracts for the sale or other disposition*[3] *of land or any interest in land* Subject to the exceptions set out below, such a contract can only be made in writing and only by incorporating all the terms expressly agreed by the parties in one document or, where contracts are exchanged, in each document; otherwise it is invalid[4]. The exceptions are:
    i.   contracts made in the course of a public auction;
    ii. contracts to grant a lease not exceeding three years taking effect in possession at the best rent reasonably obtainable; and
    iii. contracts regulated under the Financial Services Act 1986.

Subject to these exceptions, the above rule applies to any contract for any disposition (by sale, mortgage, lease or otherwise) of any 'interest in land'. 'Interest in land' includes sporting rights and *fructus naturales* (things which are the natural, rather than cultivated, produce of the soil, such as grass and even planted trees and their fruit) unless they are to be severed by the vendor or the contract binds the purchaser to sever them at once[5].

The above rule is of relevance only in relation to executory contracts for the sale or other disposition of an interest in land; an executory contract is one which has not yet been carried out. The rule does not affect the validity or enforceability of a contract which has already been carried out[6]. Consequently, if parties choose to make an oral land contract or a contract that in some respect does not satisfy the rule, it becomes irrelevant that the contract does not accord with the rule once it has been carried out.

1   Bills of Exchange Act 1882, ss 3, 17, 73 and 83.
2   Consumer Credit Act 1974, ss 60, 61 and 65; Consumer Credit (Agreements) Regulations 1983.
3   Including a contract granting an option to purchase land: *Spiro v Glencrown Properties Ltd* [1991] Ch 537, [1991] 1 All ER 600. On the other hand, a contract whereby the vendor of land promises a prospective purchaser not to negotiate with other prospective purchasers for a short stipulated period is not a contract for the sale or disposition of an interest in land and therefore does not have to be in writing: *Pitt v PHH Asset Management Ltd* [1993] 4 All ER 961, [1994] 1 WLR 327, CA.
4   Law of Property (Miscellaneous Provisions) Act 1989, s 2(1). The terms may be incorporated in a document either by being set out in it or by reference to some other document: ibid, s 2(2). The document or, where contracts are exchanged, one of them (but not necessarily the same one) must be signed by or on behalf of each party: ibid, s 2(3). In this context, 'signed' requires that the person concerned should write his name in his own hand; the printing or typing of his name will not do: *Firstpost Homes Ltd v Johnson* [1995] 4 All ER 355, [1995] 1 WLR 1567, CA. Prior to the 1989 Act, an agreement not complying with the then rules as to the form of contracts for the disposition of land could in certain circumstances be enforceable if the party seeking to enforce it had partly performed his obligations under it. This approach appears to have been abolished by the 1989 Act, but see *Singh v Beggs* (1995) 71 P & CR 120, CA, where a surprising, contrary view was expressed obiter.
5   *Smith v Surman* (1829) 9 B & C 561; *Marshall v Green* (1875) 1 CPD 35.
6   *Tootal Clothing Ltd v Guinea Properties Management Ltd* (1992) 64 P & CR 452, CA.

Contracts which must be in Writing or Evidenced in Writing

7.6   Contracts of guarantee do not have to be written but merely be evidenced in writing before they can be enforced in legal proceedings. At one time a number of other types of contract was unenforceable unless the contract was evidenced in writing, but the law in this respect has been changed in modern times.

For the sake of completeness, it should be added that a contract of marine insurance is 'inadmissible in evidence' unless it is embodied in a marine policy signed by the insurer, specifying the name of the assured (or his agent) and containing certain particulars[1]. It is not necessary for us to concern ourselves further with this.

1   Marine Insurance Act 1906, ss 22–24.

7.7   The requirement that a contract of guarantee be evidenced in writing is made by s 4 of the Statute of Frauds 1677, which provides that no action can be brought on a promise to answer for the debt, default or miscarriage of another (ie a guarantee) unless the agreement, or some memorandum or note thereof, is in writing and signed by the party to be charged or some other person lawfully authorised by him.

Nature of a contract of guarantee

7.8   A contract of guarantee must be sharply distinguished from one of indemnity because s 4 only applies to guarantees, whether of contractual or tortious liability[1], so that an oral contract of indemnity is enforceable. The distinction between a guarantee and an indemnity is a fine one but the two terms can be expressed as follows:

A will *guarantee* B's debt to C if he makes himself liable to pay it if B fails to pay. Here, A has assumed a liability subsidiary to that of B, which continues as the primary liability.

A will *indemnify* C if he assumes primary liability to pay B's debt in any event. Here, A has assumed a sole liability to C, B's liability being discharged or never arising.

As these two statements imply, for a promise to constitute a guarantee, and therefore to be required to be evidenced in writing to be enforceable, the following criteria must be satisfied:

a.   Three parties must be involved: a creditor, a principal debtor (whose liability may be actual or prospective) and the promisor (the 'guarantor' or 'surety'), who undertakes to discharge the principal debtor's liability if the latter fails to do so himself. If there never has been a person who can be described as the principal debtor a contract cannot be one of guarantee, as is shown by *Lakeman v Mountstephen*[2]. The plaintiff, a builder, was asked by the defendant, the chairman of the Brixham Local Board of Health, whether he would connect certain drains to a sewer which he had laid. The plaintiff said he would do so if the defendant or the Board would become responsible for payment. The defendant replied: 'Go on, Mountstephen, and do the work, I will see you paid.' When sued on his promise, the defendant pleaded that it was a promise to guarantee the debt of another (the Board) and, not being evidenced in writing, was unenforceable. The House of Lords rejected this defence because the defendant's promise was an undertaking of sole liability, the Board never having been liable to the plaintiff, so that the contract between the plaintiff and defendant was not one of guarantee and did not have to be evidenced in writing.

Unlike a guarantee, only two parties need be concerned in a contract of indemnity. Thus, if A agrees to keep B immune from loss through some cause extraneous to A, such as fire or flood, or attributable to him, the contract will be one of indemnity and need not be evidenced in writing to be enforceable.

b.   To be a guarantee, the principal debtor must continue to have the primary liability towards the creditor, *the promisor being liable only in the event of his default*. Thus, if the effect of the promisor's undertaking is to determine the principal debtor's debt and substitute the indebtedness of the promisor the contract is one of indemnity, not of guarantee. An example is provided by *Goodman v Chase*[3]. The plaintiffs had been awarded damages in legal proceedings against X. X was subsequently arrested for failure to satisfy the judgment but the plaintiffs consented to his release when the defendant, X's father-in-law, promised to pay the debt in return. It was held that, since the defendant's promise had discharged X's debt and substituted his own indebtedness, his promise was one of indemnity.

The fact that a guarantor's liability is secondary to that of the principal debtor's continuing liability, whereas a promise to indemnify creates a primary liability in the promisor, is well illustrated by the following dictum in *Birkmyr v Darnell*[4]:

> 'If two come to a shop, and one buys, and the other, to gain him credit, promises the seller, "*If he does not pay you, I will*", this is a collateral undertaking, and unenforceable without writing, by the Statute of Frauds: but if he says, "*Let him have the goods, I will be your paymaster*", or "*I will see you paid*", this is an undertaking as for himself, and he shall be intended to be the very buyer, and the other to act but as his servant.'

The requirement for a guarantee, that the promisor must undertake to be liable to pay only if the principal debtor fails to do so, is crucial. Thus, if the promisor has assumed liability to pay in any event, the transaction cannot be one of guarantee, even though the principal debtor still remains obliged to pay. This is shown by *Guild & Co v Conrad*[5], which also demonstrates that it is the effect, not the wording, of the promise which is important. The plaintiff accepted a batch of bills of exchange after he had been orally promised by the defendant that 'If you accept these bills I will guarantee them'. The Court of Appeal held that, despite the defendant's use of the word 'guarantee', his promise was one of indemnity because, notwithstanding that the drawer of the bills' liability under them continued, the defendant had promised to put the plaintiff into funds in any event, regardless of whether the merchants defaulted in payment. Since the promise was one of indemnity, it was irrelevant that it was oral.

1   *Kirkham v Marter* (1819) 2 B & Ald 613.
2   (1874) LR 7 HL 17, HL.
3   (1818) 1 B & Ald 297.
4   (1704) 1 Salk 27 at 28.
5   [1894] 2 QB 885, CA.

7.9   Even where the above criteria are satisfied, and the promisor's undertaking consequently a guarantee, it is nevertheless not affected by s 4 of the Statute of Frauds (1677) unless the promisor has made his promise direct to the creditor (and not to the debtor or some other person)[1] and unless the promisor's assumption of a secondary liability is the sole object of the transaction between him and the creditor. Hence, s 4 does not apply:

a.   Where the promise made is incidental to a larger transaction between the promisor and the creditor. In *Sutton & Co v Grey*[2], the defendant orally agreed to introduce clients to the plaintiffs, a firm of stockbrokers. He was to receive half the commission earned by the plaintiffs on transactions for such clients and to pay the plaintiffs half of any loss caused by the default of such clients. Despite being oral, this last promise, although in essence a guarantee, was held enforceable because it formed part of a larger transaction.

b.   Where the main purpose of the promisor in giving his promise is to acquire or retain property, and the guarantee is given by him to relieve the property from a charge or encumbrance existing in favour of another, it is not caught by s 4. Thus, if A buys goods from B which are subject to a lien[3] in favour of C, and (in order to discharge the lien) A promises C that he will pay B's debt if B does not do so, A's promise (guarantee) need not be evidenced in writing[4].

Neither of these exceptions appears in s 4 of the Statute of Frauds (1677); instead, both are judicial glosses on it. They, and the other intricate rules which have been developed concerning what is and what is not a promise governed by the section, have resulted from the courts' reluctance to see agreements rendered unenforceable for lack of written evidence. The resulting complexity and limited extent of the section prompt us to ask whether the section is worth retention at all or, if protection of guarantors and the like is necessary, whether it should not be extended without exception to all guarantees and indemnities.

1   *Eastwood v Kenyon* (1840) 11 Ad & El 438; *Reader v Kingham* (1862) 13 CBNS 344.
2   [1894] 1 QB 285, CA.
3   A lien is a right by which a person is entitled to obtain satisfaction for a debt by retaining property belonging to the person indebted to him; see further paras 2.32–2.35, above.
4   *Fitzgerald v Dressler* (1859) 7 CBNS 374.

Formal requirements of section 4 of the Statute of Frauds (1677)

7.10   Section 4 requires that the agreement, or some memorandum or note thereof, shall be in writing and signed by the party to be charged or by some person lawfully authorised by him for that purpose. If the contract is in writing no difficulty arises. However, whether there is written evidence of an unwritten contract sufficient to constitute a signed memorandum or note (which can come into existence at any time before action is brought to enforce the contract) is a somewhat complex question because, although the section does not specify the form and contents of a signed memorandum or note, the following rules have been laid down by the judges.

Contents of the 'memorandum or note'
7.11   a. The memorandum or note must name the parties to the contract or so describe them that they can be identified with certainty[1].

b.   The memorandum or note must describe the whole subject matter[2], but may sufficiently describe it although it has to be supplemented by extrinsic evidence[3].

c.   The memorandum or note must accurately set out the material terms of the oral contract, other than any implied terms[4].

d.   The memorandum or note need not state the consideration[5].

1   *William v Jordan* (1877) 6 Ch D 517; *Rossiter v Miller* (1878) 3 App Cas 1124, HL.
2   *Burgess v Cox* [1951] Ch 383, [1950] 2 All ER 1212.
3   *Plant v Bourne* [1897] 2 Ch 281, CA.
4   *Cook v Taylor* [1942] Ch 349, [1942] 2 All ER 85.
5   Mercantile Law Amendment Act 1856, s 3.

Signature

7.12   The document must be signed by the party to be charged or by his agent lawfully authorised to sign for him. The extent of an agent's authority is determined by agreement or trade usage.

Section 4 does not require signature by both parties or their agents, merely signature by the party to be charged, ie the party against whom it is sought to enforce the contract, or his agent[1]. Thus, where there is a contract of guarantee between A and B, and B alone has signed a memorandum or note of it, A can enforce the contract against B, but B cannot enforce it against A.

The word 'signed' has been liberally interpreted in the present context[2]. Provided the name, or even the initials, of the party to be charged appears in some part of the memorandum or note in some form, whether in handwriting, stamp, print or otherwise, there will be a sufficient signature, if that party has shown in some way that he recognises the whole document as a record of the contract[3]. Thus, a memorandum in the handwriting of Crockford, the person to be charged, which began 'I, James Crockford, agree' without any other signature, was held in *Knight v Crockford*[4] to have been sufficiently signed on the ground that, by writing that, Crockford had shown that he recognised the existence of the contract mentioned in the document. However, unless there is such a recognition the mere fact that a party's name appears in the document does not make it signed by him[5].

1   *Laythoarp v Bryant* (1836) 2 Bing NC 735.
2   Cf para 7.5, fn 4.
3   *Halley v O'Brien* [1920] 1 IR 330 at 339; *Leeman v Stocks* [1951] Ch 941, [1951] 1 All ER 1043.
4   (1794) 1 Esp 190.
5   *Hubert v Treherne* (1842) 3 Man & G 743.

Purpose for which document prepared irrelevant

7.13   It is irrelevant that the document was never intended to serve as a note or memorandum but was prepared for some entirely different purpose. In *Cohen v Roche*[1], for instance, a note in an auctioneer's book was held to be an effective memorandum, and so was a letter to a third party in *Moore v Hart*[2]. Moreover, a written offer signed by the defendant and orally accepted by the plaintiff is a sufficient memorandum, even though the contract does not come into existence until after the offer has been accepted[3].

1   [1927] 1 KB 169.
2   (1683) 1 Vern 110 at 201.
3   *Reuss v Picksley* (1866) LR 1 Exch 342.

Effect of non-compliance

7.14   The effect of non-compliance with the requirements of s 4 of the Statute of Frauds (1677) is not to make a contract of guarantee void or voidable. It merely makes it unenforceable by action against a party who has not signed a sufficient memorandum or note, unless, and until, he has signed such a memorandum or note, because the agreement is incapable of proof[1]. Thus, a plaintiff is caught by the statutory provisions whenever he has to rely on an oral or insufficiently evidenced contract of guarantee covered by the Statute of Frauds, even though he is not directly claiming damages for its breach[2].

Admittedly, in depriving a party of his right to enforce a contract of guarantee by an action, the section deprives him of what is usually his most important right. Nevertheless, since the contract is valid and subsisting, a person who has received money or property in accordance with the terms of the contract obtains a good title to it and the contract can be enforced in any way other than by action. Thus, if a guarantor pays the creditor under an oral contract of guarantee, the creditor can keep the money and, if sued for its recovery, can plead the oral contract as a defence[3].

1 *Maddison v Alderson* (1883) 8 App Cas 467 at 488.
2 *Delaney v T P Smith Ltd* [1946] KB 393, [1946] 2 All ER 23, CA.
3 *Thomas v Brown* (1876) 1 QBD 714; *Monnickendam v Leanse* (1923) 39 TLR 445.

Chapter 8

Contractual Terms

8.1 The terms of a contract may be express or implied.

Express Terms

8.2 Clearly, the ascertainment of its express terms is facilitated when the contract has been reduced into writing, particularly because under the 'parol evidence'[1] rule oral or other evidence extrinsic to the document is not admissible generally to add to, vary, or contradict, the terms of the written agreement[2]. However, this rule is not as harsh as might be supposed because in a number of cases extrinsic evidence is admissible, either as an exception to the parol evidence rule or because the circumstances fall outside its bounds. The following can be mentioned as examples.

1 Parol evidence of a written document means extrinsic evidence, whether oral or otherwise: *Jowitt's Dictionary of English Law.*
2 *Jacobs v Batavia and General Plantations Trust Ltd* [1924] 1 Ch 287 at 295.

Implied terms
8.3 The fact that a contract has been reduced into writing does not prevent extrinsic evidence being given to support or rebut the implication of a term into it[1] under rules which are discussed shortly.

1 *Burges v Wickham* (1863) 3 B & S 669; *Gillespie Bros & Co v Cheney, Eggar & Co* [1896] 2 QB 59.

Conditions precedent
8.4 Extrinsic evidence is admissible to show that, although a written contract appears absolute on its face, it was not intended that a binding contract should be created (or that, although there was an immediate binding contract, a party's obligation to perform would not arise) until the occurrence of a particular event, such as a surveyor's report or the availability of finance[1].

1 *Pym v Campbell* (1856) 6 E & B 370; para 5.29, above.

Invalidating factors
8.5   Extrinsic evidence of a factor, such as mistake or misrepresentation, which invalidates the written contract is, of course, admissible.

Written contract not the whole contract
8.6   While a document which looks like a contract is presumed to include all the terms of the contract, this presumption may be rebutted by evidence that the parties did not intend all the terms of their contract to be contained in the document[1]. If the presumption is rebutted, extrinsic evidence is admissible to prove the other terms of the contract. An example is provided by the case of *J Evans & Son (Portsmouth) Ltd v Andrea Merzario Ltd*, which is discussed in para 8.12, below.

1   *Gillespie Bros & Co v Cheney, Eggar & Co* [1896] 2 QB 59 at 62.

Collateral contracts
8.7   The parol evidence rule will also be circumvented if the court finds that the parties have made two contracts, the main written one and an oral one collateral to it. An example is provided by *Birch v Paramount Estates (Liverpool) Ltd*[1], where the defendants, who were developing a housing estate, offered a house they were then building to the plaintiff, stating orally that it would be as good as the show house. Subsequently, the plaintiff agreed to buy the house but the written contract of sale made no reference to this statement. The completed house was not as good as the show house. The Court of Appeal held that there was an oral contract, to the effect that the house would be as good as the show house, collateral to the contract of sale and upheld the award of damages for its breach.

In essence, a collateral contract exists where A promises B something certain[2] in return for B making the main contract. A's promise must have been intended by the parties to be legally binding and to take effect as a collateral contract, and not merely as a term of the main contract, and it must be supported by separate consideration, although this may simply be B's making of the main contract[3]. Provided these requirements are satisfied, a collateral contract will be valid and enforceable by B, even though it conflicts with a term in the main contract. This is shown by *City and Westminster Properties (1934) Ltd v Mudd*[4]. In 1941, the defendant became the tenant of a lock-up shop for three years. He was allowed by the landlords, the plaintiffs, to sleep in the shop. In 1944, a second lease for three years was granted to the defendant. In 1947, during negotiations for a new lease, the plaintiffs inserted in the draft lease a clause restricting the use of the premises to trade purposes only. The defendant objected and was told by the plaintiffs' agent that, if he accepted the new lease as it stood, the plaintiffs would not object to him residing on the premises. In consequence, the defendant signed the lease. Later, the plaintiffs sought to forfeit the lease for breach of the covenant only to use the premises for trade purposes. It was held that the defendant could plead the collateral contract as a defence to a charge of breach of the main contract, the lease.

1   (1956) 168 Estates Gazette 396, CA.
2   *Wake v Renault (UK) Ltd* (1996) Times, 1 August.

3   *Heilbut, Symons & Co v Buckleton* [1913] AC 30, HL.
4   [1959] Ch 129, [1958] 2 All ER 733.

Determination of whether a written term is a term of the contract

8.8   The determination of whether what purports to be a term of the contract is indeed a term of the contract can sometimes give rise to nice questions. It depends very much on whether or not the term is contained in a signed contractual document. If it is, the general rule is that it is a contractual term binding on a party who signed the document, even though he was unaware of it because he had not read the document[1]. This is so even though that party is, to the other's knowledge, illiterate or unfamiliar with the English language[2]. An exception is where the party seeking to rely on a term has misrepresented to the other its contents or effect. In such a case, the term is rendered ineffective to the extent that it differs from the misrepresentation[3].

Where the term is not contained in a contractual document signed by the party against whom it is being relied, eg where it is printed on a ticket or an order form or a notice, the term will only be a contractual term if adequate notice of it is given. The law in this respect has largely been developed in relation to a particular type of term, an exemption clause, and we deal with it in relation to such a clause in paras 10.28–10.31, below.

1   *L'Estrange v F Graucob Ltd* [1934] 2 KB 394, DC.
2   *Barclays Bank plc v Schwartz* (1995) Times, 2 August, CA.
3   *Curtis v Chemical Cleaning and Dyeing Co Ltd* [1951] 1 KB 805, [1951] 1 All ER 631, CA.

Contractual terms and mere representations

8.9   Where contractual terms are oral they must be proved by the evidence of the parties and other witnesses in the event of a dispute.

Problems can sometimes arise concerning whether a written or oral statement, which is made in contractual negotiations and not explicitly referred to at the time the contract is made, is nevertheless a term of the contract instead of being a mere representation. The present issue can be exemplified as follows. At the time the contract was made A may simply have said to B: 'I offer you £3,000 for the car' to which B replied 'I accept'. These two sentences will probably be the culmination of previous, and perhaps lengthy, negotiations between the parties during which B will have given A a number of assurances as to the condition of the car, its mileage and so on. Whether these pre-contractual statements are contractual terms or undertakings, or simply mere representations, is of importance for the following reason. Breach of a contractual term results in liability in damages, and certain other remedies for breach of contract may also be available to the 'injured party'. On the other hand, if a mere representation turns out to be false there can be no liability for breach of contract, although it *may* be possible for the misrepresentee to have the contract set aside (rescinded) for misrepresentation; and in certain circumstances he can recover damages for misrepresentation. Generally speaking, the remedies for misrepresentation are inferior to those for breach of contract. We discuss the subjects of breach of contract, remedies for breach and misrepresentation in chapters 10, 12 and 14. For the present we are concerned with the question of how it is ascertained whether a pre-contractual statement has become a contractual term.

8.10 A representation will be a contractual term if the parties intended that the representor was making a binding promise as to it[1]. Whether the parties did so intend can only be deduced from all the evidence. Of course, it is always possible for the parties actually to state that a particular representation is or is not a term of their contract. If they do not, then, if an intelligent bystander would infer from the words and behaviour of the parties that a binding promise was intended, that will suffice[2]. In approaching the question of the parties' intentions the courts take into account factors such as the following.

1   *Oscar Chess Ltd v Williams* [1957] 1 All ER 325 at 327–328, [1957] 1 WLR 370.
2   Ibid. See also *Howard Marine and Dredging Co Ltd v A Ogden & Sons (Excavations) Ltd* [1978] QB 574 at 590–591, [1978] 2 All ER 1134.

Execution of a written contract
8.11 If the representation was followed by a written contract in which it does not appear, it will probably (but not necessarily) be regarded as a mere representation[1] since, because of the parol evidence rule, it can only take effect as a contractual term if the court finds that the parties intended that the contract should not be contained wholly in the written document or that the representation should form part of a collateral contract. An example of a case where a pre-contractual representation was found to be a contractual term despite the subsequent execution of a written contract is *J Evans & Son (Portsmouth) Ltd v Andrea Merzario Ltd*, which is discussed in the next paragraph.

1   *Heilbut, Symons & Co v Buckleton* [1913] AC 30 at 50; *Oscar Chess Ltd v Williams* [1957] 1 All ER 325 at 329.

The importance of the representation
8.12 The more important the subject matter of the representation the more likely it is that the parties intended a binding promise concerning it. In particular, if the representation was so important that without it the representee would not have made the contract, the court is very likely to hold that it is a contractual term. In *J Evans & Son (Portsmouth) Ltd v Andrea Merzario Ltd*[1], the plaintiffs bought some machines from an Italian company. They had previously employed the defendants to arrange transport, and the machinery had always been packed in crates or trailers and carried below deck. On this occasion the defendants' representative told the plaintiffs' that it was proposed that the machinery should be packed in containers. The plaintiffs' representative replied that if containers were used they must be stowed below, and not on, deck in case the machinery rusted. He was assured by the defendants' representative that this would be done but this oral assurance was not included in the written agreement subsequently made between the plaintiffs and the defendants. In fact, the containers were carried on deck and two fell into the sea. In the Court of Appeal, Roskill and Geoffrey Lane LJJ held that the oral

assurance had become a term of the contract between the parties, which was not wholly written, and that the plaintiffs could recover damages for its breach. Roskill LJ stated that in the light of the totality of the evidence it was clear that the plaintiffs had only agreed to contract with the defendants on the basis that the containers were stowed below deck, and therefore the defendants' assurance concerning this had become a contractual term. Similarly, in *Bannerman v White*[2], a representation that sulphur had not been used in the treatment of hops was found to have become a term of the subsequent contract. It related to a matter of great importance and the buyer would not have made the contract without it.

1   [1976] 2 All ER 930, [1976] 1 WLR 1078, CA.
2   (1861) 10 CBNS 844.

Invitation to verify
8.13   If a seller invites the buyer to check his representation it is very unlikely to be regarded as a contractual term. In *Ecay v Godfrey*[1], for instance, the seller of a boat said that it was sound but advised a survey. It was held that this advice negatived any intention that the representation should be a contractual term. Conversely, if the seller assures the buyer that it is not necessary to verify the representation since he can take the seller's word for it, the representation is likely to be found to be intended to be a term of the resulting contract if the buyer contracts in reliance on it. In *Schawel v Reade*[2], the plaintiff, who required a stallion for stud purposes, went to the defendant's stables to inspect a horse. While he was inspecting it, the defendant said: 'You need not look for anything: the horse is perfectly sound. If there was anything the matter with the horse I would tell you.' The plaintiff thereupon ended his inspection and a price was agreed three weeks later, the plaintiff relying on the defendant's statement. The House of Lords held that the jury's finding that the defendant's statement was a contractual term was correct.

1   (1947) 80 Ll L Rep 286.
2   (1913) 2 IR 64, HL. Cf *Hopkins v Tanqueray* (1854) 15 CB 130.

Statements of fact, of opinion or as to the future
8.14   A statement of fact is more likely to be construed as intended to have contractual effect than a statement of opinion or as to future facts (eg a forecast)[1]. A statement about something which is, or should be, within the promisor's control is very likely to be construed as a contractual term[2].

1   *Esso Petroleum Co Ltd v Mardon* [1976] QB 801 at 825, [1976] 2 All ER 5 at 20.
2   *Oscar Chess Ltd v Williams* [1957] 1 All ER 325 at 329, [1957] 1 WLR 370 at 375.

Ability of the parties to ascertain the accuracy of the statement
8.15   If the representor had a special skill or knowledge, or was otherwise in a better position than the representee to ascertain the truth of the representation, this strongly suggests that the representation was intended to be a contractual term, and vice versa. An example is provided by *Dick Bentley (Productions) Ltd v Harold Smith (Motors) Ltd*[1]. The plaintiff purchased a Bentley car from the defendants in reliance on their statement that the car had been fitted with a

new engine and gear box and had done only 20,000 miles since then. The representation as to mileage, although honestly made, was untrue. The Court of Appeal held that the representation had become one of the terms of the contract because it had been made by a dealer who was in a position to know or find out the car's history, and it could therefore be inferred that the representation was intended to have contractual effect. The court distinguished its previous decision in *Oscar Chess Ltd v Williams*[2]. There, Williams, a private person, represented in negotiations for the part-exchange of his Morris car that it was a 1948 model. This representation was based on the logbook which had been falsified by a person unknown. The representation was held not to have become a contractual term on the ground that Williams had no special knowledge as to the car's age, while the other party, who were car dealers, were in at least as good a position to ascertain whether the representation was true.

1   [1965] 2 All ER 65, [1965] 1 WLR 623, CA. Cf *Gilchester Properties Ltd v Gomm* [1948] 1 All ER 493.
2   [1957] 1 All ER 325, [1957] 1 WLR 370, CA.

8.16   It must be emphasised that the factors mentioned above are only guides, not decisive tests or the only factors, to determining the parties' intentions[1]. Sometimes, they can point in different directions.

On many occasions, judges, having found that the parties intended a pre-contractual representation to have contractual effect, have found that it has taken effect under a collateral contract rather than as a term of the main contract.

1   *Heilbut, Symons & Co v Buckleton* [1913] AC 30, HL.

Implied Terms

8.17   In addition to its express terms, the contract may contain certain terms implied by custom or by statute or by the courts.

Terms implied by custom or usage

8.18   Terms may be implied by the custom of a particular locality, as in *Hutton v Warren*[1], or by the usage of a particular trade, as in *Harley & Co v Nagata*[2]. Although the terms are often used interchangeably, 'usage' differs from 'custom' in that it need not be ancient, but like custom it must be reasonable and certain in the sense that it is clearly established[3]. In *Hutton v Warren*, where a local custom was proved that a tenant was obliged to farm according to a certain course of husbandry for the whole of his tenancy and, on quitting, was entitled to a fair allowance for seeds and labour on the arable land, it was held that a term to this effect was implied in the lease. In *Harley & Co v Nagata*, it was held that, in the case of a time charterparty, a usage that the commission of a broker who negotiated the charterparty should be paid out of the hire which was earned, and should not be payable unless hire was in fact earned, was an implied term of the charterparty. Similarly, in *Cunliffe-Owen v Teather and*

Greenwood[4], a usage of the Stock Exchange was held to be an implied term of an option to sell shares at a future date.

A term cannot be implied by custom or usage if the express wording of the contract shows that the parties had a contrary intention. This is shown by *Les Affréteurs Réunis SA v LeopoldWalford (London) Ltd*[5]. Walford acted as a broker in effecting the time charter of a ship. The charterparty provided that commission should be payable to Walford 'on signing this charter (ship lost or not lost)'. Before the charterparty could be operated, and therefore before any hire could be earned, the French government requisitioned the ship. The House of Lords held that Walford could recover his commission because the commercial usage referred to above (commission payable only in respect of hire earned) could have no application since it was inconsistent with the express terms of the charterparty.

1   (1836) 1 M & W 466. For the requirements of a valid local custom, see para 4.61, above.
2   (1917) 23 Com Cas 121.
3   *Cunliffe-Owen v Teather and Greenwood* [1967] 3 All ER 561 at 572.
4   [1967] 3 All ER 561, [1967] 1 WLR 1421.
5   [1919] AC 801, HL.

Terms implied by statute

Sale of Goods Act 1979
8.19   The best known examples of statutorily implied terms are those implied into contracts for the sale of goods by ss 12 to 15 of the Sale of Goods Act 1979.

Section 55 of the 1979 Act provides that any of these terms may be excluded or varied:

a.   by the course of dealings between the parties (which means that the past dealings between the parties may raise the implication of a term prevailing over a term implied by the Act, in the absence of an express provision); or
b.   by such usage as binds both parties (which means that, if both parties intended to contract according to the usage of a particular trade or market, that usage prevails over the terms implied by the Act); or
c.   by express agreement between the parties.

However, as we explain in chapter 10[1], the exclusion or restriction of liability for breach of these implied terms by a term of the contract is limited by the Unfair Contract Terms Act 1977, especially in the case of a consumer sale.

The terms implied by ss 12 to 15 of the 1979 Act are as follows.

1   Paras 10.50 and 10.51, below.

8.20   *Implied undertakings as to title*   Section 12(1) and (2) provides that the following undertakings as to title are implied in every contract of sale, other than one in which there appears from the contract or is to be inferred from its circumstances an intention that the seller should transfer only such title as he or a third person may have in the goods:

a.   an implied condition[1] on the part of the seller that in the case of a sale he has a right to sell the goods, and in the case of an agreement to sell he will have a right to sell the goods at the time when the property is to pass (s 12(1)); and

b.   an implied warranty[1] that the goods are free, and will remain free until the time when the property is to pass, from any charge or encumbrance not disclosed or known to the buyer before the contract is made and that the buyer will enjoy quiet possession of the goods except so far as it may be disturbed by the owner or other person entitled to the benefit of any charge or encumbrance so disclosed or known (s 12(2)).

1   This classification is made by the Sale of Goods Act 1979, s12(5A). As to conditions and warranties, see paras 10.16 and 10.17.

8.21   The implied warranty under s 12(2) of quiet possession and freedom from encumbrance adds little to the implied condition but will be useful in the following situations:

a.   Where the seller has the right to sell, but only subject to the rights of a third party which have not been disclosed to the buyer before the contract is made. Thus, if D, an execution debtor, sells goods which have been seized by the sheriff under a writ of execution, without disclosing this, D will be in breach of the implied warranty because, although he had the right to sell the goods and is therefore not in breach of the implied condition, the title passed is not free from the rights of the sheriff[1].

b.   Where the seller had the right to sell but a third party has subsequently acquired the benefit of any charge or encumbrance not disclosed or known to the buyer before the contract was made. Thus, if S sells goods to B and after the sale T acquires a patent involving interference with B's use, S will be in breach of the implied warranty but not in breach of the implied condition because he had the right to sell when the contract was made[2].

1   *Lloyds and Scottish Finance Ltd v Modern Cars and Caravans (Kingston) Ltd* [1966] 1 QB 764, [1964] 2 All ER 732.
2   *Microbeads AC v Vinhurst Road Markings Ltd* [1975] 1 All ER 529, [1975] 1 WLR 218, CA.

8.22   *Sale by description*   Section 13 of the 1979 Act provides:

'(1) Where there is a contract for the sale of goods by description, there is an implied term [a condition][1] that the goods shall correspond with the description.

(2) If the sale is by sample[2] as well as by description it is not sufficient that the bulk of the goods corresponds with the sample if the goods do not also correspond with the description.'

The term 'description' refers to any words used in relation to the goods which identify them. It covers not only words which go to the nature of the goods, such as their size or age, but also other attributes expressed or implied in the contract, such as the origin or mode of packing of the goods, which are a substantial ingredient in identifying the goods sold[3].

151

The fact that a description is applied to goods either in the course of negotiations or in the contract itself does not necessarily make the contract one for sale by description for the purposes of s 13(1).

The reason given by the majority of the Court of Appeal in *Harlingdon & Leinster Enterprises Ltd v Christopher Hull Fine Art Ltd*[4] is that, for a sale to be 'by' description, the description has to be so influential in the sale as to have become a term of the contract. For it so to have become, the majority held, the parties, viewed objectively, must have intended that it should be a term of the contract. In determining whether or not they had that intention, the presence or absence of reliance on the description on the part of the buyer is a very relevant factor. In theory it is possible for a description of goods to be a term of the contract if it is not relied on, but in practice it is very difficult in such a case to impute the necessary common intention that the description should be a term of the contract. If there can only be a sale 'by' description if the description has become a term, an express term, of the contract, what is the point of s 13? The answer is that it makes it clear that the term relating to description is a condition, and not some lesser term, by implying a term to that effect. Classification of the term as a condition is important in terms of the legal consequences which flow from its breach, as we explain in the next chapter.

1   By the Sale of Goods Act 1979, s 13(1A), the term is classified as a condition. As to conditions, see paras 10.17–10.20.
2   Para 8.35, below.
3   Eg *Re Moore & Co and Landauer & Co's Arbitration* [1921] 2 KB 519, CA.
4   [1991] 1 QB 564, [1990] 1 All ER 737, CA.

8.23   It is particularly likely to be held that there has been a contract for sale by description where the buyer has not seen the goods described before making the contract, since reliance on the description will be particularly easy to prove. In *Varley v Whipp*[1], for instance, S offered to sell to B a second-hand reaping machine, which he described as new the previous year and to have been used only to cut 50–60 acres. B agreed to buy on the faith of this description without having seen the machine. When the machine was delivered, B discovered that it was of extreme antiquity. It was held that there had been a sale by description, that the machine did not correspond with the description, and that B was therefore entitled to reject it for breach of the condition implied by s 13(1).

If the buyer has seen the goods before buying them there can nevertheless be a sale by description, provided that any discrepancy between the goods and the description was not apparent on a reasonable examination. In *Nicholson and Venn v Smith Marriott*[2], a set of linen napkins and table cloths put up for auction by the defendants was described in the sale catalogue as dating from the seventeenth century. The plaintiffs, who were antique dealers, read the description, saw the linen and bought it. It later transpired that the set dated from the eighteenth century. It was held that, notwithstanding their inspection of the set, the plaintiffs had relied, not on its appearance, but on the catalogue description, with the result that there was a sale by description and the defendants were liable for breach of the term implied by s 13(1). This case can be contrasted with *Harlingdon & Leinster Enterprises Ltd v Christopher Hull Fine Art Ltd*[3], where both the buyer and seller of a painting later found to be a 'forgery' were art dealers. S offered for sale two paintings which had previously been described in an auction catalogue as being by the German expressionist, Gabriele Munter. In a telephone conversation S had told B that the paintings were by that artist. An employee of B then visited S's gallery and was told that S knew little or nothing about German expressionists or Gabriele Munter. B bought one of the paintings without making any further detailed inquiries. The invoice described the painting as being by Gabriele Munter. The majority of the Court of Appeal, however, held that since, viewed objectively, it could not be said that B was relying on S's description of the painting as being by Munter, the trial judge had been correct in holding that the sale had not been a sale by description for the purposes of s 13(1).

A sale can be by description even though the goods may have been selected by the buyer[4], as in a self-service shop, in which case the description will be implied from the words on the packaging or labelling of the goods.

1   [1900] 1 QB 513.
2   (1947) 177 LT 189.
3   [1991] 1 QB 564, [1990] 1 All ER 737, CA.
4   Section 13(3).

8.24   *Implied condition as to satisfactory quality*   Normally, there is no implied term in a contract of sale as to the quality of the goods sold or their fitness for a particular purpose[1]. This is in accordance with the general principle of caveat emptor (let the buyer beware). However, in addition to terms implied by usage[2], other important exceptions to this general principle are provided by ss 14(2), 14(3) and 15 of the 1979 Act, which we propose to consider in turn after we have dealt with an element common to s 14(2) and s 14(3).

1   Section 14(1).
2   Section 14(4).

8.25   Unlike ss 12 and 13 of the 1979 Act, sub-ss (2) and (3) of s 14 only apply where goods are sold *in the course of a business*. 'Business' is not limited to commercial activities in the ordinary sense because it is defined to include 'a profession and the activities of any government department or local or public authority'[1].

For the purposes of provisions in the Unfair Contract Terms Act 1977, the phrase 'in the course of a business' has been explained as follows: '[T]here are some transactions which are clearly integral parts of the businesses concerned, and these should be held to have been carried out in the course of those businesses; this would cover, apart from much else, the instance of a one-off adventure in the nature of trade where the transaction itself would constitute a trade or business. There are other transactions, however, such as the purchase of the car in the present case, which are at the highest only incidental to the carrying on of the relevant business; here a degree of regularity is required before it can be said that they are an integral part of the business carried on and so entered into in the course of that business.'[2]. There can be no doubt that the same interpretation will be applied to the phrase in s 14(2) and (3). Consequently, if an accountant sells one of his office typewriters which is surplus to requirements, the two subsections are not applicable[2], whereas the two subsections do apply to the sale of a typewriter by the proprietor of an office equipment shop. However, if a private individual sells goods through an agent acting in the course of a business, such as an auctioneer, the two subsections apply to the sale by him, unless the buyer knows that the seller is a private individual or reasonable steps have been taken to bring that fact to the buyer's notice before the contract is made[3]. This rule applies whether the private individual is a disclosed or undisclosed principal.[4]

1   Section 61(1).
2   *R & B Customs Brokers Co Ltd v United Dominions Trust Ltd* [1988] 1 All ER 847 at 854, [1988] 1 WLR 321. Also see *Davies v Sumner* [1984] 3 All ER 831, [1984] 1 WLR 1301, HL, and *Devlin v Hall* [1990] RTR 320, DC (dealing with 'in the course of a business' in the Trade Descriptions Act 1968).
3   Section 14(5).
4   *Boyter v Thomson* [1995] 2 AC 628, [1995] 3 All ER 135, HL. As to 'disclosed' and 'undisclosed' principals, see paras 23.45 and 23.46.

8.26   The implied condition as to satisfactory quality is provided by s 14(2) to 14(2C) of the 1979 Act, as substituted by s1(1) of the Sale and Supply of Goods Act 1994. Section 14(2) provides that:

> 'Where the seller sells goods in the course of a business, there is an implied term [a condition[1]] that the goods supplied under the contract are of a satisfactory quality.'

Goods are of satisfactory quality if they meet the standard that any reasonable person would regard as satisfactory, taking account of:

a.   *Any description of them.*   If word processors are sold as 'new' but it transpires that they are dented and scratched, they will not be of satisfactory quality, but if they are sold as 'second hand' or 'shop soiled', they will be, unless there is something radically wrong with them.

b.   *The price (if relevant).*   If the goods are sold at market price, a higher standard of quality can properly be expected than if they are sold at a 'cut' price.

c.   *All the other relevant circumstances.*   For instance, if there is a clause in the contract giving the buyer an allowance off the price for particular shortcomings, regard must be had to that in deciding whether they are of satisfactory quality[2].

1   By the Sale of Goods Act, 1979, s 14(6), the term is classified as a condition. As to conditions, see paras 10.17–10.20, above.
2   Ibid, s 14(2A).

8.27   For the purpose of s14(2), the quality of goods includes their state and condition and the following (among others) are in appropriate cases aspects of the quality of the goods:

a.   fitness for all the purposes for which goods of the kind in question are commonly supplied;

b.   appearance, and finish;
c.   freedom from minor defects;
d.   safety; and
e.   durability.[1]

1   Sale of Goods Act 1979, s 14(2B).

8.28   The term implied by s 14(2) does not extend to any matter making the quality of goods unsatisfactory:

a.   which is specifically drawn to the buyer's attention before the contract is made;
b.   where the buyer examines the goods before the contract is made, which *that* examination ought to reveal; or
c.   in the case of a contract for sale by sample, which would have been apparent on a reasonable examination of the sample.[1]

For b. to apply there must have been an actual examination. A mere invitation or opportunity to examine is not enough, whereas under c. it is in the case of a 'sale by sample' (as to which see para 8.35, below) if the matter would have been apparent on a reasonable examination of the sample.

1   Sale of Goods Act 1979, s 14(2C)

8.29   *Implied condition of fitness for purpose*   Section 14(3) of the 1979 Act provides:

> 'Where the seller sells goods in the course of a business and the buyer, expressly or by implication, makes known:
>
> (a) to the seller, or
>
> (b) where the purchase price or part of it is payable by instalments and the goods were previously sold by a credit-broker to the seller, to that credit-broker,[1]
>
> any particular purpose for which the goods are being bought, there is an implied term [a condition[2]] that the goods supplied under the contract are reasonably fit for that purpose, whether or not that is a purpose for which such goods are commonly supplied, except where the circumstances show that the buyer does not rely, or that it is unreasonable for him to rely, on the skill or judgment of the seller or credit-broker.'

The implied condition of fitness for a particular purpose does not simply relate to the goods at the time of delivery since it is a continuing term that the goods will continue to be fit for that purpose for a reasonable time after delivery, so long as they remain in the same apparent state as that in which they were delivered, apart from normal wear and tear[3].

1   A 'credit-broker' is defined by s 61(1) as a person acting in the course of a business of introducing *individuals* desiring to obtain credit to persons carrying on any business so far as it relates to the provision of credit, or to other credit-brokers.

2   By the Sale of Goods Act 1979, s14(6), the term is classified as a condition. As to conditions, see paras 10.17–10.20, below.
3   *Lexmead (Basingstoke) Ltd v Lewis* [1982] AC 225 at 268, [1981] 1 All ER 1185.

8.30   The implied condition under s 14(3) is that the goods supplied are reasonably fit for the *particular purpose for which they are being bought*, and it can only apply where the buyer makes that purpose known to the seller or (where relevant) the credit-broker, expressly or by implication. Where the purpose for which the goods are bought is obvious, because they only have that one ordinary purpose, it need not be made known expressly because it is clearly implied. If a person buys a bath bun, his particular purpose, to eat it, is impliedly made known to the seller, so that if it contains a stone which breaks the buyer's tooth the seller will be in breach of the condition implied into the contract of sale by s 14(3)[1]. Similarly, a buyer of underpants need not specify his particular purpose – viz to wear them next to the skin – because this is the only purpose for which anyone would ordinarily want underpants; thus, if they contain an excess of sulphite which gives the buyer dermatitis, the seller would be in breach of the implied condition as to fitness for purpose[2]. On the other hand, if the goods can be used for a variety of ordinary purposes, or if they are bought for a special or extraordinary purpose, the implied condition under s 14(3) can only apply if the particular purpose for which they are bought is made known expressly to the seller[3].

1   *Chaproniere v Mason* (1905) 21 TLR 633, CA.
2   *Grant v Australian Knitting Mills Ltd* [1936] AC 85, PC.
3   *Griffiths v Peter Conway Ltd* [1939] 1 All ER 685, CA. The approach taken in this paragraph was confirmed by the House of Lords in *Henry Kendall & Sons v William Lillico & Sons Ltd* [1969] 2 AC 31, [1968] 2 All ER 444, HL.

8.31   The implied condition of fitness for purpose is not broken simply because the goods supplied under the contract are not absolutely fit but only if they are *not reasonably fit for the particular purpose* for which they are bought. In *Heil v Hedges*[1], pork chops, which were infested with a parasite worm but would have been harmless if cooked properly, were held to be reasonably fit for their purpose, so that the seller was not liable to the buyer who had only had them partly cooked and had become ill.

1   [1951] 1 TLR 512.

8.32   In addition, the implied condition of fitness for purpose is not broken where the failure of the goods to meet the intended purpose arises from an abnormal feature or idiosyncrasy, not made known to the seller, in the buyer or in the circumstances of the use of the goods by the buyer, irrespective of whether the buyer was aware of that abnormal feature or idiosyncrasy.[1] Suppose, for example, that a new front wheel tyre is purchased for a car which, unknown to the buyer, has a defect in its steering mechanism and that as a result the tyre wears out after a few hundred miles, instead of the many thousand which would normally be expected. In such circumstances there would not be a breach of the implied condition of fitness for purpose.[2]

1   *Slater and Slater v Finning Ltd* [1996] 3 All ER 398, HL.

2   Ibid, at 405–406.

8.33   The implied condition as to fitness for purpose does not apply where the circumstances show that the buyer does not rely, or that it is unreasonable for him to rely, on the skill or judgment of the seller or credit-broker. The fact that the buyer discovers the defect before the contract is concluded does not mean that he has ceased to rely on the seller's skill or judgement if he relies on the seller to rectify the defect in the near future[1].

1   *R & B Customs Brokers Co Ltd v United Dominions Trust Ltd* [1988]1 All ER 847, [1988] 1 WLR 321, CA.

8.34   It may be noted that the insertion of the phrase 'bought as seen' into the contract will not be construed by the courts as purporting to exclude liability under s 14(2) or s 14(3)[1].

1   *Cavendish Woodhouse Ltd v Manley* (1984) 82 LGR 376, DC.

8.35   *Sale by sample*   By s 15(1) of the 1979 Act, a contract of sale is a contract of sale by sample where there is a term in the contract, express or implied, to that effect. The mere display of sample during negotiations does not make the contract one of sale by sample: there must, at least, be evidence that the parties intended the sale to be by sample.

Two conditions[1] are implied into contracts of sale by sample by s 15(2):

'a. that the bulk shall correspond with the sample in quality;

b. that the goods shall be free from any defect, rendering them unsatisfactory, which would not be apparent on reasonable examination of the sample.'

Implied condition a. is broken if the bulk does not correspond completely with the sample in quality, even though only a small amount of work or expense is required to achieve complete correspondence[2].

The seller is in breach of implied condition b. if the goods have a latent defect, but not if the defect could have been discovered by a reasonable examination of the sample (whether or not the buyer made any examination).

1   By the Sale of Goods Act 1979, s 15(3), the terms implied by s 15(2) are classified as conditions. As to conditions, see paras 10.17–10.20, above.
2   *E and S Ruben Ltd v Faire Bros & Co Ltd* [1949] 1 KB 254, [1949] 1 All ER 215.

Other statutes
8.36   Terms modelled on those implied into sale of goods contracts are implied:

a.   into contracts of hire purchase, by ss 8 to 11 of the Supply of Goods (Implied Terms) Act 1973;
b.   into contracts of hire, by ss 7 to 10 of the Supply of Goods and Services Act 1982; and
c.   into contracts analogous to sale under which a person transfers or agrees to transfer to another the property (ie ownership) in goods, by ss 2 to 5 of the Supply of Goods and Services Act 1982. One example of a contract

analogous to sale is a contract for work and materials, such as a contract for double glazing; another is a contract of exchange.

Although the exclusion or restriction by the contract of one of the implied terms referred to in this paragraph, or of liability for its breach, is permissible[1], there are strict limitations on this under the Unfair Contract Terms Act 1977 (paras 10.50–10.53, below).

1   Supply of Goods and Services Act 1982, s 11, expressly states this in relation to contracts governed by ss 2–10 thereof.

8.37   By way of a further example, it may be noted that in a 'contract for the supply of a service' certain terms are implied by the Supply of Goods and Services Act 1982. Such a contract includes, for example, a contract for dry cleaning or for professional services (but does not include a contract of employment or apprenticeship[1]). The fact that goods are transferred or hired under the contract does not prevent it being a contract for the supply of a service[2]. Consequently, for example, while a contract for work and materials will be subject to the implied terms under ss 2 to 5 of the 1982 Act in relation to the materials element, the work element will be subject to the terms implied into a contract of service by that Act.

The following terms are implied by the 1982 Act into a contract for the supply of a service:

a.   by s 13, where the supplier of the service is acting in the course of a business[3], there is an implied term that he will carry out the service with reasonable care and skill[4];

b.   by ss 14 and 15, where the time for the service to be carried out (s 14), or the consideration for the service (s 15), is not stated by the contract, or left to be determined in a manner agreed by the contract, or determined by the course of dealings between the parties, there is an implied term that the service will be carried out within a reasonable time or, as the case may be, that a reasonable charge will be paid. The implied term as to the time of performance only applies where the contract is for the supply of a service by a supplier *acting in the course of a business*[3].

Section 16 of the Act of 1982 permits the rights, duties and liabilities which may arise by virtue of ss 13 to 15 to be negatived or varied, subject to the relevant provisions of the Unfair Contract Terms Act 1977 (paras 10.43–10.48, below).

1   Supply of Goods and Services Act 1982, s 12(2).
2   Ibid, s 12(3).
3   'Business' includes a profession and the activities of any government department or local or public authority: Supply of Goods and Services Act 1982, s 10. As to 'in the course of a business', see para 8.25, above.
4   There are very limited exceptions under the Supply of Services (Exclusion of Implied Terms) Orders 1982, 1983 and 1985, the most notable being that the implied term under s 13 does not apply to the services rendered by an advocate in court or before any tribunal, inquiry or arbitrator or in carrying out certain preliminary work, nor to the services rendered by a company director to his company.

Terms implied by the courts

8.38   In *Liverpool City Council v Irwin*[1], the House of Lords recognised that terms could be implied by the courts in two distinct situations:

a.   where the term was a necessary incident of the kind of contract in question, and

b.   where it was necessary to give 'business efficacy' to the particular contract.

1   [1977] AC 239, [1976] 2 All ER 39, HL.

Implication of a term which is a necessary incident of the type of contract in question

8.39   When a court implies this type of term for the first time it lays down a general rule for contracts of the same type, eg employment contracts and contracts between banker and customer, so that the term will be implied in subsequent cases concerning that type of contract[1], subject to the rules of precedent, unless it is inconsistent with the express terms of the contract[2] or the contract validly excludes it[3]. In implying a term of the present type, the court is not trying to put the parties' intentions, actual or presumed, into effect but is implying it as a necessary incident of the type of contractual relationship in question[4]. In deciding whether to make such an implication, the courts take into account the reasonableness of the suggested term and whether it is called for by the nature of the subject matter of the type of contract in question[5].

1   *Lister v Romford Ice and Cold Storage Co Ltd* [1957] AC 555 at 576; *Liverpool City Council v Irwin* [1976] 2 All ER 39 at 46; *Shell UK Ltd v Lostock Garage Ltd* [1977] 1 All ER 481 at 487.
2   The Unfair Contract Terms Act 1977 (paras 10.43–10.56, below) may have the effect of invalidating an inconsistent express term, in which case the implication can be made: *Johnstone v Bloomsbury Health Authority* [1992] QB 333, [1991] 2 All ER 293, CA.
3   *Lynch v Thorne* [1956] 1 All ER 744, [1956] 1 WLR 303, CA.
4   *Shell UK Ltd v Lostock Garage Ltd* [1977] 1 All ER 481 at 487; *Tai Hing Cotton Mill Ltd v Liu Chong Hing Bank Ltd* [1986] AC 80, [1985] 2 All ER 947, PC.
5   *Liverpool City Council v Irwin* [1977] AC 239, [1976] 2 All ER 39, HL.

8.40   It is only possible here to refer to a few of the terms implied into contracts under the present heading. In contracts of employment a number of obligations on the employee are implied. The fundamental implied duty is that the employee will faithfully serve his employer (the implied duty of fidelity)[1]. A number of more specific implied duties to which an employee is subject are merely instances of the duty of fidelity, for example: not to use or disclose confidential information relating to his employer's business contrary to his employer's interests[2]; not to copy or memorise such information for use after his employment has ceased[2]; not to act against his employer's interests[3]; to use reasonable care and skill in performing his duties[4]; and to indemnify his employer against any liability incurred by the employer as a result of his wrongful acts[5]. There is a separate implied duty whereby an ex-employee must not use or disclose a trade secret or information relating to the former employer's business which is so confidential that it requires the same protection as a trade secret[6]. Reciprocal terms are implied in the employee's favour, the employer being obliged, for instance, not to require the employee to do any unlawful act[7], and to use reasonable care to ensure the safety of the employee (for example by providing a safe system of work)[8].

In a contract between banker and customer, the courts have, for instance, implied as necessary incidents a duty on a customer to take reasonable precautions in drawing a cheque to prevent fraud or forgery[9] and a duty on the customer to inform the bank of any forgery of a cheque as soon as the customer has discovered it[10].

Another example of an implied term of the present type is provided by *Liverpool City Council v Irwin*[11]. In that case, the House of Lords held that, where parts of a building have been let to different tenants (the case concerned a high-rise block of flats) and essential rights of access over parts of the building, such as stairs, retained by the landlord have been granted to the individual tenants, a term could be implied into the tenancy agreements that the landlord would take reasonable care to keep them reasonably safe and reasonably fit for use by tenants, their families and their visitors.

1   *Hivac Ltd v Park Royal Scientific Instruments Ltd* [1946] Ch 169, [1946] 1 All ER 350, CA.
2   *Fowler v Faccenda Chicken Ltd* [1987] Ch 117, [1986] 1 All ER 617, CA. This duty of non-disclosure of confidential information does not extend so as to bar disclosures to the Inland Revenue or a regulatory body of confidential matters which it is in the province of such an authority to investigate: *Re A Company's Application* [1989] Ch 477, [1989] 2 All ER 248.
3   *Wessex Dairies Ltd v Smith* [1935] 2 KB 80, CA.
4   *Lister v Romford Ice and Cold Storage Co Ltd* [1957] AC 555, [1957] 1 All ER 125, HL.
5   Ibid.
6   *Fowler v Faccenda Chicken Ltd*, above.
7   *Gregory v Ford* [1951] 1 All ER 121.
8   *Lister v Romford Ice and Cold Storage Co Ltd*, above.
9   See, eg, *London Joint Stock Bank Ltd v Macmillan* [1918] AC 777, HL.
10 Ibid.
11 [1977] AC 239, [1976] 2 All ER 39, HL.

Implication to give business efficacy

8.41   The implication of a term under this heading is less common and can only be made when it is necessary in the particular circumstances to imply a term to fill an obvious gap in a contract[1] and thereby to give it business efficacy and make it a workable agreement in such manner as the parties would clearly have done if they had applied their minds to what has occurred. This power of judicial implication was recognised in *The Moorcock*[2], which concerned a contract permitting the plaintiff to unload his ship at the defendants' jetty. A term was implied into the contract that the defendants had taken reasonable care to see whether the berth was safe so that the ship would not be damaged when she grounded at low tide, as both parties realised she would. Bowen LJ stated that, where the parties had not dealt with the burden of a particular peril, a court could imply a term which would give such efficacy to the contract as both parties must have intended it to have.

The test which the courts apply in deciding whether to imply a term to give the contract business efficacy is a strict one. A term cannot be implied unless it is *necessary* to give business efficacy to the contract and it can be formulated with a *sufficient degree of precision*; it is not enough that it is reasonable in all the circumstances to imply the term[3]. A classic statement of the test is that of Scrutton LJ in *Reigate v Union Manufacturing Co (Ramsbottom) Ltd*[4]:

> 'A term can only be implied if it is necessary in the business sense to give efficacy to the contract, ie if it is such a term that it can confidently be said that if at the time the contract was being negotiated someone had said to the parties: "What will happen in such a case?" they would both have replied: "Of course, so and so will happen; we did not trouble to say that; it is too clear".'

1   *Adams Holden and Pearson Ltd v Trent Regional Health Authority* (1989) 47 BLR 34 and 39, CA.
2   (1889) 14 PD 64, CA.
3   *Liverpool City Council v Irwin* [1977] AC 239, [1976] 2 All ER 39, HL; *Shell UK Ltd v Lostock Garage Ltd* [1977] 1 All ER 481, [1976] 1 WLR 1187, CA.
4   [1918] 1 KB 592 at 605, CA. See also *Shirlaw v Southern Foundries (1926) Ltd* [1939] 2 KB 206 at 227, [1939] 2 All ER 113 at 124.

8.42   Pursuant to these principles, the courts have, for instance, refused to imply terms in the following cases: where tariff booklets were supplied free to a hotel in consideration of its proprietors undertaking to circulate or display them for a specified period, a term to the effect that the proprietors' obligation should cease if the business was sold was not implied[1]; where a petrol company subsidised two neighbouring filling stations during a price cutting war, a term to the effect that it would not abnormally discriminate against the plaintiff's filling station in favour of competitors was not implied into a contract for the exclusive supply of petrol by the petrol company to the plaintiff[2]; where a variety artiste's clothes were stolen from his dressing room during rehearsals, a term was not implied into the contract between him and the theatrical producer that the latter would take reasonable care to ensure that the artiste's effects were not stolen[3]; where a sterilisation operation turned out not to have rendered the patient absolutely or permanently sterile, a term was not implied into the contract between surgeon and patient that it would[4].

In contrast, the courts have, for example, implied a term: into a contract between a driving school and its client, that any car provided under the contract would be covered by insurance[5]; into a contract of transfer of a footballer, which provided that an additional sum be paid when he had scored 20 goals for the first team, that he was entitled to a reasonable opportunity to score the goals[6]; and into a contract for a loan of money by an employer to an employee, which made no reference to interest, although the employee knew that the employer was financing it by borrowing from a bank, an implied term that the employee would indemnify the employer in respect of any interest payable on the loan[7]. In addition, the courts have held that generally a term is necessarily implied in any contract that neither party shall prevent the other from performing it[8].

Since the implication of a term under *The Moorcock* principle is always dependent on the particular circumstances of the case, the implication of a term under it does not lay down a general rule for the future.

1   *General Publicity Services Ltd v Best's Brewery Co Ltd* [1951] 2 TLR 875, CA.

2   *Shell UK Ltd v Lostock Garage Ltd* [1977] 1 All ER 481, [1976] 1 WLR 1187, CA.
3   *Deyong v Shenburn* [1946] KB 227, [1946] 1 All ER 226, CA.
4   *Eyre v Measday* [1986] 1 All ER 488, CA; *Thake v Maurice* [1986] QB 644, [1986] 1 All ER 497, CA. In neither case was the surgeon in breach of the implied term that he would use reasonable care and skill; in relation to that type of implied term, see para 8.37, above.
5   *British School of Motoring Ltd v Simms* [1971] 1 All ER 317.
6   *Bournemouth and Boscombe Athletic Football Club Co Ltd v Manchester United Football Club Ltd* (1980) Times, 22 May, CA.
7   *Baylis v Barnett* (1988) Times, 28 December, CA.
8   *William Cory & Son Ltd v London Corpn* [1951] 2 KB 476 at 484, [1951] 2 All ER 85 at 88. But see para 23.31, below, in relation to a contract of agency.

Distinction between the two types of terms implied by the courts
8.43   The distinction between the two types of implication by the courts is shown by *Scally v Southern Health and Social Services Board*[1]. Under their contracts of employment, the plaintiffs were required to contribute to a superannuation scheme and were entitled to its benefits. To qualify for a full pension under the principal regulations, as originally enacted, it was necessary for an employee to complete 40 years' contributory service. The scheme was amended in 1974 so as to give employees the right to purchase 'added years' of pension entitlement on certain terms in order to make up the full 40 years' contributions to qualify for maximum pension. This right, however, was only exercisable within a specified 12-month period.

The plaintiffs claimed damages from their employer alleged to flow from the employer's failure to bring to the plaintiffs' notice the right to enhance their pension entitlement, by the purchase of added years, on the terms available under the 1974 amendment.

On an appeal by the employer to the House of Lords, one question was whether the employer owed a duty to bring to the plaintiffs' notice the right to enhance a pension. The House of Lords held that such a term could not be implied as necessary to give business efficacy to the contract of employment as a whole. A clear distinction was to be drawn between the search for an implied term necessary to give business efficacy to a particular contract and the search, based on wider considerations, for a term which the law would imply as a necessary incident of a definable category of contractual relationship. The House held that a term of the latter type could, however, be implied. Its reasoning was that, where the following circumstances exist in a particular relationship of employer and employee:

a.   the terms of the contract of employment have not been negotiated with the individual employee but result from negotiation with a representative body or are otherwise incorporated by reference;
b.   a particular term of the contract makes available to the employee a valuable right contingent upon action being taken by him to avail himself of its benefit, and
c.   the employee cannot, in all the circumstances, reasonably be expected to be aware of the term unless it is drawn to his attention,

it is necessary to imply an obligation on the employer to take reasonable steps to bring the term of the contract in question to the employee's attention, so that he may be in a position to enjoy its benefit.

1 [1992] 1 AC 294, [1991] 4 All ER 563, HL. See also *Spring v Guardian Assurance* [1995] 2 AC 296, [1994] 3 All ER 129, HL.

Unfair Contract Terms

8.44 Under the Unfair Contract Terms Act 1977 and the Unfair Terms in Consumer Contracts Regulations 1994, which implement the EC Directive on Unfair Terms in Consumer Contracts, Directive 93/13, there are special provisions relating to contract terms which are unfair. In some cases, these provisions render an unfair term of no effect. We deal with these provisions later[1].

1 Paras 10.43–10.57 and 14.63–14.68, below.

Interpretation of Terms

8.45 Once the terms of a contract have been identified, they must be construed (ie interpreted) to ascertain their meaning. Many contractual disputes involve the construction of terms. The principles of interpretation set out below have been developed by the courts in relation to written terms but a similar approach is applicable to oral terms.

8.46 In interpreting a contract, a court is seeking to ascertain, and put into effect, the intentions of the parties. The general rule (part of the parol evidence rule referred to at the start of this chapter) is that the parties' intentions must be discovered from the document itself, giving the words used their ordinary grammatical meaning[1]. However, evidence is admissible to show that a word is to be understood in some special or technical sense, and the ordinary meaning can also be ignored if it would give rise to inconsistency with the rest of the document[2] or to absurdity[3].

The parties themselves cannot give direct evidence to show that their true intentions were different from what the terms of the document as construed indicate[4]. If the words of the contract are clear and unequivocal, a court cannot re-write it in the light of what the parties might (or might not) have contemplated when they contracted[4]. It follows that evidence of pre-contractual negotiations cannot be received to assist in the construction of a contractual document[5]. There is an exception where the document contains an ambiguity; here evidence of pre-contractual negotiations is admissible to resolve the ambiguity[6]. Evidence of post-contractual conduct is also inadmissible[7]. On the other hand, the court must seek to discover the parties' intentions in the light of the same factual background as existed at or before the time the contract was made. Thus, evidence of such background, including evidence of the object (as it appears from the background) of the transaction is admissible[8].

1 *Lovell and Christmas Ltd v Wall* (1911) 104 LT 85, CA.
2 *Watson v Haggitt* [1928] AC 127, PC.
3 *Abbott v Middleton* (1858) 7 HL Cas 68 at 69.
4 *British Movietonews Ltd v London and District Cinemas Ltd* [1952] AC 166, [1951] 2 All ER 617, HL.

5   *Prenn v Simmonds* [1971] 3 All ER 237, [1971] 1 WLR 1381, HL.
6   *Partenreederei MS Karen Oltmann v Scarsdale Shipping Co Ltd, The Karen Oltmann* [1976] 2 Lloyd's Rep 708.
7   *Schuler AG v Wickman Machine Tool Sales Ltd* [1974] AC 235, [1973] 2 All ER 39, HL.
8   *Prenn v Simmonds* [1971] 3 All ER 237, [1971] 1 WLR 1381, HL.

8.47   A number of other rules have been evolved to aid the interpretation of a contract. First, words capable of two meanings will be given the meaning which will make the contract valid and effective, rather than void or ineffective[1]. Second, where a contract refers to a list of specific things forming a class and ends the list with some more general words, it is rebuttably presumed that the general words were intended to be limited to things of the same class as the specific things. For example, in *Tillmanns v SS Knutsford*[2], the words 'any other cause' in a charterparty provision excluding liability to deliver cargo if delivery was impossible through 'war, disturbance, or any other cause' were construed as restricted to causes of the same type as war and disturbance; consequently ice was not within 'any other cause'. Third, and last, all ambiguities are construed against the person benefiting from the term in question. *Houghton v Trafalgar Insurance Co*[3] provides an example. A car with seating for five was involved in a crash while carrying six people. The driver's insurance policy exempted the insurance company from liability if the car was carrying 'any load in excess of that for which it was constructed'. 'Load' was ambiguous since it might have referred to an excess amount of passengers or goods or it might have been limited to goods. It was construed against the insurance company as not extending to an excessive number of passengers.

We deal with some other points relating to interpretation when we come to discuss exemption clauses in chapter 10.

1   *Steele v Hoe* (1849) 14 QB 431.
2   [1908] 2 KB 385, CA; affd [1908] AC 406, HL.
3   [1954] 1 QB 247, [1953] 2 All ER 1409, CA. For a recent example of the application of this principle, see *Commission for the New Towns v Cooper (Great Britain) Ltd* [1995] Ch 259, [1995] 2 All ER 929, CA.

8.48   So far, our discussion of the law of contract has concentrated on the formation and enforceability of a contract. In the next three chapters we shall be concerned principally with how a contract is discharged.

A contract can be discharged in four ways:

by agreement (which we discussed in paras 6.35–6.41, above);
by performance;
by breach;
by frustration.

Chapter 9

Discharge by Performance—

9.1 A contract is normally discharged by both parties performing their obligations under it, both parties being released from further liability thereby. If only one party performs his contractual obligations he alone is discharged and he acquires a right of action against the other for breach of contract, a subject which we discuss in the next chapter. Special rules govern the discharge of a party who has unsuccessfully tendered performance.

Performance

9.2 For a party to be discharged by performance he must have precisely performed all his obligations under the contract. Thus, to decide whether a party is discharged by performance, one must first ascertain and construe the terms of the contract, express and implied, to see what his contractual obligations were, and then look at what has happened to see whether what he has done precisely corresponds with those obligations. The requirement of precise performance is a strict one and, if it is not met, it is irrelevant that the performance effected is commercially no less valuable than that which was promised. In *Arcos Ltd v E A Ronaasen & Son*[1], the plaintiffs contracted to supply the defendants with a certain quantity of timber which, as they knew, was to be used for constructing cement barrels. The contract specified that the timber should be half an inch thick but when it was delivered the defendants discovered that 95% of it was over half an inch thick, although none of it exceeded three quarters of an inch in thickness. It was still perfectly possible for the defendants to use the wood, as it had been delivered, for the construction of cement barrels but the House of Lords held that they were entitled to reject the whole consignment since the plaintiffs had not performed a contractual obligation which was a condition of the contract[2]. Lord Atkin stated, obiter, that only if a deviation from the terms of the contract was 'microscopic' could the contract be taken to have been correctly performed. An example of this is provided by *Shipton, Anderson & Co v Weil Bros & Co*[3], where a contract requiring the delivery of 4,950 tons of wheat was held to have been performed by the seller although he had delivered 4,950 tons 55lbs.

165

Generally, no demand for performance is necessary to render an obligation to perform operative[4]. Thus, a debtor is bound to seek out his creditor and pay him.

1   [1933] AC 470, HL.
2   The contractual obligation broken was the condition implied by the Sale of Goods Act 1979, s 13(1) and (1A), that in a sale of goods by description the goods must correspond with that description. See paras 8.22, above, and 10.17–10.20, below.
3   [1912] 1 KB 574.
4   A demand will be necessary if there is an express agreement or trade usage requiring it.

Payment

9.3   Where the obligation of one party to the other consists in the payment of a sum of money, the contract is discharged by the payment of that sum. Payment should, primarily, be made in legal tender[1] but may, with the consent of the creditor, be made by cheque or other negotiable instrument[2].

1   Para 9.15, below.
2   For the meaning of this term, see para 22.20, below.

9.4   Where a cheque or other negotiable instrument is given, and accepted[1], in payment, its effect may be absolutely to discharge or only conditionally to discharge the debtor. The discharge will be *absolute* if the creditor promises expressly or impliedly, in accepting the cheque, to discharge the debtor from his existing obligations. If this occurs the creditor loses his right of action on the original contract but can sue on his rights under the instrument if it is dishonoured[2]. However, the presumption is that the creditor only accepts a cheque as a *conditional* discharge, in which case the debtor is not discharged unless, and until, the instrument is honoured; if it is dishonoured, the debtor may be sued on the original contract or on the dishonoured instrument[3].

1   *Official Solicitor v Thomas* [1986] 2 EGLR 1, CA.
2   *Sard v Rhodes* (1836) 1 M & W 153.
3   *Sayer v Wagstaff* (1844) 5 Beav 415; *Re Romer and Haslam* [1893] 2 QB 286, CA.

9.5   The presumption is different in the case of payment by a credit card or a charge card. We shall explain this by reference to payment under a contract of sale, but the explanation is equally applicable to payment under other contracts. Credit card or charge card transactions involve an underlying contractual scheme which pre-dates an individual contract of sale in which a credit card or charge card is used for payment. This underlying scheme is established by two separate bilateral contracts:

a.   between the credit company and the seller, the latter agreeing to accept payment by use of the card by a cardholder and the credit company agreeing to pay to the seller the price of the goods, less commission;
b.   between the credit company and a cardholder, the cardholder being provided with a card enabling him to pay the price by its use in return for agreeing to pay the credit company the full amount owed by him.

A third bilateral contract is then made between the buyer and seller for the purchase of goods. Tendering and accepting the credit or charge card in payment is made on the tacit assumption that the legal consequences will be regulated by the separate underlying scheme[1].

In *Re Charge Card Services Ltd*[2] the Court of Appeal held that, where a credit or charge card is used for payment, there is a presumption that it is accepted by a seller as an absolute discharge, and not simply as a conditional discharge. This presumption will be rebutted if there is an express or implied term in the contract of sale that the card is only being accepted as conditional payment, which will not normally be the case. In the *Charge Card Services* case it was held that, where a charge card was used to pay for fuel at a filling station and the charge card company had subsequently become insolvent before paying the filling station for the fuel, the filling station could not recover the price directly from the cardholder since his liability to pay had been discharged absolutely, there being no express or implied term in his contract with the filling station to indicate that the card had only been accepted as conditional payment.

1 *Re Charge Card Services Ltd* [1989] Ch 497, [1988] 3 All ER 702, CA.
2 [1989] Ch 497, [1988] 3 All ER 702, CA.

9.6 If, but only if, the creditor requests payment through the post, a payment put in the post will be deemed to have been duly made even though it is lost in transit[1], unless it was sent in a manner inappropriate to the amount in question (eg sending a substantial sum in cash)[2]. A request for postal payment may be express or implied, but the mere fact that remittances have been posted over a number of years without any objection by the creditor does not normally raise such an implication[3].

1 *Thairlwall v Great Northern Rly Co* [1910] 2 KB 509, DC.
2 *Mitchell-Henry v Norwich Union Life Insurance Society* [1918] 2 KB 67, CA.
3 *Pennington v Crossley & Son* (1897) 77 LT 43, CA. Cf *Beevers v Mason* (1978) 37 P & CR 452, CA.

Proof of payment
9.7 It is commonly, but mistakenly, believed that payment of a debt can only be proved by producing a written receipt. In fact, payment may be proved by any evidence from which payment may be inferred[1]. In particular, s 3 of the Cheques Act 1957 provides that an unindorsed cheque which appears to have been paid by the banker on whom it is drawn shall be evidence of the receipt by the payee of the sum payable on the cheque.

A debtor is not entitled to insist on a receipt when paying a debt and if he does obtain a receipt it is only prima facie, not conclusive, evidence that a debt has been paid[2]. Therefore, it is always possible for the person who has given the receipt to show either that he has not received payment or that the receipt was given by mistake, or obtained by fraud, or that it was given on certain terms.

1 *Eyles v Ellis* (1827) 4 Bing 112.
2 *Wilson v Keating* (1859) 27 Beav 121; *Cesarini v Ronzani* (1858) 1 F & F 339; *Skaife v Jackson* (1824) 3 B & C 421; *Re W W Duncan & Co* [1905] 1 Ch 307.

Appropriation of payments

9.8   We are concerned here with the case where a debtor who owes two or more debts to the same creditor makes a payment which is insufficient to discharge the whole of his indebtedness to that creditor. In some cases it may be of vital importance to know to w hich of the debts payment relates (or, to use technical language, is appropriated). Suppose that X owes Y two debts, one of which is unenforceable for some reason and the other not, and X pays Y a sum which is insufficient to cover both debts. If it is permissible for Y to appropriate the payment to the unenforceable debt, he will thereby have succeeded in getting an unenforceable debt paid, leaving the other debt still payable; this is a matter to which we return in para 9.10, below. Similarly, if one debt is guaranteed or secured and the other is not, it will be of advantage to Y if it is permissible for him to appropriate the payment to the unsecured debt, because he can enforce his guarantee or security to obtain payment of the other.

The following three rules govern the appropriation of payments.

Appropriation by the debtor

9.9   The debtor may appropriate his payment to a particular debt or debts, *provided he does so at the time of payment*. The debtor's intention to appropriate payments in a particular way must either expressly be communicated to the creditor or be capable of being inferred from the circumstances of the case as known to both parties[1]. Thus, if a debtor who owes a creditor two debts makes a payment denying the existence of one of them, an appropriation to the debt which is not denied can be inferred[2]. Similarly, if he makes a payment which exactly corresponds to the amount owing under one of the debts, an appropriation to that debt can be inferred[3]. The debtor must appropriate at the time of payment; if he does so the creditor is bound, assuming he accepts the payment, to apply it in the manner directed by the debtor[4]. Therefore, if the creditor does not agree with the debtor's appropriation, he must refuse to accept payment and stand upon his legal rights[5] .

1   *Leeson v Leeson* [1936] 2 KB 156, [1936] 2 All ER 133, CA.
2   *Burn v Boulton* (1846) 2 CB 476.
3   *Marryatts v White* (1817) 2 Stark 101.
4   *Peters v Anderson* (1814) 5 Taunt 596; *Croft v Lumley* (1855) 5 E & B 648.
5   *Croft v Lumley* (1855) 5 E & B 648.

Appropriation by the creditor

9.10   *In the absence of an appropriation by the debtor*, the creditor may appropriate the payment as he chooses, *at any time*. The creditor's choice of appropriation need not be made in express terms: it may be declared by bringing an action on a debt to which he has decided not to appropriate the payment or in any other way which indicates his choice of appropriation[1]. Moreover, until he has declared his appropriation to the debtor he may alter it[2].

The important point is that, unlike an appropriation by the debtor, an appropriation by the creditor can be made at any time (provided he has not already made an appropriation which he has communicated to the debtor, and provided nothing has happened which would make it inequitable for him to exercise it)[3]. Thus, it was held in *Seymour v Pickett*[4] that a creditor who had been owed two debts could make his appropriation for the first time in the witness box. If he wishes, the creditor may appropriate the payment to a debt which, though valid, is unenforceable because it is statute-barred, or because the contract should have been evidenced in writing, or for some other reason. In *Seymour v Pickett*, for example, the plaintiff creditor was an unregistered dentist who, by statute, could not recover any fee for performing dental surgery (although the debt was not an illegal one) but could recover the price of material supplied. The plaintiff treated the defendant and the bill came to £45, £24 for services and £21 for material (including a bridge and gold fillings). The defendant gave the plaintiff two cheques, one for £20, and the other, which was post-dated, for £25, without appropriating either. The £25 cheque was dishonoured, the defendant having stopped payment of it by his bank. In an action by the plaintiff, it was held that he could appropriate the £20 to the payment of his professional fees, and had done so by a declaration in the witness box, and therefore could recover the £21 relating to materials supplied which thus remained unpaid. On the other hand, the creditor cannot appropriate payment to an illegal debt or to a 'debt' under a void contract[5].

1   *The Mecca* [1897] AC 286, HL.
2   *Simson v Ingham* (1823) 2 B & C 65.
3   *Cory Bros & Co Ltd v Turkish SS Mecca (Owners)*, *The Mecca* [1897] AC 286, HL; *Seymour v Pickett* [1905] 1 KB 715, CA.
4   [1905] 1 KB 715, CA.
5   *Wright v Laing* (1824) 3 B & C 165; *Keeping v Broom* (1895) 11 TLR 595.

9.11   It should be noted that, in many cases where money is owed under agreements regulated by the Consumer Credit Act 1974, the creditor has no right of appropriation. Section 81 of the 1974 Act provides that, while a debtor or hirer who is liable to a creditor under two or more regulated consumer credit or consumer hire agreements is entitled to appropriate a payment towards a particular debt or debts, a failure by him to do so results in a special rule applying where one or more of the agreements is a hire purchase or conditional sale agreement or a consumer hire agreement or an agreement in relation to which any security has been provided. This special rule is that the payment is automatically appropriated towards the sums due under the several agreements respectively in the proportions which those sums bear to one another.

Payments into a current account
9.12   A special rule, the rule in *Clayton's Case*[1], applies to payments into a current account. This rule of convenience, based on so-called presumed intention, is that each payment into a current account is appropriated to the earliest debt which is not statute-barred[2]. The rule is limited to cases where there is a current account (ie an unbroken account between the parties into which all receipts and payments out are carried in order of date, so that all sums paid in form a blended fund[3]), such as a current account at a bank or a current account between traders 'for goods supplied and work done rendered periodically with a balance carried forward'[4]. The rule does not apply where there is no unbroken account, but merely an account containing distinct and separate debts[5].

Since the rule is based on presumed intention, it is excluded if the parties otherwise agree or if a contrary intention appears from the circumstances[6]. It is insufficient, however, simply to show that a bank refused to allow cheques to be drawn on an overdrawn account unless credits of an equivalent amount were paid in. The rule will not be excluded if such credits are paid in, and they will therefore go in reduction of the oldest debts and not in offsetting newly drawn cheques.

Despite the rule, the balance owed on an unbroken account is a single and undivided debt, and for that reason payment constitutes part payment of that debt within the meaning of the Limitation Act 1980 and starts the limitation period running again in relation to the whole outstanding balance[7] (with the exception of debts which are already statute-barred[8]).

1   *Devaynes v Noble, Clayton's Case* (1816) 1 Mer 529.
2   *Re Sherry* (1884) 25 Ch D 692 at 702; *Nash v Hodgson* (1855) 6 De GM & G 474.
3   *Hooper v Keay* (1875) 1 QBD 178.
4   *Albemarle Supply Co Ltd v Hind & Co* [1928] 1 KB 307 at 319.
5   *The Mecca* [1897] AC 286, HL.
6   *The Mecca; Mutton v Peat* [1899] 2 Ch 556 reversed on the facts [1900] 2 Ch 79, CA.
7   *Re Footman, Bower & Co Ltd* [1961] Ch 443, [1961] 2 All ER 161.
8   This exception results from the Limitation Act 1980, s 29(7), whereby a right of action, once statute-barred, is not revived by subsequent part payment; see para 12.39, below.

Tender of Performance

9.13   If a party makes a valid tender (ie offer) of performance of his contractual obligations and the other party refuses to accept performance, the party making the tender is freed from liability for non-performance of those obligations, provided that the tender is made under such circumstances that the other party has a reasonable opportunity of examining the performance tendered, eg the goods tendered, in order to ascertain that it conforms with the contract[1].

1 *Startup v Macdonald* (1843) 6 Man & G 593 at 610. See also Sale of Goods Act 1979, s 29.

Tender of payment
9.14   If a party makes a valid tender of payment of money which he owes but the other party refuses to accept it, this does not discharge his debt but there is no obligation to make a further tender. If an action is brought for non-payment against a party who has tendered unsuccessfully, all he has to do is to pay the money into court, whereupon, if he has pleaded and proved a valid tender:

a.   a right of lien[1] is generally extinguished; and
b.   he is not liable for his non-performance.

Thus, a creditor who refuses a valid tender of payment can eventually obtain nothing but the amount originally tendered to him and a debtor who has validly tendered payment is not prejudiced by a refusal to accept it.

1   Paras 2.32–2.35, above.

9.15 A valid tender requires the following:

a. The money must actually be produced[1]: it is not enough for the debtor to offer to pay and simply put his hand in his pocket[2]. The sole exception to the requirement of production is where the creditor expressly or impliedly dispenses with it[3]. The creditor will impliedly dispense with the need for production if, when the debtor tells him that he has come to pay a specified amount, the creditor says it is too late or otherwise indicates that he will not accept the money[3].

b. The tender must be in legal currency: a creditor is not obliged to accept a cheque or other negotiable instrument or payment in currency which is not legal tender[4]. By the Currency and Bank Notes Act 1954 and the Coinage Act 1971, legal tender is as follows:

    i.   Bank of England notes, to any amount;
    ii.   gold coins of the Mint, to any amount;
    iii. silver and cupro-nickel coins of the Mint of more than 10p, up to £10;
    iv. silver and cupro-nickel coins of the Mint of not more than 10p, up to £5;
    v.   bronze coins, up to 20p.

c. Where the amount tendered is greater than the debt due, the tender is invalid if the creditor is required to give change[5]. However, a tender of an excess payment will be valid if, though change is requested, the creditor refuses the tender for some other reason, or if the debtor is happy for the creditor to keep the excess amount[6].

d. The tender must not be made on any condition. Thus, in *Finch v Miller*[7], it was held that a tender, made on condition that a receipt for a full discharge be given, was invalid. On the other hand, a valid tender may be made under protest so as to reserve the right of the debtor to dispute the amount, provided it does not impose conditions on the creditor[8].

e. Where a debt is expressly made payable on a particular day, a tender made after that date is not strictly a valid tender. However, provided it is made before the commencement of an action for the recovery of the debt, it will generally have the same effect as a valid tender[9].

f. The tender must be in exact accordance with any other special terms of the contract, for example, as to place of payment.

1   *Thomas v Evans* (1808) 10 East 101.
2   *Finch v Brook* (1834) 1 Bing NC 253.
3   *Farquharson v Pearl Assurance Co Ltd* [1937] 3 All ER 124.
4   *Blumberg v Life Interests and Reversionary Securities Corpn* [1897] 1 Ch 171; upheld on appeal [1898] 1 Ch 27, CA.
5   *Robinson v Cook* (1815) 6 Taunt 336.
6   *Bevans v Rees* (1839) 5 M & W 306; *Wade's Case* (1601) 5 Co Rep 114a.
7   (1848) 5 CB 428.
8   *Greenwood v Sutcliffe* [1892] 1 Ch 1, CA.
9   *Briggs v Calverly* (1800) 8 Term Rep 629.

Tender of acts

9.16   Where a party is obliged to perform some act, other than the payment of something, he will make a valid tender of performance if he attempts to perform the act in precise accordance with the terms of the contract. In the case of a contract for the sale of goods, the tender of them must be made at a reasonable hour[1].

If a party (A) makes a valid tender of an act, but the other (B) refuses to accept the tendered performance, A is entitled to maintain an action for breach of contract[2]. Moreover, if B's refusal is absolute and unqualified it will constitute a renunciation of the contract, in which case A will also be entitled to treat the renunciation as discharging him from his obligation to perform the contract[3]. In the case of a valid tender of goods by the seller under a contract for the sale of goods, these rules are given statutory effect by s 37 of the Sale of Goods Act 1979.

An invalid tender does not, as a rule, prevent the party who made it from subsequently making a valid tender[4]. However, it may be impossible to make a subsequent, valid tender simply because performance had to be made on a particular day and that day is now past. In addition, if the invalid tender amounts to a repudiatory breach of the contract and this is treated by the other party as discharging his obligations under the contract, a subsequent tender cannot be valid.

1   Sale of Goods Act 1979, s 29.
2   *Startup v Macdonald* (1843) 6 Man & G 593, Ex Ch.
3   Para 10.10, below. In such a case A is said to terminate the contract for repudiatory breach. For the full effects of such termination, see paras 10.4–10.7, below.
4   *Tetley v Shand* (1871) 25 LT 658.

Time for Performance

9.17   When a contract does not stipulate a time within which a party's contractual obligations must be performed, they must be performed within a reasonable time[1].

1   *Postlethwaite v Freeland* (1880) 5 App Cas 599, HL. The Sale of Goods Act 1979, s 29, gives this rule statutory effect in relation to a seller's obligation to send goods to a buyer. The Supply of Goods and Services Act 1982, s 14, has the like effect in relation to the provision of services by a supplier acting in the course of a business; see para 8.37, above.

9.18   Whether a time is stipulated for performance of a party's obligations by the contract or whether it is implied that they must be performed within a reasonable time, the question arises whether time is 'of the essence of the contract'. If it is, the stipulation or implied obligation as to time will be classified as a condition[1] and a party's failure to perform in that time will not only constitute a breach of contract entitling the other party to maintain an action for damages but also a repudiatory breach of the contract, which the other party can accept as discharging him from his contractual obligations[2].

If time is not of the essence but a party delays in performing the contract, it may be possible to infer that he does not intend to carry out his obligations under it. In such a case, the other party will be entitled to accept this implied renunciation as discharging him from his contractual obligations[3].

1 This point was made by the majority of the Court of Appeal in *Bunge Corpn v Tradax SA* [1981] 2 All ER 513 at 523, 536 and 539 and is implicit in the leading speeches of the House of Lords in that case: [1981] 2 All ER 513, [1981] 1 WLR 711. With regard to conditions, see para 10.17, below.
2 See, in particular, *Bunge Corpn v Tradax SA* [1981] 2 All ER 513, [1981] 1 WLR 711, HL. See also paras 10.3–10.8, below.
3 *Graham v Pitkin* [1992] 2 All ER 235, [1992] 1 WLR 403, PC. See para 10.10, below.

9.19 Whether time is of the essence of a contract, other than a contract which is specifically enforceable (see para 9.20, below), depends on the parties' intentions when the contract is made. If they are not expressed in the contract, they must be inferred from the nature of the subject matter of the contract and of the obligation which has not been performed in time. In this context certain presumptions have been established. For instance, a stipulation as to time in a commercial contract is presumptively of the essence of the contract[1]. However, s 10(1) of the Sale of Goods Act 1979 provides that a term as to the time of *payment* for goods is deemed not to be of the essence of the contract, unless the contrary intention appears from the contract.

1 *Bunge Corpn v Tradax SA* [1981] 2 All ER 513, [1981] 1 WLR 711, HL; *Cie Commerciale Sucres et Denrées v C Czarnikow Ltd, The Naxos* [1990] 3 All ER 641, [1990] 1 WLR 1337, HL. See further para 10.18, below.

9.20 Before the Judicature Act 1873, common law and equity had different rules about when the time for completion was of the essence in a contract which was specifically enforceable[1], such as a contract for the sale of an interest in land or for the sale of a unique chattel or shares, but since that Act the equitable rules prevail[2]. The result is that time is not of the essence in such a contract unless it falls within one of the following three categories where equity treated it as of the essence:

a. Where the contract expressly states that obligations as to time must be strictly complied with. In *Harold Wood Brick Co Ltd v Ferris*[3], for instance, a stipulation that the purchase of a brickfield should be completed by 31 August which added that 'the purchase shall in any event be completed not later than 15 September' was held to make time (15 September) of the essence of the contract.
b. Where the contract does not expressly make time of the essence of the contract, but the stipulated or impliedly required time has passed by, the party who has been subjected to delay can make time of the essence by invoking a period of notice for performance if one is specified in the contract or, if one is not specified, by giving a notice fixing a reasonable time for performance[4].
c. Where the subject matter of the contract, or the circumstances surrounding it, makes punctual compliance with an obligation as to time imperative, time must be taken to be of the essence of the contract. For example, under this heading time has been held to be of the essence of a contract for the sale of business premises as a going concern[5].

Even if time is not of the essence of a contract for the sale of an interest in land or of some other specifically enforceable contract, a party who fails to complete within the required time is, of course, in breach of that term and liable in damages, provided that the failure was not due to some conveyancing difficulty or some difficulty with regard to title[6]. Inability to raise the necessary finance is no defence[6].

1 Paras 12.27–12.29, below.
2 Law of Property Act 1925, s 41.
3 [1935] 2 KB 198, CA.
4 *Stickney v Keeble* [1915] AC 386, HL; *Behzadi v Shaftesbury Hotels Ltd* [1992] Ch 1, [1991] 2 All ER 477, CA.
5 *Lock v Bell* [1931] 1 Ch 35. See also *Harold Wood Brick Co Ltd v Ferris* [1935] 2 KB 198, CA.
6 *Raineri v Miles* [1981] AC 1050, [1980] 2 All ER 145, HL.

Chapter 10

Breach

10.1 Breach of contract occurs where a party does not perform one or more of his contractual obligations precisely, in the sense discussed in para 9.2, above, and this failure is without lawful excuse. Thus, a breach will occur where a party without lawful excuse refuses to perform one or more of his contractual obligations, or simply fails to perform them, or incapacitates himself from performing them, or performs them defectively. Consequently, to decide whether a party is in breach of contract, one must first ascertain and construe the terms of the contract, express and implied, to see what his contractual obligations were, and then look at what has happened to see whether he has failed without lawful excuse to perform one or more of them precisely.

A person has a lawful excuse for failing to perform his contractual obligations precisely in the following cases:

a. If the contract has been discharged by frustration, a matter which we discuss in the next chapter;
b. If there is impossibility of performance less than frustration; for instance, a temporary illness preventing an employee working provides a lawful excuse for his failure to work during the period of the illness[1];
c. If he has validly tendered performance of his obligations in accordance with the rules set out in paras 9.13–9.16, above, but this has been rejected by the other party;
d. If the other party has made it impossible for him to perform his obligations.

1 *Poussard v Spiers and Pond* (1876) 1 QBD 410.

10.2 Subject to a valid exemption clause to the contrary, whenever a party to the contract is in breach of contract he is liable to pay compensation (ie damages) to the other party (the 'injured party') for the loss sustained by him in consequence of that breach, but, unless the breach can be classified as a repudiatory breach and the injured party elects to terminate the contract, the contractual obligations of the parties so far as they have not been fully performed remain unchanged. The injured party may claim damages for breach either by

175

an action of his own or by way of a counterclaim in an action brought against him by the defaulting party, and even where no actual loss or damage to the injured party can be proved nominal damages (usually in the region of £2 to £20) will be awarded. Quite apart from damages, the injured party may be entitled, additionally or alternatively, to claim an order of specific performance of the contract or an injunction or to recover an agreed sum. We consider the question of remedies in chapter 12.

In the case of certain serious breaches of contract, which are commonly described as repudiatory breaches, the injured party can elect to treat the contract as repudiated by the other, accept the repudiation, and recover damages for breach, both parties being discharged from performance of their primary obligations under the contract which would have been due thereafter. If the injured party does this, he is said to terminate (or rescind[1]) the contract for repudiatory breach.

1   Termination for repudiatory breach should not be confused with rescission for misrepresentation (discussed in Chap 14), the effects of which (and the rules concerning which) are different.

Repudiatory Breach

Option to terminate or affirm

10.3   A repudiatory breach does not automatically discharge the contract. Instead, the injured party has an option to terminate the contract or to affirm it[1]. We shall see in paras 10.19 and 10.20 that in one type of case an injured party can lose the option to terminate, even though he has not affirmed the contract.

1   *Heyman v Darwins Ltd* [1942] AC 356, [1942] 1 All ER 337 at 340; *Johnson v Agnew* [1980] AC 367 at 397, [1979] 1 All ER 883 at 889; *Fercometal SARL v Mediterranean Shipping Co SA* [1989] AC 788, [1988] 2 All ER 742, HL; *Vitol SA v Norelf Ltd* [1996] AC 800, [1996] 3 All ER 193, HL. Despite an earlier conflict of authorities, it is now settled that this option applies even in the case of a repudiatory breach of contract of employment: *Rigby v Ferodo Ltd* [1988] ICR 29, [1987] IRLR 516, HL.

Termination

10.4   The injured party will terminate the contract if he notifies the defaulting party that he regards himself as discharged by the repudiatory breach. No particular form of notification is required[1]. It is sufficient that by words or conduct the injured party clearly and unequivocally conveys to the repudiating party that he is treating the contract as at an end[1]. Thus, the contract will be terminated if the injured party refuses to accept defective performance, or refuses to accept further performance, or simply refuses to perform his own contractual obligations. Moreover, termination can occur even if the injured party does not notify the defaulting party that he regards himself as discharged, since termination can be inferred if the injured party simply does something incompatible with his own continued performance of the contract, or simply fails to perform his side of the contract, provided that this unequivocally points to the fact that he is treating the contract as at an end[1]. Suppose, for example, that an employer at the end of a day tells a contractor that he, the employer, is renouncing the contract and that the contractor need not return the next day. This would constitute a repudiatory breach of contract by the employer[2].The contractor does not return the next day or at all. The contractor's failure to return may, in the absence of any other explanation, convey a decision to terminate the contract[3]. The injured party need not personally, or by an agent, notify the guilty party of his election to terminate. It is sufficient that the election comes to the guilty party's attention. For example, notification by an unauthorised intermediary can suffice[3].

1   *Vitol SA v Norelf Ltd* [1996] AC 800, [1996] 3 All ER 193, HL
2   Para 10.10, below.
3   *Vitol SA v Norelf Ltd* [1996] AC 800, [1996] 3 All ER 193 at 200.

10.5   If the injured party elects to terminate the contract, he is discharged for the future from his obligations under the contract which would otherwise have been due or continuing thereafter. One result is that he is not obliged to accept or pay for further performance. Another result is that an injured party who has terminated a contract for breach can resist successfully any action for failing thereafter to observe or perform a continuing obligation or an obligation due thereafter[1]. Consequently, for example, a wrongfully dismissed employee who has indicated that he regards himself as discharged by the repudiatory breach from his employment contract is no longer bound by terms in that contract restraining his future employment[2]. On the other hand, an injured party who has terminated is not generally discharged from his obligations which are already due at the time of termination, since rights and obligations which arise from the partial execution of the contract – as well as causes of action which have accrued from its breach – continue unaffected[3]. However, an injured party who has terminated may be entitled:

a.   to refuse to pay for partial or defective performance already received by him (see paras 10.12 and 10.13, below); or
b.   to reclaim any money which he has paid to the defaulting party if there has been a total failure of consideration on the part of the latter.
     Where the injured party plaintiff has deposited or paid money in pursuance of a contract which is rendered ineffective by a total failure of consideration on the part of the defaulting party (ie the injured party has not received any part of what he bargained for under the contract)[3], and the injured party terminates the contract for breach, he can recover back under the law of restitution the money which he has paid[4].
     Thus, if P pays D £500 as a deposit on a car but D fails to supply the car, P can terminate the contract and recover back the £500 which he paid.
     If the failure of consideration is not total but only partial, the action for the recovery of money paid is not available, so that, whether the contract is terminated or not, the appropriate remedy is an action for damages for breach of contract. There will only be a total failure of consideration if the plaintiff has not got any part of what he bargained for under the contract. Thus, if P employs D to build a house for him and pays in advance, and D abandons the work before it is finished, P cannot recover any part of his payment and must claim damages for breach of contract[5]. However, if:
     a.   the partial performance is such as to entitle the plaintiff to terminate the contract, and he elects to do so, and

b.   he is able to restore what he has received under the contract, and does so before he has derived any benefit from it[6],

he will bring about a total failure of consideration and be entitled to recover back any money which he has paid[7]. A common example of this is where the buyer of defective goods rejects them immediately and claims back his payment. It must be emphasised that the test of total failure of consideration is whether or not the plaintiff has received any part of the benefit he bargained for under the contract. If he has not received any part of the performance of the actual thing promised, as determined by the contract, there is a total failure of consideration, even though he may have received some other benefit. For example, in a contract for the sale of goods or of hire purchase, there will be a total failure of consideration if the seller or bailor fails to pass a good title to the goods to the buyer or bailee, even though the buyer or bailee has derived benefit from them before being deprived of them by the true owner[8]. It follows that the buyer or bailee can recover back what he has paid for the goods. In *Rowland v Divall*[9], the plaintiff bought a car from the defendant for £334 and used it for four months. It then transpired that the car had been stolen, although the defendant had dealt with it in good faith, and the plaintiff had to surrender it to the true owner. The Court of Appeal held that the defendant was in breach of the implied condition in s 12(1) of the Sale of Goods Act 1979, viz, that the seller has the right to sell the goods[10], and that the plaintiff was entitled to recover the £334 which he had paid. Its reasoning was that the plaintiff had not received what he had contracted to receive, viz the property (ie ownership) and right to possession of the car, and therefore there was a total failure of consideration entitling him to recover back the whole purchase price without any set-off for his use of the car.

As a final point, it should be noted that, if the injured party has started to perform his contractual obligations but is unjustifiably prevented from completing them by the other party, he can bring an action for reasonable remuneration. This is called suing on a quantum meruit[11].

1   *General Billposting Co Ltd v Atkinson* [1909] AC 118, HL; *Rock Refrigeration Ltd v Jones* [1997] 1 All ER 1, CA (cf the view of Phillips LJ that a term restraining future employment could survive after a wrongfully dismissed employee has accepted the repudiatory breach as discharging him if this is what the parties intended, just like the terms referred to in para 10.7).

2   *General Billposting Co Ltd v Atkinson* [1909] AC 118, HL.

3   *McDonald v Dennys Lascelles Ltd* (1933) 48 CLR 457 at 476–477; *Damon Cia Naviera SA v Hapag-Lloyd International SA, The Blankenstein* [1985] 1 All ER 475, [1985] 1 WLR 435, CA.

4   *Wilkinson v Lloyd* (1845) 7 QB 27.

5   *Whincup v Hughes* (1871) LR 6 CP 78.

6   *Hunt v Silk* (1804) 5 East 449.

7   *Baldry v Marshall* [1925] 1 KB 260, CA.

8   *Rover International Ltd v Cannon Film Sales Ltd (No 3)* [1989] 3 All ER 423, [1989] 1 WLR 912, CA.

9   [1923] 2 KB 500, CA. See also *Warman v Southern Counties Car Finance Corpn Ltd* [1949] 2 KB 576, [1949] 1 All ER 711 (a hire purchase case).

10 See para 8.20, above.

11 Para 12.26, below.

10.6   After termination by the injured party, the defaulting party's position is as follows:

a.   He is not discharged from his contractual obligations which are due at the time of the termination and have not been performed (so that, for instance, he is still obliged to pay a sum of money then due[1]); and he is also liable to pay damages to the injured party for loss sustained by him in consequence of the breach of any such obligation[2].

b.   His obligations under the contract, so far as they are due or continuing after the termination, are discharged and there is substituted for them an obligation to pay damages to the injured party for the loss sustained by him in consequence of their non-performance in the future[2].

1   *McDonald v Dennys Lascelles Ltd* (1933) 48 CLR 457 at 476–477; *Hyundai Heavy Industries Co Ltd v Papadopoulos* [1980] 2 All ER 29, [1980] 1 WLR 1129, HL.
2   *R V Ward Ltd v Bignall* [1967] 1 QB 534, [1967] 2 All ER 449, CA; *Moschi v Lep Air Services Ltd* [1973] AC 331, [1972] 2 All ER 393, HL; *Photo Production Ltd v Securicor Transport Ltd* [1980] AC 827, [1980] 1 All ER 556, HL.

10.7   Termination for repudiatory breach does not necessarily extinguish the contract completely in relation to obligations whose performance is due after the time of the election to terminate, since obligations relating to matters such as arbitration or jurisdiction may continue in existence if it was the intention of the parties, when they made the contract, that this should be so[1]. In addition, terms which validly 'liquidate' damages or which validly exclude or restrict liability remain in force[2].

1   *Heyman v Darwins Ltd* [1942] AC 356, [1942] 1 All ER 337, HL; *Photo Production Ltd v Securicor Transport Ltd* [1980] 1 All ER 556 at 567.
2   *Photo Production Ltd v Securicor Transport Ltd* [1980] AC 827, [1980] 1 All ER 556, HL; *Port Jackson Stevedoring Pty Ltd v Salmond & Spraggon (Australia) Pty Ltd, The New York Star* [1980] 3 All ER 257, [1981] 1 WLR 138, PC. For liquidated damages provisions, see para 12.18, below, and for exemption clauses, see paras 10.25–10.56, below. The proposition in the text has been given statutory force in relation to exemption clauses which must satisfy the requirement of reasonableness under the Unfair Contract Terms Act 1977 (see paras 10.43–10.53, below) by s 9 of that Act.

Affirmation
10.8   The injured party will affirm the contract if, with full knowledge of the facts and of his right to terminate the contract[1], he decides to treat it as still in existence, as where he decides to keep the defective goods delivered or, if the defaulting party has not completed performance, where he calls on him to perform. The injured party does not affirm a contract simply because he does not immediately terminate the contract but delays while he considers whether or not to terminate it[2].

If the injured party elects to affirm, the contract remains in force, so that both parties are bound to continue performing any outstanding contractual obligations. Each party retains the right to sue for past or future breaches. Thus, if a seller of goods affirms the contract after a repudiatory breach by the buyer, the seller remains liable to deliver possession of the goods to the buyer and the buyer remains liable to accept delivery of the goods and pay the contract price³. Another example is provided by *Bentsen v Taylor, Sons & Co (No 2)*⁴, where a charterparty described the ship as 'now sailed or about to sail' from a port to the United Kingdom. In fact, she did not sail for another month. This constituted a repudiatory breach of contract by the shipowner⁵ but, instead of electing to terminate the contract, the charterers intimated to the shipowner that he was still bound to send the ship to the port of loading and that they, the charterers, would load her there, thereby affirming the contract. When the ship arrived, the charterers refused to load her. The Court of Appeal held that, since the contract had been affirmed, the shipowner was entitled to payment of freight, subject to a set-off for the charterers for damages for the breach of contract by the ship owner referred to above.

1   *Peyman v Lanjani* [1985] Ch 457, [1984] 3 All ER 703, CA.
2   *Bliss v South East Thames Regional Health Authority* [1987] ICR 700, [1985] IRLR 308, CA.
3   *R V Ward Ltd v Bignall* [1967] 1 QB 534, [1967] 2 All ER 449, CA.
4   [1893] 2 QB 274, CA.
5   Because the term broken was a condition, see paras 10.16–10.18, below.

Is an election irrevocable?

10.9   If the injured party elects to terminate a contract for repudiatory breach he cannot thereafter affirm it, by seeking specific performance or otherwise calling on the other party to perform, since both parties are discharged from further performance by the termination¹.

An election is also irrevocable where the injured party elects unconditionally to affirm the contract, as where he elects to keep defective goods: in such a case he cannot subsequently elect to terminate for repudiatory breach. However, if his affirmation is conditional on the other party rectifying his breach, and this is not done, the injured party can change his mind and proceed to terminate the contract and claim damages for repudiatory breach. Where the injured party obtains an order of specific performance of the contract his affirmation of the contract is conditional, and, if the order becomes impossible of performance or is otherwise not complied with, he can elect to ask the court to terminate the contract and (if the court accedes) recover damages for repudiatory breach².

1   See, eg, *Johnson v Agnew* [1980] AC 367 at 393, [1979] 1 All ER 883 at 889.
2   *Austins of East Ham Ltd v Macey* [1941] Ch 338, CA; *Johnson v Agnew* [1980] AC 367, [1979] 1 All ER 883, HL.

Types of repudiatory breach

Renunciation

10.10   Where one party renounces his contractual obligations the other party is entitled to terminate the contract. A party is said to renounce his contractual obligations if he has evinced an unconditional intention not to perform them or otherwise no longer to be bound by the contract or one of its essential terms¹. Such an intention is easily established where there has been an express and unequivocal refusal to perform. Thus, if an employee unqualifiedly refuses to carry out his contractual duties (or to carry out a duty which is an essential contractual term) his employer is entitled to dismiss him (ie terminate the contract of employment)[2]. However, express refusal is not necessary; an intent no longer to be bound by the contract (or one of its essential terms) can also be implied by the words or conduct of a party. The actual intention of the party is not the crucial issue in such a case; the test is whether his words and conduct were such as to lead a reasonable person to believe that he did not intend to be bound by the contract[3].

1   *Mersey Steel and Iron Co v Naylor Benzon & Co* (1884) 9 App Cas 434, HL; *Woodar Investment Development Ltd v Wimpey Construction UK Ltd* [1980] 1 All ER 571, [1980] 1 WLR 277, HL.
2   *Gorse v Durham County Council* [1971] 2 All ER 666, [1971] 1 WLR 775.
3   *Woodar Investment Development Ltd v Wimpey Construction UK Ltd* [1980] 1 All ER 571, [1980] 1 WLR 277, HL; *André et Cie SA v Marine Transocean Ltd* [1981] QB 694, [1981] 2 All ER 993, CA.

Incapacitation
10.11   Even though he has not evinced an intention not to be bound by the contract, a party who, *by his own act or default*, incapacitates himself from performing his contractual obligations is treated as if he had refused to perform them[1]. As Devlin J said in *Universal Cargo Carriers Corpn v Citati*[2], 'To say "I would like to but cannot" negatives intent to perform as much as "I will not".' Where a party has incapacitated himself from performing, it is no defence to show that he might be able to recover the capacity to perform[3]. One example of a case where a party has made performance of his obligations impossible is where A has contracted to sell a specific thing to B but then sells it to C[4].

1   *Torvald Klaveness A/S v Arni Maritime Corpn, The Gregos* [1994] 4 All ER 998, [1994] 1 WLR 1465, HL.
2   [1957] 2 QB 401 at 437, [1957] 2 All ER 70 at 85.
3   *Omnium D'Enterprises v Sutherland* [1919] 1 KB 618, CA.
4   But see *Jones v Lipman* [1962] 1 All ER 442, [1962] 1 WLR 832; para 25.10, below.

Failure to perform an entire obligation
10.12   An entire obligation is one whose complete and precise performance is a condition precedent[1] (ie a precondition) of the performance by the other party of his obligations. A particular obligation may be entire:

a.   *By statute* For instance, in contracts for the sale of goods the obligation to deliver the *quantity* specified in the contract is entire[2].
b.   *By express agreement between the parties.*
c.   *By implication* This occurs where, on the true construction of the contract, the parties intended that complete and precise performance by a party of a particular obligation should be a precondition of performance by the other party of his obligations. The cases show that, if B is to pay a lump sum for A's work *after* it has been completed, A's obligation to do the work is impliedly entire[3]. Because of the harsh consequences of finding an obligation to be entire, the courts lean against construing a contract so as to require complete performance of an obligation before the other party's obligations become operative[4]. Thus, if a lump sum is payable for work,

but the contract does not say when it is payable, the court is likely to construe the obligation as not being entire but severable[5].

If a party does not completely and precisely perform an entire obligation in breach of contract, the injured party can terminate the contract and the defaulting party cannot claim any performance by him. This is exemplified by *Sumpter v Hedges*[6], where the plaintiff agreed to build two houses and a stable on the defendant's land for a lump sum of £565. The plaintiff did part of the work to the value of about £333 and then abandoned the contract because of lack of money. It was held that the plaintiff's obligation to build the two houses and a stable was entire and, having failed to do so, he could not recover the contract price nor reasonable remuneration for the work done.

1   The present type of 'condition precedent' must be distinguished from that discussed in para 5.29, above, which arises where the parties make an agreement subject to some contingent future event on the basis that no immediate binding contract shall exist until the contingency occurs. The present type of 'condition precedent' does not negative the immediate existence of a binding contract but suspends the liability of one party to perform his obligations until the other party has performed something which he has promised (and is therefore obliged) to do.
2   Sale of Goods Act 1979, s 30. This rule does not apply where the contract provides for delivery by instalments: *Regent OHG Aisenstadt und Barig v Francesco of Jermyn Street Ltd* [1981] 3 All ER 327 (see para 10.15, below). Moreover, where there is a delivery of a quantity, other than that specified in the contract, and the buyer does not deal as consumer, the buyer may not reject the goods (ie terminate the contract) if the shortfall or, as the case may be, excess is so slight that it would be unreasonable for him to do so: Sale of Goods Act 1979, s30(2A). It is for the seller to show that a shortfall or excess falls within s30(2A): ibid, s30(2B).
3   Eg *H Dakin & Co Ltd v Lee* [1916] 1 KB 566, CA; *St Enoch Shipping Co Ltd v Phosphate Mining Co* [1916] 2 KB 624.
4   *Roberts v Havelock* (1832) 3 B & Ad 404.
5   Ibid. Severable obligations are discussed in para 10.15, below.
6   [1898] 1 QB 673, CA.

10.13   By way of exception, a party who has not completely and precisely performed an entire obligation in breach of contract can recover in respect of any partial performance if the other party has accepted such partial performance *voluntarily*. Such acceptance gives rise to an inference that there is a fresh agreement by the parties that payment of a reasonable sum or pro rata be made for the work already done or the goods supplied under the original contract[1].

Since the right of recovery depends on the inference of a fresh agreement, it is essential that the party from whom payment is demanded has not just received a benefit but has voluntarily accepted it. He must have had an opportunity, at the time when it became clear that there would not be complete performance of the entire obligation, to accept or reject the partial or defective performance. Thus, in *Sumpter v Hedges*[2], it was held that the builder could not recover reasonable remuneration for the work done because the defendant had no option but to accept the partial performance, viz the partly erected buildings.

1   *Christy v Row* (1808) 1 Taunt 300; *Sumpter v Hedges* [1898] 1 QB 673 at 674; Sale of Goods Act 1979, s. 30.
2   [1898] 1 QB 673, CA.

10.14   *It is important to retain a sense of proportion about entire obligations because they are the exception rather than the rule, as we now propose to demonstrate.*   Although a contract containing an entire obligation is known as an entire contract, this is usually something of a misnomer because a contract usually comprises a complex of obligations and, even though one of a party's obligations is entire, the rest may not be. Thus, if A agrees to build a house for B for a lump sum payable on completion, his obligation to build the house is impliedly entire, but his other obligations as to time of performance, quality of work etc are not entire, unless, very exceptionally, the contract expressly provides that precise performance of them is a precondition of payment[1]. Similarly, if C agrees to sell goods to D, his obligation to deliver the correct quantity is entire by statute, but his obligations as to the quality of the goods and so on are not normally entire. It follows that, if A builds the house but does so defectively or if C delivers the goods but they are defective, B and D are not entitled to terminate the contract for breach of an entire obligation, no such obligation having been broken; nor, unless the obligation broken is sufficiently important or the effects of its breach sufficiently serious, can they terminate under the ground which we discuss next (paras 10.16–10.22, below). If the contract cannot be terminated, A and C are entitled to their contractual payment, subject to a set-off or counterclaim in favour of B and D. In *H Dakin & Co Ltd v Lee*[2], for example, the plaintiff builders agreed to repair the defendant's house for £264, payable on completion, in accordance with a specification. They did the repairs but these were defective in three ways: a. only two feet of concrete had been put in in underpinning a wall, whereas four feet had been specified; b. four-inch iron columns had been fitted in a bay window, instead of five-inch ones; c. certain joists in the bay window had not been bolted together in the manner specified. These defects were relatively unimportant. The Court of Appeal held that the plaintiff builders were entitled to recover the £264, less a reduction in respect of the defective work.

1   *Eshelby v Federated European Bank Ltd* [1932] 1 KB 423, CA.
2   [1916] 1 KB 566, CA. Also see *Hoenig v Isaacs* [1952] 2 All ER 176, CA. Cf *Bolton v Mahadeva* [1972] 2 All ER 1322, [1972] 1 WLR 1009, CA.

10.15   *Severable obligations*   It would be wrong to think that an obligation to build or do some other thing is always an entire obligation. It is only so if the parties expressly or impliedly agree to the effect that, or statute provides that, complete performance of the obligation is a precondition of the other party's obligations becoming operative. Otherwise an obligation to do something is known as a 'severable' obligation, and the contract containing it as a severable contract. A clear example of a severable obligation is provided by a contract for sale and delivery by instalments; the seller's obligation in respect of each instalment is severable[1]. Moreover, if payment is required at a fixed rate per item the seller's obligation is severable, even though the contract does not refer to instalments and even though payment is not due until after performance has been completed.

Partial or defective performance of a severable obligation gives the injured party a right of action in damages but it does not entitle him to terminate the contract unless it amounts to a renunciation or falls within one of the grounds of termination which we discuss next. The defaulting party is entitled to recover payment at the stipulated rate for each item or instalment which he has provided, subject to a set-off or counterclaim for damages for breach[2].

1   *Regent OHG Aisenstadt und Barig v Francesco of Jermyn Street Ltd* [1981] 3 All ER 327.
2   *Jackson v Rotax Motor and Cycle Co* [1910] 2 KB 937, CA.

Failure to fulfil an obligation which is not an entire obligation
10.16   Failure to fulfil an obligation which is not an entire obligation is the most common type of breach of contract. Unless the party in default has a lawful excuse the injured party can, of course, recover damages for breach of contract but, leaving aside termination for renunciation[1] or incapacitation[2], he can only terminate for failure to perform an obligation which is not an entire obligation in two cases:

a.   where it involves breach of a term of the contract which is a condition;
b.   where it involves breach of an 'intermediate term' and the effect of the breach deprives the injured party of substantially the whole of his intended benefit under the contract.

1   Para 10.10, above.
2   Para 10.11, above.

10.17   *Breach of condition*   Some contractual terms can be classified as conditions, others as intermediate terms, and others as warranties. A condition is an *essential* term of the contract[1], or, as it is sometimes put, one which goes to the root of the contract. If it is broken, the injured party may[2] terminate the contract for breach of condition, as well as claiming damages, whether the effect of the breach is serious or trivial. In this context the word 'condition' is used in yet another sense. It does not bear its orthodox meaning, discussed in paras 5.29, 5.30 and 10.12, above, of an event by which an obligation is suspended or cancelled but is used to describe a particular type of contractual term. It is certainly an odd word to use for this purpose.

An intermediate term is one whose breach may entitle the injured party to terminate the contract, depending on how serious the effect of the breach is. We explain this further in para 10.21, below.

A warranty is a contractual term concerning a less important or subsidiary statement of fact or promise[3]. If a warranty is broken this does not entitle the other party to terminate the contract. It simply entitles him to sue for damages or make a set-off and the party in breach is entitled to the contractual price less the damages or set-off[4].

In the case of sales of goods, the distinctions between a condition and a warranty have been given statutory effect, the relevant statute now being the Sale of Goods Act 1979[5].

1   *Heyworth v Hutchinson* (1867) LR 2 QB 447 at 451.
2   Unless the failure in performance is microscopic; para 9.2, above.
3   *Oscar Chess Ltd v Williams* [1957] 1 All ER 325 at 328, [1957] 1 WLR 370 at 374; Sale of Goods Act 1979, s 11(3).

4   *Gilbert Ash (Northern) Ltd v Modern Engineering (Bristol) Ltd* [1974] AC 689, [1973] 3 All
    ER 195, HL; Sale of Goods Act 1979, s 53(1).
5   Sections 11(3) and 61(1).

10.18   The classification of a term as a condition depends on the following
considerations:

a.   Sometimes statute provides that particular terms are conditions or
     warranties, eg the implied conditions in sale of goods contracts, hire
     purchase contracts, contracts analogous to contracts for the sale of goods
     and hire contracts under ss 12 to 15 of the Sale of Goods Act 1979, ss 8 to
     11 of the Supply of Goods (Implied Terms) Act 1973 and ss 7 to 10 of the
     Supply of Goods and Services Act 1982, respectively[1].
b.   In other cases, a term which has been classified as a condition in judicial
     decisions will be so classified thereafter[2], subject to the rules of precedent.
c.   In the absence of classification by statute or case authority, a court has to
     decide whether the broken term is a condition by ascertaining the intention
     of the parties *as at the time the contract was made*[3]. The parties' intentions
     are particularly important and it is open to them to agree that what is a
     condition according to a previous judicial decision shall not be so treated
     in their contract, and vice versa. Because of the drastic consequences, the
     courts lean against construing a term as a condition: in fact, they are
     increasingly reluctant so to construe a term unless compelled by clear
     evidence of the parties' intentions[4].
     The approach of the courts is as follows:
     First, the court must seek to ascertain the intention of the parties as
     expressed in the contract. If the wording *clearly* reveals that the parties
     intended that any breach of the term should give rise to a right to terminate,
     that term will be regarded as a condition. But if the parties clearly did not
     so intend, the term will not be regarded as a condition even though it is
     described as a 'condition' in the contract. This is shown by *Schuler AG v
     Wickman Machine Tool Sales Ltd*[5]. A four-year distributorship agreement
     provided that the distributor should visit six named customers every week.
     The agreement described this provision as a 'condition'. The House of
     Lords held that the contract could not be terminated simply because of
     breach of this 'condition'. Its reasoning was that the parties could not
     have intended a mere failure to make one visit to result in a right to
     terminate. It thought that more probably 'condition' had been used simply
     to mean 'term'.
     Second, if the wording of the contract does not indicate the parties'
     intentions, the court must ascertain them by inference from the nature,
     purpose and circumstances of the contract. If, in the context of the whole
     contract, it is *clear* that the term was so important that a party would
     always want to terminate if it was broken it will be regarded as a condition.
     An example is *Behn v Burness*[6], where one term of a charterparty was that
     the ship was 'now in the port of Amsterdam': the ship was not then there.
     The statement was held to be a condition because of the commercial

importance attached to such a statement. Another example is that a stipulation as to time in a commercial contract (other than one as to the time of payment in a sale of goods contract[7]) is presumptively a condition of the contract because such a term is normally of major commercial significance[8]. On the other hand, a term in a charterparty that a ship is seaworthy has not been construed as a condition because it can be broken in a number of ways, in some of which the parties would clearly not intend that the charterer should be entitled to terminate[9].

1   Paras 8.19–8.36, above.
2   *Maredelante Cia Naviera SA v Bergbau-Handel GmbH, The Mihalis Angelos* [1971] 1 QB 164, [1970] 3 All ER 125, CA.
3   *Bunge Corpn v Tradax SA* [1981] 2 All ER 513, [1981] 1 WLR 711, HL.
4   *Cehave NV v Bremer Handelsgesellschaft mbH, The Hansa Nord* [1976] QB 44, [1975] 3 All ER 739 at 755; *Bunge Corpn v Tradax SA* [1981] 2 All ER 513 at 542 and 551, [1981] 1 WLR 711.
5   [1974] AC 235, [1973] 2 All ER 39, HL.
6   (1863) 3 B & S 751, Ex Ch.
7   The effect of the Sale of Goods Act 1979, s 10, is that a term as to the time of payment in a sale of goods contract is deemed not to be a condition, unless a contrary intention appears from the terms of the contract.
8   *Bunge Corpn v Tradax SA* [1981] 2 All ER 513, [1981] 1 WLR 711, HL; *Cie Commerciale Sucres et Dencrées v C Czarnikow Ltd, The Naxos* [1990] 3 All ER 641, [1990] 1 WLR 137, HL; para 9.19, above. The presumption is, of course, a rebuttable one. It was rebutted, for example, in *State Trading Corpn of India Ltd v M Golodetz Ltd* [1989] 2 Lloyd's Rep 277, CA, because the time limit term lacked sufficient commercial significance in that case.
9   *Hong Kong Fir Shipping Co Ltd v Kawasaki Kisen Kaisha Ltd* [1962] 2 QB 26, [1962] 1 All ER 474, CA.

10.19   In the case of a contract for the sale or supply of goods, the right to terminate for breach of condition is subject to statutory limitations.

First, s 15A of the Sale of Goods Act 1979 provides that, where in the case of a contract of sale:

a.   the buyer would otherwise have the right to reject goods (ie terminate the contract) by reason of a breach by the seller of one of the terms implied by ss 12 to 15 of the Act, but

b.   the seller proves that the breach is so slight that it would be unreasonable for him to do so,

then, if the buyer does not deal as consumer, the breach is not to be treated as a breach of condition but only as a breach of warranty (with the result that there is no right to reject the goods).

This provision does not apply if a contrary intention is expressed in, or is to be implied from, the contract.

Similar provision is made by s 11A of the Supply of Goods (Implied Terms) Act 1973 and s 5A of the Supply of Goods and Services Act 1982 in relation to hire purchase contracts and contracts analogous to contracts for the sale of goods, respectively.

10.20   Second, there is a special rule which (where it is applicable) prevents a buyer of goods terminating the contract of sale for breach of a condition of it, even though he has not affirmed it because he lacks the knowledge of the breach necessary for affirmation. This rule – which only applies to contracts for the sale of goods – is provided by s 11(4) of the Sale of Goods Act 1979. This states that, where a contract for the sale of goods is not severable and the buyer has accepted the goods or part of them, he can only treat a breach of condition as a breach of warranty, 'and not as a ground for rejecting the goods and treating the contract as repudiated', unless there is a term of the contract, express or implied, to that effect.

Section 11(4) only applies where the contract of sale is not severable, so that it is inapplicable to a contract under which goods are to be delivered by instalments, each of which is to be separately paid for, because this is a severable contract[1]. On the other hand, a contract for a lump sum price payable after the completion of delivery is not severable where the seller has an option to fulfil his obligations by one delivery or two or more[2], unless the seller exercises that option (whereupon what was an entire contract becomes a severable one).

By s 35(1) of the Sale of Goods Act 1979, a buyer is deemed to have accepted goods:

a.   *When he intimates to the seller that he has accepted them*; or
b.   *When the goods have been delivered to him and he does any act in relation to them which is inconsistent with the ownership of the seller.*

However, by s35(2), where goods are delivered to the buyer and he has not previously examined them, he is not deemed to have accepted them under s35(1) until he has had a reasonable opportunity of examining them to see whether they conform with the contract or, in the case of a contract for sale by sample, to compare the bulk with the sample.

Section 35(4) of the 1979 Act provides that a buyer is also deemed to have accepted the goods *when, after the lapse of a reasonable time, he retains the goods without intimating to the seller that he has rejected them.* In determining whether a reasonable time has elapsed, account must be taken of whether the buyer had a reasonable opportunity to examine the goods[3].

What constitutes a reasonable time varies according to the nature of the goods: 'What is a reasonable time for a bicycle would scarcely be adequate for a nuclear submarine'[4].

A buyer may be deemed to have accepted goods under this heading even though the defect has not manifested itself during the 'reasonable time' and even though he has not had a reasonable time to *discover* the defect[5].

By s35(6) of the 1979 Act, a buyer is not deemed to have accepted the goods merely because:

a.   he asks for, or agrees to, their repair by or under an arrangement with the seller, or

b.   the goods are delivered to another under a sub-sale or other disposition.

If there has been a breach of the implied condition under s 12(1) of the Sale of Goods Act 1979 that the seller has the right to sell the goods[6], the buyer who is forced to hand them over to the true owner is entitled to recover back the price he has paid, on the grounds that there has been a total failure of consideration[7], *notwithstanding that he has used the goods for some time*. Section 11(4) has no application to a breach of s 12(1) because there is not really a contract of sale at all if the seller has no right to sell the goods[8].

1   Para 10.15, above.
2   *J Rosenthal & Sons Ltd v Esmail* [1965] 2 All ER 860, [1965] 1 WLR 1117, HL.
3   Sale of Goods Act 1979, s35(5).
4   *Bernstein v Pamson Motors (Golders Green) Ltd* [1987] 2 All ER 220 at 230.
5   Ibid.
6   Para 8.20, above.
7   Para 10.5, above.
8   *Rowland v Divall* [1923] 2 KB 500, CA.

10.21   *Breach of an intermediate term*   If the term broken is not a condition, it must not be assumed that it is a warranty for which the only remedy is damages, unless statute[1] or a judicial decision[2] compels such a classification[3]. Instead, the contract must be construed and, unless the contract makes it clear (either by express provision or by necessary implication from its nature, purpose and circumstances) that the parties intended that no breach of the term should entitle the injured party to terminate the contract, the term will be classified as an intermediate (or innominate) term and not as a warranty. If it is so classified, one must then ask whether *the nature and effect of the breach which has occurred are such as to deprive the injured party of substantially the whole benefit which it was intended that he should obtain under the contract*[4]. If it is, the injured party is entitled to terminate the contract, as well as claiming damages. In applying this test, account must be taken not only of the actual consequences of the breach but also of those whose occurrence is reasonably foreseeable[5]. There is high judicial authority in a number of cases that the present doctrine, whereby termination for breach of a term depends on the effects of the breach, is preferable to making a termination dependent on whether the term itself is classified as a condition or a warranty, since it is far more likely to ensure that termination is possible when it is appropriate[6].

A leading authority for the present doctrine is *Hong Kong Fir Shipping Co Ltd v Kawasaki Kisen Kaisha Ltd*[7]. The plaintiffs chartered a ship to the defendants for 24 months. The ship was old and needed to be maintained by an adequate and competent engine room crew but the plaintiffs did not provide such a crew and thereby were in breach of a term of the charterparty to provide a ship 'in every way fitted for ordinary cargo service' (otherwise called a 'seaworthiness clause'). Because of the incompetence and inadequacy of the engine room crew and the age of the engines, the ship was held up for repairs for five weeks on her first voyage, and when she reached her destination it was found that further repairs, which would take 15 weeks, were necessary to make her seaworthy. The defendants purported to terminate the charterparty and the plaintiffs sued for breach of contract on the ground that the termination was wrongful. The defendants pleaded that the seaworthiness clause was a condition of the contract, and that therefore they could terminate the contract for breach of it. Having held that the clause was not a condition for the reason set out at the end of para 10.18, above, the Court of Appeal held that the effect of the plaintiffs' breach of the clause was not sufficiently serious to justify the defendants in terminating the charterparty. One reason which it particularly relied on was the fact that after the repairs the ship was still available for 17 of the original 24 months. The defendants' termination had therefore been wrongful.

The same decision was reached in *Cehave NV v Bremer Handelsgesellschaft mbH, The Hansa Nord*[8]. Citrus pulp pellets were sold by a German company to a Dutch company, delivery to be made in Rotterdam. The contract included a term that shipment was to be made in good condition. Some of the pellets arrived damaged. The buyers rejected the whole consignment (ie terminated the contract) and the goods were sold by the order of a Dutch court to a third person. Subsequently, they were re-sold at one-third the original contract price to the original buyers who then used the whole consignment for a purpose (cattle food) similar to that for which they had originally bought it (animal feed) – though at a lower rate of inclusion in the case of the damaged pellets. The Court of Appeal held that the 'shipment in good condition' term was not a condition of the contract because it could not have been intended that any breach of it should entitle the buyers to terminate the contract[9]. The court then turned to the present doctrine and held that the buyers were not entitled to terminate under it because, particularly in the light of the subsequent events, the effect of the breach was not sufficiently serious to justify termination. Thus, the buyers were only entitled to damages and could not treat themselves as discharged from their obligation to accept the pellets and pay the contract price.

1   Eg the warranties implied into contracts of sale of goods, hire purchase and analogous contracts by statute, see paras 8.19–8.36, above.
2   An example of a judicial decision which compels the classification of a term as a warranty is *Hain SS Co Ltd v Tate and Lyle Ltd* [1936] 2 All ER 597, HL, in which it was held that the implied undertaking by a shipper of goods that they are not dangerous is a warranty of the contract of carriage between the shipper and the shipowner.
3   *Hong Kong Fir Shipping Co Ltd v Kawasaki Kisen Kaisha Ltd* [1962] 2 QB 26 at 63–64, [1962] 1 All ER 474; *Reardon Smith Line Ltd v Hansen-Tangen* [1976] 3 All ER 570 at 573–575, [1976] 1 WLR 989.
4   *Hong Kong Fir Shipping Co Ltd v Kawasaki Kisen Kaisha Ltd* [1962] 2 QB 26 at 70, [1962] 1 All ER 474.
5   Ibid, at 64.
6   Eg *Reardon Smith Line Ltd v Hansen-Tangen* [1976] 3 All ER 570 at 577, [1976] 1 WLR 989.
7   [1962] 2 QB 26, [1962] 1 All ER 474, CA.
8   [1976] QB 44, [1975] 3 All ER 739, CA.
9   The court also held that there was no breach of the implied condition of satisfactory quality under the Sale of Goods Act 1979, s 14(2); see para 8.24, above.

10.22   These two cases can be contrasted with *Aerial Advertising Co v Batchelors Peas Ltd (Manchester)*[1]. The plaintiffs agreed to conduct an aerial advertising campaign for the defendants. One term of the contract was that the pilot of the aeroplane should telephone the defendants each day and obtain their approval for what he proposed to do. On Armistice Day 1937, the pilot, in breach of this term, failed to contact the defendants and flew over Salford during the two minutes' silence. The aeroplane was towing a banner saying 'Eat Batchelors Peas'. Of course, the term broken was not a condition since breach of it might well only have had trivial consequences, so that the parties could not have intended that its breach should always entitle the defendants to terminate the contract. However, the effect of the particular breach was disastrous since it aroused public hostility towards the defendants and their products. It was held that the defendants were entitled to terminate the contract.

1   [1938] 2 All ER 788.

Anticipatory breach

10.23   So far we have been concerned with actual breaches of contract, ie breaches of contractual obligations whose performance is due at the time of the breach. An anticipatory breach of contract occurs where a party renounces[1] his contractual obligations, or incapacitates himself[2] from performing them, *before the time fixed for their performance*. If a party commits such an anticipatory breach, the injured party can accept the breach as discharging the contract (ie terminate it) and immediately bring an action for damages for breach of contract or a quantum meruit action: he does not have to wait for the time of performance to become due. A leading authority is *Hochster v De La Tour*[3]. The defendant agreed to employ the plaintiff as a courier from 1 June 1852. On 11 May, the defendant informed the plaintiff that his services would no longer be required. The plaintiff brought an action for damages before 1 June and succeeded.

If the injured party validly terminates the contract for anticipatory breach, the other party is not permitted to change his mind and seek to perform his contractual obligations[4], but he may do so at any time before there is a valid termination by the injured party[5].

1   Para 10.10, above.
2   Para 10.11, above.
3   (1853) 2 E & B 678.
4   *Xenos v Danube and Black Sea Rly Co* (1863) 13 CBNS 825.
5   *Norwest Holst Group Administration Ltd v Harrison* [1985] ICR 668, [1985] IRLR 240, CA.

10.24   As in the other situations where a party can terminate a contract for the other's failure to perform, a contract is never automatically discharged by anticipatory breach; instead, the injured party has an election to terminate or affirm the contract. If he refuses to accept the anticipatory breach as discharging the contract and continues to insist on performance, he will affirm it. When a contract is affirmed after anticipatory breach the effects are as follows:

a.   The injured party loses his right to bring an action for damages for anticipatory breach.

b.   The contract remains in force. Each party remains liable to perform his obligations when they become due and will be liable if he fails to perform them then. Thus, the party who committed the anticipatory breach is given an opportunity to perform his obligations, and only if he fails to do so will he be liable. The contract remains in existence at the risk of both parties; consequently, if the party who has affirmed after anticipatory breach subsequently commits a breach of contract he will be liable[1], and either party can take advantage of any supervening circumstance which would justify him in declining to perform[2].

c. As opposed to the case where the injured party immediately sues for damages for anticipatory breach, a party who affirms is under no duty to mitigate his loss before performance is due[3] with the result that he may recover larger damages in the event of ultimate non-performance by the other. This is an important exception to the rules about mitigation of loss, which we discuss in paras 12.15 and 12.16, below.

1 *Fercometal SARL v MSC Mediterranean Shipping Co SA, The Simona* [1989] AC 788, [1988] 2 All ER 742, HL.
2 *Avery v Bowden* (1855) 5 E & B 714.
3 *Tredegar Iron and Coal Co Ltd v Hawthorn Bros & Co* (1902) 18 TLR 716, CA.

Exemption Clauses

10.25   A contract may contain an exemption clause. An exemption clause may purport to exclude or modify the obligations of a party which would normally be implied by law from the legal nature of the contract. Alternatively, it may purport to exclude or restrict one of the parties' liability for breach of contract, or some other liability, such as for misrepresentation or for the tort of negligence, or both.

Because exemption clauses could operate very unfairly in the case of standard form contracts, where one party has no real option but to accept the terms offered by the other, a number of restrictive rules have been applied to exemption clauses by the courts and, more important, statutory limitations on the validity of many exemption clauses have been introduced.

10.26   Before a defendant can rely on an exemption clause in his favour he must show that it is a term of the contract and that, as a matter of construction, it covers the damage in question. We will look at these matters, as well as certain general limitations on the application of exemption clauses, before turning to the crucial question of their validity.

Term of the contract

10.27   As in the case of any purported contractual term, the determination of whether what purports to be an exemption clause is a term of the contract depends very much on whether or not the clause is contained in a signed contractual document. If it is, it is a contractual term, binding on a party who signed the document, even though he was unaware of it (eg because he had not read it)[1].

1 *L'Estrange v F Graucob Ltd* [1934] 2 KB 394, DC. For an exception, see para 10.36, below.

10.28   In other cases, eg where the clause is printed on a ticket or an order form or a notice, the clause will only be a contractual term if reasonable notice of it is given. If reasonable notice of it is given, it is irrelevant that the party affected by the term is unaware of it. The following rules apply in this connection.

Notice must be given before or at the time of the contract
10.29   The exemption clause is ineffective unless it was brought to the party's notice before or at the time the contract was made. This is shown by *Olley v Marlborough Court Ltd*[1]. The plaintiff and her husband were accepted as guests at a hotel. They paid for a week in advance and went to their room, on the wall of which was a notice exempting the hotel proprietors from liability for the loss or theft of property. Due to the negligence of the hotel staff, property was stolen from the plaintiff's room. The Court of Appeal held that the hotel was not protected by the exemption clause because the contract had been made before the exemption clause was communicated so that it formed no part of the contract.

There are two exceptions to the present rule. The first is that, if there has been a course of dealings between the parties on the basis of documents incorporating similar terms exempting liability, then, provided those dealings have been of a consistent nature[2], the court may imply the exemption clause into a particular contract where express notice is given too late. In *J Spurling Ltd v Bradshaw*[3], the defendant had dealt with the plaintiff warehousemen for many years. He delivered barrels of orange juice to them for storage. Later, he received a document from them which acknowledged receipt and referred to clauses on its back, one of which excluded the plaintiffs from any liability for loss or damage occasioned by their negligence. Subsequently, the defendant refused to pay the storage charges because the barrels were empty on collection. He was sued for these charges and counter-claimed for negligence. The Court of Appeal held that the exemption clause was incorporated into the contract, and the defendant was therefore bound by it, because in previous dealings he had received a document containing the clause, although he had never read it. Since incorporation of an exemption clause in this way depends on a previous consistent course of dealings between the parties it is less likely to occur in the case of contracts to which a private individual is a party, because normally he will have had insufficient dealings with the other party to constitute a course of dealings; three or four dealings over a five-year period, for instance, have been held insufficient to constitute a course of dealings[4].

The second exception to the rule that an exemption clause is ineffective unless brought to the notice of the party affected before or at the time the contract was made is as follows. An exemption clause may be implied into a contract if both parties are in a particular trade and the clause is used so frequently in dealings in that trade that the party affected must (as a reasonable person in that trade) have known that it would be included in the contract[5].

1   [1949] 1 KB 532, [1949] 1 All ER 127, CA.
2   *McCutcheon v David MacBrayne Ltd* [1964] 1 All ER 430, [1964] 1 WLR 125, HL.
3   [1956] 2 All ER 121, [1956] 1 WLR 461, CA.
4   *Hollier v Rambler Motors (AMC) Ltd* [1972] 2 QB 71, [1972] 1 All ER 399, CA.
5   *British Crane Hire Corpn Ltd v Ipswich Plant Hire Ltd* [1975] QB 303, [1974] 1 All ER 1059, CA.

The notice must be contained in a contractual document
10.30   An exemption clause is ineffective if it, or notice of it, is contained in a document which a reasonable person would not assume to contain contractual terms. Thus, in *Chapelton v Barry UDC*[1], it was held that an exemption clause contained in a ticket for a deck chair on a beach was ineffective because no reasonable person would expect the ticket to be more than a receipt whose object was to enable a hirer to show that he had paid: he would not assume it contained contractual terms. The same decision was reached concerning a cheque book cover in *Burnett v Westminster Bank Ltd*[2].

1 [1940] 1 KB 532, [1940] 1 All ER 356, CA.
2 [1966] 1 QB 742, [1965] 3 All ER 81.

Reasonable notice of the exemption clause must be given
10.31   A leading authority is *Parker v South Eastern Rly Co*[1]. The plaintiff left his bag at a station cloakroom. He received a ticket which said on its face: 'See back'. On the back were a number of terms, one of which limited the railway company's liability to £10 per package. The plaintiff's bag was lost and he claimed its value of £24.10s (£24.50). It was held that the plaintiff would be bound by the exemption clause, even though he had not read it, if the railway company had given reasonable notice of its terms. Notice can be reasonable even though it involves reference to other documents or to a notice[2]. The test laid down in *Parker v South Eastern Rly Co* is objective and, if reasonable notice has been given, it is irrelevant that the party affected by the exemption clause was blind or illiterate or otherwise unable to comprehend its meaning[3].

What amounts to reasonable notice depends in part on the nature of the exemption clause. If it is particularly onerous or unusual and would not generally be known to the other party, more will be required (eg that the clause be printed in different type or colour from the other terms)[4] than would be required in a clause of a less onerous or unusual type.

1 (1877) 2 CPD 416, CA.
2 *Watkins v Rymill* (1883) 10 QBD 178; *Thompson v London, Midland and Scottish Rly Co* [1930] 1 KB 41, CA.
3 *Thompson v London, Midland and Scottish Rly Co* [1930] 1 KB 41, CA.
4 *Thornton v Shoe Lane Parking Ltd* [1971] 2 QB 163, [1971] 1 All ER 686, CA; *Interfoto Picture Library Ltd v Stiletto Visual Programmes Ltd* [1989] QB 433, [1988] 1 All ER 348, CA.

Interpretation
10.32   If an exemption clause is a term of the contract the next question is whether it applies to the loss or damage in question.

It must be emphasised that there is no rule of law that an exemption clause is eliminated, or deprived of effect, regardless of its terms by a breach of contract, however fundamental that breach may be. The question whether, and to what extent, an exemption clause applies in the event of any breach of contract is answered by interpreting the contract to see whether the parties intended that the clause should apply to the loss or damage which has occurred in the circumstances in which it has occurred. This was stated by the House of Lords in *Photo Production Ltd v Securicor Transport Ltd*[1].

In the *Photo Production* case, the plaintiff company employed the defendant company to check against burglaries and fires at their factory at night. One night, the defendant's patrolman deliberately started a fire in the factory. It got out of control and a large part of the premises was burnt down. The loss and damage suffered amounted to £615,000. By way of defence to the plaintiff's action to recover this amount as damages, the defendant relied principally on an exemption clause in its contract with the plaintiff, which purported to exempt the defendant from liability for any injurious act by an employee unless it could have been foreseen and avoided by due diligence on its part. The clause added that the defendant was not to be liable for any loss suffered by the plaintiff through fire, except in so far as such loss was solely attributable to the negligence of the defendant's employees acting within the scope of its employment. The House of Lords held that, although the defendant would otherwise have been liable to the plaintiff, on its true interpretation the exemption clause clearly and unambiguously applied to what had occurred, and protected the defendant from liability[2].

In case it should be thought that the rule that the application of an exemption clause depends on the interpretation of the contract is liable to cause injustice in consumer contracts and other contracts based on standard terms, we would point out that exemption clauses in such a contract made nowadays are rendered either totally invalid or invalid unless fair and reasonable by the Unfair Contract Terms Act 1977, as we explain in paras 10.43–10.56, below, even though on their true interpretation they were intended to apply to what has occurred. It follows that the interpretation of an exemption clause is now generally of crucial importance only where the contract has been negotiated between businessmen capable of looking after their own interests and of deciding how the risks inherent in the performance of the contract can most economically be borne, which is usually by one or other party insuring against such risks.

We set out below certain rules of interpretation which are applied to exemption clauses by the courts and which tend to favour the party affected by such a clause.

1   [1980] AC 827, [1980] 1 All ER 556, HL. See also *George Mitchell (Chesterhall) Ltd v Finney Lock Seeds Ltd* [1983] 2 AC 803, [1983] 2 All ER 737, HL.
2   The contract in this case was a standard form contract, but, since it was entered into before the Unfair Contract Terms Act 1977, the House of Lords was not concerned with the validity of the exemption clause under that Act.

Liability can only be excluded or restricted by clear words
10.33   The liability in question must be precisely covered by the exemption clause relied on. In *Andrews Bros (Bournemouth) Ltd v Singer & Co Ltd*[1], the plaintiffs entered into a contract to buy 'new Singer cars' from the defendants. One of the cars delivered by the defendants was not a new car, having run a considerable mileage. A clause in the contract exempted the defendants from liability for breach of all 'conditions, warranties and liabilities *implied* by common law, statute or otherwise' but the Court of Appeal held that this did not protect the defendants against liability for breach of an *express* term. A similar decision was reached in *Wallis, Son and Wells v Pratt and Haynes*[2]. The defendants sold by sample to the plaintiffs seed described as 'common English sainfoin'. The contract

stated that the defendants gave 'no *warranty* express or implied' as to any matter concerning the seed. The seed turned out to be the inferior and cheaper 'giant sainfoin'. The House of Lords held that the exemption clause did not apply because there had been a breach of the *condition* implied by s 13 of the Sale of Goods Act 1979 (that goods sold by description correspond with it) and the clause did not purport to exclude liability for breach of condition.

This rule of interpretation is applied more rigorously in the case of clauses purporting to exclude liability than in the case of those purporting to restrict it[3].

1   [1934] 1 KB 17, CA.
2   [1911] AC 394, HL.
3   *Ailsa Craig Fishing Co Ltd v Malvern Fishing Co Ltd* [1983] 1 All ER 101, [1983] 1 WLR 964, HL; *George Mitchell (Chesterhall) Ltd v Finney Lock Seeds Ltd* [1983] 2 AC 803, [1983] 2 All ER 737, HL.

All ambiguities in the exemption clause are interpreted against the party relying on it
10.34   This is in accordance with the rule normally applied in the interpretation of contracts[1].

1   *Houghton v Trafalgar Insurance Co* [1954] 1 QB 247, [1953] 2 All ER 1409, CA; para 8.47, above.

Exclusion of liability for negligence
10.35   The nature of liability for a breach of contract depends on the term broken. In the case of most terms, liability for their breach is strict (ie a party who does not comply with the term is liable despite the absence of any negligence on his part); in the case of others, liability for their breach only arises if the party in question has been negligent (ie has failed to show reasonable care). This distinction depends upon whether the term broken simply imposes an obligation about something or whether it imposes an obligation to take reasonable care (or the like) in relation to something. It should also be borne in mind that, where contractual liability for the breach in question is strict, the guilty party may also be liable in tort if he can be proved to have been negligent.

If an exemption clause clearly purports to exclude *all* liability, effect must be given to it[1] (subject to the general rules as to the validity of exemption clauses), but if the clause is not so clearly drafted the law is as follows:

Where contractual liability for the breach in question is strict, the clause is normally construed as being confined to that contractual liability, and not as extending to any tortious liability for negligence, with the result that the guilty party is not protected by it if he is proved to have been negligent[2]. A leading example is *White v John Warrick & Co Ltd*[3]. The plaintiff hired a tricycle from the defendants. While he was riding it the saddle tilted forward and he was injured. The contract of hire stated: 'nothing in this agreement shall render the owners liable for any personal injury'. The Court of Appeal held that the exemption clause would not protect the defendants from liability in tort if they were found to have been negligent. Its reason was that, in the absence of the exemption clause, the defendants could have been liable for breach of contract in supplying a defective tricycle[4] irrespective of negligence and the operation of the clause had to be restricted to that strict liability.

Where liability can be based on negligence and nothing else, the exemption clause will normally be interpreted as extending to that head of damage, because if it were not so construed it would lack subject matter[5]. This is shown by *Alderslade v Hendon Laundry Ltd*[6]. The defendants contracted to launder the plaintiff's handkerchiefs, the contract limiting their liability 'for lost or damaged articles' to 20 times the laundering charge. The handkerchiefs were lost through the defendants' negligence. The Court of Appeal held that the only way in which the defendants could be made liable for the loss of the handkerchiefs would be if they could be shown to have been guilty of negligence. It held that the exemption clause applied to limit the defendants' liability for negligence because otherwise the clause would be left without any content at all.

Both these rules are only rules of interpretation and, although they will normally be adopted, the court is free to interpret the clause in another way if, on its wording or other evidence, it considers that the parties had some other intention[7].

1   *Joseph Travers & Sons Ltd v Cooper* [1915] 1 KB 73, CA.
2   *Alderslade v Hendon Laundry Ltd* [1945] KB 189 at 192, [1945] 1 All ER 244.
3   [1953] 2 All ER 1021, [1953] 1 WLR 1285, CA.
4   The term broken would have been an implied term that the tricycle was reasonably fit for the purpose for which it was hired: para 8.36, above.
5   *Alderslade v Hendon Laundry Ltd* [1945] KB 189, [1945] 1 All ER 244, CA; *Hollier v Rambler Motors (AMC) Ltd* [1972] 2 QB 71, [1972] 1 All ER 399, CA.
6   [1945] KB 189, [1945] 1 All ER 244, CA.
7   *J Archdale Ltd v Comservices Ltd* [1954] 1 All ER 210, [1954] 1 WLR 459, CA; *Hollier v Rambler Motors (AMC) Ltd* [1972] 2 QB 71, [1972] 1 All ER 399, CA; *Mineralimportexport v Eastern Mediterranean Maritime, The Golden Leader* [1980] 2 Lloyd's Rep 573.

General limitations on the application of an exemption clause

Misrepresentation
10.36   If the party favoured by an exemption clause induced the other party to accept it by misrepresenting its contents or effect, the clause is rendered ineffective to the extent that it is wider than the misrepresentation, even though the contract was signed by the other party and even though the misrepresentation was innocent. In *Curtis v Chemical Cleaning and Dyeing Co Ltd*[1], the plaintiff took a dress to the defendants' shop for cleaning. The dress was trimmed with beads and sequins. The plaintiff was asked to sign a receipt exempting the defendants from all liability for any damage to articles cleaned. The plaintiff asked why her signature was required and was told that the receipt exempted the defendants from liability for damage to the sequins and beads. When the dress was returned it was badly stained. It was held that the defendants were not protected by the clause because, through their employee, they had innocently induced the plaintiff to believe that the clause only referred to damage to the beads and sequins and therefore the clause only protected them against liability for such damage.

1   [1951] 1 KB 805, [1951] 1 All ER 631, CA.

Inconsistent undertakings
10.37   If, at or before the time the contract was made, the party favoured by an exemption clause gives an undertaking which is inconsistent with it, the

exemption clause is rendered ineffective to the extent that it is inconsistent with the undertaking, even though the undertaking does not form part of the contract or of a contract collateral to it. In *Mendelssohn v Normand Ltd*[1], the plaintiff left his car in the defendants' garage on terms contained in a ticket, one of which was that the defendants would not accept any responsibility for any loss sustained by the vehicle or its contents, however caused. The car contained valuables and the plaintiff wanted to lock it, but the attendant told him that this was not permissible. The plaintiff told the attendant about the valuables and the attendant promised to lock the car after he had moved it. On his return, the plaintiff discovered that the valuables had been stolen. The Court of Appeal held that the defendants were not protected by the exemption clause because their employee had in effect promised to see that the valuables were safe, and this oral undertaking took priority over the exemption clause.

1   [1970] 1 QB 177, [1969] 2 All ER 1215, CA.

Third party generally not protected by an exemption clause
10.38   As part of the doctrine of privity of contract[1], a person who is not a party to a contract containing an exemption clause is generally not protected by the clause, even though it purports to have this effect. In *Cosgrove v Horsfall*[2], the Court of Appeal held that a clause in a bus pass, exempting the London Passenger Transport Board and its employees from liability for injury, was ineffective to protect the employees from liability in tort for negligence since they were not parties to the contract between the Board and the pass-holder. This decision was approved by the House of Lords in *Scruttons Ltd v Midland Silicones Ltd*[3], although the clause in that case did not expressly purport to exclude or restrict the liability of the third parties in question. A drum containing chemicals was shipped from New York to London. It was consigned to the plaintiffs under a bill of lading which restricted the carriers' liability to $500 (then about £180). While the drum was being handled by the defendants, who were stevedores employed by the carriers, it was damaged through the defendants' negligence; the damage amounted to £593. The contract between the *carriers* and the defendants stated that the defendants should have the benefit of the exemption clause in the bill of lading, but the majority of the House of Lords held that the defendants could not limit their liability to the plaintiffs for negligence by relying on the exemption clause because they were not parties to the bill of lading.

These two decisions show that it will sometimes be possible to circumvent an exemption clause by bringing proceedings against an employee or sub-contractor on the ground of his negligence. This may be desirable in the case of a standard form contract, particularly because the employee will usually be reimbursed by his employer for, and a sub-contractor insured against, any damages awarded. However, the reliance on the technical rule of privity of contract is harder to justify in the case of a freely negotiated contract in which one party has agreed to assume the risk of damage, particularly where the contract purports to exempt an employee or sub-contractor of the other party.

1   Para 6.24, above.
2   (1945) 175 LT 334, CA.
3   [1962] AC 446, [1962] 1 All ER 1, HL.

10.39   The position is different where one of the parties, whom we will call A, contracts with B as agent for the third person. In that case the third person is brought into contractual relations with B on the terms of the exemption clause provisions in the main contract and is protected by the clause. This was recognised by the Privy Council in *New Zealand Shipping Co Ltd v A M Satterthwaite & Co Ltd, The Eurymedon*[1], which shows that there are four prerequisites for the validity of a contract between the third party and B:

a.   the main contract must make it clear that the third person is intended to be protected by the exemption clause;
b.   the main contract must make it clear that A, in addition to contracting for the exemption clause on his own behalf, is also contracting as agent for the third person that these provisions should apply to the third person;
c.   A must have authority from the third person to do that (or the third person can subsequently ratify the agency provided he was indentifiable at the time it was made[2]); and
d.   the third person must have provided consideration for the promise as to exemption made to him, through A as his agent, by B.

In *New Zealand Shipping Co* the Privy Council explained how the third person can provide consideration for B's promise as to exemption. The main contract brings into existence a bargain initially unilateral but capable of becoming mutual, between B and the third person, made through A as agent. This will become a full contract when the third person performs services under the main contract. The performance of these services for the benefit of B is the consideration for the promise by B that the third person should have the benefit of the exemption clause contained in the main contract.

New Zealand Shipping Co is of limited effect because:

a.   Consideration can only be furnished if the third person does something after the main contract has been made. If he has already performed his services, there can be no unilateral contract of the above type and he will not have furnished the consideration necessary to make enforceable any promise as to exemption.
b.   The third person cannot be said to accept the offer of a unilateral contract unless he knows of the main contract, which may depend on whether (as in the case of bills of lading) it is a well-known commercial practice to insert into the main contract a provision conferring the benefit of an exemption clause on the third person (the stevedores, in the case of a bill of lading).
c.   The principles laid down by the Privy Council are limited to terms providing for the exclusion or restriction of liability and similar terms protecting and benefitting only one of the parties to the contract. In *The Mahkutai*[3] the Privy Council declined to extend the principles in *New Zealand Shipping Co* to a clause giving exclusive jurisdiction over any dispute to the Indonesian courts, because it did not benefit only one party, but created mutual rights and obligations.

1   [1975] AC 154, [1974] 1 All ER 1015, PC. See also *Port Jackson Stevedoring Pty Ltd v Salmond and Spraggon (Australia) Pty Ltd, The New York Star* [1980] 3 All ER 257, [1981] 1 WLR 138, PC.
2   Para 23.11, below.
3   [1996] AC 650, [1996] 3 All ER 502, PC.

10.40   Although a person cannot directly take the benefit of an exemption clause if he is not a party to a contract entitling him to do so, he may indirectly benefit from it in some cases. The reason is that an exemption clause in such a case may limit his duty of care to one of the contracting parties, and hence his liability in tort for negligence. For example, in two cases where an exemption clause in a building contract placed the risk of damage by fire on the employer (rather than the building contractor), it was held that it would not be just and reasonable to impose on a sub-contractor hired by the building contractor a duty of care to avoid causing damage by fire[1].

1   *Southern Water Authority v Carey* [1985] 2 All ER 1077; *Norwich City Council v Harvey* [1989] 1 All ER 1180, [1989] 1 WLR 828, CA.

Third party not bound by an exemption clause
10.41   Because of the doctrine of privity of contract a third party cannot be deprived of his right to sue in tort by an exemption clause contained in a contract between others, even though it purports to have that effect. An authority is *Haseldine v C A Daw & Son Ltd*[1]. The owners of a block of flats employed the defendants to repair a lift in the block. The defendants repaired the lift negligently and the plaintiff was injured when the lift fell to the bottom of the lift shaft. The defendants were held liable to the plaintiff, it being irrelevant that the contract between the defendants and the owners of the block purported to exempt the defendants from liability for personal injury. Likewise, in *Leigh and Sillivan Ltd v Aliakmon Shipping Co Ltd, The Aliakmon*[2], where a contract of carriage by sea contained an exemption clause, the buyers of the goods were not bound by it because they were not parties to that contract (whose only parties were the sellers and the shipowners).

1   [1941] 2 KB 343, [1941] 3 All ER 156, CA.
2   [1986] AC 785, [1986] 2 All ER 145, HL.

10.42   The above rule can be avoided in the following cases:

a.   If one of the parties to a contract containing an exemption clause in favour of the other contracted as agent for a third person, that person is bound by the clause.

b.   It sometimes happens, where T has handed goods to X for repair, cleaning, carriage, loading or the like, that X sub-contracts the work to Y. If the contract between X and Y contains an exemption clause in favour of Y it will not bind T under the law of contract, as we have just seen, and T will normally be able to recover damages from Y for the tort of negligence should Y carry out the sub-contracted work negligently. However, T will not have the right to sue Y for the tort of negligence if he has expressly or impliedly authorised X to make the sub-contract on terms including the exemption clause in question[1]. This is because, where X (who is called the bailee) sub-contracts the work on the goods to Y with the authority of T (who is called the bailor), not only does X make a sub-bailment with Y but also brings into effect the relationship between T and Y of bailor and bailee and T is bound by the terms of the sub-bailment if he has expressly or impliedly consented to X making the sub-bailment on those terms[2].

1   *Morris v C W Martin & Sons Ltd* [1966] 1 QB 716 at 728, [1965] 2 All ER 725; *Singer Co (UK) Ltd v Tees and Hartlepool Port Authority* [1988] 1 FTLR 442.
2   *K H Enterprise v Pioneer Container, The Pioneer Container* [1994] 2 AC 324, [1994] 2 All ER 250, PC.

Validity

10.43   The Unfair Contract Terms Act 1977 contains a number of provisions greatly limiting the extent to which it is possible to 'exclude or restrict liability'. Generally these provisions only apply to the clauses seeking to exclude or restrict 'business liability', which is defined as liability (whether in tort or for breach of contract) which arises *from things done or to be done in the course of a business or from the occupation of premises used for business purposes of the occupier*[1]. In the 1977 Act, '*business*' includes a profession and the activities of any government department or public or local authority[2]. The phrase 'in the course of a business' is discussed in para 10.45. The main impact of the 'business liability limitation' on the effect of the Act is that its provisions do not generally apply to exemption clauses in contracts made between private individuals. The exceptions are indicated at the appropriate points below.

Although the Act uses the words 'contract term', we propose generally to use the more familiar expression 'exemption clause'.

1   Unfair Contract Terms Act 1977, s 1(3).
2   Ibid, s 14.

Avoidance of liability for negligence

10.44   Section 2(1) of the Act provides that a person cannot, by reference to an exemption clause or notice, exclude or restrict his liability for death or personal injury (including any disease or impairment of physical or mental condition) resulting from negligence.

In the case of other loss or damage, s 2(2) provides that a person cannot, by reference to an exemption clause or notice, exclude or restrict his liability for negligence, except *in so far as the clause or notice satisfies the 'requirement of reasonableness'*.

These provisions do not extend to a contract of employment, except in favour of the employee[1].

'Negligence' in this context means the breach of:

a.   any obligation, arising from the express or implied terms of a contract, to take reasonable care or exercise reasonable skill in the performance of the contract; or

b.   any common law duty to take reasonable care or exercise reasonable skill; or

c.   the common duty of care imposed by the Occupiers' Liability Act 1957[2].

The Act does not prevent the parties to a contract (eg for the hire of industrial plant) agreeing between themselves which of them should bear liability in negligence for any injury to a third party (eg injury arising from the negligent use of the plant), since this merely *allocates* liability (as opposed to excluding or restricting it)[3].

1   Unfair Contract Terms Act 1977, Sch 1.
2   Ibid, s 1(1). The duties mentioned in b. and c., above, are discussed in Chaps 18 and 19.
3   *Thompson v T Lohan (Plant Hire) Ltd* [1987] 2 All ER 631, [1987] 1 WLR 649, CA; para 17.20, below.

Avoidance of liability for breach of contract

10.45   Section 3 lays down special rules which apply *as between the contracting parties where one of them deals as consumer or on the other's written standard terms of business*[1].

In the present context, a party to a contract 'deals as consumer' in relation to another party if he neither makes the contract in the course of a business nor holds himself out as doing so, and the other party does make the contract in the course of a business[2]. A dictum by Dillon LJ in *R & B Customs Brokers Co Ltd v United Dominions Trust*[3] provides an explanation of the meaning of the phrase 'in the course of a business':

> 'There are some transactions which are *clearly integral parts of the business* concerned, and these should be held to have been carried out in the course of those businesses; this would cover, apart from much else, the instance of a one-off adventure in the nature of trade where the transaction itself would constitute a trade or business. There are other transactions, however, ... which are at the highest *only* incidental to the carrying on of the relevant business; *here* a degree of *regularity* is *required* before it can be said that they are an integral part of the business carried on and so entered into in the course of that business.'

In *R & B Customs Brokers* the Court of Appeal held that a company operating as a freight forwarding agent, which had bought a car for the business and personal use of its two directors and sole shareholder, a husband and wife, had not made the purchase in the course of a business. The purchase was *not clearly* an *integral* part of the freight forwarding agency business. It was *only incidental* to it and there was *no regularity* of purchases of the type in question.

In the case of contracts for the sale, hire purchase or other supply[4] of goods, there is an additional requirement in order for a party to be 'dealing as consumer', viz that the goods are of a type ordinarily supplied for private use or consumption (see further para 10.51, below).

A buyer at an auction or by competitive tender is never regarded as dealing as consumer[5].

It is for those claiming that a party does not deal as a consumer to show that he does not[6].

Section 3 provides that, *as against the party dealing as consumer or on the other's written standard terms of business*, the other party cannot by reference to any contract term:

a.   exclude or restrict his liability for breach of contract; or
b.   claim to be entitled:
    i.   to render a contractual performance substantially different from that which was reasonably expected of him, or
    ii. in respect of the whole or any part of his contractual obligation, to render no performance at all,

except in so far as the contract term satisfies the 'requirement of reasonableness'. This provision is widely drawn; for example, under b.i., a term permitting a dealer unilaterally to alter certain terms in the contract may be held invalid, and under b.ii., a term excusing non-performance or entitling a party to cancel the contract may be held invalid.

1   Unfair Contract Terms Act 1977, s 3(1).
2   Ibid, s 12(1).
3   [1988] 1 All ER 847, [1988] 1 WLR 321, CA. Also see *Davies v Sumner* [1984] 3 All ER 831, [1984] 1 WLR 1301, HL; *Devlin v Hall* [1990] RTR 320, DC.
4   Ie those described in para 10.52, below.
5   Unfair Contract Terms Act 1977, s 12(2).
6   Ibid, s 12(3).

10.46   *Unreasonable indemnity clauses* Contracts often contain terms requiring one party to indemnify the other against liability incurred by that other in performing the contract. Section 4(1) makes such an indemnity clause void *as against a person dealing as consumer* unless reasonable. It states that a person dealing as consumer cannot by reference to any contract term be made to indemnify another person (whether a party to the contract or not) in respect of liability that may be incurred by the other for negligence or breach of contract, *except in so far as the contract term satisfies the 'requirement of reasonableness'*. This provision applies whether the liability in question is that of the person to be indemnified or is incurred by him vicariously, and whether that liability is to the person dealing as consumer or to someone else[1]. 'Person dealing as consumer' has the same meaning as in s 3[2].

1   Unfair Contract Terms Act 1977, s 4(2).
2   Ibid, s 12.

Matters common to sections 2 to 4
10.47   *Excepted agreements*[1] Sections 2 to 4 do not extend to:

a.   any contract of insurance;
b.   any contract *so far as* it relates to the creation, transfer or termination of an interest in land or of any right or interest in any patent, trade mark, copyright or the like;
c.   any contract *so far as* it relates:

i.   to the formation or dissolution of a company (which means any body corporate or unincorporated association and includes a partnership), or

ii.   to its constitution or the rights or obligations of its corporators or members;

d.   any contract *so far as* it relates to the creation or transfer of securities or of any right or interest in securities.

Contracts of insurance are totally excepted from the Act, but the other contracts are only excepted *so far as* they relate to the *specified* matters. Consequently, only those parts of such a contract which relate to the specified matters (such as the transfer of an interest in land) are excepted from ss 2 to 4 and the rest of the contract is subject to those sections.

Sections 2(2), 3 and 4 do not extend to charterparties of ships or hovercraft, to contracts of marine salvage or towage or to contracts for the carriage of goods by sea, *except in favour of a person dealing as consumer*.

1 Unfair Contract Terms Act 1977, Sch 1.

10.48   *The 'requirement of reasonableness'*   In relation to an exemption clause, the requirement of reasonableness is that the clause itself must have been a fair and reasonable one to be included having regard to the circumstances which were, or ought reasonably to have been, known to or in the contemplation of the parties when the contract was made[1].

Where a party seeks to restrict liability to a specified sum in reliance on an exemption clause, then, in determining whether the clause satisfies the requirement of reasonableness, regard must be had in particular to:

a.   the resources which that party could expect to be available to him for the purpose of meeting the liability should it arise; and

b.   how far it was open to him to cover himself by insurance[2].

It is for the party claiming that an exemption clause satisfies the requirement of reasonableness to show on the balance of probabilities that it does[3].

In *Smith v Eric S Bush; Harris v Wyre Forest District Council*[4] Lord Griffiths was of the opinion that the following matters should always be considered in relation to the requirement of reasonableness:

a.   Were the parties of equal bargaining power? If they were, the requirement of reasonableness is more easily discharged than if they were not.

b.   How difficult is the task being undertaken to which the exemption clause applies? If the task is very difficult or dangerous there may be a high risk of failure, which would be a pointer to the requirement of reasonableness being satisfied.

c.   What are the practical consequences of the decision on the requirement of reasonableness? This involves the amount of money potentially at stake and the ability of the parties to bear the loss involved, which in turn raises the question of insurance.

It cannot be over-emphasised that it is the clause as a whole which must be reasonable in relation to the particular contract; the question is not whether its particular application in the particular case is reasonable. If a clause is drawn so widely as to be capable of applying in unreasonable circumstances it will not be held to be unreasonable, even though in the actual situation which has arisen its application would not be unreasonable[5]. A clause may well have various parts to it but, because the whole clause must be subjected to the test of reasonableness, it is not permissible to look only at that part of it which is relied on[6]. A court will be particularly unwilling to find a clause reasonable if it purports to exclude all potential liability[7].

1   Unfair Contract Terms Act 1977, s 11(1).
2   Ibid, s 11(4).
3   Ibid, s 11(5); *Phillips Products Ltd v Hyland* [1987] 2 All ER 620, [1987] 1 WLR 659n, CA.
4   [1990] 1 AC 831, [1989] 2 All ER 514, HL.
5   *Walker v Boyle* [1982] 1 All ER 634, [1982] 1 WLR 495; *Phillips Products Ltd v Hyland* [1987] 2 All ER 620 at 628.
6   *Stewart Gill Ltd v Horatio Myer & Co Ltd* [1992] QB 600, [1992] 2 All ER 257, CA.
7   *Lease Management Services Ltd v Purnell Secretarial Services Ltd* (1994) 13 Tr LR 337.

Avoidance of liability arising from sale or supply of goods
10.49   Sections 6 and 7 of the 1977 Act contain additional provisions dealing with attempts to avoid liability where the ownership or possession of goods has passed.

10.50   *Sale and hire purchase*   By s 6(1), liability for breach of the obligations arising from:

a.   the Sale of Goods Act 1979, s 12 (seller's implied undertakings as to title etc)[1];
b.   the Supply of Goods (Implied Terms) Act 1973, s 8 (the corresponding things in relation to hire purchase),

cannot be excluded or restricted by reference to an exemption clause.

1   These terms are described in paras 8.20 and 8.21, above.

10.51   Section 6(2) provides that, *as against a person dealing as consumer*, liability for breach of the obligations arising from:

a.   the Sale of Goods Act 1979, ss 13, 14 or 15 (seller's implied undertakings as to conformity of goods with description or sample, or as to their quality or fitness for a particular purpose)[1];
b.   the Supply of Goods (Implied Terms) Act 1973, ss 9, 10 or 11 (the corresponding things in relation to hire purchase),

cannot be excluded or restricted by reference to an exemption clause. It must be emphasised that this provision is limited to the implied terms specified. The validity of a clause excluding or restricting liability for breach of any express term will depend on the application of the principles which we have mentioned in para 10.45, above.

Unlike s 6(1), s 6(2) only vitiates the exemption clause as against a person dealing as consumer. The definition of such a person is obviously of great importance. In the present context, a party to a contract 'deals as consumer' in relation to another party if:

a. he neither makes the contract in the course of a business nor holds himself out as doing so; and
b. the other party does make the contract in the course of a business; and
c. the goods passing under or in pursuance of the contract are of a type ordinarily supplied for private use or consumption[2].

We dealt with the meaning of 'in the course of a business' in para 10.45, above. The upshot of the above provision is that, if a company buys from a dealer a Rolls-Royce or a yacht for its chairman, it will 'deal as consumer', and liability for breach of the implied terms just mentioned cannot be excluded or restricted.

A buyer at an auction or by competitive tender is never regarded as dealing as consumer[3].

It is for those claiming that a party does not deal as consumer to show that he does not[4].

Where a party does not deal as consumer, s 6(3) is the operative provision. Section 6(3) provides that, *as against a person dealing otherwise than as consumer*, liability for breach of the obligations arising from the Sale of Goods Act 1979, ss 13 to 15, or the Supply of Goods (Implied Terms) Act 1973, ss 9 to 11, can be excluded or restricted by an exemption clause, but *only in so far as the clause satisfies the 'requirement of reasonableness'*.

The provisions of s 6(1) and (3) are exceptional in that they are not limited to liabilities arising in the course of business.

1 These terms are described in paras 8.22–8.35, above.
2 Unfair Contract Terms Act 1977, s 12(1).
3 Ibid, s 12(2).
4 Ibid, s 12(3).

10.52 *Miscellaneous contracts under which the ownership or possession of goods passes* Section 7 of the 1977 Act deals with exemption clauses purporting to exclude or restrict liability for breach of obligations implied by law[1] into contracts such as those of hire or exchange or for work and materials. Section 7 applies to these contracts a regime which is broadly similar to that just mentioned in relation to sale of goods and hire purchase.

Section 7(2) provides that, *as against a person dealing as consumer* (in the same sense as in sale of goods and hire purchase), liability in respect of the goods' correspondence with description or sample, or their quality or fitness for any particular purpose, cannot be excluded or restricted by an exemption clause.

On the other hand, *as against a person dealing otherwise than as consumer*, s 7(3) provides that such liability can be excluded or restricted by reference to such a clause, but *only in so far as the clause satisfies the 'requirement of reasonableness'*.

In relation to an exemption clause purporting to exclude or restrict liability for breach of the various terms as to title etc which are implied into contracts of exchange, contracts for work and materials or analogous contracts by s 2 of the Supply of Goods and Services Act 1982, the position is as follows. Section 7(3A) of the 1977 Act provides that liability for breach of these terms cannot be excluded or restricted by reference to an exemption clause. Section 7(3A) does not apply in the case of a contract for the transfer of goods in the case of which there is an intention that the transferor should transfer only such title as he or a third party may have.

On the other hand, by s 7(4), liability in respect of breach of the various terms as to title etc which are implied into other contracts under which ownership or possession passes cannot be excluded or restricted by an exemption clause, *except in so far as the clause satisfies the 'requirement of reasonableness'*. Thus, a different rule applies where such a clause appears in a contract of hire from that which applies where it appears in a contract for, say, work and materials.

1   Supply of Goods and Services Act 1982, ss 2–5 and 7–10; see para 8.36, above.

10.53   *The 'requirement of reasonableness' in relation to ss 6 and 7*   The provisions which we mentioned in para 10.48, above, concerning the requirement of reasonableness also apply where that requirement is relevant under ss 6 and 7. However, in addition, in determining for the purposes of these two sections whether a contract term satisfies the requirement of reasonableness, regard must be had in particular to the guidelines specified in Sch 2 of the Act[1], viz:

a.   the strength of the bargaining positions of the parties relative to each other;
b.   whether the customer received an inducement to agree to the term, or in accepting it had an opportunity of entering into a similar contract with other persons, but without having to accept a similar term;
c.   where the term excludes or restricts any relevant liability if some condition is not complied with, whether it was reasonable at the time of the contract to expect that compliance with that condition would be practicable;
d.   whether the goods were manufactured, processed or adapted to the special order of the customer;
e.   whether the customer knew or ought reasonably to have known of the existence and extent of the term (eg because it was in small print or was unlikely to be read in full by the customer). We saw in paras 10.27 to 10.31, above, that an exemption clause may be a term of the contract even though the customer was unaware of it, especially if he has signed a contractual document containing it. This provision enables the court to hold an exemption clause which is undoubtedly a term of the contract unreasonable, and therefore invalid, because, for instance, the customer could not reasonably have known of its existence.

Although Sch 2 does not apply to the requirement of reasonableness as it applies to ss 2, 3 or 4, it is clear that the courts rely on similar factors to those in Sch 2 when considering the requirement of reasonableness in relation to those sections[2].

1   Unfair Contract Terms Act 1977, s 11(2).
2   *Phillips Products Ltd v Hyland* [1987] 2 All ER 620, [1987] 1 WLR 659n, CA; *Stewart Gill Ltd v Horatio Myer & Co Ltd* [1992] QB 600, [1992] 2 All ER 257, CA.

General

10.54   *International supply contracts*   The limits mentioned above on the exclusion or restriction of liability by an exemption clause do not apply to liability arising under international supply contracts[1].

An 'international supply contract' means a contract of sale of goods or a contract under which the possession or ownership of goods passes, which is made by parties whose places of business are in different states, provided:

a.   the goods are, at the time of the conclusion of the contract, in the course of carriage, or will be carried, from one state to another; or
b.   the acts constituting the offer and acceptance were effected in different states; or
c.   the contract provides for the goods to be delivered to a state other than that within whose territory the acts constituting the offer and acceptance were effected[2].

1   Unfair Contract Terms Act 1977, s 26(1) and (2).
2   Ibid, s 26(3) and (4).

10.55   *Evasion by means of a secondary contract*   Section 10 makes provision to prevent a possible way of evading the Act's limits on the exclusion or restriction of liability. It deals with the case where X, who has rights under (or in connection with the performance of) a contract with Y, makes another contract with Y (or some other person) containing a term which excludes or restricts a prospective liability under the first contract[1]. Section 10 provides that a person, X, is not bound by any term in the second contract prejudicing or taking away rights of his which arise under (or in connection with the performance of) the first contract, so far as those rights extend to the enforcement of Y's liability which the Act prevents Y from excluding or restricting.

1   *Tudor Grange Holdings Ltd v Citibank NA* [1992] Ch 53, [1991] 4 All ER 1.

10.56   *Varieties of exemption clauses*   As we have shown, the Act repeatedly refers to the 'exclusion or restriction of liability'. These words are given a wide interpretation by s 13(1), which provides that, to the extent that the provisions mentioned prevent the exclusion or restriction of any liability, they also prevent:

a.   making the liability or its enforcement subject to restrictive or onerous conditions (eg a term requiring 14 days' notice of loss);
b.   excluding or restricting rules of evidence or procedure (eg a term that failure to complain within 14 days is deemed to be conclusive evidence of proper performance of the contract);

c.   excluding or restricting any right or remedy in respect of the liability[1], or subjecting a person to any prejudice in consequence of his pursuing any such right or remedy.

Section 13(1) also provides that, to the extent that ss 2, 6 and 7 prevent the exclusion or restriction of liability, they also prevent excluding or restricting liability by reference to terms which exclude or restrict the relevant obligation or duty. It follows that a clause purporting to disclaim any potential liability is caught by the provision, even though it purports to prevent a duty arising in the first place (as opposed simply to disclaiming liability for breach of an acknowledged duty)[2].

Whether or not a contract term has the effect of excluding or restricting liability within the above formulation is determined by looking at its effect and substance, and not at its form[3].

1   Eg a term which allows recovery of damages but which purports to remove any right to terminate the contract for repudiatory breach, or a term which excludes a right to set off a claim by a buyer for damages for breach against a claim for the price by a seller: *Stewart Gill Ltd v Horatio Myer & Co Ltd* [1992] QB 600, [1992] 2 All ER 257, CA.
2   *Smith v Eric S Bush; Harris v Wyre Forest District Council* [1990] 1 AC 831, [1989] 2 All ER 514, HL.
3   *Phillips Products Ltd v Hyland* [1987] 2 All ER 620, [1987] 1 WLR 659n, CA; *Smith v Eric S Bush; Harris v Wyre Forest District Council* [1990] 1 AC 831, [1989] 2 All ER 514 at 530; *Johnstone v Bloomsbury Health Authority* [1992] QB 333, [1991] 2 All ER 293, CA.

Unfair Terms in Consumer Contracts Regulations 1994
10.57   These Regulations, which give effect to the EC Directive on Unfair Terms in Consumer Contracts, Directive 93/13, are intended to harmonise the law relating to unfair terms in contracts between a seller or supplier and a consumer.

We deal in more detail with the Regulations in chapter 14 but it should be noted here that they cover matters already covered by the Unfair Contract Terms Act 1977. However, as will be seen, in some respects the Act is wider than the Regulations since:

a.   the Regulations are limited to contracts made by a 'consumer', whereas the Act is not;
b.   to the extent that the Act has special provisions relating to 'consumers', 'consumer' has a wider meaning under the Act, since under the Regulations a 'consumer' means 'any natural person who . . . is acting for purposes outside his business' (so that, for example, a company entering into a one-off contract which was not integral to its business would not be a 'consumer' under the Regulations, although it would be under the Act[1]);
c.   in the case of consumer contracts for the sale or supply of goods, liability for breach of statutorily implied terms as to description or quality cannot be excluded under the Act regardless of whether they are reasonable or not, nor can liability for breach of the implied term as to title in any sale or supply contract, whereas under the Regulations an exemption clause of such a type in a consumer contract will only be invalid if it is unfair.

As will be seen in chapter 14, in some respects the Regulations are wider than the Unfair Contract Terms Act, since they are not limited to exemption clauses, but extend to any 'unfair term' (as defined by the Regulations).

Despite these differences, there is a substantial area of overlap between the Act and the Regulations. It follows that, in many cases involving exemption clauses, the application of the Act and of the Regulations must be considered.

1 Para 10.45, above.

Chapter 11

Discharge by Frustration

11.1 Under the doctrine of frustration a contract is automatically discharged: 'whenever the law recognises that, without default of either party[1], a contractual obligation has become incapable of being performed because the circumstances in which performance is called for would render it a thing radically different from that which was undertaken by the contract'[2]. This classic statement of the doctrine of frustration has been approved in a substantial number of cases[3].

1 For a qualification, see para 11.10, below.
2 *Davis Contractors Ltd v Fareham UDC* [1956] AC 696 at 729, [1956] 2 All ER 145 at 160.
3 See, eg, *National Carriers Ltd v Panalpina (Northern) Ltd* [1981] AC 675, [1981] 1 All ER 161, HL; *Pioneer Shipping Ltd v BTP Tioxide Ltd, The Nema* [1982] AC 724, [1981] 2 All ER 1030, HL; *Paal Wilson & Co A/S v Partenreederei Hannah Blumenthal, The Hannah Blumenthal* [1983] 1 AC 854, [1983] 1 All ER 34, HL.

Scope

11.2 Under this heading, we propose to illustrate the scope of the classic statement we have just quoted by reference to some of the circumstances in which a contract may be frustrated. A contract may be frustrated if, for example, *subsequent to its formation*:

a thing essential to its performance is destroyed or becomes unavailable; or
a fundamental change of circumstances occurs; or
a party to a contract of a personal nature dies or is otherwise incapacitated from performing it; or
performance of it is rendered illegal; or
a basic assumption on which the parties contracted is destroyed.

The doctrine of frustration does not apply to cases where one of these circumstances existed at the time the contract was made: there the legal position must be answered by reference to the law relating to mistake[1] and illegal contracts[2].

In addition, a contract is not discharged by frustration simply because a subsequent event makes its performance more costly or difficult than envisaged when the contract was made. This is shown by *Davis Contractors Ltd v Fareham UDC*[3]. In 1946, the contractors entered into a contract with the council to build 78 houses for the fixed sum of £94,000. Owing to an unexpected shortage of skilled labour and of certain materials, the contract took 22 months to complete instead of the anticipated eight months and cost £115,000. The contractors contended that the contract had been frustrated by the long delay and that they were entitled to a sum in excess of the contract price on a restitutionary basis (ie reasonable recompense for the benefit which they had conferred). The House of Lords disagreed, holding that the mere fact that unforeseen circumstances had delayed the performance of the contract and made it more costly to perform did not discharge the contract.

1   Paras 13.2–13.12, below.
2   Paras 15.23–15.39, below.
3   [1956] AC 696, [1956] 2 All ER 145, HL.

Supervening destruction or unavailability

11.3   A contract is discharged by frustration if performance of it is rendered impossible by the subsequent destruction or unavailability of a specific thing contemplated by the contract as essential to its performance. A leading authority is *Taylor v Caldwell*[1]. The defendants agreed to hire a music hall and gardens to the plaintiffs on specified days for the purpose of concerts. Before the first of the specified days, the music hall was destroyed by fire without the fault of either party. The defendants were held not liable for breach of contract because performance of the contract had become impossible through the destruction of the hall and they were not at fault. The contract was therefore frustrated and both parties discharged from their contractual obligations.

The subsequent unavailability of a thing will frustrate a contract if it renders performance of the contract in accordance with its terms impossible. This is shown by *Nickoll and Knight v Ashton Edridge & Co*[2]. The defendants sold the plaintiffs a cargo of cotton seed to be shipped 'per steamship *Orlando* during the month of January'. Before the time for shipping arrived, the ship was so damaged by stranding as to be unable to load in January. It was held that the contract was discharged by frustration.

In order that a contract be frustrated under the present heading, the thing which has been destroyed or is otherwise unavailable must have been expressly or impliedly required by the contract for its performance. This point is well illustrated by *Tsakiroglou & Co Ltd v Noblee Thorl GmbH*[3], which concerned a contract for the sale of groundnuts which were to be shipped from the Sudan to Hamburg during November or December 1956. Both parties contemplated that the ship would proceed via the Suez Canal but this was not stated in the contract. On 2 November 1956, the canal was closed (and remained so for five months). The House of Lords held that the unavailability of the canal did not frustrate the contract, one of its reasons being that there was no express provision in the contract for shipping via the canal, nor could a provision be implied to that effect, because the route was immaterial to the buyers. A fortiori, unavailability of a thing does not frustrate the contract if it merely affects the method of performance contemplated by one of the parties[4]. In *Nickoll and Knight v Ashton Edridge & Co*, for instance, the contract would not have been frustrated if, instead of the name of the ship on which the cargo was to be loaded being stated in the contract, the defendant sellers had merely intended to load on that ship.

1   (1863) 3 B & S 826.
2   [1901] 2 KB 126, CA.
3   [1962] AC 93, [1961] 2 All ER 179, HL.
4   *Blackburn Bobbin Co Ltd v TW Allen & Sons Ltd* [1918] 2 KB 467, CA.

Fundamental change of circumstances
11.4   A contract is frustrated if an event occurs of such gravity that, although technically the contract could still be performed, it would be the performance of a radically different contract from that contemplated. In *Jackson v Union Marine Insurance Co Ltd*[1], a ship was chartered to sail from Liverpool to Newport and there to load rails and then sail to San Francisco with them. She ran aground en route to Newport on 3 January and was not re-floated until 18 February, repairs not being completed until August. It was held that the charterparty had been discharged by frustration because it was found as a fact that the particular voyage contemplated by the parties had become impossible through the ship's temporary unavailability; that a voyage undertaken after the ship had been repaired would have been a different voyage – a voyage for which the shipowner had not contracted and for which the charterers had not the cargo; a voyage as different as though it had been described as intended to be a spring voyage, while the one after repair would be an autumn voyage. A similar decision was reached in *Metropolitan Water Board v Dick Kerr & Co Ltd*[2]. The company contracted with the board to construct a reservoir within six years, subject to a proviso that time could be extended if delay was caused by difficulties, impediments or obstructions. After two years had elapsed the Minister of Munitions, acting under statutory powers, required the company to stop work on the contract and remove and sell their plant. The House of Lords held that the interruption created by the prohibition was of such a nature and duration that the contract, if resumed, would in effect be radically different from that originally made. Therefore it was frustrated.

These cases can be contrasted with *Tsakiroglou & Co Ltd v Noblee Thorl GmbH*. In that case, the House of Lords held that the contract was not frustrated by the closure of the Suez Canal because a voyage round the Cape of Good Hope would not be commercially or fundamentally different from shipping via the canal, albeit it was more expensive for the sellers.

1   (1874) LR 10 CP 125.
2   [1918] AC 119, HL.

Death or other personal incapacity
11.5   A contract of employment, or any other contract which can only be performed by a party personally, eg a contract to paint a portrait, is discharged

by frustration if that party dies[1] or is otherwise rendered permanently incapable of performing it[2].

If a person becomes *temporarily* incapable of performing such a contract, it may be discharged. Whether or not the temporary incapacity frustrates a contract depends on whether, in the light of the probable duration of the incapacity at its inception, performance after it has ceased would be radically different from what was envisaged by the contract and in effect be the substitution of a new contract. In *Morgan v Manser*[3], the defendant, a comedian, entered into a contract with the plaintiff in 1938 whereby he engaged the plaintiff's services as manager for ten years. In 1940, the defendant was called up and was not demobilised until 1946. It was held that the contract was discharged by frustration in 1940 since it was then likely that the defendant would have to remain in the forces for a very long time. Similarly, if the duration of an employee's illness is likely to be so lengthy as to make performance of a contract of employment radically different from that undertaken by him and accepted by his employer, the contract will be discharged by frustration, and so will a contract to perform at a concert on a specified day by an illness of short duration[4]. Conversely, a contract of a personal nature is not frustrated by the illness of a party where this is likely to last for only a small part of the period of the contract: further performance after the party becomes available again will not be the performance of a radically different contract.

1   *Stubbs v Holywell Rly Co Ltd* (1867) LR 2 Exch 311.
2   *Notcutt v Universal Equipment Co (London) Ltd* [1986] 3 All ER 582, [1986] 1 WLR 641, CA.
3   [1948] 1 KB 184, [1947] 2 All ER 666.
4   *Robinson v Davison* (1871) LR 6 Exch 269.

Supervening illegality
11.6   A change in the law or in the circumstances may make performance of the contract illegal. If the change is such as to make it impossible to perform the contract legally it is discharged by frustration.

In *White and Carter Ltd v Carbis Bay Garage Ltd*[1], for instance, it was held that a contract made in 1939 to display advertisements for three years was frustrated by wartime Defence Regulations prohibiting advertisements of the type in question. On the other hand, in *Cricklewood Property and Investment Trust Ltd v Leighton's Investment Trust Ltd*[2], the House of Lords held that a 99-year building lease was not frustrated by Defence Regulations prohibiting building for only a small part of that term: performance had merely been suspended, not made impossible.

1   [1941] 2 All ER 633, CA.
2   [1945] AC 221, [1945] 1 All ER 252, HL.

Supervening destruction of a basic assumption on which the parties contracted
11.7   A contract is discharged by frustration if, although it is physically and legally possible for each party to perform his obligations under the contract, a change of circumstances has destroyed a *basic assumption* on which *the parties* contracted. In *Krell v Henry*[1], the defendant agreed to hire a flat in Pall Mall from the plaintiff for 26 and 27 June 1902, on one of which days Edward VII

was to be crowned. To the plaintiff's knowledge, the defendant hired the flat in order to view the coronation processions, but this was not mentioned in their written contract. The processions were postponed because of the King's illness. The Court of Appeal held that a view of the processions was not simply the purpose of the defendant in hiring the flat but the basis of the contract for both parties, and that since the postponement of the processions prevented this being achieved the contract was frustrated.

It is not enough that the purpose of one party in making the contract cannot be fulfilled; the basis on which both parties contracted must have been destroyed. This is shown by *Herne Bay Steamboat Co v Hutton*[2], which also reveals the difficulty in drawing the distinction. The defendant chartered a ship from the plaintiffs for 28 and 29 June 1902, for the express purpose of taking fare paying passengers to see the coronation naval review at Spithead and to cruise round the Fleet. The review was cancelled, but the Fleet remained. The Court of Appeal held that the charterparty was not frustrated because the holding of the review was not the basis on which both parties had contracted and it was irrelevant that the purpose of the defendant was defeated.

1   [1903] 2 KB 740, CA.
2   [1903] 2 KB 683, CA.

Limits

Express provision for frustrating event
11.8   The doctrine of frustration does not apply if the parties have made provision to deal with the frustrating event which has occurred. There is one exception: a contract is frustrated by supervening illegality despite an express provision to the contrary[1].

A provision concerned with the effect of a possible future event is narrowly construed and, unless on its true construction it covers the frustrating event in question, the doctrine of frustration is not ousted. This is shown by *Metropolitan Water Board v Dick Kerr & Co Ltd*[2], discussed above, where the contract for the reservoir provided that in the event of delays 'however caused' the contractors were to be given an extension of time. The House of Lords held that this provision did not prevent the doctrine of frustration applying because it did not cover the particular event which had occurred. Although the event was literally within the provision, the provision could be construed as limited to temporary difficulties, such as shortage of supplies, and not as extending to events which fundamentally altered the nature of the contract and which could not have been in the parties' contemplation when they made the contract.

1   *Ertel Bieber & Co v Rio Tinto Co Ltd* [1918] AC 260, HL.
2   [1918] AC 119, HL.

Foreseen and foreseeable events
11.9   If, by reason of special knowledge, the risk of the particular frustrating event was foreseen or foreseeable by only *one* party the doctrine of frustration

cannot apply. It is up to that party to provide against the risk of that event, and if he fails to do so and cannot perform the contract he is liable for breach[1].

On the other hand, where the risk of the frustrating event was foreseen or foreseeable by both parties, but they did not make provision to deal with it, the doctrine of frustration can apply[2]. In each case, however, it is a question of construction whether the failure to make provision for the event means that each party took the risk of it rendering contractual performance impossible or whether, in the absence of any such intention, the doctrine of frustration should apply to discharge the contract[3].

1   *Walton Harvey Ltd v Walker and Homfrays Ltd* [1931] 1 Ch 274, CA.
2   *Tatem Ltd v Gamboa* [1939] 1 KB 132, [1938] 3 All ER 135; *Ocean Tramp Tankers Corpn v V/O Sovfracht, The Eugenia* [1964] 2 QB 226, [1964] 1 All ER 161, CA.
3   *Chandler Bros Ltd v Boswell* [1936] 3 All ER 179, CA; *Ocean Tramp Tankers Corpn v V/O Sovfracht, The Eugenia* [1964] 2 QB 226, [1964] 1 All ER 161, CA.

Fault of a party

11.10   A party cannot rely on the doctrine of frustration if the frustrating event was brought about by his fault, but (assuming that he has not also contributed to the event by his fault) the other party can[1].

A deliberate election to pursue a course of conduct which renders performance of the contract impossible or illegal is clearly established as fault in this context; that conduct may in itself be a breach of contract[2], but it is not necessary that it should be[3]. In *Maritime National Fish Ltd v Ocean Trawlers Ltd*[4], the plaintiffs chartered to the defendants a trawler fitted with an otter trawl. Both parties knew that use of an otter trawl without a licence from a minister was illegal. Later, the defendants applied for licences for five trawlers which they were operating, including the plaintiffs'. They were only granted three licences and were asked to specify the three trawlers which they wished to have licensed. The defendants named three trawlers other than the plaintiffs'. They then claimed that they were no longer bound by the charterparty because it had been frustrated. The Privy Council held that the frustration was due to the defendants' deliberate act in not specifying the plaintiffs' trawler for a licence and that therefore they could not rely on the doctrine of frustration. Consequently, the plaintiffs could recover the hire under the charterparty.

Any deliberate choice of conduct which renders performance of the contract impossible or illegal suffices for present purposes, however reasonable it is to make that choice. This was held by the Court of Appeal in *J Lauritzen AS v Wijsmuller BV, The Super Servant Two*[5], where the defendants agreed to transport the plaintiffs' drilling rig on one of two named submersible barges, *Super Servant Two* and *Super Servant One*. The choice of vessel rested with the defendants who allocated the task to *Super Servant Two*. The defendants made contracts with other parties which could only be performed by using *Super Servant One*. *Super Servant Two* sank before the time that the rig was to be delivered. The defendants, faced with a choice between using *Super Servant One* on the contract in question or using it on the other contracts for which it alone had been specified, chose the latter course and claimed that the contract in question was frustrated. The Court of Appeal held that the contract was not frustrated by the sinking of *Super Servant Two* because the contract had not contemplated the use of *Super Servant Two* and *Super Servant Two* only. Nor, it held, was the contract frustrated by the sinking of *Super Servant Two* coupled with the defendants' election to use *Super Servant One* on the other contracts, thereby rendering the contract impossible of performance by either of the vessels specified in it. The reason was that that election had been a deliberate choice on the defendants' part and it was irrelevant whether or not they had acted reasonably in making that choice.

It would seem that a negligent act by a party, as opposed to a deliberate choice of conduct, which renders performance of the contract impossible or illegal prevents him relying on the doctrine of frustration[6].

The onus of proof where fault is alleged is on the party alleging it[7].

1   *F C Shepherd Co Ltd v Jerrom* [1987] QB 301, [1986] 3 All ER 589, CA.
2   As in *Ocean Tramp Tankers Corpn v V/O Sovfracht, The Eugenia* [1964] 2 QB 226, [1964] 1 All ER 161, CA. In fact, the deliberate conduct in question may constitute a breach by both parties: *Paal Wilson & Co A/S v Partenreederei Hannah Blumenthal, The Hannah Blumenthal* [1983] 1 AC 854, [1983] 1 All ER 34, HL.
3   *Denmark Productions Ltd v Boscobel Productions Ltd* [1969] 1 QB 699, [1968] 3 All ER 513, CA; *J Lauritzen AS v Wijsmuller BV, The Super Servant Two* [1990] 1 Lloyd's Rep 1, CA.
4   [1935] AC 524, PC.
5   [1990] 1 Lloyd's Rep 1, CA.
6   It was assumed by the House of Lords in *Joseph Constantine SS Line Ltd v Imperial Smelting Corpn Ltd* [1942] AC 154, [1941] 2 All ER 165, HL, that it does.
7   *Joseph Constantine SS Line Ltd v Imperial Smelting Corpn Ltd* [1942] AC 154, [1941] 2 All ER 165, HL.

Effect

11.11   Frustration does not merely make the contract terminable at the election of a party: the frustrating event *automatically* discharges the contract at the time that it is frustrated[1] (except that provisions intended by the parties to apply in the event of frustration, such as one dealing with its consequences, remain in force)[2]. Where a contract is severable[3], part may be discharged by frustration and part remain in force[4]. As explained in the previous paragraph, where the frustrating event is brought about by the fault of one party, the other party may rely on it as discharging the contract but the party at fault cannot[5].

Leaving aside the complicated question of the effect of frustration on money paid or payable under the contract, the effect of frustration on other obligations under the contract is governed by the common law and is as follows: the discharge of a contract by frustration releases both parties from further performance of any such obligations due after the frustrating event[6] but not from any such obligations due before that time, which remain enforceable[6].

Turning to the effect of frustration on money paid or payable under the contract, the position is as follows.

1   *Hirji Mulji v Cheong Yue SS Co Ltd* [1926] AC 497, PC.
2   *Heyman v Darwins Ltd* [1942] AC 356, [1942] 1 All ER 337, HL; *BP Exploration Co (Libya) Ltd v Hunt (No 2)* [1982] 1 All ER 925 at 978, CA; affd [1982] 1 All ER 925, HL.
3   Para 10.15, above.

4   *Denny Mott and Dickson Ltd v James B Fraser & Co Ltd* [1944] AC 265 at 278–280, [1944] 1
    All ER 678 at 685–686; *The Nema* [1982] AC 724, [1981] 2 All ER 1030, HL.
5   *F C Shepherd Co Ltd v Jerrom* [1987] QB 301, [1986] 3 All ER 589, CA.
6   *Chandler v Webster* [1904] 1 KB 493, CA.

*Money paid or payable under the contract before the occurrence of the frustrating
event*

11.12   At common law, the original position was that an obligation to pay
money due before the frustrating event remained enforceable and money paid
under the contract before that event was irrecoverable[1]. However, in 1942, in
Fibrosa Spolka Akcyjna v Fairbairn Lawson Combe Barbour Ltd[2], a case where
money payable in advance for machinery had been paid but the contract had
been frustrated before any of the machinery had been delivered, the House of
Lords held that the money could be recovered back under the law of restitution
on the ground of a total failure of consideration, in the sense that the buyers
had got nothing of what they had bargained for.

The decision in *Fibrosa* left the law unjust in two ways:

a.   The decision only permitted recovery if there had been a total failure of
     consideration. This could be unjust to the payer of the money because, if
     he had received any part, however small, of the contractual performance,
     he could not recover a penny of what he had paid.
b.   The decision could also be unjust to a payee who was ordered to return a
     pre-payment because he might have incurred expenses in seeking to
     perform the contract.

1   *Chandler v Webster* [1904] 1 KB 493, CA.
2   [1943] AC 32, [1942] 2 All ER 122, HL.

11.13   These injustices were removed by the Law Reform (Frustrated
Contracts) Act 1943. Section 1(2) of the Act provides:

a.   All sums *payable* under the contract *before* the frustrating event *cease to be
     payable* whether or not there has been a total failure of consideration.
b.   All sums *paid* under the contract *before* the frustrating event are *recoverable*
     whether or not there has been a total failure of consideration.
c.   The court has a discretionary power to allow the payee to set off against
     the sums so paid or payable a sum not exceeding the value of the expenses
     he has incurred before the frustrating event in, or for the purpose of, the
     performance of the contract.

If the court exercises the power referred to in c., it allows the payee to retain
the amount stipulated by it (if he has been paid) or to recover the stipulated
amount (if money was payable but not paid). The stipulated amount, which
may include an element in respect of overhead expenses and of any work or
services performed personally by the payee[1], cannot exceed the sums paid or
payable to him[2]. The following illustrates the operation of these provisions. X
contracts with Y to manufacture and deliver certain machinery by 1 March for

£5,000, £1,000 to be paid on 1 January and the balance of £4,000 on delivery. The contract is discharged by frustration on 1 February before the machinery is delivered but after X has incurred expenses of £500 in making the machinery. Pursuant to s 1(2), Y need not pay the £1,000 if he has not paid it before 1 February or, if he has, he can recover the £1,000, but the court may order Y to pay X up to £500 for his expenses or may allow X to retain up to £500, as the case may be.

1   Law Reform (Frustrated Contracts) Act 1943, s 1(4).
2   There is no scope for adding to these sums something extra to represent the time value of money (sometimes referred to by accountants as discounted net cash flow): *BP Exploration Co (Libya) Ltd v Hunt (No 2)* [1982] 1 All ER 925 at 978, CA; affd ibid 986, HL.

Money payable under the contract after the occurrence of the frustrating event
11.14   Such money is not recoverable by the party to whom it was due, in accordance with the rule that frustration releases both parties from performing any contractual obligation due after the frustrating event. Thus, in *Krell v Henry*[1], it was held that the owner of the flat could not recover a sum payable for the hire of the flat because it was not due until a time after the processions had been postponed (the frustrating event). Likewise, the balance of £4,000 referred to in the example in the previous paragraph is not recoverable by X because it was not due until after the frustrating event.

In further contrast to the rules outlined in para 11.13, above, the courts do not have power to allow a claim in respect of his expenses by a party to whom money was payable only after the frustrating event.

1   [1903] 2 KB 740, CA; para 11.7, above.

Award for valuable benefit obtained
11.15   At common law, a party who had benefited another by partly performing the contract before it was frustrated could not recover any sum of money for this[1]. This rule was particularly harsh where payment was not due to him until after the occurrence of the frustrating event because where money was paid or payable before that time he could retain or recover it, as the case might be.

Section 1(3) of the Law Reform (Frustrated Contracts) Act 1943 now makes a monetary award available to either party for a valuable benefit conferred on the other. It provides that where a party to a frustrated contract has, by reason of anything done by any other party in, or for the purpose of, the performance of the contract, obtained a valuable benefit before the frustrating event (other than the payment of money to which s 1(2) applies), that other party may recover from him such sum, if any, as the court considers just, having regard to all the circumstances of the case.

In assessing the amount of an award under s 1(3), the court must first identify and value the benefit obtained by the benefited party (whom we will call B). Where services rendered by the other party (whom we will call A) have an end-product, B's benefit is the end-product of those services[2]. It follows, for example, that, in the case of a building contract which is frustrated when the building is partially completed, the benefit to be valued is the uncompleted building, not the work put in by the builder. This is important because occasionally a relatively small service performed under a contract may confer a substantial benefit, and vice versa. Sometimes services will have no end-product, as where the work is transporting goods. In such a case the benefit is the value of the services[2]. Generally speaking, valuation of the benefit must be made as at the date of the frustration and not at an earlier time when the benefit was received[2] . In particular, the court must take into account the effect in relation to the benefit of the circumstances giving rise to the frustration[3], so that if a builder (A) contracts to do building work on B's house and, when he has nearly finished, the house (including A's work) is seriously damaged by fire, and the building contract is thereby frustrated, the valuation of the benefit relates to the value of what remains of A's work as at the date of frustration. From the benefit valued in the above way there must be deducted any expenses incurred by the benefited party (B) before the contract was frustrated, including any sums paid or payable by him to A under the contract and retained or recoverable by A under s 1(2)[3].

The value of the benefit assessed by the court under the above principles forms the upper limit of an award under s 1(3) but not the award itself. This is because the court, having identified and valued the benefit, must then decide on a 'just sum' within that upper limit to award to A in respect of his *performance*. Here, the court should take into particular account the contract consideration, since in many cases it will be unjust to award more than that consideration or a rateable part of it. The fact that A has broken the contract in some way before the frustration has no bearing on the just sum to be awarded to him, although B's claim to damages for the breach may be the subject of a counterclaim or set-off if not statute-barred[2]. It is not the judge's task to draw up a balance sheet showing on one side how A benefited from the contract, on the other how B benefited, and making an award in favour of A if B has benefited more than A. Section 1(3) does not require this or any other accountancy exercise; all that it requires is that the judge should fix a sum which he considers just[2]. The time value of money is not taken into account in assessing the value of the benefit or the just sum[2].

1   *Appleby v Myers* (1867) I.R 2 CP 651.
2   *BP Exploration Co (Libya) Ltd v Hunt (No 2)* [1982] 1 All ER 925; affd [1982] 1 All ER 986, HL.
3   Law Reform (Frustrated Contracts) Act 1943, s 1(3).

11.16   The operation of the Act of 1943 can be illustrated as follows: A, a jobbing decorator, contracts with B to paint the outside of B's house for £900, £300 to be paid on 1 September and the rest on completion. B pays A the £300 on 1 September. After A has painted most of the house the contract is frustrated, A having been seriously incapacitated in a car crash. Under s 1(2), A must return the £300 to B, unless and to the extent that the court exercises its discretion to allow A to retain some or all of it. Suppose that A's expenses were £50 and the court allows him to retain this – only £250 will be recoverable by B. The obligation as to the further £600 is, of course, discharged by frustration and A cannot claim this from B. However, as A has conferred a valuable benefit on B before the frustrating event, s 1(3) comes into play. Suppose that the value of the paintwork completed by A is £525 as at the date of the frustration, the court must then deduct what it has allowed A to retain under s 1(2) and the resulting sum (ie £475) will be the upper limit of the 'just sum' awarded by the court under s 1(3).

Scope of the Law Reform (Frustrated Contracts) Act 1943

11.17   Where a contract to which the Act applies is severable, eg a contract to work for a year at £2,400 a month[1], and a severable part of it is wholly performed before the frustrating event, or wholly performed except in respect of payment of sums which are or can be ascertained under the contract, that part is to be treated as if it were a separate contract and had not been frustrated, and the Act is only applicable to the remainder of the contract[2]. The result is that, if the employee under the above contract works for two months and two weeks and then dies before any salary has been paid, his executors can recover the two months' salary owing to him (each month being treated as a separate contract) *plus* an award under s 1(3) of the Act for any valuable benefit conferred by the deceased on the employer during the remaining two weeks.

1   Para 10.15, above.
2   Section 2(4).

11.18   Where a contract contains a provision (such as one precluding any recovery of any award under the Act or one limiting such an award) which is intended to have effect in the event of circumstances arising which operate, or would but for the provision operate, to frustrate the contract, or is intended to have effect whether such circumstances arise or not, the court must give effect to that provision and only give effect to s 1(2) and (3) of the Act to such extent, if any, as is consistent with that provision[1].

1   Section 2(3). See, further, *BP Exploration Co (Libya) Ltd v Hunt (No 2)* [1982] 1 All ER 925; affd [1982] 1 All ER 986, HL.

11.19   The Act applies to contracts to which the Crown is a party[1].
The Act does not apply to the following types of contract:

a.   Any charterparty, except a time charterparty (ie one for a definite period) or a charterparty by way of demise (ie one where the possession and control over the ship, as well as the use of her, are transferred to the charterer for the specified duration of the charter). Nor does the Act apply to any contract (other than a charterparty) for the carriage of goods by sea[2]. Where the Act does not apply, freight paid in advance is not recoverable even though completion of the voyage is frustrated.

b.   A contract of insurance[3]. Generally, a premium is not returnable once the risk has attached.

c.   A contract to which s 7 of the Sale of Goods Act 1979 applies[4]. Section 7 provides that where there is an agreement to sell specific goods, and subsequently, without any fault on the part of the seller or buyer, the goods *perish before the risk passes to the buyer*, the agreement is thereby avoided[5]. Where a contract is avoided under s 7, the principles laid down by the House of Lords in the *Fibrosa* case[6] apply. Under these, a buyer who has paid for the goods before they perished can recover back his payment only

if there has been a total failure of consideration, in which case the seller
has no right of set-off for any expenses he may have incurred in seeking to
perform the contract before the goods perished.

1   Section 2(2).
2   Section 2(5)(a).
3   Section 2(5)(b).
4   Section 2(5)(c).
5   'Perishing' of goods includes cases not only where they have been destroyed or stolen, but
    also cases where they have been so damaged as to have ceased to exist commercially as goods
    of the description under which they were sold: *Asfar & Co v Blundell* [1896] 1 QB 123, CA.
    'Specific goods' are goods identified and agreed on at the time a contract of sale is made: Sale
    of Goods Act 1979, s 61(1). The term also includes an undivided share, specified as a fraction
    or percentage, of goods identified and agreed on at the time a contract of sale is made: ibid.
    Goods generally remain at the seller's risk until ownership of them is transferred to the buyer,
    after which they are at the buyer's risk (whether delivery has been made or not): Sale of
    Goods Act 1979, s 20.
6   Para 11.12, above.

Chapter 12

Remedies for Breach of Contract

12.1 In the event of a breach of contract, the injured party may, subject to any applicable and effective exemption clause, have one or more of the following remedies:

a. He may, subject to the rules discussed in paras 12.2–12.22, below, recover damages for any loss suffered as a result of the breach by bringing an action for damages for breach of contract.

b. However, if a breach consists of the other party's failure to pay a debt, ie the contractually agreed price or other remuneration, which *is* due under the contract, the appropriate course for the injured party is to bring an action for the agreed sum to recover *that* amount, rather than an action for damages. We discuss this further in paras 12.23–12.25, below. A person who recovers an agreed sum may also recover damages for any further loss which he has suffered.

c. In the case of a repudiatory breach, he may terminate the contract for breach, ie accept the breach as discharging the contract, thereby discharging himself from any obligation to perform the contract further. If the injured party elects to terminate for repudiatory breach, he may also bring an action for damages for any loss suffered. We have already discussed termination for repudiatory breach in detail in paras 10.3–10.24, above.

d. Where he has performed part of his own obligations, but is unjustifiably prevented from completing them by the other party, he may sue under the law of restitution for the value of what he has done *if he terminates the contract for breach*. We discuss this further in para 12.26, below.

e. Where he has paid the contractual price, but he has not received any part of the benefit he bargained for under the contract, the injured party may sue under the law of restitution for the return of the money paid *if he terminates the contract for breach*. If the failure of consideration is not total but only partial, an action for the return of money paid is not available. However if:

　　i. the partial performance is such as to entitle the plaintiff to terminate the contract, and he elects to do so, and

ii. he is able to restore what he has received under the contract, and does so before he has derived any benefit from it,

he will bring about a total failure of consideration and be entitled to recover back what he has paid. A common example of this is where the buyer of defective goods rejects them immediately and claims back his payment. We dealt with these matters in more detail in para 10.5, above.

f. In appropriate cases, he may seek a decree of specific performance or an injunction in addition to, instead of, damages. We discuss this further in paras 12.27–12.34, below.

Damages

12.2 Damages for breach of contract are not awarded to punish the defendant (with the result that the amount awarded is not affected by the manner of the breach or the motive behind it[1]) but to compensate the plaintiff for the loss or damage which he has suffered as a result of the breach of contract[2].

This means that, where he has not suffered any loss or damage as a result of the breach, the damages recoverable by him will normally be purely nominal (usually in the region of £2 to £20). However, in a few exceptional cases, a plaintiff can recover substantial damages for a loss which he has not suffered. One exception is where the plaintiff made the contract as agent or trustee for another[3]. If the contract is broken in such a case and the plaintiff sues for damages on the other's behalf he can recover substantial damages for the loss suffered by the other as a result of the breach[4]. Another exception relates to a contract concerning land or goods where the parties contemplated when they contracted that the proprietary interest in the property might be transferred, before the time for contractual performance, by one party to a third party who would not have a right of action for breach of the contract. Here, unless they had some other intention, the parties are treated as having made the contract on the footing that the party who subsequently transfers his interest would be entitled to enforce his contractual rights for the benefit of the third party transferee[5]. Thus, if A makes a contract with B for B to do some repair work to a building, which (as B knows) A may transfer to a third party before the time the contract is to be performed, and B in breach of contract does the work defectively after the property has been transferred to C, A can sue B for substantial damages for the loss caused to C by the defective work, since A and B are treated as having contracted on the basis that A would be entitled to enforce his contractual rights for the benefit of the third party transferee who has no contractual right of action.

1 *Addis v Gramophone Co Ltd* [1909] AC 488, HL.
2 For a modern authority for this well-established rule, see *Surrey County Council v Bredero Homes Ltd* [1993] 3 All ER 705, CA.
3 Paras 6.27 and 6.30, above.
4 *Lloyd's v Harper* (1880) 16 Ch D 290, CA; *Woodar Investment Development Ltd v Wimpey Construction (UK) Ltd* [1980] 1 All ER 571, [1980] 1 WLR 277, HL.

5   *Linden Gardens Trust Ltd v Lenesta Sludge Disposals Ltd* [1994] 1 AC 85, [1993] 3 All ER 417,
     HL; *Darlington Borough Council v Wiltshier Northern Ltd* [1995] 3 All ER 895, [1995] 1 WLR
     68, CA.

For what can compensation be awarded?

12.3   The principal function of damages for breach of contract is to put the
plaintiff into the same position, so far as money can, *as if the contract had been
performed as agreed*[1].

In achieving this, damages are awarded to compensate the plaintiff for the
loss of his expectations (or loss of bargain) under the contract. Such damages
can be illustrated as follows. Suppose that X agrees to sell some computing
equipment to a firm of accountants but fails to deliver it. The firm can get
damages, subject to the rules discussed later in this chapter, to compensate it
for being deprived of the computer and for losing the opportunity to make a
profitable use of it until it can acquire a substitute. Another example of damages
for loss of expectations is where, because of the breach of contract, the thing
contracted for is worth less than it would have been if there had been no
breach of contract. Assuming that he cannot, or does not, terminate the contract
by rejecting the defective thing, the injured party can recover damages for loss
of expectations and they will be the difference between the thing's actual value
and what it would have been worth if it had been in accordance with the
contract.

In some cases, damages are awarded to compensate the plaintiff for
expenditure which he has incurred in reliance on the contract and which has
been wasted as a result of its breach. Damages of this type, damages for reliance
loss, put the plaintiff into the position in which he would have been if *the
contract had never been made*. By way of an extension, damages can even be
recovered for expenses incurred prior to, and in anticipation of, the contract
and wasted as a result of the breach. In *Lloyd v Stanbury*[2], for instance, the
plaintiff, who had made a contract to buy a farm, which was broken by the
defendant's failure to complete, was awarded damages for (inter alia) the
following losses incurred before there was a binding contract of sale: legal
expenses incurred in carrying out pre-contract searches and drafting the
contract, and the cost of moving a caravan to the farm, as a temporary home
for the defendant, prior to and in anticipation of the contract.

Because they compensate for expenditure which has been *incurred in reliance
on the contract and wasted as a result of its breach*, damages for reliance loss
cannot be awarded if this would make the plaintiff better off than if the contract
had been performed, as where the plaintiff has made a bad bargain by agreeing
to pay more for something than it was worth. *C and P Haulage (a firm) v
Middleton*[3] provides an example of the operation of this limitation. A was granted
by B a contractual licence (on a six-month renewable basis) to occupy premises
as a workshop. A spent money in making the premises suitable, although the
contract provided that fixtures installed by him were not to be removed. Ten
weeks before the end of a six-month term, A was ejected in breach of the
contractual licence. As a temporary measure, A was permitted by his local
authority to use his own home as a workshop, which he did until well after the

six-month term had expired. The Court of Appeal held that A could only recover nominal damages. He could not recover, as reliance loss, his expenditure in equipping the premises, because, it was held, if the contract had been lawfully terminated at the end of the six-month term, there would have been no question of him recovering that expenditure and, therefore, to award him such damages would leave him better off than if the contract had been wholly performed. In order to defeat a plaintiff's claim for wasted expenditure, the onus is on the defendant to prove that the expenditure would not have been recovered if the contract had been performed[4].

A plaintiff has an unfettered right to frame his claim as one for loss of expectations or as one for reliance loss. Although a claim for reliance loss is particularly appropriate where a plaintiff cannot prove any loss of expectations or can only prove a small loss of this type or where the contract is aborted too early for the value of the eventual loss of bargain to be properly assessed, a claim for reliance loss is not limited to such cases[4].

Although damages for loss of expectations and damages for reliance loss are not mutually exclusive, claims for both cannot be combined if this has the effect of compensating the plaintiff twice over for the same loss. For example, in *Cullinane v British Rema Manufacturing Co Ltd*[5], the defendants sold a machine to the plaintiffs. A term of the contract related to the machine's output rate. The plaintiffs claimed damages for breach of this term under two headings: a. loss of profits (loss of expectations), and b. the capital cost of the machine and its installation (reliance loss). It was held that the plaintiffs could not recover damages for both types of loss, as a claim for loss of profits could only be based on the fact that money had been spent on acquiring and installing the machine.

1   *Wertheim v Chicoutimi Pulp Co* [1911] AC 301, PC.
2   [1971] 2 All ER 267, [1971] 1 WLR 535. See also *Anglia Television Ltd v Reed* [1972] 1 QB 60, [1971] 3 All ER 690, CA.
3   [1983] 3 All ER 94, [1983] 1 WLR 1461, CA.
4   *CCC Films (London) Ltd v Impact Quadrant Films Ltd* [1985] QB 16, [1984] 3 All ER 298.
5   [1954] 1 QB 292, [1953] 2 All ER 1257, CA.

12.4   Subject to the rules of remoteness, a plaintiff can recover not merely for the above types of economic loss resulting from the breach of contract, but also for personal injury (including pain and suffering), injury to property, or physical inconvenience or discomfort[1], resulting from the breach.

Damages for disappointment or distress brought about by breach of contract may also be awarded, but only:

a.   where it is a consequence of physical inconvenience or discomfort caused by the breach[2]; or
b.   where an object of the contract was the giving of pleasure or enjoyment or the prevention of disturbed peace of mind or of distress.

In *Jarvis v Swans Tours Ltd*[3], for instance, the plaintiff booked a 15-day winter sports holiday with the defendants. He did so on the faith of the defendants' brochure, which described the holiday as a house party and promised a number of entertainments including excellent skiing, a yodeller evening, a bar, and afternoon tea and cakes. In the first week there were 13 guests; in the second the plaintiff was entirely alone. The entertainments fell far short of the promised standard. The Court of Appeal held that the plaintiff was entitled to damages for mental distress and disappointment due to loss of enjoyment caused by the breach of contract. A similar decision was reached in *Heywood v Wellers*[4], where a solicitor's client suffered distress as a result of the solicitor's incompetent handling of an injunction designed to prevent molestation of the client.

In contrast, damages for emotional distress cannot be awarded where the breach is of an employment contract (eg wrongful dismissal[5]) or of a commercial contract, since pleasure or peace of mind or the like is not the object of such a contract[6]. For example, in *Hayes v James & Charles Dodd (a firm)*[7] a married couple, who suffered anxiety and distress when their car repair business failed because their solicitors had incorrectly advised them (in breach of contract) that there was a right of access to the rear of the workshop they were purchasing, were held by the Court of Appeal not to be entitled to damages for that distress (although they recovered damages for the financial loss which they had suffered). This case makes an interesting contrast to *Heywood v Wellers* where the object of the contract was to prevent the client suffering distress.

Damages for injury to existing reputation are not as a general rule recoverable in a breach of contract action[8] but, where damages for distress are recoverable, that distress (and therefore the amount recoverable for it) may be increased by the mental anguish suffered by the plaintiff as a result of his loss of reputation[9]. There are some exceptions to the general rule. For example, damages for loss of reputation can be recovered if the object of the contract is to preserve or enhance the plaintiff's reputation[10].

1   *Hobbs v London and South Western Rly Co* (1875) LR 10 QB 111; *Bailey v Bullock* [1950] 2 All ER 1167.
2   *Perry v Sidney Phillips & Son* [1982] 3 All ER 705, [1982] 1 WLR 1297, CA; *Watts v Morrow* [1991] 4 All ER 937, [1991] 1 WLR 1421, CA.
3   [1973] QB 233, [1973] 1 All ER 71, CA.
4   [1976] QB 446, [1976] 1 All ER 300, CA.
5   *Addis v Gramophone Co Ltd* [1909] AC 488, HL.
6   *Bliss v South East Thames Regional Health Authority* [1987] ICR 700, [1985] IRLR 308, CA; *Hayes v James & Charles Dodd (a firm)* [1990] 2 All ER 815, CA.
7   [1990] 2 All ER 815, CA.
8   *Addis v Gramophone Co* [1909] AC 488, HL; *Malik v Bank of Credit and Commerce International SA* [1995] 3 All ER 545, CA.
9   *McLeish v Amoo-Gottfried & Co* (1993) 10 PN 102.
10 This and other exceptions were recognised in *Malik v Bank of Credit and Commerce International SA* [1995] 3 All ER 545, CA.

Remoteness of damage

12.5   In order to succeed in his action for damages, the plaintiff must, of course, prove that the loss or damage (hereafter simply referred to as 'loss') which he has suffered resulted from the defendant's breach of contract[1]. This requires that the plaintiff's loss would not have occurred but for the defendant's breach. The defendant's breach need not be the only cause of the loss, since the conduct of others or the occurrence of extraneous events may also contribute to it, but it must be an effective or dominant cause of the loss[2].

Proof of a causal link between breach and loss is not in itself enough to entitle the plaintiff to damages for that loss, because a defendant will only be liable for it if it was not too 'remote'. Whether or not loss suffered is too remote is determined by applying the rule in *Hadley v Baxendale*[3] (as explained in *Victoria Laundry (Windsor) Ltd v Newman Industries Ltd*[4] and *Koufos v C Czarnikow Ltd, The Heron II*[5]).

The rule, as explained, provides that damage is not too remote if one of the two following sub-rules is satisfied:

a.   if the loss arises naturally, ie according to the usual course of things, from the breach of contract as a seriously possible result of it; or

b.   if the loss could reasonably be supposed to have been in the contemplation of the parties, when they made the contract, as a seriously possible result of the breach of it.

Sub-rule a. deals with 'normal' damage which arises in the ordinary course of events, while sub-rule b. deals with 'abnormal' damage which arises from special circumstances.

1   *Weld-Blundell v Stephens* [1920] AC 956, HL.
2   See, for example, *Galoo Ltd v Bright Grahame Murray* [1995] 1 All ER 16, [1994] 1 WLR 1360, CA; *County Ltd v Girozentrale Securities* [1996] 3 All ER 834, CA.
3   (1854) 23 LJ Ex 179.
4   [1949] 2 KB 528, [1949] 1 All ER 997, CA.
5   [1969] 1 AC 350, [1967] 3 All ER 686, HL.

12.6   In the light of subsequent cases, a number of things can be said about both sub-rules.

First, the plaintiff can only recover for such loss as would, *at the time of the contract,* have been within the reasonable contemplation of the parties as a serious possibility as a result of its breach, *had they had their attention drawn to the possibility of the breach which has in fact occurred*[1]. It must be emphasised that the particular breach itself need not have been contemplated. Suppose that the loss has been caused by some defect in the subject matter of the contract which was unknown, or even unknowable, when the contract was made. The court has to assume, even though it is contrary to the facts, that the parties had in mind the breach which has occurred when it considers whether the plaintiff's loss was within their reasonable contemplation[1].

Second, what was within the parties' reasonable contemplation depends on the knowledge 'possessed' by them at that time. For this purpose, knowledge 'possessed' is of two kinds: one imputed, the other actual. Under sub-rule a., everyone is taken to know (ie knowledge is imputed) the 'ordinary course of things' and, consequently, what loss is a serious possibility as a result of a breach of contract in that ordinary course. In addition, 'knowledge possessed' may, in a particular case, include knowledge which the guilty party (and the other party) actually possess of special circumstances, outside the ordinary course of things, of such a kind that the breach in these special circumstances would as a serious possibility be liable to cause more loss. Such a case attracts sub-rule b. so as to make the additional loss recoverable[2].

Third, provided the *type* of loss caused by a breach of contract was within the reasonable contemplation of the parties when the contract was made, the loss is not too remote, and damages can therefore be recovered for it, even though its *extent* was much greater than could have been reasonably contemplated[3] and even though it occurred in a way which could not have been reasonably contemplated as a serious possibility[4]. An example is provided by *H Parsons (Livestock) Ltd v Uttley Ingham & Co Ltd*[5]. The defendants supplied the plaintiffs with a hopper in which to store pig nuts. The hopper was not properly ventilated, and this constituted a breach of contract by the defendants; as a result, the pig nuts became mouldy and many of the plaintiffs' pigs suffered a rare intestinal disease (E coli) from which 254 of them died. The plaintiffs were awarded damages by the Court of Appeal for the loss sustained by the death and sickness of the pigs. The reasoning of the majority of the Court of Appeal was that, if the breach had been brought to the parties' attention and they had asked themselves what was likely to happen as a result, they would have contemplated the serious possibility that the pigs would become ill, and that, since the *type* of loss caused (physical harm) was within the parties' reasonable contemplation, it was irrelevant that its extent and the way in which it occurred were not.

1   *H Parsons (Livestock) Ltd v Uttley Ingham & Co Ltd* [1978] QB 791, [1978] 1 All ER 525, CA.
2   *Victoria Laundry (Windsor) Ltd v Newman Industries Ltd* [1949] 2 KB 528, [1949] 1 All ER 997, CA.
3   *Wroth v Tyler* [1974] Ch 30, [1973] 1 All ER 897; *H Parsons (Livestock) Ltd v Uttley Ingham & Co Ltd* [1978] QB 791, [1978] 1 All ER 525, CA.
4   *H Parsons (Livestock) Ltd v Uttley Ingham & Co Ltd* [1978] QB 791, [1978] 1 All ER 525, CA.
5   [1978] QB 791, [1978] 1 All ER 525, CA.

12.7   The degree of risk which is required to have been within the parties' reasonable contemplation in order to satisfy the test of remoteness has been variously described in the cases. In *Koufos v C Czarnikow Ltd, The Heron II*[1], which can be taken as settling the point, the House of Lords made it clear that the degree of risk is more than mere possibility or a risk that is 'on the cards'. However, they were not unanimous in their terminology as to the degree of risk required. Lords Pearce and Upjohn favoured 'serious possibility' or 'real danger'; Lord Reid favoured 'not unlikely' (ie 'considerably less than even chance, but nevertheless not very unusual and easily foreseeable'). With the exception of Lord Reid, the House was prepared to accept the phrase 'liable to result', a rather colourless and vague term which two of them thought was a convenient term to describe 'serious possibility' or 'real danger'. We have used 'serious possibility' in this book on the basis that it best conveys the degree of risk required which emerges from the speeches in the House of Lords.

1   [1969] 1 AC 350, [1967] 3 All ER 686, HL.

12.8   The application of the contractual rule of remoteness can best be illustrated by reference to past decisions. In *Hadley v Baxendale*[1], the plaintiffs' mill at Gloucester was brought to a halt when a crankshaft broke. The shaft had to be sent to its makers in Greenwich as a pattern for a new one. The defendant carriers undertook to deliver it at Greenwich the following day, but in breach of contract delayed its delivery so that the duration of the stoppage at the mill was extended. The plaintiffs' claim to recover damages for loss of profits caused by the defendants' delay was unsuccessful since this loss was held to be too remote. The basis of the court's decision was that the defendants only knew that they were transporting a broken shaft owned by the plaintiffs. The court applied the two sub-rules in turn, and held:

a.   the plaintiffs might have had a spare shaft or been able to borrow one, and therefore the loss of profits did not arise in the usual course of events from the defendants' breach; and

b.   on the facts known to the defendants (they were unaware of the lack of a substitute shaft), the loss of profits could not be supposed to have been within the reasonable contemplation of the parties at the time they made the contract as the probable result of the breach.

1   (1854) 23 LJ Ex 179.

12.9   In *Victoria Laundry (Windsor) Ltd v Newman Industries Ltd*[1], the defendants agreed to sell to the plaintiffs, who were launderers and dyers, a boiler to be delivered on a certain date. The boiler was damaged in a fall and was not delivered until five months after the agreed delivery date. The plaintiffs claimed damages for loss of profits that would have been earned during the five-month period through the extension of their business, and also for loss of several highly lucrative dyeing contracts which they would have obtained with the Ministry of Supply. The Court of Appeal held that the plaintiffs could recover for the loss of 'normal' profits (ie those which would have been earned through an extension of the business) but not for the loss of 'exceptional' profits (ie loss of the highly lucrative contracts), which it treated as a different type of loss. This decision was based on the following application of the two sub-rules:

a.   the defendants knew at the time of the contract that the plaintiffs were laundrymen and dyers and required the boiler for immediate use in their business and, with their technical experience and knowledge of the facts, it could be presumed that loss of 'normal' profits was foreseeable by them, and therefore within both parties' reasonable contemplation, as liable to result from the breach; but

b.   in the absence of special knowledge, the defendants could not reasonably foresee the loss of the 'exceptional' profits under the highly lucrative contracts as liable to result from the breach.

The case was, therefore, remitted to an official referee for a decision as to the amount of 'normal' profits which had been lost in the circumstances.

1   [1949] 2 KB 528, [1949] 1 All ER 997, CA.

12.10   In *Koufos v C Czarnikow Ltd,The Heron II*[1], the plaintiff sugar merchants chartered a ship from the defendant to carry a cargo of sugar from Constanza to Basrah. The ship deviated in breach of contract and arrived in Basrah nine days later than expected. Because of a fall in the market price of sugar, the plaintiffs obtained £3,800 less for the cargo than would have been obtained if it had arrived on time. The defendant did not know of the plaintiffs' intention to sell the sugar in Basrah, but he did know that there was a market for sugar at Basrah and that the plaintiffs were sugar merchants. The House of Lords held that the plaintiffs' loss of profits (£3,800) was not too remote under sub-rule a., since knowledge could be imputed to the defendant that the goods might be sold at market price on their arrival in Basrah and that market prices were apt to fluctuate daily, and therefore the loss of profits was within the reasonable contemplation of the parties at the time of the contract as a serious possibility in the event of the breach in question.

1   [1969] 1 AC 350, [1967] 3 All ER 686, HL.

Measure of damages
12.11   Assuming that the loss is not too remote from the breach of contract, the next question which the court has to consider is the measure (ie quantification) of damages for that loss.

Generally, there are no specific rules for the quantification of damages. One exception relates to contracts for the sale of goods, where the Sale of Goods Act 1979 provides a number of rules, such as the following.

Sections 50(2) and 51(2) of the 1979 Act deal respectively with the measure of damages where the buyer wrongfully neglects or refuses to accept and pay for the goods, and the measure where the seller wrongfully neglects or refuses to deliver the goods to the buyer. They state that the measure of damages is the estimated loss directly and naturally resulting, in the ordinary course of events, from the breach. Sections 50(3) and 51(3) go on to provide that, where there is an available market for the goods in question (ie they can be freely and readily sold), the measure of damages is prima facie the difference between the contract price and the market or current price at the time or times when the goods ought to have been accepted or delivered, or, if no time was fixed for acceptance or delivery, then at the time of refusal[1]. Consequently, in the case of a failure to accept by the buyer, for example, if there is an available market for the goods and:

a.   their market price is *lower* than their contract price, the seller is entitled to substantial damages representing the difference; but if
b.   their market price is the *same as or even higher* than the contract price, the seller is only entitled to nominal damages.

Sections 50(3) and 51(3) only lay down a prima facie rule which can be displaced if it would work injustice or otherwise be inappropriate[1].

Where there is no available market, the court has to rely on the basic provision, ss 50(2) and 51(2), and determine the loss directly and naturally resulting from the buyer's breach.

The rules just stated are concerned with valuing one element of the injured party's loss, his expectation of having the goods accepted and being paid or his expectation of getting the goods, as the case may be. In addition, he can recover for any other loss which is not too remote[2]. For example, where the buyer of goods which have not been delivered would have resold them at a profit, he can recover special damages for loss of profit if that loss is not too remote.

1   *W L Thompson Ltd v Robinson (Gunmakers) Ltd* [1955] Ch 177, [1977] 1 All ER 154.
2   Sale of Goods Act 1979, s 54.

12.12   Other rules for the measure of damages have emerged from judicial decisions. A detailed exposition of these is outside the scope of this book. In laying down a rule for the quantification of damages, the court will often be faced with a choice, as is shown by *Ruxley Electronics Ltd v Forsyth*[1]. The defendant contracted with the plaintiffs for the construction by the defendant of a swimming pool at the plaintiff's house. A term of the contract specifically required the pool to be 7'6" deep at its deepest point. However, the defendant constructed a pool which was, at most, 6' deep. More importantly, at a point where the diving board was situated, the pool was less than 6' deep. The House of Lords was faced with a choice of two options as to the quantification of damages in respect of the defect:

a.   Capital value of pool in a non-defective state minus its value in its defective state. This is the so-called 'diminution in value' measure; it was favoured by the trial judge, who found that there had been no diminution in value because, despite its defects, the pool still enhanced the value of the plaintiff's property.
b.   Cost of repair/reinstatement. This is the so-called 'reinstatement measure', which was favoured by the Court of Appeal and involved an award of damages in line with the expensive cost of digging up and extensively re-constructing the pool.

The House of Lords took the same view as the trial judge and simply awarded the plaintiff £2,500 for loss of amenity and nothing as damages in respect of the defect to the pool itself. In the major judgment in the House, it was indicated that, where the cost of reinstatement was *less* than the difference in value, the measure should be the cost of reinstatement. (By claiming diminution in value measure, the plaintiff would be failing to take reasonable steps to mitigate his loss; see mitigation of loss in para 12.15, below.) On the other hand, where the cost of reinstatement was *out of all proportion* to the good to be obtained, the appropriate measure was the diminution in value measure, and if there was no diminution in value substantial damages could not be awarded in respect of the defect in the pool itself.

The award of £2,500 for loss of amenity was justified on the basis that the object of the contract was the provision of a pleasurable amenity and that the plaintiff's pleasure was not as great as it would have been if the pool had been 7'6" deep. The trial judge had awarded £2,500, and this had not been attacked in the House of Lords, who were consequently reluctant to interfere with that amount. The one Law Lord who considered the matter further justified an award for loss of amenity on the basis that it was a logical adaptation or application of the existing exceptions to the rule that generally damages for distress or disappointment cannot be awarded[2].

1   [1996] AC 344, [1995] 3 All ER 268, HL.
2   [1995] 3 All ER 268 at 289.

12.13   Apart from any specific rules, it is up to the court to quantify adequate compensation for the plaintiff's loss as best it can. The fact that the precise assessment of damages is difficult does not prevent an award being made, as is shown by *Chaplin v Hicks*[1]. The defendant advertised that he would employ, as actresses, 12 women to be selected by him out of 50 chosen as the most beautiful by the readers of various newspapers, in which the candidates' photographs appeared. The plaintiff was one of the 50 chosen by the readers but the defendant, in beach of contract, made an unreasonable appointment for an interview with her, and selected 12 out of the 49 who were able to keep the appointment. In an action for breach of contract, the defendant contended that only nominal damages were payable, since the plaintiff would only have had a one in four chance of being selected. Nevertheless, the Court of Appeal refused to disturb an award of £100 damages for the loss of her chance of being selected. Where damages are claimed for a lost chance, the plaintiff must prove that the chance was a real or substantial, and not merely speculative, one. The value of the lost chance will depend on where the chance lay on a range between a real or substantial one and a virtually certain one[2].

1   [1911] 2 KB 786, CA.
2   *Allied Maples Group Ltd v Simmons & Simmons* [1995] 4 All ER 907, [1995] 1 WLR 1602, CA; *Stovold v Barlows* [1995] NPC 154, CA.

12.14   Where damages are awarded to compensate the plaintiff for loss of his expectations they are normally assessed as at the date of the breach. However, this is not an absolute rule since, if its observance would give rise to injustice, the court has power to fix such other date as may be appropriate in the circumstances[1]. Thus, for example, where a breach of a contract of sale of land has occurred and, having reasonably sought an order for specific performance of the contract, the plaintiff elects to claim damages in lieu of specific performance or specific performance becomes impossible (without his default), damages should be assessed as at the date of the election[2] or of specific performance becoming aborted[3], as the case may be. As another example, where the plaintiff could only reasonably have been expected to mitigate his loss at a point of time after the breach, damages should be assessed as at that point of time or, if that point of time is not earlier, at the date of the hearing[4].

In the case of an anticipatory breach of contract, damages for loss of expectations are assessed by reference to the time when performance ought to have been made, and not by reference to the time of the anticipatory breach[5].

1   *Johnson v Agnew* [1980] AC 367 at 400, [1979] 1 All ER 883, HL.
2   *Domb v Isoz* [1980] Ch 548, [1980] 1 All ER 942, CA.
3   *Johnson v Agnew* [1980] AC 367, [1979] 1 All ER 883, HL.

4 *Radford v de Froberville* [1978] 1 All ER 33, [1977] 1 WLR 1262; *William Cory & Son Ltd v Wingate Investments (London Colney) Ltd* (1978) 248 Estates Gazette 687, CA. For mitigation of loss, see paras 12.15 and 12.16, below.
5 *Tai Hing Cotton Mill Ltd v Kamsing Knitting Factory* [1979] AC 91, [1978] 1 All ER 515, PC; *Gebruder Metelmann GmbH & Co KG v NBR (London) Ltd* [1984] 1 Lloyd's Rep 614, CA.

Mitigation
12.15 The plaintiff cannot recover for loss which he could reasonably have avoided. Thus, the seller of goods which have been wrongly rejected by the buyer must not unreasonably refuse another's offer to buy them. Similarly, an employee who has been wrongfully dismissed must not unreasonably refuse an offer of employment from another[1]. If such refusals occur, the plaintiff is said to be in breach of his duty to mitigate his loss and cannot recover his unmitigated loss but only the loss which he would have suffered if the damage had been mitigated. If he would have suffered no loss at all, only nominal damages are recoverable[1].

A leading case on the duty to mitigate is *Payzu Ltd v Saunders*[2]. A contract for the sale of goods by the defendant to the plaintiffs provided that delivery should be as required over a nine-month period and that payment should be made within one month of delivery. The plaintiffs failed to make prompt payment for the first instalment and the defendant, in breach of contract, refused to deliver any more instalments under the contract. He did, however, offer to deliver goods at the contract price if the plaintiffs would pay cash with each order. The plaintiffs refused to do so and brought an action for breach of contract, claiming the difference between the contract price and the market price (which had risen). The Court of Appeal held that the plaintiffs should have mitigated their loss by accepting the defendant's offer. Consequently, the damages which they could recover were to be measured by the loss which they would have suffered if the offer had been accepted (a month's credit on each order), not by the difference between the contract and market prices.

The following points may be noted about the duty to mitigate:

a.   The phrase 'duty to mitigate' is somewhat misleading because the plaintiff is not legally obliged to do so. He is free to act as he judges to be in his best interest, but if he does so he cannot recover for loss which he could reasonably have avoided[3].
b.   The duty to mitigate may require the plaintiff to do something positive. In the examples given above, the seller and the employee would equally have been in breach of their duty to mitigate if they had not made reasonable efforts to seek other offers to buy the goods or alternative equivalent employment: it would not necessarily excuse them that no one had spontaneously made them an offer. Damages cannot be recovered for any loss which would have been avoided if such reasonable steps had been taken[4].
c.   The duty to mitigate only requires the plaintiff to take reasonable steps to minimise his loss. He is not required to act with lightning speed, nor to accept the first or, indeed, any offer that is made (unless it is a reasonable one). For example, a wrongfully dismissed managing director is not

expected to mitigate his loss by taking a job sweeping floors. Indeed, in one case it was held that it was reasonable for a person who had wrongfully been dismissed as managing director in an arbitrary and high-handed fashion to refuse the company's offer of a slightly lower post at the same salary[5].

1 *Brace v Calder* [1895] 2 QB 253, CA.
2 [1919] 2 KB 581, CA.
3 *Sotiros Shipping Inc v Sameiet Solholt, The Solholt* [1983] 1 Lloyd's Rep 605 at 608.
4 *British Westinghouse Electric and Manufacturing Co Ltd v Underground Electric Rlys Co of London Ltd* [1912] AC 673 at 689.
5 *Yetton v Eastwoods Froy Ltd* [1966] 3 All ER 353, [1967] 1 WLR 104.

12.16 Where there is an anticipatory breach of contract, the injured party has an option *either* to terminate the contract and sue immediately for damages *or* to affirm the contract and await the time fixed for performance, in which case he can then bring an action for damages if the other party is still in breach. If the injured party elects to terminate he is under a duty to mitigate his loss[1]. On the other hand, the injured party is under no duty to mitigate his loss before performance is due if he affirms the contract[2].

1 *L Roth & Co Ltd v Taysen, Townsend & Co* (1895) 1 Com Cas 240; *Gebruder Metelmann GmbH & Co KG v NBR (London) Ltd* [1984] 1 Lloyd's Rep 614, CA.
2 Para 10.24, above.

Contributory negligence
12.17 Where a plaintiff has by his own fault contributed to his loss or the event causing it, his damages for breach of contract are not generally reduced in proportion to his degree of responsibility for that loss or event[1]. The doctrine of contributory negligence, which (by virtue of the Law Reform (Contributory Negligence) Act 1945) has this effect in the case of an action in tort for negligence or breach of statutory duty[2], does not generally apply to an action for breach of contract[3]. There is one exception. If the defendant is liable in tort for negligence independently of the contract and also for breach of a contractual obligation to take reasonable care which was the same as the common law duty in the tort of negligence[4], a court may apportion the blame and reduce the damages awarded to the plaintiff for breach of contract by reason of his contributory negligence[5]. Suppose that an accountant's client negligently gives the accountant incorrect information and is then negligently given incorrect advice by the accountant. As a result of a combination of his and the accountant's negligence, the client suffers economic loss. The doctrine of contributory negligence would apply to an action by the client for breach of contract because the accountant's liability to the client in the tort of negligence and for breach of contract would be based on the same obligation to take reasonable care.

Of course, in any breach of contract case, if the plaintiff's contribution to his loss is so great as to prevent the defendant's breach of contract being an effective cause of the plaintiff's loss, the plaintiff will not be able to recover any damages at all for it[6]. Moreover, if the defendant successfully brings a counterclaim to a successful claim by the plaintiff, the effect on the damages awarded to each party may be the same as if there was an apportionment of liability on grounds of contributory negligence. In *Tennant Radiant Heat Ltd v Warrington Development Corpn*[7], for instance, the plaintiffs leased a unit in a warehouse owned by the defendants. Goods stored there by the plaintiffs were damaged when the roof collapsed under an accumulation of rainwater. The roof would not have collapsed but for the facts that the plaintiffs, in breach of covenant, had failed to repair the roof over their unit and that the defendants had failed to keep clear the water outlets on the roof as a whole and were therefore liable in tort for negligence and nuisance[8]. The Court of Appeal held that the damages recoverable on the claim and counterclaim should be assessed on the basis of the extent to which the damage to the goods (plaintiffs' claim) and to the roof (defendants' counterclaim) were caused, respectively, by the defendants' tortious behaviour and by the plaintiffs' breach of covenant.

1 *Basildon District Council v J E Lesser (Properties) Ltd* [1985] QB 839, [1985] 1 All ER 20.
2 Law Reform (Contributory Negligence) Act 1945. See paras 21.11–21.15, below.
3 *Basildon District Council v J E Lesser (Properties) Ltd* [1985] QB 839, [1985] 1 All ER 20; *Marintrans AB v Comet Shipping Co Ltd* [1985] 3 All ER 442, [1985] 1 WLR 1270; *Barclays Bank plc v Fairclough Building Ltd* [1995] QB 214, [1995] 1 All ER 289, CA.
4 As to when there may be concurrent liability in tort and in contract, see para 18.67.
5 *Forsikringsaktieselskapet Vesta v Butcher* [1989] AC 852, [1988] 2 All ER 43, CA; affd on other grounds [1989] AC 852, [1989] 1 All ER 402, HL.
6 Para 12.5, above; *Marintrans AB v Comet Shipping Co Ltd*, above.
7 [1988] 1 EGLR 41, CA.
8 See Chap 18 and paras 20.21–20.25, below.

Liquidated damages and penalties

12.18 So far we have been concerned with *unliquidated damages*, ie damages which are assessed by the court and not by the agreement of the parties. It is, however, possible for the parties to agree in their contract that in the event of a breach of it the damages shall be a fixed sum or be calculated in a specific way. Such damages are called *liquidated damages*. Liquidated damages have the obvious advantage that the amount recoverable as damages is always certain, whereas in the case of unliquidated damages it is uncertain until the court has decided the matter. Provision for liquidated damages is often found in contracts which have to be completed within a certain time. Thus, contracts for building or civil engineering work normally provide for a specified sum to be paid for every day or week of delay. Similarly, most, if not all, voyage charterparties of ships contain a provision for a specified sum per day to be paid by the charterer to the shipowner if the ship is detained by the charterer's failure to load or unload within a stipulated period of time; the specified sum is known as 'demurrage'.

It is customary to refer to penalty clauses and liquidated damages clauses as involving the payment of a sum of money, and for convenience we shall discuss them mainly in that context. However, it should not be forgotten that penalty clauses and liquidated damages clauses may involve the transfer of property, and not the payment of money[1].

If a contract containing a liquidated damages provision is broken, the injured party can recover the specified sum, whether this is greater or less than the actual loss suffered. This rule may benefit a plaintiff who has suffered little or no loss but can be to his disadvantage if the loss suffered greatly exceeds the specified sum. In *Cellulose Acetate Silk Co Ltd v Widnes Foundry (1925) Ltd*[2], the defendants agreed to build machinery for the plaintiffs in 18 weeks and, in the event of taking longer, to pay 'by way of penalty £20 per working week'. The machinery was completed 30 weeks late and the plaintiffs lost £5,850 in consequence. The House of Lords held that the provision was one for liquidated damages and that the plaintiff could only recover 30 x £20, ie £600.

1 *Jobson v Johnson* [1989] 1 All ER 621, [1989] 1 WLR 1026, CA.
2 [1933] AC 20, HL.

12.19 Liquidated damages provisions must be distinguished from two other provisions:

a. *Exemption clauses restricting liability* A liquidated damages clause is not an exemption clause limiting liability because it fixes the sum payable for breach whether the actual loss is greater or less, whereas (assuming it is valid) such an exemption clause merely fixes the maximum sum recoverable and, if the actual loss is less than that sum, only the actual loss can be recovered.
b. *Penalty clauses* Where the sum fixed by the contract is a genuine pre-estimate of the loss which will be caused by its breach, the provision is one for liquidated damages, but if instead the sum is intended to operate as a threat to hold a potential defaulter to his bargain it is a penalty[1]. The distinction between a penalty and liquidated damages is crucial because their effects are different.

1 *Law v Redditch Local Board* [1892] 1 QB 127 at 132.

Penalty
12.20 If the actual loss by a plaintiff is less than the sum specified in a penalty clause, he can only recover his actual loss[1]. Suppose that a broken contract contains a penalty clause providing for a £1,000 penalty but the plaintiff's actual loss is only £100, the plaintiff can only recover £100 (whereas if the clause had been one for liquidated damages the plaintiff could have recovered £1,000). On the other hand, if the penalty is less than the actual loss suffered by the plaintiff, eg because of inflation since the contract was made, he cannot recover more than the penalty if he sues for it, although if he sues instead for (unliquidated) damages he can recover the whole of his loss[2]. This option is not, of course, open in the case of a liquidated damages provision.

1 *Wilbeam v Ashton* (1807) 1 Camp 78. A similar principle applies where the penalty involves the transfer of property whose value exceeds the plaintiff's actual loss: *Jobson v Johnson* [1989] 1 All ER 621, [1989] 1 WLR 1026, CA.
2 *Wall v Rederiaktiebolaget Luggude* [1915] 3 KB 66.

Parties' intention
12.21 Whether an agreed sum is liquidated damages or a penalty depends on the parties' intention and, as is shown by the *Cellulose Acetate* case[1], the use

of the words 'penalty' or 'liquidated damages' in the contract is not conclusive. The crucial question is whether the parties intended the specified sum to be a genuine pre-estimate of the damage likely to be caused by the breach or to operate as a fine or penalty for breach. This intention is to be gathered from the terms and inherent circumstances of the contract at the time it was made, not at the time of its breach[2]. This does not mean that what has happened subsequently is irrelevant, since it can provide valuable evidence as to what could reasonably have been expected to be the loss when the contract was made[3].

The determination of the parties' intention is aided by a number of rebuttable presumptions of intention summarised by Lord Dunedin in *Dunlop Pneumatic Tyre Co Ltd v New Garage and Motor Co Ltd*[4]:

a. 'It will be held to be a penalty if the sum stipulated for is extravagant and unconscionable in amount in comparison with the greatest loss that could conceivably be proved to have followed from the breach.'

b. 'It will be held to be a penalty if the breach consists only in not paying a sum of money, and the sum stipulated is a sum greater than the sum which ought to have been paid.'

c. 'There is a presumption (but no more) that it is a penalty when a single lump sum is made payable by way of compensation, on the occurrence of one or more or all of several events, some of which may occasion serious and others but trifling damage.' In *Kemble v Farren*[5], for example, the defendant agreed with the plaintiff to appear at Covent Garden for four seasons at £3.6s.8d (£3.33) a night. The contract provided that if either party refused to fulfil the agreement, or any part of it, he should pay the other £1,000 as 'liquidated damages'. The defendant refused to act during the second season. It was held that the stipulation was a penalty. The obligation to pay £1,000 might have arisen simply on the plaintiff's failure to pay £3.6s.8d and was therefore quite obviously a penalty. It has been held that the court should be careful not to set too stringent a standard and should bear in mind that what the parties have agreed should normally be upheld, since any other approach would lead to undesirable uncertainty, especially in commercial contracts[3].

d. 'It is no obstacle to the sum stipulated being a genuine pre-estimate of damage, that the consequences of the breach are such as to make precise pre-estimation almost an impossibility.' This is illustrated by the *Dunlop* case itself. The plaintiffs supplied tyres to the defendants subject to an agreement that the defendants would not sell below the list price and would pay £5 by way of liquidated damages for every tyre sold in breach of the agreement. The House of Lords held that the stipulated sum was one for liquidated damages. (The agreement would now be void under the Resale Prices Act 1976.) Clearly, the figure of £5 was, at most, only a rough and ready estimate of the possible loss which the plaintiffs might suffer if their price list was undercut.

1   Para 12.18, above.
2   *Dunlop Pneumatic Tyre Co Ltd v New Garage and Motor Co Ltd* [1915] AC 79 at 86–87.

3 *Philips Hong Kong Ltd v A-G of Hong Kong* (1993) 61 BLR 41, PC.
4 [1915] AC 79 at 86.
5 (1829) 6 Bing 141.

12.22 In *Jobson v Johnson*[1], a similar approach was taken to a clause providing for the re-transfer of property at a fixed price in the event of a breach. The plaintiff contracted to sell to the defendant 45% of the shares in Southend United Football Club for a total of £350,000, £311,000 of which was payable by six instalments. The contract contained a clause providing for the re-transfer of the shares at a fixed price (£40,000) if the defendant defaulted in payment of the second or any subsequent instalment. It was held that this was a penalty clause since it was equally applicable if the defendant defaulted on the second instalment (when the plaintiff's loss would be great) or on the last (when his loss would be relatively small); the provision that in the event of default the defendant should re-transfer to the plaintiff the shares at a fixed price could therefore not be regarded as a genuine pre-estimate of the plaintiff's loss.

1 [1989] 1 All ER 621, [1989] 1 WLR 1026, CA.

Action for Price or Other Agreed Sum

12.23 If a breach consists of a party's failure to pay a debt, ie the contractually agreed price or other remuneration, which is due under the contract, the appropriate course for the injured party is to bring an action for the agreed sum to recover that amount.

Limitation: sale of goods contracts

12.24 There is an important limitation on an action for the agreed sum in the case of a contract for the sale of goods. Section 49 of the Sale of Goods Act 1979 provides that, unless the agreed price is payable on a specified date irrespective of delivery, an action for it only lies if the property (ie ownership) in the goods has passed to the buyer.

Limitations: repudiatory breach

12.25 Where a repudiatory breach is committed, the injured party may, of course, recover an agreed sum already due at the time of the breach, whether he terminates or affirms the contract.

The position is more complicated where the agreed sum is not due at the time of the repudiatory breach but may become due subsequently:

a. If the injured party elects to terminate the contract, he cannot claim an agreed sum which might have become due to him subsequently[1].
b. If the injured party elects to affirm the contract, then, as we have already said[2], the contract remains in force, so that both parties are bound to perform any outstanding contractual obligations. Consequently, if the injured party affirms the contract, he may be able to recover the agreed

sum when it becomes due in the future. Whether or not he will be able to recover that sum depends on the rules discussed in the rest of this paragraph.

It was recognised by the majority of the House of Lords in *White and Carter (Councils) Ltd v McGregor*[3] that, if further performance on the part of the injured party is required in order for the sum to become due, he will be unable to recover the agreed sum if his further performance depends on the co-operation of the other party and it is withheld. It is for this reason that a wrongfully dismissed employee cannot sue for his wages payable thereafter, even though he has subsequently indicated his willingness to go on working under the employment contract[4]. Instead he must sue for damages for breach of contract (in respect of which he must take reasonable steps to mitigate his loss by obtaining other employment) or seek payment under the law of restitution on a quantum meruit basis (see below) for the value of work already done.

· It will not be often that the injured party can perform his side of the contract without the co-operation of the other party, although it was possible in *White and Carter (Councils) Ltd v McGregor*[3]. The plaintiffs were advertising contractors. They carried on a business of supplying free litter bins to local authorities, the bins being paid for by businesses which hired advertising space on them. The plaintiffs agreed with the defendant garage proprietor to display advertisements for his garage on bins for three years. On the same day, the defendant renounced the contract and asked the plaintiffs to cancel it. They refused, thereby affirming the contract, and proceeded to prepare advertisement plates which they attached to bins and displayed. When the defendant failed to pay at the appropriate time, the plaintiffs sued for the full contract price. The House of Lords held that they could recover the full contract price despite the fact that they had made no effort to mitigate their loss by getting other advertisers in substitution for the defendant and had increased their loss after the renunciation by performing their side of the contract.

Even if he can perform his side of the contract without the co-operation of the other party, and does so, an injured party cannot recover an agreed sum when it becomes due in the future (as opposed to such damages as would be available) if it is shown that he had no legitimate interest, financial or otherwise, in performing the contract rather than claiming damages. This was stated by one of the Law Lords in *White and Carter*[5], where a lack of a legitimate interest was not shown, and has subsequently been adopted in other cases[6]. What is a 'legitimate interest' in this context remains to be fully determined, although it has been held that a commitment to a third party is such an interest[7]. The term is difficult to define since it is arguable that most injured parties have a legitimate interest in seeing their contract performed. Some judges have stated a corresponding, substitute limitation in terms of whether the injured party's conduct in performing the contract was wholly unreasonable (which would prevent him recovering an agreed sum), as opposed to merely unreasonable (which would not)[8]. This test would seem to be easier to apply than that of 'legitimate interest'.

1   Para 10.5, above.
2   Paras 10.8 and 10.24, above.
3   [1962] AC 413, [1961] 3 All ER 1178, HL.
4   *Denmark Productions Ltd v Boscobel Productions Ltd* [1969] 1 QB 699, [1968] 3 All ER 513,
    CA; *Gunton v Richmond-upon-Thames London Borough Council* [1981] Ch 448, [1980] 3 All
    ER 577, CA.
5   [1962] AC 413 at 431.
6   *Attica Sea Carriers Corpn v Ferrostaal Poseidon Bulk Reederei GmbH, The Puerto Buitrago* [1976]
    1 Lloyd's Rep 250, CA; *Gator Shipping Corpn v Trans-Asiatic Oil Ltd SA, The Odenfeld* [1978]
    2 Lloyd's Rep 357; *Clea Shipping Corpn v Bulk Oil International Ltd, The Alaskan Trader* [1984]
    1 All ER 129, [1983] 2 Lloyd's Rep 645.
7   *Gator Shipping Corpn v Trans-Asiatic Oil Ltd SA, The Odenfeld* [1978] 2 Lloyd's Rep 357.
8   *Attica Sea Carriers Corpn v Ferrostaal Poseidon Bulk Reederei GmbH, The Puerto Buitrago* [1976]
    1 Lloyd's Rep 250 at 255; *Gator Shipping Corpn v Trans-Asiatic Oil Ltd SA, The Odenfeld*
    [1978] 2 Lloyd's Rep 357 at 374; *Clea Shipping Corpn v Bulk Oil International Ltd, The Alaskan
    Trader* [1984] 1 All ER 129 at 136.

Restitutionary Claim: Quantum Meruit

12.26   In a particular situation set out below, a claim on what is called a
quantum meruit basis is available to a plaintiff as an *alternative* to a claim for
damages for breach of contract.

If a party to a contract unjustifiably prevents the other party performing his
contractual obligations, as where he states that he will not accept performance
or renders performance impossible, his conduct will normally constitute a
repudiatory breach of contract and the injured party can recover damages for
breach of contract, whether he elects to terminate or to affirm the contract.
Alternatively, if the injured party has partly performed his obligations under
the contract he can claim under the law of restitution the reasonable value of
the work done, provided he has elected to terminate the contract[1]. These rules
apply even though the obligation which has not been wholly performed by the
injured party is entire[2]. *Planché v Colburn*[3] is a leading authority. A had agreed
to write for 'The Juvenile Library', a series published by B, a book on costume
and ancient armour. After A had written part of the book, B abandoned the
series. It was held that A could recover 50 guineas (£52.50) as reasonable
remuneration on a quantum meruit.

One distinction between these two types of remedy is that, whereas an award
of damages depends on the existence of a contract and its breach, the right to
claim on a quantum meruit does not arise under the law of contract but by
virtue of the law of restitution. Another distinction relates to the amount
recoverable. As we have already stated, damages are compensatory, their object
generally being to put the plaintiff into the same position, so far as money can
do it, as if the contract had been performed. Thus, if the injured party in a case
like *Planché v Colburn* decides to sue for damages, the damages awarded will be
equivalent to the sum payable to him on completion of his work, less any savings
(eg on labour and materials) made through not completing performance.
However, if it is shown that the plaintiff would in any event have been unable to
perform his entire obligation, he will at most be entitled to nominal damages[4].
On the other hand, a quantum meruit award is restitutory, its object being to
restore the plaintiff to the position in which he would have been if the contract

had never been made by awarding him an amount equivalent to the value of the work which he has done. Generally, an award of damages will be more generous than a quantum meruit award, but the converse may be true if the plaintiff originally made a bad bargain or if only nominal damages would be awarded.

1   *Planché v Colburn* (1831) 8 Bing 14; *Lusty v Finsbury Securities* (1991) 58 BLR 66, CA.
2   Paras 10.12–10.14, above.
3   (1831) 8 Bing 14.
4   *The Mihalis Angelos* [1971] 1 QB 164, [1970] 3 All ER 125, CA.

Specific Performance

12.27   The court may grant a decree of specific performance to the injured party, instead of, or in addition to, awarding him damages. Such a decree orders the defaulting party to carry out his contractual obligations.

12.28   Specific performance will not be granted in the following cases:

a.   *Where damages are an adequate remedy*   It is for this reason that specific performance of a contract to sell goods is not normally ordered; the payment of damages enables the plaintiff to go out into the market and buy the equivalent goods[1]. On the other hand, in exceptional cases, where damages would be inadequate, eg where the contract is for the sale of specific goods of a unique character or of special value or interest, the contract is specifically enforceable[2]. In *Cohen v Roche*[3], an order of specific performance of a contract for the sale of eight Hepplewhite chairs was refused because they were 'ordinary articles of commerce and of no special value or interest'; the plaintiff was merely awarded damages for non-delivery. On the other hand, in *Behnke v Bede Shipping Co Ltd*[4], an order for specific performance of a contract of sale of a ship was made because the ship was of 'peculiar and practically unique value to the plaintiff'.

By way of contrast, every plot of land is unique, with the result that contracts for the sale or lease of land are always specifically enforceable. This has produced the rule that, since the contract is specifically enforceable in favour of the purchaser or lessee, a vendor or lessor of land can obtain an order of specific performance even though, in the particular case, damages would be an adequate remedy[5].

It is because damages are normally adequate that a contractual obligation to pay money is not normally specifically enforceable. However, in addition to the exception just mentioned, there are other exceptions, for instance:
i.   as the House of Lords held in *Beswick v Beswick*[6], a contract to pay money to a third party can be specifically enforced where, as is normally the case, any damages awarded would be nominal; and
ii.   where the contract is for an annuity or other periodical payment it can be specifically enforced (thereby avoiding the need to sue for damages every time a payment is not made)[7].

b.   *Where consideration has not been provided*   The remedy of specific performance is an equitable one and, since equity does not recognise the making of a contract by deed as an effective substitute for consideration, specific performance cannot be awarded in favour of a person who has not provided consideration ('equity will not assist a volunteer') and he is left to his common law remedy of damages[8].

c.   *Where the court's constant supervision would be necessary to secure compliance with the order*   An example is provided by *Ryan v Mutual Tontine Westminster Chambers Association*[9]. In the lease of a flat in a block of flats the lessors agreed to keep a resident porter, who should be in constant attendance and perform specified duties. The person appointed got his duties done by deputies and was absent for hours at a time at another job. The court refused to order against the lessors specific performance of the agreement relating to the performance of the specified duties by the porter because such an order would have required its constant supervision. On the other hand, in *Posner v Scott-Lewis*[10], specific performance was ordered against a lessor of a covenant to appoint a porter because what had to be done to comply with the order (appointing a porter) could be defined with sufficient certainty and enforcement of the order would not require the constant supervision of the court. In *Co-operative Insurance Society Ltd v Argyll Stores (Holdings) Ltd*,[11] where the House of Lords allowed an appeal against the Court of Appeal's order for specific performance of a covenant in a lease of a supermarket which required it to be kept open for trade, the House of Lords held that specific performance should not be ordered if it would require a defendant to run a business (save in exceptional circumstances). One of the House's reasons was that to order someone to carry on a business would require the court's constant supervision.

d.   *Where the contract is for services of a personal nature*   The obvious example of such a contract is one of employment. Section 236 of the Trade Union and Labour Relations (Consolidation) Act 1992 prohibits an order of specific performance against an *employee* to compel him to do any work or to attend at any place for the doing of any work. It is well established by the cases that contracts for personal services not covered by the Act (for example, an agency contract)[12] cannot be specifically enforced either, nor can an order of specific performance be made against an employer (except, possibly, in very exceptional circumstances). Reasons given are that such contracts would require constant supervision and that it is contrary to public policy to force one person to submit to the orders of another.

e.   *Lack of mutuality*   There is a rule that a plaintiff who has not performed his contractual obligations cannot obtain specific performance against the defendant if, in the circumstances, it would not be available to the defendant against the plaintiff. In *Flight v Bolland*[13], for instance, it was held that a minor could not be awarded specific performance of the contract in question because such an order could not be made against him in the circumstances. While there is no doubting the present rule, its extent is uncertain.

1 Apart from its inherent jurisdiction to order the specific recovery of goods, the court has power under the Sale of Goods Act 1979, s 52, to order the specific performance of contracts for the sale of specific or ascertained goods. This power has not been used more liberally than the inherent power.
2 *Behnke v Bede Shipping Co Ltd* [1927] 1 KB 649; *Phillips v Lamdin* [1949] 2 KB 33, [1949] 1 All ER 770; *Sky Petroleum Ltd v VIP Petroleum Ltd* [1974] 1 All ER 954, [1974] 1 WLR 576.
3 [1927] 1 KB 169.
4 [1927] 1 KB 649.
5 *Cogent v Gibson* (1864) 33 Beav 557.
6 [1968] AC 58, [1967] 2 All ER 1197, HL; para 6.31, above.
7 *Beswick v Beswick* [1968] AC 58, [1967] 2 All ER 1197, HL.
8 *Cannon v Hartley* [1949] Ch 213, [1949] 1 All ER 50.
9 [1893] 1 Ch 116, CA.
10 [1987] Ch 25, [1986] 3 All ER 513.
11 [1997] 2 WLR 898, HL.
12 *Clarke v Price* (1819) 2 Wils Ch 157.
13 (1828) 4 Russ 298.

12.29   If the case does not fall within one of the above cases, specific performance may be ordered, but it must not be forgotten that, since specific performance is an equitable remedy, its award does not lie as of right (unlike the common law remedy of damages) but lies in the court's discretion. Factors which make it unlikely that the court will exercise its discretion in favour of specific performance include:

a.   mistake on the part of the defendant, such that it would be unjust specifically to enforce the contract against him[1];
b.   delay in bringing an action for specific performance which resulted in the defendant so changing his position that it would be unjust specifically to enforce the contract against him[2];
c.   exceptional severity of the hardship to the defendant if the contract is specifically enforced against him[3];
d.   breach by the plaintiff of his contractual obligations in circumstances where the grant of specific performance would be unjust to the defendant[4].

1 Paras 13.11 and 13.20, below.
2 *Stuart v London and North Western Rly Co* (1852) 1 De GM & G 721; *Lazard Bros & Co Ltd v Fairfield Properties Co (Mayfair) Ltd* (1977) 121 Sol Jo 793.
3 *Patel v Ali* [1984] Ch 283, [1983] 1 All ER 978.
4 *Walsh v Lonsdale* (1882) 21 Ch D 9, CA.

Injunction

12.30   An injunction is a court order restraining a party to a contract from acting in breach of a negative stipulation contained in it. By way of comparison, specific performance is concerned with the enforcement of positive contractual stipulations.

12.31   While it is correct to say that injunctions are concerned with restraining breaches of negative contractual stipulations, it would be erroneous to assume that only an express negative stipulation can be remedied by an injunction. Generally, a breach of a positive stipulation can be enjoined if the stipulation can properly be construed as impliedly being a negative stipulation. Thus, in *Manchester Ship Canal Co v Manchester Racecourse Co*[1], a stipulation for the grant of a 'first refusal' was construed as a stipulation, enforceable by injunction, not to sell to anyone else in breach of the stipulation. Similarly, in *Metropolitan Electric Supply Co Ltd v Ginder*[2], where the defendant had undertaken to take all the electricity required for his premises from the plaintiffs, it was held that this was impliedly an undertaking not to take electricity from any other person, which could be enforced by an injunction.

1 [1901] 2 Ch 37, CA.
2 [1901] 2 Ch 799.

12.32 Although the courts are prepared to enforce negative stipulations in a contract for personal services, consistency with the rule that such a contract cannot normally be the subject of a decree of specific performance means that an injunction will not be issued to restrain an employee or the like from breaking a promise not to work for any other person, if this would indirectly amount to compelling him to perform his contract with his employer[1]. This is given statutory force in relation to contracts of employment by s 236 of the Trade Union and Labour Relations (Consolidation) Act 1992, which provides that no court may, by an injunction restraining a breach or threatened breach of a contract of employment, compel an employee to do any work or to attend at any place of work.

On the other hand, a negative promise by an employee or the like will be enforced against him by injunction if it does not indirectly force him to work for his employer. For example, in *Lumley v Wagner*[2], the defendant, an opera star, agreed to sing at the plaintiff's theatre for three months and in no other theatre during that time. An injunction was granted restraining her from singing for another theatre owner during the three-month period. The approach taken in *Lumley v Wagner* was followed in *Warner Bros Pictures Inc v Nelson*[3]. The defendant, whose stage name was Bette Davis, agreed with the plaintiff company not to work in a film or stage production for any other company for a year nor to be engaged in any other occupation. During the year she contracted to work for another film company. The judge stated that, while an injunction enforcing all the negative stipulations in the contract could not be granted (because it would force Bette Davis either to be idle or to perform her contract with the plaintiff company), the injunction requested would be granted because it was limited to prohibiting her from working in a film or stage production for anyone other than the plaintiff company; she would still be free to earn her living in some other less remunerative way. The judge was unimpressed by the argument that the difference between what the plaintiff could earn acting and what she could earn in any other capacity would be so substantial that the injunction would drive her to work for the plaintiff company. An argument of this type did, however, persuade the judge in *Page One Records Ltd v Britton*[4], an employee against employer case referred to in para 12.33, below. In *Warren v Mendy*[5], the Court of Appeal was also persuaded by such an argument on grounds of realism and practicality. Consequently, it is now the law that, contrary to the view of the judge in *Warner Bros v Nelson*, the question of whether an injunction against him would compel the defendant to work for the plaintiff is not answered in the negative merely because the defendant is not debarred from doing other work. If the nature of, or remuneration for, that work is so different that effectively the defendant would be driven to work for the plaintiff, it will be held that an injunction would so compel him and an injunction will not be ordered. Thus, if the facts in *Warner Bros v Nelson* arose today the decision on them would no doubt be against an injunction being ordered.

1   *Rely-a-Bell Burglar and Fire Alarm Co Ltd v Eisler* [1926] Ch 609.
2   (1852) 1 De GM & G 604.
3   [1937] 1 KB 209, [1936] 3 All ER 160.
4   [1967] 3 All ER 822, [1968] 1 WLR 157.
5   [1989] 3 All ER 103, [1989] 1 WLR 853, CA.

12.33   The law is similar where an employee seeks to enforce a negative stipulation against his employer. Thus, generally, an injunction will not be issued if its effect is to compel the employer to continue employment. But an injunction may be granted in exceptional cases where employer and employee retain their mutual confidence.

In *Page One Records Ltd v Britton*[1], The Troggs, a pop group, appointed the plaintiff as their manager for five years, agreeing not to let anyone else act as their manager during that time. After a year, The Troggs dismissed the plaintiff, who sought an injunction restraining them from appointing anyone else as their manager. It was held that an injunction would indirectly compel The Troggs to continue to employ the plaintiff because pop groups could not operate successfully without a manager, and it would be bad to pressure The Troggs into continuing to employ a person in whom they had lost confidence. Therefore the injunction sought was not granted. In comparison, one may note *Hill v C A Parsons & Co Ltd*[2]. The defendant employers were forced by union pressure to dismiss the plaintiff in breach of contract. An injunction was granted to restrain this breach, even though its effect was to compel the reinstatement of the plaintiff. As the Court of Appeal pointed out, the circumstances were special, in particular because the parties retained their mutual confidence. Mutual confidence has been stressed as a precondition in other cases; it can be shown either by evidence that the employer and employee have expressed confidence in each other or by inference from evidence of an established and satisfactory employment relationship[3].

Despite the general reluctance of the courts to grant specific performance or an injunction in respect of a contract of employment, there are increasing signs that, in cases where the employee's contract requires a specified procedure to be followed before dismissal can take place, the courts will grant an injunction to restrain a proposed dismissal in breach of that procedure[4].

1   [1967] 3 All ER 822, [1968] 1 WLR 157.
2   [1972] Ch 305, [1971] 3 All ER 1345, CA.
3   *Powell v Brent London Borough Council* [1988] ICR 176, [1987] IRLR 466, CA; *Wishart v National Association of Citizens Advice Bureaux* [1990] ICR 794, [1990] IRLR 393, CA.

4   *Irani v Southampton and South West Hampshire Health Authority* [1985] ICR 590, [1985] IRLR 203; *R v BBC, ex p Lavelle* [1983] 1 All ER 241, [1982] IRLR 404; *Jones v Lee* [1980] ICR 310, [1980] IRLR 67, CA.

12.34   An injunction is like specific performance in that:

a.   it may be granted with or without an order for damages;
b.   where it is applicable, the grant of an injunction is discretionary (since it is an equitable remedy) and is likely to be refused where, for example, the plaintiff is guilty of delay or is in breach of his own obligations under the contract. In particular, an injunction will normally be refused if damages would be an adequate remedy.

On the other hand, an injunction is a much wider remedy than specific performance, partly because it can be ordered in many situations other than contractual situations, and partly because it can be ordered in contractual situations where specific performance could not, eg where enforcement of the contract would require the court's constant superintendence or where the contract is one for personal services.

Limitation of Actions

12.35   An action will be barred if it is not brought within the relevant limitation period. The rules relating to these periods are statutory, the relevant Act being the Limitation Act 1980. If an action is statute-barred this does not extinguish the plaintiff's substantive right but simply bars the procedural remedies available to him. Two consequences of this are that if a debtor pays a statute-barred debt, he cannot recover the money as money not due[1], and that if a debtor who owes a creditor two or more debts, one of which is statute-barred, pays money to the creditor without appropriating it to a debt which is not statute-barred, the creditor is entitled to appropriate it to the statute-barred debt[2].

1   *Bize v Dickason* (1786) 1 Term Rep 285 at 287.
2   *Mills v Fowkes* (1839) 5 Bing NC 455. See also paras 9.9 and 9.10, above.

Limitation periods
12.36   Under the Limitation Act 1980:

a.   Actions founded on a simple contract (ie one not made by deed) cannot be brought after the expiry of six years from the date on which the cause of action accrued, which is normally when the breach of contract occurs and never when the damage is suffered[1]. However, if the damages claimed consist of or include damages for personal injuries caused by a breach of contract, the time limit is reduced to three years[2], although this period may be extended in certain circumstances.

b. Actions founded on a contract made by deed cannot be brought after the expiry of 12 years from the date on which the cause of action accrued[3]. The special rules mentioned above concerning personal injuries claims also apply here.

1   Limitation Act 1980, s 5. Also see para 21.20, below. For a special rule in relation to actions on certain contracts of loan, see Limitation Act 1980, s 6. If the plaintiff can establish a cause of action in tort for negligence, a cause of action accrues (and time runs from) when the damage is suffered, although there are numerous exceptions, eg in personal injury cases and claims based on the negligent construction of buildings; see further paras 21.18–21.24, below.
2   Limitation Act 1980, s 11(4).
3   Limitation Act 1980, s 8.

Minors and the mentally ill
12.37   If a plaintiff is a minor (ie under 18) or mentally unsound when the cause of action accrues, the action may be brought within six years of the removal of the disability or of his death, whichever event happens first[1]. On the other hand, if the limitation period has begun to run, the fact that the plaintiff subsequently becomes of unsound mind does not suspend the running of time, and, if a person is under a disability when his cause of action accrues but dies and is succeeded by someone who also is under a disability, there is no extension of time by reason of the latter's disability[2].

1   Limitation Act 1980, ss 28 and 38(2). The period is three years if damages for personal injuries are claimed: Limitation Act 1980, s 28(6).
2   Limitation Act 1980, s 28(3).

Fraud, concealment or mistake
12.38   Generally, the fact that the plaintiff is unaware that he has a cause of action does not prevent the limitation period starting to run, even if the plaintiff does not know that he has a cause of action until after the limitation period has expired. However, s 32(1) of the Limitation Act 1980 provides that if:

a. the action is based on the fraud of the defendant or someone for whom he is responsible; or
b. any fact relevant to the plaintiff's right of action has been deliberately concealed from him by such a person; or
c. the action is for relief from the consequences of a mistake,

the limitation period does not begin to run until the plaintiff has discovered the fraud, deliberate concealment or mistake (as the case may be) or could with reasonable diligence have discovered it[1]. Section 32(2) goes on to provide that a deliberate breach of duty in circumstances in which it is unlikely to be discovered for some time amounts to deliberate concealment of the facts involved in breach of that duty.

1   If a deliberate concealment starts only after the limitation period begins to run, a second limitation period begins to run after the plaintiff has discovered, or could with reasonable diligence have discovered, the concealment: *Sheldon v RHM Outhwaite (Underwriting Agencies) Ltd* [1996] AC 102, [1995] 2 All ER 558, HL.

Extending the limitation period

12.39   An acknowledgement or part payment of a debt or other liquidated pecuniary claim may start time running again, provided that the right of action has not previously become statute-barred (ie the acknowledgement or part payment must be made during the currency of the relevant limitation period)[1]. The basic provision is s 29(5) of the Limitation Act 1980, which provides that where any right of action has accrued to recover any debt or other liquidated pecuniary claim and the person (or his agent) liable or accountable therefor acknowledges the claim or makes any payment in respect thereof, the right of action is deemed to have accrued on the date of the acknowledgement or the payment. Such an extension of a current limitation period may be continually repeated by further acknowledgements or part payments[1].

It must be emphasised that an extension of a limitation period under s 29(5) is only possible in the case of a debt or other liquidated sum and that, in the case of an acknowledgement, the claim must be acknowledged as existing (since an acknowledgement that there might be a claim is not enough)[2]. However, it is not essential that an acknowledgement should quantify the amount due since it suffices if that amount can be assessed by extrinsic evidence without further agreement of the parties[3]. A cause of action for unliquidated damages cannot be extended by an acknowledgement or part payment.

1   Limitation Act 1980, s 29(7).
2   *Good v Parry* [1963] 2 QB 418, [1963] 2 All ER 59, CA; *Kamouh v Associated Electrical Industries International Ltd* [1980] QB 199.
3   *Dungate v Dungate* [1965] 3 All ER 818, [1965] 1 WLR 1477, CA.

Acknowledgement

12.40   The acknowledgement must be in writing and signed by the person making it (or his agent), and must be made to the person (or his agent) whose claim is acknowledged[1]. An acknowledgement is only sufficient to start time running again if it amounts to an admission of legal liability to pay the debt in question[2], but it is not necessary that a promise to pay should be implied. An acknowledgement by one debtor does not bind a joint debtor[3], unless the acknowledgor can be regarded as an agent for himself and the joint debtor, which will happen, for instance, if they are partners.

1   Limitation Act 1980, s 30.
2   *Surrendra Overseas Ltd v Government of Sri Lanka* [1977] 2 All ER 481, [1977] 1 WLR 565.
3   Limitation Act 1980, s 31(6).

Part payment

12.41   In order to start time running again, part payment must be clearly referable to the debt. Part payment must be made to the person (or his agent) in respect of whose claim the payment is made. If part payment is made by a joint debtor time starts running again against all the joint debtors[1].

1   Limitation Act 1980, s 31(7).

Equitable relief
12.42   The provisions of the Limitation Act do not apply to claims for equitable relief[1]. However, in cases where, before the Judicature Act 1873, the claim for relief could have been entertained in either the common law courts or in the Court of Chancery, the limitation periods under the Limitation Act 1980 are applied to equitable claims by analogy[2]. The position is different in the case of purely equitable claims, ie claims which could only have been entertained by the Court of Chancery before the Act of 1873, such as claims for specific performance or an injunction. Here, the claim may fail under the equitable doctrine of laches (delay). Traditionally, the rule has been that the plaintiff must show himself to be 'ready, desirous, prompt and eager' to assert his rights[3]; otherwise he may be barred from claiming the equitable relief. But there is authority that, at least where the claim is for specific performance, even gross delay will not bar the claim for equitable relief if it has done the defendant no harm at all[4]. The avoidance of fixed limitation periods in this area is obviously more appropriate to the discretionary nature of equitable remedies.

1   Limitation Act 1980, s 36(1).
2   Ibid; *Knox v Gye* (1872) LR 5 HL 656 at 674.
3   *Millward v Earl of Thanet* (1801) 5 Ves 720n.
4   *Lazard Bros Co Ltd v Fairfield Properties Co (Mayfair) Ltd* (1977) 121 Sol Jo 793.

Chapter 13

Mistake

13.1   In certain cases a contract[1] is void if it is made in circumstances where one or both parties are labouring under a mistake as to the facts existing at the time of their agreement. If a contract is void for mistake it has no legal effect; consequently, it is unenforceable by either party, money paid under it is recoverable back[2] and title to property cannot pass under it. A party who has received goods under a void contract will be liable to the transferor in tort if he wrongfully interferes with them, for example, by selling them, and so will a third party who has bought them from him.

Because of the serious consequences of finding a contract void for mistake, the law defines the situations in which a mistake will render a contract void very narrowly. It follows from this that many mistakes made by a party in concluding a contract are legally irrelevant. Even mistakes which are induced by the other contracting party rarely render the contract void, although there may be a remedy for misrepresentation (which we discuss in the next chapter).

A contract *may* be void for mistake:

a.   if the parties have reached an agreement, but have done so on the basis of some fundamental mistake which they share; or
b.   if, because of a mistake which the parties do not share, they are fundamentally at cross-purposes.

As a preliminary point, it should be noted that a mistake of law will generally be held to be legally irrelevant[3].

1   It is traditional, although perhaps inaccurate, to describe agreements void for mistake as contracts.
2   Assumed in *Bell v Lever Bros Ltd* [1932] AC 161, HL. See also *Griffith v Brymer* (1903) 19 TLR 434; *Nicholson and Venn v Smith Marriott* (1947) 177 LT 189.
3   *Solle v Butcher* [1950] 1 KB 671, [1949] 2 All ER 1107, CA.

Shared Mistake

Common law

Construction

13.2 If the parties have reached an agreement on the basis of a misapprehension as to the facts, which is shared by both of them, the contract may be void for mistake. Whether the rules relating to mistake come into play depends on whether or not the general law relating to the type of contract in question allocates the risk as between the parties in relation to a particular fact or event, or whether or not the contract, on its true construction, expressly or impliedly does so or provides some other solution[1]. If the risk is allocated in one of these ways or the contract provides some other solution, the court will give effect to this. In such a case, the contract is not void but enforceable, and the rules relating to mistake do not come into play. In either case, the position is as follows: if, to take as an example the case of a contract for the sale of specific goods which it turns out have never existed, the buyer assumed the risk of the goods' existence, he must pay the contractual price; but if the seller assumed that risk he will be liable in damages for breach of contract.

In the Australian case of *McRae v Commonwealth Disposals Commission*[2], the Commission sold to McRae the right to salvage a tanker which was, they claimed, lying on a specified reef. There was no reef of that name at the map reference given, nor was there any tanker. The court found as a matter of construction that the Commission had impliedly undertaken that the tanker existed and thus McRae could claim damages for breach of this undertaking. This case can be contrasted with *Clark v Lindsay*[3], which shows that a contract may also provide a solution, other than placing the risk on one of the parties, should a jointly assumed fact not exist. In *Clark v Lindsay*, A had agreed with B to hire a room along the route of Edward VII's coronation procession. When they made the contract both parties were unaware that the coronation had been postponed because of the King's illness, but the contract expressly provided that, if the procession was postponed, A should have the use of the room on any later day on which it took place. Consequently, it was held that the contract was not void for mistake and both parties were bound to perform their obligations on the re-arranged day.

The approach of first construing the contract to see whether it allocates the risk in, or otherwise provides a solution for, the matter about which the parties shared a mistake was adopted also by the House of Lords in *Couturier v Hastie*[4]. Here, a cargo of grain being shipped to the UK was sold after, unknown to the parties, it had 'perished' in the legal sense, in that it had deteriorated and had already been sold by the ship's captain. The seller demanded payment for the cargo. The House of Lords held that on a true construction of the contract the risk that the cargo did not exist had not been placed on the buyer and therefore he did not have to pay for the goods. It was not necessary for the House to decide whether the risk was placed on the seller, who could thus have been sued for non-delivery, or whether the contract was void.

251

13.2–13.6 *Mistake*

1 *Associated Japanese Bank (International) Ltd v Crédit du Nord SA* [1988] 3 All ER 902 at 912, [1989] 1 WLR 255; *William Sindall plc v Cambridgeshire County Council* [1994] 3 All ER 932, [1994] 1 WLR 1016, CA.
2 (1950) 84 CLR 377.
3 (1903) 88 LT 198.
4 (1856) 5 HL Cas 673, HL. For a more recent case where this approach was adopted, see *Associated Japanese Bank (International) Ltd v Crédit du Nord SA* [1988] 3 All ER 902, [1989] 1 WLR 255; para 13.7.

Rules relating to shared mistake

13.3   If the law or, on its true construction, the contract does not allocate the risk in, or otherwise provide a solution for, the matter concerning which the parties shared a mistake, the rules relating to mistake must be looked at. Under them, not every shared mistake renders a contract void: the mistake must be fundamental. If it is not fundamental the contract is enforceable at common law.

13.4   *Shared mistake as to existence of subject matter*   One example of a fundamental mistake in this context is a shared mistake as to the existence of the subject matter of the contract. In *Galloway v Galloway*[1], for instance, a separation agreement based on a marriage which, unknown to the parties, was invalid (and therefore non-existent) was held void. Clearly, in such a case, the separation agreement would not attempt to throw the risk of the marriage being invalid on either party and so it is not surprising that the court did not first consider the question of construction.

1 (1914) 30 TLR 531.

13.5   If the facts in *Couturier v Hastie* occurred today, the basis of the decision would almost certainly be different (although the buyer would still not be liable) because there is now a special statutory provision dealing with the *perishing of specific* goods unknown to the seller before a contract for their sale is made[1]. Section 6 of the Sale of Goods Act 1979 provides that in such a case the contract is void. Presumably, this provision can be displaced if the contract expressly places the risk as to the goods' continued existence on one of the parties or provides some other solution. Section 6 does not apply to specific goods which have never existed. In such cases, the contract is first construed. If the risk is placed on either party, expressly or impliedly, or some other solution is provided by the contract, the contract governs; but if the risk is not allocated, the contract is void.

1 'Perishing' of goods includes not only cases where they are destroyed or stolen but also cases where they are so damaged as to cease to exist commercially as goods of the description under which they were sold: *Asfar & Co v Blundell* [1896] 1 QB 123, CA. 'Specific goods' are goods identified and agreed on at the time the contract of sale is made: Sale of Goods Act 1979, s 61. The term also includes an undivided share, expressed as a fraction or percentage, of goods identified and agreed on at the time the contract of sale is made: ibid.

13.6   *Shared mistake as to possibility of performing contract*   A contract is void if it is made under a shared mistaken belief that it is possible to perform it, unless the risk of impossibility of performance is allocated to a party or the contract provides some other solution to deal with the problem. Thus, a contract, whereby X agrees to lease land to Y, which Y already owns, is void at common law[1], and so is a contract whereby X agrees with Y to cut and process a certain tonnage of a particular crop on land, when there is not that tonnage to be cropped[2]. It would be different, however, if X had warranted (as a seller normally does) that he had title to the land or had guaranteed the yield (in that case, X would be liable for breach of contract) or if Y had agreed to run the risk (ie to pay in any event).

Another example is provided by *Griffith v Brymer*[3]. As in *Clark v Lindsay*, this case concerned an agreement for the hire of a room along the route of Edward VII's coronation procession, which had been made by the parties in ignorance of the postponement of the procession. The court did not specifically deal with the construction of the contract, but presumably the contract had not provided for the risk of the postponement. It held that the contract was void for mistake and that the plaintiff could recover back money he had paid under it.

1   *Bell v Lever Bros Ltd* [1932] AC 161 at 218; *Norwich Union Fire Insurance Society Ltd v Price* [1934] AC 455 at 463.
2   *Sheikh Bros v Ochsner* [1957] AC 136, [1957] 2 WLR 254, PC.
3   (1903) 19 TLR 434.

13.7   *Shared mistake as to quality*   A vexed question is whether a shared mistake as to the *quality* (as opposed to the *existence*) of the subject matter of the contract can ever be sufficiently fundamental to render it void. Frequently, of course, the risk that the goods etc lack that quality is borne by the seller because the supposed quality of the goods is a term, express or implied, of the contract. If this occurs, the law of mistake is irrelevant because the contract provides that the seller shall be liable for breach of contract if the quality is absent. But if the risk that the quality is lacking is not allocated, is the contract *ever* void for mistake?

Dicta in *Bell v Lever Bros Ltd*[1] suggest that in some cases a contract can be void for a shared mistake as to quality. In that case, Bell was employed by Lever Bros under a contract of employment for five years at £8,000 per annum. Lever Bros agreed to pay Bell £30,000 to relinquish this contract. Subsequently, they discovered that they could have terminated the contract without compensation because of breaches of it by Bell. Bell had forgotten about these breaches and he and Lever Bros were treated as being under a shared mistake as to the *quality* of the contract of employment, in that they had believed it was only determinable with Bell's agreement when in truth it was immediately determinable by Lever Bros without his agreement. Lever Bros' claim to recover back the compensation paid, as money paid under a void contract, failed before the House of Lords, who held the contract of compensation valid despite the shared mistake, although three of their Lordships stated that a sufficiently fundamental mistake as to quality might render a contract void. Lords Atkin and Thankerton stated that, to be sufficiently fundamental, the mistake would have to be as to a quality which made the thing *essentially* different from the thing which it was believed to be. The reader may think that, if the mistake as to quality in *Bell v Lever Bros* was not sufficiently fundamental, it is hard to imagine when a mistake as to quality will be[2].

No case has actually been decided on the basis that a contract was void because of a fundamental mistake as to quality. However, it has been held, obiter, in two first instance decisions, that the contract in issue was, or could have been held, void for mistake on this ground.

The first case was *Nicholson and Venn v Smith Marriott*[3], where a set of linen napkins and table cloths was put up for sale, described as dating from the seventeenth century. Unknown to both the buyers and the sellers, it was in fact Georgian, and the buyers were able to recover for breach of contract since the sellers were in breach of the implied condition under s 13(1) of the Sale of Goods Act 1979 that the goods corresponded with their description. Strangely, the judge added as an obiter dictum that, had the buyers sought to recover the whole of the price paid, as money paid under a void contract[4], he would have been disposed to hold the contract void for mistake as to quality. The judge did not enlarge on this view.

Associated Japanese Bank (International) Ltd v Crédit du Nord SA[5] is a more impressive authority since the judge discussed the rules relating to mistake at some length. X made two contracts with the plaintiffs. The first was for the sale by X to the plaintiffs of four specified packaging machines. The second was for the lease of the four machines by the plaintiffs to X. By these two contracts the plaintiffs effected in favour of X what is called a leaseback arrangement. X's obligations under the leasing contract were guaranteed by the defendants under a contract of guarantee between them and the plaintiffs. In fact, the specified machines did not exist and the arrangement was a fraud perpetrated by X. The plaintiffs claimed from X the outstanding balance under the leasing contract but X was made bankrupt and the plaintiffs were not paid. They then sued the defendants on the contract of guarantee.

The judge held that, on the construction of the contract of guarantee, the defendants were excused from liability under it by the non-fulfilment of a condition precedent of it, viz the existence of the machines. However, he went on to consider whether, alternatively, the contract of guarantee was void for shared mistake. By his own admission, the judge's views on this matter were obiter, because, as we said in para 13.2 and as he pointed out himself, if the contract itself resolves the matter, the rules relating to mistake do not come into play.

Relying on the speeches of Lords Atkin and Thankerton in *Bell v Lever Bros Ltd*, the judge held that, to render a contract void, a shared mistake as to quality must render the subject matter of the contract essentially different from the subject matter which the parties believed to exist. Applying this test to the particular facts, the judge held that, for both parties, the guarantee of obligations under a lease with non-existent machines was essentially different from a guarantee of a lease with four machines which both parties reasonably believed to exist. Thus, since the parties had had a shared mistake as to an essential quality of the subject matter (the leasing contract) of the contract of guarantee, the contract of guarantee was void.

1 [1932] AC 161, HL.
2 An unconvincing attempt was made to rationalise the statements of principle in *Bell's* case with the decision in that case in *Associated Japanese Bank (International) Ltd v Crédit du Nord SA* [1988] 3 All ER 902, [1989] 1 WLR 255.

3   (1947) 177 LT 189.
4   Para 13.1, above.
5   [1988] 3 All ER 902, [1989] 1 WLR 255.

13.8   The dicta in support of the proposition that a contract can be void for a fundamental mistake as to quality can be contrasted with the actual decisions in a number of cases. In *Solle v Butcher*[1], a Court of Appeal decision, the fact that both parties to a lease mistakenly believed that the premises were free from rent control did not render the contract void. Similarly, in *Magee v Pennine Insurance Co Ltd*[2], another Court of Appeal decision, a compromise of a claim under an insurance policy which both parties mistakenly believed to be valid, when in fact the policy was voidable, was held not to be void for mistake. Again, we are prompted to ask, if these mistakes were not fundamental, what sort of mistake would have been? Another example of a mistake as to quality which was not legally relevant occurred in *Harrison and Jones Ltd v Bunten and Lancaster Ltd*[3]. In this case, the parties bought and sold 'Sree brand' kapok. Both parties believed 'Sree brand' to be pure kapok, when in fact it contained other substances. The judge admitted that the purchasers considered it vital that the kapok was pure but refused to hold that the contract was void for mistake.

1   [1950] 1 KB 671, [1949] 2 All ER 1107, CA. See also *Grist v Bailey*, para 13.12, below.
2   [1969] 2 QB 507, [1969] 2 All ER 891, CA.
3   [1953] 1 QB 646, [1953] 1 All ER 903.

13.9   Our conclusion is that, despite the dicta to the contrary, a contract can never be void at law because of a mistake as to quality, however fundamental.

13.10   *Effect of unreasonable mistake*   According to the judge in *Associated Japanese Bank (International) Ltd v Crédit du Nord SA*[1], a party to a contract cannot rely on a shared mistake which would otherwise render the contract void against him if he had no reasonable ground for his mistaken belief. The judge gave as an extreme example of a case falling within this exception that of the person who makes a contract with minimal knowledge of the facts to which the mistake relates but who is content that it is a good speculative risk. This qualification is part of the obiter dictum which has already been referred to. If it is subsequently held to represent the law it will duplicate the approach under the equitable rules[2] on shared mistake, whereby fault on the part of a mistaken party precludes the granting to him of relief.

1   [1988] 3 All ER 902, [1989] 1 WLR 255.
2   Para 13.11, below.

Equity
13.11   If a contract is void at law for mistake, it is of no legal effect and no damages can be awarded for non-performance or faulty performance. Further, equity, following the law, will not grant specific performance. Moreover, to put the matter beyond doubt, the equitable remedy of rescission (ie setting aside) of the contract can be obtained. Since the contract is void this is not

necessary, but it is a useful remedy where there is a formal contractual document, such as a lease.

Even though the shared mistake in question does not make the contract void at common law, equitable relief may be available. Such relief lies in the court's discretion. It will not be granted, for example, in favour of a party who has been at fault in making the mistake[1]. Equitable relief may take the form of refusing specific performance (which will not affect liability in damages), or of awarding specific performance on terms which do justice, or of rescinding the contract for mistake.

1   *Solle v Butcher* [1950] 1 KB 671 at 693.

13.12   Where a contract which is not void for mistake is rescinded, the rescission sets aside a contract which previously existed, and the parties are restored to their former positions. In addition, the court may impose terms on the parties in the interests of justice and equity. Thus, if a contract of sale of goods is rescinded for mistake, this may be done on terms that the buyer is compensated for any improvements which he has made to the goods. Rescission for mistake is not possible if the law or the contract allocates the risk in respect of the 'mistaken matter'[1].

It is not certain what mistakes are sufficient to enable a contract to be rescinded under the equitable power. Certainly, all mistakes which the law considers sufficient will suffice in equity and so will other types of mistake, although the limits are not clearly established.

Some examples of where equity has set aside a contract are *Solle v Butcher*[2] and *Grist v Bailey*[3], both of which involved mistakes of quality.

In *Solle v Butcher*, a lease was granted at a specified rent in the shared mistaken belief that the nature of the flat had been so changed as not to be a rent-controlled property. As we have said, the Court of Appeal refused to hold the contract void but it set it aside in equity. At the time there was a housing shortage and rescission was ordered on terms that the tenant should have an option either to surrender the lease or to stay in the premises under a new lease at the maximum rent which the landlord could charge under the statutory provisions then in force.

In *Grist v Bailey*, the plaintiff agreed to buy a house from the defendant at approximately one-third of its value because the house was sold subject to an existing tenancy which both parties mistakenly believed was protected by the Rent Acts (which would have given the tenant a right to remain in the property indefinitely). On discovering that the tenancy was not protected, the plaintiff sought specific performance and the defendant sought to have the agreement set aside because of the mistake. The contract was not void at law but the mistake was held to be a sufficient mistake as to quality to allow equitable intervention. The action for specific performance was dismissed and the agreement to sell set aside, but only on the term that the defendant should give the plaintiff a chance to enter into a new contract of sale at the full value of the property.[4]

The rescission of a contract for shared mistake is subject to similar bars to those which apply to rescission for misrepresentation and which we outline in para 14.16, below.

1 *William Sindall plc v Cambridgeshire County Council* [1994] 3 All ER 932, [1994] 1 WLR 1016, CA.
2 [1950] 1 KB 671, [1949] 2 All ER 1107, CA.
3 [1967] Ch 532, [1966] 2 All ER 875. For another example, see *Magee v Pennine Insurance Co Ltd* [1969] 2 QB 507, [1969] 2 All ER 891, CA.
4 The decision in *Grist v Bailey* is open to objection, in that the judge did not first advert to the contractual allocation of risk: *William Sindall plc v Cambridgeshire County Council* [1994] 3 All ER 932 at 952.

Mistake not Shared by the Parties

Common law
13.13 The fact that one party entered into an apparent contract under a mistake does not normally render the contract void, and the same is true if both parties were labouring under *different* mistaken beliefs. However, a contract will be void if a mistake which is not shared by the parties relates to:

a. the identity of the other party; or
b. the essence of the subject matter of the contract; or
c. whether a particular matter is a term of the contract,

and the mistake is an operative mistake in the sense discussed in para 13.19, below.

Mistake as to identity
13.14 A mistake as to identity can make an apparent contract void; a mistake which merely relates to an attribute, eg creditworthiness, of the other party can never do so.

In *Cundy v Lindsay*[1], a rogue, Blenkarn, who had hired premises at 37 Wood Street, wrote to the plaintiffs, offering to buy some goods. Blenkarn deliberately signed his letter 'A Blenkarn & Co' in such a way that the signature appeared to be that of A Blenkiron & Co. A Blenkiron & Co were a well-known firm which had traded for many years at 123 Wood Street. The plaintiffs accepted the offer and sent their letter of acceptance to 'Messrs Blenkiron, 37 Wood Street'. Later, goods were delivered under the contract to the same address. The House of Lords held that the plaintiffs had purported to accept an offer made by Blenkiron and had never intended to contract with Blenkarn at all. In consequence, the apparent contract with Blenkarn was void and the innocent party to whom Blenkarn had resold the goods was held liable to the plaintiffs for the tort of conversion. The plaintiffs could, of course, have sued Blenkarn for the torts of conversion and deceit[2] if they could have traced him.

In *Cundy v Lindsay*, the plaintiffs were able to establish that they meant to deal only with Blenkiron and not with the writer of the letter; there was thus a mistake as to identity. On the other hand, in *King's Norton Metal Co Ltd v Edridge, Merrett & Co Ltd*[3], the mistake made by the plaintiffs who sold goods to a rogue who resold them to the defendants before the plaintiffs discovered the truth was one as to attribute, not identity. In this case, a rogue, one Wallis, offered to buy goods in a letter written on paper headed 'Hallam & Co' and embellished with references to depots and a picture of a factory. The plaintiffs mistakenly believed Hallam & Co to be a respectable firm but they did not think that they were dealing with someone other than the writer of the letter. Their mistake was as to the credit and reliability of the writer of the letter, and not as to the identity of the other party. Thus, their contract with the rogue was not void and he had passed title to the defendants. Consequently, the defendants were not liable to the plaintiffs for conversion of the goods.

The important distinguishing feature between these two cases is that in *Cundy v Lindsay* there was an actual separate entity, 'A Blenkiron & Co', with whom the plaintiffs wished to contract, whereas in *King's Norton* there was not.

1   (1878) 3 App Cas 459, HL.
2   Paras 20.18 and 14.20, below.
3   (1897) 14 TLR 98, CA.

13.15   When the parties contract face to face, it is much more difficult to establish that a mistake relates to the identity, as opposed to attributes, of the other party, and it can normally be presumed that a party intended to deal with the person in front of him. However, every case turns on its facts and it may be possible to establish a mistake as to identity if the identity of one party was of vital importance to the other.

In *Phillips v Brooks Ltd*[1], a rogue, named North, entered the plaintiff's shop and selected some jewellery, including a ring. He then wrote out a cheque for the full amount. As he did so, he announced that he was Sir George Bullough of St James' Square. The plaintiff had heard of Sir George Bullough; he consulted a directory and found that Sir George Bullough did live at the address given. He therefore allowed North to take away the ring without first having the cheque cleared. North pledged the ring with the defendant, who was wholly innocent. The cheque was dishonoured and the plaintiff sued the defendant in tort for the conversion of the ring. He could only succeed if the contract was void for mistake. The judge held that it was not; his reason was that he found that the plaintiff had intended to contract with the person in the shop. The plaintiff's mistaken belief related to an attribute of the customer (his credit-worthiness), not his identity. It would have been different if the plaintiff had established that the identity of his customer was of vital importance to him. He had, it is true, consulted a directory to see whether there was a Sir George Bullough of St James' Square, but this was not sufficient to rebut the presumption that he intended to deal with the customer before him, whoever he was.

A similar case is that of *Lewis v Averay*[2], where a rogue, claiming to be Richard Greene, a well-known actor, bought from the plaintiff a car which he then sold to the defendant, who was innocent. The plaintiff sued the defendant for the conversion of his car but failed to establish that he had made a mistake as to the identity of the other party to the agreement. He had to be presumed to intend to deal with the person in front of him, said the Court of Appeal, unless he could establish that the identity of the buyer was of vital importance to him. In this case, the only attempt to check whether the rogue was Richard

Greene was the perusal of a Pinewood Studio pass in the name of Richard Green, which was produced by the rogue, and this was insufficient to establish that he intended to deal only with Richard Greene, the actor.

1   [1919] 2 KB 243.
2   [1972] 1 QB 198, [1971] 3 All ER 907, CA.

13.16   Two cases where the plaintiff was able to establish a mistake as to the identity of the other party are *Ingram v Little*[1] and *Sowler v Potter*[2]. In *Ingram v Little*, the plaintiffs, two elderly sisters, were confronted by a rogue who called himself Hutchinson. They agreed to sell him their car but refused to continue the sale when the rogue proposed to pay by cheque. He then announced himself to be P G M Hutchinson of Stanstead House, Caterham. One sister slipped out to the Post Office, consulted the telephone directory and found that there was a P G M Hutchinson of Stanstead House, while the other sister plied the rogue with conversation. They accepted the cheque, which was dishonoured, and the rogue sold the car to the defendant, whom the sisters sued in conversion. The Court of Appeal found that on the facts of the case the plaintiffs had done sufficient to establish that they intended to deal only with P G M Hutchinson of Stanstead House and not with the person in front of them. This decision has been greatly criticised but, since all cases turn on their own facts, it may have been correctly decided.

In *Sowler v Potter*[2], the lease of a café was granted to Potter, who had previously been convicted of keeping a disorderly café under another name, Robinson. The judge held that the lease was void because of the lessor's mistaken belief that Potter was not Robinson. The judge found that the lessor's agent, who had concluded the contract, only intended to deal with the person in front of him if that person was not Robinson, a convicted criminal. This case has also been doubted.

1   [1961] 1 QB 31, [1960] 3 All ER 332, CA.
2   [1940] 1 KB 271, [1939] 4 All ER 478.

Mistake as to the essence of the subject matter
13.17   A mistake as to the essence of the subject matter of a contract can render it void. An example of such a mistake would be where A agrees to buy B's car, mistakenly believing that it is a Ford Escort, whereas in fact it is a Vauxhall Nova. In such a case, there would be no genuine agreement, for the parties are at cross-purposes. Similarly, if X agrees to buy a consignment of wheat from Y, thinking that it is a consignment of oats, his mistake is as to the essence of the subject matter[1]. In both cases, of course, the contract would only be void if A's or X's mistake was operative in the sense explained in para 13.19, below.

On the other hand, a mistake which simply relates to a quality, but not the essence, of the thing is not sufficiently fundamental to render the contract void. Thus, if X agrees to buy oats from Y, mistakenly believing that they are old oats, the contract cannot be void for mistake[2].

1   *Scriven Bros & Co v Hindley & Co* [1913] 3 KB 564; *Raffles v Wichelhaus* (1864) 2 H & C 906.
2   *Smith v Hughes* (1871) LR 6 QB 597.

Mistake as to the terms of the contract

13.18   A contract may be void if a party mistakenly believes that a particular matter is a term of the contract, even though the mistake does not relate to the identity of the other party or the essence of the subject matter. Thus, if X mistakenly believes that Y warrants that the oats which he is selling him are old oats, the contract may be void for mistake[1]. Whether or not it is depends on whether or not the mistake is operative.

In *Hartog v Colin and Shields*[2], the sellers mistakenly offered to sell goods at a given price per pound when they had intended to offer to sell at that given price per piece, there being about three pieces to the pound. The buyer accepted the offer. The contract was apparently held void because of the sellers' mistake as to the price (a term of the contract). All the preliminary negotiations had been on the basis of price per piece and trade custom also related to price per piece. The effect of this was that the court found that the buyer must have realised that the sellers had made a mistake and could not rush in and accept what would have been a most advantageous offer.

1   *Smith v Hughes* (1871) LR 6 QB 597.
2   [1939] 3 All ER 566.

Operative mistake

13.19   It is not enough that a party was mistaken as to the identity of the other party, or as to the essence of the subject matter, or as to a term of the contract. Such a mistake must be operative to render the contract void and it will only be so if:

a.   the other party knew of the mistake, as in *Cundy v Lindsay*, *Ingram v Little*, *Sowler v Potter* and *Hartog v Colin & Shields*; or
b.   the circumstances are so ambiguous that a reasonable person could not say whether the contract meant what one party thought it meant or what the other party thought it meant.

It is only in exceptional cases that the circumstances are so ambiguous. The approach taken by the courts is that if, whatever A's real intention may be, A so conducts himself that a reasonable person would believe that A was assenting to the contract proposed by the other party (B), and B contracts with A in that belief, there is a contract with the meaning and terms understood by B[1]. In *Wood v Scarth*[2], the defendant wrote to the plaintiff, offering to let him a public house at £63 a year. After an interview with the defendant's clerk the plaintiff accepted the offer by letter. The defendant had intended also to take a premium for the tenancy and thought that the clerk had made it clear to the plaintiff that this was a term of the contract. The plaintiff accepted the offer, thinking that his only financial obligation was to pay the rent. It was held that there was a contract in the sense understood by the plaintiff.

Wood v Scarth can be contrasted with *Scriven v Hindley*[3], where the defendants successfully bid at an auction sale for a lot which consisted of tow, thinking that they were bidding for hemp, an infinitely superior product. Both tow and hemp were sold at the auction and samples of each were on display, although the defendants had not inspected them because they had already seen samples of hemp at the plaintiff's showroom. However, the lot in question was misleadingly described in the auctioneer's catalogue and the samples were confusingly marked. It was held that the contract was void. Clearly, in the special circumstances a reasonable person could not say whether there was a contract for the sale of hemp or for the sale of tow.

1   *Smith v Hughes* (1871) LR 6 QB 597 at 607; *Centrovincial Estates plc v Merchant Investors Assurance Co Ltd* [1983] Com LR 158, CA.
2   (1858) 1 F & F 293.
3   [1913] 3 KB 564.

Equity
13.20   Where a contract is void at common law because of an operative mistake not shared by the parties, equity follows the law and will not grant specific performance[1] of the contract and may, to put the matter beyond doubt, rescind the contract.

In addition, the equitable remedy of specific performance may be refused if justice so demands, and it is reasonable to do so, even though the contract is not void for mistake at common law. It was refused, for instance, in *Wood v Scarth*[2], although the plaintiff was able to obtain the common law remedy of damages. On the other hand, in *Tamplin v James*[3], where the defendant had successfully bid for a property under the mistaken belief as to its extent, specific performance was ordered: the defendant's mistake was his own fault since he had failed to check the plans to which the auctioneer had drawn attention.

1   *Webster v Cecil* (1861) 30 Beav 62.
2   (1855) 2 K & J 33, (1858) 1 F & F 293; para 13.19, above.
3   (1880) 15 Ch D 215, CA.

Mistake and Documents

Rectification
13.21   We are concerned here with the case where the parties have made a perfectly valid oral agreement but it is later embodied in a document which *records their agreement inaccurately*. In such a case, the equitable remedy of rectification is available. This enables a court to rectify the document so that it embodies the agreement of the parties accurately. Oral evidence is admissible to show that the written document does not represent the agreement of the parties even if the contract at issue is one which must be made or evidenced in writing.

Rectification will normally only be ordered if the document does not represent the intentions of *both* parties. However, rectification can be ordered where one party (A) mistakenly believed that a particular term was (or was not) included in the document to give effect to that intention, if:

a.   the other party (B) knew of[1] that mistake but nevertheless failed to draw the mistake to A's notice and allowed the document to be executed[2], or conducted himself as to divert A from discovering the mistake[3]; *and*

b.   the mistake would inequitably benefit B or be detrimental to A[4].

On the other hand, if the document simply fails to mention an obligation which one party, but not the other, had intended to be a term of the contract rectification cannot be ordered[5].

There is no right to rectification; it will only be ordered where it is just and equitable to do so. Certain written documents cannot be rectified[6].

1   Knowledge here includes wilfully shutting one's eyes to the obvious or wilfully and recklessly failing to make reasonable enquiries: *Commission for the New Towns v Cooper (Great Britain) Ltd* [1995] 2 All ER 929 at 947. Cf *J J Huber (Investments) Ltd v Private DIY Co Ltd* [1995] NPC 102 (mere suspicion not enough).
2   *A Roberts & Co v Leicestershire County Council* [1961] Ch 555, [1961] 2 All ER 545; *Thomas Bates & Son Ltd v Wyndham's (Lingerie) Ltd* [1981] 1 All ER 1077, [1981] 1 WLR 505, CA.
3   *Commission for the New Towns v Cooper (Great Britain) Ltd* [1995] 2 All ER 929 at 946.
4   *Thomas Bates & Son Ltd v Wyndham's (Lingerie) Ltd* [1981] 1 All ER 1077, [1981] 1 WLR 505, CA.
5   *Riverlate Properties Ltd v Paul* [1975] Ch 133, [1974] 2 All ER 656, CA.
6   Eg the articles of association of a company, although the company may alter the articles under the Companies Act 1985 (see para 25.25, below).

Documents mistakenly signed
13.22   Where a person signs a document which contains a contract he is bound by that contract. This is so even if it is not the contract which he expected and whether or not he has read or understood the document. An exception to this has been established; it is the plea of non est factum (it is not my deed), which, if proved, renders the contract void and permits the signatory of a written contract to deny liability under it.

To succeed in his plea of non est factum, the signatory must prove:

a.   that the signed document was radically different in character or effect from that which he thought he was signing; and
b.   that he was not careless in signing the document.

The leading case is the House of Lords' decision in *Saunders v Anglia Building Society*[1]. Mrs Gallie, an elderly widow, occupied a house under a lease. Her nephew, Parkin, wished to raise money using the house as security. Mrs Gallie was happy for this to happen, provided she could live in the house rent-free until her death[2]. Because Parkin did not want to pay maintenance to his estranged wife, he adopted a circuitous method of raising money so as to appear not to have any funds. The scheme was to induce Mrs Gallie to assign the property by way of sale to a friend of Parkin, Lee, who would mortgage it and pay the money to Parkin. A document which assigned the property to Lee by way of sale was drawn up and Mrs Gallie signed it without reading it; she had, in fact, broken her glasses. She thought the document was a deed of gift transferring the house to Parkin so that he could mortgage it. Lee mortgaged the property to the Building Society but paid Parkin nothing. Mrs Gallie, pleading non est factum, subsequently sought a declaration that the assignment to Lee was void, so that the Building Society could not enforce the mortgage.

The House of Lords rejected Mrs Gallie's plea of non est factum. They found that the document she had signed was not radically different in character or effect from what she had intended to sign. Legally, there may be a great difference between an assignment by way of sale and a deed of gift, but the effect in this case was the same – to enable Parkin to raise money on the security of the house. Even if the signed document had been radically different from what was intended, Mrs Gallie had failed to establish that she had not been careless. She had not read the document nor asked for it to be read to her; she had consulted no professional advisers and she had not acted sensibly.

In deciding whether a party has established that he was not careless, the standard of the reasonable man applies to those of full age and understanding. On the other hand, the House of Lords' decision suggests that, if the party is illiterate or is mentally handicapped or is blind, that characteristic should be taken into account in deciding whether it has been established that he was not careless. On this basis, a court dealing with a case involving an 'incapable' signatory would have to consider whether he used such care as a reasonable man with his incapacity would have used. If a blind man is proposing to sign a document, he should ask for it to be read to him by a trustworthy person, and, if he fails to do so, he cannot rely on non est factum.

Since *Saunders v Anglia Building Society*, it seems unlikely that non est factum will be pleaded successfully in more than a few cases.

1   [1971] AC 1004, [1970] 3 All ER 961, HL.
2   Mrs Gallie died before the case was heard by the House of Lords. Saunders was her executrix.

Money Paid under a Mistake of Fact

13.23   This aspect of the law of restitution is dealt with here for convenience, since it is not limited to a situation of actual or supposed contractual relationship. It is for this reason that the relevant rules are part of the law of restitution, and not of the law of contract. Money paid under a mistaken belief in the truth of a fact which, if true, would have entitled the payee to payment is recoverable back by the payer, subject to the exceptions set out later. In *Kelly v Solari*[1], for example, the plaintiff was the director of a life insurance company which had paid out insurance money to the defendant under her husband's life insurance policy. The policy had, in fact, lapsed because the last premium had not been paid. The company had noted this, but the lapse had been overlooked when the defendant claimed the money. It was held that the plaintiff could recover back the money because it had been paid under a mistaken belief in facts which, if true, would have entitled the defendant to payment.

A vexed question is whether, as in *Kelly v Solari*, the mistake must have led the plaintiff to believe a fact which, if true, would have meant that he was *legally* obliged to pay. Although this requirement has been reiterated in a number of cases[2], the Court of Appeal in *Larner v LCC*[3] held that money paid under a mistake of fact which, if true, would have morally (but not legally) obliged its payment was recoverable back. The LCC passed a resolution to make up the pay of their employees who were on war service to the amount of their civil salaries. L was one of their employees and he joined the RAF. Although he had agreed to inform the LCC of any increase in his service wages, he failed to do so and, consequently, was overpaid by the LCC. If the facts had been as supposed, the LCC would only have been morally, not legally[4], obliged to make the payments, but the mistake was held to be sufficient to entitle the Council to recover back the amount of the overpayment. It may be that the decision in this case can be justified on its special facts and goes no further than holding that a mistake as to moral liability to honour a promise to pay made for reasons of *national policy* (a matter emphasised by the Court of Appeal) is to be equated with mistakes as to legal liability to pay. On this view, the Court of Appeal did not lay down a wider rule that, whenever a person pays money to another under a mistake of fact which causes him to make the payment, he is entitled to recover it back as money paid under a mistake of fact. However, in *Barclays Bank Ltd v W J Simms, Son and Cooke (Southern) Ltd*[5], the judge stated the law in these broad terms, relying on an impressive list of authorities; but an examination of them suggests that he misinterpreted them, so that his statement of the law must be viewed with suspicion and cannot be regarded with confidence as representing the current state of the law in the light of the authority to the contrary.

Subject to what we have just said, a payment can be recovered back from the payee even though the mistake was not shared by the payer and payee[6], and even though the mistake was induced by a third person[7].

1   (1841) 9 M & W 54.
2   Eg *Aiken v Short* (1856) 1 H & N 210 at 215; *Maskell v Horner* [1915] 3 KB 106, CA.
3   [1949] 2 KB 683, [1949] 1 All ER 964, CA.
4   Para 6.3, above.
5   [1980] QB 677, [1979] 3 All ER 522.
6   *Barclays Bank Ltd v W J Simms, Son and Cooke (Southern) Ltd* [1980] QB 677, [1979] 3 All ER 522.
7   *R E Jones Ltd v Waring and Gillow Ltd* [1926] AC 670, HL.

13.24   The mistake must be one of fact: money paid under a mistake of law is not recoverable, generally. A mistake as to the construction of a statute[1], or of regulations[2], or of a contract[3], is one of law. On the other hand, a mistake as to the existence of a private right, such as a person's title to property, is, oddly enough, regarded as a mistake of fact[4].

The recovery back of money paid under a mistake of fact is subject to the following limits:

a.   Where the money was paid under a contract which had been induced under a mistake on the payer's part, there can be no recovery back of the money on the ground that it was paid under a mistake of fact, unless the contract itself is void for mistake or is rescinded by the payer[5].

b.   Where the payer intends that the payee should have the money at all events, whether the fact be true or false[6], or is deemed in law so to intend (which is the case where a bookmaker pays or overpays a betting debt by mistake), he cannot recover it back[7].

c.   Where the payee has altered his position in good faith, as where an agent without notice of the payer's mistake hands the money (or part of it) over to his principal, so that it would be inequitable in all the circumstances to require him to make restitution (or to make restitution in full), the payer cannot recover it back from him (or cannot recover it back in full, as the case may be)[8].

1   *National Pari-Mutuel Association Ltd v R* (1930) 47 TLR 110, CA.
2   *Holt v Markham* [1923] 1 KB 504, CA.
3   *Ord v Ord* [1923] 2 KB 432.
4   *Cooper v Phibbs* (1867) LR 2 HL 149, HL.
5   *Norwich Union Fire Insurance Society Ltd v William H Price Ltd* [1934] AC 455, PC; *Barclays Bank Ltd v W J Simms, Son and Cooke (Southern) Ltd* [1980] QB 677, [1979] 3 All ER 522 at 535.
6   *Kelly v Solari* (1841) 9 M & W 54 at 58.
7   *Morgan v Ashcroft* [1938] 1 KB 49, [1937] 3 All ER 92, CA, as explained in *Barclays Bank Ltd v W J Simms, Son and Cooke (Southern) Ltd* [1980] QB 677, [1979] 3 All ER 522.
8   *Lipkin Gorman v Karpnale Ltd* [1991] 2 AC 548, [1992] 4 All ER 512, HL.

Payment of unlawful tax etc

13.25   Money paid to a public body in the form of taxes or other levies pursuant to an unlawful demand is normally recoverable back under the law of restitution, with interest[1]. While the tax etc will normally have been paid in such a case under a belief that the public body is legally entitled to payment, the present principle applies regardless of whether there has been any form of duress or mistake[2].

1   *Woolwich Building Society v IRC (No 2)* [1993] 1 AC 70, [1992] 3 All ER 737, HL.
2   Ibid.

Chapter 14

Misrepresentation, Duress and Undue Influence

Misrepresentation
14.1 A misrepresentation is a false or misleading statement. Unless, as rarely happens, a mistake induced by a misrepresentation is such as to render the contract void under the rules discussed in the previous chapter, it is the rules which follow which govern the situation. These rules are somewhat involved, and different rules apply depending on whether there has been an active misrepresentation or a misrepresentation through non-disclosure.

Active Misrepresentation
14.2 When one is faced with a situation involving an 'active misrepresentation' one must first ask whether the representation has become a term of the contract or not, applying the rules set out in paras 8.9 to 8.16, above. The division between active misrepresentations which have remained pre-contractual representations (mere representations) and those which have become terms of a resulting contract is fundamental since the remedies are different.

Active misrepresentations which have remained mere representations
14.3 If the misrepresentation has not become a contractual term, and provided certain requirements are satisfied, two remedies may be available to the misrepresentee: rescission of the contract (unless this is barred) and (in many cases) damages. The requirements mentioned above are that:

the misrepresentation must be one of fact;
it must have been addressed to the person misled; and
it must have induced the contract.

Misrepresentation of fact
14.4 There must be a misrepresentation by words or conduct of a past or existing fact. An example of a misrepresentation by conduct would be where

the vendor of a house covered up dry rot in it[1]. It follows from the requirement that there must be a misrepresentation of a past or existing fact that there are many misrepresentations for which no relief is available. The following must be distinguished from misrepresentations of fact.

1 See *Gordon v Selico* (1986) 278 Estates Gazette 53, CA.

14.5 *Mere puffs*   A representation which is mere vague sales talk is not regarded as a representation of fact, as is shown by *Dimmock v Hallett*[1]. At a sale of land by auction, it was said to be 'fertile and improvable'; in fact it was partly abandoned and useless. The representation was held to be a 'mere flourishing description by an auctioneer' affording no ground for relief. It is a question of fact whether a particular statement is merely vague sales talk or the assertion of some verifiable fact.

1   (1866) 2 Ch App 21.

14.6 *Statements of opinion*   A statement which merely expresses an opinion or belief does not give grounds for relief if the opinion or belief turns out to be wrong. In *Bisset v Wilkinson*[1], the vendor of a farm which had never been used as a sheep farm told a prospective purchaser that in his judgment the land would support 2,000 sheep. It was held that this statement was one of opinion, given that the farm had never been used for sheep, and that, since it was an honest statement, no relief was available.

What has been said in the last paragraph must be qualified by pointing out that in two cases statements of opinion can involve an implied misrepresentation of fact and so give rise to relief:

a.   Where a person represents an opinion which he does not honestly hold he will at the same time make a misrepresentation of fact, viz that he holds the opinion[2].
b.   Where a person represents an opinion for which he does not have reasonable grounds, he will at the same time make a misrepresentation of fact if he impliedly represents that he has reasonable grounds for his opinion.
A classic example is *Smith v Land and House Property Corpn*[3]. The vendor of a hotel described it as let to 'Mr Frederick Fleck (a most desirable tenant) . . . for an unexpired term of 27^1/$_2$ years, thus offering a first-class investment'. Fleck had not paid the last quarter's rent and had paid the previous one by instalments and under pressure. The Court of Appeal held that the above statement was not merely of opinion but also involved a misrepresentation of fact because the vendor impliedly stated that he had reasonable grounds for his opinion. Too much should not be read into this decision because the court will only find such an implied representation where the facts on which the opinion is based are particularly within the knowledge of the person stating the opinion, and not when the facts are equally known to both parties[4].

1   [1927] AC 177, PC. See also *Hummingbird Motors Ltd v Hobbs* [1986] RTR 276, CA.
2   *Brown v Raphael* [1958] Ch 636 at 641, [1958] 2 All ER 79 at 81; *Hummingbird Motors Ltd v Hobbs*.

3 (1884) 28 Ch D 7, CA.
4 *Smith v Land and House Property Corpn* (1884) 28 Ch D 7 at 15. See also *Brown v Raphael* [1958] Ch 636, [1958] 2 All ER 79, CA.

14.7 *Statements as to the future* Such statements, the best example of which is a statement of intention, are obviously not statements of fact in themselves and no remedy is available if the future event does not occur. However, a statement as to the future will involve a misrepresentation of fact if its maker does not honestly believe in its truth. In the case of a misrepresentation of intention this rule is well summarised by the statement of Bowen LJ in *Edgington v Fitzmaurice*[1], that the state of a man's mind is as much a fact as the state of his digestion. In this case the plaintiff was induced to lend money to a company by representations made in a prospectus by the directors that the money would be used to improve the company's buildings and to expand its business. The directors' true intention was to use the money to pay off the company's debts. They were held liable in deceit (fraudulent misrepresentation) on the basis that their misrepresentation of present intentions was a misrepresentation of fact.

1 (1885) 29 Ch D 459, CA.

14.8 *Statements of law* A person who is induced to contract by a misrepresentation of law has no remedy[1]. The only exceptions are:

a. where, as in the case of a statement of opinion or intention, the representor wilfully misrepresents the fact that he does not believe his statement of the law[2]; and
b. where the misrepresentation relates to the existence or meaning of a foreign law, since such a misrepresentation is regarded by our courts as one of fact[3].

A difficulty in this area is distinguishing a statement of law from a statement of fact. Clearly, a representation as to the *meaning* of a statute is one of law. However, in *West London Commercial Bank v Kitson*[4], it was held that a misrepresentation of the *contents* of a Private Act was one of fact. The directors of a company represented that the company had power to accept bills of exchange and that they had authority to accept on its behalf. There was a misrepresentation since, under the Private Act which incorporated it, the company had no power to accept bills or authorise anyone to do so. It was held that the misrepresentation was one of fact since it related to the contents of a Private Act. It is doubtful whether this decision would be extended to a misrepresentation as to the contents of a Public Act because such a misrepresentation seems clearly to be one as to the general law.

A misrepresentation as to the contents or meaning of a document is one of fact. One authority is *Wauton v Coppard*[5]. The plaintiff contracted to buy a house from the defendant for use as a preparatory school. He made the contract after the defendant's agent had told him that there was nothing in the deed of restrictive covenants to prevent the running of a school. When the plaintiff received the deed he discovered that it prohibited any business or occupation whereby disagreeable noise or nuisance might be caused and he sought to rescind the contract. It was held that the misrepresentation made by the defendant's agent was one of fact, and that the contract would be set aside, because it concerned the contents of the deed. Likewise, in *Horry v Tate & Lyle Refineries Ltd*[6], it was held that a misrepresentation as to the nature and effect of a contract for the settlement of a claim for compensation for personal injuries was one of fact.

1   *Beattie v Lord Ebury* (1872) 7 Ch App 777.
2   The point has not yet been decided by a court. It was left open for future decision in *West London Commercial Bank v Kitson* (1884) 13 QBD 360 at 362–363.
3   *André & Cie SA v Ets Michel Blanc & Fils* [1979] 2 Lloyd's Rep 427, CA.
4   (1884) 13 QBD 360, CA.
5   [1899] 1 Ch 92.
6   [1982] 2 Lloyd's Rep 416.

14.9   *Silence*   Not surprisingly, silence cannot generally constitute an active misrepresentation[1]. However, there are two exceptions:

a.   Where silence distorts a positive assertion of fact there will be an active misrepresentation of fact. Thus, in *Dimmock v Hallett*[2], it was said that if a vendor of land states that farms on it are let, but omits to say that the tenants have given notice to quit, his statement will be a misrepresentation of fact.
b.   Where a representation of fact is falsified by later events, before the conclusion of the contract, there will be an active misrepresentation if the representor fails to notify the other of the change. This is shown by *With v O'Flanagan*[3]. Negotiations for the sale of a medical practice were begun in January 1934. The defendant vendor represented to the plaintiff that the practice was producing £2,000 per annum, which was then true. Between January and May, the defendant was seriously ill and the practice was looked after by a number of substitutes with the result that the receipts had fallen to £5 per week by 1 May 1934. On 1 May 1934, the plaintiff, who had not been informed of the change of circumstances, signed a contract to purchase the practice. The Court of Appeal rescinded the contract on the ground that the defendant ought to have communicated the change of circumstances to the plaintiff. It said that the representation made to induce the contract must be treated as continuing until the contract was signed and what was initially a true representation had turned into a misrepresentation.

1   See further paras 14.38–14.43, below.
2   (1866) 2 Ch App 21.
3   [1936] Ch 575, [1936] 1 All ER 727, CA.

The misrepresentation must have been addressed by the misrepresentor to the person misled[1]
14.10   The present requirement is not as stringent as may appear at first sight because:

a.   It is possible for a representation to be made to the public in general, as in the case of an advertisement.

b.   A representation need not be made directly to the person misled, or his agent, in order to satisfy the present requirement. It suffices that the representor knew that the person to whom he made the misrepresentation would pass it on to the plaintiff. This is shown by *Pilmore v Hood*[2]. The defendant wished to sell a public house to X and fraudulently misrepresented that the annual takings were £180. X was unable to buy and with the defendant's knowledge persuaded the plaintiff to buy by repeating the defendant's misrepresentation. The defendant was held liable in damages to the plaintiff for the tort of deceit (fraudulent misrepresentation). An important limit on the rule in *Pilmore v Hood* is that, if the person (A) to whom the misrepresentation is originally made by the defendant (D) contracts with D as a result, the misrepresentation is deemed to be exhausted. Thus, if A then contracts to sell the property to B, repeating D's misrepresentation, as D knew he would, B has no redress against D because D's misrepresentation, being exhausted, is not regarded as addressed to B[3]. Of course, in such a case B is not remediless because he can pursue the normal remedies for misrepresentation against A who passed on the misrepresentation.

1   *Peek v Gurney* (1873) LR 6 HL 377, HL.
2   (1838) 5 Bing NC 97. See also *Yianni v Edwin Evans & Sons* [1982] QB 438, [1981] 3 All ER 592.
3   *Gross v Lewis Hillman Ltd* [1970] Ch 445, [1969] 3 All ER 1476, CA.

The misrepresentation must have induced the misrepresentee to make the contract
14.11   The question of inducement is one of fact but, if the misrepresentor made a statement of a nature likely to induce a person to contract and with a view to inducing this, it will normally be inferred that it did induce the misrepresentee to contract. However, this inference is rebuttable and will, for example, be rebutted in the following three cases:

a.   If the misrepresentee actually knew the truth[1], or if an agent acting for him in the transaction knew the truth as a result of information received in the course of it (since such knowledge is imputed to the misrepresentee)[2].
b.   If the misrepresentee was ignorant of the misrepresentation when the contract was made. In *Re Northumberland and Durham District Banking Co, ex p Bigge*[3], the plaintiff, who had bought some shares in a company, sought to have the purchase rescinded on the ground that the company had published false reports of its financial state. He failed and one of the reasons was because he was unable to prove that he had read any of the reports or that anyone had told him of their contents.
c.   If the misrepresentee did not allow the representation to affect his judgment. Thus, if the misrepresentee investigates the truth of the representation (as where a prospective purchaser has a house surveyed) and relies on his investigation, rather than the representation, in making the contract the inference of inducement is rebutted, except in the case of fraud. In *Attwood v Small*[4], the defendant offered to sell a mine, making exaggerated representations as to its earning capacity. The plaintiffs agreed to buy if the defendant could verify his representations and appointed

agents to investigate the matter. The agents, who were experienced, visited the mine and were given every facility. They reported that the representations were true and the contract was made. The House of Lords held that the contract could not be rescinded for misrepresentation because the plaintiffs had not relied on the misrepresentations but on their own independent investigations. By way of contrast, the inference of inducement is not rebutted where the misrepresentee could have investigated and discovered the falsity of the representation but chose not to do so[5].

1 *Begbie v Phosphate Sewage Co* (1875) LR 10 QB 491; *Redgrave v Hurd* (1881) 20 Ch D 1, CA.
2 *Strover v Harrington* [1988] Ch 390, [1988] 1 All ER 769.
3 (1858) 28 LJ Ch 50.
4 (1838) 6 Cl & Fin 232, HL.
5 *Redgrave v Hurd* (1881) 20 Ch D 1, CA; *Laurence v Lexcourt Holdings Ltd* [1978] 2 All ER 810, [1978] 1 WLR 1128.

14.12 Before leaving the requirement of inducement two general points must be noted. First, provided that it was one of the inducements, the misrepresentation need not be the sole inducement. This is shown by *Edgington v Fitzmaurice*[1], where the plaintiff was induced to take debentures in a company partly by a misrepresentation in the prospectus and partly by his own mistaken belief that debenture holders would have a charge on the company's property. He was held entitled to rescission.

Second, the misrepresentation must not only have induced the misrepresentee to contract but it must also have been material, in that it related to a matter which would have influenced the judgment of a reasonable person[2]. The point is not an important one because an immaterial misrepresentation is unlikely to cause substantial loss, with the result that any damages awarded are likely to be nominal and rescission is likely to be refused under the court's discretion to do so (which is described in para 14.29, below).

1 (1885) 29 Ch D 459, CA.
2 *Container Transport International Inc v Oceanus Mutual Underwriting Association (Bermuda) Ltd* [1984] 1 Lloyd's Rep 476, CA; *Pan Atlantic Insurance Co Ltd v Pine Top Insurance Co Ltd* [1995] 1 AC 501, [1994] 3 All ER 581, HL (see especially pp 600–610); Marine Insurance Act 1906, s 20(1) and (2).

Remedies for active misrepresentations which have remained mere representations

14.13 Provided the above requirements are satisfied one or more of the remedies set out below is or are available to the misrepresentee. Alternatively, the misrepresentee can refuse to carry out the contract and, provided (generally) that he returns what he obtained under it, successfully resist any claim for damages or specific performance.

Rescission
14.14 The effect of a misrepresentation is to make the contract voidable – not void – so that it remains valid unless and until the misrepresentee elects to

271

rescind it on discovering the misrepresentation. Rescission entails setting the contract aside as if it had never been made, the misrepresentee recovering what he transferred under the contract but having to restore what he obtained under it. The effect of a misrepresentation is important in relation to the rights of third parties. If A sells a car to B under a contract which is voidable for B's misrepresentation, a voidable title passes to B and, if C (an innocent purchaser) buys the car from B before A has decided to rescind, A loses the right to rescind and C obtains a valid title[1]. This must be distinguished from the situation where the contract is void for mistake. There, title to the goods never passes and they can always be recovered, or damages obtained in lieu, from the other party or a third person to whom they have been transferred[2].

1   *White v Garden* (1851) 10 CB 919.
2   *Cundy v Lindsay* (1878) 3 App Cas 459, HL.

14.15   Rescission can be effected in two ways. First, by bringing legal proceedings for an order for rescission. This may be necessary where a formal document or transaction, such as a lease, has to be set aside by a court order. In other cases a court order is not essential but may be advantageous if the misrepresentor is likely to prove unwilling to return what he has obtained under the contract.

Second, rescission can be effected by the misrepresentee making it clear that he refuses to be bound by the contract. Normally, communication of this decision to the misrepresentor is required, but there is an exception. If a fraudulent misrepresentor absconds, it suffices that the misrepresentee records his intention to rescind the contract by some overt act that is reasonable in the circumstances. This was decided by the Court of Appeal in *Car and Universal Finance Co Ltd v Caldwell*[1]. The defendant sold his car to N in return for a cheque which was dishonoured when he presented it the next day[2]. The defendant immediately informed the police and the Automobile Association of the fraudulent transaction. Subsequently, N sold the car to X who sold it to Y who sold it to Z who sold it to the plaintiffs who bought it in good faith. It was held that in the circumstances the defendant had done enough to rescind the contract before the plaintiffs bought the car, title had therefore re-vested in him and the plaintiffs had not got title.

1   [1965] 1 QB 525, [1964] 1 All ER 290, CA.
2   By his conduct in drawing the cheque, N had fraudulently misrepresented that the existing state of facts was such that in the ordinary course of events the cheque would be honoured: *R v Hazelton* (1874) LR 2 CCR 134 at 140.

14.16   There are five bars to the right to rescind:

a.   *Affirmation of contract by misrepresentee*   This occurs if, after discovering that the misrepresentation is untrue and knowing of his right to rescind[1], the misrepresentee declares his intention to waive his right to rescission or behaves in a way that such an intention can be inferred. An inference of such an intention was drawn in *Long v Lloyd*[2]. The plaintiff bought a lorry as the result of the defendant's misrepresentation that it was in excellent condition. On the plaintiff's first business journey the dynamo broke and he noticed several other serious defects. On the next business journey the lorry broke down and the plaintiff, realising that it was in a very bad condition, sought to rescind the contract. The Court of Appeal held that the second journey constituted an affirmation because the plaintiff knew by then that the representation was untrue. Similarly, if a person, who has applied for, and been allotted, shares in reliance on a misrepresentation, subsequently discovers the falsity but nevertheless attempts to sell them, or retains dividends paid on them, or neglects to have his name removed from the register of shareholders, an intention to affirm will be inferred[3]. Once the election to rescind or affirm has been made it is irrevocable[4].

b. *Lapse of time* This can provide evidence of affirmation where the misrepresentee fails to rescind for a considerable time after discovering the falsity[5]. In addition, lapse of time can operate as a separate bar to rescission in cases where the misrepresentee has not delayed after discovering the falsity. This is shown by *Leaf v International Galleries*[6], where the plaintiff bought from the defendant a picture of Salisbury Cathedral which the latter had innocently represented to be by Constable. Five years later, the plaintiff discovered that this was a misrepresentation and immediately sought to rescind the contract. The Court of Appeal held that his right to rescind had been lost through lapse of a reasonable time to discover the falsity. This bar probably does not apply in the case of a fraudulent misrepresentation.

c. *Inability to restore* The main objects of rescission are to restore the parties to their former position and to prevent unjust enrichment[7]. Thus, if either party has so changed or otherwise dealt with what he has obtained under the contract that he cannot restore it, rescission is barred[8]. So, for example, the purchaser of a cake cannot rescind the contract if he has eaten the cake.

There are three qualifications on the present bar:

i.   A fraudulent misrepresentor cannot rely on his own dealings with what he has obtained as a bar to rescission by the misrepresentee[9].
ii. The fact that a seller has spent the money which he has received does not make restitution impossible since one bank note is as good as another and the seller can restore what he obtained under the contract by handing over other notes.
iii. Precise restitution is not required for rescission. Provided the property in question can substantially be restored, rescission can be enforced even though the property has deteriorated, declined in value or otherwise changed. For example, in *Armstrong v Jackson*[10], a broker fraudulently sold shares to the plaintiff. Later, when the shares had fallen to one-twelfth of their value at the time of sale, the plaintiff claimed rescission. It was held that, since the plaintiff could return the actual shares, rescission would be ordered, subject to the defendant's repayment of the purchase price being credited with the dividends received by the plaintiff. Likewise, in *Cheese v Thomas*[11], where the contract had involved the plaintiff contributing

£43,000 to the purchase of a house at a price of £83,000 but, because of a fall in property values, the house had subsequently been sold for only £55,400, rescission of the contract was ordered on the basis that the plaintiff and defendant should share the loss brought about by the fall in value in the same proportions (43:40) as they had contributed to the price, and not on the basis of the plaintiff's contribution of £43,000 being repaid.

The Court of Appeal emphasised that the basic object of rescission was to restore each party as near as possible to his original position. Where a deterioration or loss of value results from the voluntary dealings with it by the person who obtained it under the contract, he must not only account for any profits derived from it but also pay compensation for such deterioration or loss of value.[12]

d.   *Bona fide purchaser for value*   As has been indicated in para 14.14, above, if, before the misrepresentee elects to rescind, a third party has innocently purchased the property, or an interest in it, for value from the misrepresentor, his rights are valid against the misrepresentee, who loses the chance to rescind. This is illustrated by *White v Garden*[13], where a rogue bought 50 tons of iron from Garden by persuading him to take in payment a fraudulent bill of exchange. The rogue then sold the iron for value to White who acted in good faith (ie was unaware of the rogue's fraudulent misrepresentation) and Garden delivered the iron to White. The bill of exchange was subsequently dishonoured and Garden seized and removed some of the iron. Garden was held liable for what is now the tort of conversion; he had purported to rescind the contract with the rogue too late, the rogue's voidable title having been made unavoidable when White innocently bought the iron from him. In *Car and Universal Finance Co Ltd v Caldwell*[14], on the other hand, rescission was not barred because it occurred before the intervention of a bona fide purchaser for value.

e.   *The wound-up company*   Under the rule in *Oakes v Turquand*[15], if a shareholder wishes to rescind his contract to take up shares in a company on the ground of misrepresentation, he must begin an action to do so before a winding-up of the company commences.

1   *Peyman v Lanjani* [1985] Ch 457, [1984] 3 All ER 703, CA.
2   [1958] 2 All ER 402, [1958] 1 WLR 753, CA.
3   *Re Scottish Petroleum Co* (1883) 23 Ch D 413 at 434.
4   *Re Hop and Malt Exchange and Warehouse Co, ex p Briggs* (1866) LR 1 Eq 483; *Re Scottish Petroleum Co* (1883) 23 Ch D 413, CA.
5   *Clough v London and North Western Rly Co* (1871) LR 7 Exch 26 at 35.
6   [1950] 2 KB 86, [1950] 1 All ER 693, CA.
7   *Spence v Crawford* [1939] 3 All ER 271 at 288-289.
8   *Clarke v Dickson* (1858) EB & E 148; *MacKenzie v Royal Bank of Canada* [1934] AC 468, PC.
9   *Spence v Crawford* [1939] 3 All ER 271 at 280-282.
10 [1917] 2 KB 822.
11 [1994] 1 All ER 35, [1994] 1 WLR 129, CA.
12 *Erlanger v New Sombrero Phosphate Co* (1878) 3 App Cas 1218 at 1278-1279.
13 (1851) 10 CB 919.
14 Para 14.15, above.
15 (1867) LR 2 HL 325.

14.17 Before leaving the bars to rescission it should be noted that the courts have power, in the case of non-fraudulent misrepresentations, to refuse rescission, or to refuse to recognise a purported rescission, and to award damages in lieu. This power is discussed in para 14.29, below.

Damages
14.18 We are concerned here with damages for misrepresentation and not with damages for breach of contract, discussed in chapter 12, which are a different species. Sometimes damages for misrepresentation can be recovered under the common law rules of tort: sometimes under the Misrepresentation Act 1967. Rescission and damages are alternative remedies in many cases, but if the victim of a fraudulent or negligent misrepresentation has suffered consequential loss he may rescind *and* sue for damages. The duty to mitigate loss referred to in para 12.15, above, in respect of the assessment of damages from breach of contract also applies to damages for misrepresentation; the duty arises when the misrepresentee discovers the truth[1]. The same provisions as to limitation periods apply as in the case of an action for breach of contract[2]; the cause of action for damages for misrepresentation accrues (and the limitation period begins to run) when the misrepresentation is made, except in the case of the tort of negligent misrepresentation where it accrues when loss results from the misrepresentation.

1 *Smith New Court Securities Ltd v Scrimgeour Vickers (Asset Management) Ltd* [1996] 4 All ER 769, HL.
2 Para 12.35, above.

14.19 The discussion of the rules of assessment of damages for misrepresentation requires the division of the relevant law into five classes.

14.20 *Fraudulent misrepresentation* Fraudulent misrepresentation gives rise to an action for damages for the tort of deceit. The classic definition of fraud in this context was given by Lord Herschell in *Derry v Peek*[1]. Lord Herschell stated that fraud is proved where it is shown that a misrepresentation has been made:

a. knowingly, or
b. without belief in its truth, or
c. recklessly, careless whether it be true or false.

A misrepresentation would not be fraudulent if there was an honest belief in its truth when it was made, even though there were no reasonable grounds for that belief[2]. Motive was irrelevant: an intention to cheat or injure was not required.

1 (1889) 14 App Cas 337, HL.
2 See also *Thomas Witter Ltd v TBP Industries Ltd* [1996] 2 All ER 573.

14.21 *Negligent misrepresentation under the Misrepresentation Act 1967* Section 2(1) of the 1967 Act provides that where a person has entered into a contract after a misrepresentation has been made to him by another party thereto and as a result of it has suffered loss, then, if the misrepresentor would be liable to damages for misrepresentation if it had been made fraudulently, he is to be so liable notwithstanding that the misrepresentation was not made fraudulently, unless he proves that he had reasonable grounds to believe and did believe up to the time the contract was made that the facts represented were true. In other words, the misrepresentor is deemed negligent, and liable to pay damages, unless he proves in the stated way that he was not negligent. Whether the misrepresentor can prove this will depend, for instance, on whether he was an expert or not, the length of the negotiations and whether he himself had been misled by another. The misrepresentor's burden of proof is a difficult one to discharge. This is shown by *Howard Marine and Dredging Co Ltd v A Ogden & Sons (Excavations) Ltd*[1]. During negotiations for the hire of two barges, Howard's agent misrepresented their capacity in reliance on an error in Lloyd's Register. The Court of Appeal held that the burden of proof had not been discharged, since a file in Howard's possession disclosed the real capacity.

Section 2(1) applies where the misrepresentation was made on behalf of a party to the subsequent contract by his agent[2], but in such a case the misrepresentee only has an action under s 2(1) against that party and not against his agent[3].

1   [1978] QB 574, [1978] 2 All ER 1134, CA.
2   *Gosling v Anderson* (1972) 223 Estates Gazette 1743, CA.
3   *Resolute Maritime Inc v Nippon Kaiji Kyokai* [1983] 2 All ER 1, [1983] 1 WLR 857; an agent may be liable for a fraudulent misrepresentation or for negligent misrepresentation at common law.

14.22   *Remoteness and measure of damages*   In the tort of deceit and under s 2(1)of the 1967 Act the rule of remoteness of damage is that the defendant is liable for all actual damage or loss directly flowing from the misrepresentation[1]. This is a more liberal rule than that of reasonable foreseeability of the possibility of the damage which applies in other torts, and also more liberal than the rule of remoteness which applies in the case of damages for breach of contract, where damages are limited to compensation for loss which was within the parties' reasonable contemplation, when the contract was made, as a seriously possible result of its breach[2].

1   *Doyle v Olby (Ironmongers) Ltd* [1969] 2 QB 158, [1969] 2 All ER 119, CA; *East v Maurer* [1991] 2 All ER 733, [1991] 1 WLR 461, CA; *Smith New Court Securities Ltd v Scrimgeour Vickers (Asset Management) Ltd* [1996] 4 All ER 769, HL (action for deceit); *Royscot Trust Ltd v Rogerson* [1991] 2 QB 297, [1991] 3 All ER 294, CA (action under Misrepresentation Act 1967, s 2(1)).
2   See para 18.62, below (other torts) and paras 12.5–12.7, above (breach of contract).

14.23   Damages for deceit or under s 2(1) of the 1967 Act are assessed according to the 'out of pocket rule'[1], ie an amount is awarded which puts the misrepresentee into the position in which he would have been had the misrepresentation never been made.

Where he has been induced to buy something by a misrepresentation, the plaintiff is entitled to recover as damages the full price paid by him, but he must give credit for any benefits which he has received as a direct result of the transaction[2]. As a general rule, the benefits received by him include the market value of the property acquired as at the date of acquisition, with the result that the damages awarded will be the difference between the price paid and the real value of the property at the date of the acquisition by the plaintiff[2]. However, this general rule is not inflexibly applied; it will not be applied where to do so would prevent the misrepresentee obtaining full compensation for the wrong suffered[2]. Examples of cases where the general rule will not apply are where:

a. the misrepresentation has continued to operate after the date of the acquisition of the asset so as to cause the misrepresentee to retain the asset; or
b. the circumstances are such that the plaintiff is, by reason of the fraud, locked into the property[2].

One case where the general rule did not apply is *Smith New Court Securities Ltd v Scrimgeour Vickers (Asset Management) Ltd*[3], where the plaintiffs were induced to buy some shares in company X for £23m by the defendants' fraudulent misrepresentation. Because a fraud had been practised on company X before the plaintiffs acquired the shares, the shares were doomed to tumble in value and were therefore a flawed asset. There was a slump in their value and the plaintiffs were only able to sell them by degrees and only received £11m for them in total. The plaintiffs were awarded as damages the difference between what they had paid for the shares and what they had obtained by their sale of the shares, since the latter amount was to be regarded as the benefit received by them as a result of the transaction, because they could not have sold the shares at the value they had when they acquired them.

The principles set out above were stated in *Smith New Court* in relation to damages for fraudulent misrepresentation, but they are of equal application to damages under s 2(1) of the Misrepresentation Act 1967. In *Royscot Trust Ltd v Rogerson*[4] the Court of Appeal held that damages under s 2(1) should be assessed as if the misrepresentation had been made fraudulently.

The 'out of pocket rule' should be contrasted with the measure of damages for breach of contract. Here the 'loss of expectations rule' normally applies, as has been explained in para 12.3, above, and the injured party recovers an amount which puts him into the position in which he would have been if the representation had been true. Where the breach relates to the thing's quality, this amount is the difference between the 'represented value' and the actual value. The application of the 'out of pocket rule' does not mean that recovery as damages for deceit or under s 2(1) can never be made in respect of loss of profits. This is shown by *East v Maurer*[5], where the seller of a hairdressing salon fraudulently represented that he would no longer be working at another salon in the area, in order to induce the plaintiff to contract to buy the salon. The plaintiff was induced by the representation to buy the salon. As a result of the untruth of the representation, the plaintiff was unable to run a successful business at the salon. He was unable to sell it for three years. The Court of Appeal held that the damages for deceit were to be assessed on the basis that the plaintiff should be compensated for all losses which he had suffered, including his loss on the resale *and his loss of profits.* The profits lost were assessed not on the basis of the profits which would have been earned if the representation had been true (which would have been the amount under the 'loss of expectations' rule) but on the basis of the profits which the misrepresentee would have made if he had not been induced into buying the salon but had bought a different one in the area (because this was the amount by which he was out of pocket as a result of the defendant's deceit).

1   *Smith New Court Securities Ltd v Scrimgeour Vickers (Asset Management) Ltd* [1996] 4 All ER 769, HL (action for deceit); *Royscot Trust Ltd v Rogerson* [1991] 2 QB 297, [1991] 3 All ER 294, CA (action under Misrepresentation Act 1967, s 2(1)).
2   *Smith New Court Securities Ltd v Scrimgeour Vickers (Asset Management Ltd* [1996] 4 All ER 769, HL.
3   [1996] 4 All ER 769, HL.
4   [1991] 2 QB 297, [1991] 3 All ER 294, CA.
5   [1991] 2 All ER 733, [1991] 1 WLR 461, CA.

14.24   A person who has been induced into a contract by a misrepresentation which is fraudulent or which is negligent under s 2(1) of the Misrepresentation Act may also recover damages for any consequential loss or damage, such as expenses, personal injury, damage to his property[1], which he may have suffered, provided it is not too remote.

1   Damages for distress or disappointment are also recoverable in an action in deceit: *Archer v Brown* [1985] QB 401, [1984] 2 All ER 267.

14.25   The contributory negligence of the misrepresentee is not a ground for reducing damages awarded for deceit[1], but it is such a ground if damages are awarded under s 2(1) of the Misrepresentation Act, provided that the defendant is also liable in tort for negligence, since the Law Reform (Contributory Negligence) Act 1945[2] applies in such a case[3].

1   *Alliance and Leicester Building Society v Edgestop* [1994] 2 All ER 38, [1993] 1 WLR 1462; affd in another point [1995] CLY 2828, CA.
2   Para 21.11, below.
3   *Gran Gelato Ltd v Richcliff (Group) Ltd* [1992] Ch 560, [1992] 1 All ER 865.

14.26   Given that, where a fraudulent misrepresentation has been made, an action may normally be brought for the same amount of damages under s 2(1) of the Misrepresentation Act 1967 without the need to prove fraud, or indeed negligence, it makes sense in many cases of suspected fraudulent misrepresentation for an action to be brought under s 2(1) rather than for deceit.

14.27   *Negligent misrepresentation at common law*   The victim of a negligent misrepresentation may be able to sue the misrepresentor under the principles of the tort of negligence, particularly those enunciated in *Hedley Byrne & Co Ltd v Heller & Partners Ltd*[1] which we discuss in paras 18.13–18.19, below. If the misrepresentee sues under the *Hedley Byrne* principles, he must prove:

a. that the misrepresentor owed him a duty to take reasonable care in making the representation, which duty arises if there is an 'appropriate (or special) relationship';
b. that the misrepresentor was in breach of that duty; and
c. that damage resulted from that breach.

The circumstances in which a court may find an 'appropriate relationship' are not entirely clear, as we explain in para 18.16, below.

The *Hedley Byrne* principles were applied to a representation made in pre-contractual negotiations by the Court of Appeal in *Esso Petroleum Co Ltd v Mardon*[2]. In negotiations in 1963 for the tenancy of a filling station, Esso negligently told Mr Mardon that the station had an estimated annual through-put of 200,000 gallons. Mr Mardon was induced to take the tenancy but the actual annual throughput never exceeded 86,000 gallons and Mr Mardon was awarded damages against Esso. One reason for its decision given by the Court of Appeal was that Esso, having special knowledge and skill in estimating petrol throughput, were under the duty of care imposed by *Hedley Byrne* – which applied to pre-contractual statements – and were in breach of that duty. In this case, Mr Mardon could not have relied on s 2(1) of the Misrepresentation Act 1967 because the misrepresentation had occurred before the Act came into force.

In practice, it is normally better to rely on s 2(1) in the case of a negligent misrepresentation because the plaintiff does not have the onus of proving negligence under s 2(1), unlike the position at common law. In addition, no appropriate relationship is required under s 2(1). However, the *Hedley Byrne* principles are still important in cases of pre-contractual misrepresentation in three situations: where the misrepresentation is made by a third party to the contract; where the contractual negotiations do not result in a contract between the defendant and the plaintiff but the plaintiff nevertheless suffers loss in reliance on the misrepresentation; and where the limitation period for an action under s2(1) has expired but that for negligence at common law (which runs from the suffering of loss, and not the misrepresentation) has not. In these cases, assuming their requirements are satisfied, there can be tortious liability under the principles in *Hedley Byrne*, although there can be no rescission for misrepresentation or damages under the 1967 Act.

The measure of damages under *Hedley Byrne* is governed by the 'out of pocket rule'[3] and questions of remoteness of damage by the test of reasonable foreseeability at the time of the breach of duty[4]. This is a narrower test of remoteness than that under s 2(1) of the Misrepresentation Act 1967, which is another reason for an action under s 2(1) being preferable to a claim based on negligent misrepresentation at common law when both actions are available.

1   [1964] AC 465, [1963] 2 All ER 575, HL.
2   [1976] QB 801, [1976] 2 All ER 5, CA.
3   See, eg, *JEB Fasteners Ltd v Marks, Bloom & Co (a firm)* [1983] 1 All ER 583 at 587.
4   Paras 18.61–18.66, below.

14.28 *Innocent misrepresentation*   Subject to what is said in para 14.29, below, damages cannot be awarded for a misrepresentation which is not fraudulent or negligent, as defined above. However, an indemnity – which is different from damages – may be awarded.

14.29   *Damages in lieu of rescission*   Section 2(2) of the Misrepresentation Act 1967 provides that, where a person has entered into a contract after a non-fraudulent misrepresentation has been made to him which would entitle him to rescind the contract, then, if it is claimed in proceedings arising out of the contract that the contract ought to be or has been rescinded, the court or arbitrator may declare the contract subsisting and award damages in lieu of rescission, if of the opinion that it would be equitable to do so. The rationale for this power is that rescission may be too drastic in some cases, eg where the misrepresentation was trifling. An award of damages under s 2(2) is discretionary. In exercising his discretion, a judge or arbitrator is required by s 2(2) to have regard to the nature of the misrepresentation and the loss that would be caused by it if the contract was upheld, as well as the loss that rescission would cause to the other party.

A literal interpretation of s 2(2) might be thought to suggest that the power to award damages in lieu of rescission can only be exercised if rescission has not been barred, eg by affirmation of the contract, and cannot be exercised in the case of a fraudulent misrepresentation. However, it has been held by a judge in the Chancery Division that this is not so and that the power to award damages under s 2(2) does not depend on an extant right to rescind, but only on a right having existed at some time after the contract was made[1].

Important distinctions between s 2(1) and s 2(2) are that damages cannot be awarded under s 2(1) if lack of negligence is proved, whereas they can be awarded in such a case under s 2(2); that damages under s 2(1) can be awarded in addition to rescission; that an award of damages under s 2(1) is not discretionary; and that s 2(3), described below, contemplates that the measure of damages under s 2(1) is different from, and more generous than, an award under s 2(2)[2].

In the light of this, obiter dicta in the Court of Appeal that, unlike damages under s 2(1), damages under s 2(2) cannot include damages for consequential loss, is not surprising, although the other part of the obiter dicta, that damages under s 2(2) in respect of the value of the thing are assessed on the basis of 'loss of expectations' is surprising and doubtful in the light of the generally less generous rule which applies to damages under s 2(1)[3].

Where a person has been held liable to pay damages under s 2(1) of the 1967 Act, the judge or arbitrator, in assessing damages thereunder, is required by s 2(3) to take into account any damages in lieu of rescission under s 2(2).

1   *Thomas Witter Ltd v TBP Industries Ltd* [1996] 2 All ER 573; cf *The Lucy* [1983] 1 Lloyds Rep 188 at 202.
2   *William Sindall plc v Cambridgeshire County Council* [1994] 3 All ER 932 at 954; *Thomas Witter Ltd v TBP Industries Ltd* [1996] 2 All ER 573 at 591.
3   For differing views, see *William Sindall plc v Cambridgeshire County Council* [1994] 3 All ER 932 at 954 and 961.

Indemnity
14.30   It has already been noted that the object of rescission is to restore the contracting parties to their former position as if the contract had never been

made. As part of this restoration the misrepresentee can claim an indemnity against any *obligations necessarily created by the contract*[1]. The italicised words must be emphasised since they indicate that an indemnity is far less extensive than damages, as was recognised by the Court of Appeal in *Newbigging v Adam*[2]. A classic example of this distinction is provided by *Whittington v Seale-Hayne*[3]. The plaintiffs, breeders of prize poultry, were induced to take a lease of the defendant's premises by his innocent misrepresentation that the premises were in a thoroughly sanitary condition. Under the lease, the plaintiffs covenanted to execute all works required by any local or public authority. Owing to the insanitary condition of the premises the water supply was poisoned, the plaintiffs' manager and his family became very ill, and the poultry became valueless for breeding purposes or died. In addition, the local authority required the drains to be renewed. The plaintiffs sought an indemnity for the following losses: the value of the stock lost; loss of profit on sales; loss of breeding season; rent, and medical expenses on behalf of the manager. The trial judge rescinded the lease and held that the plaintiffs could recover an indemnity for what they had spent on rent, rates and repairs under the covenants in the lease, because these expenses arose necessarily out of the occupation of the premises or were incurred under the covenants in the lease and were thus obligations necessarily created by the contract. However, the judge refused to award an indemnity for the loss of stock, loss of profits, loss of breeding season or the medical expenses, since to do so would be to award damages, not an indemnity, there being no obligation created by the contract to carry on a poultry farm on the premises or to employ a manager, etc.

1   *Whittington v Seale-Hayne* (1900) 82 LT 49, adopting the view of Bowen LJ in *Newbigging v Adam* (1886) 34 Ch D 582, CA.
2   (1886) 34 Ch D 582, CA.
3   (1900) 82 LT 49.

14.31   Two further points may be made concerning the award of an indemnity:

a.   Being ancillary to rescission, an indemnity cannot be awarded if rescission is barred.
b.   The remedy of an indemnity is redundant where the court can, and does, award damages for misrepresentation. However, where there has merely been an innocent misrepresentation and the court decides not to award damages in lieu of rescission, the availability of an award of an indemnity is very important.

Active misrepresentations which have become contractual terms
14.32   Whether a misrepresentation made during pre-contractual negotiations has become a term of the resulting contract, or of a contract collateral to it, is determined in accordance with the rules set out in paras 8.9–8.16, above.

If the misrepresentation has become a contractual term the misrepresentee has a choice between two courses of action.

Breach of contract
14.33   As in the case of the breach of any other contractual term, the misrepresentee can sue for breach of contract. If he does so, he can recover damages for breach of contract (as opposed to damages for misrepresentation). Where the misrepresentation relates to the subject matter of the contract, damages will be assessed according to the normal contractual rule, the 'loss of the expectations' rule, and recovery can also be had for all consequential loss, provided the loss was within the parties' reasonable contemplation, at the time the contract was made, as a seriously possible result of the breach. The relevant law has already been discussed in detail in chapter 12. In addition, if the misrepresentation has become a condition of the contract, or an 'intermediate term' and there has been a sufficiently serious breach of it, the misrepresentee can also terminate the contract for *breach*, a matter which we discussed in paras 10.3–10.22, above.

Misrepresentation Act 1967, s 1(a)
14.34   The misrepresentee's alternative course of action is to make use of s 1(a) of the Misrepresentation Act 1967. Under this provision a person who is induced to enter into a contract by a misrepresentation of fact, which has become a term of the contract, can elect to rescind the contract for *misrepresentation* subject to the bars to rescission mentioned in para 14.16, above. However, if he does so rescind he cannot recover damages for breach of contract since rescission for misrepresentation sets aside the contract, including his right to claim damages for its breach, although he may be able to claim damages for misrepresentation, depending on the circumstances, in accordance with the rules set out in paras 14.18–14.29, above.

14.35   The choice of a particular course of action will depend very much on whether greater damages will be obtained for breach of contract or for misrepresentation and on whether the plaintiff wishes, and is able, to rescind for misrepresentation.

Avoidance of provision excluding or limiting liability for misrepresentation
14.36   Section 3 of the Misrepresentation Act 1967 provides that if a contract contains a term which would exclude or restrict:

a.   any liability to which a party to a contract may be subject by reason of any misrepresentation made by him before the contract was made; or
b.   any remedy available to another party to the contract by reason of such a misrepresentation,

that term is of no effect, except in so far as it satisfies the requirement of reasonableness. It is for the person claiming that it satisfies that requirement to show that it does. The requirement of reasonableness is that the term must have been a fair and reasonable one to be included having regard to the circumstances which were, or ought reasonably to have been, known to or in the contemplation of the parties when the contract was made[1].

1   Unfair Contract Terms Act 1977, s 11. See, further, para 10.48, above.

14.37   Section 3 not only applies where the relevant misrepresentation has remained a mere representation but also where it has become a contractual term – at least, as far as rescission for misrepresentation and damages for misrepresentation are concerned, although it is uncertain whether it applies if the misrepresentee elects to treat it as a breach of contract.

Misrepresentation through Non-disclosure

14.38   Generally, mere silence as to a material fact or tacit acquiescence in another's erroneous belief concerning such a fact does not constitute a misrepresentation. Thus, in *Turner v Green*[1], where two solicitors arranged a compromise of certain legal proceedings, the failure of the plaintiff's solicitor to inform the defendant's of a material fact was held not to be a ground for relief, even though the defendant would not have made the compromise if he had known of that fact.

1   [1895] 2 Ch 205.

14.39   However, in certain situations there is a duty to disclose material facts, breach of which gives rise to relief. Two of these situations have been referred to already: where silence distorts a positive assertion and where a positive assertion is falsified by later events (see para 14.9, above). In these cases silence is deemed to be an active misrepresentation. In addition, in the case of contracts *uberrimae fidei* – of the utmost good faith – a duty to disclose fully all material facts is imposed, breach of which is regarded as a misrepresentation through non-disclosure for which relief is available.

Contracts uberrimae fidei can be divided into three types:

a.   insurance contracts;
b.   contracts preliminary to family arrangements; and
c.   contracts where one party is in a fiduciary relationship with the other.

Insurance contracts
14.40   An intending insurer or insured is under a duty to disclose all material facts known to him[1]. In the case of marine insurance, an insured's duty of disclosure is now imposed by s 18(1) of the Marine Insurance Act 1906 but otherwise it rests on the common law. In the case of an intending insured, a material fact is one which would have an effect, not necessarily a decisive influence, on the mind of a prudent insurer in deciding whether to accept the risk or as to the premium to be charged[2]. In the case of an intending insurer, a material fact is one relating to the nature of the risk to be covered or the recoverability of a claim, which a prudent insured would take into account in

deciding whether or not to place the risk in question with that insurer[3]. In marine insurance an intending insured is deemed by s 18(1) of the 1906 Act to know every fact which ought to be known to him, but otherwise the duty of disclosure only extends to those material facts which are actually known to an intending insurer or insured[4]. If a material fact is not disclosed as required, the other party cannot rely on it as a ground to avoid the contract if it did not induce him to make the contract[5].

1   *Carter v Boehm* (1766) 3 Burr 1905; *Banque Financière de la Cité SA v Westgate Insurance Co Ltd* [1990] 1 QB 665, [1989] 2 All ER 952, CA; affd [1991] 2 AC 249, [1990] 2 All ER 947, HL.
2   *Lambert v Co-operative Insurance Society* [1975] 2 Lloyd's Rep 485, CA; *Container Transport International Inc v Oceanus Mutual Underwriting Association (Bermuda) Ltd* [1984] 1 Lloyd's Rep 476, CA; *Pan Atlantic Insurance Co Ltd v Pine Top Insurance Co Ltd* [1995] 1 AC 501, [1994] 3 All ER 581, HL; Marine Insurance Act 1906, s 18(2).
3   *Banque Financière de la Cité SA v Westgate Insurance Co Ltd* [1990] 1 QB 665, [1989] 2 All ER 952, CA; affd [1991] 2 AC 249, [1990] 2 All ER 947, HL.
4   *Joel v Law Union and Crown Insurance Co* [1908] 2 KB 863, CA.
5   See, for example, *Pan Atlantic Insurance Co Ltd v Pine Top Insurance Co Ltd* [1995] 1 AC 501, [1994] 3 All ER 581, HL (marine insurance contract).

Contracts preliminary to 'family arrangements'
14.41   Examples of 'family arrangements' are the settlement of land between members of a family and the surrender by one member of a family of some proprietary right to another member. People making contracts for such purposes are under a duty imposed by equity to make full disclosure of all material facts known to them[1].

1   *Gordon v Gordon* (1821) 3 Swan 400.

Contracts where one party is in a confidential or fiduciary relationship with the other
14.42   Where one prospective contracting party stands in a confidential relationship with the other (such as parent and child; solicitor or accountant and client; trustee and beneficiary; partner and partner, and principal and agent)[1] he is under a duty to disclose any material fact known to him. The same duty of disclosure applies where one person has placed himself in such a position that he becomes obliged to act fairly and with due regard to the interests of the other party[2].

1   See Chaps 23 and 24 in respect of the last two relationships.
2   *Tate v Williamson* (1866) 2 Ch App 55.

14.43   The effect of a breach of the duty of disclosure in contracts uberrimae fidei is that the person to whom the duty was owed can have the contract rescinded, in which case an indemnity can be awarded where appropriate. The same bars to rescission apply as described above. Alternatively, the person to whom the duty was owed can refuse to carry out the contract and, provided (generally) that he returns what he obtained under it, successfully resist any claim for damages for breach of duty[1]. The Misrepresentation Act 1967 does not apply to misrepresentation through non-disclosure in contracts uberrimae fidei, nor do the common law rules relating to liability for negligent misrepresentation.

1   *Banque Financière de la Cité SA v Westgate Insurance Co Ltd* [1990] 1 QB 665, [1989] 2 All ER 952, CA; affd [1991] 2 AC 249, [1990] 2 All ER 947, HL.

Duress and Undue Influence

14.44   In some situations a contract can be avoided on the ground that it has been procured by illegitimate pressure or that unfair influence over a contracting party has been proved or may be presumed. The first case is governed by the common law of duress, and the second by principles of equity relating to undue influence and to what may be called 'unconscionable bargains'.

Duress

14.45   At one time only duress to the person, ie actual or threatened personal violence or imprisonment, sufficed for duress at common law[1]. In recent times, however, it has been held that economic duress, eg a threat to goods or to a person's business or a threat to break a contract, can also constitute duress at common law[2].

To constitute duress at common law, the pressure must be 'illegitimate'. Legitimate commercial pressure cannot constitute duress[3]. Pressure will be illegitimate if what is threatened is unlawful (ie a breach of contract, tort or crime)[4]. Pressure can also be illegitimate, even though the threat is of lawful action, because of the nature of the pressure and of the demand to which it relates. Consequently, a threat to assault someone can amount to duress (because what is threatened is unlawful) and so can a threat to report a crime to the police unless a demand is complied with (because the pressure is illegitimate on the second ground)[5]. Cases where a threat of lawful action amounts to illegitimate pressure will be rare in commercial dealings. The Court of Appeal has held that where parties are traders dealing at arm's length and one threatens lawful action (eg not to grant credit) thinking in good faith that his demand is valid, it will be particularly difficult to establish illegitimate pressure, and relatively rare if he did not consider his demand valid[6].

Even if there is illegitimate pressure, it will not constitute duress unless the victim has been coerced by that pressure into doing something because he had no practical alternative to submission to the pressure, so that he cannot be regarded as having given his true consent to that act[3].

If duress is proved, it is irrelevant that it was not the sole or predominant cause inducing the contract, provided that it was a cause[7].

It appears that duress renders a contract voidable, so that it is valid unless and until rescinded by the coerced party[8], not void.

1   Co Litt 353b; *Cumming v Ince* (1847) 11 QB 112 at 120.
2   *Occidental Worldwide Investment Corpn v Skibs A/S Avanti, The Siboen and The Sibotre* [1976] 1 Lloyd's Rep 293; *Pao On v Lau Yiu Long* [1980] AC 614, [1979] 3 All ER 65, PC; *B & S Contracts and Designs Ltd v Victor Green Publications Ltd* [1984] ICR 419, CA; *Atlas Express*

Ltd v Kafco (Importers and Distributors) Ltd [1989] QB 833, [1989] 1 All ER 641.
3   *Occidental Worldwide Investment Corpn v Skibs A/S Avanti, The Siboen and The Sibotre; Pao On v Yau Yiu Long; Hennessy v Craigmyle & Co Ltd* [1986] ICR 461, CA; *Enimont Overseas AG v RO Jugotanker Zadar, The Olib* [1991] 2 Lloyd's Rep 108.
4   *Barton v Armstrong* [1976] AC 104 at 121; *Universe Tankerships Inc of Monrovia v International Transport Workers Federation, The Universe Sentinel* [1983] 1 AC 366, [1982] 2 All ER 67, HL.
5   *Universe Tankships Inc of Monrovia v International Transport Workers Federation, The Universe Sentinel; B & S Contracts and Designs Ltd v Victor Green Publications Ltd; Atlas Express Ltd v Kafco (Importers and Distributors) Ltd.*
6   *CTN Cash and Carry Ltd v Gallaher Ltd* [1994] 4 All ER 714, CA.
7   *Barton v Armstrong* [1976] AC 104, [1975] 2 All ER 465, PC.
8   *Pao On v Yau Yiu Long* [1980] AC 614 at 634; *Universe Tankships Inc of Monrovia v International Transport Workers Federation, The Universe Sentinel.*

Undue influence

14.46   A contract which falls within the equitable doctrine of undue influence is voidable at the instance of the party influenced. Two types of case fall within the equitable doctrine:

a.   where actual undue influence is proved;
b.   where there is a confidential relationship between the parties, in which case undue influence is presumed provided that the contract is manifestly disadvantageous to the weaker party.

Actual undue influence

14.47   The party alleging undue influence must prove that the other party actually exerted unfair or improper influence over him and thereby procured a contract that would not otherwise have been made, as where a bank procured a mortgage from a father by a threat to prosecute his son for forgery otherwise[1]. There is no need for him to prove that the contract is manifestly disadvantageous to him[2].

Developments in the common law rules of duress mean that there is now little difference in coverage between those rules and the equitable rules on actual undue influence.

1   *Williams v Bayley* (1866) LR 1 HL 200.
2   *CIBC Mortgages plc v Pitt* [1994] 1 AC 200, [1993] 4 All ER 433, HL.

Presumed undue influence

14.48   A presumption of undue influence arises if the party alleging undue influence proves:

a.   that there was a confidential relationship between him and the other party to the contract, in which the other was the dominant party; and
b.   that the contract is manifestly disadvantageous to him.

Once the presumption of undue influence has arisen, the contract can be set aside at the instance of the weaker party, unless the presumption is rebutted by the dominant one.

14.49 *Confidential relationship* What is required here is a relationship in which one party places confidence in the other who thereby has the opportunity to exercise overt or subtle influence over him: undue influence cannot be presumed where the parties are in an ordinary, everyday business relationship.

14.50 In the case of some relationships, it is presumed that the relationship is a confidential one. Examples are the relationships of: parent and child[1]; solicitor or accountant and client[2]; and trustee and beneficiary[3], in each of which the first-named party is presumed to be in a position to influence the other. While the list of relationships which can be presumed to be confidential is not closed, it has been held that the relationships between husband and wife[4] and between employer and employee[5] are not presumed to be confidential.

1 *Bainbrigge v Browne* (1881) 18 Ch D 188.
2 *Wright v Carter* [1903] 1 Ch 27, CA.
3 *Beningfield v Baxter* (1886) 12 App Cas 167, PC.
4 *Howes v Bishop* [1909] 2 KB 390, CA; *Kingsnorth Trust Ltd v Bell* [1986] 1 All ER 423, [1986] 1 WLR 119, CA.
5 *Mathew v Bobbins* (1980) 124 Sol Jo 479, CA.

14.51 Where a confidential relationship cannot be presumed, undue influence may be presumed if it is positively proved that one party actually had a position of personal ascendancy[1] and influence over the other at the material time. For example, although the relationships of banker and customer and of creditor and debtor are not normally confidential[2], they will be held be so if special facts exist which justify such a finding. This is shown by *Lloyds Bank v Bundy*[3]. The defendant was an elderly farmer. A company which was run by his son got into difficulties and the defendant guaranteed its overdraft with the plaintiff bank, mortgaging his farmhouse, which was his home and only asset, to the bank as security for the guarantee. In relation to this transaction he had placed himself entirely in the hands of the assistant bank manager who not only explained the legal effects of the transaction *but also advised on more general matters germane to the wisdom of the transaction*. In the light of this special fact it is not surprising that the Court of Appeal held that there was a confidential relationship between the bank and the defendant and that not only could the mortgage not be enforced but it, and the guarantee, should be set aside.

Another case where a confidential relationship was proved is *O'Sullivan v Management Agency and Music Ltd*[4] where the relationship between a young, unknown composer and performer of pop music and his manager was held to be a confidential one for the purpose of the rules on undue influence.

1 Domination is not required; a relationship of trust will do: *Goldsworthy v Brickell* [1987] Ch 378, [1987] 1 All ER 853, CA.
2 *National Westminster Bank plc v Morgan* [1985] AC 686, [1985] 1 All ER 821, HL.
3 [1975] QB 326, [1974] 3 All ER 757, CA.
4 [1985] QB 428, [1985] 3 All ER 351, CA.

Manifestly disadvantageous contract
14.52 Even if a confidential relationship is presumed or proved, this is not in itself enough to give rise to the presumption that the dominant party actually

exercised undue influence over the other. That presumption can only be drawn if the contract between them is manifestly disadvantageous to the weaker party.

This was held by the House of Lords in *National Westminster Bank plc v Morgan*[1]. Mr and Mrs M got into difficulties with the repayments to a building society of the mortgage on their house. Consequently, Mr M sought a bank rescue operation, asking the bank to refinance the building society loan. The bank agreed and Mr M executed a legal charge in favour of the bank to secure a loan from it sufficient to redeem the mortgage. Because the house was in joint names, the bank required Mrs M's signature to the legal charge, and the bank manager called on Mrs M to obtain it. She told him that she did not wish the legal charge to extend to the husband's business liabilities. The bank manager assured her in good faith, but incorrectly, that the charge did not extend to those liabilities but was limited to securing the amount financed for the refinancing of the mortgage[2]. Without taking any independent legal advice, Mrs M signed the legal charge. Subsequently, Mr and Mrs M fell into arrears with their repayments to the bank, which obtained a possession order on the house. Mr M died soon afterwards without any business debts owing to the bank. Mrs M appealed against the possession order, contending that she had signed the legal charge because of undue influence from the bank via its manager.

The House of Lords rejected this. It held that the case was not one in which there was a presumption of undue influence, not only because the relationship between the parties was merely that of bank and customer, and not a confidential relationship, but also because the legal charge was not manifestly disadvantageous to Mr and Mrs M; in fact, it provided a desperately urgent rescue of their house from the building society.

In *Woodstead Finance Ltd v Petrou*[3], the Court of Appeal held that the fact that the interest rate on a loan was high did not make the contract of loan manifestly disadvantageous if it was the normal rate for the type of loan in question.

1   [1985] AC 686, [1985] 1 All ER 821, HL.
2   No claim based on misrepresentation was made.
3   [1986] BTLC 267, CA.

Rebutting the presumption
14.53   The presumption that undue influence has been exercised can only be rebutted by proof that the party presumed to have been influenced has been placed in such a position as will enable him to form an entirely free and unfettered judgment, independent altogether of any sort of control[1]. The onus of proving this is on the party presumed to have exercised undue influence. The best, but not the only[2], way of doing so is by proving that the other party received independent and informed advice, particularly legal advice, before making the contract[3].

1   *Archer v Hudson* (1844) 7 Beav 551 at 560.
2   *Inche Noriah v Shaik Allie Bin Omar* [1929] AC 127, PC.
3   See *Credit Lyonnais Bank Nederland NV v Burch* [1997] 1 All ER 144, CA. One member of the Court of Appeal went further, obiter, and held that taking independent legal advice is not

in itself enough to rebut the presumption. It must also be proved that the party concerned has acted on that legal advice, that the legal adviser was satisfied that the transaction was one that that party could sensibly enter into, and that the legal adviser advised the party concerned that he was under no obligation to enter into the transaction: ibid, at 155–156.

Where the other party to the contract was not the person who exercised undue influence, actual or presumed

14.54   It can happen that a person under the undue influence of a third party (or of a co-contracting party) makes a contract with another person who is not involved in that undue influence. An example would be where a person under the domination of a third party contracts with a bank to guarantee a loan by the bank to the third party. The unduly influenced person can have the contract rescinded if:

a.   the third party was an agent of the other party to the contract, which is normally unlikely; or
b.   when making the contract, the other party had actual notice (ie actually knew) or constructive notice (ie would have discovered if reasonable steps had been taken) that there had been undue influence[1].

Whether or not there was constructive notice depends on whether the other contracting party knew of facts (for example, the confidential relationship between the person concerned and the third party or that the contract was manifestly disadvantageous to the person concerned) which should have put him on enquiry. If he did, he will have constructive notice unless he took reasonable steps to satisfy himself that the agreement of the party in question had been properly obtained. For example, suppose that a wife agrees with a bank to act as surety for her husband's debt to the bank. The bank will have constructive notice of any undue influence (because the transaction is not of financial benefit to the wife and is of a type where there is a substantial risk that the husband has procured the wife's agreement by undue influence) unless it takes reasonable steps to bring home to the wife the risk she was running by standing as surety and to ensure that she takes independent advice before entering into the transaction[1].

The same rules apply where a dominant person in a relationship has by misrepresentation induced the weaker one to contract with another[1].

1   *Barclays Bank plc v O'Brien* [1993] 4 All ER 417, HL; *CIBC Mortgages plc v Pitt* [1994] 1 AC 200, [1993] 4 All ER 433, HL. Also see *Banco Exterior Internacional SA v Thomas* [1997] 1 All ER 46, CA; *Credit Lyonnais Bank Nederland NV v Burch* [1997] 1 All ER 144, CA.

Unconscionable bargains

14.55   Acting under equitable principles, a court will rescind a contract on the basis that unfair advantage has been taken by one party (or his employee or agent) of the other party who was poor, ignorant, weak-minded, illiterate, unfamiliar with the English language, or otherwise in need of *special* protection[1]. Unfair advantage will have been taken if the party at risk has not received independent legal advice[2].

The law on unconscionable bargains has the same basis as the other areas of equitable intervention which have just been mentioned: inequality of bargaining power. Although there are dicta in some cases to the effect that this 'common thread' permits the courts to intervene in contractual situations other than those involving pressure or influence, or the taking of an unfair advantage of a poor, ignorant or weak-minded party or one otherwise in need of special protection, fairly recent decisions have rejected the argument that inequality of bargaining power is in itself a ground for rescinding a contract[3].

1   *Evans v Llewellin* (1787) 1 Cox Eq Cas 333; *Barclays Bank plc v Schwartz* (1995) Times, 2 August, CA.
2   *Fry v Lane* (1888) 40 Ch D 312.
3   *Pao On v Lau Yiu Long* [1980] AC 614, [1979] 3 All ER 65, PC; *Alec Lobb (Garages) Ltd v Total Oil GB Ltd* [1985] 1 All ER 303, [1985] 1 WLR 173, CA.

Bars to rescission[1]

14.56   Where a contract is voidable for duress or undue influence, or because it is an unconscionable bargain, it is valid unless and until it is rescinded. Rescission will be barred in three cases.

1   These bars also apply to gifts made in similar circumstances.

Affirmation

14.57   Rescission is barred if, after the pressure or influence, or relationship giving rise to a presumption of undue influence, has ceased, the party influenced expressly or impliedly affirms the contract[1]. An unreasonable lapse of time after removal of the influence before seeking rescission of the contract is a particularly important evidential factor suggesting affirmation[2], and so is the fact that the party influenced performs obligations under the contract without protest[3]. A secret mental reservation not to affirm in such cases is irrelevant[3]. A person can be held to have affirmed even though he has not had independent advice after the removal of the influence[4] and did not know that he could have the contract rescinded, provided he was aware that he might have rights and deliberately refrained from finding out[5].

1   *Allcard v Skinner* (1887) 36 Ch D 145, CA; *Fry v Lane* (1888) 40 Ch D 312.
2   *Allcard v Skinner.*
3   *The Atlantic Baron* [1979] QB 705, [1978] 3 All ER 1170.
4   *Mitchell v Homfray* (1881) 8 QBD 587, CA.
5   *Allcard v Skinner* (1887) 36 Ch D 145 at 192.

Inability to restore

14.58   Since, as in the case of misrepresentation, the party seeking to rescind must restore what he obtained under the contract, an inability to do so is a bar to rescission[1]. However, precise restitution is not necessary; where precise restitution is not possible the same principles apply as in the case of rescission for misrepresentation[2].

If restitution is not possible under the above principles, the court may order that the party influenced be paid compensation by the other party to the value of what the party influenced surrendered under the contract, less anything which he received under it[3].

1   *O'Sullivan v Management Agency and Music Ltd* [1985] QB 428, [1985] 3 All ER 351, CA.
2   Para 14.16, above.
3   *Mahoney v Purnell* [1996] 3 All ER 61.

Purchasers without notice
14.59   The right to rescission is lost if a third party acquires an interest for value in the property transferred by the party influenced, without notice of the pressure or influence, or facts giving rise to a presumption of undue influence, in question[1]. Rescission is, of course, not barred if the third party does not provide consideration or has notice of the facts[2].

1   *Bainbrigge v Browne* (1881) 18 Ch D 188; *O'Sullivan v Management Agency and Music Ltd* [1985] QB 428, [1985] 3 All ER 351, CA.
2   *Lancashire Loans Ltd v Black* [1934] 1 KB 380, CA.

Unfair Terms in Consumer Contracts

14.60   We saw in para 10.57, above, that the Unfair Terms in Consumer Contracts Regulations 1994, which give domestic effect to an EC directive on unfair terms in consumer contracts, Directive 93/13, are concerned not only with exemption clauses but with unfair terms in general in *consumer* contracts relating to the sale or supply of goods or the supply of a service. In para 10.57, above, we contrasted the coverage of the Unfair Contract Terms Act 1977 with that of the directive in relation to exemption clauses.

The Regulations deal with two separate issues:

a.   unfair terms in consumer contracts; and
b.   interpretation of written terms in consumer contracts,

provided in each case that the term is one to which the Regulations apply.

Terms to which the Regulations apply
14.61   Regulation 3(1) provides that the Regulations apply to any term[1] in a contract, whether written or oral, between a *seller of goods or supplier of goods or services* and a *consumer* where the term has *not been individually negotiated*, with the exception of the following types of contract excluded by Schedule 1 of the Regulations:

a.   any contract relating to employment;
b.   any contract relating to succession rights;
c.   any contract relating to rights under family law;
d.   any contract relating to the incorporation and organisation of companies or partnerships; and

e. any term incorporated in order to comply with or which reflects –
    i   statutory or regulatory provisions of the United Kingdom; or
    ii the provisions or principles of international conventions to which the
        Member States or the Community are party.

1 Including a term which constitutes an 'arbitration agreement' (ie an agreement to submit
   to arbitration a present or future dispute, whether or not contractual): Arbitration Act 1996,
   s 89.

14.62 Regulation 2(1) provides the following important definition for the
purposes of the Regulations:

A '*seller*' is defined as meaning a person who sells goods and who, in making
a contract to which the Regulations apply, is acting for purposes relating to his
business.

A '*supplier*' is defined as meaning a person who supplies goods or services
and who, in making a contract to which the Regulations apply, is acting for
purposes relating to his *business*.

A '*person*' in both definitions includes a company or other corporate body.

A '*consumer*' is defined as meaning a natural person who, in making a contract
to which the Regulations apply, is acting for purposes which are *outside* his
business. As this definition indicates, a 'legal person' (ie a company or other
corporate body) cannot be a 'consumer' for the purposes of the Regulations[1].

Lastly, a 'business' includes a trade or profession and the activities of any
government department or local or public authority.

As reg 3(1) indicates, the Regulations only apply to a term which has not
been individually negotiated. By reg 3(3), a term is always to be regarded as
not having been individually negotiated where it has been *drafted in advance
and the consumer has not been able to influence the substance of the term*. Regulation
3(4) adds that, notwithstanding that a specific term or certain aspects of it in
a contract has been individually negotiated, the Regulations apply to the rest
of a contract if an overall assessment of the contract indicates that it is a pre-
formulated standard contract.

If a *seller or supplier* claims that a term was *individually negotiated*, he has the
burden of proving this.[2]

1 There is one exception. Where the term constitutes an 'arbitration agreement', the Regulations
   apply where the 'consumer' is a legal person as they apply where the consumer is a natural
   person: Arbitration Act 1996, s 90.
2 Reg 3(5).

Unfair terms

14.63 The Regulations subject any term to which they apply to a test of
fairness, save for an exception set out in reg 3(2). This provides that, *in so far as
it is in plain, intelligible language*, no assessment shall be made of the fairness of
any term which:

a. defines the main subject matter of the contract, or
b. concerns the adequacy of the price or remuneration, as against the goods
    or services sold or supplied.

The meaning of these exceptions, especially the first is obscure. If they are given a liberal interpretation by the courts, the efficacy of the Regulations as a consumer-protection measure will be limited.

14.64   *The test of fairness*   Regulation 4(1) sets out the test of fairness[1]. It provides that, subject to reg 4(2) and (3), 'unfair term' means any term which contrary to the requirement of good faith causes a significant imbalance in the parties' rights and obligations under the contract to the detriment of the consumer.

From these two elements of unfairness can be derived:

a.   The term must cause significant imbalance to the parties' rights and obligations to the detriment of the consumer; and

b.   this 'significant imbalance' must be 'contrary to the requirement of good faith'.

1   There is a special test of unfairness in respect of terms which constitute an 'arbitration agreement'. A term which constitutes an agreement to refer a claim to arbitration is unfair for the purposes of the 1994 Regulations so far as it relates to a claim for a pecuniary remedy which does not exceed £3,000: Arbitration Act 1996, s 91.

14.65   Regulation 4(3) provides that, in determining whether a term satisfies the requirement of good faith, regard must be had in particular to the matters specified in Schedule 2, viz:

a.   the strength of the bargaining positions of the parties;

b.   whether the consumer had an inducement to agree to the term;

c.   whether the goods or services were sold or supplied to the special order of the consumer, and

d.   the extent to which the seller or supplier has dealt fairly and equitably with the consumer.

The first three of these factors are similar to those in Sch 2 of the Unfair Contract Terms Act 1977[1].

As with the test of reasonableness under Unfair Contract Terms Act, the test of fairness is assessed as at the time of the conclusion of the contract. Regulation 4(2) provides as assessment of the unfair nature of a term must take into account the nature of the goods or services for which the contract was concluded and referring, as at the time of the conclusion of the contract, to all circumstances attending the conclusion of the contract and to all the other terms of the contract or of another contract on which it is dependent.

1   Para 10.53, above.

14.66   The application of the test of fairness is greatly assisted by Sch 3 which contains an indicative, non-exhaustive and lengthy list of terms which may be regarded as unfair. These are terms which have the object or effect of, for example:

a.   excluding or limiting the legal liability of a seller or supplier in the event of the death of a consumer or personal injury to the latter resulting from an act or omission of that seller or supplier;

b.   inappropriately excluding or limiting the legal rights of the consumer vis-à-vis the seller or supplier or another party in the event of total or partial non-performance or inadequate performance by the seller or supplier of any of the contractual obligations, including the option of offsetting a debt owed to the seller or supplier against any claim which the consumer may have against him;

c.   making an agreement binding on the consumer whereas provision of services by the seller or supplier is subject to a condition whose realisation depends on his own will alone;

d.   permitting the seller or supplier to retain sums paid by the consumer where the latter decides not to conclude or perform the contract, without providing for the consumer to receive compensation of an equivalent amount from the seller or supplier where the latter is the party cancelling the contract;

e.   requiring any consumer who fails to fulfil his obligation to pay a disproportionately high sum in compensation;

f.   irrevocably binding the consumer to terms with which he had no real opportunity of becoming acquainted before the conclusion of the contract;

g.   enabling the seller or supplier to alter unilaterally without a valid reason any characteristics of the product or service to be provided;

h.   giving the seller or supplier the right to determine whether the goods or services supplied are in conformity with the contract, or giving him the exclusive right to interpret any term of the contract;

i.   obliging the consumer to fulfil all his obligations where the seller or supplier does not perform his;

j.   giving the seller or supplier the possibility of transferring his rights and obligations under the contract, where this may serve to reduce the guarantees for the consumer, without the latter's agreement.

Unlike the provisions relating to the requirement of reasonableness in the Unfair Contract Terms Act 1977[1], no provision is made concerning the burden of proof. Thus, it is for the consumer to prove that the test of fairness is not satisfied.

1   Para 10.48, above.

14.67   *Consequence of inclusion of unfair term*   An unfair term under the provisions of the Regulations is not binding on the consumer.[1] However, the rest of the contract continues to bind the parties if it is capable of continuing in existence without the unfair term.[2]

1   Reg 5(1).
2   Reg 5(2).

Interpretation of written terms in consumer contracts

14.68   By reg 6, a seller or supplier must ensure that any written contractual term to which the Regulations apply is expressed in plain, intelligible language. The only effect of a breach of this requirement is that, where there is doubt about the meaning of a written term, the interpretation most favourable to the consumer prevails, a rule akin to *contra proferentem* rule[1]; the term is not rendered ineffective.

1 Para 8.47, above.

Chapter 15

Void and Illegal Contracts

15.1   A contract which would otherwise be valid may be invalid on the ground that it is void on grounds of public policy or illegal. For convenience, such contracts will be dealt with in the following order:

Wagering and gaming contracts.
Other contracts void on grounds of public policy.
Illegal contracts.

Wagering and Gaming Contracts

15.2   Under the Gaming Act 1845, all wagering and gaming contracts are void[1] and, therefore, unenforceable by either party. A fresh promise, supported by fresh consideration, to pay an unsuccessful bet is also unenforceable[2]. No more need be said about contracts of this type, but the other two types of contract mentioned in the previous paragraph require a more detailed discussion.

1   Gaming Act 1845, s 18.
2   Ibid; *Hill v William Hill (Park Lane) Ltd* [1949] AC 530, [1949] 2 All ER 452, HL.

Other Contracts Void on Grounds of Public Policy

15.3   Contracts which are void on grounds of public policy can be divided into three types:

Contracts prejudicial to the married state[1].
Contracts ousting the jurisdiction of the courts.
Contracts in restraint of trade.

The last two types call for further explanation.

1   *Hermann v Charlesworth* [1905] 2 KB 123, CA.

Contracts purporting to oust the jurisdiction of the courts

15.4 For the purposes of this book, it is only appropriate to refer here to agreements relating to arbitration.

An agreement to refer a dispute to arbitration[1] for settlement as a condition precedent to an action in the courts is perfectly valid. This was held in *Scott v Avery*[2]. An insurance policy provided that if there was a dispute relating to the policy the assured could not bring any action in the courts in relation to it until the dispute had been referred to arbitrators and the arbitrators had reached a decision. The House of Lords held that the clause was valid since it did not purport to oust the jurisdiction of the courts but simply laid down a condition which had to be satisfied before the courts might exercise jurisdiction. On the other hand, an agreement, whether contained in an arbitration agreement or made thereafter, which excludes the courts' power to give a final decision on a question of law, is void on grounds of public policy[3]. A clause which simply makes the arbitrator the final arbiter on questions of fact is always valid[4].

1 Also see paras 3.39–3.48.
2 (1856) 5 HL Cas 811, HL.
3 Para 3.48, above.
4 *Lee v Showman's Guild of Great Britain* [1952] 2 QB 329 at 342, [1952] 1 All ER 1175 at 1181.

Contracts in restraint of trade

15.5 Contracts in restraint of trade may be void at common law or, in some cases (which are outside the scope of this book), by statute.

Contracts in restraint of trade which are void at common law can be divided into four principal categories:

a. agreements restricting the subsequent occupation of an employee;
b. agreements restricting the subsequent occupation of a partner;
c. agreements between the vendor and purchaser of the goodwill of a business restricting competition by the vendor; and
d. exclusive dealing agreements.

This list is not exhaustive. Other types of agreement in restraint of trade are, or may be, void unless they satisfy the tests mentioned in the next paragraph[1].

1 *Esso Petroleum Co Ltd v Harper's Garage (Stourport) Ltd* [1968] AC 269, [1967] 1 All ER 699, HL.

15.6 The general tests of validity applicable to contracts falling within the restraint of trade doctrine are as follows:

A contract in restraint of trade is prima facie void. But–

such a contract will be valid and enforceable if –

first, the person seeking to enforce it shows that the restraint is reasonable between the parties to the contract; *and*, second, the other party does not show that the restraint is unreasonable in the public interest[1].

The tests of reasonableness must be applied as at the date the contract was made and in the light of the then existing facts and of what might possibly happen in the future. Anything else which has occurred subsequently must be ignored[2]. The tests must also be applied by reference to what the terms of the restraint entitle or require the parties to do, and not by reference to what they have actually done or intend to do[3]. The application of the tests can be demonstrated by reference to the four categories of agreement mentioned above.

A restraint of trade which is valid is most commonly enforced by an injunction restraining the defendant from breaking it.

1   These tests have their foundation in *Nordenfelt v Maxim Nordenfelt Guns and Ammunition Co* [1894] AC 535, HL and *Herbert Morris Ltd v Saxelby* [1916] 1 AC 688, HL.
2   *Putsman v Taylor* [1927] 1 KB 637 at 643; *Gledhow Autoparts Ltd v Delaney* [1965] 3 All ER 288 at 295.
3   *Watson v Prager* [1991] 3 All ER 487, [1991] 1 WLR 726.

Agreements restricting the subsequent occupation of an employee
15.7   A contract between employer and employee, normally the contract of employment, may contain a covenant (promise) by the employee that he will not be employed in, or conduct, a business competing with his employer's after leaving his employment. Although this is the common form of a covenant restricting subsequent occupation, such a covenant need not be framed in these terms. A covenant is also in restraint of trade where it contains a restriction which provides that after leaving his employer's employment an employee shall be paid a pension or arrears of commission provided that he does not take employment with a competitor of the employer[1]. A covenant restricting the subsequent employment of an employee will normally be limited in duration and area. Being in restraint of trade, it is prima facie void and will only be valid and enforceable if the tests of reasonableness referred to above are satisfied.

1   *Wyatt v Kreglinger and Fernau* [1933] 1 KB 793, CA (facts set out in para 15.9); *Sadler v Imperial Life Assurance Co of Canada Ltd* [1988] IRLR 388.

15.8   *Reasonable between the parties*   Two things must be proved to satisfy this test:

a.   The restriction must protect a legally recognised interest of the employer. Only two types of interest are so recognised:

i.   *Protection of employer's trade secrets or other confidential information equivalent to a trade secret concerning employer's affairs*   An example of a case involving the protection of trade secrets is provided by *Forster & Sons Ltd v Suggett*[1]. The defendant was the plaintiff company's works manager. He was instructed in secret methods relating to the production of glass which the plaintiff company produced. He agreed that, during the five years after the end of his employment with the plaintiff company, he would not carry on in the United Kingdom, or be interested in, glass bottle manufacturing or any other business connected with glass making as carried on by the company. It was held that this restriction was reasonable to protect the plaintiff company's trade secrets and an injunction was ordered to restrain breach of it. Examples of information equivalent to a trade secret concerning the employer's affairs are detailed information on costing, customer accounts, profit margins and development plans.[2]

ii. *Protection of employer's business connections* An employer is entitled to prevent an employee misusing influence which he has obtained over the employer's customers and thereby enticing them away[3]. Thus, in *Fitch v Dewes*[4], where the contract provided that a Tamworth solicitor's managing clerk (who was himself a solicitor) should never practise within seven miles of Tamworth Town Hall, the House of Lords held that the restriction was valid because it constituted a reasonable protection of the employer's business connections against an employee who could gain influence over his clients.

It is not enough merely to show that the restriction purports to protect trade secrets or connections: it must also be shown that they require protection against the particular employee. Thus, the restriction will be invalid if the employee did not know enough about a trade secret to be able to use it or was insufficiently acquainted with customers to be able to influence them. This is shown, for example, by *SW Strange Ltd v Mann*[5], where a restriction imposed on a bookmaker's manager was held to be void because the business was mostly conducted by telephone and the manager had no chance to get to know his employer's customers or to influence them.

No other interests can be protected validly by the present type of restriction[6]; consequently, a restriction whose object is simply to protect the employer against competition is invalid[6].

b. Reasonableness. To be reasonable between the parties, the restriction must be no wider than is reasonably necessary to protect the employer's trade secrets (or other equivalent information) or business connections. Reasonableness is a matter of degree: the terms of the restriction must be measured against the degree of knowledge or influence which the employee has gained in his employment. A fortiori, a restriction will be void if it relates to a wider range of occupations than is reasonably necessary to protect the relevant protectable interest. Two other factors which are particularly important are the duration and area of the restriction.

i. *Duration* In *M and S Drapers v Reynolds*[7], a collector-salesman of a credit drapery firm covenanted not to canvass his employers' customers for a period of five years after leaving their employment. The restriction was held to be void: in view of the lowly position of a collector-salesman it was for a longer period than was reasonably necessary to protect the employers' business connections. On the other hand, the restriction in *Fitch v Dewes* was upheld, even though it was to last for life, because of the degree of influence which the solicitor's managing clerk would gain over his employer's clients.

ii. *Area* In *Mason v Provident Clothing and Supply Co Ltd*[8], a canvasser in the plaintiff company's Islington branch district covenanted not to work in any similar business for three years within 25 miles of London. The restriction was held to be void because it extended further than was reasonably necessary to protect the plaintiff company's business connections. On the other hand, a covenant by a sales representative employed by a small company that, for two years after leaving his employment, he would not canvass (in the same goods) people *who had been customers of his employer during his employment*, was upheld in *G W Plowman & Son Ltd v Ash*[9], even though it was unlimited in area.

1   (1918) 35 TLR 87.
2   *Poly Lina Ltd v Finch* [1995] FSR 751.
3   *Herbert Morris Ltd v Saxelby* [1916] 1 AC 688 at 709.
4   [1921] 2 AC 158, HL.
5   [1965] 1 All ER 1069, [1965] 1 WLR 629.
6   *Herbert Morris Ltd v Saxelby* [1916] 1 AC 688 at 710.
7   [1956] 3 All ER 814, [1957] 1 WLR 9, CA.
8   [1913] AC 724, HL.
9   [1964] 2 All ER 10, [1964] 1 WLR 568, CA.

15.9 *Reasonable in the public interest* The operation of this test is demonstrated by *Wyatt v Kreglinger and Fernau*[1]. The employers of a wool broker promised to pay him a pension on his retirement provided he did not re-enter the wool trade and did nothing to their detriment (fair competition excepted). The broker subsequently sued for arrears of pension but the Court of Appeal held that he could not succeed since the contract was void for two reasons:

a.   the restriction was unreasonable as between the parties;
b.   the contract was unreasonable in the public interest because the permanent restriction on the broker working anywhere in the wool trade deprived the community of services from which it might benefit.

Provided the restriction is reasonable between the parties, employer-employee restrictions will rarely be invalidated on the ground that they are unreasonable in the public interest. However, where the employee has a special skill of particular value to the community, the restriction may well be found unreasonable in the public interest even though it affords reasonable protection for the employer's trade secrets or business connections[2].

1   [1933] 1 KB 793, CA.
2   *Bull v Pitney-Bowes Ltd* [1966] 3 All ER 384, [1967] 1 WLR 273.

15.10 It may be noted in passing that, even in the absence of an express restraint, where an employee uses or discloses an employer's trade secrets or confidential information concerning his employer's affairs, or where an employee solicits an employer's customers, the employer can obtain an injunction to restrain this[1]. An employer can also obtain an injunction, even in the absence of an express restraint, to restrain an ex-employee from using or disclosing a trade secret of the employer or confidential information relating to the employer's business equivalent to a trade secret[2].

The basis on which such conduct is restrained is that there has been a breach of an implied term of the contract of employment whereby the employee is obliged not to engage in such conduct[3].

1   *Wessex Dairies Ltd v Smith* [1935] 2 KB 80, CA; *Fowler v Faccenda Chicken Ltd* [1987] Ch 117, [1986] 1 All ER 617, CA.
2   *Printers and Finishers Ltd v Holloway* [1964] 3 All ER 731, [1965] 1 WLR 1; *Fowler v Faccenda Chicken Ltd* [1987] Ch 117, [1986] 1 All ER 617, CA; *Roger Bullivant Ltd v Ellis* [1987] ICR 464, [1987] IRLR 491, CA; *Johnson & Bloy (Holdings) Ltd v Wolstenholme Rink plc* [1987] IRLR 499, CA.
3   Para 8.40, above.

Agreements restricting the subsequent occupation of a partner

15.11   Partnership agreements commonly provide that a partner who ceases to be a partner shall not, for a specified period, act for or deal with any client of the firm in the professional capacity in which he was a partner. Such a restraint is valid and enforceable only if it is reasonable as between the parties to protect some legitimate interest of the firm and is not unreasonable in the public interest[1]. What is a legitimate interest of the firm depends largely on the nature of its business and on the ex-partner's position in the firm, but an example of such an interest is a firm's connections with its clients. This was held in *Bridge v Deacons (a firm)*[2], which was concerned with a covenant in a Hong Kong solicitors' partnership agreement whereby a partner who ceased to be a partner was restricted for five years thereafter from acting as a solicitor in Hong Kong for anyone who had been a client of the firm when he ceased to be a partner or during the preceding three years. The Privy Council held that the covenant, which applied to all the partners, was reasonable as between the parties, since it went no further in extent or time than was reasonable to protect the firm's connections with its clients, and was not unreasonable in the public interest; the covenant was therefore held enforceable against an ex-partner.

1   *Bridge v Deacons (a firm)* [1984] AC 705, [1984] 2 All ER 19, PC; *Edwards v Worboys* [1984] AC 724n, CA.
2   [1984] AC 705, [1984] 2 All ER 19, PC.

Agreements between the vendor and purchaser of the goodwill of a business restricting competition by the vendor

15.12   The goodwill of a business means its commercial reputation, its customer connections and its potential customers through referrals by existing customers[1]. An agreement of the present type is prima facie void for restraint of trade but will be valid and enforceable if it is reasonable between the parties and not unreasonable in the public interest. The following can be said concerning the requirement of reasonableness between the parties:

a.   *The restriction must protect the goodwill of the business sold*   An agreement whereby one business surrenders to another its liberty to trade in a particular field is void since mere competition is not a protectable interest[2]. The restriction must relate to an actual business which has been sold. Thus, even though it is contained in what purports to be a contract for the sale of a business, a restriction will be void if there is no actual business to protect. This is shown by *Vancouver Malt and Sake Brewing Co Ltd v Vancouver Breweries Ltd*[3]. The appellants held a licence to brew beer and other liquors but the only trade actually carried on by them under the licence was brewing sake. They purported to sell the goodwill of their licence, so far as it related to brewing beer, to the respondents and covenanted not to brew beer for 15 years thereafter. The Privy Council held that the covenant was void because, if there was a sale, it was merely a sale of the appellants' liberty to brew beer since there was no goodwill of a beer brewing business to be transferred and the covenant was simply a bare restriction on competition.

Other aspects of the rule that the covenant must protect the goodwill of the business actually sold are demonstrated by *British Reinforced Concrete Engineering Co Ltd v Schelff*[4]. The defendant, who ran a small business for the *sale* of 'Loop' road reinforcements, sold it to the plaintiff company, a large company which manufactured and sold 'BRC' road reinforcements. In the contract of sale the defendant covenanted that, for three years after the end of the First World War, he would not 'either alone or jointly or in partnership with any other person or persons whomsoever and either directly or indirectly carry on or manage or be concerned or interested in or act as servant of any person concerned or interested in the business of the manufacture or sale of road reinforcements in any part of the United Kingdom'. It was held that this covenant was too wide because it extended to the manufacture of road reinforcements as well as their sale, and thus it sought to protect more than the actual business sold (the *sale* of road reinforcements) in that it sought to protect the purchaser's existing business (the sale and *manufacture* of road reinforcements).

b.   *The restriction must go no further than is reasonably necessary to protect the business sold*   As was pointed out in the *Schelff* case, the reasonableness of the restriction must be judged by reference to the extent and circumstances of the business sold, and not by the extent and range of any business already run by the purchaser. Reasonableness is judged from the standpoint of both parties. For example, in the *Schelff* case it was held that the 'servant clause' was unreasonable because it would preclude the defendant from becoming the servant of a trust company which, as part of its investments, held shares in a company manufacturing or selling road reinforcements. The amount of the consideration for the agreement is a relevant factor in assessing the reasonableness of the restriction[5]. In addition, the duration and area of the restriction are particularly important factors to be taken into account in assessing its reasonableness. The approach of the courts is more liberal here than in the case of employer-employee restrictions because buyers and sellers of businesses are more obviously equal bargaining partners. A good example of this liberality is provided by *Nordenfelt v Maxim Nordenfelt Guns and Ammunition Co Ltd*[6]. The defendant, who had obtained patents for improving quick-firing guns, carried on, among other things, business as a maker of such guns and of ammunition. He sold the goodwill and assets of the business to a company, entering into a covenant which restricted his future activities. The company later merged with another to become the plaintiff company and the defendant's earlier covenant was substantially repeated with it. This covenant provided that for 25 years the defendant would not engage, except on behalf of the company, directly or indirectly in the trade or business of a manufacturer of guns, gun mountings or carriages, gunpowder, explosives or ammunition, or in any business competing or liable to compete in any way with that for the time being carried on by the plaintiff company. The first part of the covenant, relating to engaging in a business manufacturing guns etc, was held by the House of Lords to provide reasonable protection for the business acquired by the company, even though the restriction was world-wide and was to last for 25 years, and was therefore valid. It was recognised, however, that the second part of the covenant, relating to engaging in any business competing with that carried on by the company, was void because it went further than was reasonable to protect the business acquired by the company. Similarly, the restriction in the *Schelff* case, even as it related to the management, etc of a business selling reinforcements, was held void because it applied to the whole of the United Kingdom, which was regarded as a wider area than was necessary to protect the actual business sold.

1   *Allied Dunbar (Frank Weisinger) Ltd v Weisinger* [1988] IRLR 60.
2   *Vancouver Malt and Sake Brewing Co Ltd v Vancouver Breweries Ltd* [1934] AC 181, PC.
3   [1934] AC 181, PC.
4   [1921] 2 Ch 563.
5   *Nordenfelt v Maxim Nordenfelt Guns and Ammunition Co Ltd* [1894] AC 535 at 565.
6   [1894] AC 535, HL.

Exclusive dealing agreements
15.13   One type of agreement under this heading is a 'solus agreement' whereby A agrees to buy all his requirements of a particular commodity from C. In *Esso Petroleum Co Ltd v Harper's Garage (Stourport) Ltd*[1], the House of Lords held that such exclusive purchasing agreements were subject to the restraint of trade doctrine and were prima facie void. However, as their Lordships recognised, there are exceptions. The House of Lords held that where a person acquires land by conveyance or lease, and an exclusive purchasing agreement relating to the land is inserted into the conveyance or lease, it is not subject to the restraint of trade doctrine. Thus, if an oil company sells or leases a filling station to X, inserting a covenant into the conveyance or lease that X shall only buy petrol supplies from the company, the covenant falls outside the restraint of trade doctrine and is valid. Lord Reid said that the reason for this was that the restraint of trade doctrine only applied where a person gave up a freedom which he would otherwise have enjoyed, and a person buying or leasing land had no previous right to trade there and thus gave up no previously held freedom. The courts will not allow this exception to be used as a device to evade the restraint of trade doctrine, as is shown by the decision of the Court of Appeal in *Alec Lobb (Garages) Ltd v Total Oil GB Ltd*[2]. In that case, L Ltd which owned the freehold of land on which it carried on a garage and filling station business, leased the land to T Ltd to raise capital; the lease was followed immediately by a lease-back by T Ltd to the proprietors of L Ltd at an annual rent. If the lease-back had been to L Ltd it would clearly have been subject to the restraint of trade doctrine, because L Ltd would have given up its previously enjoyed freedom to buy fuel for the filling station as it pleased. The Court of Appeal held that it could pierce the corporate veil, recognise a continued identity of occupation and hold that T Ltd could be in no better position with regard to the restraint of trade doctrine by granting the lease-back to the proprietors than if it had granted the lease-back to the company. Therefore, the exclusive purchasing agreement was subject to the restraint of trade doctrine.

1   [1968] AC 269, [1967] 1 All ER 699, HL.
2   [1985] 1 All ER 303, [1985] 1 WLR 173, CA.

15.14   Where the restraint of trade doctrine applies to an exclusive purchasing agreement, the restraint is, of course, valid only if it is reasonable between the parties and is not shown to be unreasonable in the public interest. It appears that, as opposed to the heads of agreements in restraint of trade already mentioned, an exclusive purchasing agreement can be valid even though its object is simply to protect a party against competition. This also appears true of the other types of exclusive dealing agreements. The operation of the restraint of trade doctrine to exclusive purchasing agreements is demonstrated by *Esso Petroleum Co Ltd v Harper's Garage (Stourport) Ltd*. Harper's agreed to buy all their petrol requirements from Esso. They also agreed to operate their two garages in accordance with the 'Esso co-operation plan', under which they had to keep the garages open at all reasonable hours and not sell them without getting the purchaser to enter into a similar agreement with Esso. In return, Harper's got a 1d rebate per gallon off the list price of petrol. In the case of one garage, the agreement was to last for four years five months. The agreement relating to the other garage was to last for 21 years, being contained in a mortgage of the garage to Esso for 21 years which was not redeemable before that time had expired. The House of Lords held that both agreements were prima facie void since neither fell within an exception to the restraint of trade doctrine, even though one was contained in a mortgage. The question was therefore whether the restrictions in the two agreements were reasonable:

a.   The House held that the agreement for four years five months was reasonable between the parties. It was reasonably required to protect Esso's legitimate interest in securing continuity of their sales outlets, their system of distribution and the stability of their sales. In return, Harper's not only got a rebate on the price of the petrol which they purchased but could also rely on the financial backing of a big company if they were short of funds. The agreement was also not unreasonable in the public interest.
b.   The House held that the agreement for 21 years was unreasonable between the parties, because its duration was longer than necessary to protect Esso's interests, and therefore void.

The public interest in this context refers to the interest of the public that a person should not be subjected to unreasonable restrictions on his freedom to work or trade, and not to any ultimate economic or social or other advantage to the public at large[1].

1   *Texaco Ltd v Mulberry Filling Station Ltd* [1972] 1 All ER 513, [1972] 1 WLR 814.

15.15   Too much should not be read into the *Esso Petroleum* decision because, as the Court of Appeal held in *Alec Lobb (Garages) Ltd v Total Oil GB Ltd*[1], every case turns on its facts; the court also pointed out that the adequacy of the consideration received by the party restrained is relevant to the question of the reasonableness of the restraint. In the *Lobb* case, L Ltd, which was insolvent and seriously under-capitalised, leased its garage and filling station for 51 years in consideration of a premium of £35,000 to T Ltd. T Ltd then leased back the premises to Mr and Mrs L (the proprietors of L Ltd) for a period of 21 years, with a right of either party to terminate the lease-back after seven or fourteen years, at an initial rent of £2,250 pa with upwards only rent reviews after eight and fifteen years. The lease-back also contained a tie provision requiring Mr and Mrs L to take all supplies of petrol from T Ltd exclusively.

The Court of Appeal upheld the tie provision as being in reasonable restraint of trade. It took into account, in particular:

a.   that the consideration (£35,000) for the lease, and thus the consideration by T Ltd for the tie (since the lease-back was part of the same transaction as the lease), was the market value of the lease, whereas the initial rent under the lease-back was nominal;
b.   that under the lease-back Mr and Mrs L were not locked into trading with T Ltd's products from the property for 21 years since they were free to exercise the break-clause in the lease-back after seven or fourteen years; and
c.   that L Ltd was insolvent and the sum of £35,000 was designed to enable it to pay its debts and continue in business, and to save Mr and Mrs L from personal bankruptcy, and that the rescue operation had been undertaken reluctantly by T Ltd to preserve the site as an outlet for its petrol.

In the light of these factors, the Court of Appeal held that the tie did not go further than reasonably necessary to provide adequate protection for T Ltd and was reasonable in the interests of Mr and Mrs L because of the benefits which they derived in return. Moreover, the court held, the tie was not unreasonable in the public interest.

1   [1985] 1 All ER 303, [1985] 1 WLR 173, CA.

15.16   Another type of agreement which may be said to fall under the heading of exclusive dealing agreements is an agreement whereby A agrees to provide his services solely to B for the duration of the agreement. Normally, such a contract does not fall within the restraint of trade doctrine, even though it necessarily involves the restriction of one party's right to exercise any lawful activity he chooses, but if the contractual restriction appears to be unnecessary or to be reasonably capable of enforcement in an oppressive manner it is prima facie void and its validity depends upon the twin tests of reasonableness[1]. An example of an exclusive services contract which fell within the restraint of trade doctrine for the reasons just given is *Schroeder Music Publishing Co Ltd v Macaulay*[2]. M, a young and unknown song writer, entered into a contract with S Ltd, who were music publishers, whereby they engaged his exclusive services for five years. Under the contract M assigned to S Ltd full copyright for the whole world in anything composed by him during the period of the contract or before it. If M's royalties exceeded £5,000 during the five-year period the contract was to be automatically extended for another five years. S Ltd reserved the right to terminate the contract with one month's notice, but M had no such rights. S Ltd were not obliged by the contract to publish anything composed by M. The House of Lords held that the contract fell within the restraint of trade doctrine and was void, the main reason for its decision being that the agreement was unreasonable between the parties because, while S Ltd were given the sole right to publish M's songs, they were not bound to do so and could simply leave them lying in a drawer.

1   *Schroeder Music Publishing Co Ltd v Macaulay* [1974] 3 All ER 616, [1974] 1 WLR 1308, HL; *Clifford Davis Management Ltd v WEA Records Ltd* [1975] 1 All ER 237, [1975] 1 WLR 61, CA; *O'Sullivan v Management Agency & Music Ltd* [1985] QB 428, [1985] 3 All ER 351, CA; *Watson v Prager* [1991] 3 All ER 487, [1991] 1 WLR 726.
2   [1974] 3 All ER 616, [1974] 1 WLR 1308, HL.

15.17   One type of exclusive dealing agreement is exempt from the restraint of trade doctrine because it has gained general commercial acceptance[1]. This is a 'sole agency agreement', ie an agreement giving a person the sole right to supply a manufacturer's goods.

1   *Esso Petroleum Co Ltd v Harper's Garage (Stourport) Ltd* [1968] AC 269 at 336, [1967] 1 All ER 699 at 731.

15.18   Before leaving exclusive dealing agreements it should be noted that, if they affect trade between two or more members of the European Community, exclusive dealing agreements may also be void under art 85 of the Treaty establishing the European Economic Community, unless exempted by the EC Commission.

Effects of a contract void on grounds of public policy

15.19   Provided that the part of the contract which is void on grounds of public policy can be severed from the rest of the contract, the latter, as opposed to the void part, is enforceable. However, if the void part cannot be severed the whole contract is void and unenforceable. Severance can operate in two ways.

15.20   *Severance of the whole of an objectionable promise*   If this can be done the rest of the contract is valid and enforceable. Severance of a whole promise is not possible if it is the whole or the main part (ie substantially the whole) of the consideration furnished by the party who wishes to enforce the contract. Thus, in *Wyatt v Kreglinger and Fernau*, which we discussed in para 15.9, above, it was held that the ex-employee could not enforce the promise to pay him a pension since he had given no valid consideration for it, his only promise – not to compete – being void under the restraint of trade doctrine. This can be contrasted with *Marshall v N M Financial Management Ltd*[1], where the plaintiff's contract of employment stated that commission should be payable to him after the termination of his employment, provided that he did not compete with his former employer. This proviso was void under the restraint of trade doctrine. It was held, however, that the plaintiff could enforce his right to commission because in substance the consideration given by him for the former employer's promise to pay it was his provision of services during the period of his employment, and not his promise not to compete.

1   [1995] 4 All ER 785, [1995] 1 WLR 1461.

15.21   *Severance of the objectionable part of a promise*   This is particularly relevant in restraint of trade contracts. If severance of part of a promise is possible, the rest of the contract, including the unsevered part of the promise, can be enforced. Severance of this type is only possible if two tests are satisfied:

a.   The 'blue pencil' test. This test is only satisfied if the objectionable words can be struck out of the promise *as it stands*. This was possible in relation to the offending part of the promise in the *Nordenfelt* case, which has been discussed in para 15.12, above. Another example is provided by *Goldsoll v Goldman*[1]. The defendant sold his imitation jewellery business in Old Bond Street to the plaintiff, another jeweller. The defendant covenanted that for two years he would not 'either solely or jointly with or as agent or employee for any person or company . . . carry on or be interested in the business of a vendor of or dealer in real or imitation jewellery in the county of London, England, Scotland, Ireland, Wales, or any part of the United Kingdom and the Isle of Man or in France, the United States of America, Russia or Spain, or within 25 miles of Potsdamerstrasse, Berlin, or St Stephan's Kirche, Vienna'. The defendant joined a rival jeweller's in New Bond Street within two years and the plaintiff sought an injunction to restrain breach of the covenant. The Court of Appeal held that the covenant was unreasonably wide in respect of subject matter (for the defendant had not dealt in real jewellery) and also in respect of area (because the defendant had not traded abroad), but that the references to foreign places and real jewellery could be severed because it was possible to delete them from the covenant *as it stood*. After severance, the covenant merely prohibited dealing in imitation jewellery in the United Kingdom and the Isle of Man, and an injunction was granted to prevent such dealing.

If the unreasonable part of the promise cannot be deleted from the promise as it stands, severance of it is not possible. The court cannot rewrite the promise by adding or altering even one word so as to make it reasonable. Thus, in *Mason v Provident Clothing and Supply Co Ltd*[2], which has already been referred to[3], where the contract in question contained a promise that the employee would not work within 25 miles of London after leaving his employment, the House of Lords held that the promise was too wide in area, and therefore unreasonable, and refused to re-draft the clause so as to make it reasonable and enforceable. The whole promise was therefore held void and unenforceable.

b.   Severance of the objectionable part must not alter the nature (as opposed to the extent) of the original contract. This means that severance of part of a promise is impossible unless it can be construed as being divisible into a number of separate and independent parts. This rule is sensible – otherwise the mechanical deletion of the objectionable part of the promise could radically change the whole contract – but difficult to apply.

The application of this test can be illustrated by two cases. In *Attwood v Lamont*[4], the plaintiffs owned a general outfitter's business in Kidderminster. The business was divided into a number of departments. The defendant was the head of the tailoring department but had no concern with any other department. In his contract of employment the defendant had undertaken that, after the termination of his employment, he would not 'be concerned in any of the following trades or businesses, that is to say, the trade or business of a tailor, dressmaker, general draper, milliner, hatter, haberdasher, gentlemen's, ladies' or children's outfitter' within ten miles of Kidderminster. Later the plaintiffs sought to enforce this covenant. They admitted that it was too wide in terms of the trades covered but argued that the references to aspects of the business other than tailoring could be severed, leaving the tailoring restraint enforceable. The Court of Appeal rejected this course because such severance would have altered the whole nature of the covenant: the covenant as it stood was one indivisible covenant (or promise) for the protection of the whole of the plaintiffs' business, not several covenants for the protection of the plaintiffs' several departments, and to alter it would be to alter its nature.

This case can be contrasted with *Putsman v Taylor*[5]. The plaintiff carried on business as a tailor at three places in Birmingham: Snow Hill, Bristol Road and Aston Cross. He employed the defendant at his Snow Hill branch, although under the defendant's contract of employment he could have been directed to work at any of the three branches. The defendant covenanted that, for five years after leaving the plaintiff's employment, he would 'not carry on any business similar to that of the employer ... or be employed in any capacity by any person ... carrying on a business similar to that of the employer in Snow Hill ... or within half-a-mile radius of Aston Cross ... or Bristol Road'. A divisional court held that the Aston Cross and Bristol Road restrictions were unreasonable to protect the plaintiff's business connections but could be severed from the Snow Hill part of the covenant. Presumably, the restrictions were divisible in substance into several covenants.

1   [1915] 1 Ch 292, CA.
2   [1913] AC 724, HL.
3   Para 15.8, above.
4   [1920] 3 KB 571, CA.
5   [1927] 1 KB 637, DC.

Other effects
15.22   If money is paid under a contract which is wholly void on grounds of public policy, or under a severable part which is void on such grounds, it is recoverable back, even though the contract has been performed by the other party[1].

1   *Hermann v Charlesworth* [1905] 2 KB 123, CA.

Illegal Contracts
15.23   A contract may be illegal in one of three ways, in that:

it is prohibited by statute; or
it is performed in a manner which is prohibited by statute; or
it involves an element which is unlawful, immoral or prejudicial to the interests of the state.

These three types of illegality, with their effects on the enforcement of a contract, will be discussed in turn, followed by a discussion of the question of the recovery back of money or property transferred under an illegal contract.

Contracts prohibited by statute

15.24   A contract is illegal in itself if a statute expressly or impliedly prohibits it. In this context a 'statute' includes a piece of subordinate legislation.

15.25   An example of a contract which was *expressly* so prohibited is provided by *Re Mahmoud and Ispahani*[1]. Under wartime delegated legislation it was forbidden to buy or sell linseed oil without a licence. A agreed to sell and deliver some linseed oil to B but B subsequently refused to accept delivery because, unknown to A, he did not have a licence to buy linseed oil. The Court of Appeal held that, there being a clear statutory prohibition of the making of such a contract without a licence, it was illegal and unenforceable by A.

A modern example of a statute expressly prohibiting a contract is provided by s 1 of the Resale Prices Act 1976. This makes *illegal* agreements for the *collective* enforcement of price maintenance conditions. Section 1 strikes at such agreements between suppliers and at such agreements between dealers. It provides that any agreement, or even any arrangement, between two or more persons carrying on business in the United Kingdom as suppliers of goods is illegal if it provides:

a.   that goods shall be withheld from dealers who have infringed a condition as to the prices at which those goods may be sold (this includes putting a dealer's name on a stop-list); or

b.   that goods shall not be supplied to such dealers except on terms which are less favourable than those applicable to similar dealers (eg by cancellation of a trade discount); or

c.   that goods will only be supplied to persons who undertake to withhold or refuse supplies of goods in the above two ways.

In addition, agreements or arrangements authorising the recovery of penalties from offending dealers are illegal.

The consequences of a contract which is illegal under s 1 are not simply that it is unenforceable. In addition, the Crown may obtain an injunction 'or other appropriate relief', and a person affected by the agreement can bring an action for damages for breach of statutory duty.

1   [1921] 2 KB 716, CA.

15.26   If a statute prohibits one party from entering into the contract, without expressly prohibiting its making, the contract may be *impliedly* prohibited. This depends partly on whether the statute simply prohibits a party from *making* the contract or whether it not only prohibits a party from making the contract but also prohibits him from *carrying it out*. In the latter case the contract is prohibited by necessary implication since otherwise a party would be legally obliged to do something forbidden by statute[1].

In the former case, ie where a statute simply prohibits a party from making the contract, the question whether the contract is impliedly prohibited is productive of uncertainty since its answer depends on the judicial interpretation of the statute to ascertain whether the legislation was intended to forbid the particular contract. Because of the harsh consequences of such a finding, a contract will not be held to be prohibited unless there is a clear implication that this was Parliament's intention[2]. One factor which is particularly relevant is whether the object of the statute is to protect the public or a class of persons, eg to protect the public against unqualified persons or to protect licensed persons from competition[2]. If so, this suggests that Parliament intended a contract made in breach of the statute to be prohibited. In *Cope v Rowlands*[3], for instance, a statute provided that anyone who acted as a broker in the City of London without a licence should pay a penalty for each offence. The plaintiff, who was unlicensed, acted as a broker for the defendant whom he later sued for the work which he had done for him. The action was dismissed because, although the statute did not expressly prohibit the contract in question, Parliament had intended to protect the public in stockbroking transactions. The statute therefore had to be taken as impliedly prohibiting stockbroking contracts by unlicensed persons.

On the other hand, the fact that the statute's object is sufficiently served by the imposition of the statutory penalty suggests that Parliament did not intend a contract made in breach of the statute to be prohibited. In *Smith v Mawhood*[4], the plaintiff, a tobacconist, sued the defendant for the price of tobacco which he had delivered to him. The defendant pleaded that the contract was illegal because the plaintiff did not have a licence to sell tobacco, nor was his name painted on his premises, as required by statute. It was held that, although the plaintiff had committed a statutory offence, the contract was not illegal because the object of the statute was the imposition of a penalty for revenue purposes, and not the prohibition of contracts of sale by unlicensed dealers.

Another factor to which regard may be made is the inconvenience and injury which would be caused by holding the contract to be illegal[5].

The approach of the courts is well demonstrated by the decision of the Court of Appeal in *Archbolds (Freightage) Ltd v S Spanglett Ltd*[6]. The defendants contracted with the plaintiffs to carry whisky from Leeds to London. The whisky was stolen en route through the negligence of the defendants' driver and the plaintiffs claimed damages for its loss. The defendants raised the defence that, under the Road and Rail Traffic Act 1933, it was illegal for a person to use a vehicle to carry goods for another for reward unless the vehicle held an 'A' licence, that the vehicle used did not hold an 'A' licence (in fact none of their vehicles held an 'A' licence), and that therefore the contract was illegal and unenforceable. The trial judge dismissed this defence and awarded the plaintiffs damages. The Court of Appeal dismissed the defendants' appeal. It held that if, as had been found, the contract merely provided for the carriage of whisky from Leeds to London, the *formation* of that contract could not be illegal because, even had both parties contemplated that an unlicensed vehicle would be used, this would not be a contractual term. Moreover, the Court continued, even if the contract was to carry goods in a vehicle which did not in fact have an 'A' licence, the contract would still not be illegal in its formation. This was because the 1933 Act did not expressly prohibit such a contract; nor did it impliedly prohibit it, since its object was not to interfere with the owner of goods or his facilities for transport but to control competition between transport firms and improve efficiency, and that object was sufficiently served by the penalties prescribed for the transport undertaking using the unlicensed vehicle.

1   *Phoenix General Insurance Co of Greece SA v Administration Asigurarilor de Stat* [1988] QB 216, [1987] 2 All ER 152 at 176; *Re Cavalier Insurance Co Ltd* [1989] 2 Lloyd's Rep 430.
2   *St John Shipping Corpn v Joseph Rank Ltd* [1957] 1 QB 267, [1956] 3 All ER 683.
3   (1836) 2 M & W 149.
4   (1845) 14 M & W 452.
5   *St John Shipping Corpn v Joseph Rank Ltd* [1957] 1 QB 267, [1956] 3 All ER 683.
6   [1961] 1 QB 374, [1961] 1 All ER 417, CA. Also see *Hughes v Asset Managers plc* [1995] 3 All ER 669, CA.

15.27   Where a contract is statutorily illegal, neither party can enforce it, subject to the exceptions mentioned below, even though he was unaware of the facts constituting the illegality. Thus, in *Re Mahmoud and Ispahani*[1], the seller could not sue the buyer for refusing to take delivery of the linseed oil; this was so despite the facts that he was unaware that the buyer did not have the necessary licence and that, between the contract and attempted delivery, he had been assured by the buyer that he had a licence.

A contract which is statutorily illegal can be enforced in part if the illegal portions are severable. The rule is that where a party makes a number of promises, one of which is illegal and the rest legal, the illegal promise can be severed and the rest of the agreement enforced provided that:

a.   the illegal promise does not constitute the main or only consideration given by that party for the other's promises; and
b.   the illegal promise and the legal ones are not inseparable from, and not dependent upon, one another; and
c.   the nature of the illegality is not such as to preclude on grounds of public policy the enforcement of the rest of the agreement[2].

If the statute under which a contract is illegal is a 'class protecting statute', a party to the contract who is a member of the protected class can enforce it[3]. A 'class protecting statute' is one which has been passed to protect a particular class of persons, rather than simply to impose a penalty and prohibit the contract[4].

1   [1921] 2 KB 716, CA; para 15.25, above.
2   *Kearney v Whitehaven Colliery Co* [1893] 1 QB 700, CA; *Carney v Herbert* [1985] AC 301, [1985] 1 All ER 438, PC.
3   *Nash v Halifax Building Society* [1979] Ch 584, [1979] 2 All ER 19.
4   *Green v Portsmouth Stadium Ltd* [1953] 2 QB 190, [1953] 2 All ER 102, CA.

Contracts which become illegal because they are performed in a manner which constitutes a statutory offence

15.28   The fact that a statutory offence is committed in performing an initially lawful contract does not necessarily make the contract illegal[1], and generally it does not have that effect. Thus, for reasons which will become apparent shortly, the fact that an employee of a road haulage company exceeds the speed limit while delivering goods does not render illegal the contract of carriage made by the company.

1   *St John Shipping Corpn v Joseph Rank Ltd* [1957] 1 QB 267, [1956] 3 All ER 683.

15.29   Some statutes (or pieces of subordinate legislation) expressly state whether breach of their provisions does or does not invalidate a contract. However, generally, it depends on the interpretation of the statute to see whether Parliament intended that the particular type of contract in question should be prohibited if performed in contravention of the statute. The approach here is the same as that to the question whether a contract is impliedly illegal as formed. Breach of a statute in performing a contract will only be held to invalidate it if there is a clear implication that Parliament so intended. A statute whose object is the protection of the public or a class of persons is likely to give rise to such an implication, as will a statute which says that the type of contract in question can only be performed in one way. In *Anderson Ltd v Daniel*[1], for instance, the statute made it an offence for a person to sell artificial fertilisers without giving the buyer an invoice stating the percentage of certain chemicals. The plaintiffs sold ten tons of artificial fertiliser to the defendants but did not provide the necessary invoice. It was held that, since the statute had specified the only way in which the contract could be performed, and since this had not been done, the contract was rendered illegal and the plaintiffs could not recover the price of the fertiliser. On the other hand, if the purposes of the statute are sufficiently served by the prescribed penalties, the statute is unlikely to be construed as prohibiting a contract performed in breach of it. Another factor to be taken into account is the inconvenience or injury to a party which would result from a finding that the contract is prohibited.

These factors were taken into account by Devlin J in *St John Shipping Corpn v Joseph Rank Ltd*[2]. By statute it is an offence to load a ship to such an extent that the load line is below water. The plaintiffs chartered their ship to X to carry grain from the United States to England. The plaintiffs overloaded the ship so that the load line was submerged. The defendants, who were consignees of part of the cargo, withheld part of the freight charge (the equivalent of the amount due on the excess cargo), contending that the plaintiffs could not enforce the contract because they had performed it unlawfully. The judge held that the plaintiffs could recover the amount due. He held that the illegal performance of the contract of carriage did not render it illegal, because the Act merely punished infringements of the load line rules and was not intended to prohibit a contract of carriage performed in breach of them.

1   [1924] 1 KB 138, CA.
2   [1957] 1 QB 267, [1956] 3 All ER 683.

Enforcement

15.30   Where a contract has become illegal through performance in breach of a statute, the party who has so performed it cannot enforce the contract, as is shown by *Anderson Ltd v Daniel*[1], where the plaintiffs' claim for the price of the fertiliser which they had delivered was dismissed because of their illegal performance.

A limited exception was recognised in *Frank W Clifford Ltd v Garth*[2], namely that, if the performance was initially legal but became illegal and the legal and illegal parts of the performance can be precisely valued, the illegal part can be severed and the party who has illegally performed the contract can recover the amount of the contractual price which is attributable to the legal performance. In this case, the defendant engaged the plaintiffs to convert premises into a coffee bar for her. At the time in question, it was illegal to do more than £1,000 worth of such work on any single property in any year without a licence. The defendant had already had £146 worth of work done that year by another contractor. Her contract with the plaintiffs was not for a fixed figure but on a 'cost-plus' basis, and because of various difficulties the plaintiffs' bill was far in excess of £1,000. The Court of Appeal held that, although the plaintiffs could not recover the full amount claimed, they could recover £854 because, until the work in the particular year exceeded £1,000 in value, it was perfectly lawful and only became unlawful in relation to the excess. Thus, the plaintiffs could recover the amount which fell within the free limit.

Another exception is that, where the party who has performed the contract in breach of a statute did not intend to do so when he made the contract, he may enforce it if he does not have to rely on the illegal act to establish his right to enforce the contract. This was held in *Skilton v Sullivan* [3], where a seller of koi carp had committed an offence under VAT legislation by presenting an invoice describing the fish as trout (which were zero-rated, whereas koi carp were not). The Court of Appeal held that the sellers could enforce the contract of sale and recover the price, because he had formed the illegal intent after making the contract and did not have to rely on his illegal act to establish his right to recover from the buyer.

Some modern cases suggested that, where the enforcement of the contract by the party concerned would not be an affront to the public conscience, he can enforce the contract[4]. This is a vague test and difficult to apply. For this reason, its subsequent disapproval by the House of Lords in *Tinsley v Milligan*[5] is to be welcomed.

1   [1924] 1 KB 138, CA.
2   [1956] 2 All ER 323, [1956] 1 WLR 570, CA.
3   [1994] 21 LS Gaz R 41, CA.
4   *Euro-Diam Ltd v Bathurst* [1990] 1 QB 1, [1988] 2 All ER 23, CA; *Howard v Shirlstar Container Transport Ltd* [1990] 3 All ER 366, [1990] 1 WLR 1292, CA.
5   [1994] 1 AC 340, [1993] 3 All ER 65, HL.

15.31   The other party to a contract which is illegal as performed can sue on it. There is one exception. Where the party who has illegally performed the contract could not enforce the contract, the other party cannot enforce it if he knew of the mode of performance adopted (although he need not have known that it was illegal[1]) and *allowed* the performance to proceed. It is for him to establish his innocence. In *Marles v Philip Trant & Sons Ltd (No 2)*[2], for instance, the Court of Appeal held that although a contract for the sale of wheat was illegal, because the seller had not given the buyer certain written details as required by statute, the buyer could nevertheless sue the seller for breach of contract (the wheat having been misdescribed as 'spring wheat') because of his innocence. Similarly, in the *Archbolds (Freightage)* case[3], the Court of Appeal did not find it necessary to pursue the question whether the hauliers' unlawful performance of the contract rendered it illegal, because the plaintiffs had been ignorant that it was to be so performed and could have sued on the contract of carriage anyway. On the other hand, the plaintiffs failed to recover damages for breach of contract in *Ashmore Benson Pease & Co Ltd v A V Dawson Ltd*[4], where a contract of carriage performed by the defendants in breach of maximum load regulations was held to be illegal, because their transport manager had watched the lorries being overloaded and, by allowing it, had participated in the illegal performance of the contract.

1 *Archbolds (Freightage) Ltd v S Spanglett Ltd* [1961] 1 QB 374, [1961] 1 All ER 417, CA.
2 [1954] 1 QB 29, [1953] 1 All ER 651, CA.
3 [1961] 1 QB 374, [1961] 1 All ER 417, CA. The facts are set out in para 15.26, above.
4 [1973] 2 All ER 856, [1973] 1 WLR 828, CA.

15.32 If a party, who cannot sue on the illegal contract because he has illegally performed it, can prove that a collateral contract existed whereby the other party assumed responsibility for ensuring that the performance would be lawful, as by obtaining a necessary licence, he can recover damages for breach of that collateral contract[1].

1 *Strongman (1945) Ltd v Sincock* [1955] 2 QB 525, [1955] 3 All ER 90, CA.

Contracts involving an element which is unlawful, immoral or prejudicial to the interests of the state
15.33 Sometimes, a contract will be overtly for an unlawful, immoral or state-prejudicial purpose: at other times, an overtly proper contract, or its subject matter, will be intended by one or both of the parties, when the contract is made, to be exploited for such a purpose. Both types of contract are illegal ab initio but their consequences differ.

15.34 Any agreement to commit a crime or tort falls within this head, so that an agreement to defraud X is illegal[1], as is an agreement to publish a libel about X[2]. The width of the present head may be demonstrated by reference to *Miller v Karlinski*[3] and *Alexander v Rayson*[4]. In the former, the terms of an employment contract were that the employee should be paid £10 a week plus travelling expenses. The contract also provided that he could recover the amount of income tax payable on the £10 by claiming it as travel expenses. The employee later claimed ten weeks' arrears of salary plus 'expenses', most of which related to what was payable in income tax. It was held that since the contract was overtly for an illegal purpose – to defraud the Revenue – it could not be enforced by the employee and his action was dismissed. In contrast, the contract in *Alexander v Rayson*, which was not overtly for an unlawful purpose, was held to be illegal because it was intended to be exploited for such a purpose. The plaintiff let a flat to the defendant at £1,200 pa. The transaction was effected by two documents: a lease of the flat at £450 pa which provided for certain services to be rendered by the plaintiff, and an agreement that in consideration of £750pa the plaintiff would render certain services, which were substantially the same as in the lease. Subsequently, the defendant refused to pay an instalment due under the documents. When sued for this, the defendant raised the defence that the object of the two documents was that only the lease was to be disclosed to the local authority to deceive them into reducing the rateable value of the property. The Court of Appeal held that, if the documents were intended to be used for such an unlawful purpose, the plaintiff could not enforce either the lease or the service agreement.

1   *Taylor v Bhail* (1995) Independent, 27 November, CA.
2   *Apthorp v Neville & Co* (1907) 23 TLR 575.
3   (1945) 62 TLR 85, CA. See also *Corby v Morrison* [1980] ICR 564, [1980] IRLR 218.
4   [1936] 1 KB 169, CA.

15.35   Turning to agreements involving immorality, a contract to pay a woman in return for her agreeing to become a mistress is an obvious example of a contract which is illegal on the ground that its purpose is overtly immoral[1]. Likewise, a contract of employment will be held illegal if one of its terms is that the employee should procure prostitutes for his employer's clients, because its purpose is overtly immoral[2]. A contract to hire to a prostitute a car which is intended for use in her profession will be held illegal because the subject matter of the contract is intended to be used for an immoral purpose[3].

1   *Walker v Perkins* (1764) 1 Wm Bl 517.
2   *Coral Leisure Group v Barnett* [1981] ICR 503 at 508.
3   *Pearce v Brooks* (1866) LR 1 Exch 213.

15.36   Agreements which involve an element prejudicial to the interests of the state include agreements which are hostile to a friendly foreign state[1], agreements which tend to injure the public service (under which heading an agreement to assign a salary earned in a public office is illegal)[2] and agreements prejudicial to the administration of justice.

An agreement not to appear at the public examination of a bankrupt, nor to oppose his discharge, is an example of an agreement which has been held illegal as prejudicial to the administration of justice.

Two other types of agreement which are prejudicial to the administration of justice are those tainted by maintenance or champerty. Maintenance occurs if a person without just cause or excuse supports litigation by another in a case in which he has no legitimate interest. Champerty is maintenance plus a further agreement that the person giving such support shall have a share in anything recovered as a result of the litigation, including an agreement for a differential fee dependent on the outcome of litigation[3]. However, by s 58 of the Courts and Legal Services Act 1990, an agreement may in some cases be validly made in writing, by which a client promises to pay a 'conditional fee' to a person providing him with advocacy or litigation services. The condition may be that the litigation ends in the client's favour, and the 'conditional fee' may be the normal fee plus an uplift (of up to 100% of it). The agreement must comply with any requirements prescribed by the Lord Chancellor[4]. Conditional fee agreements are currently only valid in relation to proceedings in respect of a claim for damages for personal injury, proceedings by a company which is being wound up or in respect of which an administration order is in force, proceedings by the liquidator or administrator of a company, or by a trustee in bankruptcy of an individual, and proceedings before the European Commission, or European Court, of Human Rights, provided in each case that the client does not have legal aid[5].

1   *Foster v Driscoll* [1929] 1 KB 470, CA.
2   *Re Mirams* [1891] 1 QB 594.
3   *Aratra Potato Co v Taylor Joynson Garrett* [1995] 4 All ER 695.
4   Conditional Fee Agreements Regulations 1995.
5   Conditional Fee Agreements Order 1995.

Enforcement
15.37   The enforceability of a contract which is illegal because it involves an element which is unlawful, immoral or prejudicial to the interests of the state depends on whether or not it overtly involves such an element. If it does, neither party can enforce it however innocent he may be[1]. On the other hand, where the contract is not overtly for one of the above purposes but is intended to be, or its subject matter is intended to be, exploited for such a purpose the situation is as follows:

a.   the contract cannot be enforced by a party who intended to exploit it unlawfully, immorally or 'prejudicially'[2]; nor
b.   can it be enforced by a party who knew the other had such an intention[3]; but
c.   it can be enforced by a party who did not know of the other's unlawful, immoral or 'prejudicial' intentions before he performed or tendered performance of his contractual obligations[4].

Thus, in *Cowan v Milbourn*[5], where the defendant, who had agreed to let a room to the plaintiff but later refused to fulfil the agreement on learning that the plaintiff intended to use the room for an unlawful purpose (a blasphemous lecture), was sued for breach of contract, it was held that the plaintiff's action failed because of his unlawful intention in relation to the subject matter of the contract. On the other hand, it was said, the defendant could have sued the plaintiff for the hire charge if he had let him into possession not knowing of his unlawful intentions, but not if he had previously learnt of them. In *Archbold (Freightage)*[6], the Court of Appeal held that the fact that the hauliers had intended ab initio to carry out the contract of carriage in an unlawful way did not prevent the other party to the contract suing on it because they were ignorant of that intention. A party will have sufficient knowledge in the present context if he has full knowledge of what the other party intends to do; he need not know that it is unlawful[7].

Modern cases suggested an exception to the rules in a. and b., above, viz where the enforcement of the contract by the party concerned would not be an affront to the public conscience[8]. This is a vague test and difficult to apply. Consequently, its disapproval by the House of Lords in *Tinsley v Milligan*[9] is welcome.

In contracts involving an element of unlawfulness, immorality or prejudice to the interests of the state it is not possible to sever the illegal part and enforce the rest of the contract[10].

1 *Miller v Karlinski* (1945) 62 TLR 85, CA; *Keir v Leeman* (1846) 9 QB 371, Ex Ch; *Corby v Morrison* [1980] ICR 564, [1980] IRLR 218.
2 *Alexander v Rayson* [1936] 1 KB 169, CA; *Corby v Morrison* [1980] ICR 564, [1980] IRLR 218.
3 *Pearce v Brooks* (1866) LR 1 Exch 213; *Corby v Morrison* [1980] ICR 564, [1980] IRLR 218.
4 *Cowan v Milbourn* (1867) LR 2 Exch 230.
5 (1867) LR 2 Exch 230.
6 [1961] 1 QB 374, [1961] 1 All ER 417, CA; the facts are set out in para 15.26, above.
7 *J M Allan (Merchandising) Ltd v Cloke* [1963] 2 QB 340, [1963] 2 All ER 258, CA; cf *Waugh v Morris* (1873) LR 8 QB 202.
8 *Euro-Diam Ltd v Bathurst* [1990] 1 QB 1, [1988] 2 All ER 23, CA; *Howard v Shirlstar Container Transport Ltd* [1990] 3 All ER 366, [1990] 1 WLR 1292, CA.
9 [1994] 1 AC 340, [1993] 3 All ER 65, HL.
10 *Bennett v Bennett* [1952] 1 KB 249 at 252-254, [1952] 1 All ER 413 at 416-417; *Miller v Karlinski* (1945) 62 TLR 85, CA; *Kuenigl v Donnersmarck* [1955] 1 QB 515, [1955] 1 All ER 46; *Corby v Morrison* [1980] ICR 564, [1980] IRLR 218. Cf *Fielding and Platt Ltd v Najjar* [1969] 2 All ER 150 at 153.

Recovery back of money or property transferred under an illegal contract

15.38   The general rule is that a person cannot recover back money or property which he has transferred under an illegal contract. With one important exception (see para 15.39f, below), that general rule applies even if the other party has completely failed or refused to perform his contractual obligations. The general rule is particularly harsh where a party to an illegal contract is not permitted to enforce it, since not only are damages for its breach irrecoverable by him but also he cannot successfully claim back what he has transferred under it instead. An authority is *Parkinson v College of Ambulance Ltd*[1]. The secretary of the defendant charity promised the plaintiff that, if he would make a certain donation to the charity, he would procure a knighthood for him. The knighthood did not materialise and the plaintiff sought to recover the £3,000 he had paid. It was held that the contract was illegal (as tending to injure the public service) and that the plaintiff's action, being based on it, must fail.

1 [1925] 2 KB 1.

15.39   In the following exceptional cases a party to an illegal contract can recover back from the other what he has transferred under it.

a.   *Fraudulent misrepresentation by the other party that the contract was lawful*   Instead of suing for damages for deceit[1], the party deceived can recover back what he has transferred under the contract. This is shown by *Hughes v Liverpool Victoria Legal Friendly Society*[2], where a woman, who had been induced to take out an insurance policy by a fraudulent misrepresentation that it was valid, was held able to recover the premium which she had paid. The present exception does not apply where the misrepresentation as to the legality of the contract was not fraudulent[3]. However, where a person has been induced to enter into an illegal contract by a misrepresentation of *fact*, he can *rescind the contract for misrepresentation* and recover back what he transferred under it, *provided rescission is not barred*, even though the misrepresentation was innocent[4].

b.   *Contract procured through oppression by the other party*   In *Atkinson v Denby*[5], for example, the plaintiff, a debtor, offered his creditors five shillings (25p) in the pound. The defendant, who was one of the creditors, told the plaintiff that he would only accept this dividend if the plaintiff first paid him £50 and gave him a certain bill of exchange. The plaintiff agreed and did so. The contract was illegal because of the fraud on the other creditors, but it was held that the plaintiff could recover the £50 because the contract to defraud had been procured by oppression, since the other creditors would not have accepted the composition if the defendant had not. The basis of this exception, like the previous one, is that the parties are not equally guilty.

c.   *No reliance on the illegal contract*   A party to an illegal contract can recover back what he has transferred under it if he can establish his right to it without relying on the terms of the illegal contract or its illegality[6].

This exception is of limited application. This is partly because the ownership of property can pass under an illegal contract if the parties so intend[7], and where this occurs, as in the case of goods sold under an illegal contract of sale, the transferor cannot recover the property back.

However, where an owner of property has merely transferred some limited interest to another under an illegal contract, as by pledging goods with him or hiring them to him, any rights which he may have independent of his illegal contract will be recognised and enforced. Thus, if A hires goods to B under an illegal contract he can recover them back, or recover damages in lieu, when B's right to possess them has ended. This is because A's right to immediate possession will have revived thereby and consequently he will be entitled to sue B in tort for conversion of the goods without having to base his claim in any way on the terms of the illegal contract or its illegality[8]. On the other hand, if E deposits property with F to secure payment of charges under an illegal contract the property is irrecoverable, unless the charges have been paid, because, once F has pleaded that the property has been pledged with him, E can only base his claim to possession by showing that the pledge was invalid because of the illegality of the contract[9].

d.   *Unlawful purpose not yet carried into effect*   This exception is relevant to contracts which are illegal because their purpose is unlawful. A party can recover back what he has transferred under an illegal contract if he genuinely repents (which he will not do if his change of mind is brought about by the other's failure to perform the contract or because the illegality has been discovered by the authorities)[10] and withdraws from the contract before the unlawful purpose is partially performed in a substantial way[11] .

e. *Class protecting statutes* If a statute which makes a particular type of contract illegal as formed was passed to protect a particular class of persons, rather than simply to impose a penalty and prohibit the contract[12], a member of that class who is a party to such a contract can recover back money or property which he has transferred under it, even though the contract has been completely performed[13]. The basis of this exception is that the parties are not equally guilty[13]. Some class protecting statutes which make particular contracts illegal expressly provide for recovery by a member of the protected class of what he has transferred under them. For example, s 125 of the Rent Act 1977 provides that where an unlawful premium has been paid under any agreement it is recoverable back by the person who paid it (eg the tenant).

f. *Total failure of consideration: recovery back of money by innocent party* There is recent authority that, where there has been a total failure of consideration by the payee party under an illegal contract (ie the payer party has not received any part of what he bargained for under the contract), the payer party can recover back the money paid on the ground of that failure *if he is an innocent party*[14]. Otherwise the payee party could benefit from the illegality at the expense of the innocent payer party because he could refuse to carry out the contract and benefit by retaining the money paid.

1 Para 14.20, above.
2 [1916] 2 KB 482, CA.
3 *Harse v Pearl Life Assurance Co* [1904] 1 KB 558, CA.
4 *Edler v Auerbach* [1950] 1 KB 359, [1949] 2 All ER 692. For these bars see para 14.16, above.
5 (1862) 7 H & N 934.
6 *Tinsley v Milligan* [1994] 1 AC 340, [1993] 3 All ER 65, HL.
7 *Sajan Singh v Sardara Ali* [1960] AC 167, [1960] 1 All ER 269, PC; *Belvoir Finance Co Ltd v Stapleton* [1971] 1 QB 210, [1970] 3 All ER 664, CA.
8 *Bowmakers Ltd v Barnet Instruments Ltd* [1945] KB 65, [1944] 2 All ER 579, CA.
9 *Taylor v Chester* (1869) LR 4 QB 309.
10 *Bigos v Bousted* [1951] 1 All ER 92; *Alexander v Rayson* [1936] 1 KB 169 at 190.
11 *Kearley v Thomson* (1890) 24 QBD 742, CA; cf *Taylor v Bowers* (1876) 1 QBD 291, CA.
12 *Green v Portsmouth Stadium Ltd* [1953] 2 QB 190, [1953] 2 All ER 102, CA.
13 *Browning v Morris* (1778) 2 Cowp 790; *Kiriri Cotton Co Ltd v Dewani* [1960] AC 192, [1960] 1 All ER 177, PC.
14 *Re Cavalier Insurance Co Ltd* [1989] 2 Lloyd's Rep 430.

Chapter 16

Capacity to Contract

Minors
16.1   The age of majority was reduced from 21 to 18 by s 1 of the Family Law Reform Act 1969. Persons under that age are known as minors.

Minors' contracts can be divided into three types:

valid contracts;
voidable contracts;
other contracts.

It should be noticed at the outset that a parent or guardian is never liable for a minor's contract unless the minor acts as his agent, nor can a minor's invalid contract be validated by subsequent parental ratification.

Valid contracts
16.2   Three types of contract made by a minor fall within this heading: contracts for necessary goods for the minor; contracts for necessary services for the minor, and contracts of employment or apprenticeship (and analogous contracts) which are beneficial to the minor.

Contracts for necessary goods for the minor
16.3   Proof that goods were necessaries requires two conditions to be satisfied:

a.   *The goods must be suitable to the minor's position in life*   Necessaries are not limited to the necessities of life but they do not extend to mere luxuries[1]. They can include anything fit to maintain the minor in his station in life[2].

b.   *The goods must be necessaries according to the minor's actual requirements at the time of delivery*   In *Nash v Inman*[3], the defendant minor was an undergraduate at Cambridge. The plaintiff, a tailor, supplied him with clothes, including 11 waistcoats. The plaintiff's action for the price of the clothes failed because, the evidence showing that the defendant was amply provided already with clothes suitable to his position, there was no proof of the present condition.

320

1 *Peters v Fleming* (1840) 6 M & W 42.
2 *Bryant v Richardson* (1866) 14 LT 24 at 26; *Ryder v Wombwell* (1868) LR 3 Exch 90 at 96.
3 [1908] 2 KB 1, CA.

Contracts for necessary services for the minor
16.4   These must satisfy the same tests as contracts for necessary goods. In *Chapple v Cooper*[1], the following examples of necessary services were given: education, training for a trade, and medical advice. Of course, as was emphasised in that case, whether services are necessaries in a particular case depends on the state and condition of the minor.

1 (1844) 13 M & W 252.

General points concerning contracts for necessaries
16.5   a.   A contract which would otherwise be enforceable against the minor as a contract for necessaries cannot be so enforced if it contains terms which are harsh or onerous on him[1].

b.   A question of some importance is whether a contract for necessaries can be enforced against a minor if it is still executory. In other words, can a minor be sued if he repudiates the contract before the necessary goods have been delivered or the necessary services performed?

Although the matter is not entirely free from doubt, it seems that, in the case of contracts for necessary goods, a minor is only liable if the goods have actually been delivered; he is not liable if he repudiates the contract before delivery[2]. In this context it may also be noted that s 3(2) of the Sale of Goods Act 1979 provides that, where necessary goods are sold and delivered to a minor, he must pay a reasonable price for them, which is not necessarily the contract price.

Unlike a contract for necessary goods, a contract for necessary services is enforceable against a minor even though it is executory when the minor repudiates it[3].

1 *Fawcett v Smethurst* (1914) 84 LJKB 473.
2 *Nash v Inman* [1908] 2 KB 1 at 8 (contrast p 12); *Pontypridd Union v Drew* [1927] 1 KB 214 at 220.
3 *Roberts v Gray* [1913] 1 KB 520, CA.

Contracts of employment or apprenticeship and analogous contracts[1]
16.6   Such a contract is valid and enforceable against the minor even though executory, provided that, on the whole, it is beneficial to him. In *Clements v London and North Western Rly Co*[2] a minor undertook in his employment contract to accept the terms of an insurance scheme to which the employer contributed and to forego any statutory claims he might have against the employer. The terms of the scheme were in some ways more beneficial to him, and in other ways less beneficial, than those of the statute. It was held that the contract, taken as a whole, was for his benefit and that he was bound by it. This case can be contrasted with *De Francesco v Barnum*[3]. Under an apprenticeship deed made between a minor, aged 14, and the plaintiff, the minor bound herself apprentice to the plaintiff for seven years to learn dancing. In the deed she

agreed not to take any professional engagement without the plaintiff's consent, nor to marry. She was to be paid for any performance she might give, but there was no provision for other pay, nor did the plaintiff undertake to find her other work. It was held that the deed was unenforceable because, on the whole, it was not beneficial to the minor, being unreasonably harsh and oppressive.

1 'Analogous contracts' in this context include contracts whereby a minor earns a fee in his occupation, or obtains a licence to follow his occupation.
2 [1894] 2 QB 482, CA.
3 (1889) 43 Ch D 165.

16.7 For no apparent reason, a minor's trading contract does not fall within the present heading and is not binding on him[1] however beneficial to him it may be. For instance, in *Cowern v Nield*[2], it was held that a contract to deliver hay could not be enforced against a hay and straw dealer who was a minor.

1 Such a contract will, however, become binding if once he reaches 18 the ex-minor ratifies it within a reasonable time of reaching that age; see para 16.11, below.
2 [1912] 2 KB 419.

Voidable contracts
16.8 There are five types of voidable contract[1]:

a. A contract by a minor to buy or sell land.
b. A contract by a minor to lease land.
c. A contract by a minor to buy shares.
d. A contract to bring property into a marriage settlement.
e. A partnership agreement.

1 *Whittingham v Murdy* (1889) 60 LT 956; *Davies v Beynon-Harris* (1931) 47 TLR 424; *North Western Rly Co v M'Michael* (1850) 5 Exch 114; *Edwards v Carter* [1893] AC 360, HL; *Goode v Harrison* (1821) 5 B & Ald 147.

16.9 A person who makes one of these voidable contracts while he is a minor is bound by it, unless and until he expressly repudiates it during minority or within a reasonable time of attaining his majority.

A repudiation during minority is not conclusive and can be withdrawn within a reasonable time of majority[1].

An adult party to one of these voidable contracts cannot repudiate it[2] but, of course, he will no longer be bound by the contract if the person who contracted as a minor makes a valid repudiation.

1 *North Western Rly Co v M'Michael* (1850) 5 Exch 114 at 127.
2 *Clayton v Ashdown* (1714) 2 Eq Cas Abr 516.

Effect of repudiation
16.10 Repudiation relieves the minor or former minor from contractual liabilities accruing after his repudiation[1] but it is uncertain whether repudiation relieves him from liabilities which have accrued before repudiation[2].

A person who exercises the right to repudiate the voidable contract cannot recover back money paid under it unless there has been a total failure of consideration, which will not occur unless he has not received any part of what he has bargained for[3]. This is demonstrated by *Steinberg v Scala (Leeds) Ltd*[4]. The plaintiff, a minor, applied for, and was allotted, shares in a company. She received no dividends and after 18 months claimed to repudiate the allotment and recover back the money she had paid in respect of the shares. The Court of Appeal held that, while she could repudiate the contract and thereby avoid liability for future calls, she could not recover back what she had already paid because she had got the shares she bargained for and it was immaterial that she had not received any real benefit by way of dividends: there had been no total failure of consideration.

1   *Steinberg v Scala (Leeds) Ltd* [1923] 2 Ch 452, CA.
2   Contrast *North Western Rly Co v M'Michael* (1850) 5 Exch 114 at 125 (retrospective) with *Blake v Concannon* (1870) IR 4 CL 323 (not retrospective). There are dicta in support of both views in the Court of Appeal decision in *Steinberg v Scala (Leeds) Ltd*.
3   *Corpe v Overton* (1833) 10 Bing 252.
4   [1923] 2 Ch 452, CA.

Other contracts

16.11   Contracts made by a minor, other than those previously described, do not bind the minor unless he ratifies them within a reasonable time of reaching 18.

The following types of contract are included under this heading:

a.   contracts for the loan of money to or by a minor;
b.   contracts for non-necessary goods or services supplied or to be supplied to a minor;
c.   contracts of employment of a minor which are not beneficial to him;
d.   trading contracts made by a minor.

16.12   The effect of a contract of the present type is:

a.   It does not bind the minor party, except that it does become binding on him if he ratifies it within a reasonable time of reaching 18[1].
b.   It binds the adult party but, although the minor party may recover damages, the minor party cannot obtain specific performance of the contract[2].
c.   The minor party cannot recover back money paid, or property transferred, under the contract simply because the contract does not bind him[3]. However, he can recover it back on any ground which would be available to an adult party. For example, he can recover back money if there has been a total failure of consideration, which will only occur if the minor party has not received any part of what he bargained for[4].
d.   It appears that the property in (ie the ownership of) goods may pass to or from the minor party under the present type of contract[5].

1   *Bruce v Warwick* (1815) 6 Taunt 118.

2   *Flight v Bolland* (1828) 4 Russ 298. This limitation would not apply after a ratification by the
     minor party after reaching 18.
3   *Corpe v Overton* (1833) 10 Bing 252 at 259.
4   Para 10.5, above.
5   The Minors' Contracts Act 1987, s 3, seems to assume this in relation to property passing to
     the minor; para 16.15, below.

Guarantees

16.13   A guarantee given in respect of an obligation of a party which is not
binding on him (whether from the start or by virtue of a subsequent repudiation
by him) because he was a minor when the contract was made is not thereby
rendered unenforceable against the guarantor[1].

1   Minors' Contracts Act 1987, s 2.

Liability for torts connected with contracts

16.14   Generally, a minor is liable for his torts, but he is not so liable if he
commits a tort in performing or procuring a contract which is not binding on
him. Otherwise such a contract could be indirectly enforced by means of a
tortious action. Thus, in *Jennings v Rundall*[1], a minor who had hired a mare
and injured her by excessive and improper riding was held not liable in tort,
and, in *R Leslie Ltd v Sheill*[2], a minor who obtained a loan of money by a
fraudulent misrepresentation as to his age was held not to be liable in the tort
of deceit.

The only exception to the above rule is where the minor does something
which is not simply a wrongful performance of something authorised or
contemplated by the contract, but is the performance of something prohibited
by the contract or not contemplated by it. An example is *Burnard v Haggis*[3]. A
minor hired a mare for riding and was given strict instructions 'not to jump or
lark with her'. He lent her to a friend who jumped her, causing fatal injuries.
The minor was held liable in tort because the jumping was a prohibited act,
Jennings v Rundall being distinguished on the ground that the minor there had
not done a prohibited act but merely an authorised act (riding) improperly. A
more modern case is *Ballett v Mingay*[4], where the plaintiff hired to a minor a
microphone and amplifier. The minor delivered these improperly to X. The
Court of Appeal held that the minor was liable in tort because parting with
possession of the goods fell outside the scope of the contract.

1   (1799) 8 Term Rep 335.
2   [1914] 3 KB 607, CA.
3   (1863) 14 CBNS 45.
4   [1943] KB 281, [1943] 1 All ER 143, CA.

Restitution of property acquired under contract by minor

16.15   Where a party (A) has entered into a contract with a minor (M) and
the contract does not bind M (whether from the start or by virtue of a
subsequent repudiation by him) because he was a minor when the contract

was made, the court may, if it is just and equitable to do so, order M to transfer to A any property acquired by M under the contract, or any property representing it[1].

This is aimed particularly at preventing minors obtaining goods under a contract which is not from the start binding on them and then refusing to pay for them or to return them. However, there need be no fraud or impropriety on the minor's part in order for this power to be exercised. Of course, the major limitation with it is that, if the minor has consumed the goods or given them away, there is nothing which he can be ordered to restore. In contrast, if he has sold or exchanged the goods, he can be ordered to restore their proceeds, ie what he has received for them.

1   Minors' Contracts Act 1987, s 3.

Mentally Disordered and Intoxicated Persons

16.16   If the Court of Protection[1] has assumed jurisdiction to manage the property and affairs of a person suffering from mental disorder, its powers include making contracts for the benefit of that person and carrying out contracts already made by him[2]. It is possible that such a person is absolutely incapable of entering into a contract which binds him; certainly, he is not bound if he makes one purporting to dispose of property since this would interfere with the Court's jurisdiction[3].

Apart from this, mentally disordered persons generally have full contractual capacity, although their contracts may be voidable in the circumstances outlined next.

If a person proves that, because of mental disorder or intoxication, he was incapable, at the time of making the contract, of understanding its nature *and* that the other party knew of this, the contract is voidable at his option[4]. This option can only be exercised when the person is of sane and sober understanding, and if he decides to affirm the contract rather than avoid it he is bound by it[5]. Where the other party did not know of the mental disorder, the contract is valid. It cannot be avoided simply on the ground that it was unfair to the mentally disordered party because its terms were more favourable to the other[6]. Of course, if there is unfairness in circumstances which would have enabled him to avoid the contract if he had been sane[7], the contract is voidable by him.

1   Para 3.35, above.
2   Mental Health Act 1983, s 96.
3   *Re Walker* [1905] 1 Ch 160, CA; *Re Marshall, Marshall v Whateley* [1920] 1 Ch 284.
4   *Imperial Loan Co v Stone* [1892] 1 QB 599, CA.
5   *Matthews v Baxter* (1873) LR 8 Exch 132.
6   *Hart v O'Connor* [1985] AC 1000, [1985] 2 All ER 880, PC.
7   Paras 14.50–14.55, above.

16.17   A person who is not contractually liable under the above rules is nevertheless liable to pay a reasonable price for necessary goods sold *and delivered* to him since s 3(2) of the Sale of Goods Act 1979, which has already been mentioned in relation to minors' contracts[1], also applies to persons who are incompetent to contract 'by reasons of mental incapacity or drunkenness'.

1   Para 16.5, above.

Companies, Partnerships and Unincorporated Associations

16.18   The contractual capacity of companies and of partnerships is dealt with in paras 25.29–25.30 and 24.36, below. We dealt with the contractual capacity of unincorporated associations other than partnerships in paras 2.11 and 2.17, above.

Part III

Elements of the
Law of Tort

Chapter 17

Introduction and Vicarious Liability

Introduction

17.1 The law of tort (or torts) seeks to define those circumstances in which a person whose interests (physical or economic) have been harmed by another can seek compensation from that other irrepective of a contractual or other relationship with him[1]. The harm caused will generally involve damage but there are a few torts where an action can be brought without any actual damage occurring[2].

A difficulty that can be encountered in determining whether a person who has suffered harm has a tortious remedy is that the law recognises some losses which can be attributed to the actions of another as compensatable by that other while other losses also caused by another are not. It is not always easy to see why some losses attract a tortious remedy and others do not. There are certain general principles which provide some guidance as to whether a loss may be compensatable in tort, which we discuss in paras 17.4 and 17.5, below.

In this chapter we begin by discussing the imposition of tortious duties in general. We go on to consider certain procedural matters including joint tortfeasors (a tortfeasor being a person who has committed a tort). We then consider vicarious liability and related matters. In the following two chapters (18 and 19) we consider negligence and torts closely related to it. We then consider a number of other torts in Chapter 20. In Chapter 21 we discuss defences and remedies available in tort actions.

The usual remedy levied for the commission of a tort is damages, although in a limited number of circumstances other remedies are available[3]. We refer, sometimes, to a law of 'torts' rather than a law of 'tort', because there are a variety of different torts which protect either different interests or similar interests in different ways although there are themes common to all or many torts.

---

1 The existence of a contractual or other relationship between a person suffering harm and the peron inflicting it does not preclude the existence of a tortious duty.
2 The most important example is trespass to property; an action is generally brought in such circumstances to establish the legal position of the parties for the future.

17.2   The vast majority of successful tort claims, whether they are litigated or settled out of court (which applies to 99% of tort claims), are in respect of road accidents or accidents at work, both areas where insurance is compulsory and hence there is a defendant capable of satisfying any judgment. However, it should not be forgotten that the victim of a tort may receive compensation for his injuries from the state, in the form of social security benefits, or from his own private insurance.

The principal function of the law of tort is to compensate the victim for any harm which he has suffered as the result of the act or omission of another (whom we shall call X). However, the mere fact that X has harmed the victim will not necessarily entitle him to be compensated by X. A tortious remedy will only lie if X owed a legal obligation (a duty) not to cause the victim the particular type of harm in question and was in breach of it. Moreover, a victim who can prove that his harm was caused by X, in breach of a duty owed to him by X, will not necessarily receive full (or, indeed, any) compensation in tort for his injuries. First, while the harm may in fact have been caused by X the law may regard that harm as too remote in law[1]. Second, the alleged tortfeasor, X, may be able to establish a total or partial defence to the action[2]. Third, the victim's claims may be statute-barred in that the action has not been commenced within the legal time limits[3]. Even when the victim has a good cause of action, it will avail him little if X has disappeared and cannot be found or if X has no funds to satisfy any judgment against him and is uninsured. Where a loss is not caused by a tortious act or omission the victim has to rely on other sources of compensation. It has been argued that individuals should insure themselves against loss or harm rather than relying on finding a person who owes them a tortious duty who may provide a source of compensation

The law of tort also has an 'educational' aim. It seeks to encourage people to modify their behaviour to avoid causing harm to others. The sanction for failing to learn the lesson being an award of damages against a person in breach of a tortious duty or, in a limited number of cases, an order requiring a person to modify their behaviour in the future.

1   Paras 18.61–18.66, below.
2   Paras 21.2–21.17, below.
3   Paras 21.18–21.25, below.

Imposition of a tortious duty
17.3   As we have already indicated, a tortious remedy will lie only if there is a legal obligation (a duty) not to cause that particular type of harm, if the defendant owed that duty to the plaintiff and if the defendant has, in breach of that duty, caused that type of harm.

A tortious duty (in common with the duty to obey the criminal law) is imposed by law independently of the wishes of the person owing the duty. However, it may be possible to modify the scope of a tortious duty, for example, by the use of a notice restricting or excluding liability[1]. Tort liability can be distinguished from contractual liability in two main areas. First, parties choose whether to enter into a contract and undertake contractual duties, the law of tort is imposed on persons irrespective of any prior agreement. Second, damages are awarded in tort to restore the staus quo, ie to put the victim back into the position he was before, whereas damages are generally awarded in contract to compensate for the other party's failure to perform, ie to compensate for loss of expectations. There is, however, an uncertain overlap between contract and tort which we discuss in paras 18.67–18.70, below

The law of tort is not static; existing torts extend their ambit and new torts appear, albeit rarely. The difficulty lies in determining the basis on which the court will determine whether a tortious duty exists in a novel situation.

1 For a situation where liability may be excluded or modified see para 18.15, below.

17.4 How then do the courts decide whether liability should be imposed upon a particular defendant? This is a two-stage process. First, the court must decide whether a duty not to cause the injury complained of could be owed by one person to another – a question of law. Second, the court must determine whether this defendant owed this plaintiff a duty not to cause the relevant injury – a question of fact.

At the outset it must be noted that the courts have held that:

a.   Tortious liability cannot be imposed unless the claim for breach of duty could give rise to an award of unliquidated damages, that is damages measured by reference to a plaintiff's loss and not a predetermined sum, even if the particular plaintiff in the case before the court is seeking a remedy other than damages.

b.   Where a previous case has found a duty to exist (or not to exist) in respect of harm comparable to that before the court, then that decision will apply unless there is a very good reason why it should not be followed[1]. For example, it is clearly established that we must all exercise reasonable care in the way we conduct our lives to avoid causing physical injury to others.

c.   The defendant's motive or intention in acting as he did is not usually legally relevant to the question of liability. If he is not under a duty a bad motive or intention will not render him liable. Thus, if a defendant acts maliciously and thereby harms the plaintiff, but he is under no duty not to cause that harm, malice will not render his conduct tortious[2]. However, in the tort of nuisance, where the issue is whether there was an unreasonable interference with the plaintiff's use or enjoyment of his property, the motive of the defendant may be relevant in deciding if his interference was 'unreasonable'[3].

1 This can be regarded as an application of the doctrine of precedent which we discuss in Chap 2.
2 *Bradford Corpn v Pickles* [1895] AC 587, HL.
3 See para 20.22, below.

17.5 It is generally accepted that there is no one underlying principle by which the courts decide whether a duty in law does exist (or does not exist). There are, however, a number of factors which may be used by the courts in determining this question.

a.   *Fault*   A very important principle for determining whether a legal duty arises is the negative one that no duty can arise (and thus there can be no liability) without fault[1]. Fault does not mean merely the deliberate infliction of harm but also includes the negligent infliction of injury. However, the importance of fault in determining the vital question of the imposition of a duty can be criticised. It is argued that, since damages are assessed by reference to the degree of harm suffered by the plaintiff and not the relative culpability of the defendant, the fault or otherwise of the defendant should be irrelevant. In reply, it is argued that to have liability without fault would encourage people to be careless – because there is no advantage in taking due care (the educational function of tort). It may be doubted, however, whether people mould their conduct to avoid tortious liability. For example, drivers use due care because they wish to avoid damage to themselves and their cars and to escape criminal liability, not because they will avoid liability in tort if they drive with due care.

b.   *Balancing of interests*   The courts, in deciding whether to impose a legal duty, may try to effect a compromise between competing legitimate interests. The tort of defamation, for example, seeks to balance the right of free speech and the right of an individual not to have his reputation besmirched. The interests of society may be advanced by the building of a power station, the interests of those living in the locality are likely to be impaired, the tort of nuisance may have to balance those interests. In one recent example of this balancing of interests[2], the House of Lords refused to impose a duty to cargo owners on a society which classified ships as seaworthy or not. The general utility of society's conduct outweighed the interests of cargo owners whose goods had been lost on a ship wrongly classified as seaworthy – cargo owners should insure their own property. It could have been argued that the task of the defendants in this case was so important, it affected the safety of those that sailed on the ships and not just the owners of goods, that the decision should have been to impose a duty.

   This balancing of interests, to which greater prominence has lately been given, is influenced by previous decisions and long term social and political factors. The importance of some interests has led to the courts holding that infringement of those interests, even if it causes no loss to the plaintiff, constitutes a tort; trespass to goods is one example. Conversely, the courts have held some interests to be so important that they have been upheld even where their exercise has caused harm to others; for example, a businessman can cut his prices even if it harms (and was designed to harm) his trade rivals[3].

c.   *Justice and policy*   The courts also accept that there are some cases where, on a conventional analysis, a tortious duty would arise but there are policy arguments against the imposition of a duty. For example, it has been held that the law of tort should not be used to try and outflank a decision in other legal proceedings. For example, a person convicted of a criminal offence cannot sue his barrister for negligently conducting the case since this is an indirect challenge on his conviction[4]. There is considerable overlap between arguments based on policy and those based on a balancing of interests but where the court balances interests it is determining *whether* a tortious duty can arise whereas arguments based on policy permit the court to reject a duty which has arisen.

d.   *Alternative liability*   It had been thought that where a person owed another a contractual duty he could not owe a concurrent duty in tort. For example, it was thought that, if X had a contract with his accountant and the accountant gave X negligent financial advice in breach of that contract, liability to X arose for breach of contract but not for the tort of negligence. This view is now much less prevalent and, apart from certain special cases and where statute requires otherwise, there is no reason why a person should not have an action in both contract and tort in respect of the same facts[5]. The advantages of dual liability from the point of view of the plaintiff are that damages are assessed differently (although the plaintiff does not get double damages) and the possible differences in the commencement of limitation periods[6]. It is generally thought that where there is concurrent liability the standard of care is determined by reference to the terms of the contract[7] rather than that which would arise in tort although the other benefits of tortious liability, for example, the differences in the limitation periods, can still operate.

1   Fault may be important in determining whether a duty exists. It is also required in some cases to establish breach of a duty, although some torts are actionable without proof of fault. See, for example, paras 20.9–20.15, below.
2   *Marc Rich & Co v Bishop Rock Marine Co Ltd* [1996] AC 211, [1995] 3 All ER 307, HL.
3   Although it may be tortious to combine with others to force a rival out of business.
4   See para 18.35, below.
5   For cases recognising that concurrent duties can be owed see, for example, *Midland Bank Trust Co Ltd v Hett, Stubbs and Kemp* [1979] Ch 384, [1978] 3 All ER 571; *Esso Petroleum Co Ltd v Mardon* [1976] QB 801, [1976] 2 All ER 5, CA; *Punjab National Bank v de Boinville* [1992] 3 All ER 104, [1992] 1 WLR 1138, CA; *Henderson v Merrett Syndicates Ltd* [1995] 2 AC 145, [1994] 3 All ER 506, HL. See further on this point paras 18.67–18.70, below.
6   Paras 12.2–12.17 and 12.35–12.41, above, and 21.18–21.25, below.
7   *Johnstone v Bloomsbury Health Authority* [1992] QB 333, [1991] 2 All ER 293, CA.

Breach of a tortious duty

17.6   Once a court has determined that the defendant owed a tortious duty to the plaintiff it must then determine whether he broke that duty and thereby caused the injury of which the plaintiff complains.

Breach of duty arises in respect of some torts only if the defendant was at fault. Fault in this context embraces not only intentional conduct (conduct in the context of fault generally includes inaction) causing foreseen and desired harm, but also intentional conduct causing foreseeable[1] but undesired harm and also objectively careless conduct (ie conduct adjudged careless by reference to the standards expected of the reasonable man) causing foreseeable harm.

In other torts, liability arises simply because the defendant engaged in conduct which caused the injury; torts of this type are called torts of strict liability. Some torts which may be committed without fault derive from statute, for example, the Factories Act 1961, the Animals Act 1971 and most importantly the Consumer Protection Act 1987[2]. Other strict liability torts derive from the common law, for example, defamation[3] and trespass. Even in respect of strict liability torts, the defendant cannot incur liability if he did not *cause* the harm about which the plaintiff complains. The courts have construed 'cause' in such a way as to limit it to voluntary conduct by the defendant. For example, a person who, without permission, enters onto land belonging to another commits the tort of trespass. However, if the reason that he entered onto that land was that he was knocked onto it from the pavement by a hit-and-run driver, he has not caused the prohibited incursion and is not liable in tort.

1   Foreseeability is assessed objectively but there is some inconsistency between different torts as to how likely the foreseen event must be. Generally, the foreseen event must be reasonably probable or must be a 'real risk'; in the tort of nuisance it seems that where an event is a remote possibility it may still be a 'real risk'. For nuisance see paras 20.21–20.25, below.
2   Paras 20.9–20.15, below.
3   Paras 20.29–20.35, below.

Who can sue in tort?
17.7   Any victim of a tort has a cause of action in respect of his harm, although an action for harm suffered by a minor is brought by the minor's 'next friend' (usually the child's parent or guardian).

A minor has a cause of action for injuries incurred before birth, for example, physical deformities which can be proved to have been caused by a road accident. However, the right of a child to sue for injuries received before birth is limited to those cases where the alleged tortfeasor was responsible for an event affecting a parent of the child (obviously this is most likely to be the mother) and would have been liable to that parent in tort[1].

1   Congenital Disabilities (Civil Liability) Act 1976.

17.8   The death of a tort-victim does not preclude a tort claim which arose before death being continued by the deceased's estate[1]. The only exception to this is defamation when, for unconvincing reasons, the death of the victim or the tortfeasor terminates any action for defamation even if legal proceedings have already begun. If formal legal proceedings have not been begun before the death of the victim, the deceased's representatives have six months from the death in which to commence proceedings[2].

Causing death does not in itself give rise to any claim in tort. However, if the death of a person is attributable to a tortious act, the Law Reform (Miscellaneous Provisions) Act 1934 provides that the death of the victim does not preclude an action for damages. In addition to any liability under the 1934 Act to his victim, a tortfeasor who causes death may incur liability to the dependants of the deceased under the Fatal Accidents Act 1976.

1   Law Reform (Miscellaneous Provisions) Act 1934, s 1.
2   As with most tort claims, the representatives will seek to settle the action out of court but it may be wise to issue a protective writ or summons in good time lest settlement proves elusive.

The Law Reform (Miscellaneous Provisions Act) 1934
17.9   As we have mentioned above, this Act provides that almost every existing cause of action in tort survives the death of the tort victim. However, most claims under this Act are actions by the estate of a person whose death was

caused by a tortious act or omission in respect of that tort. Thus, if P is knocked down and killed by a negligent driver, D, P's estate can seek damages from D (any award of damages being paid by D's insurers if he has insurance, and otherwise by the MIB) and any damages paid are distributed in accordance with P's will or under the rules of intestacy. In assessing the damages payable, sums are awarded for the pain and suffering[1] and expenses incurred by the victim and for any loss of earnings suffered by the deceased between the date of the tort and his death. Hence, if death is instantaneous nothing is awarded to the estate. Thus, in *Hicks v Chief Constable of the South Yorkshire Police*[2], it was held that the pain and mental agony suffered by the deceased victims in the seconds leading up to their deaths by crushing did not give rise to an actionable head of loss; they were part of the death itself.

Any damages awarded under this Act can be reduced if the deceased contributed to his own death[3].

1 For assessment of damages see paras 21.29–21.39, below; exemplary damages cannot be awarded.
2 [1992] 2 All ER 65, HL; one of the 'Hillsborough Disaster' cases.
3 For contributory negligence as a defence see paras 21.11–21.15, below.

The Fatal Accidents Act 1976

17.10   This Act provides that dependants[1] whose breadwinner has been killed by the tortious acts of another can recover damages from the tortfeasor. Damages are recoverable only if the deceased could have sued for his injuries had he survived. Their purpose is to compensate the dependants for the disappearance of the person on whom they were dependent[2]. It must be stressed that damages are not awarded to dependent relatives simply because they fall into that category. Recovery is possible only where they were actually dependent on the deceased. Hence, damages are not awarded to dependants for any pain and suffering of the deceased but are awarded for that portion of future earnings which he would have expended on his dependent relatives.

In awarding damages the Act provides that no reduction is to be made in respect of any benefits accruing to dependants because of the death. Thus, insurance moneys, pensions and sums awarded to the deceased's estate under the Law Reform (Miscellaneous Provisions) Act 1934, for example, are ignored in assessing damages under this Act. Damages awarded to dependent relatives will be reduced if the deceased contributed to his own death[3].

1 Dependants are defined in s 1 and include a spouse, certain long-term cohabitees, children (including illegitimate children) and parents.
2 A claim may also be brought, but only by a spouse or parents of the deceased, for 'bereavement'. An award is not conditional upon proof of dependency. The sum awarded for bereavement is fixed by statute; at present it is £7,500.
3 For the defence of contributory negligence see paras 21.11–21.15, below.

Who can be sued in tort?

17.11   As a general rule any tortfeasor, whether a natural or legal person[1], is capable of being sued in tort, although there are exceptions[2], and the death of a tortfeasor does not prevent an action subsisting at his death (except one for defamation) from continuing against his estate.

In addition to the ability to sue a tortfeasor, it may be possible to sue a person who, while not a tortfeasor himself, is regarded in law as responsible for the tortfeasor. It is this latter principle, vicarious liability, by virtue of which the victim of a tort may be able to recover damages from a person other than the tortfeasor. In particular, the principle of vicarious liability permits tort-victims to sue employers (who are generally insured) for certain torts committed by their employees.

1   A company is a legal person; see para 2.5, above.
2   See, eg, para 2.3, above, paras 18.33–18.36, below.

Joint tortfeasors
17.12   Apart from vicarious liability, there may be joint liability for damage caused tortiously so that there is more than one potential defendant. If two or more persons, acting in pursuance of a common design or in the same incident, cause injury they are joint tortfeasors. For example, if D and D2 jointly contribute a defamatory article or jointly conduct a negligent audit, they are joint tortfeasors. Similarly, if D driving carelessly collides with D2, who is also driving carelessly, with the result that a passenger in D's car is injured, both D and D2 are liable.

However, if more than one person inflicts damage upon a victim but their torts are independent, each is responsible for the damage he has inflicted. For example, if D knocks down and injures P through negligent driving and D2 publishes a defamatory statement alleging that P's injuries were caused in a drunken brawl, D and D2 both incur liability in respect of their own torts but there are no joint tortfeasors and there is no joint liability[1].

1   See also paras 17.28–17.35, below, for a situation where two defendants incur separate liability in respect of the same incident.

17.13   Where there is joint liability, the tortfeasors are jointly and severally liable to their victim. Thus, the victim of a joint tort can sue all (or some) of the tortfeasors in a joint action with one sum being awarded by way of damages[1]. When the plaintiff sues all potential joint tortfeasors, the judge must determine whether the plaintiff has a cause of action and, if he has, assess the amount of damages to which the plaintiff is entitled, taking into account any contributory negligence manifested by the plaintiff. Having arrived at a figure for damages[2], the judge will, if the defendants so desire, determine the relative responsibility of the defendants for the injuries caused and order that responsibility for the payment of damages be similarly split[3].

Because the liability of joint tortfeasors is several as well as joint it is possible, if unusual, for a plaintiff to sue each joint tortfeasor in turn until he has recovered his damages. However, such a plaintiff would probably be required to pay the costs of any actions after the first.

1   *Wah Tat Bank Ltd v Chan* [1975] AC 507, [1975] 2 All ER 257, PC. Suing all potential defendants in one action is the usual practice.
2   This amount being reduced, where appropriate, to reflect any contributory negligence on the part of the plaintiff; see paras 21.11–21.15, below.
3   *Fitzgerald v Lane* [1989] AC 328, [1988] 2 All ER 961, HL. When the judge apportions responsibility for payment of the damages he is determining the issue of contribution which we discuss in the next paragraph.

17.14   Instead of suing all (or some) of the defendants in one action (or all of them in turn) the victim of a joint tort may choose to sue and successfully obtain damages from one tortfeasor (the richest or the one who carries insurance perhaps). In such a situation, that tortfeasor can subsequently obtain contribution from his fellow tortfeasors provided that they too were liable in respect of the same damage to the plaintiff[1]. The amount of contribution payable by any joint tortfeasor can be fixed by the court at such level (anything from nought to 100%) as it considers just and equitable, having regard to the relative responsibility of that tortfeasor for the injuries caused to the victim. However, the sum awarded as contribution cannot exceed the sum which the joint tortfeasor would have been liable to pay the plaintiff had the plaintiff sued him directly[2].

A joint tortfeasor against whom an award has been made may have a right to an indemnity (a right to have the sum reimbursed) from a third party and this is not lost where the third party is also a joint tortfeasor.

A claim for contribution is statute-barred after two years.

1   Civil Liability (Contribution) Act 1978, s 1. 'Liable' in this context means that the person from whom contribution is sought has been or could potentially be held liable (disregarding any technical procedural bars which might preclude actual liability) in an English court applying English or any appropriate foreign law, see *Birse Construction Ltd v Haiste Ltd* [1996] 2 All ER 1, [1996] 1 WLR 675, CA.
2   For example, D2's liability to pay damages might be restricted by a valid exemption clause or by a provision of foreign law.

Vicarious Liability

17.15   Vicarious liability enables the victim of a tort to sue a person standing in a particular relationship to the tortfeasor, provided that the commission of the tort is referable to that relationship. An example of a relationship giving rise to vicarious liability is that of employer and employee; an employer is vicariously liable for torts committed by an employee in the course of his employment. To a lesser extent, a principal may be vicariously liable for the torts of his agent. An employer is not vicariously liable for the torts of his independent contractor. However, in a limited number of situations an employer is personally liable for the tortious conduct of his appointed, independent contractor[1].

In addition to vicarious liability, an employer who specifically authorises or ratifies a tortious act committed by an employee of his is also personally liable for that tort. Whether an employer has authorised or ratified his employee's tort is a question of fact.

Further, a person, such as an employer, who owes a duty to an employee, X, will incur tortious liability for a breach of that duty which results in injury to X. This is so even where the breach of duty consists of failing to ensure that other employees do not jeopardise the safety of X. This is not vicarious liability for the acts of the other employees but primary liability for failing to operate a safe workplace[2].

If a person is vicariously liable for the torts of the tortfeasor this does not make him a tortfeasor, nor does it exempt the tortfeasor from liability; it merely enables the victim to choose the person whom he wishes to sue. Since an employer or principal will generally be better able (perhaps because of insurance) to satisfy a judgment made against him than would the tortfeasor, the victim of the tort will usually choose to sue the employer or principal. Where there is no vicarious liability at common law, responsibility for the torts of another may be imposed by statute. Police officers are not the employees of their chief constable but, by virtue of the Police Act 1996[3], he is liable for torts committed by them in the performance of their duties. Any damages awarded against a chief constable are payable out of public funds.

1   See paras 17.28–17.35, below.
2   For employers' liability see, paras. 19.2–19.9, below.
3   Section 88.

17.16   The advantages for the plaintiff in being able to sue a person better able than the tortfeasor to satisfy any judgment are obvious. Moreover, it is arguably more sensible for an employer to bear the responsibility of paying for damage caused by his employees, in that the employer can spread the cost among his customers or take out insurance for his complete workforce at relatively modest cost.

Furthermore, since it is the employer who chooses his staff, controls the workplace and the organisation of his business and has overall charge of safety, it seems appropriate that he should be responsible, either personally or vicariously, when things go awry.

Employers and employees
17.17   Because employers are vicariously liable for the torts of their employees committed in the course of their employment in situations when they would not incur liability for the torts of their independent contractors, it is necessary to determine whether a particular tortfeasor is or is not an employee. Additionally, it is necessary to determine who is the employer of the tortfeasor and whether the tortfeasor was or can be deemed to have been acting in the course of his employment when he committed the tort. It is to these three issues which we now turn.

Who is an employee?
17.18   In many cases there is no difficulty in deciding whether a person is an employee. The courts have stressed that, while each case turns on its own facts, it is usually obvious whether or not a person is an employee (employed under a contract of employment) rather than an independent contractor (engaged under a contract for services). Where the nature of the relationship is not clear, various factors may be considered, particularly what the parties call their relationship.

In early cases, the courts sought to identify the contract of employment by reference to the 'control test': if the employer controls not only where and when the work is done, but also *how* it is done, the contract is one of employment. Control in this sense is not nowadays regarded as a decisive test of general application, because it is inappropriate when one is dealing with a man with some particular skill[1]. While the employer of a labourer may be in a position to control the manner in which he carries out his tasks, the employer of someone such as a ship's captain or an engineer will rarely have the expertise to do so. There remain, however, other circumstances surrounding a contract of employment in which control in the broad sense may be expected to be found, such as control over what the employee is to do and when and where it is to be done[2].

The trend today is away from the test of control and in favour of the test of whether the work is integrated into the employer's business, or whether it is only accessory to it, being done by the worker as a person in business on his own account[3]. When deciding whether a particular worker is performing his work as a person in business on his own account, the court should consider all aspects of the relationship, including the element of control, whether the person provides his own equipment, whether he hires his own helpers, what degree of financial risk he takes, what degree of responsibility for investment and management he has, and whether and how far he has an opportunity of profiting from sound management in the performance of his task[4]. In the leading case of *Ready Mixed Concrete (South East) Ltd v Minister of Pensions and National Insurance*[5], the court held that a driver who worked for the company was not an employee and that therefore the company was not liable to pay national insurance contributions in respect of him. Considerations which influenced the court were that, by arrangement with the company, the driver hire-purchased the vehicle he operated; that, although the vehicle was in the company's livery and could only be used on the company's business, the driver was responsible for repairs; and that the driver could delegate his task and was paid by reference to mileage and deliveries.

An illustration of the difficulty which may be encountered in determining the status of a person is provided by considering the case of a ship's pilot. In *Esso Petroleum Co Ltd v Hall Russell & Co Ltd*[6], the House of Lords held that a ship's pilot was an independent professional man who navigated a ship as a principal and not as an employee of his general employer.

1   *Morren v Swinton and Pendlebury Borough Council* [1965] 2 All ER 349, [1965] 1 WLR 576.
2   *Wickens v Champion Employment* [1984] ICR 365, EAT.
3   *102 Social Club and Institute Ltd v Bickerton* [1977] ICR 911, EAT.
4   *Market Investigations Ltd v Minister of Social Security* [1969] 2 QB 173, [1968] 3 All ER 732; *Lee Ting Sang v Chung Chi-Keung* [1990] 2 AC 374, PC.
5   [1968] 2 QB 497, [1968] 1 All ER 433.
6   [1989] AC 643, [1989] 1 All ER 37, HL. Followed in *The Cavendish* [1993] 2 Lloyd's Rep 292, despite the obligation imposed on the Port of London by the Pilotage Act 1987 to provide a properly authorised pilot.

Who is the employer?

17.19   Identifying the employer of an employee who has committed a tort is rarely a problem. However, an employee who works for employer A, his usual or general employer, may be lent or hired to employer B, his temporary employer, for a period of time or for a particular purpose. If the employee commits a tort while working for employer B, the courts have to decide which employer is to compensate the tort-victim. In *Mersey Docks and Harbour Board v Coggins and Griffiths (Liverpool) Ltd*[1], the House of Lords attempted to formulate some guidelines for the courts. In this case, a crane driver and his crane were hired by the Harbour Board to Coggins under a contract which provided that the crane driver was to be the employee of Coggins, although the Harbour Board continued to be responsible for paying his wages. Coggins told the crane driver what they required to be done but did not attempt to instruct him how to operate his crane. In carrying out Coggins' instructions, the crane driver injured X when he operated his crane negligently. The Harbour Board, the general employer, was held vicariously liable for its crane driver's tort. The House of Lords held that, unless the general employer clearly established otherwise, he should be the employer held vicariously liable to the tort-victim. Further, the general employer does not necessarily avoid vicarious liability by providing in his contract with the temporary employer that the employee is the employee of the temporary employer. The House stated that the most important factor, in determining who is to be vicariously liable, is who controlled the way the employee was to work; but other relevant factors are who paid his wages and who was entitled to dismiss him. Obviously, the less skilled the employee, the more likely it is that the temporary employer controls the way in which the employee works and therefore the more likely it is that the temporary employer is vicariously liable.

1   [1947] AC 1, [1946] 2 All ER 345, HL.

17.20   The effect of a clause in the contract which 'lends' the employee, providing either that the borrowed employee shall be the employee of the temporary employer or that the employee's actions are the sole responsibility of the temporary employer, must be construed by the court. As we have said in the previous paragraph, such a clause will generally not absolve the general employer from liability to the tort-victim. However, such a clause may be construed either as an indemnity clause which permits the general employer to seek an indemnity from the temporary employer, or as an exemption clause which, being subject to the Unfair Contract Terms Act 1977, may be ineffective against the temporary employer[1]. In *Thompson v T Lohan (Plant Hire) Ltd*[2], the Court of Appeal held that where the clause clearly displayed an intention by the parties to transfer liability to the temporary employer for an employee's negligence it was effective in so doing between the parties. Hence, in this case, the general employer, who was liable to compensate the widow of an employee killed by the negligence of a fellow employee, could claim an indemnity from the temporary employer for whom the tortfeasor was working at the time of the accident, on the basis that the contract under which the employee was lent clearly manifested such an intention[3]. However, even where the contract does manifest such an intention, the general employer will not be able to obtain an indemnity from the temporary employer if he was himself in breach of the contract by supplying an incompetent employee[4].

1   Paras 10.43–10.48, above.
2   [1987] 2 All ER 631, [1987] 1 WLR 649, CA.
3   Compare *Phillips Products Ltd v Hyland* [1987] 2 All ER 620, [1987] 1 WLR 659n, CA, in which the relevant clause was construed as being an exemption clause which was unreasonable

and therefore ineffective under the Unfair Contract Terms Act 1977, s 2(2). In this case it was the temporary employer's premises which had been damaged by the employee's negligence and had the clause been construed as an indemnity clause it would have deprived the tort-victim (the temporary employer) of any remedy.

4 *McConkey v Amec plc* (1990) 27 Con LR 88, CA.

Course of employment

17.21 An employer is only vicariously liable for torts committed by his employees while they were acting in the course of their employment. An employee is acting in the course of his employment if the act which constitutes the tort is committed in the course of a *task*:

a. expressly authorised by his employer[1]; or
b. impliedly authorised by his employer; or
c. incidental to the performance of an authorised task; or
d. which was being performed by a method, even if an improper method, of carrying out an authorised task.

If an employee departs so radically from what he is authorised to do, or adopts a method of performance which is so totally different from that authorised that he can no longer be regarded as acting in the course of his employment, his employer ceases to be vicariously liable for his torts; the employee is 'on a frolic of his own'. For example, when firemen, in pursuance of an industrial dispute, drove to a fire to which they had been summoned, both with innumerable stops and extremely slowly, the Privy Council ruled that the firemen had departed so radically from their authorised task (to drive to fires as expeditiously as possible) that they were no longer acting in the course of their employment. In consequence, their employer was not liable to the person whose premises had burnt down and which might have been saved had the fire brigade attended the fire at normal speed[2].

1 The employer is vicariously liable when he has expressly authorised his employee to undertake a particular act or task and the employee commits a tort in carrying out his instructions. The employer is personally liable (jointly with the employee) if he expressly authorises his employee to commit a tort.

2 *General Engineering Services Ltd v Kingston and St Andrew Corpn* [1988] 3 All ER 867, [1989] 1 WLR 69, PC.

17.22 *Authorised task* While engaged on tasks expressly authorised by his employer, an employee is acting in the course of his employment.

An employee also acts in the course of his employment if he is doing something impliedly authorised by his employer. Whether he is or not, is a question of fact and previous cases can do no more than illustrate the type of approach adopted by the courts.

In *Staton v National Coal Board*[1], a first-aid attendant was held to have been acting in the course of his employment while cycling across his employer's premises to collect his pay. Similarly, an employee may be impliedly authorised to go to the lavatory, have tea-breaks and meals etc. In such cases he is almost certainly acting in the course of his employment while engaged on these activities if they are undertaken on the employer's premises. Indeed, an employer may be vicariously liable for torts committed by employees during such activities while not on his premises if it is reasonable for the employee to be off-site, for example to go for meals etc. In *Harvey v R G O'Dell Ltd²*, an employee who had been sent on an all-day job was held to have been acting in the course of his employment when driving off to lunch. However, in *Hilton v Thomas Burton (Rhodes) Ltd³*, employees who took a tea-break seven miles from their work-site were not so acting when they had an accident in their employer's van on the return journey. The tea-break was authorised and so was use of the van but, on the facts, particularly the fact that the employees had decided to finish working for the day and fill in the time before going home by taking a break, this journey was not in the course of their employment.

Normally, an employee is not acting in the course of his employment when he is travelling to work but an employee who is 'on duty' while travelling to or between particular places of work, for example, a travelling salesman, is acting in the course of his employment. Whether an employee is 'on duty' while travelling depends upon the facts of the case. In *Smith v Stages⁴*, X and the defendant, S, were employed by D Ltd as peripatetic laggers. X and S were working at one site when D Ltd instructed them to carry out urgent work at another site in South Wales. They were paid wages for their travelling time (there and back) and given their train fare for the journey but were not required to travel by train. S gave X a lift to and from Wales in his car and, during the return journey, and because of S's negligence, the car crashed and X was injured. S was uninsured and the question was whether D Ltd was vicariously liable for S's negligence. The House of Lords held that, on the facts, particularly that travelling was in the employer's time, S was acting in the course of his employment when the accident occurred and that consequently D Ltd was liable to X. Receipt of wages for travelling time was, the House of Lords held, indicative that the employee was travelling in the employer's time.

1 [1957] 2 All ER 667, [1957] 1 WLR 893.
2 [1958] 2 QB 78, [1958] 1 All ER 657.
3 [1961] 1 All ER 74, [1961] 1 WLR 705.
4 [1989] AC 928, [1989] 1 All ER 833, HL.

17.23 *Authorised task in an unauthorised manner* In determining whether an employee was carrying out an authorised task in an unauthorised manner the court must determine what the employee was engaged to do and then decide whether the tort was committed while performing that task. As with impliedly authorised tasks, whether the employee is merely doing an authorised task in an unauthorised manner or whether he has ceased to do the task at all is a question of fact and differentiating between cases is not always easy, as is shown by comparing the two following cases.

In the first¹, the employer of a petrol-tanker driver was held vicariously liable for a fire caused by its driver casting aside a match, which he had used to light a cigarette, while delivering petrol to a garage. The driver was engaged to deliver petrol and the tort was committed while performing this task even though his method of performance was patently not what his employers had authorised². In contrast, a bus conductor who caused an accident while negligently driving a bus was held not to have been acting in the course of his employment; he was not authorised to drive buses at all[3]. However, the bus company could have been liable if its driver had negligently allowed the conductor to drive the bus, because then the *driver* could have been performing his authorised task in an unauthorised manner[4].

1 *Century Insurance Co Ltd v Northern Ireland Road Transport Board* [1942] AC 509, [1942] 1 All ER 491, HL.
2 See also *General Engineering Services Ltd v Kingston and St Andrew Corpn* [1988] 3 All ER 867, [1989] 1 WLR 69, PC, discussed in para 17.21, above.
3 *Beard v London General Omnibus Co* [1900] 2 QB 530, CA.
4 In *Ilkiw v Samuels* [1963] 2 All ER 879, [1963] 1 WLR 991, the Court of Appeal held vicariously liable the employer of a lorry driver who had negligently allowed an incompetent person to drive the lorry.

17.24 Disregard of the express instructions of the employer does not necessarily take an employee out of the course of his employment. In every case the court must decide whether ignoring instructions means that the employee is merely doing an authorised task in an unauthorised manner or has ceased to do an authorised task. Thus, in *Limpus v London General Omnibus Co Ltd*[1], the employer was held vicariously liable for damage to the plaintiff's bus, which had been caused by its employee (a bus driver) racing his bus contrary to the employer's express instructions. The employee was employed to drive buses and, therefore, the employer was liable for torts committed while he was driving buses, even if his method of driving was not an authorised method. Similarly, in *Rose v Plenty*[2], the employers of a milkman were vicariously liable for the injuries caused to the plaintiff by their employee's negligent driving of his milk-float. This was so even though the plaintiff was a child whom the milkman, contrary to express instructions, was using as an assistant. The Court of Appeal held that the milkman, by disregarding his instructions, had not ceased to be acting on behalf of his employer and was still seeking to benefit the employer.

On the other hand, in *Kooragang Investments Pty Ltd v Richardson and Wrench Ltd*[3], the defendant employer was held not to be vicariously liable for the negligent survey reports produced for X Ltd by its employee, R. R had not produced the report in the course of his employment because he had been specifically instructed by his employer not to do work for X Ltd. This instruction was known to X Ltd, of whom R was a director, and indeed all the paperwork surrounding the survey had been done by staff of X Ltd on X Ltd's premises.

1 (1862) 1 H & C 526, Ex Ch.
2 [1976] 1 All ER 97, [1976] 1 WLR 141, CA.
3 [1982] AC 462, [1981] 3 All ER 65, PC.

17.25 Determining whether the employer is vicariously liable for an employee's torts when the employee committed the tort intentionally or for his own benefit or purpose is a difficult question of fact.

An employer has been held vicariously liable for a blow given by a carter to a boy whom he suspected of stealing sugar from his employer's cart[1] (a misplaced attempt to do his job) and for assaults by bouncers who attacked a person after he had kicked and broken a door at the employer's premises[2]. In contrast, the employer was not vicariously liable for an assault committed by a bus conductor on a passenger who had remonstrated with the conductor for swearing at him[3].

Vicarious liability can arise when an employee, in purporting to do his job steals money or property from the employer's clients. However, it cannot be stressed enough that it is always a question of fact as to whether the employee was purporting to do his job at the relevant time and was thus acting in the course of his employment. In *Lloyd v Grace, Smith & Co*[4], a clerk, who defrauded clients of the solicitors for whom he worked, had been held out by them as having authority to engage in the type of transaction which he misused for his own purposes; it was held that, when defrauding the clients, the clerk had been acting in the course of his employment. In contrast, in *Heasmans v Clarity Cleaning Co Ltd*[5], the employer of a cleaner who illegally used the telephone at offices which he was employed to clean was not vicariously liable. Using the telephone was not something the cleaner was authorised to do at all.

1   *Poland v John Parr & Sons* [1927] 1 KB 236, CA.
2   *Vasey v Surrey Free Inns* [1995] CLY 3735, CA; the court regarded the employees acts as a reaction to the damage to the employer's property and not a private quarrel.
3   *Keppel Bus Co Ltd v Sa'ad Bin Ahmad* [1974] 2 All ER 700, [1974] 1 WLR 1082, PC. This was regarded as effectively a private quarrel.
4   [1912] AC 716, HL.
5   [1987] ICR 949, [1987] IRLR 286, CA.

Principal and agent[1]

17.26   A principal is vicariously liable for torts committed by his agent when the agent is acting within his actual, usual or ostensible authority (which can be equated with acting within the course of employment)[2].

Difficult questions arise when the conduct of the agent benefits the agent but not his principal. A case in point is *Armagas Ltd v Mundogas SA, The Ocean Frost*[3]. In this case the House of Lords held that the defendant company was not vicariously liable for the fraudulent misrepresentation made to the plaintiff by the defendant company's employee/agent, X, that he had authority to negotiate tanker-charters. The appropriate test for the imposition of vicarious liability on a principal in respect of torts committed solely to benefit the agent was held to be whether the principal had by words or conduct induced the tort victim to believe that the agent was acting in the lawful course of his employment. If the belief that the agent has authority is induced by the agent himself (as in this case) there can be no liability imposed upon the principal.

1   Chap 23.
2   Paras 23.38–23.44, below; *Lloyd v Grace, Smith & Co* [1912] AC 716, HL; *Armagas Ltd v Mundogas SA, The Ocean Frost*, [1986] AC 717, [1986] 2 All ER 385, HL.
3   [1986] AC 717, [1986] 2 All ER 385, HL.

17.27   A vexed question is that of the relationship of a vehicle owner and a person who drives the vehicle with his permission but is not a named driver on the owner's insurance policy. If the driver is an agent, the principal (the car owner) is vicariously liable for an accident involving the vehicle, which was caused by the driver's negligence (so that the owner's insurers will have to pay any damages). It appears that the car driver is the agent of the car owner if he drives the car with the owner's permission and the owner has some interest or concern in the journey[1].

1   *Morgans v Launchbury* [1973] AC 127, [1972] 2 All ER 606, HL; *Ormrod v Crosville Motor Services Ltd* [1953] 2 All ER 753, [1953] 1 WLR 1120, CA.

Employers and independent contractors

17.28   An employer is not vicariously liable for torts committed by independent contractors whom he has engaged. However, *personal* liability is imposed on the employer in three situations when an independent contractor, commits a tort while undertaking the task which he was engaged to perform. Such liability is comparable with the vicarious liability of an employer for the torts of his employees, in that the employer is liable to pay the tort-victim for the damage arising from the tortious acts of his independent contractor. However, this liability is not vicarious. Liability arises because the employer himself is deemed to be in breach of a tortious duty; in other words, the employer is not merely (as with vicarious liability) responsible for the payment of damages because of the tort of another but is himself liable for his own wrong-doing. Just as with true vicarious liability (where the employee can be sued), the tort victim can choose to sue the independent contractor for his injuries if he wishes to do so.

17.29   The three situations in which an employer incurs personal liability in respect of torts caused by his independent contractor are:

a.   when the employer has failed to take adequate care to ensure that the contractor whom he has engaged is competent to undertake the task he is required to do;
b.   when the task which the independent contractor is engaged to undertake is a 'non-delegable duty';
c.   when the employer condones the commission of a tort by his independent contractor[1]. In this case, the employer is a joint tortfeasor.

In the first two cases, which we discuss in the following paragraphs, the employer incurs liability only if the tort was caused while the contractor was engaged on the task he was employed to perform.

1   *D & F Estates Ltd v Church Comrs for England* [1989] AC 177, [1988] 2 All ER 992, HL. It is not certain whether an employer's knowledge of the commission of a tort by his independent contractor in carrying out the relevant task is in itself condonation.

Negligent selection of contractor

17.30   An employer may incur personal liability to a tort victim injured by his independent contractor if he failed to take adequate care in the selection and instruction of that contractor.

An employer will be in breach of his duty (to select and instruct with adequate care) if:

a.   he does not use due care to see that his contractor is properly qualified for the task entrusted to him;
b.   he fails to give the contractor adequate instructions in relation to matters not within the contractor's professional knowledge but incidental to the task for which the contractor is engaged[1]; and
c   he fails adequately to supervise the work being done. The degree of supervision required depends upon the expertise of the contractor and the complexity of the task but it is generally permissible to assume a properly selected contractor knows what he should be doing.

A person may be contractually obliged to undertake a particular task and engage a sub-contractor to perform it for him; for example, a builder may employ specialist plasterers. Having selected the sub-contractor with due care, there is no further obligation imposed on the builder in such cases to instruct or supervise the sub-contractor and hence no liability if the sub-contractor does his job negligently[2]. However, a builder's contract with his client may expressly or impliedly provide for a continuing degree of instruction or supervision and failure to provide this, if it results in the sub-contractor performing his task negligently, will mean that the builder is personally in breach of contract.

1   *Robinson v Beaconsfield RDC* [1911] 2 Ch 188, CA.
2   *D & F Estates Ltd v Church Comrs for England* [1989] AC 177, [1988] 3 All ER 992, HL.

Non-delegable duties
17.31   The expression 'non-delegable duty', while hallowed by time, is extremely misleading. 'Non-delegable' in this context does not mean that *performance* of the relevant duty cannot, in fact, be delegated but that if performance *is* delegated the employer cannot escape liability if the duty is not properly performed by his independent contractor[1]. What constitutes improper performance by the independent contractor, and hence what may render the employer liable, varies depending on the duty involved.
There appears to be no consistent principle which determines whether a duty (or more accurately liability for breach of the duty) is non-delegable or not; in the following paragraphs we discuss some examples of such duties.

1   For an important re-statement of this fundamental point, see *McDermid v Nash Dredging and Reclamation Co Ltd* [1987] AC 906, [1987] 2 All ER 878, HL.

17.32   *Operations on a highway*   If an independent contractor is engaged to work on or under the highway, the employer is liable for any tortious activities or omissions of the contractor which are referable to the task for which he was engaged and which cause damage[1]. This liability does not extend to activities carried on near a highway[2], even if the negligence of the independent contractor results in injury to road users[2].

1   *Tarry v Ashton* (1876) 1 QBD 314.
2   *Salsbury v Woodland* [1970] 1 QB 324, [1969] 3 All ER 863, CA.

17.33   *Employer's liability*   We shall see in para 19.3, below, that an employer owes a duty of care in negligence to his employees. This duty, to see that the employees are reasonably safe, is not held to be discharged simply by entrusting the organisation of safety at work to an independent contractor, however competent. The employer remains liable if there is a breach of such duty either by himself or his employees or his independent contractors. Thus, if an employee is injured the general employer remains liable to him[1].

1 *Johnson v Coventry Churchill International Ltd* [1992] 3 All ER 14.

17.34 *Rylands v Fletcher and extra-hazardous activities* The conduct of his independent contractor may involve the employer in liability under the rule in *Rylands v Fletcher*[1], which we discuss in paras 20.26–20.28, below. This rule imposes liability on people who are responsible for things which the law defines as dangerous, which escape and cause injury.

By analogy with the rule in *Rylands v Fletcher*, an employer owes a duty of care to those likely to be affected by his pursuance of acts which clearly involve danger to others because of the dangerous equipment used or the inherently dangerous nature of the task to be performed. This duty, which involves a duty to see that care is taken, cannot be discharged merely by employing a competent independent contractor. In *Honeywill and Stein Ltd v Larkin Bros Ltd*[2], the plaintiffs engaged the defendant to take flashlight photographs of the interior of X's cinema; they were held liable when the defendant's negligent use of magnesium flash powder resulted in fire damage to the cinema.

1 (1866) LR 1 Exch 265.
2 [1934] 1 KB 191, CA.

17.35 *Strict statutory duties* Certain statutes impose liability on an employer for the defaults of his independent contractor. Examples may be seen in the Factories Act 1961 and the Consumer Protection Act 1987[1].

1 Paras 20.9-20.15, below.

Chapter 18

Negligence

18.1 Negligence is both a method of committing some torts and a tort in its own right. In this chapter we consider the tort of negligence, which is the most common tort.

To render the defendant liable for negligence, the plaintiff must prove three things:

a. that the defendant owed him a legal duty of care;
b. breach of that duty for which the defendant is responsible; and
c. that the harm suffered by him was caused by that breach.

For ease of exposition we divide the chapter into three sections reflecting these issues but there is considerable overlap between them and they should not be seen as watertight categories.

Duty of Care

18.2 In practice, the theoretical issue of whether a duty of care can be owed by the defendant to the plaintiff rarely arises in negligence actions, since once a court has determined that a legal duty of care does or does not arise in a particular context, a duty of care is imposed or denied in all subsequent cases on similar facts.

For example, normally a motorist or pedestrian who has suffered personal injury or damage to his property in a traffic accident can successfully sue the motorist who negligently caused the harm, since it is long established that motorists owe a duty of care to other road users and their property. Of course, in some cases an action may fail on the ground that a *particular* road user was not owed a duty of care[1].

In the immediately following paragraphs (18.3–18.7, below) we consider the general criteria for the imposition of a duty of care.

---

1 Perhaps because the pedestrian sprang out from behind a parked car; this could lead to a finding of no duty.

18.3 In determining whether the defendant owed the plaintiff a legal duty of care, the starting point must be the case which is the basis of the modern law of negligence: *Donoghue v Stevenson*[1]. In this case, while in a café, a friend of the appellant purchased a bottle of ginger beer which the appellant began to consume. It was then discovered that the bottle contained a partially decomposed snail: this occasioned shock to the appellant who claimed later to have developed gastro-enteritis. She could not sue in contract (since she had not bought the ginger beer), so she sued the manufacturers in tort. The House of Lords held that manufacturers of products could owe a duty of care not merely to those who bought the product but also to its user or consumer.

While this decision can be seen as the foundation of manufacturers' liability for products[2], the principal importance of the case is that Lord Atkin attempted to formulate general principles to determine when a duty of care could exist, the so-called 'neighbour test'. Lord Atkin said[3] that to found a duty of care there must be foreseeability of harm:

> 'you must take reasonable care to avoid acts or omissions which you can reasonably foresee would be likely to injure your neighbour. Who, then, in law is my neighbour? The answer seems to be – persons who are so closely and directly affected by my act that I ought reasonably to have them in contemplation as being so affected when I am directing my mind to the acts or omissions which are called in question.'

He also said[4] that for a duty to arise there must be a close and direct relationship of proximity between the person causing the harm and the person who suffers injury:

> 'I think that this sufficiently states the truth if proximity be not confined to mere physical proximity, but be used . . . to extend to such close and direct relations that the act complained of directly affects a person whom the person alleged to be bound to take care would know would be directly affected by his careless acts.'

Later cases have stressed that these dicta are not a statute and should not be construed as if they were[5], but they do provide broad general guidelines on the imposition of a duty of care.

A problem is whether Lord Atkin's dicta should apply whenever the issue of the existence or non-existence of a duty of care arises or whether it is limited to novel factual situations not previously litigated. Recent cases have held that the issue of whether there is a duty can be approached from first principles only when a novel situation is before the court[6].

They show that there are two concepts necessary for the creation of a duty: reasonable foreseeability and neighbourhood (which is now generally called proximity). Hence, in determining whether a duty of care exists a court should first consider whether there is a case in point which determines the existence or non-existence of a duty. If there is that determines the question. If there is no such case the plaintiff must establish that the harm suffered was reasonably foreseeable. If he fails to establish this, there is no duty. If he succeeds in establishing that the harm was reasonably foreseeable, he must then prove that he was sufficiently proximate. If the plaintiff can establish reasonable foreseeability and proximity, the court may still deny the existence of a duty (or modify it) on policy grounds[7].

The current trend is to consider novel situations as part of a process of incremental development by analogy with established categories.

1   [1932] AC 562, HL.
2   Paras 19.7–19.15, below.
3   [1932] AC 562 at 580.
4   Ibid, at 581.
5   *Home Office v DorsetYacht Co Ltd* [1970] AC 1004, [1970] 2 All ER 294, HL.
6   See particularly, *D & F Estates Ltd v Church Comrs for England* [1989] AC 177, [1988] 2 All ER 992, HL and *Murphy v Brentwood District Council* [1991] 1 AC 398, [1990] 2 All ER 908, HL.
7   *Caparo Industries Ltd v Dickman* [[1990] 1 AC 605, [1990] 1 All ER 568, HL. Policy arguments are sometimes deployed at the proximity stage to deny the existence of a duty.

Reasonable foreseeability

18.4   The first issue for consideration in determining whether the plaintiff was owed a duty of care, that of reasonable foreseeability, involves a consideration of whether a reasonable man, in the defendant's position, would have foreseen that his acts or omissions might adversely affect others. This test is an objective one; it is based on the foresight of the reasonable man.

For a duty of care to arise it is not necessary reasonably to foresee the particular plaintiff; it is sufficient that the plaintiff belongs to a reasonably foreseeable class, for example, pedestrians or the blind[1]. What is not entirely clear is what constitutes *reasonable* foreseeability; the cases are not consistent, some reasonable men are far-sighted, others are myopic but the weight of authority would seem to require the harm to be at least possible.

1   *Haley v London Electricity Board* [1965] AC 778, [1964] 3 All ER 185, HL.

Proximity

18.5   If the harm suffered is reasonably foreseeable, the plaintiff must then show that he was sufficiently proximate to be owed a duty of care. Proximity is not measured in geographical terms[1] but rather by reference to whether a reasonable man could have expected a particular person (the plaintiff) or class of persons to be adversely affected by any want of care on his part.

If the reasonably foreseeable harm suffered is physical injury, directly inflicted on the plaintiff (or his property) by the defendant, the courts are likely to find the plaintiff was sufficiently proximate[2]. However, where the defendant's alleged negligence is in failing to prevent a third party inflicting physical harm, foreseeability alone is not sufficient to establish a duty of care[3]; a strong degree of proximity between the defendant and the plaintiff must be proved.

When the harm suffered is economic loss, foreseeability alone is manifestly not sufficient and proximity is crucial. Obviously, a negligent act causing physical damage is likely to affect a limited number of people, whereas negligence, perhaps negligent advice, could, potentially, affect a large number. Hence, the courts have used proximity to limit the number of persons to whom a duty may be owed. For example, in *Yuen KunYeu v A-G of Hong Kong*[4], the

Privy Council refused to find that the Commissioner of Deposit-taking Companies in Hong Kong, whose statutory duty it was to register and license bodies who sought deposits, owed a duty of care to potential depositors. Thus, the plaintiff, who had invested money in a licensed company which had gone into liquidation, could not recover from the Hong Kong government the sum lost. The loss suffered might have been reasonably foreseeable in that the Commissioner could foresee that the continued registration of an uncreditworthy company might lead to the loss of investors' money but an unspecified group of potential investors could not be regarded as sufficiently proximate in the circumstances.

1 Although physical proximity may be relevant in deciding if the parties are 'neighbours', see *Home Office v Dorset Yacht Co Ltd* [1970] AC 1004, [1970] 2 All ER 294, HL.
2 *Mobil Oil Hong Kong Ltd v Hong Kong United Dockyards Ltd* [1991] 1 Lloyds Rep 309, PC; but see *Marc Rich & Co v Bishop Rock Marine Co Ltd* [1996] AC 211, [1995] 3 All ER 307, HL, where the court held that it was not fair, just and reasonable to find proximity between the parties. In this case the physical damage to property was classified as indirect.
3 For liability for omissions see para. 18.27, below.
4 [1988] AC 175, [1987] 2 All ER 705, PC. The Privy Council thought that it was not fair, just and reasonable to find proximity.

Policy
18.6 Proximity embraces a strong policy element, in that the courts may treat a plaintiff as insufficiently proximate where it is not fair, just or reasonable to impose a duty on the defendant[1]. However, even when the application of the proximity requirements seems to indicate the existence of a duty, the courts will deny its existence if policy so demands[2]. Thus, judges will use policy as a limiting factor, ie as a reason for limiting or negating a duty which prima facie arises by applying the tests of reasonable foreseeability and proximity.

In *McLoughlin v O'Brian*[3], for example, the majority of the House of Lords held that it is reasonably foreseeable that anyone who witnesses a car accident or the aftermath of a car accident will suffer nervous shock, in other words such persons are potentially owed a duty of care. However, the House then ruled that, on policy grounds, that the class who could sue a car driver who caused the accident was restricted. One Law Lord preferred to find that the reasonable man in such a case would reasonably foresee injury by nervous shock only to that restricted class and thus used policy to negate the existence of a duty at all. We return to the whole question of nervous shock in paras 18.20–18.23, below. More recently, in *Mulcahy v Ministry of Defence*[4], a soldier, who sued for injuries suffered during the Gulf War caused by the negligence of a fellow soldier rather than by the enemy, was denied a remedy. It was said that public policy requires that, when members of the armed forces of the Crown are engaged in the course of hostilities, they are under no duty of care in tort to each other.

1 See, for example, *Marc Rich & Co v Bishop Rock Marine Co Ltd* [1996] 1 AC 211, [1995] 3 All ER 307, HL. See also, para 17.5, above.
2 See for example, *Rondel v Worsley* [1969] 1 AC 191, [1967] 3 All ER 993, HL; para 18.34, below, (the judicial process), and *Calveley v Chief Constable of the Merseyside Police* [1989] AC 1228, [1989] 1 All ER 1025, HL, para 18.36, below (the police) are examples.

3   [1983] 1 AC 410, [1982] 2 All ER 298, HL. See also *Alcock v Chief Constable of the South Yorkshire Police* [1992] 1 AC 310, [1991] 4 All ER 907, HL.
4   [1996] 2 All ER 758, CA.

18.7   The principles enunciated in *Donoghue v Stevenson* and subsequently refined by the courts provide general guidance for determining whether a duty of care exists. However, the courts have identified a wide range of factors which may be regarded as relevant in determining whether a duty (or a modified duty) exists. It is not always clear whether these factors are relevant to the question of proximity (ie proximity will be denied if it is not fair, just and reasonable to find proximity) or to the general issue of whether policy requires the denial of a duty. Policy may also have a part to play in deciding if a harm is 'reasonably' foreseeable. Factors which may be relevant to a policy argument (wherever it arises) negating a duty are many. An example would be where the plaintiff is arguing that he should have been saved from his own folly[1] by the defendant. Another relevant factor would be whether the imposition of duty would lead to public bodies making decisions not in the public interest but with an eye to the avoidance of negligence claims[2]. Similarly, the courts have considered whether imposition of a duty on a public body would have such an effect on the finances of that body so that it was less able to carry out its functions for the benefit of all[3]. Other factors have included the existence of alternative remedies[4], and the existence of a public system of regulation of the acts or omissions of which the plaintiff complains. The existence of a web of contractual dealings which embrace the plaintiff and defendant, while not providing a direct contract between them, has also been treated as relevant[5].

A case which encapsulates foreseeability, proximity and policy is *Marc Rich & Co v Bishop Rock Marine Co Ltd*[6]. In this case, a ship owned by the defendants and carrying cargo belonging to the plaintiff developed a crack during a voyage. The ship was inspected by a surveyor acting for the ship's classification society, NKK, allowed to proceed after temporary repairs, but sank when the repairs failed; the cargo was lost. The issue for the House of Lords was whether a classification society owed a duty of care to the cargo owners. Classification societies are independent, non-profit-making entities, created and operating for the sole purpose of the collective welfare of mariners and ships, which inspect ships during building and at subsequent times to determine if a vessel reaches certain standards. Without classification a ship is economically uninsurable. The House, after considering foreseeability, proximity and policy, held no duty was owed.

We now turn to some areas where the existence, or not, of a duty of care has proved particularly problematic. They are three types of situation which have given rise to difficulties although they cannot be seen as watertight categories. In some cases the harm suffered is of a particular sort; in others the loss has been caused in a particular manner, and in others the defendant is regarded as particularly worthy of protection from suit. In some cases, it is a combination of factors which leads to the rejection of the existence of a duty of care.

1   For example, *Barrett v Ministry of Defence* [1995] 3 All ER 87, CA, para 21.4, below.
2   *Skinner v Secretary of State for Transport* (1995) Times, 3 January (no duty on coastguards), compare the fire brigade cases, para 18.27, below.

3   *X v Bedfordshire County Council* [1995] 2 AC 633, [1995] 3 All ER 353, HL, para 18.31, below.
4   *Olotu v Home Office* [1997] 1 All ER 385, CA. The possibility of alternative remedies did not preclude a duty of care in *Spring v Guardian Assurance plc* [1995] 2 AC 296, [1994] 3 All ER 129, HL, see para 18.9, below.
5   See para 18.70, below.
6   [1996] AC 211, [1995] 3 All ER 307, HL.

Economic loss

18.8   When a plaintiff sues successfully in negligence for injury to himself or his property, he is also entitled to recover damages for *consequential* economic loss, such as loss of earnings or the cost of repairing damaged goods. However, *pure* economic loss (financial loss unassociated with damage to property or person)[1] is generally irrecoverable[2]. The courts traditionally limit recovery for pure economic loss by finding that there was no duty not to cause the plaintiff such loss[3].

A case which illustrates the difference between pure economic loss and consequential loss is *Spartan Steel and Alloys Ltd v Martin & Co (Contractors) Ltd*[4]. In this case, the defendant's employees negligently severed an electricity cable leading to the plaintiff's factory. At the time when the electricity failed, the plaintiff was melting material in a furnace, and the melt was ruined. The plaintiff was able to recover for damage to the materials in the furnace (direct physical loss) and for the loss of profit on that melt (consequential economic loss) but not for the loss of profit on melts which could not take place because of the power failure (pure economic loss).

An illustration of the basic rule is provided by *Weller & Co v Foot and Mouth Disease Research Institute*[5]. The defendants negligently permitted the escape of foot and mouth virus; in consequence local cattle-markets were closed. The plaintiff cattle auctioneer's claim against the defendants for its foreseeable lost profits was dismissed by the court.

In the light of recent cases, particularly the decisions discussed in paras 18.11 and 18.12 below, the basis of some cases permitting recovery for pure economic loss, particularly *Ross v Caunters*[6], seem difficult to support. In *Ross v Caunters*, a beneficiary under a will, who was not entitled to her bequest because the deceased's solicitor had negligently failed to warn the deceased not to allow a spouse of a beneficiary to witness the will, succeeded in an action in negligence against the solicitor. However, in *White v Jones*[7], which has some factual similarities, the House of Lords held *Ross v Caunters* to be good law but indicated that they considered the case explicable on a different basis from that relied on by the judge, that is the application of the principles relating to negligent misstatements[8].

1   *Cattle v Stockton Waterworks Co* (1875) LR 10 QB 453; approved by the House of Lords in *Simpson v Thomson* (1877) 3 App Cas 279.
2   The most important exception concerns pure economic loss caused by negligent misstatements, see *Hedley Byrne & Co Ltd v Heller & Partners Ltd* [1964] AC 465, [1963] 2 All ER 575, HL discussed in paras 18.13–18.19, below.
3   It should be noted, however, that certain statutes, for example, the Fatal Accidents Act 1976, discussed in para 17.10, above, permit recovery for pure economic loss.

4   [1973] QB 27, [1972] 3 All ER 557, CA. See also *SCM (UK) Ltd v Whittal & Son Ltd* [1971]
    1 QB 337, [1970] 3 All ER 245, CA.
5   [1966] 1 QB 569, [1965] 3 All ER 560.
6   [1980] Ch 297, [1979] 3 All ER 580.
7   [1995] 2 AC 207, [1995] 1 All ER 691, HL
8   See paras 18.13–18.19, below.

18.9   There are two principal arguments put forward to justify the rule
disallowing recovery for pure economic loss. The first is that to permit actions
by persons who suffer only in the economic sense would be to open the
floodgates of litigation since, whereas physical damage resulting from an
incident will normally be limited in its extent, the financial consequences of a
single incident may well affect a large number of people. For example, an
incident which results in a failure in the supply of electricity may have serious
financial consequences for a large number of factories in the affected area,
their employees and their customers. However, it could be argued that the
rules concerning remoteness of damage[1] would adequately restrict the class of
potential plaintiffs.

The second justification is that the extent of any economic loss is not
foreseeable by the potential tortfeasor, whereas the potential victim will be
able to assess, and thus insure against, such loss. In reply, it could be argued
that it is illogical to distinguish between careless acts or omissions causing
physical damage to person or property and those causing economic damage, if
both types of harm are foreseeable.

It could be argued that the requirement that a duty of care can be owed
only to those who are sufficiently proximate would sufficiently restrict
recoverability for pure economic loss and that to have a special rule for such
cases is unjustifiable. In this respect, it is noteworthy that the major exception
at common law to non-recoverability for pure economic loss, which concerns
negligent misstatements, (paras 18.13–18.19, below), does not open up liability
to an indeterminate number but restricts recoverability to plaintiffs who have
an appropriate relationship with the defendant (a form a proximity test). The
'proximate' status of the plaintiff was also a factor in *Spring v Guardian Assurance
plc*[2] which was not argued on the basis of negligent misstatement. In this case,
the plaintiff, who was engaged in the financial services industry, sought
employment with X. X sought a reference from the plaintiff's former employer,
the defendant company. The defendant negligently provided an inaccurate
and damning reference. As a result, X (and others) declined to employ the
plaintiff. The House of Lords had no difficulty in finding that the loss of
employment (pure economic loss) was foreseeable and that the plaintiff was
sufficiently proximate, and it saw no reason of policy to prevent the success of
an action against the defendant by the plaintiff. Obviously, the plaintiff, and
perhaps the recipient of the reference, were the only parties proximate to the
defendant's wrongdoing – there was no unlimited class of potential litigants.

In the light of *Spring v Guardian Assurance plc* and *Henderson v Merrett
Syndicates Ltd*[3], which we discuss in paras 18.12 and 18.70, below, it could be
argued that general principles of negligence are applicable to pure economic
loss cases, albeit proximity and policy are enforced rigorously. Moreover, these

cases (and *White v Jones* which we discuss in paras 18.8 and 18.16) might be regarded as suggesting that, where a defendant assumes responsibility towards a plaintiff, a duty of care arises, which extends to a duty not to cause the plaintiff pure economic loss, by negligent acts or words. However, the extent to which the principles applicable to the imposition of liability based on the assumption of responsibility extend beyond cases involving negligent misstatements are not yet certain.

We now consider two areas where the force of the general rule at common law, that damages for pure economic loss are not recoverable, has been reiterated.

1   Discussed in paras 18.61–18.66, below.
2   [1995] 2 AC 296, [1994] 3 All ER 129, HL.
3   See paras 18.12 and 18.70, below.

Physical damage to property

18.10   Where a person's property (real or personal) is foreseeably damaged by a want of care and he has a cause of action in negligence and he can recover damages not merely for the cost of replacing or repairing the property but also for consequential economic loss[1]. However, this physical damage may cause economic loss only to a third party or to the person suffering physical injury and to a third party. In such cases, the third party so affected cannot recover in negligence.

Hence, for example, if a shipper negligently damages in transit goods which belong to X, but which are in the course of being sold to Y, who intends to resell them, Y will suffer loss of profit through inability to complete a sub-sale but Y has no cause of action. The House of Lords in *Leigh and Sillivan Ltd v Aliakmon Shipping Ltd*[2] held that a person in the position of Y has no cause of action against the shipper since he is not the owner of the goods even though his loss might be thought to be reasonably foreseeable and he is the only possible plaintiff, since the person suffering physical damage has no cause of action. In *Candlewood Navigation Corpn Ltd v Mitsui OSK Lines Ltd*[3], the Privy Council affirmed the principle that a person (in this case charterers of a ship) who is not the owner of a chattel but who has a right to use it has no cause of action for economic loss against a person who negligently damages that chattel[4].

Similarly, if X negligently damages Y's property so that Y's employees are laid off or suffer a reduction in wages, the employees cannot recover their losses from X.

1   Subject to the rules of remoteness, paras 18.61–18.66, below.
2   [1986] AC 785, [1986] 2 All ER 145, HL.
3   [1986] AC 1, [1985] 2 All ER 935, PC.
4   The High Court of Australia has permitted recovery when there was a close degree of proximity between the chattel-user and the tortfeasor: *Caltex Oil (Australia) Pty Ltd v Dredge Willemstad* (1976) 136 CLR 529.

Defective products

18.11   *Donoghue v Stevenson*[1] permitted a plaintiff to recover damages from a manufacturer of a defective product (ginger beer containing a snail) which had caused her injury. The House of Lords did not have to determine whether a plaintiff could recover damages if a product was defective, for example flat ginger beer, but had not caused physical injury to a person or to other property. The traditional view has always been that in such a case recovery of damages for defects in goods or services (pure economic loss) is limited to those cases where there is a contract between a supplier and consumer of those goods or services and that the only appropriate cause of action is for breach of contract[2].

After a period of uncertainty, the traditional view has been approved by the House of Lords in two cases – *D & F Estates Ltd v Church Comrs for England*[3] and *Murphy v Brentwood District Council*[4]. In *D & F Estates Ltd v Church Comrs for England*, a block of flats was discovered to have been built with inadequately keyed plaster which would inevitably fall off the walls unless replaced. The House of Lords held that the cost of repairing a defective chattel or structure was not recoverable in tort if the defect was discovered before it had caused damage to the person or property other than the product subject to the defect; the cost was irrecoverable pure economic loss. Hence, there could be no recovery for the cost of remedying the defective plaster-work. In reaching this decision the House of Lords distinguished one of its own decisions – *Junior Books Ltd v Veitchi Co Ltd*[5], which we discuss in para 18.12, below.

In *Murphy v Brentwood District Council*, the plaintiff had, in 1970, purchased from the construction company a house built on an in-filled site. The house had been built on a concrete raft foundation to guard against settlement and the plans for the foundations had been approved by the defendant local authority after advice from consulting engineers. In 1981, serious cracks developed in the house and it was discovered that the raft foundation had distorted due to differential settlement. The plaintiff could not afford the cost of repairs (£45,000) and in 1986 sold the house for £35,000 less than the market value of a comparable house in sound condition. The plaintiff's insurers compensated him and sued the local authority alleging negligence in approving the design. The House of Lords held that the local authority did not owe a duty of care to the plaintiff (or his insurers) for the cost of remedying a dangerous defect in a product – the house – before it caused physical injury. The House held that the damage suffered by a building owner or occupier in such circumstances was not physical damage but purely economic loss (since that damage consisted of the cost of either remedying the defect or abandoning the property as unfit for habitation). Furthermore, the House of Lords thought that, since a dangerous product becomes merely a defective product, once the risk of physical injury is discovered, to permit the owner (or occupier) to recover his economic loss would lead to an unacceptably wide category of claims in respect of products which were defective in quality. To allow such claims would, in effect, introduce product liability and transmissible warranties of quality into the law of tort when such issues were a matter for the law of contract.

The House did, however, hold in these cases that, where there was actual damage to persons or other property, the cost of repairing the defective product and rendering it safe was recoverable.

1 [1932] AC 562, HL.
2 See, eg, *Simaan General Contracting Co v Pilkington Glass Ltd (No 2)* [1988] QB 758, [1988] 1 All ER 791, CA; no recovery by contractors in tort for supply of usable but wrongly coloured glass; the contractor should sue sub-contractor in contract and sub-contractor should sue supplier.

3   [1989] AC 177, [1988] 2 All ER 992, HL.
4   [1991] 1 AC 398, [1990] 2 All ER 908, HL.
5   [1983] 1 AC 520, [1982] 3 All ER 201, HL.

18.12   There are some cases on pure economic loss which do not seem to fit into the conventional pattern. The leading example is *Junior Books Ltd v Veitchi Co Ltd*[1]. In this case the defendants were sub-contractors engaged to lay a floor in a factory; they had been nominated as sub-contractors by the plaintiffs (the factory owners) but the contract engaging their services was with the main contractor and not the plaintiffs. The floor was defective and had to be replaced (pure economic loss). The plaintiff claimed that the defendants owed them a duty of care and that, if a want of care could be proved, they could recover the cost of its replacement. A majority of the House of Lords held that a duty of care existed; there was a sufficient degree of proximity between plaintiffs and defendants. Their Lordships stressed that the defendants were not akin to a manufacturer producing goods for an unknown consumer. They were producing goods for a particular person whose identity was known to them, and who was relying on their skill and judgement as flooring contractors, and they must have realised the loss which the plaintiffs would suffer if the floor was, through a want of care on their part, defective. The situation was described as 'akin to contract'. Various attempts have been made to explain *Junior Books,* but none can be regarded as satisfactory; it is generally distinguished although it has not been overruled.

The idea that it was the almost contractual nature of the relationship which led to the imposition of liability must be treated with extreme caution. It is difficult to see why it could not apply in *Murphy* if this is the test. Further, in *Greater Nottingham Co-operative Society Ltd v Cementation Piling and Foundations Ltd*[2] the Court of Appeal regarded the existence of a contract between the owner of a building and a contractor as tending to militate against the existence of a tortious duty between them. The view was that the contract can be presumed to define the scope of any duty owed by the contractor and, since the contract imposed no liability for pure economic loss, the law of tort could not do so. As the Court of Appeal postulated, if there was no liability between contracting parties how could the existence of a relationship 'akin to contract' avail the plaintiff?

The existence of a chain of contracts embracing the plaintiff and defendant was, however, held not to preclude the creation of a tortious duty, in *Henderson v Merrett Syndicates Ltd*[3]. In this case, the plaintiffs were Lloyd's names (ie investors in the Lloyd's insurance market) who were members of syndicates managed by the defendant underwriting agents. They argued that they were owed a duty of care by the defendant underwriting agents. In some cases the names had a direct contract with the defendant underwriting agent, and in such cases it was held that a duty of care was owed to the names despite the existence of a contractual relationship. In other cases the names had a contract with members' agents who then placed business with the defendant underwriting agents who acted as sub-agents. It was held that the defendant underwriting agents acting as sub-agents had undertaken responsibility for the interests of the plaintiffs, who had relied on their professional expertise, and that there was no reason for the defendant underwriting agents' contract with the members' agents to limit the tortious duty which would otherwise be owed to the plaintiffs. The House of Lords based the defendant underwriting agents' liability on the fact that they had assumed responsibility towards the plaintiffs in rendering professional services to them and that the plaintiff had relied upon the defendant underwriting agents. The imposition of a duty of care on this basis[4] derives from the principles formulated in cases of negligent misstatements to which we now turn.

1   [1983] 1 AC 520, [1982] 3 All ER 201, HL.
2   [1989] QB 71, [1988] 2 All ER 971, CA. See, also, *Simaan General Contracting Co v Pilkington Glass Ltd (No 2)* [1988] QB 758, [1988] 1 All ER 791, CA, where there was a contract in respect of the supply of glass bricks between A and B and then between B and C – A was held to owe no duty of care to C.
3   [1995] 2 AC 145, [1994] 3 All ER 507, HL. See further, para 18.70, below.
4   It is arguable that general principles of negligence would have led to the same conclusion.

Negligent misstatements
18.13   There is no reason in principle why liability for negligent words should differ from liability for negligent conduct since both may give rise to a loss which is both reasonably foreseeable and suffered by a proximate plaintiff. Indeed, where negligent words cause physical injury, no difficulty has been experienced in finding that the person who uttered the words owed a duty of care to someone who suffered reasonably foreseeable physical injury after relying on them[1].

If negligent words cause pure economic loss, the rules on pure economic loss which we have just discussed would seem to preclude the existence of a duty of care. The policy arguments against a duty of care are obvious. Words are capable of wide dissemination and many may suffer from relying on negligent words. Consequently the courts at one time restricted[2] liability for words causing pure economic loss to cases where the defendant had committed the tort of deceit[3] or had a fiduciary[4] or contractual relationship with the victim of the loss, lest there would be a flood of litigation by those who had suffered economic loss in reliance on advice or information.

1   *Sharp v Avery and Kerwood* [1938] 4 All ER 85, CA.
2   See particularly *Derry v Peek* (1889) 14 App Cas 337, HL, and *Candler v Crane, Christmas & Co* [1951] 2 KB 164, [1951] 1 All ER 426, CA.
3   *Derry v Peek* (1889) 14 App Cas 337, HL; see para 14.20, above.
4   *Nocton v Lord Ashburton* [1914] AC 932, HL.

Hedley Byrne v Heller 1964
18.14   A major change of policy in respect of pure economic loss following negligent words occurred in 1963 in *Hedley Byrne & Co Ltd v Heller & Partners Ltd*[1]. In this case, the plaintiffs' bankers, on their clients' behalf, addressed inquiries to the defendant bankers as to the financial standing of a company called Easipower Ltd (who were clients of the defendants). The plaintiffs initiated these inquiries because they had entered into contracts on behalf of Easipower and, in the event of Easipower failing to meet their contractual obligations, the plaintiffs would be liable on them. The defendants' replies,

though somewhat non-committal, were sufficient to encourage the plaintiffs to continue their dealings with Easipower. Easipower went into liquidation and the plaintiffs became liable to pay some £17,661 due on the contracts. The replies made by the defendants to the inquiries as to the financial standing of Easipower were found to have been made carelessly and the House of Lords had to decide:

a.   whether the defendants could owe the plaintiffs a duty of care not to cause economic loss caused by negligent advice; and
b.   if such a duty of care could exist, whether such a duty actually existed in this case.

The House of Lords held, by a majority, that a duty of care could exist in relation to economic loss caused by negligent misstatements provided:

a.   that such a loss was reasonably foreseeable; and
b.   that there was also a 'special relationship' between the parties.

A 'special relationship' (now more commonly called an 'appropriate relationship') is a particular type of proximity and it embodies the idea that the plaintiff reasonably relied upon the advice given by the defendant.

However, the House held that on the facts no duty of care actually existed because the advice given by the defendants was prefaced by a disclaimer of responsibility for the accuracy of their replies.

1   [1964] AC 465, [1963] 2 All ER 575, HL.

18.15   *The disclaimer*   Since the Unfair Contract Terms Act 1977, such a disclaimer of responsibility for negligent advice made in the course of business is only effective to prevent a duty of care arising in respect of pure economic loss, and hence to exclude liability, in so far as such exclusion is reasonable[1].

In *Smith v Eric S Bush*[2], the House of Lords held that a surveyor, instructed and paid for by a potential lender of money on mortgage, owed to the potential purchaser of the property, who would be likely to rely on his report, a duty not to cause economic loss. The House then considered the effect of a disclaimer of responsibility and held that, on the facts of the case, the disclaimer was unreasonable. Factors which influenced their Lordships included the recognition that the purchase was at the lower end of the housing market where, it is well known, purchasers rarely seek surveys of their own, the recognition that the purchaser was, albeit indirectly, paying the fee of the surveyor instructed by the potential lender, the high cost of houses and the high interest rates payable by borrowers. The House indicated that in some circumstances, for example where the property purchased was commercial property or very expensive houses, where it would be prudent for the purchaser to obtain his own survey, it might be reasonable for the surveyor to limit or exclude his liability.

Consequently, it was not surprising that in *McCullagh v Lane Fox and Partners Ltd*[3], estate agents who had mis-described the size of the garden of a house sold for £875,000, were able to rely on a disclaimer of liability contained in the sale particulars.

1   Unfair Contract Terms Act 1977, s 2. The requirement of reasonableness is the same as that discussed in para 10.48, above.
2   [1990] 1 AC 831, [1989] 2 All ER 514, HL.
3   [1995] EGCS 195, CA.

When does an appropriate relationship arise?
18.16   There is a lack of judicial unanimity as to what is necessary to constitute an appropriate (or special) relationship which imposes liability on an advice-giver. The critical elements necessary for an appropriate relationship, and hence a duty of care, to arise delineated in *Hedley Byrne* were that:

a.   one person relies on the skill, judgement or advice of another, provided that such reliance is reasonable[1]; and
b.   the person giving the advice realises or should realise that his advice will be relied on by a particular person in a particular transaction and that, if the advice is given without due care, loss will be suffered.

In *Hedley Byrne* itself, the House of Lords found that the defendants could owe a duty of care to the plaintiffs, even though the plaintiffs did not address their request for information directly to the defendants, because the defendants realised that someone intended to rely on their replies.

Recent cases on negligent misstatements have stressed another element of the judgments in *Hedley Byrne* as determinative of the question of whether a duty of care has arisen – that is, was there a voluntary assumption of responsibility by the defendant. For example, in *Henderson v Merrett Syndicates Ltd*[2], it was said that:

'if a person assumes responsibility to another in respect of certain services, there is no reason why he should not be liable in damages for that other in respect of economic loss which flows from the negligent performance of those services.[3]'

Subsequently, in *White v Jones*[4], in which a solicitor was held to owe a duty of care to the intended beneficiaries of a will so that he was liable to compensate those intended beneficiaries who lost legacies as a result of his negligent delay in the drawing of his client's will[5], it was stated (though not by all members of the House) that the *Hedley Byrne* principle was based upon an assumption of responsibility. The approach taken in *White v Jones* manifests some difference of approach from that displayed in *Caparo Industries plc v Dickman*[6], a case of considerable importance for accountants.

In *Caparo Industries plc v Dickman*, Touche Ross were the auditors of a company, F Ltd, of which Dickman was a director and in which Caparo was a shareholder; they produced audited accounts for the year 1983–84. On the basis of those accounts, Caparo purchased further shares in the company and subsequently took it over. Caparo then discovered that the accounts were inaccurate and that F's financial position was less favourable than that shown. Caparo sued, alleging that they were owed a duty of care by the auditors which

Touche Ross had broken. The House of Lords decided that Touche Ross did not owe a duty of care to Caparo. It ruled that no duty is owed by an auditor to persons who use information provided by the audit unless it can be shown that the auditor knew the information so provided would be communicated to the person who has relied on it for a particular transaction and that that person would be very likely to rely on it for the purpose of deciding whether to enter into the transaction. Unless the auditor is aware that a particular shareholder or group of shareholders will rely on the accounts in respect of a particular transaction he does not owe them a duty. The mere fact that he is the auditor of a company does not create a relationship of proximity with potential investors or existing shareholders. Their Lordships made it plain that an auditor owes no duty to potential investors in the company since there is insufficient proximity between the auditor and the investor. Further, the auditor owes no duty to an existing shareholder in the relevant company who wishes to buy more shares, since the purpose of an audit is not to facilitate investment decisions but to enable the shareholders as a group to exercise informed control of the company.

In reaching their decision their Lordships stressed that a high degree of 'specificity' was required to impose a duty on the provider of negligently inaccurate information. Where information was put into circulation by a person which might be relied upon by persons unknown to him for any one of a number of purposes, which the maker of the statement had no specific reason to anticipate, there can be no relationship of proximity between the maker of the statement and anyone relying on it, unless the maker knew his statement would be communicated to the *specific* person relying on it, *specifically* in connection with a *particular* transaction of a *particular* kind and that that person would be *very likely* to rely on it for the purpose of entering into that *specific* transaction.

1   *Ashmore v Corpn of Lloyd's* [1992] 2 All ER 486, [1992] 1 WLR 446, HL.
2   [1995] 2 AC 145, [1994] 3 All ER 507, HL. See also *Spring v Guardian Assurance plc* [1995] 2 AC 296, [1994] 3 All ER 129, HL, and paras 18.12, above and 18.70, below.
3   Ibid at p 521.
4   [1995] 2 AC 207, [1995] 1 All ER 691, HL.
5   Note that this case does not impose a duty of care which is owed to all persons who might be affected by a negligent performance of a client's instructions. The House was influenced by the fact that to deny a remedy would lead to an irrecoverable loss since the deceased client could not amend his will, but had suffered no loss himself, while the beneficiaries had no contractual claim against the solicitor.
6   [1990] 2 AC 605, [1990] 1 All ER 568, HL.

18.17 Whether the approach in *White v Jones* will, in practice, lead to significantly different results from an application of the more detailed approach in *Caparo* is uncertain. What is clear is that the determination of whether a duty arises depends upon a consideration of all the circumstances of the relationship between the plaintiff and defendant. Factors which may be taken into account in deciding whether a duty arose include the circumstances in which the statement was made. For example, if it was made to a specific person or a group of people rather than generally a duty is more likely to arise; in contrast, where it made on a social occasion or clearly made informally a duty is unlikely. Other factors include the status of the advisor or informer, is he a professional or in a particularly good position to provide the information or not. However, this is less important if the critical issue is whether the advisor assumed responsibility towards the plaintiff since a person who assumes an advisory role cannot then automatically negate liability by arguing than the advisee should not have relied on a non-professional adviser. Another factor is and whether it was reasonable for the plaintiff to rely on the person who provides the advice or information, although again this may be less important if the critical issue is whether the advisor undertook the responsibility.

Caparo Industries left open the question of whether an appropriate relationship can exist only when the adviser chooses to give advice, or whether there can be an appropriate relationship, and hence a duty, even when there is a statutory obligation to give that advice[1]. This issue has not been settled by *White v Jones*.

1 In *Ministry of Housing and Local Government v Sharp* [1970] 2 QB 223, [1970] 1 All ER 1009, CA, a duty arose when there was a statutory duty.

18.18 Cases in which there has been recovery for pure economic loss caused by negligent misstatements include, *Punjab National Bank v de Boinville*[1], where the Court of Appeal held that the defendant insurance brokers who placed insurance policies on behalf of a client owed a duty to the client's bank which, to the brokers' knowledge, had participated actively in urging that insurance be obtained and which, as the brokers' knew, was intended to become assignee of the policies.

Another example is provided by *Esso Petroleum Co Ltd v Mardon*[2]. The Court of Appeal held that the defendant company (an expert in the petrol trade) which had given the potential tenant of a new filling station advice as to its expected annual throughput, owed him a duty of care. Indeed, in one case[3], a duty was imposed on a friend of the plaintiff in respect of his negligent advice as to the selection of a second-hand car, because he was acting as the plaintiff's unpaid agent and thus in a business context.

The outcome of two other cases was also entirely predictable. In *Al Saudi Banque v Clarke Pixley*[4], the auditors of a company were held to owe no duty to a bank which lent money[5] to the company since, even if it was foreseeable that the bank might seek a copy of the audited accounts and rely on them when making an advance, there was not a sufficiently close or direct relationship between the auditors and the bank to give rise to the degree of proximity necessary to establish a duty of care. In *Al-Nakib Investments (Jersey) Ltd v Longcroft*[6], the directors of a company were held to owe no duty to potential investors, including existing shareholders, who purchased shares on the *stock market* on the faith of a prospectus issued to existing shareholders for the particular purpose of enabling them to decide whether to acquire further shares in the company by *subscription*. Since the prospectus was not relied on by the investor for the particular purpose for which the directors had issued it, the relationship of the directors and the investor was insufficiently proximate. In contrast, in the earlier case of *JEB Fasteners Ltd v Marks, Bloom & Co*[7], a firm of accountants, who negligently prepared the accounts of company X, were held to owe a duty of care to the plaintiffs. This decision can be supported because the accountants knew that the plaintiffs were considering investing in or taking over company X and thus were likely to rely on the published accounts. The decision in *JEB Fasteners*, that a duty may be owed to a potential take-over bidder, must be regarded as applicable only if the identity of the bidder and his intention were known to the auditor prior to the preparation of the accounts[8].

A solicitor acting for a vendor owes no duty of care to the purchaser in replying to 'inquiries before contract', even though the vendor may incur liability to the buyer for any negligent misrepresentation made by his solicitor[9].

1   [1992] 3 All ER 104, [1992] 1 WLR 1138, CA.
2   [1976] QB 801, [1976] 2 All ER 5, CA.
3   *Chaudhry v Prabhakar* [1988] 3 All ER 718, [1989] 1 WLR 29, CA; see para 23.18, below.
4   [1990] Ch 313, [1989] 3 All ER 361.
5   Whether the loan was a further advance to an existing debtor or a loan to a person previously unconnected with the bank.
6   [1990] 3 All ER 321, [1991] BCLC 7.
7   [1981] 3 All ER 289; the defendants were not liable because the plaintiffs' loss was not caused by their negligence. The decision was affirmed by the Court of Appeal which accepted the judge's findings on duty of care: [1983] 1 All ER 583.
8   A view accepted in *Morgan Crucible Co plc v Hill Samuel & Co Ltd* [1991] Ch 295, [1991] 1 All ER 148, CA, but compare *James McNaughton Papers Group Ltd v Hicks Anderson & Co* [1991] 2 QB 113, [1991] 1 All ER 134, CA; see para 19.17, below, for a discussion of both cases.
9   *Gran Gelato Ltd v Richcliff (Group) Ltd* [1992] Ch 560, [1992] 1 All ER 865; see also para 22.17, below.

Breach of duty

18.19   The standard of care which the person owing a duty of care under *Hedley Byrne* is expected to satisfy is a requirement to act honestly and exercise reasonable care. It is not a duty to give correct advice. This is illustrated by *Stafford v Conti Commodity Services Ltd*[1]. The plaintiff made certain investments in the commodity markets, which dealings were not successful; he lost £19,000. The brokers who had advised him were held not to be negligent; the judge stressed that an error of judgment, especially concerning a wayward and rapidly changing market, is not necessarily negligent.

The precise nature of the obligation depends upon the facts of each case. In *Esso Petroleum Co Ltd v Mardon*[2], the defendants gave accurate advice which, to their knowledge, became inaccurate because of changed circumstances. Their duty of care was held to require them to inform the plaintiff of this inaccuracy. With this case can be compared *Argy Trading Development Co Ltd v Lapid Developments Ltd*[3]. In this case the tenants of a property were obliged to insure it; the landlord took out a block fire insurance policy on their behalf and informed them that it had done so. The landlord was held not to be liable for failing to inform the tenants that the policy had lapsed. Its duty was a duty to give information about insurance which was accurate at the time the policy was taken out and not a duty to give information about changed circumstances.

1   [1981] 1 All ER 691.
2   [1976] QB 801, [1976] 2 All ER 5, CA.
3   [1977] 3 All ER 785, [1977] 1 WLR 444.

Nervous shock

18.20   A plaintiff who seeks to recover for nervous shock (or perhaps more aptly, psychiatric illness) suffered as result of a negligent act, omission or statement attributable to the defendant faces two hurdles:

a.   the harm suffered must be of an appropriate type; and
b.   the requirement of proximity is rigorously enforced.

As to the harm which suffered, cases indicate that to recover for reasonably foreseeable nervous shock, the plaintiff must prove that he has suffered not mere mental upset or grief or sorrow[1] as a consequence of the shocking event but physical or mental injury or illness[2]. The courts recognise post-traumatic stress disorder and pathological grief[3] as psychiatric illness[4]. Obviously, nervous shock cases can give rise to particularly difficult issues of causation[5].

Sums awarded for psychiatric illness can be considerable[6]. For example in *Brice v Brown*[7], in which the plaintiff suffered a complete breakdown of her personality, the plaintiff was awarded £22,500, and in arbitration following the Zeebrugge ferry disaster awards ranged from £1,750 up to £30,000[8].

For no very obvious reason, the courts limit recovery for foreseeable nervous shock to victims who are proximate to a 'shocking event'. Thus if a parent witnesses the gradual death of a child over a period of time from injuries received in an accident negligently caused by the defendant, the parents cannot recover for any mental illness caused by the slow death[9].

1   *Vernon v Bosley* [1997] 1 All ER 577, CA. Of course where a person has himself suffered physical injury, damages for grief and stress may also be recoverable under the heading of pain and suffering.
2   *Alcock v Chief Constable of the South Yorkshire Police* [1992] 1 AC 310, [1991] 4 All ER 907, HL and *McLoughlin v O'Brian* [1983] 1 AC 410, [1982] 2 All ER 298, HL.
3   *Vernon v Bosley* [1997] 1 All ER 577, CA.
4   *Re Herald of Free Enterprise* (1989) Independent, 5 May, arbitration to assess damages for nervous shock following the Zeebrugge ferry disaster. See also *Vernon v Bosley* [1997] 1 All ER 577, CA.
5   For causation see paras. 18.52–18.60, below.
6   See, for example, *Vernon v Bosley (No 2)* [1997] 1 All ER 614, CA in which the plaintiff, who had witnessed attempts to salvage the car, in which his young daughters were passengers, from the river into which it had been negligently driven, and who suffered pathological grief disorder as a result of the incident, which led to the breakdown of his marriage and the loss of his business was awarded £37,500.
7   [1984] 1 All ER 997.
8   *Re Herald of Free Enterprise* (1989) Independent, 5 May, arbitration to assess damages for nervous shock following the Zeebrugge ferry disaster.
9   See, for example, *Taylorson v Shieldness Produce Ltd* [1994] PIQR P329, CA.

18.21   Even if the plaintiff has suffered psychiatric illness as a result of the defendant's negligent conduct[1], recovery is possible[2] only if:

a.   he was a rescuer who suffered the illness as a result of witnessing the shocking event at which he attended[3]; or
b.   his injuries were reasonably foreseeable and he was sufficiently proximate (discussed in paras 18.22 and 18.23, below).

The rationale for the rescuer cases (apart from an understandable sympathy for such persons) is unclear; they are perhaps 'secondary victims' (a term defined below) who are reasonably foreseeable and proximate on a basis other than that outlined in para 18.23, below. What does seem clear is that there is no reason why a professional rescuer (eg ambulance personnel) could not recover if he can establish that witnessing the incident caused his illness[4].

Another supposed situation where liability for psychiatric illness can arise, namely where the tortfeasor had a pre-existing obligation towards the property of the plaintiff[5], seems unsupportable. The fact that a person owes another a duty in respect of *one* type of damage does not mean he owes a duty in respect of a different type of damage which the plaintiff has suffered.

In terms of when someone other than a rescuer covered by a. can recover damages for psychiatric illness suffered as a result of the defendant's negligence, a distinction must be drawn between a primary victim (a person who is directly involved in the events which occasion the shock) and a secondary victim (a person who is not directly involved in the events occasioning the shock but who witnesses events in which another person is put at risk).

1   Where the defendant acted intentionally or recklessly, as opposed to negligently, the plaintiff can recover damages for psychiatric illness. See *Wilkinson v Downton* [1897] 2 QB 57; in which the plaintiff was awarded £100 for psychiatric illness suffered after she was told by the defendant, as a joke but untruthfully, that her husband has suffered a serious injury.
2   Where a plaintiff is owed a duty to ensure his safety, for example an employee by an employer, exposure to risk of psychiatric injury is, of course, as much a breach of duty as exposure to a risk of physical injury; for employers' liability see paras 19.2–19.9, below.
3   *Chadwick v British Transport Commission* [1967] 2 All ER 945, [1967] 1 WLR 912. Approved in *McLoughlin v O'Brian* [1983] 1 AC 410, [1982] 2 All ER 298, HL.
3   See *Frost v Chief Constable of the South Yorkshire Police* [1997] 1 All ER 540, CA., para. 19.5, below, and *Hale v London Underground Ltd* [1993] PIQR Q30.
4   In *Attia v British Gas plc* [1988] QB 304, [1987] 3 All ER 455, CA, the plaintiff recovered £16,409 for the illness occasioned by the shock of seeing her house damaged by fire. The defendant, which was installing central heating in the house, owed her a pre-existing duty of care (to take proper care for the safety of the premises) and the court held the only live issue was that of remoteness.

18.22   *Primary victims* Where the person who has sustained the shock also sustained physical injury in an incident caused by the defendant's negligence, the plaintiff can recover for the shock element as well as the physical injury. Indeed, it is now clear that where physical injury to a person is foreseeable he can recover for shock even if he did not suffer any physical injury[1]. When it is a primary victim who seeks to recover for psychiatric illness it does not matter that the plaintiff is a person who is particularly susceptible to some form of psychiatric reaction; the critical issue is whether the defendant's conduct caused the harm suffered[2].

1   *Page v Smith* [1996] AC 155, [1995] 2 All ER 736, HL.
2   Ibid.. In this case, the plaintiff who had mild ME which was then in remission, recovered £162,153 when the ME was exacerbated by the defendant's negligent act. This is an example of the 'eggshell-skull' rule which we discuss in para. 18.66, below.

18.23   *Secondary victims* Where the person suffering psychiatric illness is a secondary victim the position is more complicated. The leading case of *Alcock v Chief Constable of the South Yorkshire Police*[1]. In this case, the police had allowed an excessively large number of spectators into a football stadium, Hillsborough, shortly before the commencement of a major football match. As a result, 95 spectators were crushed to death and many more were injured; scenes of the incident (but not individual victims) were broadcast on television and there was extensive news coverage of the tragedy. A number of people some, but not all, of whom were at the ground, and who were related to spectators in the relevant part of the ground, suffered psychiatric illness from seeing or hearing news of the disaster. They sued the police. The House of Lords held that a person who sustained psychiatric illness as a result of apprehending the infliction of physical injury (or the risk of such injury) to *another* person could only recover from the person who negligently put the primary victim at risk if he satisfied two requirements. He must establish that:

a.   it was reasonably foreseeable that he would be affected by psychiatric illness as a result of the consequences of the incident because of his close relationship of love and affection with a primary victim; and

b.   he satisfied the test of proximity in relation to the tortfeasor in terms of physical and temporal connection between the plaintiff and the incident; and

c.   he is a person of reasonable fortitude and not unduly susceptible to some form of psychiatric reaction[2].

Applying these tests, the House ruled, first, that a plaintiff could recover only if his relationship to the primary victim was sufficiently close that it was reasonably foreseeable that he might sustain nervous shock if he feared the primary victim had or might have been injured. Where there was a close family tie, for example, parent and child or husband and wife, a close relationship would be assumed, in other cases such a relationship could be proved to exist. Second, a plaintiff must be sufficiently close in time and space to the incident or its immediate aftermath. Hence, to see an incident on television or to be told of it by a third party was not sufficient to render a victim proximate. In consequence, none of the plaintiffs recovered, none was sufficiently proximate to the events.

In addition, in *Alcock* a majority of the House also accepted that a bystander who has no prior relationship with the direct victims of the shocking event, and who suffers psychiatric illness after witnessing a particularly horrific catastrophe close to him may be able to recover if a reasonably strong-minded person would have been so affected (this explanation has been given in some of the rescuer cases[3]). However, the issue of whether a person could recover for nervous shock from witnessing horrific injuries suffered by another as a result of *that* other's negligence, was left open. Further, in *McFarlane v EE Caledonia Ltd*[4], the Court of Appeal rejected a claim for damages for nervous shock from a seaman present on a ship which attended the Piper Alpha disaster. The plaintiff was insufficiently close to the horrific events and had no pre-existing relationship with any of the victims; he was insufficiently proximate.

Many cases decided prior to *Alcock* fit neatly within its analysis[5].

1   [1992] 1 AC 310, [1991] 4 All ER 907, HL.
2   Approving on this point, *Bourhill v Young* [1943] AC 92, [1942] 2 All ER 396, HL and *McLoughlin v O'Brian* [1983] 1 AC 410, [1982] 2 All ER 298, HL.
3   The Court of Appeal in *Frost v Chief Constable of the South Yorkshire Police* [1997] 1 All ER

540, CA, suggested that this was one ratio of *Chadwick v British Transport Commission* [1967] 2 All ER 945, [1967] 1 WLR 912.

4 *McFarlane v EE Caledonia Ltd* [1994] 1 All ER 1.
5 For example, *Hinz v Berry* [1970] 2 QB 40, [1970] 1 All ER 1074, CA where a wife recovered £4,000 for the nervous shock caused by seeing her husband and foster-children injured by a negligent car driver and *Boardman v Sanderson* [1964] 1 WLR 1317, CA, in which a father who heard his son screaming as he was run over recovered £75. Following *Alcock* there is some doubt about the correctness of *Dooley v Cammell Laird & Co Ltd* [1951] 1 Lloyd's Rep 271 in which a crane driver who, wrongly but reasonably, thought a workmate had been crushed by falling cargo recovered £377 for nervous shock in that the relationship of the victim and the plaintiff was, arguably, not 'close'.

Acts of third parties

18.24 If a person owes a duty of care to another, he may break it by his own acts or omissions or by virtue of his responsibility for the acts or omissions of others[1]. However, as a general rule, a defendant does not owe a duty of care in relation to the acts or omissions (deliberate or negligent) of third parties which cause harm to others[2]. An example is provided by *Smith v Scott*[3], where a local authority was held not to owe a duty of care to neighbours of a known problem family whom it had rehoused next to them.

There is a diversity of approach as to why there is no duty of care in respect of the acts of third parties. In *Smith v Littlewoods Organisation Ltd*[4], where the defendant was held not to be liable for acts of vandalism by third parties who, unknown to it, had broken into a cinema it had purchased for conversion and had started a fire which destroyed adjoining property, a dichotomy of views was apparent. However, Lord Mackay's speech appears to represent current thinking; he said that he agreed with counsel for both sides:

'. . .that what the reasonable man is bound to foresee in a case involving injury or damage by independent human agency . . . is the probable consequence of his own act or omission, but that, in such a case, a clear basis will be required on which to assert that the injury or damage is more than a mere possibility.'

In this case the risk of fire damage was found not to be a reasonably probable consequence of the defendant's actions; the defendant did not know of previous acts of vandalism and it had no reason to suppose that a fire would be started in its property.

Many of the cases on the acts of third parties involve an accusation that the defendant omitted to prevent something happening and are, thus, often closely linked to the cases on omissions which we discuss in para 18.27, below.

1 Vicarious liability is discussed in paras 17.15–17.27, above, and personal liability may be incurred by the employer of negligent independent contractors (see paras 17.28–17.35, above).
2 *Deyong v Shenburn* [1946] KB 227, [1946] 1 All ER 226, CA.
3 [1973] Ch 314, [1972] 3 All ER 645.
4 [1987] AC 241, [1987] 1 All ER 710, HL.

18.25 A defendant may owe a duty of care to a foreseeable and proximate plaintiff in respect of the acts or omissions of third parties if two conditions are satisfied:

a. a third party causes reasonably foreseeable harm to the plaintiff or his property; and

b. the defendant has control over, or responsibility for, either the plaintiff (or his property) or the third party who causes the harm.

Thus, in *Stansbie v Troman*[1], a painter, contrary to the instructions of the plaintiff, left the plaintiff's house on which he was working unlocked during a two-hour absence. He was held liable in negligence when property was stolen from the house. The painter had sufficient control over the house and theft from it was held to be a reasonably foreseeable and probable consequence of his omission. In *Home Office v Dorset Yacht Co Ltd*[2], the Home Office was held responsible for the damage caused to yachts by borstal boys during their escape by sea from a camp on Brownsea Island. The duty of care to people whose property might foreseeably be damaged in any escape was based on the control which the Home Office had over the borstal boys. In *Carmarthenshire County Council v Lewis*[3], a teacher was held to exercise 'control' over school children and was, thus, liable to a lorry driver injured in a road accident negligently caused during school hours by a child who had been let out early.

More recently, in *Smoldon v Whitworth*[4], a referee in a colts rugby match was held to owe a duty of care to players to ensure that their safety was not jeopardised by other participants. The standard of care in this case was held to require the referee to exercise an appropriate degree of control over the game in the context arising. The referee was held liable to the plaintiff, who suffered serious spinal injury when a scrum collapsed (acts of third parties), in that such injury was a foreseeable consequence of a scrum collapsing, that the rules governing colts matches required particular attention to be paid to the risks of such incidents, and that a very considerable number of collapses had already occurred in the game before the one in which the plaintiff had been injured.

1   [1948] 2 KB 48, [1948] 1 All ER 599, CA.
2   [1970] AC 1004, [1970] 2 All ER 294, HL.
3   [1955] AC 549, [1955] 1 All ER 565, HL.
4   (1996) Times, 18 December, CA.

18.26   In the absence of sufficient control over, or responsibility for, the tortfeasor or relevant property, it is extremely unlikely that a defendant would be held liable for the acts or omissions of a third party[1]. For example, in *P Perl (Exporters) Ltd v Camden London Borough Council*[2], thieves gained access to the plaintiff's premises through adjoining, unoccupied council-owned property. The local authority had no control over the thieves and were not liable for their depredations. Similarly, in *Topp v London Country Bus (South West) Ltd*[3], the Court of Appeal refused to hold the bus company liable for the actions of a third party who stole a bus and drove it negligently thereby killing the plaintiff's wife, even though the company's employees had left the vehicle unattended with the key in its ignition.

In several cases the courts have had to consider whether the police could be liable to the plaintiff for loss which he has suffered as a result of deliberate wrongdoing by a third party. The general view[4] is that, in the absence of any special characteristic or ingredient, the police owe no duty of care to an individual plaintiff. Although the police owe a duty to the general public to enforce the criminal law, that duty does not extend to a duty to arrest and identify an unknown criminal. For example, in *Alexandrou v Oxford*[5], the Court of Appeal held that the police owed no duty to prevent thieves from robbing the plaintiff's premises. Clearly there is a large policy element in such cases as well as issues of liability for third parties and of whether a public body can be liable for failing to carry out its appointed task impeccably, an issue to which we turn in para 18.29, below.

1 But see *Ward v Cannock Chase District Council* [1986] Ch 546, [1985] 3 All ER 537. Notice, however, that leaving property unoccupied for a considerable period, resulting in its natural decay or damage by third parties, may render the property an actionable nuisance. See paras 20.21–20.25, below.
2 [1984] QB 342, [1983] 3 All ER 161, CA.
3 [1993] 3 All ER 448, [1993] 1 WLR 976, CA.
4 See particularly *Hill v Chief Constable for West Yorkshire* [1989] AC 53, [1988] 2 All ER 238, HL, in which the House of Lords rejected a claim by the mother of a victim of the 'Yorkshire Ripper' who claimed that had the police acted properly the killer would have been arrested before he killed her daughter.
5 [1993] 4 All ER 328, CA.

Omissions

18.27   Lord Atkin in *Donoghue v Stevenson*[1] said that 'you must take reasonable care to avoid acts or omissions which you can reasonably foresee would be likely to injure your neighbour' but great care must be taken in determining whether a person incurs liability for failing to act. It is clear that, if a pre-existing duty of care exists, failure to reach the standard imposed constitutes negligence whether the failure consists of acting carelessly or of carelessly failing to act. It is as much negligence for an accountant carelessly to omit relevant material as it is carelessly to insert inaccurate material.

However, in cases in which there is no pre-existing duty of care, it is rare for a court to find an obligation to take positive action, in other words no duty is imposed. For example, a stranger who observes a child drowning in a shallow pond is under no legal duty to go to its aid, even though it is reasonably foreseeable that his omission will cause injury. The fact that the damage is foreseeable is not enough to create a duty. On the other hand, there will be an obligation to take positive action if there is a recognised relationship with the victim, as where the defendant is the parent of the victim or has control over him[2].

Recently, in the case of public service bodies, the issue of whether a duty of care arises has been much influenced by the fact that there has an omission, rather than a positive act of misfeasance[3]. That the harm suffered has been caused by an omission has been a factor which tends to negate the existence of a duty. Hence, in the bundle of cases reported as *Capital and Counties plc v Hampshire County Council*[4], it was held that the fire service is not under a duty to answer a call for help or take care to do so.

1   [1932] AC 562, HL.
2   *Home Office v Dorset Yacht Co Ltd* [1970] AC 1004, [1970] 2 All ER 294, HL; see para 18.25, above. Liability may also arise for failure to prevent naturally occurring hazards on land causing harm to others, see *Goldman v Hargrave* [1967] 1 AC 645, [1966] 2 All ER 989, PC.
3   See particularly *Stovin v Wise* [1996] AC 923, [1996] 3 All ER 801, HL.
4   [1997] NLJR 599, CA. See particularly *Stovin v Wise* [1996] 3 All ER 801, HL.

Voluntary undertakings
18.28   We have seen in para 18.16, above, that, in determining whether a duty of care is owed to the recipients of advice or information, it may be relevant whether or not the person giving that advice or information assumed responsibility for it. In cases other than those involving negligent advice, the question of whether a person assumed responsibility for a particular task has also been treated as having some relevance to the question of whether a duty of care exists. The assumption of responsibility for a situation, even if it is not one of the defendant's making, may be a relevant factor in imposing a duty on the defendant in cases where there is no initial duty to act but the defendant has chosen to intervene.

Bodies exercising statutory duties and powers
18.29   Local authorities and other public bodies, such as the police, the fire services, bodies overseeing the regulation of financial markets, the Charity Commissioners etc, have duties and powers delegated to them by Parliament. The question arises as to whether a body which possesses statutory duties and powers owes a duty of care in negligence to a person whom it is reasonably foreseeable could be affected either by a failure to exercise that power or duty or by a careless exercise of it.

There is no doubt that failure to exercise, or careless exercise, of a statutory power may give rise to an action for breach of statutory duty, provided the conditions necessary for such an action (paras 20.2–20.7, below) are satisfied.

In the absence of an action for breach of statutory duty can a common law action for negligence arise? The cases on bodies exercising statutory duties and powers are not consistent in their approach and at various times different reasons have been given in determining if such a body has broken a common law duty of care. A remedy to a person aggrieved by the conduct of a public body has been denied a remedy because:

a.   the plaintiff was not reasonably foreseeable or was insufficiently proximate[1], applying justice and reason (ie no duty); or
b.   dictates of policy required the negation of any duty[2]; or
c.   the duty did not extend to the type of harm of which the plaintiff complained (usually pure economic loss)[3]; or
d.   the conduct did not constitute a breach of the standard of care required of public bodies.

1   *Yuen Kun Yeu v A-G of Hong Kong* [1988] AC 175, [1987] 2 All ER 705, PC.
2   *Hill v Chief Constable for West Yorkshire* [1989] AC 53, [1988] 2 All ER 238, HL; no duty is owed to individuals to apprehend unidentified criminals.
3   *Murphy v Brentwood District Council* [1991] 1 AC 398, [1990] 2 All ER 908, HL.

Duty of care

18.30 A body in *exercising* statutory powers or duties *may* be liable for direct harm negligently inflicted applying the general principles which derive from *Donoghue v Stevenson* (including the restrictions on the ability to recover for pure economic loss). Thus, a plaintiff who can establish that he has suffered foreseeable harm and that he is proximate may be owed a duty of care even if his complaint is against a public body, provided it is appropriate to impose a common law duty on that body and there are no policy arguments which outweigh the interests of individuals and negate a duty of care. The financial consequences of the imposition of a duty with its impact upon the wider community to whom the public duty is responsible is a powerful argument against the imposition of a duty.

In determining whether a duty of care is owed by a public body the decision of the House of Lords in *Home Office v Dorset Yacht Co Ltd*[1], is an appropriate starting point. In this case, the House found that the Home Office, whose powers include the management of prisons, owed a duty of care to yacht owners whose yachts were moored adjacent to a camp for borstal boys on Brownsea Island. The Home Office had an obligation to operate custodial facilities with due regard to those who might be immediately affected by an escape in that such persons were at particular risk, even if it had a discretion as to how to run the prison service. The fact that an escape occurred was not in itself actionable but the Home Office was liable in permitting this escape because there had been inadequate supervision of the inmates by the staff. It could be said that the Home Office had undertaken a special responsibility to those whose property was adjacent to penal facilities. Once a duty was established, it was irrelevant the breach of it was an omission, failure to supervise, rather than a positive act of negligence. Thus, it is clear that the negligent *exercise* of a statutory power, whether by act or omission may give rise to liability. However, it will not necessarily do so.

Examples of where a public authority has been liable include, where police officers caused a traffic accident through a want of care[2] and, in a recent case, where a fire officer negligently decided to turn off a sprinkler system, which exacerbated a fire at which the fire service was attending[3]. Similarly, a school which inadequately supervised sporting activities could be liable for injuries suffered by a participant even though the school operated pursuant to a statutory duty. A local authority has been held liable for negligently advising a person that he could proceed with building works without waiting for the outcome of an application for planning permission[4] From these cases, and others[5], we can conclude that one factor which may influence the determination of whether a duty of care arises include whether the alleged breach of duty is a positive act rather than an omission.

Whether the exercise of a power or duty gives rise to a duty of care seems to be decided on a case by case basis. However, the fact that the alleged negligence is in connection with the exercise, as opposed to the formulation, of a statutory power is clearly of considerable significance. For example, in *Anns v Merton London Borough Council*[6], a local authority which had the power (but not a duty) to inspect the foundations of buildings chose not to do so. A flat-dweller who occupied premises which suffered damage due to the inadequacy of the foundations alleged that the local authority had been negligent in failing to inspect them. The House of Lords held that the local authority must give proper consideration to the question of whether it should inspect or not but, if it had done so, it was not liable if it chose not to inspect. Hence, the House accepted that if the local authority had simply failed to inspect through oversight, rather than in pursuance of a policy, it might have been liable to those who suffered reasonably foreseeable loss as a consequence although arguments of policy might tend to negate any duty in such a case. The House also stated that had the local authority chosen to inspect the foundations, but had done so carelessly, liability could have arisen[7].

In cases where common law liability appears to arise, the liability of a body exercising public duties or powers is the same as that of a private person unless the duty is restricted by its statutory duties or powers.

1   [1970] AC 1004, [1970] 2 All ER 294, HL.
2   *Knightley v Johns* [1982] 1 All ER 851, [1982] 1 WLR 349, CA.
3   *Capital and Counties plc v Hampshire County Council* [1997] NLJR 599, CA. This was a consolidated appeal involving three cases against the fire services, the other two cases are discussed in para 18.27, above.
4   *Lambert v West Devon Borough Council* [1997] 11 LS Gaz R 35, applying the principles in *Hedley Byrne & Co Ltd v Heller and Partners* which we discuss in para 18.14, above.
5   Especially *Stovin v Wise* [1996] 3 All ER 801, HL, which we discuss in the next paragraph..
6   [1978] AC 728, [1977] 2 All ER 492, HL.
7   The actual decision in *Anns* has been overruled on the basis that the loss suffered by the plaintiff was pure economic loss but the discussion concerning the imposition of a duty valid. It remains unclear what the position is if a body charged with a statutory power formulates a policy for the discharge of that power but does so carelessly.

18.31   Even when a duty of care arises, the plaintiff has also to establish breach of that duty to sue successfully. Proving the existence of a duty and its breach has proved particularly difficult where the allegation is that the relevant body has failed to exercise its powers in a particular way and that this failure cause the harm suffered.

Consider first, *X v Bedfordshire County Council*[1]. Here it was alleged that local authorities had been negligent either in investigating allegations of child abuse or in failing to provide appropriate education for children diagnosed as suffering from learning disorders. The House of Lords, in rejecting the existence of a duty of care owed to the child victims of the councils' inadequacies (which were foreseeable and proximate), held that the councils had been given by Parliament a discretion as to the extent to which, and the methods by which, their statutory duties would be performed. Consequently, if a council made a decision which was within the ambit of its statutory discretion that decision could not be actionable at common law even if the injury which resulted was foreseeable and the plaintiff could be regarded as proximate. The House accepted that where the decision taken by a public body was so unreasonable that it could be regarded as falling outside the scope of the discretion conferred by Parliament liability might arise. However, the House was of the view that where the exercise of the statutory discretion included issues of policy, rather than operations, it was not open to a court to hold that the exercise of the discretion was outside the ambit of the statutory power. Unfortunately, it is not certain what would be regarded as a policy issue. Further, a common law duty which might arise, for example, where a local authority exercised its powers unreasonably, would not do so, concluded the House, if compliance with such a duty was inconsistent with the due implementation or performance of any statutory duties imposed by Parliament.

Where the alleged source of liability derives from an omission to exercise a discretionary power it is particularly difficult to establish a duty of care. In *Stovin v Wise*[2], for example, a local authority was not liable to a motorcyclist who collided with a car at a junction where visibility was impaired by an earth bank on adjacent property, even though it was aware that the bank made the junction dangerous. The House of Lords concluded that the statutory power conferred upon a highway authority, which would have allowed it to remove the bank, did not create a duty of care which would give rise to liability to compensate persons injured by a failure to use that power. The House was of the view that liability could arise only where it was manifestly irrational for the statutory body not to act and there were exceptional grounds for giving a right to compensation to persons who had suffered loss as a result of the failure to exercise the power.

The reluctance to impose liability for an omission was also relevant in the earlier case of *Curran v Northern Ireland Co-ownership Housing Association Ltd*[3]. In this case, the housing association, which had the power to award householders improvement grants, had made a grant available to the previous owner of the plaintiff's house in order to fund an extension to the property. The association was held not liable to the plaintiff in respect of the defective workmanship of that extension. One reason was that the powers of the association were designed to ensure the proper allocation of public money and not to protect individuals against defective workmanship. In other words the purpose of the power was not not to impose liability for failure to supervise work which it funded. Another reason was that even careful exercise of its power would not have prevented the harm which occurred (poor work by the builder), so that the plaintiff could not prove that the alleged negligence by the defendant caused his loss.

1   [1995] 2 AC 633, [1995] 3 All ER 353, HL. There were a number of actions against a variety of local authorities heard together.
2   [1996] 3 All ER 801, HL. See also the cases on omissions discussed in para 18.27, above.
3   [1987] AC 718, [1987] 2 All ER 13, HL.

Policy
18.32   Policy operates at two levels in this area. It may be a factor which precludes the existence of a duty or it may be treated as a reason to negate the existence of a duty which would otherwise arise. In recent decisions, policy has generally been deployed at the initial stage and the very existence of a duty has been denied. Thus, we have seen that the courts are reluctant to subject to judicial scrutiny matters which call for the exercise by a public body of a discretion[1] and that in deciding if a duty of care arises the fact that the the principal purpose of a statutory duty or power is to benefit the community rather than individuals is significant[2]. Further, the existence of an alternative remedy for the person aggrieved is a strong policy factor for rejecting the imposition of a duty. In *Rowling v Takaro Properties Ltd*[3], for example, the Privy

Council, in rejecting the plaintiff's claim alleging negligence on the part of a government minister who had been exercising a regulatory function, was influenced by the existence of the remedy of judicial review[3]. In *Jones v Department of Employment*[4], a claimant who had initially been denied unemployment benefit (which was granted on appeal) could not sue the initial adjudicator of his claim in negligence; there was a statutory procedure for aggrieved claimants, which the plaintiff had used.

An example of policy limiting the existence of a duty of care is provided by *Osman v Ferguson*[5]. In this case, the police had been aware that X, a school-teacher, was obsessed with the plaintiff, a former pupil, and that he was liable to do something criminally insane. Indeed, X (as they knew) had already committed a number of offences. The police, however, did not arrest X. X then shot the plaintiff and killed his father. The Court of Appeal held that the plaintiff and his family had been exposed to a risk from X over and above that of the general public and that there was an arguable case that there was a sufficient degree of proximity, arising from the special circumstances, to create a duty of care owed by the police to the plaintiff. Nevertheless, the court held that it was against public policy to impose on the police a liability to individual members of the public for damage caused by criminals whom the police had failed to apprehend and dismissed the plaintiff's claim. This case does not, however, establish that the police are automatically immune from suit on policy grounds. Hence, if the facts reveal that the police have voluntarily assumed responsibility for a particular person, negligent failure to exercise that responsibility may give rise to an action for negligence[6].

1   *X v Bedfordshire County Council* [1995] 2 AC 633, [1995] 3 All ER 353, HL.
2   *Hill v Chief Constable for West Yorkshire* [1989] AC 53, [1988] 2 All ER 238, HL.
3   [1988] AC 473, [1988] 1 All ER 163, PC.
4   [1989] QB 1, [1988] 1 All ER 725, CA. See also *Mills v Winchester Diocesan Board of Finance* [1989] Ch 428, [1989] 2 All ER 317; statutory system of appeals from decisions of The Charity Commissioners.
5   [1993] 4 All ER 344, CA.
6   *Swinney v Chief Constable of the Northumbria Police* [1996] 3 All ER 449, CA, police could owe duty to informant to keep her name secret when it was known that the persons about whom information was given were violent and ruthless, particularly since it was in the public interest that people gave information about crimes to the police.

Legal Process

18.33   We have seen that policy issues may be relevant in that the courts do not regard particular types of loss, for example pure economic loss and psychiatric damage suffered by secondary victims, as appropriate areas for the imposition of a duty of care on a defendant. The courts may also deny the existence of a duty of care on policy grounds in respect of aspects of the operation of the legal process. In such cases policy is designed to protect particular defendants in that the public interest in the proper working of the legal process must, in some cases, outweigh the interests of individuals.

We divide these cases into matters directly connected with court proceedings and issues arising in the legal process.

Court proceedings

18.34 'It is well settled that judges[1], barristers, solicitors, jurors and witnesses enjoy an absolute immunity from any form of civil action being brought against them in respect of anything they say or do in court during the course of a trial'[2]. This immunity from suit in respect of proceedings in court is a classic example of policy negating the existence of a possible duty of care; the advancement of justice in general requires possible injustice to a few.

The judicial immunity extends to those exercising quasi-judicial functions. Hence, arbitrators are, at common law, immune from actions in negligence when acting as arbitrators and valuers have a similar immunity if they are acting as an arbitrator or quasi-arbitrator[3], but not otherwise[4]. The immunity of arbitrators is now regulated by statute[5].

The immunity is not limited to those trying cases. Consequently, it was held in *Palmer v Durnford Ford*[6], that an expert witness was immune from suit in respect of his evidence in court and work related or proximate to that evidence[7]. This would apply whether the gathering of material was solely for the purposes of litigation or for that purpose and for another reason. However, the immunity is not given to everyone connected with litigation. For example, in *IRC v Hoogstraten*[8], it was held that a sequestrator owes a duty of care to the owner of property which he administers even though acting on behalf of the court.

Barristers, for a combination of policy and practical reasons, are also immune from actions in negligence in respect of work connected with litigation[9]. This immunity arises only if the work is so intimately connected with the conduct of the case that it can be regarded as a preliminary decision affecting the way the case is to be conducted in court[10] and this can include advice on whether or not to plead guilty in criminal proceedings[11]. This immunity has, by statute, been extended to any person acting as an advocate[12].

Solicitors probably owe their clients a duty of care[13] but, while acting as advocates (which may include pre-trial matters intimately bound up with the conduct of proceedings), they enjoy the same immunity as barristers[14]. A solicitor has no immunity in respect of 'non-advocacy' matters, but it appears that, where his advice concerning litigation is subsequently approved by a court or a barrister, he cannot be liable in negligence[15].

1 A judge in an inferior court, eg a magistrate, is not protected if he exceeds his jurisdiction unless he honestly believed he was acting within his jurisdiction. It is for the plaintiff to prove the defendant had no such belief.
2 *Sutcliffe v Thackrah* [1974] AC 727, [1974] 1 All ER 859, HL. This immunity is not limited to actions in negligence but extends to all civil actions, eg defamation. A solicitor does owe the court a duty to conduct the case with due propriety but this does not impose such a duty on him in respect of the opposing party: *Orchard v South Eastern Electricity Board* [1987] QB 565, [1987] 1 All ER 95, CA.
3 *Palacath Ltd v Flanagan* [1985] 2 All ER 161.
4 *Arenson v Casson Beckman Rutley & Co* [1977] AC 405, [1975] 3 All ER 901, HL.
5 Arbitration Act 1996, s 29.
6 [1992] QB 483, [1992] 2 All ER 122.
7 The immunity does not extend to advice given by the expert to the client on the merits of the claim, particularly if proceedings have not yet started; nor does it protect the expert who gives out of court advice on matters beyond his expertise.

8   [1985] QB 1077, [1984] 3 All ER 25, CA.
9   *Rondel v Worsley* [1969] 1 AC 191, [1967] 1 All ER 993, HL.
10 *Saif Ali v Sydney Mitchell & Co* [1980] AC 198, [1978] 3 All ER 1033, HL.
11 *Somasundaram v M Julius Melchior & Co* [1989] 1 All ER 129, [1988] 1 WLR 1394, CA.
12 Courts and Legal Services Act 1990, s 62.
13 In addition to any contractual liability: *Midland Bank Ltd v Hett, Stubbs & Kemp* [1979] Ch 384, [1978] 3 All ER 571; see paras 18.67–18.70, below.
14 *Saif Ali v Sydney Mitchell & Co* [1980] AC 198, [1978] 3 All ER 1033, HL.
15 *Somasundaram v M Julius Melchior & Co* [1989] 1 All ER 129, [1988] 1 WLR 1394, CA. It is not clear why this is the case but presumably it is to prevent a collateral attack on judicial findings or the barrister's immunity.

18.35   Again for reasons of policy the courts will refuse to find a duty of care in any action in which the tort of negligence is being used to make a collateral attack on a decision in a previous case if that case has been determined by a court of competent jurisdiction[1]. This denial of duty extends beyond the decision in the case to encompass matters of procedure. For example, in *Business Computers International Ltd v Registrar of Companies*[2], a petition for winding up was served on a company by a creditor at the wrong address with the result that the company did not defend the petition and was wound up by the court. The company, having had the winding up set aside, sought to recover its costs from the creditor, alleging negligence in serving the petition at the wrong address. The judge held that, even if the harm done to the company was foreseeable, policy demanded the rejection of a duty of care. One policy factor deemed relevant was that the procedure and conduct of litigation are subject to judicial control and have their own system of checks and safeguards (eg striking out petitions) which provide litigants with sufficient protection against improper actions, so that there was no need to impose parallel duties in negligence.

Whether an action is brought for the purpose of attacking the previous judgment or for some proper purpose, for example, the recovery of damages for professional negligence, the court will not permit a subsequent action which would have the effect of re-litigating an issue which has been properly determined[3]. Thus in *Smith v Linskills*[4], the plaintifff who had been convicted of burglary, was denied the right to sue his former solicitors for their alleged negligence in their conduct of his criminal case. The Court of Appeal held that it would be an affront to a coherent system of justice to have two final, inconsistent court decisions. In addition it is often impossible to reconsider a case years after the event; this was the case here in that it was some 12 years after the crime, and there should be finality to litigation.

1   *Somasundaram v M Julius Melchior & Co* [1989] 1 All ER 129, [1988] 1 WLR 1394, CA. This is also of relevance in considering the liability of barristers
2   [1988] Ch 229, [1987] 3 All ER 465. Doubt was cast upon whether a plaintiff whose case was not determined on the merits should be denied the right to litigate in *Smith v Linskills* [1996] 2 All ER 353, [1996] 1 WLR 763, CA.
3   *Walpole v Partridge & Wilson* [1994] 1 All ER 385, CA. There are recognised exceptions where further litigation is possible, for example when significant fresh evidence is admissible.
4   [1996] 2 All ER 353, CA.

Out of court proceedings
18.36   An immunity from suit which is parallel to that enjoyed by those engaged in court proceedings is enjoyed by others who are concerned in the

legal process. Hence, the police in their investigation of crime are not liable for failing to catch a criminal[1], nor are they liable for failing to warn the public of possible dangers[2]. This immunity is not absolute: it does not extend to cases where the police have undertaken some special responsibility towards a person. In *Swinney v Chief Constable of the Northumbria Police*[3], the police, negligently revealed the name of an informant (who had provided information about the killing of a police officer), to third parties who passed her name to the person she had implicated. The person she had implicated was known to be violent. Thereafter the plaintiff was subject to serious threats and suffered psychiatric harm. Holding that the police owed the informant a duty of care, the Court of Appeal accepted that the police were generally immune from suit on grounds of public policy in relation to their activities in the investigation or suppression of crime but it stated that that immunity had to be weighed against other considerations of public policy. It was in the public interest that the public gave information to the police without fear that the name of an informant would be passed to the person implicated and this policy, in this case, outweighed the immunity normally possessed by the police.

The immunity enjoyed by the police also extends to the Crown Prosecution Service (CPS)[4].

1 *Hill v Chief Constable for West Yorkshire* [1989] AC 53, [1988] 2 All ER 238, HL.
2 *Ancell v McDermott* [1993] 4 All ER 355, CA. No duty to warn motorist of fuel spilt on the road.
3 [1996] 3 All ER 449, CA.
4 *Elguzouli-Daf v Metropolitan Police Comr* [1995] 1 All ER 833, CA. It is arguable that should the CPS voluntarily assume responsibility for a person a duty of care could, subject to policy arguments, arise.

Breach of Duty

18.37 Once it is determined that a person owes another a duty of care, liability in negligence will arise if there is a breach of that duty. A breach occurs if there is a failure to reach the standard of care which the law requires. Thus breach of duty requires the determination of two issues:

a. what standard of care should the defendant have displayed – the required standard is the degree of care which could have been expected of a reasonable man faced with the circumstances confronting the defendant.
b. did the defendant's conduct, on the facts, fall below this standard.

Hence, a decision that the defendant's conduct failed to reach the required standard of care is a finding of what standard was required and a finding that the defendant did not reach that standard. Thus, identical conduct may be a breach of duty in one case but not in another. For example, to drive at 80 mph on a busy suburban road is almost certainly a breach of a driver's duty of care, whereas to do so on an empty motorway may not be. Similarly, to comply with a recognised rule or law is not necessarily to display reasonable care; to drive at 29 mph is within the speed limit but in an appropriate case, for example where traffic is practically stationary, it could be negligent.

The standard of care

18.38   The standard of care to be reached is assessed objectively and not subjectively; the defendant is not entitled to say that he did his best which was, unfortunately, inadequate in the circumstances.

While it is not open to a defendant to say that he should not be judged by the standard of the reasonable man, because he personally is very stupid or totally lacking in common sense or is old or ill[1], the courts, somewhat illogically, have sometimes held that children are judged by reference to a subjective standard, that is should the child defendant, given his age and capacity, have displayed more care? Such decisions may be defensible on another ground, namely did the child reach the standard of care demanded of the reasonable child – if such a thing exists?

The standard of care demanded by the law is reasonable care adjudged by reference to the standard of the reasonable man placed in the position of the defendant. Since even reasonable men have accidents, the fact that an accident has occurred is not automatically proof of a want of care. For example, in *Porter v Barking and Dagenham London Borough Council*[2], a school caretaker who allowed his son and the plaintiff (both aged 14) to practise putting the shot in the school grounds out of school hours was not liable for the injuries suffered by the plaintiff; he was not in breach of duty since there was no reason to treat permitting two sensible, well-behaved boys to practise shot-putting as imprudent.

In some cases, generally for policy reasons, the courts have determined that the standard of care which could be expected from the reasonable man is extremely high. For example, in formulating the standard of care demanded of car drivers, the courts have held that the 'reasonable car driver' is a paragon of all the motoring virtues who rarely makes a mistake. All car drivers are expected to be competent and experienced and reach this elevated standard, even a defendant who is a learner driver[3] or is actually an extremely incompetent driver. Of course, all car drivers should carry compulsory insurance, so that any claim against a driver can be met by a solvent backer[4].

1   For example, in *Roberts v Ramsbottom* [1980] 1 All ER 7, [1980] 1 WLR 823, the court held that a driver who had suffered a stroke at the wheel and had had an accident, must be judged by the usual standard applicable to car drivers.
2   (1990) Times, 9 April.
3   *Nettleship v Weston* [1971] 2 QB 691, [1971] 3 All ER 581, CA.
4   Claims against drivers who, in breach of the law, are not insured are met by the Motor Insurers' Bureau.

18.39   In deciding the extent of the standard of care to be achieved, a defendant may be expected to account not merely for his own actions but also for a want of care displayed by others[1] if the reasonable man would have foreseen that such want of care was likely. For example, a defendant cannot expect children to recognise and guard against dangers as well as an adult and consequently must protect them against dangers which he could expect an adult to avoid for himself.

The standard of care requires a defendant to display a degree of care which could be expected from a reasonable man faced with his circumstances. Several different courses of action may be regarded as a reasonable response to events. The courts will not find that a defendant has fallen below the standard of care for preferring one approach to a problem when other solutions were available, provided that the method selected was a reasonable one. For example, in *Robinson v Post Office*[2], a doctor, who adopted an old-fashioned, but still accepted, test to see if the plaintiff was allergic to a vaccine, was held not to be liable for the brain damage suffered by the plaintiff whose allergy to the vaccine had not been revealed by the test. Nor can the standard of care require the implementation of procedures which at the time of the incident were not recognised as necessary. In *Roe v Minister of Health*[3], for example, no liability was imposed for failing to guard against the risk that ampoules of anaesthetic had been contaminated by storage in disinfectant; the risk of such contamination was not known until after the date of incident so that the reasonable doctor would not have been expected to guard against such a risk.

The standard of care required of a reasonable man may be determined by reference to the common practice of mankind or accepted trade practice and custom. However, even an approach generally adopted by mankind or all members of a trade or industry may be ruled to set too low a standard. Hence, to achieve this standard would still be to manifest a lack of reasonable care and thus be negligent[4]. This is surely correct. To allow, for example, a trade to set itself low standards and thereby escape liability for injury by reaching this modest target would be to encourage unsafe practices.

1   *London Passenger Transport Board v Upson* [1949] AC 155, HL. Any lack of care for his own safety displayed by a plaintiff may be contributory negligence; see paras 21.11–21.15, below.
2   [1974] 2 All ER 737, [1974] 1 WLR 1176, CA.
3   [1954] 2 QB 66, [1954] 2 All ER 131, CA. Also see *Thompson v Smiths Shiprepairers (North Shields) Ltd* [1984] QB 405, [1984] 1 All ER 881: no requirement to provide ear-defenders when the risks of industrial deafness were not recognised.
4   *Thompson v Smiths Shiprepairers (North Shields) Ltd* [1984] QB 405, [1984] 1 All ER 881; *Bolitho v City and Hackney Health Authority* [1993] 4 Med LR 381, CA.

18.40   *Professional personnel*   The standard of care demanded of a professional person[1] is that which could be expected from a reasonably competent fellow professional and not merely that of the reasonable man[2]. Thus, a person who has his ears pierced by a doctor can require the doctor to carry out the task to the standard expected of a reasonably competent doctor; if a jeweller is employed, the client can only expect him to reach the standard of a reasonably competent jeweller engaged in ear-piercing[3].

Difficulty can arise in determining the appropriate standard to impose on a professional person who is carrying out a specialist function; should the standard be that of a competent professional or that of a competent professional engaged in a specialist area? In *Wilsher v Essex Area Health Authority*[4], the Court of Appeal took the view that the standard was judged by reference to competent fellow professionals occupying a similar post or carrying out similar tasks to those performed by the defendant. In other words, the standard is judged by reference to the post occupied or function performed and not the person occupying it[5]. However, in *Whiteoak v Walker*[6], an accountant/auditor, whose valuation of shares in the company was alleged to be negligent, was judged by reference to the standard of an accountant acting as an auditor and not that of a specialist valuer[6]. What is clear is that professionals are always expected to reach the standard of other competent professionals; there is no concept of the learner professional.

It must be noted that a divergence of opinion, or adherence to different schools of thought, between professionals as to the proper course of action to be followed may result in different courses of action both being regarded as valid professional practice[7].

1   For professional negligence, see paras 19.16–19.22, below.
2   *Bolam v Friern Hospital Management Committee* [1957] 1 WLR 582. In *Wilsher v Essex Area Health Authority* [1987] QB 730, [1986] 3 All ER 801, CA (reversed on appeal by the House of Lords on other grounds; see para 18.52, below) the court held that the standard was judged by reference to competent fellow professionals occupying similar posts to that held by the defendant, ie the standard is judged by reference to the post occupied not the person occupying it.
3   *Philips v William Whiteley Ltd* [1938] 1 All ER 566. However, if the jeweller had held himself out as possessing some greater skill than might be expected of a jeweller, he must meet this higher standard: *Wells v Cooper* [1958] 2 QB 265, [1958] 2 All ER 527, CA.
4   [1987] QB 730, [1986] 3 All ER 801, CA.
5   A view approved in *Harvest Trucking Ltd v Davis* (1991) 135 Sol Jo 443.
6   (1988) 4 BCC 122. In this case, the accountant had not held himself out as having specialist knowledge of valuations so that the plaintiff could be said to have taken the risk that the advice would not match that which a specialist would have provided. See also *Luxmoore-May v Messenger May Baverstock* [1990] 1 All ER 1067, CA, in which the actions of a provincial auctioneer were judged by reference to the standard of a provincial auctioneer asked to comment on the provenance of a picture and not by reference to the standards expected of experts on fine art.
7   *Maynard v West Midlands Regional Health Authority* [1985] 1 All ER 635, [1984] 1 WLR 634.

Achieving the standard of care

18.41   While always remembering that each case turns on its own facts we now turn to some factors which courts consider in assessing whether a particular defendant, in the circumstances which he faced, failed to take reasonable care.

In determining whether the defendant has reached the standard of care which could be expected of a reasonable man in his position, the courts, while applying the overall concept of reasonableness, tend to pay particular regard to the risk of harm to which the plaintiff is exposed by the defendant. The concept of risk can be regarded as a balancing of many factors, particularly:

a.   whether the conduct of the defendant was likely to cause harm;
b.   whether the harm to which the plaintiff was exposed by the defendant was likely to be serious;
c.   whether the defendant was engaged on some useful task when he placed the plaintiff at risk;
d.   the cost of guarding against (or eliminating) the harm.

Likelihood of injury

18.42   A defendant who owes a duty of care is only required to take reasonable care to guard against breach of that duty. He is not required to guard against remote possibilities of injury[1]. Two cases concerning cricket grounds may be contrasted. In *Bolton v Stone*[2], the plaintiff was struck by a cricket ball while standing in the street outside her house. 'Sixes' of such mammoth proportions had occurred about six times in the previous 30 years. The House of Lords held that a duty of care existed but that no breach of that duty had occurred; the chances of such accidents were too fantastic a possibility to require the club to guard against them. In *Miller v Jackson*[3], the plaintiffs occupied a house adjacent to a cricket ground. Balls flew into their garden and neighbouring gardens much more regularly than in *Bolton v Stone*; in the preceding season five balls had landed in their garden. The Court of Appeal held that the risk of harm to the plaintiffs or their property was a far from remote possibility and the club was held liable in negligence for damage caused by flying cricket balls.

1   *Fardon v Harcourt-Rivington* (1932) 146 LT 391, HL.
2   [1951] AC 850, [1951] 1 All ER 1078, HL.
3   [1977] QB 966, [1977] 3 All ER 338. CA.

Seriousness of harm
18.43   Where serious harm is reasonably likely to occur if there is a breach of the duty of care, the defendant will be considered to have acted reasonably only if he has exercised care appropriate to the level of possible harm. In *Paris v Stepney Borough Council*[1], the local authority was liable for the loss of sight sustained by the plaintiff while in its employment. The defendant had failed to provide the plaintiff with goggles and, while such failure might be reasonable in respect of the usual employee, it was not reasonable in the case of the plaintiff since he only had one good eye. The seriousness of the harm likely to affect the plaintiff (blindness) required a reasonable employer to provide goggles.

   If the chance of harm occurring is foreseeable, albeit slim, but the seriousness of the possible harm is considerable, the standard of care is likely to reflect the potential seriousness of any injury which might be suffered[2].

1   [1951] AC 367, [1951] 1 All ER 42, HL. A further example is provided by *Johnstone v Bloomsbury Health Authority* [1992] QB 333, [1991] 2 All ER 293, CA, a junior hospital doctor not required to work such hours as might damage his health.
2   *Wright v Dunlop Rubber Co Ltd* (1972) 13 KIR 255, CA.

Usefulness of the defendant's conduct
18.44   If the defendant causes injury while engaged on some useful or desirable activity, he may not be in breach of his duty of care. The courts have to balance two issues: social utility and the harm caused. The more worthy the object which the defendant sought to attain, the less likely is he to be held liable in negligence[1]. In *Watt v Hertfordshire County Council*[2], a fireman was injured by heavy equipment which was being carried in a lorry not designed for such equipment. The fire authorities had used the lorry because they were rushing to the scene of an accident to attempt to save someone trapped under a heavy vehicle. The risk which they took in an attempt to save life was held not to be a breach of the duty of care which they owed to the plaintiff.

Doubts may be expressed about the validity of this factor. Should a person who is engaged voluntarily, or for a living, on some socially useful task be denied a remedy if he is injured while engaged on such a task? Should a bystander mown down by a fire engine and injured be told he can have no damages because fire engines perform socially useful tasks?

1   *Daborn v Bath Tramways Motor Co Ltd and Smithey* [1946] 2 All ER 333, CA; *Rigby v Chief Constable of Northamptonshire* [1985] 2 All ER 985, [1985] 1 WLR 1242.
2   [1954] 2 All ER 368, [1954] 1 WLR 835, CA. Compare *Ogwo v Taylor* [1988] AC 431, [1987] 3 All ER 961, HL; para 19.32, below.

Cost of precautions
18.45   If the likelihood of injury is small there will probably be no liability for failing to prevent that injury, but in every case the courts must balance the likelihood of injury against the cost and practicability of preventing it[1]. A risk which it is easy to eliminate should be eliminated even if the likelihood of injury is relatively small. Conversely, if an injury is unlikely to occur and the cost or practicability of guarding against it would be large, failure to do so may not be negligent[2]. Whether precautions should have been taken is generally assessed objectively and it is not open to the defendant to allege that, while precautions were reasonable, he could not afford to take them.

1   *The Wagon Mound (No 2)* [1967] 1 AC 617 at 642, [1966] 2 All ER 709; *Latimer v AEC Ltd* [1953] AC 643, [1953] 2 All ER 449, HL.
2   *Withers v Perry Chain Co Ltd* [1961] 3 All ER 676, [1961] 1 WLR 1314, CA.

Proof of negligence
18.46   As is usual in civil cases, the plaintiff bears the burden of proof in negligence[1]. Therefore, the plaintiff must adduce sufficient evidence to convince the court that, on the balance of probabilities, the defendant was careless[2]. The plaintiff may be aided in his task by s 11 of the Civil Evidence Act 1968 or the application of res ipsa loquitur.

1   See para 1.15, above.
2   A defendant who alleges contributory negligence on the part of the plaintiff bears the burden of proof on that issue.

Civil Evidence Act 1968
18.47   Section 11 of the Civil Evidence Act 1968 provides that a subsisting criminal conviction is evidence in any subsequent civil proceedings that the person convicted committed the offence. Hence, a conviction for careless driving is evidence of negligence in a later civil action. However, s 11 only provides that the conviction is evidence, and not proof, of liability in the civil case. Thus, while the evidential value of a criminal conviction is very high[1] it is not conclusive. In a civil case the defendant may be able to adduce evidence which was not relevant in a criminal trial, such as the utility of his conduct, to disprove negligence.

An acquittal in a criminal trial is not evidence of innocence in any subsequent civil proceedings.

1   *Stupple v Royal Insurance Co Ltd* [1971] 1 QB 50, [1970] 3 All ER 230, CA.

Res ipsa loquitur

18.48   In seeking to prove negligence, the plaintiff may be assisted by the maxim res ipsa loquitur, which can be translated as 'the thing speaks for itself', that is the circumstances are such that a breach of duty can be inferred. The maxim applies if a plaintiff establishes two basic facts set out below. Such proof gives rise to a rebuttable presumption of law which has the effect of satisfying the plaintiff's obligation to prove breach of the duty of care unless and until the defendant produces sufficient evidence in rebuttal. If the defendant produces evidence to rebut the presumption, the presumption disappears and the court determines the issue of breach without reference to it[1].

The classic definition of res ipsa loquitur was given by Erle CJ in *Scott v London and St Katherine Docks Co*[2]:

> 'There must be reasonable evidence of negligence. But where the thing is shown to be under the management of the defendant or his servants, and the accident is such as in the ordinary course of things does not happen if those who have the management use proper care, it affords reasonable evidence, in the absence of explanation by the defendants, that the accident arose from want of care.'

Therefore, if the maxim is to apply, the plaintiff must show:

a.   that the thing which caused the accident was under the control of the defendant or someone for whom he was responsible; and
b.   that the incident was such that it would not normally occur unless there had been negligence.

1   *Henderson v Henry E Jenkins & Sons and Evans* [1970] AC 282, [1969] 3 All ER 756, HL.
2   (1865) 3 H & C 596, Ex Ch.

18.49   *Control*   If the thing which caused the accident was under the control of the defendant or those for whom he is responsible and no outsider has tampered with it, the maxim can apply. The defendant will still be regarded as having control of a thing if an outsider might have tampered with it but such outside interference was unlikely. For example, in *Gee v Metropolitan Rly Co*[1], the defendants were held to be in control of the doors of their train while it was in a station and immediately on its departure from the station. Consequently, a passenger who fell out while leaning against a train door could rely on the maxim. An outsider might have been responsible for the door being insecurely latched but, given that the train had just left a station, this was unlikely. In contrast, in *Easson v London and North Eastern Rly Co*[2], the defendant railway company was not liable to the plaintiff who fell through a train door some miles from the last station. The defendant was not in control of the door for it was quite likely that a passenger had been responsible for the fact that the door was insufficiently fastened.

1   (1873) LR 8 QB 161, Ex Ch.
2   [1944] KB 421, [1944] 2 All ER 425, CA.

18.50 *Likelihood of negligence* In determining whether the incident was such that it would not normally occur without negligence, the court is guided by common sense and experience.

Stones in buns[1], slippery substances on supermarket floors[2] and swabs left in a patient after an operation[3] have all been held to be incidents which would not normally happen without negligence.

1 *Chaproniere v Mason* (1905) 21 TLR 633, CA.
2 *Ward v Tesco Stores Ltd* [1976] 1 All ER 219, [1976] 1 WLR 810, CA.
3 *Mahon v Osborne* [1939] 2 KB 14, [1939] 1 All ER 535, CA.

Damage Resulting

18.51 A plaintiff can recover damages for negligence only if he can prove that any harm which he has suffered was a consequence of a breach of duty by the defendant. In deciding this issue the court must consider two things:

a. whether, as a matter of fact, the breach of duty caused the harm; and
b. whether, as a matter of law, the harm suffered is too remote.

Causation in fact

18.52 Even when the defendant admits a breach of duty, the plaintiff in an action for negligence must prove that an effective cause of any harm which he has suffered was a breach of duty by the defendant. This has been reiterated by the House of Lords in *Wilsher v Essex Area Health Authority*[1], in which the plaintiff, who had become blind shortly after birth, failed in his action for damages because, while one possible cause of his injury was negligence by medical staff, other causes were equally likely; hence there was no *proof* that careless medical treatment was a material contributory cause of the harm.

A test adopted by the courts to determine whether the defendant's breach caused the harm of which the plaintiff complains is the 'but for' test; would the harm have occurred 'but for' the defendant's breach of duty? For example, in *McWilliams v Sir William Arrol & Co Ltd*[2], the defendants failed to provide safety equipment for steel erectors whom they employed, one of the employees fell to his death. His widow was unable to recover damages because it was conclusively established that the deceased would not have used the safety equipment even if it had been provided. Thus, the House of Lords held that the sole cause of the accident was the default of the deceased, and not the employer's failure to provide safety equipment. In *JEB Fasteners Ltd v Marks, Bloom & Co*[3], the defendant accountants carelessly audited the accounts of firm X, which was then taken over by the plaintiffs. The plaintiffs' action for damages failed. They had taken over the company not on the basis of the accounts but in a desire to obtain the services of two of X's directors; but for this desire no take-over bid would have been made. In contrast, in *Kirkham v Chief Constable of the Greater Manchester Police*[4], the Court of Appeal held that the effective cause of the suicide of a person remanded in custody was a failure by the police to pass on to the remand centre information about his suicidal tendencies; 'but for' this failure the deceased would not have been able to commit suicide[5].

A difficult problem arises when the defendant admits that he has failed to take some course of action but contends, that even if he had done so, he would not have prevented the loss suffered by the plaintiff. The approach taken by the courts requires the plaintiff to prove that, had there been no omission, steps would have been taken by the defendant which would have prevented the harm suffered. If the defendant can show that, even if he had attended, the actions he would have taken, despite not being negligent, would not have prevented the harm, the failure to take the course of action is not the effective cause of the harm[6].

1   [1988] AC 1074, [1988] 1 All ER 871, HL.
2   [1962] 1 All ER 623, [1962] 1 WLR 295, HL.
3   [1983] 1 All ER 583, CA.
4   [1990] 2 QB 283, [1990] 3 All ER 246, CA.
5   Distinguishing on the facts the earlier case of *Knight v Home Office* [1990] 3 All ER 237.
6   *Joyce v Wandsworth Health Authority* [1996] PIQR P121, CA. But see *Allied Maples Group Ltd v Simmons & Simmons* [1995] 4 All ER 907, CA, where the court inclined to the view that a defendant who has failed to take a course of action, thereby denying the plaintiff a choice as to how to proceed, would be liable for the value of the chance of benefit or avoidance of detriment which the plaintiff has lost.

Loss of a chance

18.53   Particularly difficult issues of causation arise when the plaintiff alleges that the negligence of the defendant has deprived him of a chance. For example, suppose a doctor negligently fails to treat a patient who then becomes permanently disabled. If the doctor can establish that the disability would *probably* have occurred anyway, has the patient failed to prove the doctor's omission caused the harm or is he compensated for the loss of a chance that the treatment might have been successful? In *Hotson v East Berkshire Health Authority*[1], the House of Lords treated such cases as a matter of causation; only if the plaintiff can prove the omission caused the harm can he be compensated.

In contrast, in *Allied Maples Group Ltd v Simmons v Simmons*[2], solicitors, who had failed to warn the plaintiff about possible liabilities which could arise if the plaintiff entered into an arrangement under a scheme drawn up by the defendants, thereby depriving the plaintiff of the chance to avoid that liability, were held liable. The court concluded that the appropriate approach was to evaluate the chance that the plaintiff would have been able obtain indemnity cover for the possible liability and compensate for the loss of that chance. Rather than treat the loss of the chance as purely a question of causation, the court held that once there was a substantial possibility that the loss to the plaintiff could have been avoided (by G agreeing to indemnify), the issue was one of quantification of damage.

Perhaps the cases can be distinguished on the basis that in the latter case the plaintiff's loss depended upon the hypothetical action of an independent third party rather than something which was a matter of historical fact, that is that the harm would probably have arisen even if the doctor had treated the injury .

1   [1987] AC 750, [1987] 2 All ER 909, HL.
2   [1995] 4 All ER 907, CA. See also *Spring v Guardian Assurance plc* [1995] 2 AC 296, [1994] 3 All ER 129, HL, discussed in para 18.9, above, in which the plaintiff recovered for loss of the chance of employment even though there was no guarantee that the third party would have employed him even if the reference had not been given negligently.

Multiple causes

18.54   The 'but for' test cannot be applied in all situations. For example, if a plaintiff's injuries are concurrently caused by the negligence of two or more people not acting in concert they cannot evade liability by claiming that the immediate cause of the plaintiff's loss was the action of the other. Both of them are liable to the plaintiff[1]. The plaintiff can sue one or both of the tortfeasors but cannot, of course, recover damages twice.

1   *Fitzgerald v Lane* [1989] AC 328, [1988] 2 All ER 961, HL. See paras 17.13 and 17.14, above, for contribution between tortfeasors.

18.55   Another difficulty arises where tortfeasor X injures the plaintiff and the same or similar injuries are subsequently caused by tortfeasor Y. If X negligently damages the plaintiff's car so that it needs to be resprayed but, before such a respray, Y further damages the car's paintwork, X alone is liable for the cost of the respray. Y cannot be said to have caused any new damage to the car[1].

However, if the effect of Y's tort is to supersede the effect of X's tort, is X liable? In *Baker v Willoughby*[2], the defendant negligently injured the plaintiff's leg; subsequently, the plaintiff was the victim of an armed robbery and in consequence the leg had to be amputated. Nevertheless, the House of Lords required the defendant to compensate the plaintiff for his initial damage on the basis that the plaintiff still had and would continue to have an injured leg. One of the arguments accepted by the House was that, had the robbers been sued, they would have been liable to compensate the plaintiff not for the loss of a leg but for the loss of an already defective leg. Doubt has been cast upon *Baker v Willoughby* by *Jobling v Associated Dairies Ltd*[3], although the cases are distinguishable in that in *Jobling* the injury caused by the tortfeasor was superseded not by another tortious act but by the onset of illness which was unconnected with the initial injury.

In *Jobling*, the House of Lords held that the defendant employer's liability to compensate the plaintiff for lost future earnings, the employer's negligence having partially disabled the plaintiff, was limited to the amount of earnings lost between the date of disablement and the subsequent onset of illness which rendered Jobling totally disabled. Their Lordships accepted the argument that Jobling would have become totally disabled anyway and that to require his employer to compensate him for the partial disablement after the onset of illness was unjust.

1   *Performance Cars Ltd v Abraham* [1962] 1 QB 33, [1961] 3 All ER 413, CA.
2   [1970] AC 467, [1969] 3 All ER 1528, HL.
3   [1982] AC 794, [1981] 2 All ER 752, HL.

Intervening causes

18.56   If the effective cause of the ultimate harm suffered by the tort victim is not the act or omission of the defendant but the act or omission of a third party, the defendant will not be liable. Hence, in *Barnett v Chelsea and Kensington Hospital Management Committee*[1], a hospital doctor who negligently failed to examine the plaintiff's husband (who had been poisoned by someone unknown[2]) was not liable. The doctor's negligence did not cause the husband's subsequent death since, even if correct medical treatment had been forthcoming, death would have ensued.

When the effective cause of the ultimate harm is some non-tortious event which has been followed by a negligent act or omission by the defendant, the defendant is not liable. In *Hotson v East Berkshire Area Health Authority*[3], a child fell out of a tree and suffered severe leg injuries which were, initially, mis-diagnosed and hence mistreated. The leg was permanently damaged but an action for negligence failed once it was established that, given the severity of the injury caused by the fall, the ultimate damage to the leg had been more than likely to occur whatever treatment was given.

1   [1969] 1 QB 428, [1968] 1 All ER 1068.
2   This person, if he could be identified and found, would be liable for the death in tort (and in criminal law) but he might not have had sufficient funds to be worth suing.
3   [1987] AC 750, [1987] 2 All ER 909, HL.

18.57   Since the defendant will not be responsible for any harm suffered by the plaintiff, even though he is in breach of duty, if the harm was *caused* by a third party or the plaintiff himself, it is a critical question whether the actions of a third party or a plaintiff are held to be the effective cause of the plaintiff's injuries. The critical question is whether there a 'break in the chain of causation' between defendant and plaintiff sufficient to absolve the defendant from the consequences of his wrongdoing. A subsequent action which has such a causal link to the ultimate loss suffered by the plaintiff that it 'swamps' the original wrongdoing is called a novus actus interveniens (or an intervening cause).

A finding that a subsequent act was an intervening cause is a finding of fact and thus the examples given below are merely illustrative of the operation of the principle.

18.58   *Act of the plaintiff*   An act or omission on the part of the plaintiff, which, combined with the defendant's breach of duty, occasions the plaintiff injury, will normally be an act of contributory negligence[1]. Less commonly, the plaintiff's act or omission is regarded as the sole cause of his injuries as in *McWilliams v Sir William Arrol & Co Ltd*, discussed in para 18.52, above.

A defendant may also plead that the plaintiff's act or omission is the cause of some portion of the total harm which he has suffered. This could arise if, subsequent to the defendant's tort, the plaintiff behaved unreasonably and hence increased his injuries. An example is provided by *McKew v Holland and Hannen and Cubitts (Scotland) Ltd*[2]. In this case, the plaintiff who had been negligently injured by the defendant was consequently afflicted with a leg which sometimes gave way beneath him. After the accident, he visited a flat which was approached by a steep staircase without a handrail. When descending the stairs, the plaintiff felt his leg giving way and jumped to try and land upright, sustaining a fractured ankle. The House of Lords held that the defendant was not responsible for the broken ankle (as opposed to the original injury to the leg). The effective cause of the plaintiff's accident was his foolhardiness in using the stairs without any assistance, knowing that his leg was liable to give way.

What will be regarded as unreasonable behaviour on the part of the plaintiff may be difficult to determine. It is not unreasonable to refuse a late abortion following the conception of a child after a negligently performed sterilisation[3], nor to decline to undergo psychiatric treatment involving 're-living' the very incident which occasioned the harm if that incident was particularly stressful[4], but it may be unreasonable to refuse simple medical treatment which would minimise one's injuries[5].

1 Paras 21.11–21.15, below.
2 [1969] 3 All ER 1621, HL.
3 *Emeh v Kensington and Chelsea and Westminster Area Health Authority* [1985] QB 1012, [1984] 3 All ER 1044, CA.
4 *Re Herald of Free Enterprise* (1989) Independent, 5 May, arbitration to assess damages for nervous shock following the Zeebrugge ferry disaster.
5 *Selvanayagam v University of the West Indies* [1983] 1 All ER 824, [1983] 1 WLR 585, PC.

18.59   A plaintiff who, faced with a risk of injury to himself or another by the defendant's breach of duty, attempts to rectify the situation by trying to rescue himself or that other is not regarded as breaking the chain of causation unless the rescue attempt is completely unnecessary or unreasonable in the circumstances. For example, in *Haynes v Harwood*[1], the defendants, who were responsible for negligently allowing their dray-horses to bolt down a busy street, were held liable to a policeman injured in trying to stop the bolting horses; his rescue attempt was both necessary and appropriate. In contrast, a person injured in attempting to 'rescue' a person who was in no danger could not recover[2]. A rescuer who undertakes a rescue which is necessary, but who goes about it in a negligent way, may have his damages reduced on the grounds of contributory negligence[3].

1 [1935] 1 KB 146, CA.
2 *Cutler v United Dairies (London) Ltd* [1933] 2 KB 297, CA.
3 In *Harrison v British Railways Board* [1981] 3 All ER 679, the plaintiff, a railway guard who attempted to rescue an endangered passenger, could recover damages from the passenger (who had created the danger to himself) less 20% for contributory negligence. He had ignored a safe method of rescue and had adopted a more hazardous method.

18.60   *Act of a third party*   A conscious act by a third party may, but does not necessarily, operate as an intervening cause and thus break the chain of causation between the original tort and the ultimate loss suffered by the plaintiff. Certainly, if the intervening act was tortious (particularly if deliberate[1]) and unconnected with the original breach of duty, it is more likely to break the chain of causation. Judges have called for a 'robust and sensible approach to this question with the application of common sense rather than logic'.

In *The Oropesa*[2], the master of a ship which had been badly damaged in an accident launched a boat in heavy seas to cross to *The Oropesa*, which was responsible for the accident, to discuss salvage. The boat overturned and nine men drowned. *The Oropesa* was held responsible for the deaths; she had imperilled the other vessel and the master's action in launching the boat (neither tortious nor unconnected with the original accident) did not break the chain of causation. In *Rouse v Squires*[3], a motorist who negligently caused an accident which blocked the road was held responsible for the death of the plaintiff who had stopped to assist at the scene, even though the plaintiff was actually killed by another negligent motorist who had collided with the crashed vehicles. The Court of Appeal held that a motorist who causes an accident and thereby obstructs the highway is responsible for other motorists who accidentally contribute to further collisions, even though the later motorists may crash through driving too fast or not keeping a proper look out, since such subsequent collisions were connected with the original accident[4]. On the other hand, if subsequent collisions are caused by the deliberate or reckless acts of other drivers the original tortfeasor is not liable for them. Consider, for example, *Wright v Lodge, Kerek v Lodge*[5], in which the respondent's car broke down and came to a halt on the nearside lane of an unlit dual carriageway on a foggy night. While she was attempting to restart the car an articulated lorry, driven recklessly at excessive speed by the appellant, crashed into it and careered across the central reservation before halting on the opposite carriageway where it was struck by several vehicles including a car driven by X who was killed in the incident. The Court of Appeal held that while the respondent had been negligent in not removing her car from the carriageway on to the verge, the sole cause of the truck crossing the central reservation and the subsequent death of X was the appellant's reckless driving which was the only relevant legal cause of the death.

Foreseeable intervening acts by those who are not to be regarded as fully responsible for their actions (such as children) are not likely to be an intervening cause[6].

1 *Lamb v Camden London Borough Council* [1981] QB 625, [1981] 2 All ER 408, CA; no liability on the part of the council for acts of squatters in the plaintiff's house (even though the acts were foreseeable), despite council being liable in tort for rendering the house uninhabitable by the plaintiff. But see *Philco Radio and Television Corpn of Great Britain Ltd v J Spurling Ltd* [1949] 2 KB 33, [1949] 2 All ER 882, CA; defendants liable for fire caused by a typist employed by the plaintiff who deliberately set fire to material which, unbeknown to her, was dangerous (unforeseeable and unreasonable acts) and which they had, negligently misdelivered to the plaintiff's premises.
2 [1943] P 32, [1943] 1 All ER 211, CA.
3 [1973] QB 889, [1973] 2 All ER 903, CA.
4 Ibid, at 898.
5 [1993] 4 All ER 299, CA; see also *Knightley v Johns* [1982] 1 All ER 851, [1982] 1 WLR 349, CA.
6 *Haynes v Harwood* [1935] 1 KB 146, CA.

Remoteness of damage

18.61 If the defendant's breach of duty caused any harm suffered by the plaintiff, the plaintiff can recover damages for the harm suffered provided that it was not in law too remote a consequence of that breach. Judges have, on the practical ground that to do otherwise would unreasonably restrict human activity, limited the recoverability of damages to claims for injuries which are not too remote a consequence of the breach of duty. There have been two main contenders for the test to determine whether a consequence is legally too remote: first, that all direct consequences are recoverable, and, second, that only reasonably foreseeable consequences are recoverable.

In 1921, in *Re Polemis*[1], the Court of Appeal held that damages for all direct consequences were recoverable and this was the law until 1961, when, in *The Wagon Mound*[2], the Privy Council adopted the rule that damages are recoverable only for reasonably foreseeable consequences. While not binding on English courts, the *Wagon Mound* rule now represents English law.

1   [1921] 3 KB 560.
2   [1961] AC 388, [1961] 1 All ER 404, PC.

18.62   In *The Wagon Mound*[1], a ship, the *Wagon Mound*, was taking on fuel oil at a wharf in Sydney harbour. Due to the carelessness of the employees of the defendants (who were charterers of the ship), large amounts of fuel oil were spilt. Some of the oil spread to another wharf owned by the plaintiff, where welding was taking place; the plaintiff stopped welding but recommenced on receiving expert opinion that fuel oil would not burn on water. Two days later the oil was ignited by splashes from the welding falling onto the oily water. This caused extensive damage to the plaintiff's wharf. It was found as a fact that it was unforeseeable that fuel oil on water would burn, although it was reasonably foreseeable that the oil might foul parts of the plaintiff's wharf. While the damage caused by the fire was a direct consequence of the breach of duty by the defendants, it was unforeseeable and the Privy Council, therefore, rejected the plaintiff's claim for damages.

Thus, reasonable foreseeability is both an element of the test for determining whether a duty of care exists and is the test for deciding whether the harm suffered by the plaintiff is too remote[2]. There are cases in which a plaintiff has been denied a remedy by some of the court on the ground that there was no duty, while the rest of the court have denied him a remedy on the ground that the harm suffered was too remote. At present reasonable foreseeability is deployed by judges predominantly at the duty stage[3]. Once it is established that the damage suffered was a reasonably foreseeable consequence, the likelihood that it would have occurred is irrelevant. The likelihood that damage will occur is relevant in determining if there has been a breach of duty.

While 'reasonable foreseeability' appears to be a very different rule of remoteness from 'direct consequences' it has turned out in practice to be a less than revolutionary change. This can be seen by looking separately at the three identifying characteristics of any harm for which a remedy is sought: the type of harm or damage, the method of its infliction, and its extent.

1   [1961] AC 388, [1961] 1 All ER 404, PC.
2   Although it must be stressed that while the words are the same the interpretation of what it is that must be reasonably foreseen is rather different; see paras 18.63–18.66, below, in particular.
3   An exception is *Attia v British Gas plc* [1988] QB 304, [1987] 3 All ER 455, CA, in which the court held that, where the defendant owed a duty of care to the plaintiff, the plaintiff could recover for nervous shock if it was reasonably foreseeable that this might occur as a consequence of the breach.

Type of harm

18.63   An injury is reasonably foreseeable if it is of the *type* of harm, albeit not the exact type, that a reasonable man would foresee as a not wholly unlikely consequence of the breach of duty. For example, physical injury is a reasonably foreseeable consequence of a car accident even if the precise nature of those injuries is not. In *Bradford v Robinson Rentals Ltd*[1], the plaintiff, who was sent by the defendant on a long drive during very cold weather in an unheated van, recovered for frostbite since cold damage was foreseeable even if frostbite was not. However, in *Tremain v Pike*[2], the plaintiff failed to recover for catching a disease spread by rat urine because, while the defendant had exposed the plaintiff to risk (by failing to suppress a rat plague on his farm), the reasonable man would only have foreseen damage by rat bite. This decision can be doubted in that 'rat damage' was certainly foreseeable. In the recent case of *Page v Smith*[3], the House of Lords rejected the very specific approach adopted in *Tremain* and held that where physical injury was foreseeable, the plaintiff could recover for psychiatric damage; psychiatric damage was simply another form of physical injury. The court accepted that psychiatric injury itself was not a foreseeable consequence of the defendant's negligence (defective driving causing a car accident). However, since injury to the body was foreseeable, although not sustained, the plaintiff could recover for the injury to his mind which he had sustained.

The difficulty of predicting whether the court will find harm to be of a foreseeable type is further illustrated by the situation which gave rise to *The Wagon Mound* itself. In *The Wagon Mound* the plaintiff wharf-owner could not recover for fire damage but did recover for fouling of the slipways and similar damage because the latter type of damage was reasonably foreseeable. In a subsequent case concerning the same incident[4], fire damage itself was found to be reasonably foreseeable.

1   [1967] 1 All ER 267, [1967] 1 WLR 337.
2   [1969] 3 All ER 1303, [1969] 1 WLR 1556.
3   [1996] AC 155, [1995] 2 All ER 736, HL. It is important to bear in mind that the foreseeability of psychiatric harm may be relevant in determining if a duty of care is owed at all, this issue did not arise in *Page v Smith* because the plaintiff was a primary victim of the negligent incident and not simply an observer, see further para 18.22, above.
4   *The Wagon Mound (No 2)* [1967] 1 AC 617, [1966] 2 All ER 709, PC. The plaintiff wharf-owner did not plead the damage was reasonably foreseeable in *The Wagon Mound* since he had authorised the welding. In *The Wagon Mound (No 2)* the plaintiffs were ship-owners whose vessels were being welded so that a finding that fire was reasonably foreseeable did not affect their claim.

Method of infliction

18.64   A type of harm can be reasonably foreseeable even though the precise *method* of its infliction is not reasonably foreseeable. In *Hughes v Lord Advocate*[1], some workmen left an open manhole unattended but surrounded by paraffin lamps. A child playing with one of the lamps fell through the manhole and was severely burnt when the lamp exploded. It was foreseeable that a child might break a lamp and be burnt but it was totally unforeseeable that a lamp should explode. The child was able to recover damages because the type of harm, burning, was foreseeable, even if the way in which it occurred was not. In contrast, in *Doughty v Turner Manufacturing Co Ltd²*, workmen were not able to recover for injuries caused by the eruption of a cauldron of molten metal, which occurred when a cover fell into the cauldron and suffered chemical change. Injury by splashing molten metal was foreseeable, but not, held the Court of Appeal, injury by eruption of the molten metal. However, it seems possible to doubt the decision in *Doughty* and to argue that the type of harm (burns caused by molten metal) was foreseeable, even if the exact way in which it was inflicted was not. Certainly, in *Banque Financière de la Cité SA v Westgate Insurance Co Ltd³*, the Court of Appeal stated that, where economic loss was foreseeable and in fact occurred, the loss was not too remote even though its method of infliction, fraud, was not foreseeable.

1 [1963] AC 837, [1963] 1 All ER 705, HL.
2 [1964] 1 QB 518, [1964] 1 All ER 98, CA.
3 [1989] 2 All ER 952, CA. This point was not considered in the House of Lords: [1991] 2 AC 249, [1990] 2 All ER 947, HL.

Extent of injury

18.65 If the type of harm suffered is reasonably foreseeable the total *extent* of the actual injury need not be foreseeable. Hence, in *Wieland v Cyril Lord Carpets Ltd¹*, the plaintiff, whose injuries (caused by the defendant's negligence) required her to wear a surgical collar, could also recover for subsequent injuries caused by falling down some steps which she was unable to see because her angle of visibility was impaired by the collar even though those injuries were completely unforeseeable.

That the extent of injuries need not be foreseeable is illustrated by the principle that 'you take your victim as you find him' (also called the thin- or eggshell-skull rule). If a motorist negligently runs over a cyclist who, because he suffers from haemophilia, bleeds to death, the motorist is responsible for the death. He cannot argue successfully that a reasonable man could not have foreseen the extent of his victim's injuries. An application of the rule is contained in *Smith v Leech Brain & Co Ltd²*. Here, an employer negligently burnt an employee; this activated a pre-existing cancer from which the employee died three years later. The employer was held liable for this death.

1 [1969] 3 All ER 1006.
2 [1962] 2 QB 405, [1961] 3 All ER 1159.

18.66 The 'eggshell-skull' rule has been applied to a plaintiff with a personality disorder, so that she could recover for a complete personality breakdown following a minor road accident¹, as well as to victims with physical defects which rendered their injuries much more serious than would be normal. In *Meah v McCreamer²*, the plaintiff suffered head injuries in a road accident caused by the defendant. These injuries exacerbated the plaintiff's existing aggressive tendencies. This resulted in him committing two rapes for which he was sentenced to life imprisonment. The defendant was required to pay damages to compensate the plaintiff for the head injuries, the changed personality and the prison sentence³.

The House of Lords, in the *Liesbosch Dredger v SS Edison⁴*, held that the 'eggshell-skull' rule is limited to the physical state of the plaintiff and cannot be extended to his financial state. In that case, X negligently damaged Y's ship and Y, needing to replace the vessel quickly, had to hire an alternative vessel at great expense because he lacked the capital to buy a replacement. The House of Lords held that Y could not recover the hire costs but only the costs of a replacement. Y's poverty was not reasonably foreseeable and there was no eggshell-wallet rule. Doubt has been cast on the decision in *Liesbosch Dredger* and it may be that it will be reconsidered in the future. It has now been distinguished in a number of later cases; for example, where the defendant's tort caused the plaintiff's poverty, or where the plaintiff declined to ameliorate the tort (thereby increasing his losses) for sound commercial reasons[5]. In *Mattocks v Mann*[6] the plaintiff was able to recover the cost of hiring a comparable car to the one damaged by the defendant until the defendant's insurers provided funds to repair her car.

1   *Brice v Brown* [1984] 1 All ER 997. See also *Page v Smith* [1996] AC 155, [1995] 2 All ER 736, HL in which the plaintiff was able to recover for the exacerbation of a pre-existing psychiatric ailment.
2   [1985] 1 All ER 367; the defendant seems to have conceded the remoteness issue and it seems at least arguable that Meah's wrongful acts could have been treated as an intervening cause breaking the chain of causation.
3   Meah was subsequently successfully sued for damages in trespass by the victims of the rapes. He then sought to recover the damages which he had had to pay to his victims from the original tortfeasor; his claim was rejected as being too remote a consequence of the road accident: *Meah v McCreamer (No 2)* [1986] 1 All ER 943.
4   [1933] AC 449, HL.
5   See further para 21.36, below.
6   [1993] RTR 13, CA,

Interrelation of Contractual and Tortious Liability

18.67   Traditionally the law of contract protects rights and imposes duties upon parties who have entered into a voluntary agreement – a contract – whereas tort duties are imposed by law regardless of any agreement between tortfeasor and tort victim. The apparent dichotomy between contract (consensual duties) and tort (imposed duties) has never created an impermeable divide. Some tort duties can only arise in the context of a consensual relationship, for example the duty of an employer to provide safe working conditions, and some contractual duties are imposed, for example the implied terms in contracts for the sale of goods. Perhaps a more telling distinction between contract and tort lies in the possible remedy for breach of a duty rather than in the source of the duty. Tort restores the plaintiff to where he was whereas contract puts the plaintiff in the position he should have been had the duty been performed, but even here anomalies arise. The tort victim who recovers damages for lost future earnings can be seen as recovering what should have been his, rather than being restored to his original position, and the victim of a breach of contract which results in damage to his property is restored to his former position by the law of contract. However, despite the possibility of an overlap between contract and tort they remain distinct bodies of law with many points of difference. This leads to the question of how do contract and tort interrelate in situations where, potentially, both contract and tort could apply.

The majority of cases where there is a possible overlap between contract and tort involve an allegation that the defendant has displayed a lack of care, that is, an allegation of negligence. Since this is the case, we discuss the interrelation of contract and tort at this point. However, it should not be forgotten that there are other situations in which contract and tort overlap; for example, the unjustified retention of goods by an unpaid repairer of them may be both a breach of contract and the tort of wrongful interference with goods[1].

1   Paras 20.16–20.19, below.

Concurrent duties owed to the same party

18.68   Recent cases support the view that, where a person has a contract with another person (X) and would owe X a duty of care (applying the normal principles of the law of tort), there can be concurrent liability in contract and tort[1]. Hence, the existence of a contract does not require a court to apply the contractual rules on assessment of damages or limitation of actions where they are stricter than the corresponding rules for the tort of negligence[2]. It follows that a plaintiff who has available to him concurrent remedies in contract and tort can choose the remedy most advantageous to him. An exception is where the contract precludes the plaintiff from doing so[3].

What remains a contentious issue is the degree to which a duty of care which would exist in tort can be modified by a contract between the parties. There is no doubt that a contract can *increase* the duties of a party to it so that their contractual obligations exceed those which would apply in tort[4].Nor is there any doubt that the law of tort and a concurrent contract can require the same standard of care from a person. For example, a professional adviser's contract with his clients may, either expressly or impliedly[5], require him to exercise due care with regard to his clients' affairs; he owes a parallel duty in tort. What remains at issue is whether a contract can *reduce* the scope of a duty which would otherwise arise in tort. The general view is that the standard of care demanded in tort is never higher than that required by the terms of the contract so that the duties of the parties can be said to be as set out in their contract[6]. If this is the case then, if there is no breach of the express or implied terms of the contract, there is no liability in tort either[7]. However, in one case[8], the Court of Appeal stated that there was no reason in principle why the duty of care in tort could not impose wider obligations than those arising under the contract if the circumstances justified such a conclusion.

1   *Henderson v Merret Syndicates Ltd* [1995] 2 AC 145, [1994] 3 All ER 506, HL, approving *Midland Bank Trust Co Ltd v Hett, Stubbs and Kemp* [1979] Ch 384; see also *Esso Petroleum Co Ltd v Mardon* [1976] QB 801, [1976] 2 All ER 5, CA; *Forsikringsaktielskapet Vesta v Butcher* [1989] AC 852, [1988] 2 All ER 43, CA; *Punjab National Bank v de Boinville* [1992] 3 All ER 104, [1992] 1 WLR 1138, CA.
2   *Henderson v Merret Syndicates Ltd* [1995] 2 AC 145, [1994] 3 All ER 506, HL.
3   *Pirelli General Cable Works Ltd v Oscar Faber & Partners* [1983] 2 AC 1, [1983] 1 All ER 65, HL. A contrary view was expressed in *Tai Hing Cotton Mill Ltd v Liu Chong Hing Bank Ltd* [1986] AC 80 at 107, [1985] 2 All ER 947 at 957, [1985] 3 WLR 317 at 330. *Pirelli* has been approved on this point in later cases; see, for example, *Henderson v Merret Syndicates Ltd* [1995] 2 AC 145, [1994] 3 All ER 506, HL.
4   For an example see *Thake v Maurice* [1986] QB 644, [1986] 1 All ER 497, CA.

5   By virtue of the Supply of Goods and Services Act 1982, s 13; para 8.37, above.
6   *Tai Hing Cotton Mill Ltd v Liu Chong Hing Bank Ltd* [1986] AC 80, [1985] 2 All ER 947, PC.
    This case has been approved in *National Bank of Greece SA v Pinios Shipping Co No 1* [1990]
    1 AC 637, [1989] 1 All ER 213, CA.
7   *Johnstone v Bloomsbury Health Authority* [1992] QB 333, [1991] 2 All ER 293, CA, states this
    very clearly but whether a court would allow an express contractual term to reduce the degree
    of care which, in tort, the employer must display towards his employees seems doubtful.
8   *Holt v Payne Skillington* [1996] 02 LS Gaz R 29, CA.

18.69   What is also uncertain is when a contract, which purports to restrict
or exempt a tortious duty which would otherwise arise, has this effect. Obviously,
an express contractual term can restrict a tortious duty and it is thought that
where the contractual and tortious duties are inconsistent the contract must
prevail[1]. Where a tortious duty is neither contrary to an express term of the
contract, nor inconsistent with its terms, there is no reason why it should not
co-exist with the contractual duties.

In cases in which the contract between tortfeasor and tort victim contains
an exemption clause or disclaimer, that clause is subject to the usual rules for
determining its enforceability[2]. Should the exemption clause or disclaimer be
upheld by the court, then, if its effect is to exclude both contractual and tortious
liability, the party at fault escapes liability in both contract and tort. If only
liability in tort is excluded, contractual liability is unaffected and there seems
no reason in principle why the reverse should not be the case.

1   See, for example, *Greater Nottingham Co-operative Society Ltd v Cementation Piling and
    Foundations Ltd* [1989] QB 71, [1988] 2 All ER 971, CA.
2   Paras 10.25–10.56, above.

Concurrent duties owed to different parties

18.70   A contract between one person and a person causing harm does not
preclude tortious liability to a third person suffering that harm. In *Smith v Eric
S Bush*[1], the House of Lords held that a professional person, a surveyor, owed
to his client, a building society, a contractual duty to take care and owed to the
potential house purchaser a duty of care under the rules relating to the tort of
negligence. More recently, in *White v Jones*[2], the House of Lords accepted that
a solicitor who negligently failed to alter his deceased client's will was in breach
of his contractual duty to his client (any damages payable would accrue to the
estate) and in breach of his duty of care to the parties whom the deceased
would have benefited by the alteration.

It is, however, necessary to stress that the existence of a contract between a
person causing harm and someone else does not mean that a person suffering
that harm is automatically owed a tortious duty; the victim must establish that
he is owed a duty on normal principles. Where there is a chain of contracts
binding A to B and B to C etc, the courts are slow to impose an added duty
above those provided for in the contract[3]. Thus, if the owner of a building
enters into a contract for its refurbishment with a head contractor, who sub-
contracts portions of the work to third parties, there is no contract between
the owner and the sub-contractors and there is unlikely to be a tortious duty
either. However, the courts are not consistent in their approach. In *Henderson*

v Merrett Syndicates Ltd[1], the House of Lords did not regard the fact that the parties to the action chose to arrange their relationship through a chain of contracts (between Lloyd's names and agents and between agents and sub-agents) as incompatible with the existence of a tortious duty between names and sub-agents.

An exemption clause in a contract between a tortfeasor and a third party, whether it binds the third party or not, will not generally affect the tort victim[5].

1　[1990] 1 AC 831, [1989] 2 All ER 514, HL.
2　[1995] 2 AC 207, [1995] 1 All ER 691, HL, see para 18.16, above.
3　*Pacific Associates Inc v Baxter*　[1990] 1 QB 993, 1989] 2 All ER 159, CA.
4　[1995] 2 AC 145, [1994] 3 All ER 506, HL See further, para 18.12, above.
5　*Leigh and Sillivan Ltd v Aliakmon Shipping Co Ltd* [1986] AC 785, [1986] 2 All ER 145, HL; see further paras 10.41 and 10.42, above.

to protect employees against that risk will be actionable, even if it is still the practice of the relevant trade to ignore it[1].

In a situation in which the employer owes both this common law duty and a duty imposed by statute, compliance with the statutory duty is likely to be regarded as manifesting reasonable care[2].

The common law duty of care owed by the employer (but not its performance[3]) is non-delegable. The result is that, if an employer delegates performance of his duty to an independent contractor and the independent contractor causes the injury to an employee, the employer is liable for breach of the duty which he (the employer) owes to his employees.

Additionally, if an employer has failed to select his independent contractor with adequate care, or has failed adequately to brief or supervise the contractor, the employer is liable for injuries caused by the contractor[4].

1 *Thompson v Smiths Shiprepairers (North Shields) Ltd* [1984] QB 405, [1984] 1 All ER 881.
2 *Chipchase v British Titan Products Co Ltd* [1956] 1 QB 545, [1956] 1 All ER 613, CA.
3 See also paras 17.31–17.35, above.
4 See further para 17.30, above.

19.5 *Safe system of work* The employer must plan the work with due regard to the physical and mental safety of his employees.

Consequently, an employer was held to be in breach of his duty by permitting a crane to swing stones over the heads of employees working in a quarry, when this resulted in an employee being injured by falling stones. The fact that the employees continued to work knowing of the risk did not mean that they continued to work consenting to the risk of injury[1]. In planning the work, the employer must recognise that employees become careless about risks involved in their jobs, and that the fact that a practice has grown up of doing a particular job in a particular way does not necessarily mean that to adopt that practice is to employ reasonable care[2].

An experienced workman dealing with a familiar and obvious risk may not reasonably need the same attention or the same precautions as an inexperienced man[3]. In the case of the skilled and experienced worker, it may be necessary only to make available safety equipment such as goggles, belts or spats[4]; in others it may be necessary to provide the equipment into the employee's hands[5], and in the case of the inexperienced man it may be necessary actually to exhort him to use the equipment[6].

A failure to provide safety equipment for a worker will not result in an employer losing an action for breach of common law duty where it is shown that the accident would have occurred in any event because the employee would have refused to use the equipment[7].

Recent cases have stressed that the duty is not limited to physical injury. Thus, in *Walker v Northumberland County Council*[8], a social services officer employed by the defendant council recovered damages in respect of a nervous breakdown suffered as a consequence of overwork. The plaintiff had had a nervous breakdown in the past and it was found to be foreseeable that, if he was exposed to the same workload, there was a risk that his condition would recur.

1   *Smith v Baker & Sons* [1891] AC 325, HL.
2   *Cavanagh v Ulster Weaving Co Ltd* [1960] AC 145, [1959] 2 All ER 745, HL.
3   *Qualcast (Wolverhampton) Ltd v Haynes* [1959] AC 743, [1959] 2 All ER 38, HL.
4   *Smith v Scot Bowyers Ltd* [1986] IRLR 315, CA.
5   *Crouch v British Rail Engineering Ltd* [1988] IRLR 404, CA.
6   *Bux v Slough Metals Ltd* [1974] 1 All ER 262, [1973] 1 WLR 1358, CA.
7   *Cummings (or McWilliams) v Sir William Arrol & Co Ltd* [1962] 1 All ER 623, [1962] 1 WLR 295, HL; para 18.52, above.
8   [1995] 1 All ER 737; see also *Frost v Chief Constable of the South Yorkshire Police* [1997] 1 All ER 540, CA.

19.6   *Competent staff*   In *Hudson v Ridge Manufacturing Co Ltd*[1], an employee was injured by being tripped up by a fellow employee who had, to the employer's knowledge, engaged in such 'horse-play' for a number of years. The employer was held to be liable for not removing a foreseeable source of danger, the fellow employee. Clearly, the employer would not be in breach of this duty where he had no reason to expect the employee would do anything dangerous. It should be noted that the employer is liable for his own negligence in not taking reasonable care for his employees' safety; the action is not based on vicarious liability for the acts of the employee.

1   [1957] 2 QB 348, [1957] 2 All ER 229.

19.7   *Safe plant, machinery and premises*   The employer must take reasonable care to provide safe plant, machinery and premises. Thus, an employer was held liable for sending an employee on a long journey in an unheated van in cold weather whereby the employee suffered frostbite[1]. In another case, an employee slipped on a 'duck-board' which was in a slippery condition, and was injured. Although at the time she was seeking to wash a cup for her own purposes her employer was held liable. The obligation to provide safe plant etc extends to cover all acts which are normally and reasonably incidental to a day's work[2]. The employer's obligation is to take reasonable care to ensure that the place where the employee works is safe, and this includes the premises of others.

1   *Bradford v Robinson Rentals Ltd* [1967] 1 All ER 267, [1967] 1 WLR 337.
2   *Davidson v Handley Page Ltd* [1945] 1 All ER 235, CA.

19.8   *Defective equipment*   Where an employee suffers an injury *in the course of his employment* because of a defect in equipment provided by his employer for the purposes of the business, and the defect is attributable wholly or in part to the fault of a third party (eg the manufacturer or supplier of the equipment), the injury is *also* deemed to be attributable to the employer's negligence[1]. Thus, the employee may sue his employer rather than pursuing the manufacturer[2] or supplier; the employer may then seek a contribution from the third party.

1   Employer's Liability (Defective Equipment) Act 1969. 'Equipment' has been construed broadly by the courts and has been held to include a ship, see *Coltman v Bibby Tankers Ltd* [1988] AC 276, [1987] 3 All ER 1068, HL, and a flagstone being manhandled by a labourer, see *Knowles v Liverpool City Council* [1993] 4 All ER 321, [1993] 1 WLR 1428, HL.
2   An employee who is injured by defective equipment may also be able to sue the manufacturer either for negligence or for producing a defective product. See paras 19.9–19.15, below.

Defences

19.9   The usual defences to negligence are available to the employer, although the courts are reluctant to hold that an employee agreed to run the risk of no compensation (volenti) merely because he agreed to work knowing of a risk[1].

1   See further paras 21.2–21.10, below.

Manufacturers' Liability

19.10   A person injured by defective goods or disgruntled by defects in goods may have an action for breach of contract[1] but such an action may only be brought by the person who purchased the goods[2]. However, in the case of *Donoghue v Stevenson*[3], the House of Lords held that the user of a defective product might in certain circumstances have a remedy in tort for negligence against the manufacturer of a product which caused damage to the person or to property. The difficulties of proving negligence, always a problem for plaintiffs, are particularly acute in respect of defective products. In 1987, in order to comply with an EC directive, Parliament enacted the Consumer Protection Act[4] which imposes strict liability on the manufacturer of certain defective products. This Act, while not abolishing the common law claim in negligence in respect of defective products, is likely to diminish the importance of the common law action in tort[5].

1   Particularly under the Sale of Goods Act 1979, see paras 8.19–8.35, above.
2   An application of the doctrine of privity, see paras 6.24–6.34, above.
3   [1932] AC 562, HL; para 18.2, above.
4   For a more detailed discussion of this Act see paras 20.9–20.15, below.
5   The Consumer Protection Act 1987 only applies to claims for death, personal injury or damage to 'domestic' property; consequently, claims for damage to business property can be brought only at common law.

19.11   The basis of a claim for manufacturers' liability at common law still derives from *Donoghue v Stevenson*[1]. In this case the House of Lords held that the manufacturer of a product owed a duty of care to the ultimate consumer of his product, provided that the form in which the goods were sold indicated that they were not intended to be subject to any inspection between manufacture and sale and that he knew or ought to have known that a want of care in the manufacture of them could result in injury to the consumer or his property. In this case the manufacturer (of ginger beer) owed a contractual duty to the retailer of the product but this did not prevent a concomitant duty in negligence being owed to the consumer of the drink.

1   [1932] AC 562, HL.

Who is liable?

19.12   Liability in negligence for defective products was originally imposed only on manufacturers but it has been extended from manufacturers to impose liability on assemblers, fitters, repairers and inspectors and certifiers[1].

1   Liability has also been imposed upon distributors of products but such liability is probably limited to products with inherently dangerous defects, eg a car with defective brakes, which an inspection would have revealed.

Products
19.13   The 'manufacturer' rule has been extended to cover damage by a variety of products including foodstuffs, walls, clothing, motor vehicles, lifts, chemicals, houses and faulty designs. A product includes its packaging and any instructions for use[1].

1   *Distillers Co (Biochemicals) Ltd v Thompson* [1971] AC 458, [1971] 1 All ER 694, PC.

Who can sue?
19.14   Not only can an ultimate consumer recover damages from the manufacturer, but so can anyone else[1] who suffers foreseeable injury, provided, of course, that he can prove that the manufacturer failed to discharge his duty of care and that it was that breach which caused his injury[2]. There seems no reason why liability should be limited to products which are sold; a consumer injured by a negligently produced promotional free gift should be able to sue.

1   *Stennett v Hancock and Peters* [1939] 2 All ER 578.
2   Causation can be especially difficult to prove in the case of drugs which allegedly injure those who have taken them. For causation in general see paras 18.52–18.60, above.

Imposition of the duty
19.15   A duty of care to the ultimate consumer does not arise if an intermediate examination of the product is reasonably foreseeable as more than a mere possibility[1]. Just as the mere possibility of inspection will not abrogate the potential duty of care owed by a manufacturer, nor will an actual inspection of the product between manufacture and the loss or damage caused by it unless such inspection was reasonably foreseeable[2].

Whether an intermediate examination was foreseeable is determined objectively, but it is a decision influenced by policy factors. Essentially, it is a decision as to whether a manufacturer should have to bear the risk of loss or damage caused by the product he has manufactured. Absence of control by the manufacturer once the goods have left his hands does not necessarily abrogate his duty of care. However, where there is a considerable time-lag between manufacture and the causing of injury, the manufacturer is less likely to be liable, especially if the ultimate consumer, or an intermediate owner, is in a better position to know whether the product is satisfactory. In *Paine v Colne Valley Electricity Supply Co Ltd*[3], an improperly insulated housing for electrical equipment caused the death of an employee. The employers had purchased the housing more than two years previously and had themselves installed it. The employers, and not the manufacturer of the defective housing, were held responsible for the death.

If there is a reasonably foreseeable inspection after the product has left the control of the manufacturer, which is carried out so carelessly that the defect is not discovered, the manufacturer may be exempt from liability[4].

1   *Driver v William Willett (Contractors) Ltd* [1969] 1 All ER 665.
2   If an unforeseeable inspection reveals the defect and the consumer still uses the product, he may well be contributorily negligent; see paras 21.11–21.15, below.
3   [1938] 4 All ER 803.
4   The consumer may break the chain of causation by using a defective product following a careless inspection, see para. 18.57, above. This would not apply if the consumer had no

choice but to continue to use the product, see *Targett v Torfaen Borough Council* [1992] 3 All ER 27, CA.

Breach of duty and causation

19.16 The duty of care imposed upon manufacturers is not strict. Liability arises only if the plaintiff can prove that the defendant failed to take reasonable care. This may be a formidable task. In *Donoghue v Stevenson*[1] itself, the House of Lords stated (obiter) that the plaintiff must prove that the defect which caused the injury was present when the product left the defendant's control and that the defect was caused by the carelessness of the defendant. On this basis, the plaintiff's action must fail where the only available evidence is that the product was defective and the plaintiff cannot prove when or how the defect occurred. However, the Privy Council in *Grant v Australian Knitting Mills Ltd*[2] held that, in those cases in which the defect could only have occurred through fault, the plaintiff need not prove the precise act of carelessness by the manufacturer; negligence on the part of the manufacturer could be inferred from the existence of the defect taken in conjunction with all the known circumstances.

This latter decision is limited to those cases in which the defect must have arisen through fault and it merely provides that in such cases negligence on the part of the manufacturer is presumed in the absence of any further explanation[3]. The manufacturer may be able to produce further evidence to rebut the presumption of negligence. For example, establishing that production methods are practically foolproof may rebut the presumption[4].

If the defect did not cause the harm suffered the plaintiff cannot recover. Hence, if a consumer misuses a product in an unforeseeable way and is injured, the manufacturer is not liable since the product is not defective. It is uncertain whether a warning not to misuse a product in a foreseeable way is sufficient to exempt a manufacturer from liability caused by foreseeable misuse.

1 [1932] AC 562, HL.
2 [1936] AC 85, PC.
3 While not so described by the Privy Council, this may be an application of res ipsa loquitur, on which see paras 18.48–18.50, above.
4 *Daniels and Daniels v White & Sons Ltd and Tarbard* [1938] 4 All ER 258.

Defences

19.17 The usual defences to negligence – volenti and contributory negligence[1] – can be pleaded by a manufacturer of defective products. The fact that the plaintiff knew that a product was dangerous does not mean that he consented to the risk of having no claim against the manufacturer if he continues to use it; the critical question is did he have a choice whether or not to continue to use the item[2].

An attempt to exclude or restrict liability in a 'guarantee' contained in a contract term or notice is void if the goods were supplied in the course of a business and are of a type ordinarily supplied for private use or consumption. In this context anything in writing containing a promise to repair or replace defective goods is a guarantee[3].

1 Paras 21.2–21.15, below.

2   *Targett v Torfaen Borough Council* [1992] 3 All ER 27, CA, tenant of house had no choice as to whether to use external stairs which were poorly lit and had no hand-rail.
3   Unfair Contract Terms Act 1977, s 5; see also paras 10.43–10.56, above.

Damages

19.18   If a manufacturer is liable under the above rules, the consumer of the defective product is entitled to recover damages for personal injury and for damage to other chattels caused by the defect.

Until relatively recently it seemed clear that there could be no recovery of damages in tort in respect of defects in the product itself. Thus, in *Donoghue v Stevenson* the consumer of the ginger beer could complain that the presence of the snail caused her injury but could not have complained that the bottle contained flat ginger beer or water; it would be pure economic loss. The House of Lords[1] had suggested that where a product is defective and thereby dangerous, the owner could recover from the manufacturer the cost of rendering it safe but more recent cases have held that recovery is possible only if the dangerous product has actually caused damage to the person or to other property of the plaintiff[2].

In one case[3] the House of Lords went much further and held that the plaintiff was able to recover from the manufacturer the cost of replacing a defective but non-dangerous product (a factory floor). This decision has been distinguished in a number of later cases and its ambit, which we discuss in para 18.12, above, is not clear. It is noteworthy that damages for defective but non-dangerous products (and any consequential economic loss) have not been awarded in any later reported cases[4].

1   *Anns v Merton London Borough Council* [1978] AC 728, [1977] 2 All ER 492, HL.
2   *D & F Estates Ltd v Church Comrs for England* [1989] AC 177, [1988] 2 All ER 992, HL and *Murphy v Brentwood District Council* [1991] 1 AC 398, [1990] 2 All ER 908, HL.
3   *Junior Books Ltd v Veitchi Co Ltd* [1983] 1 AC 520, [1982] 3 All ER 201, HL.
4   For example, in *Muirhead v Industrial Tank Specialities Ltd* [1986] QB 507, [1985] 3 All ER 705, CA, the court refused to award damages against the manufacturer of defective products (electric motors for commercial fish breeding tanks) either for loss of profit caused by their defective product or for money wasted on buying the tanks.

Professional Negligence

19.19   The importance of the law of tort to the professional person acting in a professional capacity is that it may impose a legal obligation or duty upon him which he owes to persons who are not parties to his contract of engagement. Professional people who give advice, such as accountants and solicitors, may incur liability not only to their client (in contract or tort) but also to others who are sufficiently proximate. Such liability will almost certainly be in negligence.

Tortious liability can be more extensive than contractual liability. Contractual liability is owed to a defined (usually small) number of people for a limited period; tort liability can be owed to an unquantifiable number for a longer period of time.

The courts had, until recently, held that a professional adviser who owed his client a contractual duty could not also owe him a tortious duty. However, this view no longer represents the law[1]. and there has never been any no doubt that the existence of a contractual duty owed to a client does not preclude the existence of a tortious duty owed to others[2]. The growth in the range of tortious liability and the willingness to litigate of disgruntled clients has led to an upsurge in claims against professional advisers and concomitant sharp increases in the cost of professional indemnity insurance.

Whether there is a tortious duty not to cause the particular harm suffered by a plaintiff, generally in these types of case, economic loss, is determined by reference to the usual rules for the imposition of a duty[3].

1 See paras 18.67–18.70, above. But see *Lee v Thompson* [1989] 40 EG 89, CA.
2 See for example, *Ross v Caunters* [1980] Ch 297, [1979] 3 All ER 580, discussed in para 18.8, above, which has been approved in a spate of cases; *White v Jones* [1995] 2 AC 207, [1995] 1 All ER 691, HL, and *Henderson v Merrett Syndicates Ltd* [1995] 2 AC 145, [1994] 3 All ER 506, HL, are two illustrations.
3 See paras 17.3–17.5, above, for the general rules relating to the imposition of a tortious duty and paras 18.2–18.36, above, for a discussion of the duty of care in negligence.

Duty of care and accountants

19.20 Accountants are most likely to incur liability in tort where they have provided negligent financial advice or information[1]. Financial advice may be given in a public form; for example, when an accountant prepares an audit he is providing information not merely to his client (the business which is being audited) but also to others who may read that report (an audit being a public document). Alternatively, financial advice may be given in the form of a private report. A duty of care may be owed to a third party who relies upon a report, public or private, and suffers loss because it has been prepared negligently, *provided that it is foreseeable that he will do so and reasonable for him to do so*. The leading case on accountants is *Caparo Industries plc v Dickman*[2].

In *Caparo Industries plc v Dickman*, the plaintiff company, which was already a minority shareholder in a company (F), launched a successful take-over bid for F in reliance on F's audited accounts. The House of Lords held that the plaintiff company was not owed a duty of care by F's auditors. The House held that, while a statutory duty was owed to shareholders as a body (since they were the very body to whom, by statute, the auditors must report), no common law duty of care was owed to any individual shareholder unless the auditors were fully aware that that shareholder would rely on that report in deciding whether or not to engage in a particular transaction and that any such reliance was reasonable. The House also held that a common law duty of care owed to other potential investors (since they are not sufficiently proximate[3]) unless, perhaps, the auditors knew that a bid was in the offing from a specific person[4]. Nor do the auditors owe a duty to creditors of the company[5].

The liability of accountants for financial statements has been discussed in several other cases. In two cases[6], the courts held that the third party who relied on an inaccurate, general financial statement was insufficiently proximate to the maker of that statement, since the maker of the statement had not undertaken any obligation towards the person who used the information. Where an express representation has been made, the courts seem to ask themselves whether the maker of the statement has induced the person who used the information to rely on it or not and whether such reliance was highly likely and reasonable; each case seems to turn on its own facts. In *Morgan Crucible Co plc v Hill Samuel Bank Ltd*[1], the Court of Appeal held that accountants who, along with its directors, made express representations about the financial state of a company which was the subject of a take-over bid *after* an identified bidder had emerged, with the intention that the bidder should rely on those representations could owe the bidder a duty of care. In contrast, in *James McNaughton Papers Group Ltd v Hicks Anderson & Co*[8], the Court of Appeal held that a firm of accountants which prepared (at short notice) *draft* accounts for the chairman of a company, owed no duty of care to a bidder who took the company over after having inspected those accounts. The court found that the bidder was an experienced businessman with his own independent advisers and the defendants could reasonably expect such a person to rely on his own advisers rather than on draft accounts. The court stated that factors to be taken into account in determining whether a duty of care in respect of a financial statement arose included: the purpose for which the statement was made; the purpose for which it was communicated; the relationship of maker and giver and recipient; the size of class to which the recipient belonged; the state of knowledge of the maker or giver; and the degree of reliance by the recipient.

1   Generally in accordance with the principles enunciated in *Hedley Byrne & Co Ltd v Heller and Partners Ltd* [1964] AC 465, [1963] 2 All ER 575, HL; discussed in para 18.14, above.
2   [1990] 2 AC 605, [1990] 1 All ER 568, HL. A slightly different emphasis was placed on this case in *Henderson v Merrett Syndicates* Ltd [1995] 2 AC 145, [1994] 3 All ER 506, HL, discussed in paras 18.12 and 18.70, above.
3   For the requirement of proximity see para 18.5, above.
4   As in *JEB Fasteners Ltd v Marks, Bloom & Co* [1983] 1 All ER 583, CA; para 18.18, above.
5   *Al Saudi Banque v Clarke Pixley* [1990] Ch 313, [1989] 3 All ER 361, para 18.18, above; *Deloitte Haskins & Sells v National Mutual Life Nominees Ltd* [1993] AC 774, [1993] 2 All ER 1015, PC.
6   *Al-Nakib Investments (Jersey) Ltd v Longcroft* [1990] 3 All ER 321, para 18.18, above; (no liability to shareholders who relied on a prospectus in respect of a rights issue to make further investments); *Huxford v Stoy Hayward & Co* (1989) 5 BCC 421. Contrast *Possfund Custodian Trustee Ltd v Diamond* [1996] 2 All ER 774, [1996] 1 WLR 1351, in which it was suggested that the directors of a company who provided misleading information in a propectus might owe a duty of care to potential investors.
7   [1991] Ch 295, [1991] 1 All ER 148, CA. See also *Galoo v Bright Grahame Murray* [1995] 1 All ER 16, CA.
8   [1991] 2 QB 113, [1991] 1 All ER 134, CA.

Breach of duty
19.21   The standard of care demanded of a professional adviser in carrying out his professional activities is not that of the reasonable man engaged in such an activity but a higher standard. He must display such care and skill as could be expected from a reasonably competent practitioner in that field[1]. For example, an accountant advising a client on his tax affairs owes him a duty to use all reasonable professional skill in so doing[2].

A professional adviser is required to use reasonable care and skill; he is not required to be right. Thus, it is not negligent to fail to guard against a risk if no competent practitioner in that field would have foreseen that the risk existed. For example, in *Roe v Minister of Health*[3], an anaesthetist injected an anaesthetic into patients who subsequently developed paraplegia. This was caused by the sterilising solution in which the anaesthetic containers were stored penetrating the containers through undetectable cracks. The doctor was not liable; at the time the anaesthetic was given such a risk was unforeseeable.

Adoption of a common professional practice will generally exempt a professional adviser from an action for negligence[4]. This, of course, requires professionals to keep up to date with new techniques and practices; if not immediately, then when they become standard. However, it is always open to the courts to find to be negligent a practice commonly adopted within a profession[5].

1   This principle derives from the case of *Bolam v Friern Hospital Management Committee* [1957] 2 All ER 118, [1957] 1 WLR 582, the *Bolam* test. Expert evidence is led on this issue.
2   *Owen Investments Ltd v Bennett Nash Wolf & Co* (1984) 134 NLJ 887.
3   [1954] 2 QB 66, [1954] 2 All ER 131, CA.
4   *Whitehouse v Jordan* [1981] 1 All ER 267, [1981] 1 WLR 246, HL.
5   *Lloyds Bank Ltd v E B Savory & Co* [1933] AC 201, HL; *Bolitho v City and Hackney Health Authority* [1993] 4 Med LR 381, CA.

19.22   It seems that the standard of care owed in tort to a client cannot be higher than that imposed by the contract between adviser and client[1]. There is, however, no objection to concurrent liability in contract and tort[2]. Where a contract between professional adviser and client contains an exemption clause or disclaimer which purports to reduce the contractual duty below that which is usual in negligence, ie the taking of reasonable care, the effectiveness of such a contractual clause may be limited by the effect of the Unfair Contract Terms Act 1977[3].

The contract between adviser and client generally does not affect the scope of the duty owed to third parties.

1   *Tai Hing Cotton Mill Ltd v Liu Chong Hing Bank Ltd* [1986] AC 80, [1985] 2 All ER 947, PC, which view was adopted by the Court of Appeal in *Johnstone v Bloomsbury Health Authority* [1992] QB 333, [1991] 2 All ER 293, CA, but see *Holt v Payne Skillington* [1996] 02 LS Gaz R 29, CA. See paras 18.67–18.70, above, for a consideration of the interrelation of contract and tort. The standard of care imposed by a contract may be the same as that imposed by tort, ie reasonable care, or it could impose a higher standard.
2   *Caparo Industries plc v Dickman* [1990] 2 AC 605, [1990] 1 All ER 568, HL; *Henderson v Merrett Syndicates* Ltd [1995] 2 AC 145, [1994] 3 All ER 506, IIL, discussed in para 18.12, above.
3   *Smith v Eric C Bush* [1990] 1 AC 831, [1989] 2 All ER 514, HL; para 10.54, above.

The standard of care and accountants
19.23   In para 19.21, above, we said that adoption of a common professional practice will generally exempt a professional adviser from an action for negligence. Consequently, deviation from such practice without good reason is negligence. 'Common practice' is of particular relevance for professionals especially where statements of professional practice have been issued. For example, the governing bodies of the accountancy profession have issued 'Statements of Standard Accountancy Practice' (SSAPs) which provide guidance as to the standards to be expected of an accountant. SSAPs are not conclusive evidence of good practice but are strong evidence as to the standard

of care to be expected from an accountant. Where there are differing views within the profession, eg on the appropriate method of valuing an asset, a court will not seek to determine which is best practice but will treat compliance with either view as satisfying the duty of care unless one view can be condemned as wholly unreasonable[1].

It is clear that it is a breach of duty for a professional to fail to adopt and maintain adequate standards of management and procedure. Hence, accountants have been held liable for failing to detect fraudulent accounting, having discovered that invoices had been altered[2].

An accountant may also be in breach of the standard of care imposed upon him when the plaintiff can prove that the accountant failed to exercise an appropriate degree of care and skill in formulating his professional judgment. However, to prove such failure is extremely difficult. It must also be borne in mind that a professional advisor may not have undertaken an obligation to provide *advice* but merely to provide *information* so that any loss attributable to a shortfall in the quality of the advice cannot be recovered[3].

1   *Luxmoore-May v Messenger May Baverstock* [1990] 1 All ER 1067, [1990] 1 WLR 1009, CA.
     It would be extremely rare for a court to condemn a current accepted professional practice.
2   *Re Thomas Gerrard & Son Ltd* [1968] Ch 455, [1967] 2 All ER 525.
3   *South Australia Asset Management Corpn v York Montague Ltd* [1996] 3 All ER 365, HL,
     discussed in para 21.39, below.

19.24   The duty of care imposed upon accountants in respect of company audits includes an obligation to investigate and warn[1]. The Companies Act 1985 requires the accountant to form an independent judgment as to whether the accounts of a company (or group of companies) present a true and fair view of the company's financial position. Whether the standard of care required in carrying out this trial is that of the inquiring sceptic who takes nothing on trust, or merely that of a 'watchdog' who is entitled to assume that nothing is wrong unless there is obvious cause for suspicion, or some point in between, is not clear[2]. However, if there is cause for suspicion even a passive watchdog is required to become a 'bloodhound' and 'probe the matter to the bottom' and report his findings to the shareholders[3].

1   Companies Act 1985, s 237.
2   *Re City Equitable Fire Insurance Co Ltd* [1925] Ch 407, CA, favoured the watchdog approach
     whereas *Re Thomas Gerrard & Son Ltd* [1968] Ch 455, [1967] 2 All ER 525, seemed to
     envisage a more inquiring role (the bloodhound) for an auditor particularly if, as in that case,
     altered invoices or other suspicious circumstances were discovered.
3   *Re London and General Bank (No 2)* [1895] 2 Ch 673, CA.

Recovery of damages
19.25   The failure of a professional adviser to reach the requisite standard of care imposed by a tortious duty is actionable (usually as negligence) if loss or harm results. Hence, a person who has suffered loss after being negligently advised can recover damages only if he relied upon that negligent advice. For example, in *JEB Fasteners Ltd v Marks, Bloom & Co*[1], the defendants, who had negligently audited the books of a firm which they knew to be of interest to the plaintiff company, were not liable to the plaintiff company in negligence when

it lost money in acquiring the firm. This was because the plaintiff's decision to take over the firm was motivated by its desire to acquire the services of certain directors of the firm and it had not relied upon the audited accounts to any material degree.

1   [1983] 1 All ER 583, CA.

Liability for Dangerous or Defective Premises

19.26   Premises may, either because of their physical state or because of activities taking place on them, be a danger to their occupiers or to others. Premises may also contain some defect (latent or patent) which, while not being a present danger, renders them either potentially dangerous or less valuable than comparable premises without such a defect. In this final section of the chapter, we consider the liability of occupiers of dangerous premises and the liability of non-occupiers for dangerous or defective premises.

Occupiers' liability

19.27   The occupier of premises owes a statutory duty of care to entrants, whether lawful or non-lawful, in respect of the *state* of his premises, and both a statutory duty and a common law duty to lawful visitors in respect of *activities* which he carries on on his premises[1]. A duty in respect of activities taking place on premises is owed under the general principles of the tort of negligence, and not by statute, to non-lawful entrants. For example, in *Adams v Southern Electricity Board*[2], the Court of Appeal held the defendants liable in negligence for burns suffered by the plaintiff (a 14-year-old) who climbed up an inadequately fenced, high-voltage electrical installation erected near his home. More recently, in *Revill v Newbery*[3], the occupier of an allotment was held liable in negligence when he shot the plaintiff who was attempting to burgle a shed on the allotment without giving him a prior warning that he would fire.

1   The wording of the relevant statute could be interpreted to mean that it replaces the pre-existing common law duty in respect of activities but the cases seem to treat lawful entrants injured by activities on an occupier's land as having a choice of actions; see *Ogwo v Taylor* [1988] AC 431, [1987] 3 All ER 961, HL.
2   (1993) Times, 21 October, CA; the boy's damages were reduced by two-thirds to reflect his contributory negligence.
3   [1996] QB 567, [1996] 1 All ER 291, CA.

19.28   In addition to these statutory and common law duties owed to entrants on to his premises, the occupier of premises owes non-entrants, such as neighbours, a common law duty of care in respect of the state of his property and of activities taking place on it for which he is responsible[1].

The occupier of land is not usually responsible for unauthorised activities on his premises by third parties since he is not legally liable for their activities. However, each case turns on its own facts. In *Cunningham v Reading Football Club*[2], the plaintiff, a police officer on duty inside the ground at a football match, was able to recover from the club for injuries caused by hooligans throwing lumps of concrete. The club knew that the defective state of the ground allowed lumps of concrete to be broken off and that such conduct had occurred in the past. Consequently, the conduct of the hooligans was a foreseeable consequence of the club's breach of duty in providing handy missiles (concrete lumps).

The occupier may also incur liability to neighbouring landowners (or occupiers) in nuisance[3] or under the rule in *Rylands v Fletcher*[4]. It is settled, however, that no duty of care is owed to a neighbouring landowner whose land is adversely affected by the abstraction of percolating water[5]. Neither is there a duty to prevent natural water percolating on to land which lies lower than one's own, conversely, a person occupying low-lying land can take reasonable steps to prevent the ingress of percolating water from higher land[6].

1   See paras 18.24–18.26, above.
2   [1992] PIQR P141.
3   Paras 20.21–20.25, below.
4   Paras 20.26–20.28, below.
5   *Langbrook Properties Ltd v Surrey County Council* [1969] 3 All ER 1424, [1970] 1 WLR 161.
6   *Home Brewery Co Ltd v William Davis & Co (Leicester) Ltd* [1987] QB 339, [1987] 1 All ER 637.

19.29   *Duty owed to entrants*   If the entrant on to the occupier's property is classified by the law as a lawful visitor[1], the occupier's duty of care is imposed by s 2 of the Occupiers' Liability Act 1957 (the common duty of care).

In respect of an entrant who is not in law a lawful visitor (a non-lawful visitor[2]) a duty is imposed by s 1 of the Occupiers' Liability Act 1984.

Non-lawful visitors may or may not be trespassers[3], although the majority of cases concerning non-lawful visitors involve trespassers. We use the expression 'non-lawful visitors' in this chapter to embrace trespassers and other people not classified as lawful visitors by the Occupiers' Liability Act 1957 and the expression 'trespassers' when we are limiting the discussion to true trespassers.

1   Occupiers' Liability Act 1957, ss 1(2) and 2(6).
2   Occupiers' Liability Act 1984, s 1(3).
3   For example, visitors to National Parks and those using private rights of way are not trespassers, although they do not come within the 1957 Act's definition of lawful visitor.

Lawful or non-lawful visitor
19.30   As we have said, a different duty is owed to an entrant dependent upon whether he is a lawful visitor (the common duty of care) or a non-lawful visitor (the duty set out in s 1 of the 1984 Act). A person is a lawful visitor if:

a.   he has been invited by the occupier (or the occupier's authorised agent) on to the occupier's premises; or
b.   he has a contractual right to be on them; or
c.   he is on them as of right (eg under a statutory power of entry such as that possessed by certain officials)[1]; or
d.   because he has been expressly or impliedly permitted by the occupier (or the occupier's authorised agent) to be on them.

A lawful visitor may become a non-lawful visitor if he visits parts of the premises of the occupier to which he has not been invited or allowed to enter or if he stays beyond a specified time. It was said in one case that, when one invites visitors into one's house to use the staircase, one does not invite them to slide down the banisters; in other words, a visitor remains a lawful visitor only while within the ambit of his lawful visit. However, lawful visitors have implied permission to do certain things while on the premises, for example, in most cases to seek out a lavatory, and to do so will not render the entrant a non-lawful visitor.

1   This does not extend to those lawfully using a public right of way, see *McGeown v Northern Ireland Housing Executive* [1995] 1 AC 233, [1994] 3 All ER 53, HL.

Implied licences

19.31   Difficulty can be experienced in distinguishing between persons who enter on to premises under an implied permission to do so (implied licensees), and who are thus lawful visitors, and other entrants, who are not. For example, there is an implied licence for people visiting premises occupied by tenants to use parts of those premises still occupied by the landlord[1], such as staircases. There is an implied licence to visit public parks to take recreation or to visit public libraries to consult or borrow books.

An implied licence can also arise if the occupier of premises knows of the incursion of non-lawful visitors (almost certainly in this context trespassers) and he acts in such a way that assent to those incursions can be assumed. However, great care should be taken in relying on implied licence cases which pre-date the Occupiers' Liability Act 1984 (which extends the very limited common law duty owed to non-lawful visitors). The reason is that, prior to the passing of this Act, a finding that a person was a non-lawful visitor almost always denied a remedy to a person injured by the state of the occupier's premises. Now that such is not the case, less generosity may be extended by the courts to those who claim an implied licence.

1   *Jacobs v LCC* [1950] AC 361, [1950] 1 All ER 737, HL.

19.32   There may be an implied licence despite a notice saying 'No Trespassers', if the occupier of land makes no attempt to seek a remedy against persistent and regular unauthorised entrants[1]. In *Lowery v Walker*[2], an implied licence was found to exist in favour of people using a field as a short cut to a railway station. This short cut had been used for 35 years and, although the owner of the field had often sought to prevent its use, he had never taken proceedings against anyone. It was held that people using the short cut had an implied licence to do so, and therefore the plaintiff, who was savaged by a dangerous horse which the defendant had put in the field, could recover damages. However, the absence of a 'No Trespassers' notice does not automatically give an implied licence to enter premises[3].

Children have, prior to the passing of the 1984 Act, been held to have an implied licence if they have been 'allured' onto the occupier's premises. Among the things which have been held to be 'allurements' (which can be described as objects fascinating but potentially fatal) are poisonous shrubs[4] and a horse and cart[5].

1   *Robert Addie & Sons (Collieries) Ltd v Dumbreck* [1929] AC 358 , HL.
2   [1911] AC 10, HL.
3   *Edwards v Railway Executive* [1952] AC 737, [1952] 2 All ER 430, HL.
4   *Glasgow Corpn v Taylor* [1922] 1 AC 44, HL.
5   *Lynch v Nurdin* (1841) 1 QB 29.

Occupiers

19.33   It is the occupier of the premises who owes the common duty of care to lawful visitors[1] and the duty set out in s 1 of the 1984 Act to non-lawful visitors.

The crucial determinant of whether a person is an occupier of premises is whether he has control of them. Ownership in itself is not enough. Different parts of the same premises may be occupied by different people for the purposes of the Occupiers' Liability Acts. In *Wheat v E Lacon & Co Ltd*[2], the owners of a public house, which was managed for them by X, were held to be occupiers of it because they retained a degree of control over the premises. The House of Lords went on to point out that the owners and X were in occupation of X's flat on the premises, although X's responsibility extended only to his belongings and not to the structure of the premises. A local authority which had served a compulsory purchase notice, even though it had not taken possession of the vacant premises, has been held to be in occupation of them. The notice asserted its right to control the premises and it was because of that assertion that the premises had become vacant[3].

1   Occupiers' Liability Act 1957, s 1(1). Additionally, landlords are in a special position under the Occupiers' Liability Act 1957, s 4. They owe a duty to those likely to be affected by a want of repair in the demised premises but only if they have a duty to repair the premises or if they have a right to enter and repair those premises.
2   [1966] AC 552, [1966] 1 All ER 582, HL.
3   *Harris v Birkenhead Corpn* [1976] 1 All ER 341, [1976] 1 WLR 279, CA.

Premises

19.34   For the purposes of the two Acts, 'premises' includes not only land and buildings but also extends to fixed and movable structures[1]. This definition appears wide enough to embrace such things as tents and workmen's huts and has been held to include scaffolding[2], a ship in dry dock[3], a large mechanical digger[4] and a lift[5]. With respect to the latter three cases, all of which involved not merely movable but self-propelling objects, items of this type may be regarded as 'premises' and thus within the Acts only in respect of their defective condition and not their defective operation[5].

1   Occupiers' Liability Act 1957, s 1(3) and Occupiers' Liability Act 1984, s 1(2).
2   *Kearney v Eric Waller Ltd* [1967] 1 QB 29, [1965] 3 All ER 352.
3   *London Graving Dock Co Ltd v Horton* [1951] AC 737, [1951] 2 All ER 1, HL. This case was decided at common law but is still applicable.
4   *Bunker v Charles Brand & Son Ltd* [1969] 2 QB 480, [1969] 2 All ER 59.
5   *Haseldine v Daw & Son Ltd* [1941] 2 KB 343, [1941] 3 All ER 156, CA. This case was decided at common law but is still applicable.

The common duty of care

19.35 The common duty which the occupier of premises owes towards the person and property of his lawful visitors is defined, by s 2 of the Occupiers' Liability Act 1957, as a duty to take such care as, in all the circumstances of the case, is reasonable to see that the visitor will be reasonably safe in using the premises for the purposes for which he is invited or permitted by the occupier to be there. The common duty of care imposed by the statute closely resembles the standard and duty of care which are the bases of the common law tort of negligence. An illustration of the operation of the common duty of care is provided by *Murphy v Bradford Metropolitan Borough Council*[1], in which the plaintiff, a teacher, recovered damages for injuries suffered when he slipped on an icy path leading to the school. The Court of Appeal found that the path was known to be slippery and the actions of the school caretaker in clearing the snow and putting down salt were insufficient to discharge the common duty of care; grit and ashes, said the court, should have been used.

The common duty of care is further explained by the 1957 Act, as follows:

a. an occupier is entitled to assume that lawful visitors will display ordinary prudence while on his premises[2];

b. an occupier must expect children to be less careful than adults[3]. However, in *Phipps v Rochester Corpn*[4], the Court of Appeal held that an occupier is entitled to assume that very young children (in this case aged five and seven) will be accompanied by a responsible adult; and

c. an occupier can assume that a lawful visitor carrying out his job on the premises will, where the occupier leaves his visitor a discretion as to how to carry out his job, recognise and guard against any special risks attaching to that job[5].

1 (1991) Times, 11 February, CA.
2 Section 2(3). Thus in *Staples v West Dorset District Council* (1995) 93 LGR 536, the council was not liable to the plaintiff who slipped on a sea wall which was covered in algae and obviously slippery.
3 Ibid.
4 [1955] 1 QB 450, [1955] 1 All ER 129.
5 Section 2(3); *Roles v Nathan* [1963] 2 All ER 908, [1963] 1 WLR 1117, CA. But note that in *Ogwo v Taylor* [1988] AC 431, [1987] 3 All ER 961, HL, the occupier of premises was held liable in negligence to a fireman injured in extinguishing a blaze carelessly started by the occupier.

19.36 If an occupier warns his lawful visitors of a danger, he discharges his duty of care, provided that the notice in itself is enough to render a visitor reasonably safe[1]. Whether a notice is sufficient is a question of fact. It is generally thought that a notice must specify the nature and location of the danger so that a prudent visitor can take steps to avoid it. Hence a notice which simply said 'Danger' would not discharge the occupier's duty unless the danger was obvious. However, if the danger is extremely obvious there may be no need to warn at all since any visitor exercising reasonable care for his own safety should recognise and avoid the hazard[2].

Further, an occupier will not usually be liable for a danger caused by the faulty work of an independent contractor whom he has employed[3].

1 Occupiers' Liability Act 1957, s 2(4).
2 *Cotton v Derbyshire Dales District Council* (1994) Times, 20 June, CA.
3 Ibid; those cases where the occupier incurs liability in respect of the torts of independent contractors are discussed in paras 17.28–17.35, above.

Exclusion of the common duty of care
19.37   An occupier may seek to exclude or restrict the duty which he would otherwise owe under the Occupiers' Liability Act 1957 either by a term in a contract with his visitor or by means of a notice indicating that those who enter do so at their own risk. Section 2(1) of the 1957 Act permits an occupier to exclude or restrict the common duty of care by contract or otherwise (eg a notice).

While an occupier of premises is entitled to exclude or restrict the common duty of care, by contract or by means of a notice, there are exceptions. First, an occupier cannot exclude or restrict, by contract, the common duty of care owed to those lawful visitors who enter by virtue of a contract but who are not parties to that contract[1]. Second, any exclusion or restriction of liability must satisfy the common law rules relating to the exclusion or restriction of liability[2].

There is a third exception which is limited to an occupier of business premises. Such an occupier cannot exclude or restrict the common duty of care by contract, or otherwise, for causing death or personal injury to visitors, and he can only exclude or restrict liability for causing other types of injury, for example damage to property, if such exclusion or restriction is reasonable[3].

1 Occupiers' Liability Act 1957, ss 2(1) and 3(1).
2 See paras 10.25–10.35, above.
3 Unfair Contract Terms Act 1977, s 2; para 10.44, above.

Defences to actions by lawful visitors
19.38   The occupier can rely on the defences of volenti and contributory negligence, which we discuss in paras 21.2–21.15, below.

Common law duties owed to non-lawful visitors
19.39   It is long established that, in respect of the state of the premises or activities carried out on them, an occupier cannot deliberately seek to injure non-lawful visitors nor recklessly disregard their presence; to do so would constitute trespass to the person or negligence.

In other cases, the duty owed to non-lawful visitors is that set out in s 1 of the Occupiers' Liability Act 1984.

The statutory duty owed to non-lawful visitors
19.40   The 1984 Act creates a statutory duty which is owed to all persons other than lawful visitors[1].

Section 1(3) of the 1984 Act provides that the occupier of premises owes a duty to a non-lawful visitor if:

a.   he is aware of a danger or has reasonable grounds to believe that it exists;
b.   he knows or has reasonable grounds to believe that the non-lawful visitor is in (or may come into) the vicinity of a danger; and

c. the risk of injury is one against which he may reasonably be expected to offer the non-lawful visitor some protection.

'Reasonable grounds to believe' in a. and b. require that the occupier should actually know the relevant fact or know facts which provide grounds for a relevant belief established by evidence; it is not enough simply that he ought to have known[2]. In short, the occupier is not in breach of his duty if a non-lawful visitor is injured by a danger of which the occupier was reasonably unaware, but the occupier must protect such a person adequately from those dangers of which he is aware or ought reasonably to have been aware. Even when the occupier is aware of some danger to non-lawful visitors, his duty is not to render them safe but to take reasonable care to see that the danger does not cause injury to that non-lawful visitor[3]. Moreover, even if the occupier is in breach of his duty under this Act, a non-lawful visitor can recover damages only for certain injuries, namely, death and personal injury, and not for damage to his property[4].

The operation of s 1(3) was discussed in *White v St Albans City and District Council*[5]. In this case, the Court of Appeal held that the occupier of land which contained a danger could not be treated as knowing or having reasonable grounds to believe that a non-lawful entrant would come into the vicinity of the danger (b., above) simply because he had erected a fence to prevent people approaching the danger. The issue was one of fact and a duty arose only where the circumstances on the ground revealed the likelihood of unlawful entry. In this case, the plaintiff, who had taken a short cut across fenced land and had fallen into a trench, was not owed a duty since there was no evidence that people used the land as a short cut.

1 Section 1(2). Note that non-lawful visitors include those legitimately using a public right of way, see *McGeown v Northern Ireland Housing Executive* [1994] 3 All ER 53, HL This seems particularly unfortunate since users of the highway have limited rights to sue in respect of the defective state of the highway.
2 *Swain v Puri* [1996] 10 CL 499, CA.
3 Section 1(4).
4 Section 1(8) and (9).
5 (1990) Times, 12 March, CA.

Exclusion of the duty created by the 1984 Act
19.41 An occupier may seek to exclude or restrict the duty which he would otherwise owe under the Occupiers' Liability Act 1984 by means of a notice indicating that those who enter do so at their own risk. The 1984 Act does not indicate whether such exclusion of liability is permissible but it might be thought odd if liability to lawful visitors could be excluded[1] but not liability to non-lawful visitors. The Unfair Contract Terms Act does not apply to the s 1 duty created by the Act of 1984. Consequently, it appears that any occupier can exclude or restrict the duty owed to non-lawful visitors unless any breach of duty also constitutes common law negligence. The ability to exclude liability for negligence is concurrent with the ability to exclude the common duty of care which we discussed above.

1 Para 19.34, above.

Defences to an action for breach of the duty
19.42   In addition to the ability to discharge the duty owed to non-lawful visitors by giving them an adequate warning (or discouraging them from running the risk of injury) an occupier can rely on the defence of volenti[1] and presumably also that of contributory negligence[2].

1   Section 1(5) and (6); see paras 21.2–21.10, below.
2   See paras 21.11–21.15, below.

Liability of non-occupiers for dangerous or defective premises
19.43   While non-occupiers are not subject to the statutory duties owed to entrants onto premises, which we have just discussed[1], there is no reason why, in an appropriate case, a non-occupier of premises should not be liable in negligence, in respect of his activities on those premises, to occupiers or to other non-occupiers. For example, a builder who is constructing or altering a house owes a duty to ensure that occupants of the premises, visitors to the site and passers-by are reasonably safe[2]. Superimposed on any liability in negligence may be liability under the Defective Premises Act 1972.

We shall consider first the general rules for the imposition of liability for defective premises on non-occupiers both in negligence and under the Defective Premises Act 1972, and then consider two categories of non-occupier. Former editions of this book have also discussed the liability of local authorities in connection with their exercise of the duties and powers given to them by statute in respect of the construction of buildings. While there is no doubt that failure to exercise a statutory duty or power in relation to the construction of buildings, eg failure to inspect foundations, or its careless exercise, may in an appropriate case give rise to an action for breach of statutory duty such actions are very rare. An action for negligence could be brought against a local authority where a statutory duty is imposed or a statutory power is given to a local authority and the duty or power is either not exercised or is exercised carelessly[3], but the courts are extremely reluctant to impose such a duty of care[4].

1   But note the liability to lawful visitors owed by landlords; see para 19.33, above.
2   *A C Billings & Sons Ltd v Riden* [1958] AC 240, [1957] 3 All ER 1, HL. The builder is also liable in negligence to any future owners or occupiers of that house although, as usual, not for pure economic loss (eg the value of the property being less than non-defective property).
3   Subject to the usual rules for the imposition of a duty of care on public bodies; see paras 18.29–18.32, above.
4   See, for example, *Tesco Stores Ltd v Wards Construction (Investment) Ltd* (1995) 76 BLR 94.

General liability in negligence
19.44   In determining whether a non-occupier is liable in negligence to a person adversely affected by defects which he has caused to premises, the courts require the plaintiff to prove the three elements necessary for the imposition of liability in negligence. These are the existence of a duty not to cause the harm complained of, breach of that duty and proof that the breach caused the harm.

In this context, as with most of the tort of negligence, there is generally no recovery for pure economic loss[1]. Thus, there can be no recovery of damages in negligence from a non-occupier for any diminution in value of the premises because of the defect: damages are awarded only to compensate for personal injuries, for damage to property, not including the defective property itself[2], for example, a car damaged when a defectively constructed garage roof falls down, and for any consequential economic loss.

1 See paras 18.8–18.12, above.
2 *D & F Estates Ltd v Church Comrs for England* [1989] AC 177, [1988] 2 All ER 992, HL, and *Murphy v Brentwood District Council* [1991] 1 AC 398, [1990] 2 All ER 908, HL. See para 18.11, above.

Liability under the Defective Premises Act 1972

19.45   Section 1[1] of the Act provides that a person taking on work for or in connection with the provision of a dwelling owes a duty both to the person who ordered the dwelling to be built or enlarged and any other person who has or subsequently acquires a legal or equitable interest in the dwelling. This duty, which is owed by builders, architects and sub-contractors etc, and which cannot be contracted out of, is to provide a dwelling fit for habitation[2]. This provision is of limited value, in that it does not apply to houses covered by an 'approved scheme', eg the scheme for the remedying of defects in new houses administered by the National House-Building Council.

Section 3 of the Act provides that, where work is done to premises by their owner, any liability which he would incur (probably in negligence) if he does that work without due care does not terminate if he then sells the premises. This provision merely reiterates, but does not replace, the common law although in more restricted form. It is of limited value in that it does not create liability; rather it provides that any liability that has arisen does not terminate on sale of the property.

1 Discussed generally in *Andrews v Schooling* [1991] 3 All ER 723, [1991] 1 WLR 783, CA, which determined that the section applies to failure to do work at all as well as doing work defectively.
2 Thus there can be no recovery unless the house is unfit for habitation; *Thompson v Clive Alexander and Partners* (1992) 28 Con LR 49.

Liability of owners and owner-builders

19.46   A person who owns and then sells premises has obligations imposed upon him by the contract of sale which could include (but probably will not) liability for the dangerous or defective state of the premises. In the absence of express contractual liability, the former owner of premises can generally rely on the maxim caveat emptor – let the buyer beware. Hence, a vendor of defective premises who did not create that defect is liable, if at all, only if he is in breach of an express contractual term that the premises are free of defects[1].

A vendor of defective premises who created the defect, for example, an owner-builder who puts in inadequate foundations, will incur liability in negligence to subsequent owners or occupiers of them for any personal injury or damage to other property caused by the defect which he created[2]. Property may be 'other property' even if not physically separate. For example, if X installs a defective central heating boiler which explodes and damages the house in which it is installed, the owner of the house can recover for the damage to the house. However, in accordance with the general principles of negligence, there is no liability for pure economic loss[3], ie repairing the defect to the building itself, which is recoverable, if at all, only in contract[4]. However, in *Murphy v Brentwood District Council*[5], Lord Bridge suggested that there was one exception to the rule that economic loss was irrecoverable and that was where the defective property bordered a highway. In such a case, he said, the owner should be able to recover from the builder the cost of averting the danger to road-users.

1   *Rimmer v Liverpool City Council* [1985] QB 1, [1984] 1 All ER 930, CA.
2   *Murphy v Brentwood District Council* [1991] 1 AC 398, [1990] 2 All ER 908, HL.
3   Diminution in the value of the premises due to the builder's negligence is also pure economic loss; see paras 18.8–18.12, above.
4   *D & F Estates Ltd v Church Comrs for England* [1989] AC 177, [1988] 2 All ER 992, HL; *Murphy v Brentwood District Council* [1991] 1 AC 398, [1990] 2 All ER 908, HL. Only the first purchaser of such premises has a remedy for any breach of contract.
5   [1991] 1 AC 398, [1990] 2 All ER 908, HL; see para 18.11, above.

Chapter 20

Some Other Torts

20.1 While there can be no doubt that negligence in its many guises is the most important tort, there are many other torts recognised by English law. We discuss some of these in this chapter. Unlike the tort of negligence, some, but not all, torts discussed in this chapter are torts of strict liability. In other words, liability is imposed upon a person simply because he broke a duty not to cause the relevant harm, whether or not such was his intention or he was negligent in causing it. However, even in torts for which liability is strict, the law recognises a variety of defences.

Breach of Statutory Duty

20.2 Acts of Parliament and regulations made under them may create new torts or modify existing tortious duties in express words. Such statutory provisions, eg the Consumer Protection Act 1987 which we discuss in paras 20.9–20.15, below, will usually specify who can sue, who can be sued and what remedies are available.

Breach of such statutes is technically a breach of a statutory duty but the expression breach of statutory duty generally refers to a more general tort. Where a civil action may be brought against a person in breach of statutory duty by a person injured thereby, this has been called an 'action for breach of statutory duty *simpliciter*'[1]. Liability for such a breach is not dependent upon proof of negligence since the standard of liability is determined by the wording of the statute.

It is not every breach of a statutory duty which gives to a person injured thereby an action in tort for breach of statutory duty. The reason is that statutory provisions imposing a duty normally have a public purpose to achieve, for example, an orderly system of educational provision, and provide sanctions, criminal or otherwise, for breach of the duty and the courts may think it inappropriate to hold that such a statute also creates private rights to sue for its breach. Indeed many statutes provide a specific statutory remedy for those upset at its application and the existence of such a remedy may also militate against the concurrent existence of private law remedies. Hence, the first task of a plaintiff is to establish that breach of the particular statutory duty which has caused him injury is actionable as a tort.

In deciding this preliminary question, the courts purport to apply the intentions of Parliament. Consequently, if a statute expressly provides that failure to comply with the statute confers (or excludes) a right of action on individuals, the courts must give effect to that intention[2]. However, most statutes are silent on this issue and the courts then seek to apply Parliament's implied intention. In *R v Deputy Governor of Parkhurst Prison, ex p Hague*[3], Lord Bridge said the question a court should ask itself was, '[D]id the legislature intend to confer on the plaintiffs a cause of action for breach of statutory duty?' In this case, the House of Lords held that the Prison Rules 1964 did not give an individual prisoner a private law claim for damages; the purpose of the Prison Rules (made under the Prison Act 1952) was to deal with the administration and management of prisons and Parliament had not intended to confer private law rights on an individual prisoner who had suffered following a breach of the rules. In allegedly interpreting Parliament's unexpressed intention, judges are really deciding whether or not they think an action in tort should lie[4].

Most, but by no means all, successful actions for breach of statutory duty are actions by employees against their employers alleging that breaches of safety legislation resulted in injuries at work.

1   *X v Bedfordshire County Council* [1995] 2 AC 633, [1995] 3 All ER 353, HL.
2   For example, the Sex Discrimination Act 1975, s 60; the Data Protection Act 1984, ss 22 and 23, and the Consumer Protection Act 1987, s 41, expressly confer a right of action, whereas the Medicines Act 1968, s 133 and the Guard Dogs Act 1975, s 5, expressly preclude action. An action for breach of statutory duty may also be possible in respect of breaches of the EC Treaty: *Garden Cottage Foods Ltd v Milk Marketing Board* [1984] AC 130, [1983] 2 All ER 770, HL.
3   [1992] 1 AC 58, [1991] 3 All ER 733, HL.
4   The court applies reasoning similar to that employed in determining whether a particular plaintiff is sufficiently proximate to be owed a duty of care in negligence and whether it is fair, just and reasonable to impose such a duty, see paras 18.2–18.7, above.

20.3   At one time, the courts adopted a relatively liberal approach in determining if breach of a statute gave rise to a civil action; this is no longer the case. What is crucial is did Parliament impose a duty for the protection of a limited class of the public[1] *and* did Parliament intend to confer on members of that class a private right of action for breach of the duty. In formulating Parliament's implied intention various factors may be taken into account: none of them are conclusive and they afford only limited guidance[2]. Factors taken into account by the courts include:

a.   If there exists a common law duty in respect of particular activities the courts may be inclined to find that breach of a statute dealing with similar activities is also tortious (and vice versa)[3] in so far as the civil action for breach of statutory duty complements the common law. For example, at common law, the tort of negligence requires employers to provide safe working conditions and it has been held that breaches by employers of the Factories Act 1961 almost always confer a right to sue in tort on employees injured by that breach.

b.   If a statute is designed to prevent a particular type of injury and it is that type of injury which the plaintiff has suffered, an action in tort is likely to exist[4] (but see f., below).

c.   If a statute provides no sanction for its breach a civil action in tort may lie, because, unless such an action is available, breach of that statute would escape all punishment (but see e., below)[5]. Hence, if the statute provides for a penalty or an alternative remedy for a person adversely affected by breach of a statute, there is a presumption against giving a civil remedy to individuals[6].

d.   The fact that some part of a fine levied for breach of statutory duty can be used to compensate the victim of that breach militates against, but does not preclude, a right to sue in tort[7].

e.   Where a statute imposes an administrative function on a public body, which has a discretion as to how that function should be exercised, the court is unlikely to find that there is a cause of action for breach of statutory duty vested in individuals[8].

f.   If the loss suffered is pure economic loss it is unlikely that the court will impose civil liability on the party bearing the statutory duty[9].

1   See, for example, *X v Bedfordshire County Council* [1995] 2 AC 633, [1995] 3 All ER 353, HL. In this case, the House of Lords determined that a local authority which carelessly performed its duties relating to the education and welfare of children was not liable for breach of statutory duty. The House held that the purposes of the relevant statutes were plain and it did not extend to conferring a right on individuals to sue in tort for breach of statutory duty. This affirmed the view expressed in *Lonrho Ltd v Shell Petroleum C Ltd (No 2)* [1982] AC 173, [1981] 2 All ER 456, HL.
2   In *Ex p Island Records Ltd* [1978] Ch 122, [1978] 3 All ER 824, CA, it was suggested that tossing a coin was as reliable as these factors.
3   *Cutler v Wandsworth Stadium Ltd* [1949] AC 398, [1949] 1 All ER 544, HL; see also *West Wiltshire District Council v Garland* [1995] Ch 297, [1995] 2 All ER 17, CA. For a case where the existence of a statutory duty for the benefit of employees did not give them a civil action see *Richardson v Pitt-Stanley* [1995] QB 123, [1995] ICR 303, CA. Where the common law claim and the claim for breach of statutory duty relate to the same loss there is no double recovery of damages.
4   *Monk v Warbey* [1935] 1 KB 75, CA.
5   *Thornton v Kirklees Metropolitan Borough Council* [1979] QB 626, [1979] 2 All ER 349, CA.
6   See *Olotu v Home Office* [1997] 1 All ER 385, [1997] 1 WLR 328, CA, (alternative remedy of habeas corpus open to plaintiff who had been detained after the expiry of the custody time limit; no private law action justiciable).
7   *Groves v Lord Wimborne* [1898] 2 QB 402, CA.
8   *X v Bedfordshire County Council* [1995] 2 AC 633, [1995] 3 All ER 353, HL.
9   *Murphy v Brentwood District Council* [1991] 1 AC 398, [1990] 2 All ER 908, HL; cf *Invercargill City Council v Hamlin* [1996] AC 624, [1996] 1 All ER 756, PC.

20.4   If an action for breach of statutory duty is permitted, a particular plaintiff who has suffered injury as a result of the breach can sue successfully only if two conditions are satisfied:

a.   The statutory duty must have been owed to *him*[1]. For example, in *Knapp v Railway Executive*[2] a statute imposed a duty upon railway authorities to secure level crossing gates so that the road-using public could not collide with oncoming trains. It was held that, a train driver who was injured when an insecurely fastened gate swung across the line has no cause of action[2]. However, if a statute imposes a duty, but does not define the class whom the statute is designed to protect, the courts will tend to hold that the duty is owed to anyone adversely affected by the breach[3]; and

b.   The injury must have been of a *kind* which the statute sought to prevent[4]. In *Gorris v Scott*[5], a shipowner failed to provide pens for livestock on board his ship, which was a breach of statutory duty. In consequence, the plaintiff's sheep were washed overboard and he sued for breach of statutory duty. The plaintiff's claim failed, the court holding that the purpose of the legislation was to prevent the spread of disease among livestock and not to prevent them being swept overboard[6]. More recently, in *Pickering v Liverpool Daily Post and Echo Newspapers plc*[7], the House of Lords held that unauthorised publication of information about the plaintiff's application for discharge from a mental hospital, which was in breach of the Mental Health Tribunal Rules 1983, did not give the plaintiff a cause of action. The function of the non-publication rules was to ensure privacy for the proceedings of a Mental Health Tribunal. Publication, while adverse to the plaintiff's interests, was incapable of causing him injury of a kind for which the law awarded damages.

1   *Hartley v Mayoh & Co Ltd* [1954] 1 QB 383, [1954] 1 All ER 375, CA.
2   [1949] 2 All ER 508, CA.
3   *Westwood v Post Office* [1974] AC 1, [1973] 3 All ER 184, HL. A trespassing employee who fell through a defective trap-door could recover for breach of a statute designed to protect employees; the courts have tended to be more generous in the imposition of liability in employee cases.
4   *Hartley v Mayoh & Co Ltd* [1954] 1 QB 383, [1954] 1 All ER 375, CA.
5   (1874) LR 9 Exch 125.
6   However, provided that one injury is of the kind which the statute sought to prevent damages can be recovered at large. The plaintiff is not limited to damages for the kind of injury at which the statute was aimed but can recover for all losses: *Cynat Products Ltd v Landbuild (Investment and Property) Ltd* [1984] 3 All ER 513.
7   [1991] 2 AC 370, [1991] 1 All ER 622, HL.

Breach of the relevant duty

20.5   The standard which a person who is under a statutory duty must reach in order to avoid liability is determined by reference to the statute in issue. If a statute provides that an employer must do something, it must be done and any failure to comply with the Act in question, however innocent, is a breach of statutory duty. Thus, in *John Summers & Sons Ltd v Frost*[1], an employer was liable for breach of statutory duty when an employee was injured by an unfenced grinding wheel (fencing being required by the Factories Acts), even though he proved that fencing as required by the Act rendered the wheel unusable. Conversely, a person subject to a statutory duty need do no more than the statute requires. In *Chipchase v British Titan Products Co Ltd*[2], the defendant employer was required by statute to provide employees who were working at six and a half feet (or more) above the ground with a working platform at least 34 inches wide. The plaintiff fell from a working platform of only nine inches width but the employer was not in breach of the statute because the employee was working at a height of only six feet above the ground[3].

Because the standard of liability varies depending upon the wording of the statutory provision which has been broken, the tort of breach of statutory duty cannot be classified either as requiring fault or being a tort of strict liability[4].

Note that where a body charged with performing a statutory duty, or exercising a statutory discretion or power, does so negligently an action for negligence may, in a limited number of cases, also arise[5].

1 [1955] AC 740, [1955] 1 All ER 870, HL.
2 [1956] 1 QB 545, [1956] 1 All ER 613, CA.
3 While the absence of six inches prevented the employer being in breach of his statutory duty, his conduct might have been held to constitute common law negligence which requires him to provide reasonably safe working conditions.
4 The consumer safety provisions of the Consumer Protection Act 1987, paras 20.9–20.15, below, provide a good example of provisions breach of which gives rise to civil liability without any need of fault.
5 See paras 18.29–18.32, above.

Causation
20.6 In order to succeed in an action for breach of statutory duty, the plaintiff must establish that the breach caused his injuries[1]. If such a breach caused his injuries (at least partially) the plaintiff can recover damages even if he too is in breach of a statutory duty. Thus, if an employer fails to encourage his employees to wear safety-goggles which he has provided and this failure is a breach of statute, an employee who suffers eye injuries while not using his goggles can recover damages. This will be so even if the employee was in breach of a statutory duty owed by him to wear the goggles[2].

On the other hand, if the plaintiff's breach of statutory duty is the sole cause of his injuries he cannot recover damages; even though the defendant was also in breach of a statutory duty. In *Ginty v Belmont Building Supplies Ltd*[3], an employee, who, in breach of his statutory duty, failed to use crawling boards and consequently was injured by falling through a roof, was held to be the sole cause of his misfortune. This was the case even though his employer (who had provided crawling boards and instructions on their use) was also technically in breach of the statute which provided that, while working on fragile roofs, crawling boards 'shall be used'.

1 For a discussion of causation see paras 18.52–18.60, above.
2 *Bux v Slough Metals Ltd* [1974] 1 All ER 262, [1973] 1 WLR 1358, CA. In this case the employee's damages were reduced by 40% to reflect his partial responsibility for his injuries.
3 [1959] 1 All ER 414.

Defences
20.7 The defences of contributory negligence[1] and volenti[2] (consent) are available in actions for breach of statutory duty.

An employer can raise the defence of contributory negligence when sued by his employees for breach of statutory duty. However, it is the policy of the courts, in deciding whether an employee has contributed to his injuries:

'to give due regard to the actual conditions under which men work in a factory or mine, to the long hours and the fatigue, to the slackening of attention which naturally comes from constant repetition of the same operation, to the noise and confusion in which the man works, to his preoccupation in what he is actually doing at the cost perhaps of some inattention to his own safety[3].'

To do otherwise would be to deprive employees of the protection of much of the safety legislation which is designed to protect them.

A paternalistic approach is also adopted with respect to the defence of consent in employment cases involving breach of statutory duty. It is settled law that an employer who is personally in breach of a statutory duty, for example, by providing unfenced machinery, cannot rely on this defence at all[4]. However, an employer who is in breach of statutory duty because he is held vicariously responsible for the actions of another one of his employees can raise this defence[5].

1 Contributory negligence is discussed in paras 21.11–21.15, below.
2 Volenti is discussed in paras 21.2–21.10, below.
3 *Caswell v Powell Duffryn Associated Collieries Ltd* [1940] AC 152, [1939] 3 All ER 722 at 739.
4 *Baddeley v Earl Granville* (1887) 19 QBD 423, DC.
5 *ICI Ltd v Shatwell* [1965] AC 656, [1964] 2 All ER 999, HL.

Torts Concerning Goods

20.8   As we have seen in Chapter 19, a person who suffers an injury which was caused by defective goods may have a cause of action against the manufacturer of those goods. In respect of certain injuries a person harmed by a defective good has an alternative (and in many ways wider) cause of action for breach of the Consumer Protection Act 1987 (product liability) which we discuss in paras 20.9–20.15, below.

In addition to goods causing a person harm, a person's goods may be harmed by another. If the harm is inflicted negligently then an action for negligence can be brought. There are, however, other torts which relate solely to goods (wrongful interference with goods); we discuss these in paras 20.16–20.19, below.

Product liability
20.9   A purchaser of defective goods has a remedy against the retailer in contract both in respect of the defect and in respect of any consequential injury. However, there is no general contractual remedy for the purchaser against someone who was not a party to the contract of sale, such as a wholesaler or manufacturer of the goods, and there is no contractual remedy against anyone for the non-purchaser[1]. In the absence of an effective contractual remedy, a person injured by a defective good may be able to sue the manufacturer in negligence, which liability we discussed in paras 19.7–19.15, above. The major drawback of suing in negligence is that the plaintiff bears the burden of proving all the elements of negligence.

In 1987, in order to comply with an EC directive[2], Parliament enacted the Consumer Protection Act, which enables those injured by a defective product to sue a variety of people concerned with its manufacture and distribution, without having to prove negligence on the defendant's part.

1   This is merely an application of privity of contract; paras 6.24–6.34, above.
2   In consequence all members of the EC should have similar legislation.

20.10   In order to succeed in an action under the Consumer Protection Act 1987 the plaintiff must prove:

a.   that a defective product;
b.   caused him the requisite injury; and
c.   the defendant produced that product or otherwise falls within s 2 of the Act.

A defective product

20.11   The Act defines products in s 1 as goods[1] and electricity and also products comprised in another product, such as the wheels on a car or the bricks incorporated into a house. The Act provides that immovables are not products so that the builder of a defective house would not be liable; the manufacturer of the car and the manufacturer of the wheels would be jointly liable if the wheels on a car are defective.

Section 3 defines a defective product as a product the safety of which is not such as persons generally are entitled to expect. The court can take into account such factors as it sees fit in determining if the product's safety is not what persons are entitled to expect; factors might include the cost and ease, or otherwise, of eliminating the defect and the social value of the product, but the Act articulates some possible factors. These include the manner in which the product was marketed, the purposes for which it was marketed, any warnings in respect of use of the product and what the product might be used for. For example, the vendor of a domestic sleeping bag does not incur liability for frostbite suffered by a user on a polar expedition. A defect in design or manufacture can fall within the Act, as can a risk in the use of the product about which adequate warnings were not given, eg failure to warn that a drug can cause drowsiness.

1   The definition of goods in s 45 includes gas, growing crops (although there is no strict liability for unprocessed agricultural products, query whether this would exclude genetically modified agricultural products), things attached to land (such as railings), ships, aircraft and vehicles.

Which caused injury

20.12   The Act provides a remedy only in respect of certain injuries; namely, death, personal injury and damage to 'domestic' property (including land)[1]. There is no recovery in respect of damage to, or destruction of, the defective product itself nor in respect of any reduction in the value of the product caused by the defect. Nor is there recovery for financial loss consequential upon the injury, except perhaps loss of earnings caused by personal injury.

Domestic property is property ordinarily intended for domestic use and intended by the person suffering the injury mainly for his private use.

The injury must be caused by the defective product. Causation is discussed in relation to negligence in paras 18.52–18.60, above, and those rules are applicable here.

1 Section 5. Property damage must exceed £275.

The identity of the defendant
20.13 Liability for defective products is imposed by s 2 of the Act on:

a. producers;
b. persons who hold themselves out as producers;
c. persons who, in the course of business, import that product into the EEC, intending to supply it to another; and
d. suppliers[1] who, after a request by the person injured, fail to identify to him within a reasonable time persons listed in a. to c.

If the injury suffered by the plaintiff is of the requisite type, the liability of the above persons arises without any need for the plaintiff to prove fault by all or any of them. If liability is imposed on more than one person that liability is joint and several[2].

It should be noted that a person may be a 'producer' even though the production is not in the course of a business. However, a person who does not produce products for profit has a defence[3]. An example of a person who holds himself out as a producer might be a supermarket which sold goods manufactured by others under its own label.

1 Whether supply was to the plaintiff, a producer of a product into which the defective product was incorporated or to anyone else.
2 A defendant who is sued successfully can seek contribution from others; see paras 17.12–17.14, above.
3 Under s 4; see para 20.14, below.

Defences
20.14 The most controversial defence is set out in s 4(1)(e). This provides a 'development risks defence', under which a producer of a defective product can escape liability for injuries caused by it if he can prove that at the time the product was marketed available scientific and technical knowledge meant that he could not have discovered the defect. Thus, manufacturers of a new drug which causes injury and which is found to be defective may have a defence if they can show that they considered all relevant, available medical information and that it did not disclose any such risk.

Section 4 also provides that if products are not supplied at all, as where they are stolen, or if they are not supplied in the course of a business, there is no liability under the Act. Additionally, it is a defence for a defendant to show that the defect was not present when he supplied the product. For example, a manufacturer is not liable for people who tamper with his products when they are on the supermarket shelf unless, perhaps, that tampering was likely to occur and 'persons generally' would anticipate the use of tamper-proof packaging. Producers of component parts are not liable when their products become defective only because they have been inadequately or improperly incorporated into another product.

Section 6 provides that contributory negligence on the part of the plaintiff is a defence to an action under this Act.

426

Limitation

20.15 The Act provides that an action for an injury caused by a defective product must be brought either within three years of the injury or, if this is later, within three years of the plaintiff becoming aware of the injury[1]. However, in no circumstances can an action be brought more than ten years after the date on which the defendant supplied the defective product to another person.

1 There is a discretion to override this three-year period if the injury suffered is personal injury, subject always to the ten-year 'longstop'.

Interference with goods

20.16 Prior to 1977 there were a number of torts dealing with interference with goods[1]; these torts were partially amalgamated and codified by the Torts (Interference with Goods) Act 1977. This Act imposes tortious liability upon any person who wrongfully interferes with goods. Wrongful interference is constituted either by trespass to goods, or by conversion, or by negligence resulting in damage to goods[2] (or an interest in goods), or by any other tort resulting in damage to goods (or an interest in goods).

1 'Goods' means any chattel, except a chose in action (see para 22.2, below) or money.
2 Since this is in effect an action for negligence the principles applicable to that tort (which we discuss in Chap 19) operate.

Trespass to goods

20.17 Trespass to goods comprises any direct physical interference with goods which are in the possession of another person (whether or not the goods are damaged) unless there is lawful justification for the interference. It is trespass to scratch or beat goods in the possession of another and also to touch goods, even if this does not damage them. The interference must be deliberate or negligent but, provided that such interference is established, liability is strict and it is no defence to prove that one acted honestly. Thus, if a person genuinely but mistakenly believes that goods belong to him and removes them from the possession of another, that constitutes trespass[1].

Because trespass to goods is an injury to possession, it is possible for the owner of goods to be liable for trespass if he seizes his goods from a person who is lawfully in possession of them.

1 *Wilson v Lombank Ltd* [1963] 1 All ER 740, [1963] 1 WLR 1294, CA.

Conversion

20.18 Conversion is dealing with another person's goods in a way which, without lawful justification, denies that other person's rights in respect of the goods. Liability arises whenever a person intentionally does something which in fact denies another person's rights in respect of goods, whether or not there was an intention to deny those rights.

This denial can take many forms. One example is where a person admits that he possesses goods belonging to another but refuses to allow him to collect them[1]. If the purchaser of goods from a person who has no title to them[2] subsequently refuses to return them to the person with title, there is a denial of the rights of the true owner of those goods, even if the purchaser has acted in good faith. Hence, an innocent purchaser of stolen goods who has no title to them commits conversion if he refuses to return them to the true owner[3]. To deal with goods in a manner inconsistent with the rights of the true owner is also a denial of his rights. Thus, an auctioneer, who, however innocently, sells goods which the vendor had no right to sell, is liable for conversion[4]. It is also conversion for a bailee, eg a hirer of goods, to lose, damage or refuse to return them.

An action for conversion can be brought by anyone who has possession of goods or a right to possession of goods, whether such a person is the owner of those goods or not.

1   *Howard E Perry & Co Ltd v British Railways Board* [1980] 2 All ER 579, [1986] 1 WLR 1375. It is not wrongful interference to clamp a car, and require a release fee, if the car owner parks without authorisation on private land displaying warning signs that unauthorised vehicles would be immobilised, see *Arthur v Anker* [1996] 3 All ER 783, CA.
2   For example, because the vendor of goods acquired them under a contract void for mistake (see Chap 13) or because the vendor of goods is a thief or a person who has acquired the goods from a thief.
3   There are situations where a person can acquire title even if his vendor lacked title.
4   *R H Willis & Son v British Car Auctions Ltd* [1978] 2 All ER 392, [1978] 1 WLR 438, CA.

Remedies for wrongful interference
20.19   The remedies available are:

a.   an order to pay damages, the amount awarded being assessed so as to compensate the plaintiff for the destruction, damage or deprivation of the goods and for any consequential loss[1];
b.   at the discretion of the court, and only where the defendant is in possession or control of the goods,
   i.   an order for the return of the goods; or
   ii.   an order for the return of the goods, but giving the defendant the alternative of paying damages by reference to the value of the goods,
   together in either alternative with payment of damages for any consequential loss.

In *BBMB Finance (Hong Kong) Ltd v Eda Holdings Ltd*[2], the Privy Council ruled that the general rule which should be adopted by the courts is that where the plaintiff's property has been irreversibly converted he has a right to damages measured by the value of the property at the date of conversion. An award of damages under a. or b.ii. may be reduced to reflect any improvements made to the goods by a person who honestly believed that he had title to them. There is also a limited right to use self-help by taking back the goods from the person who has wrongfully interfered with them, but this should be exercised with great care. Contributory negligence[3] is not a defence to conversion or intentional trespass to goods.

1   Thus, if a person to whom one has lent a profit-earning chattel fails to return it, damages will include the amount of profit which the chattel would have earned: *Hillesden Securities Ltd v Ryjack Ltd* [1983] 2 All ER 184, [1983] 1 WLR 959.
2   [1991] 2 All ER 129, [1990] 1 WLR 409, PC.
3   See paras 21.11–21.15, below.

Torts Concerning Land

20.20 The ownership or occupation of land imposes an obligation on the owner and/or the occupier to take due care to ensure that the state of the land or activities carried on on it do not cause injury to others. This aspect of the tort of negligence was discussed in Chapter 19. There are two other torts (which overlap with negligence) which impose obligations on those who own or occupy land – nuisance and the rule in *Rylands v Fletcher* – and it is these which we now consider.

Private nuisance

20.21 Every occupier of property must expect his property and his enjoyment of it to be affected to some degree by the activities of his neighbours or the physical state of adjoining land. However, if this interference exceeds what one can reasonably be expected to endure, it is an actionable private nuisance.

Actions for private nuisance can be brought in respect of either material physical damage to property or in respect of 'substantial' interference with the use or enjoyment of property (amenity damage)[1].

1 Property in this context means real property, which will include things growing on the land, or chattels. The loss of even a night's sleep has been held to be substantial interference with the enjoyment of property: *Andreae v Selfridge & Co Ltd* [1938] Ch 1, [1937] 3 All ER 255, CA, but this seems doubtful.

20.22 In determining whether activities carried on on neighbouring land or its physical state are an actionable nuisance, the courts seek to balance a number of factors, particularly:

a. *The nature of the locality* In assessing whether enjoyment of property has been substantially impaired, the courts consider the overall nature of the locality. If land is in an industrial or urban area the courts require adjoining property owners or occupiers to put up with more noise, dirt and smell than those living in more rural surroundings. When the plaintiff's complaint alleges actual physical damage to his property the court disregards this factor[1].

b. *The duration of the activity* An activity which is carried on infrequently or only once (or a state of the land which is only temporary or of short duration) is unlikely, unless extremely disruptive, to be an actionable nuisance. One noisy party is not actionable; one every night is. However, it must be noted that, where an activity extends over a period of time, an action for nuisance may lie even though it causes damage or interference with enjoyment only once or infrequently[2].

c. *Reasonableness* This is the most difficult factor to analyse. Perhaps it is best summed up by the dictum 'There must be a measure of give and take, live and let live'[3]. The courts have to weigh up the nature of the defendant's conduct and assess its effect upon a reasonable member of society. In reaching this decision factors such as the social utility, or otherwise, of the defendant's actions

429

are treated as relevant[4], as is the defendant's motive. Hence, conduct motivated by malice may lead the court to find the defendant's conduct to be unreasonable[5].

1   *St Helen's Smelting Co v Tipping* (1865) 11 HL Cas 642; acid rain which damaged plants on the plaintiff's land was an actionable nuisance even in an industrial area.
2   *Miller v Jackson* [1977] QB 966, [1977] 3 All ER 338, CA.
3   *Kennaway v Thompson* [1981] QB 88 at 94, [1980] 3 All ER 329 at 333.
4   *Kennaway v Thompson* [1981] QB 88, [1980] 3 All ER 329, CA; power-boating in a rural area a nuisance.
5   *Christie v Davey* [1893] 1 Ch 316; accordingly, banging on the wall in order to disturb neighbour's music lessons and activities was a nuisance.

Who can sue?

20.23   The occupier of property affected by the nuisance is the usual plaintiff and he can recover damages for injury to the property and to his enjoyment of the property and possibly for any personal injury to himself caused by the nuisance. Alternatively, or in addition, he may seek an injunction, which is a discretionary remedy, to prevent the nuisance continuing[1].

An owner of property who is not in occupation can also sue in nuisance but only for damage to the property.

Since nuisance is essentially a tort designed to protect land and the enjoyment of land, it was generally thought that the plaintiff must have a proprietary interest in the land affected in order to sue. However, in *Khorasandjian v Bush*[2], the Court of Appeal granted an injunction against the defendant to restrain acts of harassment, carried out by means of frequent, unwanted phone calls to the plaintiff, despite the fact that the plaintiff (the intended recipient of the calls) had no such interest in land. This decision has been subject to considerable criticism and was overruled on this point by the House of Lords in *Hunter v Canary Wharf Ltd*[3].

1   For injunctions, see paras 12.30-12.34, above, and para 21.25, below.
2   [1993] QB 727, [1993] 3 All ER 669, CA.
3   [1997] 2 All ER 426, HL.

Who can be sued?

20.24   The person in occupation of the property from which the nuisance emanates is liable if either:

a.   he created the nuisance and was 'at fault' in so doing[1]. Fault in nuisance means that the creator of the nuisance deliberately engaged in conduct which caused the nuisance (whether or not he intended to cause a nuisance) and the injury suffered by the plaintiff was either reasonably foreseeable or was a 'real risk'. A 'real risk' seems to mean that the injury to the plaintiff could have been foreseen, even if it was not *reasonably* foreseeable, and the injury, if it occurred, was likely to be serious[1];

b.   the nuisance was created by a third party (eg a trespasser)[2], or arose naturally (eg a tree struck by lightning)[3], and the person in occupation cannot prove that he was not negligent in failing to prevent the nuisance affecting the plaintiff. In deciding whether the defendant has done sufficient to prevent the injury to the plaintiff, the courts have regard to the defendant's personal circumstances, such as his age, financial circumstances etc. Thus, unusually, the standard of care imposed on the defendant is that of a reasonable person in the *defendant's* circumstances – perhaps to reflect the fact that the hazard has been thrust on to the defendant through no fault of his own.

If the nuisance was created by a person other than the occupier of the property from which it emanates, that person is also liable.

1 *The Wagon Mound (No 2)* [1967] 1 AC 617, [1966] 2 All ER 709, PC.
2 *Sedleigh-Denfield v O'Callaghan* [1940] AC 880, [1940] 3 All ER 349, HL; the third party who created the nuisance was also liable.
3 *Goldman v Hargrave* [1967] 1 AC 645, [1966] 2 All ER 989, PC.

Defences
20.25 Among the defences which are available are prescription (ie that an actionable nuisance has continued for 20 years and that action has not been taken during that period), volenti[1], contributory negligence[2] and statutory authorisation[3].

1 See paras 21.2–21.10, below.
2 See paras 21.11–21.15, below.
3 See para 21.17, below; *Allen v Gulf Oil Refining Ltd* [1981] AC 1001, [1981] 1 All ER 353, HL.

The rule in *Rylands v Fletcher*
20.26 This resembles nuisance in that one landowner or occupier is entitled to bring an action against another land owner or occupier. Traditionally, however, it differed from nuisance in that a person with no interest in land could also have a cause of action[1]. In practice the restrictive interpretation placed upon this tort by the courts has rendered it practically moribund and the House of Lords, in *Cambridge Water Co Ltd v Eastern Countries Leather plc*[2], has narrowed what differences there were between this tort and the tort of nuisance.

1 This difference has been affirmed recently, see para 20.23, above.
2 [1994] 2 AC 264, [1994] 1 All ER 53, HL.

20.27 Liability under this rule arises where the defendant, for his own purposes, brings onto his land and collects and keeps there, something which constitutes a non-natural use of the land and which is likely to cause mischief if it escapes, which does escape and causes foreseeable damage of the relevant type[1]. The vital elements are the collection of potentially mischievous items and their escape from land within the occupation or control of one person to land outside his occupation or control, always providing that what is collected constitutes a non-natural use of the land and foreseeable damage is caused. This does not mean *unnatural* use but use of land which is unusual or not ordinary or one bringing with it increased danger to others having regard to modern conditions.

The owner or occupier of the land adversely affected by the escape can sue for damages for injury to the person or to property provided that such damage was foreseeable. In addition, a non-occupier can sue for physical injury.

1   *Cambridge Water Co Ltd v Eastern Counties Leather plc* [1994] 2 AC 264, [1994] 1 All ER 53, HL.

20.28   The defences available are volenti, that the collecting and keeping was partly for the defendant's benefit, that the escape was caused by the unforeseeable act of a stranger, that the plaintiff was contributorily negligent, that there was statutory authority and, in very extreme cases, that the escape was an act of God.

Defamation

20.29   Defamation is close to being unique in English law in that it is a civil action which is tried by a jury[1]. Where a jury tries a case it is the jury which fixes the amount of damages, if any. Although, as with most torts, an award of damages for defamation is designed to compensate the tort victim for the loss which he has suffered, the amount of damages for defamation awarded by a jury bears no relation to the apparent harm caused by the defamatory statement or to the award of damages made (by judges) in other cases, such as actions for personal injury. In some cases, it is hard not to conclude that the jury is expressing its disapproval of the conduct of the defendant (perhaps a newspaper) rather than seeking to compensate the plaintiff[2].

Until recently there was little that the judge could do to deter a jury from being over-generous in its award in a defamation case. However, in 1993 the Court of Appeal held that the judge may direct the jury about the level of awards made by the Court of Appeal in defamation cases[3] and in *John v Mirror Group Newspapers Ltd*[4], the Court of Appeal ruled that juries could also be referred to conventional compensation awards in personal injury cases by way of comparison. If the jury's award is excessive, in the sense that no reasonable jury could have thought that the amount was necessary to compensate the plaintiff and re-establish his reputation, the Court of Appeal can order a new trial or substitute a lower award[5].

It should not be forgotten that not all defamation cases involve statements in the press or television; it is as much defamation to write in an auditor's report 'the directors have a limited grasp of the principles of honesty and fair dealing', unless this is indeed so (in which case the defence of justification will be available).

1   Defamation Act 1996, s 8, introduces a summary procedure for disposing of defamation claims. Section 8 allows a court to dismiss a plaintiff's claim if it has no realistic chance of success and there is no reason why it should be tried. It also allows the court to give judgment for the plaintiff if it appears that there is no defence which has a realistic chance of success and there is no other reason why the claim should be heard. Section 9 limits the amount of damages awarded in summary proceedings to £10,000.
2   See para 21.31, below.

3   *Rantzen v Mirror Group Newspapers* [1994] QB 670, [1993] 4 All ER 975, CA.
4   [1996] 2 All ER 35, CA. Jury award of £75,000 by way of compensatory damages reduced to
£25,000 in that defamatory statement while false and offensive did not attack the plaintiff's
personal integrity or damage his reputation as an artist.
5   Courts and Legal Services Act 1990, s 8. This applies both the compensatory element of
damages and any exemplary damages, see para 21.31, below, awarded to punish the defendant.

20.30   Defamation consists of publishing a statement which would *tend* to
lower a living person in the estimation of right-thinking members of society
generally[1] or which would *tend* to make them shun or avoid him. It is not
necessary for anyone *actually* to think the worse of the plaintiff or to shun or
avoid him[2], nor is it necessary for the person making or transmitting the
statement to intend such a result.

1   *Sim v Stretch* [1936] 2 All ER 1237, HL.
2   *Theaker v Richardson* [1962] 1 All ER 229, [1962] 1 WLR 151, CA.

Libel and slander

20.31   Defamation is sub-divided into libel and slander. A defamatory statement
which is published in a permanent form, for example, in a film or newspaper, is
libel, and defamatory words or pictures broadcast over the radio or television
are, by statute, considered to be libel. A defamatory statement in transient form,
for example, a conversation which is not recorded, is a slander. Libel is actionable
without proof of any damage, whereas slander is only actionable if there has
been some damage caused to the plaintiff or the slander imputes:

a.   that the plaintiff has committed a criminal offence; or
b.   that he is unfit for his trade, profession or office; or
c.   where the plaintiff is a woman, that she is unchaste; or
d.   that the plaintiff suffers from a 'noxious' disease, such as VD, or perhaps,
     AIDS.

20.32   If the plaintiff is to sue successfully for defamation, he must prove
three things:

a.   that the words, picture, film or other material were defamatory, either in
     their natural and ordinary meaning or because of facts known only to
     people to whom the words were published (whether or not they believed
     them)[1]. For example, to write that X has no religious beliefs is not
     apparently defamatory, but if the recipients of that statement know that X
     is a candidate for holy orders then it is; and
b.   that the words, picture, film or other material referred to the plaintiff
     (although the reference need not be by name if the plaintiff is clearly
     indicated, eg the occupier of a particular office) or might reasonably be
     supposed to refer to the plaintiff, whether or not this was the intention of
     the maker of the statement[2]; and
c.   that the words, picture, film or other material were published to a third
     party. Publication to a single person (other than the publisher's spouse)

will suffice, but there is no publication if the alleged defamation is only revealed to the person to whom the statement refers.

1   The judge rules whether the statement is capable of being defamatory. If he rules that it is so capable, the jury decide if the statement actually is defamatory.
2   But note the defence sometimes available when a statement was not intended to refer to the plaintiff: see para 20.34, below.

20.33   Every repetition of a defamatory statement is a publication so that not only is the writer or speaker of the defamatory statement liable but so is a printer or publisher etc. Even a seller or distributor of papers and books (but not the Post Office) can be liable if he knew or ought to have known that the paper or book which he disseminated contained defamatory material (but see 20.34b, below, for a defence that may well apply to innocent disseminators of defamatory material).

20.34   The defences available to an action for defamation are:

a.   *Offer to make amends*   Sections 2 to 4 of the Defamation Act 1996 introduce this defence which allows a person who has published a statement alleged to be defamatory to offer to make amends. The party who published the allegedly defamatory material does so by issuing a suitable correction of the statement complained of, making a sufficient apology and paying the aggrieved party such compensation (if any) and such costs as are agreed or determined to be payable (s 2). The person to whom the offer is made can accept it (s 3) or reject it (s 4). If the offer is accepted any disputes about compensation can be referred to a court. If the offer is rejected the offer is a complete defence unless the plaintiff can show that when publishing the defamatory material the defendant knew, or had reason to believe, that it referred to the plaintiff and was both false and defamatory.

b.   *Responsibility for publication*   Section 1 of the Defamation Act 1996 provides that a person who is not the author, editor or commercial publisher of the statement complained of, for example, a printer or distributor, has a defence to a defamation action if he can show that he took reasonable care in relation to its publication and that he did not know, and had no reason to believe, that what he did caused or contributed to the publication of a defamatory statement.

c.   *Justification*   ie that the defamatory statement was true; this defence is not destroyed by the fact that the statement was prompted by spite or malice. An exception is the case where the defamatory statement relates to the criminal conviction of a person who has been 'rehabilitated' under the Rehabilitation of Offenders Act 1974, in which case the defence of justification is destroyed by proof of malice.

d.   *Fair comment*   The comment must be on a matter of public interest; it must be an expression of opinion on matters of fact, it must be fair and it must not be motivated by malice.

e. *Absolute privilege* A limited number of statements are absolutely privileged and cannot, normally, form the basis of an action for defamation. One example is a statement in Parliament but s 13 of the Defamation Act 1996, permits MPs and peers to waive the protection of Parliamentary privilege. Fair and accurate reports of proceedings in public before a court, if published contemporaneously with the proceedings, are also subject to absolute privilege[1].

f. *Qualified privilege* Where a statement is subject to a qualified privilege, the privilege disappears if there is malice. Section 15 of the Defamation Act 1996 provides a non-exhaustive list of statements to which qualified privilege attaches. It includes, fair and accurate report of parliamentary proceedings and fair and accurate reports of proceedings before courts anywhere in the world. Qualified privilege also exists where there is a duty (legal or moral) to make a statement and the recipient has a legitimate interest in receiving it, as for example when an existing or former employer gives a reference for an employee to a prospective employer[2].

1   Defamation Act 1996, s 14.
2   See also para 18.12, above.

20.35   Finally, it should be noted that, in the landmark case of *Derbyshire County Council v Times Newspapers Ltd*[1], the House of Lords held that a local authority could not sue for defamation since it was contrary to public policy to allow an organ of government, central or local, to have that right. The House declared that it was of the highest public importance that a government body should be open to uninhibited public criticism and that a right to sue for defamation would deter freedom of speech.

1   [1993] AC 534, [1993] 1 All ER 1011, HL.

Chapter 21

Defences and Remedies

21.1 In this chapter we discuss two things: defences to tort actions available to defendants and remedies for successful plaintiffs.

A plaintiff who can establish the basic elements necessary to found a claim in tort may fail in his action (or receive less compensation than he sought) if the defendant can rely on a specific defence. The defences discussed in this chapter apply to most torts; defamation is the principal exception.

The usual remedy awarded to a successful plaintiff is damages but, as we shall see, it is by no means the only remedy. Of course, where the defendant has no money and no insurance, a successful plaintiff may be successful in name only.

Defences

Volenti non fit injuria
21.2 A plea of volenti, which is a complete defence to a tortious action, embraces two alternative situations. It arises:

a. where the plaintiff consented to the act which caused his injury; and
b. where the plaintiff agreed to run the risk of having no legal redress for an injury.

Because volenti constitutes a complete defence to an action in tort it is very narrowly construed by the courts.

Consent
21.3 An application of the first type of volenti is in relation to the tort of trespass to the person, ie the intentional and direct application of force to a person. If a person consents to the application of force, as where a properly informed patient agrees to an operation, he cannot complain that the injury which he suffers as a *necessary* consequence of the operation, however skilfully it was performed, constitutes a trespass. The patient's consent must be freely

given although implied consent to any necessary emergency treatment may be assumed in the case of the unconscious patient. There is no effective consent if the doctor has failed to explain the nature of any treatment and any major risks attached to it[1]. Because a person may consent to an act which would otherwise be a trespass, he does not agree to run the risk of having no legal redress if the person to whom the consent has been given commits some other act of wrongdoing. The patient who consents to an operation (a trespass) does not agree to give up any legal remedy he might have if the operation is performed negligently. Further, it is the fact that he can be said to have consented to have no legal redress which generally precludes a sportsman complaining of injuries received from a fellow participant in the course of the game. However, a sportsman is not defeated by a plea of volenti if the injury of which he is complaining was inflicted in gross violation of the rules of the game; he cannot be said to have consented to that risk[2].

1   *Sidaway v Board of Governors of the Bethlem Royal Hospital* [1985] AC 871, [1985] 1 All ER 643, HL. The degree of disclosure about risks etc required is judged by reference to customary medical practice.
2   In *Condon v Basi* [1985] 2 All ER 453, [1985] 1 WLR 866, CA, the plaintiff was awarded £4,900 for a broken leg sustained in an amateur football match as the result of a reckless and dangerous, although not malicious, tackle.

Assumption of risk
21.4   A good example of the second type of volenti occurred in *Morris v Murray*[1], in which the Court of Appeal held that a passenger, who appreciated (albeit imperfectly since he was drunk) the risk he ran in embarking on an aeroplane joyride with a pilot whose drunkenness was extreme, was barred by the defence of volenti from recovering damages from the deceased pilot's estate. The court held that to embark on such an intrinsically dangerous flight was to assume to the risk of having no legal redress if disaster overtook the enterprise. The plaintiff was effectively the author of his own misfortune.

In some cases the court has used the plaintiff's own ill-judged conduct not to found a defence of volenti but to deny the existence of a duty of care. For example, in *Barrett v Ministry of Defence*[2], a naval airman choked to death on his own vomit when he became unconscious after consuming a large quantity of very cheap alcohol supplied at a foreign naval base. It was argued that the Ministry owed him a duty of care to prevent him from consuming excessive alcohol but this was firmly rejected by the Court of Appeal. The court determined that it was not fair, just and reasonable[3] for the law to place the responsibility for determining the appropriate amount of alcohol a responsible adult could consume on anyone other than the consumer. The deceased alone must be regarded as having responsibility for his actions.

1   [1991] 2 QB 6, [1990] 3 All ER 801, CA.
2   [1995] 3 All ER 87, [1995] 1 WLR 1217, CA.
3   See para 18.6, above, for a discussion of factors limiting the imposition of a duty of care.

Conditions necessary for the plaintiff to have waived his legal rights
21.5   Where the defendant alleges the plaintiff had waived his right to legal redress and in consequence volenti is a defence, he must prove, both that the

plaintiff knew of the risk of injury and that the plaintiff genuinely and voluntarily consented (expressly or impliedly) to abandon in advance any right of action.

21.6   *Knowledge of risk*   A plaintiff cannot be said to consent to run a risk unless he knows of it[1]. However, the converse is not the case; merely to know of a risk is not to consent to run it. In *Smith v Baker & Sons*[2], an employee knew and understood that he ran the risk of being injured by a stone falling from his employer's crane as it swung overhead, a practice which had continued for many months. The employee was seriously injured by a falling stone. The House of Lords held that his knowledge of the risk did not constitute consent. Similarly, in *Nettleship v Weston*[3], the Court of Appeal held that although a person giving driving lessons might have known that he ran a risk of injury, he had not thereby consented to having no legal redress if he was injured (as had happened) through the learner driver's negligence.

Since knowledge of a risk is not automatically treated as consent to run that risk, it is not surprising that the courts have held that those who are injured in attempting to rescue persons from danger are not denied a remedy against the creator of that danger merely because they knew that the rescue would expose them to the risk of injury. For example, in *Haynes v Harwood*[4], a policeman, who was seriously injured in attempting to rescue a woman and child from horses which had bolted, recovered damages from the defendant whose negligence had caused the horses to bolt. An injured rescuer can recover for any injury not only when the defendant has placed a third person at risk but also when the defendant has placed himself at risk[5]. Where it is a third party who was put at risk by the tortfeasor any tortious action by the rescuer is independent of his claim.

1   *Harrison v Vincent* [1982] RTR 8, CA.
2   [1891] AC 325, HL.
3   [1971] 2 QB 691, [1971] 3 All ER 581, CA.
4   [1935] 1 KB 146, CA. An alternative approach in rescuer cases is to find that even if a rescuer can be said to know the risk he runs he does not consent to abandon any cause of action he might otherwise have.
5   See, eg, *Harrison v British Railways Board* [1981] 3 All ER 679, in which a train guard who was injured in attempting to rescue a passenger, who had negligently attempted to board a moving train, recovered damages from the passenger.

21.7   *Genuine and voluntary consent*   Where a person who would otherwise have a claim in tort against a defendant knew of a risk he was running he can still recover unless the defendant can show that he consented to run the risk of having no legal redress in respect of the defendant's acts. Consent to the waiving of a cause of action will be ineffective if it was obtained by fraud.

In addition, there is no true consent if the potential plaintiff has no real option but to run a risk. For example, an employee may know of a risk from dangerous machinery but continue to use the machinery rather than lose his job; he would not be held to have consented to the risk of injury from the machinery. However, if an employee is injured at work, not through any tortious act or omission of his employer but because of a tortious act or omission by a fellow employee for which his employer is vicariously liable[1], the employer may be able to rely on volenti as a defence. In *ICI Ltd v Shatwell*[2], X, a shot-firer employed by ICI, tested a firing circuit improperly in breach of his statutory duty and thereby injured the plaintiff, a fellow shot-firer. The plaintiff brought an action against ICI: it would have succeeded if X was liable in tort (ICI would have been vicariously liable for X's acts). The claim failed because the plaintiff, having agreed to the improper testing, was himself in breach of statutory duty and had, thus, agreed to run the risk that he might not have any legal redress if X's actions caused him injury.

1   For vicarious liability see paras 17.15–17.27, above.
2   [1965] AC 656, [1964] 2 All ER 999, HL.

21.8   If the plaintiff has genuinely and voluntarily consented to an act by the defendant any claim in tort is subject to the defence of volenti, even if the act to which the plaintiff consented was illegal[1]. However, the court will consider carefully what it is to which the potential plaintiff can be said to have consented; to strike a person a glancing blow in a fight may be implied consent to similar treatment, but it is not consent to a disproportionate response[2].

1   *Murphy v Culhane* [1977] QB 94, [1976] 3 All ER 533, CA.
2   *Lane v Hollaway* [1968] 1 QB 379, [1967] 3 All ER 129, CA.

21.9   *Express and implied consent*   While it may be easy to envisage a person expressly consenting to some intentional act which would otherwise be tortious, it is difficult to imagine a person expressly consenting to waive his right to sue for negligence. However, such consent may arise by virtue of a contract between the parties which contains a clause exempting or restricting the liability of a party for negligence. A notice may also purport to exclude or restrict liability in negligence. Where a person has entered into such a contract or is bound by the notice, he may be said to have consented to the risk of having no redress if he is subsequently injured.

The efficacy of such an exemption clause or notice is severely restricted by statute, particularly the Unfair Contract Terms Act 1977. This Act limits the effectiveness of exemption clauses or notices in relation to negligence (which bears an extended meaning under the Act)[1]. It also provides that knowledge of (or agreement to) an exemption clause or notice purporting to exclude or restrict liability for negligence does not by itself indicate a voluntary acceptance of any risk[2].

It is extremely rare for a court to find that a person has impliedly consented to waive any cause of action which he might have in respect of another's tort, particularly where the defendant seeks to establish that the plaintiff consented to the negligent performance of an act by the defendant.

1   Discussed in paras 10.42–10.43, above, and 21.16, below.
2   Unfair Contract Terms Act 1977, s 2(3).

Consent and the standard of care[1]
21.10   In the absence of express or implied consent a person who knows of a risk cannot be said to be volenti. However, knowledge of risk, while not sufficient to constitute the defence of volenti, may have some effect. Knowledge of a particular risk may result in a lessening of the standard of care which must be

displayed towards that person; if that lesser standard is achieved no tort is committed. For example, in *Wilks v Cheltenham Home Guard Motor Cycle and Light Car Club*[2], it was held that, while competitors at a motorcycle scramble must exercise reasonable care in riding their machines, this means reasonable care in the circumstances. Thus, spectators at such events, who can clearly see the risks, cannot expect riders in a race to reach the same standard of reasonable care as can be expected from those riding motorcycles on public roads.

In *Pitts v Hunt*[3], the Court of Appeal held that the appropriate standard of care owed to a plaintiff who was injured while engaging in a joint unlawful enterprise with a defendant was to be assessed by reference to the conduct of the plaintiff and the hazards inherent in the enterprise. In this case the conduct of the plaintiff, a motorbike pillion passenger who encouraged the driver, whom he knew to be uninsured and unlicensed, to drive in a reckless manner designed to frighten the public, was held to be such as to render it impossible to find that he was owed any care at all. In the recent case of *Revill v Newbery*[4], the defendant, who was sleeping in a shed on his allotment, shot the plaintiff when he heard him trying to break in. It was held that the defendant had owed the plaintiff a duty of care which he had broken by not firing a warning shot or aiming more carefully, and that the defendant's illegal act, attempted burglary, did not debar him from all remedy. Consequently, the plaintiff recovered damages, although they were reduced by two-thirds because of the plaintiff's contributory negligence.

1   The standard of care is discussed in paras 18.36–18.50, above.
2   [1971] 2 All ER 369, [1971] 1 WLR 668, CA.
3   [1991] 1 QB 24, [1990] 3 All ER 344.
4   [1996] QB 567, [1996] 1 All ER 291, CA.

Contributory negligence
21.11   Accidents may be caused to a plaintiff by two or more persons. Where the plaintiff is one of those persons the defendant may plead contributory negligence. Unlike volenti, contributory negligence is not a complete defence to an action in tort. If successfully pleaded it leads to a reduction in the damages awarded to the plaintiff[1].

The defence is governed by the Law Reform (Contributory Negligence) Act 1945[2]. This statute, while applying to torts other than negligence, has no application to wrongful interference with goods or to deceit[3].

1   The burden of proving contributory negligence falls upon the defendant.
2   See further, para 12.17, above.
3   In the case of these torts contributory negligence is a complete defence. For deceit, see para 14.20, above, and for wrongful interference with goods, see paras 20.16–20.19, above.

Causation
21.12   A plaintiff is contributorily negligent and liable to have his damages reduced when his own conduct has contributed to the *injury* which he has suffered. Whether or not the plaintiff's conduct contributed to the *accident* is irrelevant; it is his contribution to his injury (whether the contribution is large or small) which may result in a reduction of damages. For example, failure to

wear a seat-belt is unlikely to cause an accident but if such failure contributes to the plaintiff's injuries, for example, if he is flung out of a car during a crash, then it is contributory negligence[1].

An example is provided by *Capps v Miller*[2], in which the rider of a motor cycle, who suffered head injuries in a crash which was entirely caused by the drunken defendant, had his damages reduced by 10% because he had failed to buckle his crash helmet which, had it not flown off on impact, might have cushioned his impact.

1   *Froom v Butcher* [1976] QB 286, [1975] 3 All ER 520, CA.
2   [1989] 2 All ER 333, [1989] 1 WLR 839, CA.

21.13   The plaintiff's lack of care must have contributed to the injuries which he actually suffered if his damages are to be reduced. In *Jones v Livox Quarries Ltd*[1], the plaintiff, who was injured while riding on the towbar at the back of a 'traxcavator' vehicle (which involved a clear risk of falling off and being injured), had his damages reduced by 20%, even though the actual injury suffered was sustained when another vehicle drove into the back of the 'traxcavator'. The Court of Appeal held that, while the principal risk to which the plaintiff had exposed himself was injury through falling off, he had also exposed himself to the risk of the accident which had in fact occurred. However, the Court of Appeal said that, had he been shot by a negligent sportsman while so riding, his damages would not have been reduced; negligent riding would not have contributed to such an injury.

1   [1952] 2 QB 608, CA.

Standard of care
21.14   To be contributorily negligent a plaintiff must fail to take reasonable care for his own safety. There is no need for him to owe the defendant a duty of care. In consequence, in deciding whether the plaintiff is contributorily negligent, the court has regard to the same factors as are applicable in determining if the defendant is in breach of his duty[1]. Examples of conduct likely to manifest a want of care for one's own safety, and hence to constitute contributory negligence, include: failure to wear a car seat-belt[2]; accepting a lift with a driver whom one knows to be drunk[3] or whose car one knows to be dangerously defective[4]; and crossing the road at a pelican crossing when the lights are green for cars[5]. Conduct which might be classified as contributory negligence if undertaken in normal circumstances might not be so classified if the plaintiff was faced with an emergency.

Knowledge of a risk with no attempt to avoid it is not sufficient by itself to justify a finding that the plaintiff had consented to run a risk (volenti) but may be enough to support a finding of contributory negligence.

1   See paras 18.37–18.50, above.
2   *Froom v Butcher* [1976] QB 286, [1975] 3 All ER 520, CA. Failure to wear a seat-belt, in addition to being a breach of the Road Traffic Act 1988, will result in a 15%–25% reduction in damages.
3   *Owens v Brimmell* [1977] QB 859, [1976] 3 All ER 765.
4   *Gregory v Kelly* [1978] RTR 426; failure to wear a seat-belt and knowledge that the car had faulty brakes – 40% reduction in damages.

5 *Fitzgerald v Lane* [1989] AC 328, [1988] 2 All ER 961, HL; the plaintiff's damages were reduced by 50%.

Apportionment
21.15   The Act gives the court complete discretion as to how much or how little the plaintiff should lose from the total sum awarded by way of damages to reflect his contributory negligence[1]. This issue has been treated by the courts as one of fact and appellate courts are reluctant to depart from the judge's decision unless it is manifestly incorrect[2].

Broadly speaking two factors are considered by the courts[3]:

a. the blameworthiness of the plaintiff compared with the totality of the defendant's tortious conduct[4]; and
b. to what extent the plaintiff's conduct caused or exacerbated his injuries.

1 Reductions of between 5% and 80% are common and reductions of 100% have been made although the Court of Appeal in *Pitts v Hunt* [1991] 1 QB 24, [1990] 3 All ER 344, ruled, obiter, that it was logically unsupportable to find a plaintiff 100% contributorily negligent since the premise on which the 1945 Act operated was that there was fault on the part of *both* parties which caused the plaintiff's injury.
2 *Hannam v Mann* [1984] RTR 252, CA.
3 *Stapley v Gypsum Mines Ltd* [1953] AC 663 at 682.
4 *Fitzgerald v Lane* [1989] AC 328, [1988] 2 All ER 961, HL.

Exclusion of liability
21.16   Tortious liability may be excluded or restricted by an exemption clause or notice. However, the effectiveness of clauses which seek to exclude or restrict liability for negligence has been severely restricted by s 2 of the Unfair Contract Terms Act 1977; negligence bears an extended meaning in this context[1].

All that need be said about s 2 here is that a defendant cannot by an exemption clause or notice exclude or restrict his liability for negligence (if it arises in the course of a business) which causes death or personal injury, and can exclude such liability for other damage only in so far as it is reasonable so to do.

We have already explained the requirement of reasonableness in relation to an exemption clause[2]. In relation to a notice not having contractual effect s 11(3) of the Act provides that, wherever a defendant claims to have excluded or restricted liability in tort by reference to a non-contractual notice, reliance on that notice is operative only in so far as it is reasonable in the circumstances[3]. The onus of proving reasonableness is on the defendant[4].

1 We discuss this provision in more detail in paras 10.42–10.43 and 10.47, above.
2 Para 10.47, above.
3 See also paras 10.43 and 10.47, above.
4 Unfair Contract Terms Act 1977, s 11(5). Section 11(4), referred to in para 10.48, above, also applies to non-contractual notices.

Statutory authority
21.17   When a statute authorises the commission of what would otherwise be a tort, for example, operating a power station which constitutes a nuisance[1],

a party who is injured by that authorised activity has no remedy other than that provided by the statute (if any). In determining whether the defence of statutory authority is available, the court first decides whether the commission of the tort has been authorised either expressly or impliedly and, if so, whether the statutory exemption is total or only applicable in the absence of negligence on the part of the person carrying out the authorised act[2]. In *Allen v Gulf Oil Refining Ltd*[3], for example, the House of Lords held that a statute, which authorised the construction of an oil refinery, impliedly permitted the non-negligent operation of that refinery without it thereby constituting an actionable nuisance.

The grant of planning permission which authorises a change of use, intensification of current activities, or the erection or modification of buildings or structures, does not constitute statutory authority to commit a nuisance[4]. However, a grant of planning permission may alter the character of a locality with the effect of rendering conduct which would have been a nuisance in the locality before the change of use etc no longer a nuisance given the amended nature of the neighbourhood.

1   See paras 20.21–20.25, above.
2   See *Department of Transport v North West Water Authority* [1984] AC 336, [1983] 3 All ER 273, HL.
3   [1981] AC 1001, [1981] 1 All ER 353, HL.
4   See, for example, *Hunter v Canary Wharf Ltd* [1997] 2 All ER 426, HL.

Limitation of actions
21.18   The right to initiate formal legal proceedings for damages in tort must be exercised within a specified period, the limitation period, after the cause of action has accrued. Failure so to do renders the cause of action unenforceable; it has become statute-barred. It is for the defendant to prove that an action is statute-barred.

The principal statutes governing limitation of actions are the Limitation Act 1980, which applies to most torts, and the Latent Damage Act 1986, which applies only to actions in negligence and then only if the claim is *not* in respect of personal injuries or death.

Injunctions are not subject to these Acts but an injunction will not be awarded if not sought with reasonable dispatch[1].

1   Para 12.42, above.

The time periods
21.19   The Limitation Act 1980 provides that actions in tort must generally be brought:

a.   within six years of the cause of action accruing; unless, either
b.   the claim is in respect of personal injuries[1] when the limitation period is reduced to three years; or
c.   the action is for defamation or malicious falsehood when the limitation period is one year[2].

The Latent Damage Act 1986 provides that in respect of claims in negligence, other than claims for personal injuries or death, the primary six-year limitation period may be reduced to three years. However, this Act also amends the date at which the limitation period begins[3].

Some statutes, for example the Consumer Protection Act 1987[4], have their own limitation period.

1　It remains six years when the claim is for trespass to the person: *Stubbings v Webb* [1993] AC 498, [1993] 1 All ER 322, HL.
2　Limitation Act 1980, s 4A as amended by Defamation Act 1996, s 5. There is a discretion to extend this period.
3　This alternative limitation period is subject to a 'longstop' provision, see further paras 21.22–21.24, below.
4　See para 20.15, above.

Commencement of the period

21.20　Since an action must be commenced within the limitation period, it is vital to determine when this period begins. With torts that are actionable without proof of damage, for example trespass, the limitation period begins on the date of the defendants' act. In contrast, with torts actionable only on proof of damage, for example negligence, the limitation period begins when the damage occurs, which may or may not be the date on which the defendant's breach of duty occurred[1]. Time usually starts to run against a plaintiff even if he did not then know of the breach of duty or that any damage had occurred.

In contract the cause of action accrues at the date of breach. Thus, it seems that a client, faced with the choice of suing his accountant who, in breach of contract, has negligently prepared the client's accounts, may prefer to sue in tort rather than for breach of contract because of the apparent difference in the date of the commencement of the limitation period. However, a breach of contract (particularly when the breach is an omission) may be treated as arising not merely when the initial omission occurred but as continuing to arise every day the omission is not corrected. Hence, the start date of the limitation period is rolled forward up to the moment when the breach is incapable of remedy[2].

In the majority of cases both the fact that damage has occurred and the date when it occurred are obvious. However, difficulties have arisen in two situations. First, when the loss is apparently prospective, and, second, when the damage is not discovered (or even discoverable) until after the expiry of the limitation period, ie it is latent damage.

1　If some damage was manifest to, or discoverable by, the plaintiff in respect of which a claim would now be time-barred, that does not preclude an action for damage of a different type which arises from the same breach of duty which caused the earlier damage: *Nitrigin Eireann Teoranta v Inco Alloys Ltd* [1992] 1 All ER 854, [1992] 1 WLR 498.
2　*Midland Bank Trust Co Ltd v Hett-Stubbs and Kemp* [1979] Ch 384, [1978] 3 All ER 571.

Prospective loss

21.21　Since a cause of action in tort generally arises at (and thus time starts to run from) the date the damage occurred it is necessary to decide whether a prospective loss is treated as a loss when it actually arises or when the breach of duty occurred. Consider an example: suppose a client, following negligent advice from his solicitor, entered into an imprudent and onerous mortgage;

does the damage occur when actual financial loss occurs or immediately the mortgage is executed? In one case[1] the Court of Appeal held that the damage in such a case occurred immediately (hence time started to run from the date the mortgage was granted), even though at that moment the plaintiff had suffered no actual loss. This view was approved and explained by the Court of Appeal in *DW Moore & Co Ltd v Ferrier*[2]. In this case an action in 1985 against the defendant solicitor in respect of a contract which he had drawn up in 1975, and which contained what were later discovered to be inoperative restrictive covenants, was held to be statute-barred. The court held that a negligently drafted contract caused damage at the date it was drawn (in this case 1975) if, at that time, the contract was not merely defective but was already of less commercial value than it would have been had it been drawn without negligence. The effect of these decisions is that a tort victim may be deprived of a remedy before he even realised that a tort had been committed.

Other cases have made it clear that prospective loss is not always suffered at the moment of breach of duty; each case turns on its facts. Thus in *Ross v Caunters*[3], the cause of action of beneficiaries, who lost a legacy due to negligent advice given to the deceased by his solicitor, arose on the death and not when the advice was given. It seems clear that in building cases a latent defect may cause a prospective loss which is unquantifiable until damage begins to manifest itself physically and that time starts to run only at that later date[4].

When loss, actual or prospective, occurs because of a latent defect special provision, which we discuss in paras 21.23 and 21.24, below, amend the rules on when time starts to run.

1   *Forster v Outred & Co* [1982] 2 All ER 753, [1982] 1 WLR 86, CA; approved in *Secretary of State for the Environment v Essex, Goodman & Suggitt* [1986] 2 All ER 69, [1986] 1 WLR 1432.
2   [1988] 1 All ER 400, [1988] 1 WLR 267, CA.
3   [1980] Ch 297, [1979] 3 All ER 580. See also *Hopkins v Mackenzie* [1995] 6 Med LR 26.
4   *Pirelli General Cable Works Ltd v Oscar Faber & Partners* [1983] 2 AC 1, [1983] 1 All ER 65, HL. This was a latent damage case and would now be subject to the Latent Damage Act 1986.

Latent damage
21.22   The issue of latent damage arises when damage is not discovered, or is not even discernible, or does not even occur, until some time after the causative breach of duty. Suppose that a plaintiff, due to the negligence of his employer, has contracted a disease at work which does not manifest itself until years later (eg asbestosis). Suppose that a plaintiff's house was negligently upon insubstantial foundations. Is the plaintiff in either case unable to sue the tortfeasor if the harm suffered was not discovered until after the limitation period had expired? The answer depends upon the nature of the injury.

21.23   *Personal injury*   In cases of personal injury caused by negligence, nuisance or breach of duty, the Limitation Act 1980[1] creates an alternative commencement date for the limitation period. Section 11 states that in such cases the three-year limitation period begins to operate only when the plaintiff discovers certain facts; s 14 sets out the facts which will trigger the limitation period. They are knowledge that the injury was significant, that it was attributable to negligence, nuisance or breach of duty and that it can be attributed to an identified defendant. If a plaintiff is aware of these facts, the limitation period will begin even if he did not realise that the facts disclosed a cause of action[2]. Indeed, in *Forbes v Wandworth Health Authority*[3], the court held that a plaintiff who had undergone an operation, which had not merely not ameliorated his existing medical condition but had worsened it in that his leg had had to be amputated, fell outside the limitation period because he had constructive knowledge that the cause of the amputation was tortious. The plaintiff had not acquired actual knowledge as to the cause of his injury until some nine years after the operation. However, the court held that, given the disastrous consequences of his operation, it was reasonable to expect he would have sought expert medical advice once he had recovered from the immediate trauma of the operation (a 12 to 18 month period) as to what had gone wrong. Thus, he was held to have constructive knowledge from the date when he should have known the possible cause of his injury. Consequently, the three year limitation period commenced at that time.

Difficulties arise in cases where the plaintiff is aware he has suffered injury within the limitation period but is unaware that the injury might have arisen tortiously. For example, a person might emerge from an operation in a worse state than before and only later realise that this was not simple misfortune but attributable to the negligence of the medical team. In such cases it seems that the injured person has sufficient knowledge to trigger s 14 when he knows that his injury is causally attributable to the defendant even if he did not then know that the defendant's acts or omissions were actionable or tortious[4].

1   A claim for trespass to the person causing personal injury does not fall within these sections and time starts to run at the date of the trespass: *Stubbings v Webb* [1993] AC 498, [1993] 1 All ER 322, HL.
2   *Brooks v J and P Coates (UK) Ltd* [1984] 1 All ER 702.
3   [1996] 4 All ER 881, CA.
4   *Dobbie v Medway Health Authority* [1994] 4 All ER 450, [1994] 1 WLR 1234, CA.

21.24   *Damage to goods or property*   In cases, such as damage to goods or property, the Latent Damage Act 1986[1] provides that, if the action is for negligence, the limitation period can, if the plaintiff wishes, be three years from what can be called 'the date of discoverability', ie the date at which the plaintiff had (or should have had) the necessary knowledge to bring an action rather than six years from the date of damage. This provision is modelled on the rule for personal injuries but unlike it in that it is subject to a 'longstop' provision[2]. The longstop provides that no action can be brought more than 15 years after the breach even if damage has not been discovered, could not reasonably have been discovered, or had not even occurred, in that 15-year period[3].

It appears that the Latent Damage Act does not apply to actions for breach of contract[4]. Thus, it may be crucial to discover whether a plaintiff has concurrent claims in contract and tort in a case where the damage was not discoverable within the normal six-year period. If there are concurrent claims an action in contract may be statute-barred while an action in tort is not. This is of particular relevance to professionals who give negligent advice when the damage the advice causes is not immediately discoverable[5].

1 By inserting a new s 14A in the Limitation Act 1980.
2 See also the Consumer Protection Act 1987, which creates a ten-year longstop in respect of claims against the manufacturer of defective goods; paras 20.9–20.15, above.
3 Limitation Act 1980, s 14B.
4 *Iron Trades Mutual Assurance Co Ltd v JK Buckenham Ltd* [1990] 1 All ER 808; *Société Commerciale de Réassurance v ERAS (International) Ltd* [1992] 2 All ER 82n, CA.
5 See *Henderson v Merrett Syndicates Ltd* [1995] 2 AC 145, [1994] 3 All ER 506, HL; for a discussion of when concurrent liability can arise see paras 18.67–18.70, above.

Extension of time

21.25 The limitation period can be extended:

a. if there is fraud, concealment or mistake[1]; or
b. if the plaintiff is a minor, ie under 18, or mentally ill when the cause of action accrues[2]; or
c. if it is a personal injury claim and to apply the usual rule would prejudice the defendant[3]. In this case, the court has a discretion to extend the limitation period if it is equitable so to do. In exercising its discretion, the court is directed to have regard to all the circumstances, particularly such factors as the reasons for the delay and the conduct of the parties. The discretion, which is rarely exercised, is completely unfettered. An extension of time is not precluded merely because the plaintiff has an alternative cause of action against a person other than the defendant, eg a former legal adviser for failure to bring the action within the limitation period, although each case must turn on its own facts.

In *Thompson v Brown Construction (Ebbw Vale) Ltd*[4], the discretion was exercised since the defendant was not prejudiced by the plaintiff's delay. On the other hand, in *Donovan v Gwentoys Ltd*[5], the balance of prejudice led to a refusal to exercise the discretion. In *Donovan*, the defendants would have had to face a stale claim of which they had known nothing until over five years after the accident, whereas the plaintiff had an obvious claim against her solicitors for failing to issue a protective writ.

1 See further, para 12.38, above.
2 See further, para 12.37, above. If the plaintiff is mentally ill and never recovers, the limitation period never commences.
3 Limitation Act 1980, s 33. This section does not apply to actions for trespass to the person; *Stubbings v Webb* [1993] AC 498, [1993] 1 All ER 322, HL.
4 [1981] 2 All ER 296, [1981] 1 WLR 744, HL
5 [1990] 1 All ER 1018, [1990] 1 WLR 472, HL.

Remedies

21.26 The principal remedy in tort is an award of damages. There are, however, a number of other remedies which may be more appropriate in a particular case. For example, a successful plaintiff in a nuisance action[1] may be more interested in an injunction preventing further commission of the nuisance than in damages. We discuss these other remedies, particularly injunctions, before turning to damages.

1   Paras 20.21–20.25, above.

Injunctions[1]

21.27   In cases where damages would not be an adequate remedy, the courts may be prepared to grant an injunction (an equitable remedy) requiring the defendant to cease committing his tortious acts. An injunction, like all equitable remedies, is discretionary and the court is unlikely to exercise its discretion in favour of the plaintiff if the harm he is suffering is of a transient nature, or where his conduct is regarded as improper, or where damages are an adequate remedy for the injury suffered. Injunctions are most commonly granted in actions for nuisance[2] but can be granted in other cases[3]. The court has a discretion to award damages in addition to, or in substitution for, an injunction[4].

It is possible, though very rare, for an injunction to be granted in *quia timet* proceedings, ie before the tort has been committed, if the likelihood of substantial damage is strong and imminent. A case where one might be granted would be where there is evidence that a magazine which has not yet been published contains defamatory material.

1   See also paras 12.30–12.34, above.
2   For example, in *Kennaway v Thompson* [1981] QB 88, [1980] 3 All ER 329, CA, an injunction was granted to limit the operation of motorboats (which constituted a nuisance) to specified times.
3   In *Miller v Jackson* [1977] QB 966, [1977] 3 All ER 338, the Court of Appeal said (albeit obiter) that an injunction would never be granted to restrain negligence.
4   Supreme Court Act 1981, s 50. The power to substitute damages for an injunction is rarely exercised.

Certain minor remedies

21.28   An order for the restitution of land or chattels may in some circumstances be made for the torts of trespass to land and of wrongful interference with goods[1].

A tort-victim may be able to exercise a limited amount of self-help. For example, he can abate a nuisance[2] but only when it is reasonable to do so, and probably only after notice to the tortfeasor. He may be able to retake goods wrongfully detained by another[3]. In exercising self-help great care is needed, since a tort victim who goes further than is necessary to protect his rights or who, however innocently, purports to exercise rights which he does not have may himself become liable in tort. Self-help is a summary remedy which is justified only in clear and simple cases or in an emergency. Hence, in *Burton v Winters*[4], the plaintiff was not justified in attempting to pull down her neighbour's garage wall, which had encroached on to her land by some four inches, when the courts had already refused her an injunction to instruct the removal of the wall.

1   Paras 20.16–20.19, above.
2   Paras 20.21–20.25, above.

3   Paras 20.16–20.19, above.
4   [1993] 3 All ER 847, [1993] 1 WLR 1077, CA, an extraordinary saga of litigation over the encroachment which resulted in the plaintiff being imprisoned for contempt of court.

Damages

21.29   An award of damages, the principal remedy in tort, can be made to a plaintiff who has established that the injury he has suffered was caused by the defendant and was not too remote[1]. Damages are traditionally awarded as a once and for all lump sum assessed at the date of trial but there are now provisions for provisional settlements (see para 21.37, below). In addition, in personal injury cases, it may be possible to agree a 'structured settlement'. Structured settlements provide for some of the sum awarded to the tort victim to be invested in an annuity, income from which the Inland Revenue has agreed to treat as tax-free capital payments. However, a structured settlement is not always the most advantageous method of personal injury damages for the plaintiff.

Damages are generally designed to compensate the plaintiff for the loss caused to him by the tort. Hence, if, although a tort has been committed[2], the plaintiff has suffered no loss he cannot generally recover anything other than nominal damages. The basis of an award is to try to place the plaintiff in the position in which he was before the tort was committed[3] in so far as money is capable of fulfilling this function. Plainly, money cannot replace a severed limb, restore sight, or restore a battered reputation, but it can help to ease the life of tort victims who suffer such injuries. In a limited number of cases, discussed in paras 21.31 and 21.33, below, the basis of the award of damages is not compensatory.

A book of this nature is not an appropriate place to discuss in detail the rules for the computation of damages; we touch but lightly on this highly complex subject.

1   A plaintiff who cannot recover damages in tort may recover under a scheme of private insurance or be eligible for state benefits.
2   Certain torts – for example, trespass to goods – are actionable without proof of actual damage.
3   This can be compared with the bases of assessment in contract discussed in para 12.3, above. The reliance loss basis equates with the basis of assessment in tort.

Compensatory damages

21.30   When damages are awarded to compensate the tort victim for his injury or loss, as is usually the case, they are called compensatory damages. A plaintiff cannot recover for damage suffered after the commission of the tort which is caused by his own unreasonable conduct[1].

1   See paras 18.58 and 18.59, above, for the situation where the plaintiff's post-tort negligence and consequent injury may be deemed to be attributable to the original tort.

Contemptuous damages

21.31   A plaintiff who establishes a claim in law, but who is regarded as bringing an action in some sense improperly, may be awarded contemptuous damages of a penny. A plaintiff who is awarded contemptuous damages (generally awarded only in defamation actions[1]) will probably be required to pay his own costs (and in exceptional cases may have to pay those of the defendant) and thus ends up considerably out of pocket[2].

1 Such an award is appropriate if the defendant technically has defamed the plaintiff but the plaintiff's reputation or true character is so dreadful that he can scarcely be said to have suffered any loss of reputation.
2 Particularly since legal aid is not available in defamation actions.

Nominal damages
21.32   In torts not requiring proof of damage, nominal damages may be awarded to a plaintiff who, while having a perfectly proper legal claim, has been caused no loss by the tort. For example, in *Constantine v Imperial Hotels Ltd*[1], the defendants wrongfully refused accommodation to Lord Constantine, the great West Indian cricketer. He obtained accommodation elsewhere and so suffered no real loss; an award of five guineas was made with an order for the defendants to pay the costs of the legal action.

1 [1944] 1 KB 693, [1944] 2 All ER 171; he was suing in tort for the failure by the hotel to provide accommodation in breach of its common law duty as an 'inn-keeper'.

Aggravated and exemplary damages
21.33   In assessing damages a court may take into account the conduct and motives of the defendant.

If the action is for deceit, defamation, malicious prosecution, false imprisonment or trespass, but probably not in other cases, and the defendant's conduct and motives injure the plaintiff's proper feelings of dignity, the plaintiff may receive aggravated damages in addition to any compensatory award to smooth his justifiably ruffled feathers[1]. Aggravated damages are intended as compensation for the plaintiff and *not* as a form of punishment of the defendant.

Additionally, a court may consider the defendant's conduct to be so outrageous that it awards the plaintiff exemplary damages in addition to any compensatory award. Exemplary damages are designed to punish or to deter the defendant. Because it may well be asked why the plaintiff should benefit from the court's desire to condemn the defendant's behaviour, the House of Lords has held that exemplary damages may be awarded only in three categories of cases[2]:

a. oppressive, arbitrary or unconstitutional action by employees of the government (including local government and the police); or
b. where statute expressly permits such an award; or
c. where the defendant has calculated that the amount of any compensatory award will still leave him with a profit from his tort[3]. The plaintiff must prove that such was the defendant's intention[4].

1 In *Archer v Brown* [1985] QB 401, [1984] 2 All ER 267, the plaintiff received £500 by way of aggravated damages following a blatant fraud (tort of deceit) by the defendant. In *Appleton v Garrett* [1996] PIQR P1, a dentist who carried out unnecessary dental treatment to increase his income was ordered to pay aggravated damages at a rate of 15% of the sum awarded by way of general damages.

2 *Rookes v Barnard* [1964] AC 1129, [1964] 1 All ER 367, HL.
3 In *Drane v Evangelou* [1978] 2 All ER 437, [1978] 1 WLR 455, the Court of Appeal ordered the defendant-landlord to pay £1,000 to the plaintiff-tenant whom he had sought wrongfully to evict in order to obtain the premises for his own purposes. Actions for exemplary damages arise most frequently in actions against the police, landlords and in defamation cases. Actions against the metropolitan police have proved so numerous that the courts have limited the amount that will be awarded.
4 *Riches v News Group Newspapers Ltd* [1986] QB 256, [1985] 2 All ER 845, CA.

Assessment of compensatory damages: personal injuries
21.34 Where the victim of a tort is seeking damages for personal injury any award of damages will seek to compensate the plaintiff both for his pecuniary and his non-pecuniary losses. Certain losses suffered by a plaintiff can be calculated with reasonable accuracy, for example, clothing damaged in an accident or loss of income up to the time of trial, and such claims are often called special damages. Inexact losses are compensated by an award of general damages. For example, general damages can be awarded for pain and suffering or loss of amenity.

While sums awarded to a plaintiff may be based upon calculation of future need, projected medical costs etc, there is no requirement that the money is spent on such things and the plaintiff can, if he is able and chooses so to do, invest all his damages in riotous living or gambling.

21.35 *Pecuniary loss* This head of damage includes any medical expenses, costs of care or supervision[1], costs incurred in connection with adapting the victim's home or car[2], and loss of earnings.

In assessing loss of earnings the court takes into account earnings actually lost before the trial (minus any tax or national insurance payable on those earnings) and also calculates a sum to represent any future earnings which will be lost because of any disability suffered by the tort victim due to the tort. In calculating lost future earnings a court fixes a figure which represents what the plaintiff could have expected as his annual wage (taking into account any probable promotion but ignoring inflation[3]) and from this it deducts what he would have paid by way of tax and national insurance. From this figure it further deducts any current or expected earnings; if the plaintiff is in an irreversible coma or is completely disabled this is likely to be nothing. After making any such deduction, the court multiplies the figure remaining by an appropriate multiplier. The multiplier[4] is not the difference between the plaintiff's age and his normal retirement age but some lesser figure. This is because the plaintiff is receiving a lump sum now rather than wages on a staggered basis and his life may also have been shortened by his injuries. The multipliers used also assume a particular rate of return on capital will be achieved[5].

While reduced life expectancy is taken into account in fixing the multiplier, which thus reduces the damages paid by the defendant, the court does not entirely disregard the fact that the defendant has shortened the plaintiff's life. In respect of these so-called lost years (the 'lost years' being those working years which the plaintiff will not live to see because he will die young as a result of his injuries), the court's award for lost future earnings can include a sum to represent a period when the plaintiff is expected to be dead[6]. To hold otherwise would be to absolve the defendant from paying as much in damages to a victim whom he had injured more seriously, and whose life expectancy he had thereby reduced, than to a less seriously injured victim. The lost years of child-victims are not taken into account in assessing lost future earnings[7].

As a result of very complex legislation[8] the person making a compensation payment (the 'compensator') must deduct in full from the damages assessed as a whole very many statutory benefits which the plaintiff receives as a result of his injuries and account for the deductions to the state. Earlier legislation requires partial deduction of some social security benefits from the sum awarded to the tort-victim. Moreover, the judges had ruled that certain state benefits should be deducted from an award of damages even if the benefit was not subject to either statutory regime. However, benefits derived from private insurance, benevolence or charity are not taken into account by the courts and such sums will not reduce a plaintiff's damages.

1   A sum may be awarded to represent earnings lost by a parent or relation who gives up work to look after a disabled tort-victim: *Donnelly v Joyce* [1974] QB 454, [1973] 3 All ER 475, CA, unless the parent or relative is the defendant, see *Hunt v Severs* [1994] 2 AC 350, [1994] 2 All ER 385, HL.
2   *Housecroft v Burnett* [1986] 1 All ER 332, CA; *Moriarty v McCarthy* [1978] 2 All ER 213, [1978] 1 WLR 155.
3   *Cookson v Knowles* [1979] AC 556, [1978] 2 All ER 604, HL.
4   The multiplier rarely exceeds 18.
5   The courts are entitled to consult the Ogden Tables which incorporate rates of return on capital by reference to index-linked securities, Damages Act, s 1, but in *Wells v Wells* [1997] 1 All ER 673, CA, the court rejected the idea that it should be assumed that damages would only be invested in such securities. In this case the court assumed that lump-sums would be invested 'prudently', which would include equities, in fixing the multiplier.
6   *Pickett v British Rail Engineering Ltd* [1980] AC 136, [1979] 1 All ER 774, HL. The Administration of Justice Act 1982, s 4 limits an award in respect of the lost years to a plaintiff who is alive at the time of the action.
7   *Croke v Wiseman* [1981] 3 All ER 852, [1982] 1 WLR 71, CA.
8   Social Security Administration Act 1992.

21.36   *Non-pecuniary loss*   Sums are also awarded to compensate, in so far as money can, the plaintiff for pain and suffering (including the mental pain which comes from knowing that one is scarred or that one's life expectancy is diminished) and for loss of amenity, ie loss of faculties and the inability to pursue activities and hobbies.

Nothing is awarded for pain and suffering if the plaintiff has not actually suffered it, for example, because he is in a coma[1]. Damages can, however, be awarded for loss of amenity whether or not the tort victim is capable of realising that his amenities have been reduced; damages are awarded for the fact of deprivation and not for realisation of deprivation[2]. There is a tariff system which the courts operate, with adjustments, for loss of amenity. For example, a lost leg might generally be compensated by an award of £X but this sum would be increased in the case of a keen sportsman or walker.

1   *Lim Poh Choo v Camden and Islington Area Health Authority* [1980] AC 174, [1979] 2 All ER 910, HL.
2   *H West & Sons v Shephard* [1964] AC 326, [1963] 2 All ER 625, HL.

21.37 *Provisional awards* In exceptional cases, where there is a chance that at some time in the future the plaintiff will, because of his injuries, suffer a serious deterioration in his physical or mental condition, the court can award damages to reflect the current extent of injuries but, at the request of the plaintiff, make an order allowing him to seek further damages if the projected deterioration occurs within a specified time[1]. There can only be one further application to court and it must be in respect of a disease or type of injury specified in the original action. Where the medical evidence can predict that a deterioration in the plaintiff's condition is very likely (rather than a chance) it is more apposite for a lump sum to be awarded which reflects the projected medical prognosis[2].

Where provisional damages are awarded, and the victim subsequently dies, the award to the deceased does not prevent a further claim by his dependent relatives[3] for loss of dependency provided there is no element of double compensation[4].

1 Supreme Court Act 1981, s 32A and RSC, Ord 37. See generally, *Hurditch v Sheffield Health Authority* [1989] QB 562, [1989] 2 All ER 869, CA.
2 *Willson v Ministry of Defence* [1991] 1 All ER 638.
3 See para 17.10, above for claims by dependent relatives.
4 Damages Act 1996, s 3.

Assessment of compensatory damages: damage to property
21.38 The victim of a tort who is complaining of damage to property is entitled to rely on the same principle as a person who has suffered personal injury – he is entitled to be compensated for what he has lost.

Destruction of property entitles the plaintiff to recover both the value of the property destroyed[1] and damages for foreseeable loss of profit (profits which would have been made from use of the property) or loss of use or, if it was reasonable to do so, the cost of acquiring a substitute[2]. The value of the thing destroyed is the difference in value of the thing before and after destruction, ie it is the market value of the property at the date of destruction which is payable by way of damages, and not the cost of restoration[3]. However, where the plaintiff has to replace an asset tortiously destroyed by the defendant, the Court of Appeal has held[4] that the measure of damages is fixed by reference to the cost of putting the plaintiff into the position he was prior to the tortious act, even if this means the plaintiff has to be awarded the cost of replacing the asset.

Damage to property entitles the plaintiff to recover the diminution in value of the property, foreseeable loss of profit and for loss of use while the property is being repaired[5]. Diminution in value will generally be the cost of reasonable repair assessed either at the date when the damage occurred or at the date when the plaintiff ought reasonably to have repaired the property[6]. If the cost of repair is unreasonable, for example, an expensive repair of an asset of merely sentimental value, only the market value of the property is recoverable in most cases. In very rare cases, for example where a unique chattel is damaged, the plaintiff can claim the diminution in value of the asset even though it *exceeds* the cost of repair[7].

Damage to land or buildings gives rise to particular problems. Generally, the cost of amelioration is recoverable and land or buildings are more likely to justify repair costs which exceed market value than is the case with chattels but the question of assessment may turn on the plaintiff's future intentions. Hence, it seems that where a person intends to sell the damaged property he can recover the diminution in market value (regardless of the cost of repair) but where he intends to continue using the property the cost of repair is the sum recoverable[8].

1   *Liesbosch Dredger v SS Edison* [1933] AC 449, HL.
2   In *Dominion Mosaics and Tile Co Ltd v Trafalgar Trucking Co Ltd* [1990] 2 All ER 246, CA, the plaintiff was able to recover the cost of alternative premises; acquiring new premises allowed the business to continue and reduced the claim for loss of profits, and the purchase of new machines allowed the plaintiff to continue the business.
3   *Moss v Christchurch RDC* [1925] 2 KB 750.
4   *Dominion Mosaics and Tile Co Ltd v Trafalgar Trucking Co Ltd* [1990] 2 All ER 246, CA.
5   *Mattocks v Mann* [1993] RTR 13, CA, in which the plaintiff was able to recover the cost of hiring a comparable car to the one damaged by the defendant until the insurers provided funds for repair.
6   *Martindale v Duncan* [1973] 2 All ER 355, [1973] 1 WLR 574, CA; *Dodd Properties (Kent) v Canterbury City Council* [1980] 1 All ER 928, [1980] 1 WLR 433, CA. In this latter case the court held it reasonable for the impecunious plaintiff to postpone repair until it had received damages.
7   *Lodge Holes Colliery Co Ltd v Wednesbury Corpn* [1908] AC 323, HL.
8   *Dodd Properties (Kent) v Canterbury City Council* [1980] 1 All ER 928, [1980] 1 WLR 433, CA, in this case the court also accepted that some cases might constitute an in-between situation.

Assessment of compensatory damages: pure economic loss
21.39   In those limited cases in where a plaintiff can recover for pure economic loss[1], the basic principle underlying the assessment of damages is an attempt to return the plaintiff to the financial position he occupied before the tort was committed.

For example, a client who sues his accountant in tort for negligently recommending a particular investment can recover the difference in value between the price paid for the investment and its true worth at that time and any transactional costs[2].

One type of economic loss which has recently been considered by the House of Lords is that suffered by a person who has lent money on the security of property only to discover, when the borrower defaults, that the property is inadequate to repay the loan. The shortfall in the value of the security may be attributable solely to a downturn in property prices (no tortious remedy) or may arise because the property was negligently over-valued in the first place. If there has been a negligent valuation and the plaintiff can establish that had he known the true valuation he would not have entered into the security contract, can he recover the difference between the true value of the property and the inaccurately advised figure at the time of valuation or between the *current* market value (which might have been affected by a downturn in property prices) and the figure advised? In *South Australia Asset Management Corpn v York Montague Ltd*[3], the House of Lords ruled that a valuer, who negligently over-valued property, was responsible only for the foreseeable consequences of a transaction entered into in reliance on his valuation. Hence, since it was the valuer's duty to advise on property values (not advise on the wisdom of lending on this property) he was liable only for the foreseeable consequences of breach of this duty. The importance of this decision for all professional advisors is that it makes plain that where a professional owes a duty to a client, it is the precise scope of that duty which, if broken, determines the amount of damages which are foreseeable and recoverable[4]. In *South Australia* itself (there were a number of linked actions) the valuer had negligently valued a building at £15m when its then market value was £5m. The plaintiff lent £11m on that security and ultimately the property was sold for £2.4m. The House of Lords accepted that the lender had £10m less security than they thought. Had the lender had this margin they would have suffered no loss on the sale. Consequently, the loss suffered was a reasonably foreseeable consequence of the negligent valuation and the valuers were liable for the whole of the loss. In another of the cases (*United Bank of Kuwait plc v Prudential Property Services Ltd*), the lenders advanced £1.75m on a building valued at £2.5m with a true value of £1.8m; subsequently it was sold for £0.95m. The House ruled that the foreseeable consequence of the negligent valuation was that the lenders had £0.7m less security than they thought so that the amount awarded could be no more than that sum.

In addition, where actionable negligent advice persuades a person to invest in an asset or property at an overvalue and in an attempt to improve that asset the person invests more of his money, he can recover the additional lost capital provided that such a rescue bid was reasonable and foreseeable[5]. Where bad advice is provided fraudulently all losses flowing from the transaction are recoverable.

1   See paras 18.8–18.12, above.
2   *Watts v Morrow* [1991] 4 All ER 937, [1991] 1 WLR 1421, CA, reaffirmed this point.
3   [1996] 3 All ER 365, HL.
4   See further paras 18.61–18.66, above.
5   *Esso Petroleum Co Ltd v Mardon* [1976] QB 801, [1976] 2 All ER 5, CA; in this case the asset was acquired as the basis of the plaintiff's business and all his capital was invested in it. If an asset was acquired purely as an investment it might not be reasonable to throw good money after bad.

Part IV

Commercial Law

Chapter 22

Transfer of Rights and Liabilities

22.1 In this chapter we are concerned with the circumstances in which certain rights or obligations can be transferred from one person to another. Such transfers may be voluntary or involuntary (in that they occur automatically by operation of law). We will consider first the transfer of rights, then the transfer of contractual liabilities before considering involuntary transfers.

Rights can be transferred voluntarily by a statutory or equitable assignment, by negotiation or by a novation.

Voluntary Transfer of Rights

22.2 Contractual rights may be transferred from one person to another by a process called assignment. Thus, while a contract cannot generally confer rights upon a third party[1], it is possible for a right created by a contract to be assigned by the party to the contract who is its owner to a third party. The effect of the assignment of a right is that the assignor (the person making the assignment) transfers to the assignee the right in question, which the assignee can enforce by action on his own initiative and in his own name. An assignment cannot increase the liability of a contracting party and the assignee cannot recover more than the assignor could have obtained had no assigment occurred[2].

Contractual rights are not the only rights which are assignable, since any chose (ie thing) in action can be assigned from one person to another. The term chose in action comprises all personal rights of property which can only be claimed or enforced by action, and not by taking physical possession[3]. This definition includes not only contractual rights but also rights which are not contractual, such as copyrights, rights of action in tort and rights under a trust.

1 Para 6.24, above.
2 *Darlington Borough Council v Wiltshier Northern Ltd* [1995] 3 All ER 895, [1995] 1 WLR 68, CA.
3 *Torkington v Magee* [1902] 2 KB 427 at 430.

22.3 Rights under a contract and other choses in action can generally be assigned by their owner to a third party either by statutory assignment under s 136(1) of the Law of Property Act 1925 or by an equitable assignment where s 136(1) is not complied with.

22.4   Section 136 (1) does not apply to the assignment of all choses in action. The following choses in action can be assigned only in accordance with special statutory provisions:

a.   negotiable instruments, in accordance with the Bills of Exchange Act 1882 (such an assignment is called a negotiation);
b.   bills of lading, in accordance with the Bills of Lading Act 1855;
c.   copyrights, in accordance with the Copyright, Designs and Patents Act 1988;
d.   policies of life assurance or marine insurance, in accordance with the Policies of Assurance Act 1867 or the Marine Insurance Act 1906, respectively; and
e.   shares, in accordance with the Companies Act 1985[1].

With the exception of the rules relating to negotiable instruments which we discuss in detail in paras 22.17 to 22.30, below, these special provisions fall outside the scope of this book.

We begin by considering the general rules which apply to choses in action, concentrating in particular on the assignment of ordinary contractual rights, the most common example of which is the assignment of a debt.

1   By the Companies Act 1985, s 182, shares in a registered company can normally only be transferred in the manner prescribed by the articles of association of the company. For company law in general, see Chaps 26 and 27.

Statutory assignment
22.5   The rules relating to statutory assignment are now contained[1] in s 136(1) of the Law of Property Act 1925[2], under which there are four requirements for a valid statutory assignment:

a.   the assignment must be in writing;
b.   it must be signed by the assignor;
c.   it must be absolute; and
d.   the debtor, trustee or other person from whom the assignor would have been entitled to claim the debt or other chose in action must be given written notice.

It must be emphasised that an assignee can enforce an assignment even though he has not provided any consideration[3]. If the requirements for a statutory assignment are satisfied the assignee obtains the exclusive legal right to the debt or other chose in action and can bring an action in his own name to enforce it without joining the assignor as a party to the proceedings.

Three of the four requirements require further examination.

1 General statutory provisions for the assignment of choses in action were first made by the Judicature Act 1873.
2 Although the wording of s 136 refers only to 'legal' choses, it was held in *Torkington v Magee* [1902] 2 KB 427 that equitable choses as well as legal choses can be assigned under s 136. The distinction between legal and equitable choses is outlined in para 22.10, below.
3 *Re Westerton, Public Trustee v Gray* [1919] 2 Ch 104.

Assignment in writing
22.6   The written document must purport to be an assignment but it need not be made in a particular form, nor by deed.

Assignment absolute
22.7   For an assignment to be absolute the *whole interest* of the assignor in the chose in action must be transferred unconditionally to the assignee and *placed completely under his control*. Provided these criteria are satisfied, it is not necessary that there should be an out and out transfer depriving the assignor of all further interest in the chose: the unconditional transfer for the time being of the whole of the assignor's interest in the chose is an absolute assignment. This is shown by *Tancred v Delagoa Bay and East Africa Rly Co*[1], where a debt was assigned as security for a loan, with the proviso that, if the assignor repaid the loan, the debt should be re-assigned to him. This was held to be an absolute assignment.

Absolute assignments must be distinguished from three other types of assignment which, not being absolute, cannot be made under s 136(1):

a.   *Conditional assignments*   These are assignments which automatically take effect or cease on the happening of a future uncertain event. *Durham Bros v Robertson*[2] provides an example. A firm of building contractors, to whom £1,080 was due under a building contract, borrowed money from the plaintiffs and assigned their right to the £1,080 to them as security for the loan '*until the money lent . . . be repaid to you*'. It was held that this was a mere conditional assignment and therefore it could not take effect under s 136. The distinction between this case and *Tancred v Delagoa Bay Rly Co* is that in *Durham Bros v Robertson* the assignment did not transfer the debt unconditionally to the plaintiffs, but only until the loan was repaid, on which event the plaintiffs' interest in the debt would automatically cease, with the result that the debtor would not be certain that he was paying his debt to the right person without knowing the state of accounts between assignor and assignee. On the other hand, in *Tancred v Delagoa Bay Rly Co*, the debt was transferred completely to the assignee and did not automatically revert to the assignor on repayment of the loan but required a re-assignment, of which the debtor would have notice, so that he would be in no doubt as to who was entitled to payment at any particular time without looking at the state of accounts between assignor and assignee.

b.   *Assignments by way of charge*   Assignments purporting to be by way of charge are expressly excluded from s 136. An assignment by way of charge merely gives the assignee a right to payment out of a particular fund or property without transferring that fund or property to him[3]. An example of an assignment by way of charge is provided by *Jones v Humphreys*[4]. A schoolmaster, who had borrowed £15 from a money-lender, assigned to him so much of his salary as should be necessary to repay the amount which he had already borrowed or any further sums which he might borrow. It was held that this was not an absolute assignment of a definite debt but a mere security purporting to be by way of charge.

c.   *Assignments of part of a chose*   In *Williams v Atlantic Assurance Co Ltd*[5], for instance, it was held that the assignment of part of a debt was not an absolute assignment.

1   (1889) 23 QBD 239.
2   [1898] 1 QB 765, CA.
3   *Tancred v Delagoa Bay and East Africa Rly Co* (1889) 2 QBD 239.
4   [1902] 1 KB 10, DC.
5   [1933] 1 KB 81, CA.

Written notice
22.8   Written notice of the assignment must be given to the debtor, trustee or other person from whom the assignor would have been able to claim the debt or other chose in action. The written notice need not be in any particular form but it must clearly indicate the fact of the assignment, the subject matter of the assignment and the identity of the assignee[1]. It is effective from the date on which it is received and the statutory assignment is not perfected until then[2].

1   *Denney, Gasquet and Metcalfe v Conklin* [1913] 3 KB 177; *James Talcott Ltd v John Lewis & Co Ltd and North American Dress Co Ltd* [1940] 3 All ER 592, CA.
2   *Holt v Heatherfield Trust Ltd* [1942] 2 KB 1, [1942] 1 All ER 404.

Equitable assignment
22.9   At common law, choses in action were not generally assignable, but from the early seventeenth century equity enforced assignments of choses in action. The provisions relating to statutory assignment do not supersede equitable assignment but limit its operation to cases where the requirements for statutory assignment have not been satisfied[1]. Since 1 November 1875, when the Judicature Act 1873 came into force, any equitable assignment is recognised by all divisions of the High Court, but the rules governing such assignments are based on those existing before the Act was passed and came into force.

1   *William Brandts Sons & Co v Dunlop Rubber Co Ltd* [1905] AC 454 at 461.

22.10   The effect of an equitable assignment on the enforcement of the chose in action assigned differs, depending upon whether a legal chose in action or an equitable chose in action is involved. A legal chose in action is a right which, before 1875, could be enforced by an action in a common law court, for example, a debt under a contract: an equitable chose in action is a right which, before 1875, could only be enforced by an action in the Court of Chancery, such as a right under a trust.

The effect of an equitable assignment of an equitable chose is that, as in the case of a statutory assignment, the assignee can enforce the chose by bringing an action in his own name without joining the assignor as a party[1]. The sole exception is where the assignment is not absolute, ie the assignor still has some interest in the chose in action, in which case the assignor must be joined as a party to the proceedings so that the court can make a final adjudication binding on all those concerned with the chose in action[2] and thereby protect the person against whom the chose can be enforced against other claims. If he is willing to co-operate the assignor will be joined as co-plaintiff; otherwise he will be joined as co-defendant.

The effect of an equitable assignment of a contractual right or other legal chose in action is that, while the assignee can bring an action in his own name[3] (ie the assignment is not a nullity), he can only recover damages or a debt or obtain an injunction or other remedy by joining the assignor as a party to the proceedings[4]. If the assignee does not do so initially, the action may be stayed (and not immediately struck out) to give him an opportunity to do so[4]. Where it is unnecessary to protect the debtor or the like against claims by the assignor, eg because the debtor has obtained a discharge from him, the assignor need not be joined[5]. These procedural complications make it highly desirable to ensure that the absolute assignment of a legal chose in action complies with the requirements for a statutory assignment.

1 *Donaldson v Donaldson* (1854) Kay 711.
2 *Re Steel Wing Co Ltd* [1921] 1 Ch 349.
3 The assignor may also retain a cause of action, *Three Rivers District Council v Bank of England* [1996] QB 292, [1995] 4 All ER 312, CA, although the assignee should be joined as a co-plaintiff.
4 *Performing Right Society Ltd v London Theatre of Varieties Ltd* [1924] AC 1, HL; *Weddell v J A Pearce & Major* [1988] Ch 26, [1987] 3 All ER 624.
5 *William Brandts Sons & Co v Dunlop Rubber Co Ltd* [1905] AC 454, HL, approved in *Three Rivers District Council v Bank of England* [1996] QB 292, [1995] 4 All ER 312, CA; *Weddell v J A Pearce & Major* [1988] Ch 26, [1987] 3 All ER 624.

22.11 Unlike statutory assignment, an equitable assignment need not be absolute (so that it may be conditional, or by way of charge, or of part of a debt)[1]; writing is not always required, the equitable assignment of a *legal* charge can be oral[2], and notice to the debtor is not essential. On the other hand, consideration is sometimes necessary.

1 *Durham Bros v Robertson* [1898] 1 QB 765, CA; *Re Steel Wing Co Ltd* [1921] 1 Ch 349.
2 For equitable assignment of an equitable chose see the Law of Property Act 1925, s 53(1)(c).

Notice
22.12 Notice to the debtor or other person from whom the assignor would have been entitled to claim the chose in action is not essential to perfect the assignee's title under an equitable assignment[1]. However, it is advisable to give such notice because:

a. An assignment does not bind the debtor etc until he has received notice, written or otherwise, of the assignment. Thus, if, before notice, the debtor pays the assignor he gets a good discharge of his debt[2] and the assignee will have the trouble and expense of seeking to recover the payment from the assignor.

b. Notice to the debtor etc prevents him from setting up new equities which may mature between himself and the assignor thereafter[3].

c. Notice to the debtor etc is necessary to establish priority under the rule in *Dearle v Hall*[4]. This provides that, where an assignor makes two or more assignments of the same chose in action, the priority of the respective claims of the assignees depends on the order in which they gave notice of their assignment. The notice must be clear and unequivocal and, in the case of an equitable chose in action only, must be in writing[5]. However, an assignee who at the time of the assignment actually knows, or would have known if he had made proper inquiries, of a previous assignment cannot gain priority over it by being first to give notice. The rule in *Dearle v Hall* also applies to determine priorities in statutory assignment[6].

1   *Gorringe v Irwell India Rubber and Gutta Percha Works* (1886) 34 Ch D 128, CA.
2   *Stocks v Dobson* (1853) 4 De GM & G 11.
3   Para 22.15, below.
4   (1828) 3 Russ 1.
5   Law of Property Act 1925, s 137(3).
6   *Marchant v Morton, Down & Co* [1901] 2 KB 829; *E Pfeiffer Weinkellerei-Weineinkauf GmbH & Co v Arbuthnot Factors Ltd* [1988] 1 WLR 150.

Communication to assignee
22.13   Unless it is made in pursuance of a previous agreement between assignor and assignee, an equitable assignment is not binding until it is communicated to the assignee[1]. Until then it may be revoked by the assignor.

1   *Re Hamilton, FitzGeorge v FitzGeorge* (1921) 124 LT 737, CA.

Consideration
22.14   An equitable assignment will be enforced, even though the assignee has not furnished consideration, provided the assignor has done everything required to be done by him in order to transfer the chose in action, whether the chose is legal[1] or equitable[2]. Thus, in *Holt v Heatherfield Trust Ltd*[3], an absolute written assignment of a debt, which failed to be a statutory assignment because written notice had not been given to the debtor, was held to be effective as an equitable assignment even though it was not supported by consideration.

However, consideration is a requirement for enforcement in the following cases, even though the assignment is made by deed:

a. *Future choses in action*   A future chose is a pure expectancy, such as a legacy hoped for under the will of a living person. It must be contrasted with an existing right to be paid in the future, which is an existing, not a future, chose. Examples of future choses are future royalties, future income and future book debts.

b. *Contracts to assign*   Similarly, consideration is required for a contract to assign even an existing chose in action in the future[4].

c. *Assignments by way of charge* The rights of an assignee under such an assignment are founded in contract and therefore the assignee must have provided consideration[5].

1 *Kekewich v Manning* (1851) 1 De GM & G 176.
2 *Harding v Harding* (1886) 17 QBD 442; *Holt v Heatherfield Trust Ltd* [1942] 2 KB 1, [1942] 1 All ER 404.
3 [1942] 2 KB 1, [1942] 1 All ER 404.
4 *Re McArdle* [1951] Ch 669, [1951] 1 All ER 905, CA.
5 *Re Earl of Lucan, Hardinge v Cobden* (1890) 45 Ch D 470.

Rules common to both statutory and equitable assignments

Assignee takes subject to the equities
22.15 An assignee only steps into the shoes of his assignor; consequently, he takes the right to the chose in action 'subject to the equities', that is subject to any defence or counterclaim which the debtor etc had against the assignor. This is so even though the assignee provided value for the assignment and was ignorant of the claims of the debtor etc when he took the assignment[1].

Where the debtor's claim arises directly out of the *same* contract or transaction as the subject matter of the assignment, the debtor may set it up against the assignee *whether it accrued to him before or after he had received notice of the assignment*[2]. Thus, where contractual rights have been assigned, the debtor can rescind the contract on the ground that he was induced to enter it by the assignor's fraud[3], or set off against the assignee any claim for damages for breach of the contract by the assignor regardless of when it occurred[4].

Where the debtor's claim arises out of a contract or transaction *other* than that which forms the subject matter of the assignment, the debtor may *only set it up if it accrued to him before the time when he received notice of the assignment*[5]. Thus, if X owes Y £100 under a particular contract and Y assigns this debt to Z, X can only set off against Z a debt of £50 owed to him by Y under another contract if that debt has arisen before he (X) received notice of the assignment.

A limitation which applies in both cases is that nothing in the nature of a personal claim against the assignor, such as a claim to damages for fraud, can be set up against an assignee[6].

1 Where money due on a contract is paid to the assignee in advance of the due date for payment, the party paying that sum cannot recover it from the assignee if there is defective performance of the contract and is limited to a contractual remedy against the assignor, see *Pan Ocean Shipping Co Ltd v Creditcorp Ltd* [1994] 1 All ER 470, [1994] 1 WLR 161, HL.
2 *Newfoundland Government v Newfoundland Rly Co* (1888) 13 App Cas 199, PC.
3 *Graham v Johnson* (1869) LR 8 Eq 36.
4 *Young v Kitchin* (1878) 3 Ex D 127.
5 *Roxburghe v Cox* (1881) 17 Ch D 520, CA.
6 *Stoddart v Union Trust Ltd* [1912] 1 KB 181, CA.

Choses in action incapable of assignment
22.16 We mentioned in para 22.4, above, that certain choses in action, for example negotiable instruments, can be assigned only by using a special procedure. In addition, certain choses in action are incapable of assignment .

Thus an attempt to assign such a chose is ineffective to transfer it to the assigneee. The following are non-assignable:

a. The right to the salary or pension of a public officer is not assignable[1]. A public officer is a person employed by central government. Thus, a civil servant cannot, but a local government officer can, assign the right to his pay.

b. Where a contractual right is conferred on a party for reasons personal to him, eg because of his qualifications or because of confidence reposed in him, he cannot assign it. The basis of this rule is that an assignment of a contractual right must not prejudice the party who owes the corresponding obligation[2]. Thus, an employer cannot assign his contractual right to an employee's service[3]; the identity of his employer is of obvious importance to an employee.

c. A right of litigation (eg to sue and recover damages)[4] is not assignable where it arises out of a right which is not assignable (ie one mentioned in a. and b., above). The rationale for this rule being to protect the integrity of public civil justice. Consequently, where there is no such tendency the modern trend is to treat an assignment which has no element of trafficking in litigation as valid[5]. Hence, for example, a right to litigation is assignable where it arises out a right which is assignable *and* the assignee has a genuine commercial interest in taking the assignment and enforcing it for his own benefit[6], as where an insured person assigns to his insurer (who has compensated him) his rights against the person who has caused him the loss. If an assignee of a right of litigation arising out of an assignable right does not have a genuine commercial interest in taking the assignment, the assignment will be illegal and unenforceable on the grounds of maintenance or champerty.

d. An otherwise assignable contractual right is not assignable if, or to the extent that, this is expressly forbidden by the contract[7].

1 *Grenfell v Dean and Canons of Windsor* (1840) 2 Beav 544; *Re Mirams* [1891] 1 QB 594.
2 *Tolhurst v Associated Portland Cement Manufacturers (1900) Ltd* [1903] AC 414, HL.
3 *Nokes v Doncaster Amalgamated Collieries Ltd* [1940] AC 1014, [1940] 3 All ER 549, HL.
4 A contractual right, for example a debt, can be assigned even if it seems likely that it will only be enforceable by taking legal action, see *Camdex International Ltd v Bank of Zambia* [1996] 3 All ER 431, CA.
5 *Giles v Thompson* [1994] 1 AC 142, [1993] 3 All ER 321, HL. In this case, drivers who had been involved in accidents which were almost certainly the fault of another driver were provided with cars by car-hire companies on the basis that the hire-charges would be paid from the damages paid by the party at fault. The court held that the car-hire companies might be seen as supporting litigation to which they are strangers but they were not claiming to 'share the spoils' of litigation; the agreement was not invalid.
6 *Trendtex Trading Corpn v Crédit Suisse* [1982] AC 679, [1981] 3 All ER 520, HL.
7 *Linden Gardens Trust Ltd v Lenesta Sludge Disposals Ltd* [1994] 1 AC 85, [1993] 3 All ER 417, HL.

Negotiation
22.17   As we indicated in para 22.4, above, a chose in action of a particular type, a negotiable instrument, while capable of transfer, is subject to a special type of assignment known as negotiation.

Statutory and equitable assignment and assignability differ from negotiation and negotiability in a number of ways. The specific differences between the types of assignment just discussed and negotiation fall into two broad categories. First, there are technical differences of procedure for effecting the process of negotiation. Second, the consequences of a transfer being a negotiation rather than an assignment are different[1].

It must be stressed that the transfer of a chose in action by negotiation is applicable only if the chose to be transferred is a negotiable instrument. The most common example of a negotiable instrument (we define the term in para 22.20, below) is a cheque.

1   Particularly, that a person to whom a negotiable instrument is negotiated may acquire a better title than that possessed by the transferor; see further para 22.18, below.

Negotiation and assignment

22.18   The principal differences between an assignment and negotiation are:

a.   a statutory assignment of a chose in action must be in a particular form, whereas a negotiable instrument can be transferred by indorsement and delivery[1], or by mere delivery in appropriate cases;
b.   no notice of transfer is necessary[2];
c.   a transferee of a negotiable instrument can always enforce it without joining the transferor as a party to the action;
d.   the transferee of certain negotiable instruments, if he is a holder in due course, can acquire a better title than the transferor since he takes free of any rights or claims between the creator of the instrument and the transferor[3].

The fact that a person who acquires a negotiable instrument may obtain good title, sometimes even from a thief who has stolen it, is one of the attractions of a negotiable instrument.

1   See para 22.26, below
2   Notice is essential only for a statutory assignment.
3   *Miller v Race* (1758) 1 Burr 452.

Negotiation and transfer

22.19   When discussing cheques, bills and other negotiable instruments the word 'transferable' should be regarded as meaning that ownership of the instrument (including the rights it represents) can be effected by delivery (or indorsement and delivery) of it without any separate form or document of transfer being required and with no requirement that notice of the transfer is given to the party liable. Consequently, a transfer is a change of ownership of an instrument effected by delivery (sometimes with indorsement) without notice having been given to the person liable on the relevant instrument. A negotiable instrument which is transferred to a person who takes free of equities and free from defects in title of prior holders has been 'negotiated' with the consequent advantages which negotiation brings.

Confusion can arise when the word 'negotiable' is used as a synonym for 'transfer for value by delivery'. If X sells a chose in action to Y and Y thereby become the legal owner, X has transferred it for value but, unless the instrument is negotiable, it has not been *negotiated* and Y is bound by existing equities etc. Confusion arises even in statutes relating to negotiable instruments; both the Bills of Exchange Act 1882 and the Cheques Act 1957 use the word 'negotiable' when the context makes it clear that the apposite word is 'transferable'.

What is a negotiable instrument?
22.20   A negotiable instrument is simply a document (the instrument) which:

a.   confers title to money;
b.   is capable of being transferred to another without giving notice of the transfer to the debtor; and
c.   on transfer, can pass a title to the money it represents which is free from claims (equities) available against any prior holder of the instrument and which is not affected by any defects in title of any prior holder.

A negotiable instrument which is transferred to a person who takes free of equities and free from defects in title of prior holders is said to have been 'negotiated'

22.21   It is important to note that a negotiable instrument is independent of the transaction which generates its use. For example, if X buys goods in a shop and pays for them by means of a cheque X is liable to pay for the goods *and* X also incurs liability on the cheque. If the cheque is paid by X's bank the shop would not, of course, be entitled to demand further payment for the goods. But if X was to 'stop' the cheque, ie prohibit his bank from paying, the shop would have a choice, it could either sue X for the price of the goods (a contract action) or on the cheque. Further, if the owner of the shop transferred my cheque to Y, Y could sue X on that cheque and demand its payment from X even if X had returned the goods to the vendor – perhaps because they were unsatisfactory. Any complaint about the quality of the goods purchased, does not affect his liability to honour his cheque. X should not be out of pocket because when he returned the goods he would be entitled to be reimbursed what he had paid for the goods.

22.22   Negotiable instruments developed to meet commercial need; bills of exchange (defined in para 22.24, below) have the longest history but as banks have developed, other negotiable instrument, for example, promissory notes, bank notes and cheques, have evolved. The use of bills of exchange in inland transactions (where the person liable is resident in the United Kingdom or the bill is payable here) has greatly diminished and their primary function – to provide a certain means of payment without the inconvenience of cash – has been usurped by the letter of credit or banker's confirmed credit. The use of bills of exchange in international trade is, however, still extensive.

Types of negotiable instrument
22.23   Cheques, bills of exchange and promissory notes are all recognised as negotiable instruments by the Bills of Exchange Act 1882 (referred to as the

1882 Act for the remainder of this chapter), which is the principal source of the law relating to negotiable instruments. Dividend warrants, interest warrants, bearer bonds, debentures payable to bearer, share warrants payable to bearer, Treasury bills and bankers' drafts are also recognised as negotiable instruments. Most of these are payable to bearer (ie the person who is in possession of them) from the outset. However, bills of exchange, cheques, dividend warrants and interest warrants are often drawn in favour of a specific person, and must be indorsed (signed by the specified person) in order to transfer them (and the rights they represent) to another.

On the other hand, some documents of title to money or security for money, such as postal orders, money orders, share certificates, insurance policies and debentures, and all documents of title to goods, such as bills of lading, are not negotiable. The only way of finding if a certain document of value is negotiable is to see whether all the features of negotiability are found in the instrument itself or in its use. If any one is missing then the document is not a negotiable instrument. For example, a share certificate is not negotiable because it is transferable neither by delivery nor by indorsement and delivery. A form of transfer is needed to evidence the change of ownership, and notification of the transfer has to be given to the company concerned (ie the party liable) by sending the transfer for registration.

A document of title which would appear to satisfy the general definition of a negotiable instrument may not be negotiable in fact. For example, no instrument can be called negotiable, even though it belongs to a class of documents considered negotiable, if it bears evidence on its face to destroy or negative its negotiability. For example, although cheques are recognised as negotiable, a cheque that has been marked 'not negotiable' obviously cannot be a negotiable instrument. Although use of the words 'not negotiable' means that its negotiability is lost, we must bear in mind that a cheque is still freely transferable[1]. Non-negotiability is not a synonym for non-transferability[2].

1 A transferee of a 'non-negotiable' cheque does *not* take free of claims against prior holders and is subject to any defects in title of a prior holder.
2 Although since the Cheques Act 1992 it has been possible to create non-transferable cheques.

22.24 *Bills of exchange* A bill of exchange is a negotiable instrument by which its maker agrees to pay a fixed sum of money at some future date; it is a form of credit in that the maker of the bill receives goods or services but does not have to pay the sum due until the date specified in the bill. However, the person to whom a bill is payable (the payee) can raise money on it immediately either by selling it to a third party who thereby becomes the person entitled to be paid, or by using it as a security for a loan.

22.25 *Promissory notes* A promissory note is defined in the 1882 Act[1] as unconditional promise by the maker of the note to pay a specified sum at a particular time. A bill or cheque is an order to pay, which must be presented for payment. A promissory note is a promise to pay, and its presentment is not always necessary for payment. In common with a bill or cheque, the note gives rise to no liability until issued or delivered.

Treasury bills are a form of promissory note. They are receipts for cash lent to the government which incorporate a promise to repay the loan in (usually) 91 days. Each week the Bank of England acting for the Treasury invites offers of cash, much of which will be used to repay bills maturing that week. Treasury bills are much held by commercial banks as a good short term deposit. They are payable to 'bearer' and fully negotiable. Any bank which finds itself short of cash can sell these bills in the Discount Market in minutes. Banks do not normally apply to the Bank of England for such bills but prefer the Discount Houses to take them up on issue and to re-sell to the commercial banks a few days later.

1   Section 83.

Negotiation and indorsement

22.26   The principles relating to the negotiation of bills of exchange, cheques or promissory notes are set out in the 1882 Act. We concentrate upon bills and cheques and the same rules are applicable to both types of instrument.

Negotiation is defined in the 1882 Act as the 'transfer of a bill etc to another so as to constitute the transferee the holder of the bill'. A bill etc may be transferred from one person to another but, unless that other is also constituted the holder of it, the instrument is not negotiated to him. The advantages which flow from a transfer[1] which is also a negotiation are that the transferee takes free of claims against prior holders of the instrument and that he can acquire a better title than his transferor.

Negotiation is effected differently depending upon whether the bill or cheque is a bearer bill or cheque or an order bill or cheque (we define bearer bill and order bill in paras 22.27 and 22.28, below). A bearer cheque or bill is negotiated by delivery and an order cheque or bill by delivery and indorsement (what constitutes indorsement is discussed in para 22.30, below). Therefore, anyone in possession of a bearer cheque or bill is the holder thereof, but to be the holder of an order cheque or bill the possessor of it must also be either its payee (ie the person to whom it was initially made payable) or indorsee (following a valid indorsement). Since negotiation of a bearer cheque or bill depends upon possession, a thief can be a holder (although he does not have good title) and can confer good title upon a bona fide transferee of it.

Very few cheques are transferred from one person to another so that the indorsement of cheques is not of major importance.

1   Section 8 of the 1882 Act allows the drawer of a cheque or bill to prohibit or restrict its transferability. This does not affect the validity of a bill between drawer, drawee (the bank to whom it is addressed) and payee but such a bill cannot be transferred or negotiated. The same is true of cheques, except that a cheque which is crossed 'not negotiable' can be transferred, although the transfer is not a negotiation. Section 81A allows the creation of a non-transferable cheque by use of the words 'a/c payee'.

22.27   *Order bills (or cheques)*   A cheque or bill which is payable to a specified person, eg 'to X' or 'to X or order' is valid[1]. Such a cheque or bill is called an order bill or an order cheque[2]. The name of the payee need not be used, but the payee must be indicated with reasonable clarity and the safest plan is, of course, to name the payee[3]. Parol evidence[4] is admissible to establish who is the payee where the name of the payee has been misspelt[5].

1   Section 7.
2   Section 8(4), provided there is no limitation on transfer.
3   Section 7.
4   See para 8.2, above.
5   *Willis v Barrett* (1816) 2 Stark 29.

22.28   *Bearer bills (or cheques)*   A cheque or bill which is payable 'to bearer' or 'to X or bearer' (or which is indorsed 'to bearer' or indorsed in blank[1], ie without specifying an indorsee) is also valid. Such a cheque or bill is called a bearer bill or a bearer cheque[2].

Cheques frequently specify that they are payable to 'cash or order' or 'wages or order'. This is not a sufficient specification of the payee and the bank to whom such a cheque is presented can require it to be indorsed; in practice indorsement is rarely required. It is thought that, provided it is uncrossed, a cheque payable to 'cash or bearer' can be cashed by a bearer, but a bank should be careful before cashing such a cheque. It has been suggested that, unless the bank can prove that the customer intended the cheque to be cashed by a bearer, it is not entitled to debit the customer's account.

1   For indorsement, see para 22.30, below.
2   Section 8(3).

22.29   Section 7(3) of the 1882 Act provides that, where a cheque or bill is payable to a payee who is in fact fictitious or non-existent, it is to be regarded as payable to bearer. If the payee is not fictitious but has been named as payee as a result of fraud, it is a vexed question whether the cheque or bill can be regarded as falling within the ambit of s 7(3) and therefore payable to bearer.

In *Bank of England v Vagliano Bros*[1], V's clerk forged certain instruments purporting to be bills drawn on V in favour of X, who were a perfectly respectable firm. The clerk then forged an indorsement by X in favour of M, under which name he obtained payment of the bills. The question at issue was whether the bank could debit V's account with the amount of these bills. If the payee could have been regarded as fictitious the bills would have become payable to bearer (V's clerk as the person in possession would be the bearer) and the bank could have debited V's account. The House of Lords held that a bill could be regarded as payable to bearer if the payee, while not fictitious, had not, and had never been intended to have, any rights in the cheque or bill or, in other words, if the insertion of the payee's name was a mere pretence. On the other hand, it held, if there was an intention to benefit the payee named in a cheque or bill it could not be regarded as payable to bearer, even if the payee's name had been inserted because of fraud[2]. Therefore, if V's clerk had induced V to draw up the bills in favour of X by fraudulently pretending that X was owed money by V, the bills would not have been payable to bearer. In this case the payee was held to be fictitious; the bills were, therefore, payable to bearer and the bank could debit V's account.

1   [1891] AC 107, HL.
2   *North and South Wales Bank Ltd v Macbeth* [1908] AC 137, HL.

Indorsement

22.30   Negotiation of an order cheque or bill requires delivery and indorsement. Section 32 of the 1882 Act sets out the requirements for a valid indorsement:

a.   The indorsement must be written on the cheque or bill, usually (but not necessarily) on the back of it.
b.   It must be signed by the indorser. The indorser's signature by itself is an indorsement, an indorsement in blank.

An indorsement which purports to transfer only part of the amount payable under the cheque or bill, or which purports to transfer the cheque or bill to two unconnected indorsees, does not operate as a negotiation[1]. However, such an indorsement gives the indorsee a right to retain the bill. An indorsement is not effective unless it is unconditional[2]. Under s 33 of the 1882 Act, if a bill purports to be indorsed conditionally, for example, 'pay X if he marries Y', the payer can, if he wishes, disregard the condition and payment to the indorsee will be valid whether or not the condition has been complied with.

Section 31 of the 1882 Act provides that, where the holder of an order cheque or bill transfers it for value but without indorsing it, the transferee has no better title than the transferor (since there is no negotiation) but is entitled to have the cheque or bill indorsed in his favour.

If there are two or more indorsements, the order in which they appear on the cheque or bill is deemed to be the order in which they were made unless the contrary is proved[3].

1   Section 32(2).
2   If an indorsement prohibits further transfer or expressly states that it is merely authority to deal with the cheque or bill as thereby directed, it is a restrictive indorsement which gives the indorsee the right to receive payment of the cheque or bill and to sue anyone whom the indorser could have sued, but, unless expressly authorised, he cannot transfer his rights.
3   Section 32(5).

Novation of contractual rights

22.31   Novation is another process whereby a third party to a contract can acquire a right provided by it. By a novation, contractual rights are transferred indirectly to a third party by means of a new contract between the debtor, creditor and the third party, in substitution for the original one, the new contract providing that the debt owed by the debtor to the creditor shall henceforth be owed to the third party. A novation is not enforceable by the third party unless he has provided consideration for the debtor's promise to pay him[1]. Novation is most common in the case where A owes B £x, and B owes T £x. If the three agree that A shall pay T instead of B, in discharge of his indebtedness to B and of B's to T, there will be a novation, and T can sue A for the money because he has provided consideration for A's promise to pay him by the promise to discharge B's debt.

1   *Tatlock v Harris* (1789) 3 Term Rep 174 at 180; *Wharton v Walker* (1825) 4 B & C 163.

22.32   There are three essential distinctions between assignment and novation:

a.   the process of assignment is not limited to contractual rights;
b.   in an assignment the debtor is not a party to the transaction;
c.   the debtor's consent is not necessary for the validity of an assignment.

These distinctions illustrate why assignment is far more common than novation.

Assignment of Contractual Liabilities

22.33   A party to a contract cannot assign his contractual obligations to a third party (ie he cannot transfer them without the creditor's consent)[1]. However, he can do so if the creditor consents. The transaction will be one of novation and releases the party transferring his obligations and imposes them on the third party[1]. What is required for the novation of a contractual obligation is a new contract between the creditor, debtor and third party that the obligation owed by the debtor under the original contract to the creditor shall henceforth be owed by the third party in substitution. Such a novation is only binding if supported by consideration. Usually, the creditor provides consideration for the third party's promise to perform by promising to release the debtor (and so can enforce the obligation against the third party) and the debtor provides consideration for the creditor's promise to release him by providing the third party (and so is effectively released). An example of a novation of liability is *Miller's Case*[2]. M insured his life with the N Co. The N Co became amalgamated with the O Co and ceased to carry on business. The O Co agreed to become liable on the policy if M paid future premiums to it. Subsequent premiums were paid to the O Co by M and it was held that, there being a complete novation, he could enforce the policy against the O Co.

Novation is frequently used where there is a change in the membership of a partnership, the old and new partners and the firm's creditors agreeing, expressly or by implication, that the creditors will look to the new partner (and the remaining ones), in place of the retiring partner, for payment of their debts.

1   *Tolhurst v Associated Portland Cement Manufacturers (1900) Ltd* [1902] 2 KB 660 at 668.
2   (1876) 3 Ch D 391, CA.

22.34   There is no other way in which a party can extinguish his contractual liability by transferring it to a third party. It is possible in some cases for him to arrange for a third party to perform his obligations so as to discharge him, but in such a case there is no transfer of contractual liability so that the party remains liable if the third party fails to perform or performs defectively.

Involuntary Transfer of Rights and Liabilities

22.35   A person's rights and liabilities are automatically assigned by operation of law in the event of his death or bankruptcy.

Death

22.36   On the death of a person, his property (including any choses in action which survive him) goes to his personal representatives, ie his executors (if he leaves a will) or administrators (if he dies intestate). It is the personal representatives' duty, after paying the deceased's debts and testamentary and funeral expenses, to distribute his estate in accordance with his will or, in the case of intestacy, in accordance with the Administration of Estates Act 1925.

The law of succession is a large subject but the scope of this book merely requires us to consider in more detail the devolution by death of the deceased's contractual rights and liabilities. Under s 1 of the Law Reform (Miscellaneous Provisions) Act 1934, all causes of action subsisting against or vested in a party to a contract survive against or, as the case may be, for the benefit of his estate on his death[1]. The result is that his personal representatives may sue for debts due to the deceased and recover damages for any breach committed in his lifetime, and conversely they can be sued by the other party to the contract for a breach of contract committed during the deceased's lifetime (though they are not personally liable, but only to the extent of the assets in their hands, so that there is not strictly an assignment of liability).

1   The same rule applies to causes of action in tort, with the exception of defamation.

22.37   Where a contract has not been fully performed at the time of death, the general rule is that the benefit and the burden pass to the personal representatives so that they are entitled to any outstanding performance on the part of the other party and must perform any outstanding obligation on the part of the deceased, failure to do so rendering them liable to the extent of the assets. There are two exceptions:

a.   Where the parties intended the contract to be for life only.
b.   Where the contract depends on the personal skill or service of a party, as in the case of an employment contract or a contract of agency, the death of that party frustrates the contract[1] and the deceased's contractual obligation does not devolve to his personal representatives, although of course they can sue for money earned by the deceased or sue or be sued for breaches committed before his death[2].

1   Para 11.5, above.
2   *Stubbs v Holywell Rly Co* (1867) LR 2 Exch 311.

Bankruptcy[1]

22.38   If a person is adjudicated a bankrupt, property (including choses in action) belonging to, or vested in, him at the time of his bankruptcy passes to his trustee in bankruptcy, with the exception of such tools, books, vehicles and other equipment as are necessary for the bankrupt's personal use in his trade or employment and such clothing, bedding, furniture, household equipment and provisions as are necessary to satisfy the basic needs of the bankrupt and his family[2]. Choses in action pass to the trustee without an assignment by the bankrupt and are 'deemed to have been duly assigned' by him[3].

The scope of this book only necessitates a further discussion of the effects of bankruptcy on the bankrupt's contractual rights and liabilities.

1   If a company is unable to pay its debts it can be wound up on the grounds of insolvency; see further para 26.81, below.
2   Insolvency Act 1986, s 283.
3   Ibid, s 311.

22.39   The trustee in bankruptcy is generally in the position of an assignee of all the contractual rights of the bankrupt, and he alone can recover debts due to the bankrupt and claim damages for breach of any contract with the bankrupt (even if it was committed before the bankruptcy) since the bankrupt has no further interest[1]. However, the following contractual rights do not pass to the trustee in bankruptcy:

a.   A right of action for income earned *after* the bankruptcy does not pass to the trustee but remains vested in the bankrupt, subject to the power of the trustee to intervene and retain out of the sum recovered what is not required to maintain the bankrupt and his family[2]. (Whether or not the bankrupt's right to payment of income has arisen after the commencement of the bankruptcy, the trustee in bankruptcy may apply to the court for an income payments order, requiring either the bankrupt or the person from whom payment is due to pay to the trustee so much of the income during the period of the order as may be specified in it. The court must not make an order whose effect would be to reduce the bankrupt's income below what appears necessary to meet the reasonable domestic needs of the bankrupt and his family[3].)

b.   A right of action for damages for breach of contract resulting immediately in injury to the character, feelings or reputation of a bankrupt does not pass to the trustee but remains vested in the bankrupt, whether the breach was committed before or after the bankruptcy. This is shown by *Wilson v United Counties Bank Ltd*[4]. The plaintiff, a trader, entrusted the financial side of his business to the defendant bank during his absence on military service in the First World War. The bank conducted the business so negligently that the plaintiff was adjudicated bankrupt. In an action which he and the trustee brought against the bank, damages of £45,000 were awarded for the loss to his estate and of £7,500 for the injury to his credit and reputation. It was held that the £7,500 belonged personally to the bankrupt as compensation for damages to his reputation, while the £45,000 went to the trustee for the benefit of the creditors.

1   *Farrow v Wilson* (1869) LR 4 CP 744.
2   *Bailey v Thurston & Co Ltd* [1903] 1 KB 137, CA.
3   Insolvency Act 1986, s 310.
4   [1920] AC 102, HL.

22.40   Where a contract made by the bankrupt is executory, the trustee may (subject to the provisions of the Insolvency Act 1986) perform it and claim payment from the other party[1]. However, he is not entitled to do so if the contract is one which is personal in nature, such as one whose execution requires the skill and judgment of the bankrupt. For example, in *Knight v Burgess*[2], it was held that the trustee in bankruptcy was not entitled to complete the building of a chapel because the contract involved the personal skill of the bankrupt builder.

1   Insolvency Act 1986, s 312.
2   (1864) 33 LJ Ch 727.

22.41   The bankrupt's contractual liabilities pass to the trustee in bankruptcy, in the sense that the trustee must distribute the bankrupt's assets (including those which he has acquired by enforcing the bankrupt's contractual rights) among the bankrupt's creditors. This, of course, does not strictly involve an assignment because the trustee is not personally liable but only to the extent of the bankrupt's property which he has collected.

22.42   The trustee has power to disclaim an executory contract on the ground that it is onerous or unprofitable. The effect of his doing so is to discharge the contract, but a person injured by the disclaimer can prove in the bankruptcy for any damage which he suffers by such disclaimer[1].

1   Insolvency Act 1986, s 315.

Chapter 23

Agency

23.1 The words 'agent' and 'agency' are familiar ones but we must stress that they are not, in popular speech, always used in their correct legal sense[1]. In this book references to agent and agency refer only to relationships which are legally recognised as such. Examples include company directors acting on behalf of their companies and accountants acting for their clients.

The rules relating to agency are relevant in many areas covered in different chapters of this book particularly those on partnership and company law.

1 For example, a 'motor agent' is not necessarily in law the agent of the manufacturer whose cars he sells.

23.2 Agency is the relationship between two legal persons, natural or artificial, whereby one person (the principal) appoints another (the agent) to act on his behalf in effecting a transaction. Agents are usually, although not necessarily[1], appointed by contract and they may be authorised to make contracts or undertake other tasks on behalf of their principals and their endeavours may affect the legal position of the principal vis-à-vis third parties. For example, an agent may sign documents on behalf of his principal[2], execute deeds (if authorised by deed to do so[3]), or execute a bill of sale[4]. In addition, a principal may be liable for torts committed by his agent in the course of the agency[5].

1 Paras 23.14 and 23.15, below.
2 *LCC v Agricultural Food Products Ltd* [1955] 2 QB 218, [1955] 2 All ER 229, CA.
3 *Steiglitz v Egginton* (1815) Holt NP 141.
4 *Furnivall v Hudson* [1893] 1 Ch 335.
5 *Lloyd v Grace, Smith & Co* [1912] AC 716, HL; see also paras 17.26 and 17.27, above.

Three issues
23.3 The three issues with which we are concerned in this chapter are as follows:

a. the relationship of principal and agent (ie the creation of agency, the rights and duties of principal and agent, and the termination of agency)[1];
b. the changes in the legal relationship of the principal and third parties which may be effected by an agent; and

477

c.   the legal relationship, if any, between the agent and third parties.

Commercial agents

23.4   The rights and duties of agents were traditionally governed by the general rules of agency and any modifications agreed by the parties, and the general rules of agency did not differentiate to any large degree between different types of agent. However, the position has now changed in that the Commercial Agents (Council Directive) Regulations 1993, which came into effect on 1 January 1994, provide a special regime applicable only to 'commercial agents'. It appears that the Regulations can apply to any commercial agent operating within the UK even if neither the agent nor the principal is a national of a member state of the European Union but this cannot be regarded as certain without a judicial ruling on the point. However, where the principal is operating from an EU state and the agent operates in the UK it appears that the law of the principal's state will govern the relationship (the principal's state should have its own version of the Regulations). Except where the Regulations apply the general rules of agency are equally applicable to commercial agents.

A commercial agent is defined by the regulations as a 'self-employed intermediary who has continuing authority to negotiate the sale or purchase of goods on behalf of another person (the "principal"), or to negotiate and conclude the sale or purchase of goods on behalf of and in the name of that principal'. Consequently, a person who acts as an intermediary in respect of contracts for services, perhaps a person who introduces insurance business, is not a commercial agent. The nature of commercial agency seems to envisage a long-term relationship during which the agent will try to build up a market or goodwill and will generate sales for the principal. The Regulations list several factors which may be indicative of whether a relationship is to be construed as creating a commercial agency. For example, if a manufacturer, importer or wholesaler's goods can be obtained only from an intermediary and the number of intermediaries is controlled by the manufacturer etc, the relationship is likely to be that of commercial agency. Where the intermediary merely acts as a conduit through which orders are passed to the manufacturer etc, as opposed to acting as a negotiator, the relationship is probably not within the ambit of the Regulations[1]. We indicate at relevant points where the special rules affecting only commercial agents operate.

1   Those operating mail order catalogues for consumer goods are specifically excluded from the Regulations.

Principal and Agent

Creation of agency

23.5   Agency may be created by agreement, express or implied, by ratification or by virtue of necessity. In determining whether a principal (P) has appointed another person to act as his agent (A), it is necessary to decide, first, whether P had the capacity to appoint an agent and whether A had the capacity to act as an agent and, second, how an agent is appointed.

Capacity

23.6 An agent can be appointed to effect any transaction for which the principal has capacity[1]. A minor can appoint an agent to buy necessaries or make a beneficial contract of employment[2] for him, but a minor cannot enter into trading contracts merely by the interposition of an adult agent[3]. A mentally disordered person can appoint an agent to purchase or obtain necessaries[4], and an agent who incurs expense on behalf of a mentally disordered principal is entitled to reimbursement.

Anyone not suffering from a mental disorder can act as an agent. A minor can act as agent in a transaction which he would not have capacity to effect on his own behalf. For example, a father could appoint his 17-year old son to purchase non-necessary goods on his behalf even though the son, being a minor, could not make a binding contract for non-necessary goods on his own behalf. However, an agent who lacks full contractual capacity can only be made *personally* liable on those contracts which he would have had capacity to make on his own behalf[5] and may well not be liable on the contract of agency. Companies, as well as natural legal persons, can be appointed as agents.

1 For the law relating to capacity to contract, see Chap 16 and paras 25.29 and 25.30, below.
2 *Doyle v White City Stadium* [1935] 1 KB 110, CA.
3 *G(A) v G(T)* [1970] 2 QB 643, [1970] 3 All ER 546, CA.
4 For the contractual capacity of a mentally disordered person see para. 16.17, above.
5 *Smally v Smally* (1700) 1 Eq Cas Abr 6; for when an agent is personally liable on contracts see paras 23.50–23.54, below.

Appointment by express agreement

23.7 A person may be appointed as an agent by express agreement with the principal. This agreement is usually, but not necessarily, a contract[1] and the usual rules for the formation of contracts apply. The appointment can normally be made informally, even if the agent is to transact contracts which must be in writing. All that is necessary is a desire to appoint A as agent and A's consent to act as such.

The agreement which appoints an agent will usually specify the authority (ie the powers) which the principal bestows upon him, although this may be extended by implication[2] and by the concept of ostensible authority[3].

Where an agent is appointed as a commercial agent as defined in para 23.4, above, he is entitled to receive on request a signed, written contract setting out the terms of the agency agreement and any terms subsequently agreed[4].

1 *Chaudhry v Prabhakar* [1988] 3 All ER 718, [1989] 1 WLR 29, CA, is an example of a non-contractual agency; see further para. 23.19, below.
2 Paras 23.38–23.40, below.
3 Paras 23.41–23.44, below.
4 Regulation 13; the principal has a similar right against the agent.

Appointment by implied agreement

23.8 If the parties have not expressly agreed to become principal and agent, it may be possible to find an implied agreement based on their conduct or relationship. If the parties have so conducted themselves towards one another that it would be reasonable for them to assume that they have consented to act as principal and agent, they are deemed to be principal and agent[1]. For example, the agent of a finance company or of an insurance company may also be held to be the agent of the party seeking finance or insurance if the circumstances warrant an implication of agreement to such a relationship[2]. Factors which have been found relevant in determining whether agency has been created by implied agreement are whether one party acts for the other at the other's request and whether commission is payable. The House of Lords has rejected the notion that a spouse who negotiates a loan secured on the matrimonial home is necessarily an implied agent of the lender vis-à-vis his or her spouse[3].

An implied agreement arises in the case of husband and wife by virtue of their relationship. A wife has authority to pledge her husband's credit for household necessaries even if he has not expressly appointed her his agent[4].

Since there is no express appointment in the present type of case, the authority which the principal bestows upon the agent is implied authority[5]; but, as with agents expressly appointed, agents impliedly appointed may also have the power to bind the principal to contracts with third parties by virtue of ostensible authority[6].

1 *Ashford Shire Council v Dependable Motors Pty Ltd* [1961] AC 336, [1961] 1 All ER 96, PC.
2 *Newsholme Bros v Road Transport and General Insurance Co Ltd* [1929] 2 KB 356, CA.
3 *Barclays Bank plc v O'Brien* [1994] 1 AC 180 , [1993] 4 All ER 417, HL.
4 *Debenham v Mellon* (1880) 6 App Cas 24, HL.
5 Paras. 23.38–23.40, below.
6 Paras. 23.41–23.44, below.

Ratification
23.9   In certain circumstances, the relationship of principal and agent can be created or extended retrospectively under the doctrine of ratification. What this means is that, if A purports to act as agent for B in a particular transaction (although he is not authorised to do so), B may subsequently 'ratify' or adopt what A has done. In such a case, A is deemed to have been acting as an authorised agent when he effected the transaction[1]. However, ratification only validates past acts of the 'agent' and gives no authority for the future[2], although frequent acts of ratification by a principal may create agency by implied agreement or confer ostensible authority on the person purporting to act as agent[3].

1 *Bolton Partners v Lambert* (1889) 41 Ch D 295.
2 *Irvine v Union Bank of Australia* (1877) 2 App Cas 366, PC.
3 *Midland Bank Ltd v Reckitt* [1933] AC 1, HL.

23.10   *Effects of ratification*   If a person (hereafter the principal) ratifies a transaction entered into on his behalf he must be taken to have ratified the whole transaction, and not merely those parts which are to his advantage[1]. The effect of ratification is to make the transaction (which is usually a contract) binding on the principal from the moment that it was made by the agent[2]. Since the acts of the agent are retrospectively validated, the agent cannot be liable to a third party for breach of warranty of authority (acting without authority), nor can he be liable to his principal for acting outside the scope of his authority[3], and he can claim commission and an indemnity[4]. Once a contract is ratified, the agent generally ceases to be liable on the contract[5], but ratification cannot vary rights in property which have vested before ratification. Perhaps the most controversial effect of ratification is that it allows the principal to decide whether to accept a contract or reject it. The third party may wish to repudiate an agreement with the agent because of the agent's lack of authority, but find himself bound by the contract if the principal subsequently ratifies[6]. However, if a contract is made 'subject to ratification' the third party can withdraw prior to ratification and, if he does so, ratification cannot bind him[7].

Because the effects of ratification are at least potentially unfair to third parties, ratification is only possible in some circumstances.

1   *Cornwal v Wilson* (1750) 1 Ves Sen 509.
2   *Bolton Partners v Lambert* (1889) 41 Ch D 295.
3   *Smith v Cologan* (1788) 2 Term Rep 188n. For breach of warranty of authority see para. 23.56, below.
4   *Hartas v Ribbons* (1889) 22 QBD 254, CA. For indemnities see para. 23.26, below.
5   He will continue to be liable in those cases where an agent properly authorised at the outset would retain liability; see paras 23.49–23.54, below.
6   *Bolton Partners v Lambert*(1889) 41 Ch D 295.
7   *Warehousing and Forwarding Co of East Africa Ltd v Jafferali & Sons Ltd* [1964] AC 1, [1963] 3 All ER 571, PC.

23.11   *Who can ratify?*   Only a principal can ratify the actions of his alleged agent (hereafter the agent) and then only if the latter purported to act on his behalf[1]. Therefore, if an agent has not revealed that he was acting as an agent, ie he has an undisclosed principal, the undisclosed principal cannot ratify. A leading illustration of this is the case of *Keighley, Maxsted & Co v Durant*[2]. In this case, an agent purchased wheat at a price which was higher than that which he had been authorised to pay. The agent had not revealed that he was acting as an agent when he bought the grain. Because of this the House of Lords found the defendant principal was not liable for breach of contract when he refused to accept delivery of the grain, even though he had purported to ratify the contract of sale. Provided that an agent reveals that he is acting as an agent, his principal can ratify his unauthorised actions, even though he is unnamed[3]. Generally, an unnamed principal should, be capable of being identified at the time that the unauthorised actions occurred[3]. However, when the third party has shown that he is uninterested in the identity of the principal, it is thought that the principal can ratify even if he was not capable of being identified at the time the unauthorised transaction was negotiated.

A company can only ratify an unauthorised contract or other transaction if it is in existence at the time the agent enters into it[4]. Thus, even if a company takes the benefit of a pre-incorporation contract, it is not liable on it. If a company replaces the pre-incorporation contract with a new contract, post-incorporation, on the same subject matter[5] it is liable on the new contract. A new contract will *not* be implied merely because the company continues to take the benefit of the pre-incorporation contract[6]. Any new contract is, of course, only prospective in effect. The agent who makes a pre-incorporation contract on behalf of a non-existent company is personally liable on it, unless personal liability has been excluded by agreement[7], and only the 'agent' can sue on the contract. Similarly, only the 'agent' can sue or be sued on a transaction entered into on behalf of a company when that company has been liquidated[8].

To be able to ratify, a disclosed principal must have had the capacity to make the contract himself at the date when his agent contracted[9].

1   *Wilson v Tumman* (1843) 6 Man & G 236.
2   [1901] AC 240, HL.
3   *Watson v Swann* (1862) 11 CBNS 756.
4   *Kelner v Baxter* (1866) LR 2 CP 174; see now s 36C of the Companies Act 1985, the section only applies to contracts.
5   *Howard v Patent Ivory Manufacturing Co* (1888) 38 Ch D 156.
6   *Touche v Metropolitan Railway Warehousing Co* (1871) 6 Ch App 671.
7   Companies Act 1985, s 36C. In *Phonogram Ltd v Lane* [1982] QB 938, [1981] 3 All ER 182, the Court of Appeal held the 'agent' of an unformed company liable to return money which the plaintiffs had paid to him for the use of the unformed company, even though the plaintiffs knew he was not receiving the money on his own account and he derived no benefit from the money.
8   *Presentaciones Musicales SA v Secunda* [1994] 2 All ER 737, CA.
9   *Boston Deep Sea Fishing and Ice Co Ltd v Farnham* [1957] 3 All ER 204, [1957] 1 WLR 1051.

23.12   *What can be ratified?*   Any action can be ratified, even where the purported agent was seeking to benefit himself, except a void or illegal act[1].

Considerable difficulty has arisen over forged signatures by an alleged agent. Such a forgery could simply be regarded as a void act and unratifiable, and in early cases, it was so regarded. However, subsequent interpretation of the leading case, *Brook v Hook*[2], has suggested that, while forgeries are generally regarded as unratifiable, it is for a different reason. Current opinion is that a forged signature by an alleged agent is unratifiable because in forging a signature the 'agent was not purporting to be an agent' but to be the person whose signature he forged[3]. Where an agent executes an unauthorised signature it can be ratified.

1   *Re Tiedemann and Ledermann Frères* [1899] 2 QB 66; *Bedford Insurance Co Ltd v Instituto de Resseguros do Brasil* [1985] QB 966, [1984] 3 All ER 766.
2   (1871) LR 6 Exch 89.
3   In *First Sport Ltd v Barclays Bank plc* [1993] 3 All ER 789, [1993] 1 WLR 1229, CA, a forged signature on a cheque was held capable of effecting a contractual relationship between a retailer and the bank which issued the cheque. Consequently, the courts may be changing their view of forged signatures.

23.13   *How to ratify*   Ratification may be made by express affirmation of the unauthorised actions of the agent by the principal[1]. It need not, as a rule, take any special form, except that, where the agent has without authority executed a deed, ratification too must be by deed[2].

Ratification may also be effected by conduct[3], although mere passive acceptance of the benefit of a contract may be insufficient[4]; each case turns on its own facts. Examples of ratification by conduct are provided by the following cases. In *Lyell v Kennedy*[5], A received rent from property for many years, although not authorised to do so. The owner sued him for an account of the rents; it was held that the owner's action constituted ratification of the agent's receipt of the rents. Similarly, in *Cornwal v Wilson*[6], A bought some goods in excess of the price authorised by P. P objected to the purchase but sold some of the goods; it was held that he had ratified the unauthorised act by selling the goods. An action by the principal will only constitute ratification by conduct if he had a choice of whether or not to act. Where the principal has no real choice, other than to accept the benefit of the unauthorised actions of his agent, accepting that benefit is not ratification. For example, if an agent has had unauthorised repairs done on a ship, merely retaking the ship with these repairs is not ratification by the principal; if P wished to recover his property he had to have it with the unauthorised repairs[7].

Ratification will, generally, only be implied from conduct if the principal has acted with full knowledge of the facts[8]. But, if the principal is prepared to take the risk of what his agent has done, he can choose to ratify without full knowledge. For instance, in *Fitzmaurice v Bayley*[9], an agent entered into an unauthorised contract for the purchase of property. The principal wrote a letter saying he did not know what his agent had done but would stand by all that he had done. This was an express ratification by him because he had agreed to bear the risk of being bound by the unauthorised acts of his agent, whatever they were.

Ratification must take place within a reasonable time[10]. What is reasonable is a question of fact in every case, but if the time for performance of a contract has passed ratification is impossible[11].

1 *Soames v Spencer* (1822) 1 Dow & Ry KB 32.
2 *Hunter v Parker* (1840) 7 M & W 322.
3 *Lyell v Kennedy* (1889) 14 App Cas 437, HL.
4 *Hughes v Hughes* (1971) 221 Estates Gazette 145, CA.
5 (1889) 14 App Cas 437, HL.
6 (1750) 1 Ves Sen 509.
7 *Forman & Co Pty Ltd v The Liddesdale* [1900] AC 190, PC.
8 *The Bonita; The Charlotte* (1861) 1 Lush 252.
9 (1856) 6 E & B 868.
10 *Re Portuguese Consolidated Copper Mines Ltd, ex p Bosanquet* (1890) 45 Ch D 16, CA.
11 *Metropolitan Asylums Board of Managers v Kingham & Sons* (1890) 6 TLR 217.

Agency of necessity

23.14 Agency of necessity is a limited exception to the concept that agency is based on a consensual relationship between the parties. When certain emergencies occur, immediate action may be necessary and the courts may be prepared to find that the person taking such action was thereby acting as an agent of necessity. A common example of agency of necessity is that masters of ships faced with an emergency are agents of the shipowner, and have authority to enter into contracts with third parties on the shipowner's behalf which bind the shipowner[1].

Agency of necessity arises in two rather different situations[2]. Generally it merely extends the authority of an existing agent. However, it may also create agency where none existed previously; for example, between masters of ships and cargo owners. In the latter situation such agency will only affect the relationship of the alleged principal and agent, and does not confer power on the agent to deal with third parties on behalf of the principal further than the necessity requires. For example, someone who salvages a ship cannot make contracts unrelated to that emergency on behalf of the shipowner.

Agency of necessity will only arise if:

a.   the agent has no practical way of communicating with the principal[3]; and
b.   the action of the agent is reasonably necessary to benefit the principal[4]; and
c.   the agent has acted bona fide; and
d.   there is, or at that time appears to be, some pressing reason for action[2].

1   *The Gratitudine* (1801) 3 Ch Rob 240. There is no wider implied authority: *The Choko Star* [1989] 2 Lloyd's Rep 42.
2   *The Winson* [1982] AC 939, [1981] 3 All ER 688, HL.
3   *Springer v Great Western Rly Co* [1921] 1 KB 257, CA.
4   *Prager v Blatspiel, Stamp and Heacock Ltd* [1924] 1 KB 566.

An important postscript

23.15   In some cases a person will be held to have authority to affect the legal relationship of an apparent principal and third parties even if the person whose actions thereby bind the apparent principal is not technically an agent. This is *not* a method of creating agency between principal and agent but it may result in an alleged principal being unable to deny that his apparent agent was authorised to act on his behalf and is sometimes called agency by estoppel[1].

1   Paras 23.41–23.44, below.

Duties of an agent

23.16   The duties of an agent may be set out in the contract of agency (if there is one) but the terms of such contracts are rarely comprehensive. Consequently, the duties, and also the rights, of agents, are often determined by reference to the general law of agency and any appropriate trade custom or usage, so far as these things do not conflict with any express contractual provisions. It must also be stressed that, while the implied duties which arise from the general law of agency operate only in so far as they do not conflict with the terms of the contract, they are equally independent of the existence of a contract and can continue to exist even after the contract of agency has terminated[1].

An example of a duty arising under the general law of agency is the obligation of an agent to pay over to his principal any money received for the use of the principal in the course of the agency. This liability to account arises even if the money is claimed by a third party. Thus, if an agent who has funds payable to the principal pays it to a third party, he must also pay the sum to his principal.

Failure to comply with the contractual duties or the important duties deriving from general rules of agency which are detailed below will generally disentitle the agent from remuneration and may render him liable to pay damages for breach of contract or in tort.

An agent, as a fiduciary, has a general duty to act honestly and in good faith in conducting his principal's affairs. However, but more specific duties are also recognised by the law. We now consider some of the obligations which an agent incurs irrespective of a contract of engagement as an agent, including those applicable to commercial agents (defined in para 23.4, above) set out in the Commercial Agents (Council Directive) Regulations 1993. The obligations in the Regulations *cannot* be excluded by the parties.

1   *Kelly v Cooper* [1993] AC 205, [1992] 3 WLR 936, PC; *Yasuda Fire and Marine Insurance Co of Europe Ltd v Orion Marine Insurance Underwriting Agency Ltd* [1995] QB 174, [1995] 4 All ER 211.

Duty to act

23.17   A paid agent is under a duty to do any act required by the contract of agency, other than an act which is illegal or void[1], and any loss suffered by the principal because of failure to fulfil this duty is recoverable from the agent by the principal[2]. The duty to act imposed upon a commercial agent is contained in reg 3 which requires such an agent to 'make proper efforts to negotiate and, where appropriate, conclude the transaction he is instructed to take care of.'

If A is a gratuitous agent he does not appear to be under any positive duty to act, although if he chooses to act and does so negligently he is liable in tort for his negligence[3].

The duty to act is a duty to act *personally* so that an agent cannot delegate his responsibilities to a sub-agent without the authority of his principal[4]. This does not apply to purely administrative actions which can be delegated without prior permission[5].

1   *Cohen v Kittell* (1889) 22 QBD 680.
2   *Turpin v Bilton* (1843) 5 Man & G 455.
3   *Wilkinson v Coverdale* (1793) 1 Esp 74; *Chaudhry v Prabhakar* [1988] 3 All ER 718, [1989] 1 WLR 29, CA.
4   *De Bussche v Alt* (1878) 8 Ch D 286, CA.
5   *Allam & Co v Europa Poster Services Ltd* [1968] 1 All ER 826, [1968] 1 WLR 638.

Duty to obey instructions

23.18   The primary obligation imposed on an agent is to act strictly in accordance with the instructions of his principal in so far as they are lawful and reasonable[1]. An agent has no discretion to disobey his instructions, even in what he honestly and reasonably regards to be his principal's best interests[2]. When an agent carries out his instructions he cannot be liable for loss suffered by the principal because the instructions were at fault[3]. If the instructions which an agent receives are not complied with he will be responsible to his principal for any loss thereby suffered, even if the loss is not occasioned by any fault on his part[4]. However, if the instructions received by an agent are ambiguous he is not in breach of this duty if he makes a reasonable but incorrect interpretation of them[5]. If the instructions confer a discretion on an agent, he will not be liable for failure to obey them if he exercises the discretion reasonably[6].

An agent who, in obeying instructions, conveys to a third party false information which he has been given by his principal, does not incur liability under s 2(1) of the Misrepresentation Act 1967 for negligent misrepresentation if this misstatement induces a contract between the third party and the principal[7]. However, if he knows the information to be false he may incur liability for deceit. The position where the agent should have known of the falsity is unclear[8], there seems no reason in principle why an agent who assumed the appropriate degree of responsibility for a statement should not be liable in tort for negligence[9].

1   The Regulations specify that a commercial agent must comply with reasonable instructions given by his principal.
2   *Bertram, Armstrong & Co v Godfray* (1830) 1 Knapp 381, PC.
3   *Overend, Gurney & Co v Gibb* (1872) LR 5 HL 480.
4   *Lilley v Doubleday* (1881) 7 QBD 510.
5   *Weigall & Co v Runciman & Co* (1916) 85 LJKB 1187, CA.
6   *Boden v French* (1851) 10 CB 886.
7   *Resolute Maritime Inc v Nippon Kaiji Kyokai, The Skopas* [1983] 2 All ER 1, [1983] 1 WLR 857; see para 14.21, above.
8   In *Gran Gelato Ltd v Richcliff (Group) Ltd* [1992] Ch 560, [1992] 1 All ER 865, a solicitor, acting as agent for the owner of property, did not incur liability for negligent mis-statement when he gave inaccurate replies in answering inquiries before lease relying on information provided by the client .
9   For liability for negligent mis-statements see para 18.13, above. See also para 23.56, below.

Duty to exercise care and skill

23.19   A paid agent is required to display reasonable care in carrying out his instructions and also, where appropriate, such skill as may reasonably be expected from a member of his profession[1]. Should he fail to do so, an agent will be liable for any consequential loss which his principal suffers. For example, an accountant acting as agent should acquaint himself with such relevant legislation as a competent accountant would do, as well as exercising proper care in pursuing his principal's instructions.

The standard of care which can be expected from a gratuitous agent is similar, namely, to exercise such care and skill as could reasonably be expected in the circumstances. In a relatively recent case, a knowledgeable amateur advised a friend on the purchase of a second-hand car which turned out to be a valueless insurance write-off. He conceded that he was acting as her agent in advising on the purchase. He was held to have failed to exercise sufficient care and skill in that he failed to question the vendor of the car (a car sprayer and panel beater) as to why it had a crumpled bonnet[2].

1   Supply of Goods and Services Act 1982, s 13, which affirms the previous case law, makes the exercise of reasonable care and skill an implied term of all contracts of agency.
2   *Chaudhry v Prabhakar* [1988] 3 All ER 718, [1989] 1 WLR 29, CA.

Duty to provide information

23.20   Since the agent has the ability to effect contractual relations between his principal and a third party, which may impose liability on the principal, it is important that the agent provides adequate information to the principal. Consequently, in *Yasuda Fire and Marine Insurance Co of Europe Ltd v Orion Marine Insurance Underwriting Agency Ltd*[1], the principal's claim to be entitled to inspect the books and computer records of the defendant who was its agent was upheld. In this case, the agent was entrusted with the making of insurance contracts binding on the principal; the principal was entitled to know what its personal contractual rights and duties were both in relation to the agent and third parties. This duty continues after the agency relationship has terminated in respect of contracts or other obligations which the agent entered into before the relationship was ended and which continue to bind the principal.

Regulation 3 of the provisions relating to commercial agents provide that a commercial agent must communicate to his principal 'all the necessary information available to him'.

1 [1995] QB 174, [1995] 3 All ER 211.

Fiduciary duties

23.21 Every agent owes fiduciary duties, ie duties of good faith, to his principal (unless excluded by the contract between them). These duties are based on the confidential nature of the agency relationship. It is important to appreciate that an agent may be in breach of one of these duties, and liable for the consequences, even where he acts innocently[1]. There are two main fiduciary duties – a duty to disclose any conflict of interest and a duty not to take secret profits or bribes – but even these duties may be displaced, expressly or impliedly, by the terms of the contract. For example, in *Kelly v Cooper*[2], an estate agent, whom his principal knew would be acting for competing house vendors, was not in breach of his fiduciary duties in failing to disclose to the plaintiff-principal confidential information obtained in acting for one house vendor. The reason was that circumstances of estate agency contracts give rise to an implied contractual term that the normal duty of disclosure is displaced. However, the obligation to act in good faith embodied in reg 3 for commercial agents cannot be excluded, with the result that a commercial agent's duty cannot be excluded by his contract of appointment (or otherwise).

a. *Conflict of interest* Wherever an agent's own interests come into conflict with those of his principal, he must make a full disclosure to the principal of all relevant facts, so that the latter may decide whether to continue with the transaction. It is this rule which prevents an agent, in the absence of disclosure, from selling his own property to the principal[3], purchasing the principal's property for himself[4] or acting as agent for both parties to a transaction[5]. If the agent is in breach of this duty, the principal may have any resulting transaction set aside, claim any profit accruing to the agent and refuse to pay commission[6].

b. *Secret profits and bribes* If an agent, in the course of the agency and without his principal's knowledge and consent, makes a profit for himself out of his position, or out of his principal's property, or out of information with which he is entrusted by virtue of his agency, he must account for this profit to the principal[7]. Thus, an agent may not accept commission from both parties to a transaction[8], nor keep for himself the benefit of a trade discount while charging his principal the full price[9], without the principal's informed consent. It makes no difference that the agent has acted honestly throughout, nor even that his actions have conferred substantial benefits upon the principal[10]. Where the secret profit takes the form of a payment from a third party who is aware that he is dealing with an agent, it is called a 'bribe', even if the payment is not made with any evil motive and even if the principal suffers no loss thereby[11]. The taking of a bribe entitles the principal to dismiss the agent[12], recover either the amount of the bribe or his actual loss (if greater) from the agent or third party[13], refuse to pay commission, and repudiate any transaction in respect of which the bribe was given (provided that he can return to any third party any contractual benefits he has received)[14]. Where an agent has taken a bribe and used the money to good effect so that he has increased its value, the principal is entitled to claim not merely the amount of the bribe but also any increment in its value[15].

1   *Keppel v Wheeler* [1927] 1 KB 577, CA. Although an agent may in some cases be able to recover commission when he has innocently broken his fiduciary duty.
2   [1993] AC 205, [1992] 3 WLR 936, PC.
3   *Gillett v Peppercorne* (1840) 3 Beav 78.
4   *McPherson v Watt* (1877) 3 App Cas 254, HL.
5   *Harrods Ltd v Lemon* [1931] 2 KB 157, CA.
6   Note that in *Kelly v Cooper* [1993] AC 205, [1992] 3 WLR 936, PC, the court suggested, obiter, that an agent who committed an innocent breach of fiduciary duty could recover any commission otherwise payable. Whether this would be sufficient to disentitle a commercial agent to recover commission is uncertain.
7   *Regal (Hastings) Ltd v Gulliver* [1967] 2 AC 134n, [1942] 1 All ER 378, HL. This is a particularly harsh decision in that the principal was incapable of taking advantage of the opportunity from which the agent derived his profit albeit that the agent used information available to him by virtue of his office to get the opportunity.
8   *Andrews v Ramsay & Co* [1903] 2 KB 635.
9   *Hippisley v Knee Bros* [1905] 1 KB 1.
10   *Boardman v Phipps* [1967] 2 AC 46, [1966] 3 All ER 721, HL.
11   *Industries and General Mortgage Co Ltd v Lewis* [1949] 2 All ER 573.
12   *Boston Deep Sea Fishing and Ice Co v Ansell* (1888) 39 Ch D 339, CA.
13   *Mahesan S/O Thambiah v Malaysia Government Officers' Co-operative Housing Society Ltd* [1979] AC 374, [1978] 2 All ER 405, PC; *Armagas Ltd v Mundogas SA* [1986] AC 717, [1986] 2 All ER 385, HL.
14   *Shipway v Broadwood* [1899] 1 QB 369, CA; *Logicrose Ltd v Southend United Football Club Ltd* [1988] 1 WLR 1256.
15   *A-G of Hong Kong v Reid* [1994] 1 AC 324, [1994] 1 All ER 1, PC.

Rights of agents

23.22   The rights of agents were traditionally governed by the general rules of agency and any modifications agreed by the parties. However, the position has now changed where the agent is a commercial agent in that the relationship of principal and agent is largely governed by the Commercial Agents (Council Directive) Regulations 1993. Thus, we have one set of rules for commercial agents and another for all other agents. Particular note should be taken of reg 4 which imposes a type of fiduciary duty on the *principal* in that he is required to deal with his commercial agent 'dutifully and in good faith.' We defined a commercial agent in para 23.4, above.

It should be noted that a commercial agent is entitled to request and receive from his principal a signed, written contract setting out the terms of the agency contract and any subsequent amendments[1].

In the following paragraphs we consider various rights possessed by agents. We look first at the general rules of agency and then consider, where relevant, any modification of these rules by the Regulations.

1   Regulation 13; this right cannot be waived.

Payment

23.23 An agent need not be paid by his principal[1] but in practice most agents are paid for their efforts. An agent who is paid can be remunerated in two ways. He may be entitled to be paid simply for being an agent whether he sells any goods or services on behalf of the principal or not, or he may be paid by receiving commission on goods or services sold, or he may be entitled to payment in both cases.

1 Regulation 6 of the Regulations relating to commercial agents provides that in the absence of an express agreement, a commercial agent is entitled to be paid.

23.24 *Remuneration* When there is a contract of agency it may provide for the agent to be paid for being an agent irrespective of his negotiating any transaction on behalf of his principal. The right to be paid may be an express term of the contract of agency or, in the absence of such a term, may be implied provided that it was clearly the intention of the parties that the agent was to be paid[1]. In order to imply a right to be paid it is not enough for the contract to mention remuneration; an agent is not entitled to any payment unless the contract, on its true construction, *entitles* him to payment[2].

An agent employed under a contract of agency is entitled to be paid only if he has performed, *precisely and completely*, the obligations in the agency agreement, unless the contract otherwise provides. This is because an agency contract is normally an entire one[3]. Consequently, when an agent does less than he is contractually required to do he can recover nothing, unless the contract provides for payment for partial performance.

Where the contract of agency expressly provides the amount of remuneration for a given task, this is the amount payable. However, if the contract provides that the agent is entitled to be paid but does not specify an amount, he is entitled to recover a reasonable amount[4]. When there is an implied term providing for payment, the amount of such payment must be determined by the courts. Usually it will be on the basis of what is reasonable, but it may be possible to imply the fixed scale costs of professional men[5]. Under the Regulations, a commercial agent is entitled to whatever is customary in the place where he carries out his activities (ie French rates for agents operating in France) or a reasonable amount. Even if payment is expressly or impliedly agreed that does not mean that the agent can deduct the payment from any sums in his possession to which the principal is entitled (ie reasonable remuneration for what has been done) unless the contract expressly authorises such a retention.

In the absence of a contract of agency the agent may be entitled to be paid on a quantum meruit basis. However, where an agent is to be paid on the occurrence of a certain event, such as visiting 15 potential clients, there can be no claim for a quantum meruit if the event does not occur[6], even if the agent has incurred expense or expended time in trying to bring about the desired event.

1 *Reeve v Reeve* (1858) 1 F & F 280. Supply of Goods and Services Act 1982, s 15.
2 See for example, *Kofi Sunkersette Obu v Strauss & Co Ltd* [1951] AC 243, in which the Privy Council refused to allow an agent to recover any commission in a case where the contract of agency provided that the amount of commission, *if any*, was to be fixed by the principal.

3 Para 10.12, above.
4 *Way v Latilla* [1937] 3 All ER 759, HL.
5 For when the courts will imply terms into contracts, see paras 8.38–8.42, above.
6 *Howard Houlder & Partners Ltd v Manx Isles SS Co Ltd* [1923] 1 KB 110.

23.25 Commission As we said in the previous paragraph an agent employed under a contract of agency is entitled to be paid only if he has performed, *precisely and completely*, the obligations in the agency agreement. Thus, if the agent is entitled to commission only if he effects a sale of an item he is entitled to nothing if he merely introduces a ready and willing purchaser but no sale follows (unless the contract provides for payment for partial performance).

Indeed in English law, the mere occurrence of the transaction which the agent is entrusted to effect does not entitle the agent to commission: the occurrence must be brought about by the agent unless, the contract provides that he is to be paid however the desired result occurs[1]. If the agent is a commercial agent and is remunerated wholly or in part by commission regs 7 to 10 determine when it is payable.

If the principal hinders the earning of commission by the agent, the agent cannot recover any commission thereby lost or sue the principal, unless the contract of agency contains a term that the principal will not hinder the agent in his efforts to earn his commission. If it is not an express term the courts are reluctant to imply such a term into a contract of agency[2]. It would seem that the principal of a commercial agent would be liable for hindering the earning of commission – it is surely a breach of reg 4 (the duty to act dutifully and in good faith).

Even if an agent complies with his instructions, he cannot recover any commission in respect of a transaction rendered void or illegal by statute[3]. An agent who is in breach of his duties towards his principal normally forfeits his right to commission[4], unless the breach is a technical one and the agent has acted honestly[5].

1 *Millar, Son & Co v Radford* (1903) 19 TLR 575, CA.
2 *Luxor (Eastbourne) Ltd v Cooper* [1941] AC 108, [1941] 1 All ER 33, HL; *Marcan Shipping (London) Ltd v Polish SS Co* [1988] 2 Lloyd's Rep 171; but for a case where such a term was implied see *Alpha Trading Ltd v Dunnshaw-Patten Ltd* [1980] 2 Lloyd's Rep 284. See also para 23.31, below.
3 Chap 15.
4 *Salomons v Pender* (1865) 3 H & C 639.
5 *Keppel v Wheeler* [1927] 1 KB 577, CA.

Indemnity
23.26 An agent who has suffered loss or incurred liabilities in the course of carrying out authorised actions for his principal is entitled to be reimbursed or indemnified by the principal[1]. However, he has no right to reimbursement or an indemnity for losses or liabilities arising because of breaches of duty by him, eg failing to comply with his instructions, or arising in his carrying out an illegal transaction, or a transaction rendered void by statute[2].

1 *Hooper v Treffry* (1847) 1 Exch 17.
2 *Capp v Topham* (1805) 6 East 392; *Gasson v Cole* (1910) 26 TLR 468.

Right to information
23.27 English law has not formulated an obligation whereby a principal must provide his agent with relevant information although a term to this effect might well be implied into a contract of agency. If the agent is a commercial agent, reg 4 provides that the principal must provide his agent with the necessary documentation relating to the goods concerned and the information necessary for the performance of the agency contract[1].

1 The principal has a specific obligation to warn his agent once he anticipates that the volume of transactions will be significantly lower than the commercial agent might normally have expected.

Sub-agents
23.28 Even where an agent is authorised to appoint a sub-agent to carry out his instructions[1], it is presumed that the person appointed is merely an agent of the agent; he does not, in the absence of clear evidence, become an agent of the principal[2]. As a result, the sub-agent has no claim against the principal for remuneration or indemnity, nor does he owe the principal any duty to act or to obey instructions.

In contrast it seems that a sub-agent who knew both of the existence and of the identity of the principal could owe the principal a duty of care under the normal principles of negligence[3] and might owe the principal fiduciary duties[4]. Moreover it has been suggested that, at least in relation to the principal's property[5], a duty might be owed to an unnamed principal.

1 An agent who is authorised to delegate must use reasonable care and skill in selecting the sub-agent; *Aiken v Stewart Wrightson Members' Agency Ltd* [1995] 3 All ER 449, [1995] 1 WLR 1281.
2 *Calico Printers' Association Ltd v Barclays Bank Ltd* (1931) 145 LT 51, CA.
3 *Henderson v Merrett Syndicates Ltd* [1995] 2 AC 145, [1994] 3 All ER 506, HL. For liability for negligence generally see Chap 18.
4 *Powell and Thomas v Evan Jones & Co* [1905] 1 KB 11, CA; cf *New Zealand and Australian Land Co v Watson* (1881) 7 QBD 374, CA.
5 *Balsamo v Medici* [1984] 2 All ER 304, [1984] 1 WLR 951; the sub-agent in this case was unknown to the principal who had not authorised his appointment but the judge stated, obiter, that the sub-agent owed a duty to take reasonable care of the goods of the owner whether or not he knew the owner's identity.

Termination of agency
23.29 A contract of agency may be terminated, like any other contract, by agreement[1], by performance[2], by breach[3] or by frustration[4]. It is important to remember that termination of agency between principal and agent may not terminate the agent's authority to bind his principal (see paras 23.41–23.44, below). In addition, there are certain special rules applicable to termination of agency, including some rules relating only to commercial agents, which we now discuss.

1 Paras 6.35–6.41, above
2 Chap 9.
3 Chap 10.
4 Chap 11.

Termination by the parties

23.30 A contract of agency will not be specifically enforced, because it is a contract for personal services[1]. As a corollary, either party may terminate the relationship at will albeit the termination may amount to a breach of contract. For example, where the agency was for a fixed period which has not expired, or where a required period of notice has not been given. If so, the innocent party is entitled to damages, but the relationship of agency itself is nonetheless determined[2].

As to whether termination of an agency relationship without notice amounts to a breach of contract (rendering the party in breach liable to pay damages), we have already seen[3] that if an agent accepts a bribe his contract of agency can be terminated without notice. Other contracts on their true construction allow either principal or agent to terminate the agreement without any notice[4]. For example, if an agent is employed on a commission basis, so that he is only entitled to remuneration when he does the act required by the agency agreement, for example, selling a house, such a contract can be terminated without notice[5]. Agency contracts which resemble contracts of employment, in that the agent is paid merely for being an agent rather than for facilitating a particular transaction, require notice[6].

There are some cases where the authority of an agent is irrevocable. Under s 4 of the Powers of Attorney Act 1971, a power of attorney, expressed to be irrevocable and given to secure a proprietary interest of the donee of the power, cannot be revoked by the donor of that power without the consent of the donee or by the death, insanity or bankruptcy of the donor. Also, if the agent is given authority by deed, or for valuable consideration, to effect a security or to protect an interest of the agent, that authority is irrevocable while the security or interest subsists[7]. Again, an authority coupled with an interest is not revoked by the death, insanity or bankruptcy of the donor.

1 *Chinnock v Sainsbury* (1860) 30 LJ Ch 409; para 12.26, above.
2 *Page One Records Ltd v Britton* [1967] 3 All ER 822, [1968] 1 WLR 157.
3 Para 23.21, above.
4 *Atkinson v Cotesworth* (1825) 3 B & C 647. Notice is always required for the termination of a commercial agency which is not for a fixed term.
5 *Motion v Michaud* (1892) 8 TLR 253; affd (1892) 8 TLR 447, CA.
6 *Parker v Ibbetson* (1858) 4 CBNS 346; *Martin-Baker Aircraft Co Ltd v Canadian Flight Equipment Ltd* [1955] 2 QB 556, [1955] 2 All ER 722.
7 *Gaussen v Morton* (1830) 10 B & C 731.

23.31 A problem may arise where a principal, without actually revoking his agent's authority, effectively brings the agency to an end; for example, by closing down the business to which it relates. In order to recover damages for loss of prospective earnings, the agent must be able to prove that the principal's action amounts to a breach either of an express term of the contract of agency or of one necessarily implied to give business efficacy[1]; namely that he would not deprive his agent of the chance to earn his commission. The courts are slow to imply such terms. In *Rhodes v Forwood*[2], a colliery owner appointed brokers as sole agents for the sale of his coal in Liverpool for seven years or as long as he did business there. After four years the colliery was sold. It was held that the owner had not contracted, either expressly or impliedly, to keep the brokers supplied with coal for sale, and he was therefore not liable for breach of contract. A similar example is provided by *French & Co Ltd v Leeston Shipping Co*[3]. Agents who arranged the charter of a ship for 18 months were to be paid commission on the basis of the monthly chartering fee. The charterers bought the ship after four months, thereby terminating the contract of charter. It was held that the agents were not entitled to claim the commission which they would have earned if the charter had continued for the full 18 months. On the other hand, in *Turner v Goldsmith*[4], a shirt manufacturer expressly agreed to employ a travelling salesman for five years, but his factory was destroyed by fire after only two years. It was held that the manufacturer was not released from his obligation to provide his agent with a chance to earn commission, so that the agent was entitled to damages.

Whether closing down the relevant business terminates a commercial agency is not covered by the Regulations. We assume that the principles outlined above apply.

1 Paras 8.41 and 8.42, above.
2 (1876) 1 App Cas 256, HL.
3 [1922] 1 AC 451, HL.
4 [1891] 1 QB 544, CA.

Death

23.32 The death of a principal or of an agent determines the agency[1]. The actual authority of an agent (and probably also ostensible authority) ceases on the death of his principal and any transactions entered into thereafter bind the agent, but not the principal's estate, even if the agent does not know of the death[2].

1 *Blades v Free* (1829) 9 B & C 167; *Friend v Young* [1897] 2 Ch 421. A commercial agent's estate is entitled to an indemnity or compensation when death terminates the agency contract, see para 23.36, below.
2 *Blades v Free* (1829) 9 B & C 167.

Insanity

23.33 Generally, if a principal becomes insane the agency and any actual authority are terminated[1]. However, where an agent has ostensible authority, this survives his principal's insanity, and any contract entered into by him is binding upon the principal, unless the third party knew of the insanity[2].

1 The appointment of an agent appointed in compliance with the Enduring Powers of Attorney Act 1985 does not terminate on the insanity of the principal. A commercial agent who becomes insane will be entitled to an indemnity or compensation if the insanity terminates the agency, see further para 23.36, below.
2 *Drew v Nunn* (1879) 4 QBD 661, CA.

Bankruptcy

23.34 The bankruptcy of a principal terminates a contract of agency[1]. On the other hand, the bankruptcy of an agent does not automatically determine the agency, unless it prevents the agent acting as agent[2].

1 *Elliott v Turquand* (1881) 7 App Cas 79, PC.
2 *McCall v Australian Meat Co Ltd* (1870) 19 WR 188.

Effects of termination of agency

23.35 While the termination of agency cannot deprive the agent of any rights to commission or indemnity which have already accrued[1], it prevents him from acquiring such rights in the future[2]. Furthermore, an agent who continues to act may become liable to a third party for breach of warranty of authority, even if he is unaware that his actual authority has been determined[3].

In the absence of ostensible authority, a principal is not usually bound by anything which his agent does after termination of the agency. However, where the agency is created by deed, both an agent and a third party are given statutory protection in respect of transactions effected after termination, provided that they were unaware of the termination[4].

Where the person whose agency has been terminated is a commercial agent there are special rules relating to compensation which we discuss in the next paragraph.

1 *Chappell v Bray* (1860) 6 H & N 145.
2 *Farrow v Wilson* (1869) LR 4 CP 744; *Pool v Pool* (1889) 58 LJP 67.
3 *Yonge v Toynbee* [1910] 1 KB 215, CA. If the agent retains ostensible authority and acts within the scope of it he cannot, of course, incur such liability.
4 Powers of Attorney Act 1971, s 5.

23.36 *Special rights of commercial agents* Where the principal either terminates the contract of agency, other than for one of the reasons set out in the Regulations, or a fixed term contract expires, or the agent terminates the contract due to circumstances attributable to the principal, the principal must compensate or indemnify the agent[1]. Compensation is not payable if the agent's default justifies immediate termination or if exceptional circumstances arise, but it is payable if the agent dies or is too ill to carry out his activities. It appears that the philosophy underpinning this provision is that the agent may well have established a market and goodwill for his principal within an area and that to allow the principal simply to replace the original agent (with a cheaper one it is assumed) after the hard work has been done would be unjust. It is not possible to contract out of this provision[2].

Regulation 17 provides that the commercial agent is entitled to be compensated for termination of office unless the agency contract provides for indemnification. Indemnity in this context means a sum to represent the capitalised value of the agent's lost remuneration up to a maximum of one year's remuneration calculated by reference to the average of the previous five years' remuneration. Compensation is not necessarily the equivalent of the amount which might be paid for breach of the agency contract by the principal, since these provisions apply even if the principal is not in breach[3].

1 Regulations 17 and 18.
2 Regulation 19.
3 Where the principal is in breach damages may also be claimed.

Principal and Third Parties

23.37 If an agent has *authority* to make a contract for his principal it is called an authorised contract and the principal is deemed to have made the contract.

If a principal is a disclosed principal, he alone is deemed to have entered into the contract, except in certain limited circumstances set out later. Thus, a disclosed principal alone may sue and be sued on authorised contracts made by his agent. If a principal is undisclosed then both principal and agent can sue or be sued on the authorised contract.

A contract or other transaction, such as a disposition of property, which is not authorised does *not* bind the principal but the agent may incur personal liability in respect thereof.

An agent's authority may take various forms.

The authority of agents

Actual authority

23.38 An agent who has been expressly appointed may have both express and implied actual authority. An agent appointed by implied agreement has implied actual authority.

Express authority is conferred by the agreement (which is usually a contract) creating the agency relationship. Implied authority consists of those terms which will be implied into the contract of agency by applying the usual rules for the implication of terms into contracts[1].

It should be noted that, as between principal and agent, express authority is paramount. An agent who disobeys an express instruction cannot avoid liability to his principal on the ground that his actions lay within what would otherwise be his implied authority. However, as far as third parties are concerned, they are entitled to assume, until they have notice to the contrary, that the agent has whatever authority would usually be implied into the contract of agency common in the relevant trade or business. Hence, an agent acting within the usual authority of agents of his type can bind his principal vis-à-vis a third party, even if he is disobeying the express instructions of his principal[2].

Certain types of implied actual authority are well recognised, for instance, incidental and customary authority.

1 Paras 8.18 and 8.38–8.42, above.
2 *Watteau v Fenwick* [1893] 1 QB 346; *Daun v Simmins* (1879) 41 LT 783, CA.

23.39 Incidental authority has been described as conferring authority to do 'all subordinate acts incident to and necessary for the execution of [express actual] authority'[1]. Thus, incidental authority supplements the actual authority of the agent and gives the agent authority to undertake tasks which are incidental to his authorised task. It is a question of fact in every case whether a particular action is incidental to the authorised purpose of the agent. For example, a solicitor who is engaged in litigation on behalf of a client has the power to compromise that action[2].

1 *Collen v Gardener* (1856) 21 Beav 540.
2 *Waugh v HB Clifford & Sons Ltd* [1982] Ch 374, [1982] 1 All ER 1095, CA.

23.40   Customary authority arises in two situations.

First, an agent operating in a particular market or business has the authority which an agent operating in that market or business usually has[1].

Second, an agent who occupies a particular position either in his principal's business (such as company secretary or foreman[2]) or in his own right (such as stockbroker or auctioneer) has a type of customary authority commonly called usual authority. Usual authority of this type only arises when the agent has been properly appointed by his principal to the post or office which he occupies. A person who, while not properly appointed to a post or office, is held out by a person with actual authority as being the legitimate holder of that post or office has ostensible authority which is co-extensive with the usual authority which he would have had if he had been properly appointed.

Usual authority confers on a person the authority to undertake any tasks which an agent in that position usually has authority to make[3]. For example, in *Panorama Developments (Guildford) Ltd v Fidelis Furnishing Fabrics Ltd*[4], the company appointed X its company secretary; as such he was an agent of the company. It was held that the company was liable to pay for cars hired by X in the company's name, even when he used them for his own and not the company's purposes, because hiring cars was within the customary usual authority of an agent holding the position of company secretary.

1   *Bayliffe v Butterworth* (1847) 1 Exch 425.
2   *Hely-Hutchinson v Brayhead Ltd* [1967] 2 All ER 14; affd on other grounds by the Court of Appeal.
3   What is usual is adjudged by reference to current practice in the relevant trade or business, which may change. See, eg, *United Bank of Kuwait v Hammoud* [1988] 3 All ER 418, [1988] 1 WLR 1051, CA, in which it was found to be usual for solicitors to give certain undertakings on behalf of clients.
4   [1971] 2 QB 711, [1971] 3 All ER 16, CA.

Ostensible authority

23.41   Ostensible (or apparent) authority arises when the alleged principal makes a representation of fact, often by conduct, to a third party that a person is authorised to act on his behalf (even though he may not be) and the third party relies upon that representation. It must be stressed that the effect of ostensible authority is not to create an agency relationship between the alleged principal and agent, nor does it extend the actual authority of the agent in relation to his alleged principal, but rather permits the agent to alter the legal position of his apparent principal in relation to third parties who are unaware that the intermediary does not have authority.

Ostensible authority is of great importance either where a principal has restricted (or terminated) the actual authority of his validly appointed agent or where the apparent agent has never been appointed an agent at all (in which case there can be no actual authority). As between principal and agent, a restriction (or termination) is binding and an agent will be liable to his principal should he ignore it; but third parties who are entitled to rely on ostensible authority are not bound by any restriction or termination[1] of which they are unaware.

1   The same is true when an agent has usual authority.

23.42 *Creation of ostensible authority* For ostensible authority to be created in respect of a transaction the following conditions must be satisfied.

a. There must be a *representation* or holding out[1]. For example, if a company permits X to act as its managing director although he has not been appointed to that post, the company represents that X is its managing director and cannot deny his authority to bind the company in respect of transactions normally entered into by managing directors.

b. The representation must be one of fact and it must be made by the alleged principal (or an authorised agent acting on his behalf) to the third party. Thus, the alleged agent cannot hold himself out as an agent of the alleged principal[2].

c. The third party must *rely* upon the representation. When the alleged principal has made a representation a third party who knows that the agent is not authorised cannot claim to have relied upon it[3]. This follows logically from the principle that ostensible authority is based on the belief raised in the mind of the third party by the representation of the alleged principal[4].

1 For two statutory versions of ostensible authority see in relation to partners the Partnership Act 1890, s 14, discussed in para. 24.47, below.
2 *Armagas Ltd v Mundogas SA* [1986] AC 717, [1986] 2 All ER 385, HL, in which the alleged agent made his own representation that he had authority to conclude a charterparty and the third party was unable to rely on ostensible authority. But see *First Energy (UK) Ltd v Hungarian International Bank* [1993] 2 Lloyd's Rep 194, [1993] BCLC 1409, CA, in which an intermediary who informed the third party that authority, which could have been delegated to him, had been delegated to him by his Head Office, was found to have ostensible authority.
3 *Overbrooke Estates Ltd v Glencombe Properties Ltd* [1974] 3 All ER 511, [1974] 1 WLR 1335, CA; it is thought, but not certain, that if the third party should have known that the agent did not have authority he is disentitled to rely on the representation.
4 For a particular difficulty concerning companies see para 25.35, below.

23.43 *Operation of ostensible authority* The effect of the impression created by the alleged principal in the mind of the third party may be either:

a. the extension of the authority of a properly appointed agent beyond that which is usual for an agent of that type; or

b. that a person who is not a properly appointed agent may be treated as such an agent (agency by estoppel). In this case the authority conferred upon the agent is equivalent to the usual authority of a properly appointed agent occupying a similar position or such wider authority as the principal has represented the agent as possessing[1].

Ostensible authority may operate in a single transaction. For instance, if a person stands by and watches someone acting on his behalf he conveys the impression to the third party that the intermediary is acting for him and he is bound in respect of that transaction.

Ostensible authority can also operate in a series of transactions. If a person has frequently allowed an unauthorised person to act for him, he may be unable to deny that the person had ostensible authority to act for him either in similar future transactions or in transactions which would fall within his usual authority if he had been properly appointed as an agent of the type he is held out to be. In *Swiss Air Transport Co Ltd v Palmer*[2], for example, an agent had frequently been held out as having authority to arrange shipments of wigs. It was held that he had ostensible authority to arrange further shipments of wigs and other items over the same routes without any further holding out by the principal, but that he had no ostensible authority to purchase an air ticket for himself.

1 *Freeman and Lockyer (a firm) v Buckhurst Park Properties (Mangal) Ltd* [1964] 2 QB 480, [1964] 1 All ER 630, CA.
2 [1976] 2 Lloyd's Rep 604.

23.44 Acts within the ostensible authority of an agent bind the alleged principal even if they are entered into for the agent's own purposes or are fraudulent, provided the fraud occurs while he is purporting to carry out what he is ostensibly authorised to do[1].

1 *Lloyd v Grace, Smith & Co* [1912] AC 716, HL; see also paras 17.26 and 17.27, above.

The disclosed principal
23.45 A disclosed principal is one whose existence, though not necessarily his identity, is known to the third party at the time of contracting. To put it another way, a principal is disclosed wherever the third party is aware that he is dealing with an agent.

If the agent of a disclosed principal makes an authorised contract, the principal can almost invariably sue and be sued upon it[1]. Whether the agent also can sue or be sued on the contract is a question which we discuss in paras 23.50–23.54, below.

1 *Montgomerie v United Kingdom Mutual SS Association* [1891] 1 QB 370.

The undisclosed principal
23.46 If the third party is unaware that he is dealing with an agent, the principal is called an undisclosed principal. An undisclosed principal can sue and be sued on authorised contracts entered into on his behalf[1]. The agent can also sue and be sued on such contracts[1]. For example, as we explained in Chapter 8, the Sale of Goods Act 1979[2], implies into contracts for the sale of goods, when those goods are sold in the course of a business, a requirement that the goods are of satisfactory quality. Where goods are sold by an agent both the principal and the agent incur liability if the goods are not satisfactory[2].

It may seem odd that the third party can be sued by someone with whom he did not know he was contracting and with whom he may not have wished to contract, but it is justified on grounds of commercial convenience[3]. To protect the third party certain limitations have been placed on the right of the undisclosed principal to sue.

1 *Siu Yin Kwan v Eastern Insurance Co Ltd* [1994] 2 AC 199, [1994] 1 All ER 213, PC.
2 *Boyter v Thomson* [1995] 2 AC 628, [1995] 3 All ER 135, HL; s 14 will not impose liability on a principal who is not selling in the course of a business and the buyer knows this or reasonable steps are taken to draw it to the buyer's attention.

3 In *Welsh Development Agency v Export Finance Co Ltd* [1992] BCLC 148, the Court of Appeal accepted that the historical view, that an undisclosed principal was a party to the contract made by his agent, was anomalous.

Limitations on the right of the undisclosed principal to sue

23.47 An undisclosed principal cannot sue:

a.   If he did not exist or lacked capacity at the time the agent contracted[1].

b.   If the contract expressly prohibits the intervention of an undisclosed principal[2].

c.   If the contract impliedly but clearly excludes the intervention of an undisclosed principal, as where, for example, the contract is worded in such a way as to indicate that the agent is contracting as principal[3]. Merely because the agent contracts in a manner which is *consistent* with him being a principal does not necessarily exclude the intervention of an undisclosed principal. In a recent case[4], an agent signed a policy of insurance as 'employer' of X. This did not preclude the principal, the actual employer of X, enforcing the contract of insurance. The courts will not readily find that a contract impliedly precludes the intervention of an undisclosed principal.

d.   If the third party can establish that he had some reason for wishing to deal with the agent personally. An example would be where the agent was a man of fine reputation and acknowledged skill, and the contract involved reliance on such integrity and skill[5].

e.   If the third party would have a defence to an action by the agent. This may arise when the third party has a right of set-off against the agent. However, this only prevents the undisclosed principal from suing where it is his conduct which has enabled the agent to appear to be dealing on his own account[6].

f.   If the third party's legal position would be materially worse as a result of the undisclosed principal's intervention[7]. For example, where a person became a protected tenant of a flat, it was held that evidence could not be brought to show that she had taken the lease as agent for an undisclosed principal, since this would increase the number of people who would be entitled to security of tenure under the Rent Act[8].

Apart from these cases, an undisclosed principal can intervene on the contract, even it seems where it is clear that the third party would have refused for personal reasons to deal with him, provided that there has been no positive misrepresentation as to the identity of the principal[9]. Note that payment by the third party to the agent absolves the third party from liability to the undisclosed principal.

1 Para 23.6, above.
2 *United Kingdom Mutual SS Assurance Association v Nevill* (1887) 19 QBD 110, CA.
3 *Humble v Hunter* (1848) 12 QB 310.
4 *Siu Yin Kwan v Eastern Insurance Co Ltd* [1994] 2 AC 199, [1994] 1 All ER 213, PC, approving the earlier decision in *Fred Drughorn Ltd v Rederiaktiebolaget Trans-Atlantic* [1919] AC 203, HL.
5 *Collins v Associated Greyhounds Racecourses Ltd* [1930] 1 Ch 1, CA; *Nash v Dix* (1898) 78 LT 445.
6 *Isaac Cooke & Sons v Eshelby* (1887) 12 App Cas 271, HL.

7   *Collins v Associated Greyhounds Racecourses Ltd* [1930] 1 Ch 1, CA.
8   *Hanstown Properties Ltd v Green* (1977) 246 Estates Gazette 917, CA.
9   *Dyster v Randall & Sons* [1926] Ch 932. In *Said v Butt* [1920] 3 KB 497, it was suggested
    that the undisclosed principal could not intervene when the third party could show that he
    would not have dealt with the principal even in the absence of such a representation but the
    correctness of this decision on this basis is in doubt.

Election

23.48   If an agent has acted on behalf of an undisclosed principal, or in any
other case where an agent is jointly liable on a contract with his principal, the
third party may elect to sue the principal or the agent[1]. This election may be
express or implied. An implied election will only occur if a third party with full
knowledge of all the relevant facts indicates clearly which party he intends to
hold liable on the contract[2]. What constitutes implied election is a question of
fact; beginning legal proceedings[3], demanding payment, and debiting an
account[4] are all relevant but not conclusive factors. Where principal and agent
are jointly liable, a third party can sue one of them and obtain judgment without
forfeiting his right to sue the other[5].

1   *Paterson v Gandasequi* (1812) 15 East 62.
2   *Thomson v Davenport* (1829) 9 B & C 78.
3   *Clarkson Booker Ltd v Andjel* [1964] 2 QB 775, [1964] 3 All ER 260, CA.
4   *Young & Co Ltd v White* (1911) 28 TLR 87.
5   Civil Liability (Contribution) Act 1978, s 3; see para 17.14, above.

Agents and Third Parties

23.49   As we have seen, where an agent makes an authorised contract on
behalf of an undisclosed principal, the agent can sue and be sued upon the
contract[1]. Where an agent makes an authorised contract on behalf of a disclosed
principal, the general rule is that the agent cannot sue or be sued on the
contract[2]. However, in certain cases set out below, an agent is liable under,
and can enforce, the contract either alone or jointly with his disclosed principal.

1   *Saxon v Blake* (1861) 29 Beav 438.
2   *Wakefield v Duckworth & Co* [1915] 1 KB 218, CA.

Contracts made by deed

23.50   An agent who enters into a contract made by deed is liable on it, even
if he is known to be contracting as an agent[1].

1   *Schack v Anthony* (1813) 1 M & S 573.

Trade custom

23.51   If a trade custom, not inconsistent with the contract, makes an agent
liable on a contract, the courts will give effect to that custom[1].

1   *Barrow & Bros v Dyster, Nalder & Co* (1884) 13 QBD 635, DC.

Negotiable instruments

23.52   An agent will be personally liable on a negotiable instrument if he
signs his name as a party to the instrument, unless he indicates that he is

signing on behalf of a principal[1]. Merely signing 'as agent' will not necessarily suffice to exempt the agent from personal liability.

1   Bills of Exchange Act 1882, s 26. We define negotiable instruments in para 22.20, above.

Where the agent is in fact principal

23.53   If an agent contracts on behalf of a non-existent principal then the agent must be contracting on his own behalf[1]. If X purports to contract as agent but is in fact the principal it seems that he can sue and be sued on the contract[2]. However, in cases where an 'agent' has contracted on behalf of a named person, but that person is in fact a non-existent principal, the 'agent' cannot sue or be sued on the contract[3] unless the contract merely indicates the existence of a principal and it appears that the identity of the principal is not relevant to the other contracting party[4]. The cases in this area are generally considered to be very unsatisfactory.

1   See, in relation to unformed companies, the Companies Act 1985, s 36C and para 23.11, above.
2   *Gardiner v Heading* [1928] 2 KB 284, CA; accepted without discussion in *Fraser v Thames Television Ltd* [1984] QB 44, [1983] 2 All ER 101.
3   *Fairlie v Fenton* (1870) LR 5 Exch 169. The 'agent' could be liable for breach of warranty of authority.
4   *Schmaltz v Avery* (1851) 16 QB 655.

Other cases

23.54   Apart from these special cases, an agent may be jointly or solely liable on the contract entered into on behalf of his disclosed principal, if the contract expressly or impliedly reveals this to be the intention of the parties. Under s 5 of the Partnership Act 1890[1], a partner who contracts on behalf of the partnership is jointly liable with the rest of the partners on that contract. In other cases, whether there is an implied intention that an agent shall be jointly or solely liable on the contract is a question of construction[2].

Particular note is taken of the description of the agent in a written contract and of how the agent signed a written contract. If the document describes the agent as an agent and he signs 'as agent' he is not liable on the contract[3]. If neither the document nor the signature describes him as an agent he is usually liable on the contract[4], even if he is known to be acting as an agent. If either the document or the signature reveals him to be an agent, the question of his personal liability is one of fact[5]. If the contract is oral and the agent is known to be an agent, the above rules for written contracts do not apply and every case is determined by reference to its particular facts[6]. If an agent is liable on a contract he will probably also have the benefit of that contract, unless, as a matter of construction, the contract reveals that the agent is to be liable without having the benefit of the contract.

An agent is not personally liable on a contract merely because he has entered into it without the authority of his principal.

1   Para 24.37, below.
2   But see the doctrine of election, para 23.48, above.
3   *Lucas v Beale* (1851) 10 CB 739.
4   *Basma v Weekes* [1950] AC 441, [1950] 2 All ER 146, PC; *Universal Steam Navigation Co Ltd v J McKelvie & Co* [1923] AC 492, HL.

5   *Burrell v Jones* (1819) 3 B & Ald 47.
6   *N & J Vlassopulos Ltd v Ney Shipping Ltd* [1977] 1 Lloyd's Rep 478, CA.

Rights of third parties against agents

23.55   In addition to any right to sue on the contract a third party may be able to sue an agent for breach of warranty of authority or in tort.

For breach of warranty of authority

23.56   If a person acts as agent, knowing that he has no actual authority, he is liable to the third party for breach of warranty of authority if he has represented to the third party that he had authority and the third party relied on that representation and thereby suffered loss[1]. Purporting to act as agent constitutes a representation of authority, unless the third party knew or ought to have known of the lack of authority[2].

Even if an agent who lacks authority genuinely and reasonably believes he has it, when he has not, he may be liable to the third party[3]. In *Yonge v Toynbee*[4], an agent acting on behalf of his principal was held liable for breach of warranty of authority when, entirely unknown to him, his authority had been terminated by the insanity of his principal. The third party can sue the agent even if he has not entered into a contract, provided he has altered his position in reliance on the representation.

If the representation made by an agent is one of law, not fact, he is not liable if it is untrue[5]. An action for breach of warranty cannot lie if the principal ratifies the unauthorised act.

The amount of damages which may be awarded under this head is the amount which would put the third party in the same position as if the representation (of authority) had been true[6]. Therefore, where the third party could recover nothing from the principal, even if the agent had had authority, he can recover nothing for breach of warranty of authority.

1   *Collen v Wright* (1857) 8 E & B 647. If the misrepresentation of authority is made fraudulently
    or negligently an action for damages in tort for deceit or negligence will also lie.
2   *Halbot v Lens* [1901] 1 Ch 344.
3   *Yonge v Toynbee* [1910] 1 KB 215, CA.
4   [1910] 1 KB 215, CA.
5   *Beattie v Lord Ebury* (1872) 7 Ch App 777.
6   *Richardson v Williamson and Lawson* (1871) LR 6 QB 276.

In tort

23.57   If an agent commits a tort in the course of his agency, his principal is vicariously liable for it[1]. However, an agent may also be personally liable in tort, for example, for deceit or under the rules relating to negligent misstatements[2].

1   See paras 17.26 and 17.27, above.
2   See para 14.20 above and paras 18.13–18.19, above.

Chapter 24

Partnership

24.1 In this chapter we consider the law relating to the formation and termination of partnerships, the liability of partners to third parties and the rights of partners between each other.

All statutory references in this chapter are to the Partnership Act 1890, which largely codified existing commercial practice, unless otherwise indicated. The Partnership Act applies to all partnerships except to the extent that the partners have agreed, and are permitted, to exclude its provisions. In general terms, the partners can exclude those provisions of the Act which govern their rights and duties vis-à-vis each other but cannot exclude those terms of the Act which regulate the relationship of the partnership and third parties.

Types of business organisation

24.2 A person who decides to engage in trade or business may at the outset choose to operate by himself as a sole trader, or in conjunction with others either as a partnership or as a company. Alternatively, a sole trader currently operating a business may decide to turn that business into a partnership or a company; the reverse process is rare.

A sole trader, who does not necessarily *operate* the business on his own, is subject to the usual legal rules imposed upon all of us. Thus, he is bound by the rules of contract and tort and must pay income tax. A sole trader owns his business, the responsibilities of management are his, the debts of the business are his but so are any profits.

A partnership consists of two or more persons who between them own and run the business. A partnership is subject to a legal regime that combines the law applicable to individuals (especially contract and agency) and also some special rules applicable only to partnerships. A partnership, which may be called a firm[1], is not a legal person distinct from its members[2] and the partners are each responsible for the debts of the partnership, but it can sue and be sued and enter into contracts in its own name. The profits of the partnership belong to the partners and are subject to income tax in their hands. The death of a partner automatically terminates the partnership[3].

A company is a separate legal entity subject to a complex legal regime combining common law, equity and innumerable statutory provisions. The shareholders and directors are not usually responsible for the debts of the company and there is no implied right to participate in management, nor is there any right to the profits generated by the company (which profits are subject to corporation tax). The death of a shareholder or director of a company (or even, all the shareholders and directors) does not in itself affect the existence of the company. Company law is dealt with in the next two chapters.

1 Section 4.
2 In Scotland a partnership is a separate legal entity but the partners remain liable for the debts of the partnership.
3 Section 33; the partnership agreement can exclude the operation of the section.

Formation and Termination of Partnerships

Formation of a partnership

24.3 Section 1 defines partnership as the 'relationship which subsists between persons carrying on a business in common with a view to profit'. Section 1(2) expressly excludes shareholders in a company from being in partnership, even though they may well satisfy this definition. In addition, s 2, which we discuss below, also precludes certain relationships from being partnerships.

The necessary relationship, which is almost certain to be a contract, may be based on a written, oral or even an implied agreement. There is no legal requirement that a partnership agreement must be in a particular form although it is obviously sensible, for the avoidance of disputes, for the agreement to be in writing. In the absence of an agreement to the contrary, the relationship of the partners to each other is governed by the provisions of the Act.

In the next three paragraphs (24.4–24.6, below) we consider the purpose of the partnership, the name of the partnership and the relevance of the intention of the parties in determining if there is a partnership. We then turn (paras 24.7–24.12, below) to the individual elements of the definition of a partnership given in s 1.

Purpose of formation

24.4 A partnership can be formed for any purpose which the partners choose provided that the purpose is not illegal[1]. A partnership which was formed for a purpose which was lawful but which becomes illegal is automatically dissolved[2].

Obviously, where persons have combined for an illegal purpose they are unlikely to bring their disputes to court. However, if such a 'partnership' is the subject of litigation, a court would not enforce any purported rights of the parties between themselves, for example, by requiring one partner to contribute to losses incurred by another, nor would a court adjudicate on the disposition of any ill-gotten profits.

A splendid example is provided by *Everet v Williams*[3], in which two highwaymen, E and W, having concluded a successful joint enterprise over a number of years, fell into dispute as to the division of the proceeds of their activities and were imprudent enough to petition the court for a ruling on this point. The court held that no ruling would be made, that counsel must pay the costs of the proceedings personally, that both solicitors be fined and one be transported, and that both litigants be hanged.

Where a partnership is void on the ground of illegality, a creditor, whose claim is otherwise valid and who was unaware of the illegality at the time his debt was incurred, can seek recompense from an individual 'partner'.

1   See Chap 15 for a discussion of illegality.
2   Section 34; see para 24.25, below.
3   (1725) discussed in 9 LQR 197.

Name
24.5   A partnership can generally operate under any name it chooses. However, the use of certain words is prohibited[1] and the use of other words requires permission from the government or a government-designated body[2]. The firm's name may be a combination of the names of the partners (or others), or a name descriptive of their business (eg 'Bright Sparks Electrical Contractors'), provided that the chosen name does not involve the commission of the tort of passing off[3]. Somewhat confusingly, a partnership can use the word 'company' or '& Co' in its name but cannot include the words 'limited' or 'public limited company'.

The Business Names Act 1985 requires the names of all partners, and a British address for the service of documents on them, to be stated on all business letters and documents[4]. Firms with more than 20 partners are exempt provided that anyone dealing with the firm has access to this information[4].

1   Business Names Act 1985, s 2.
2   Ibid, s 3.
3   Para 25.17, below.
4   Section 4.

Intention as a factor to determine whether a partnership has been formed
24.6   When a relationship clearly falls within the ambit of s 1 it is a partnership even if the parties seek to exclude this result[1]. Conversely, the mere fact that the relevant parties call themselves 'partners' is not conclusive evidence that they are in partnership. However, where the parties so conduct themselves that their relationship might well be construed as that of partners, their intentions (as manifested by their words and conduct) are important factors in determining if they are to be regarded as partners.

A case indicating that a declaration by the parties that they are *not* partners is not conclusive is *Malin v Customs and Excise Comrs*[2]. In *Malin*, two brothers both independently operated as builders from their own premises. They often worked together but employed no staff in common and contended that they were not partners. The VAT Tribunal held that their stated intention not to be partners was insufficient to override the clear evidence to the contrary, viz, a joint insurance policy, a joint trading name (Malins Contractors), application for council work in which they described themselves as partners, and a joint bank account with profits split equally.

The importance of the apparent intention of the parties is illustrated in the case of a person who works for a firm under the title 'salaried partner'. In *Stekel v Ellice*³, E was the only remaining member of a firm of chartered accountants. E took S into salaried partnership for seven months on the understanding that he (E) would provide all the capital, that he would take all profits and bear all the losses of the practice, and that during this period an agreement would be concluded whereby S would become a full partner. At the end of the seven months no partnership had been finalised and the temporary arrangement continued for a further 14 months, at the end of which time S and E had fallen out. Was S a partner? It was held that he was; the court was strongly influenced by the fact that S had been held out by E as a partner, for example, by the printing of his name on the firm's letterhead, which manifested an apparent intention that S was to be regarded as a partner.

1   *Weiner v Harris* [1910] 1 KB 285, CA.
2   (1993) unreported.
3   [1973] 1 All ER 465, [1973] 1 WLR 191.

Persons
24.7   Section 1 defines partnership as a relationship between 'persons'. Persons include natural and artificial legal persons (or any combination of the two¹); the only restriction on a person being a partner is that he must have capacity to enter into a partnership.

Most natural legal persons have the capacity to enter into a partnership but if a minor contracts to do so his contract is voidable at his option during his minority or within a reasonable time of attaining his majority². The liability of a minor for partnership debts is considered in para 16.9, above. A person of unsound mind who enters into a partnership and subsequently seeks to avoid the agreement can do so only if, in addition to proving his mental incapacity, he can show that his partners knew, at the time he entered into the partnership, that he was of such unsound mind as not to be capable of understanding what he was doing³. As long as a person of unsound mind is a partner he incurs liability on the firm's contracts and for its debts, unless the person seeking to enforce a contract or debt knew of his disability at the time of its creation.

Whether a company has the capacity to become a partner depends upon the terms of its objects clause⁴. The Companies Act 1985 provides that a trading partnership of more than 20 persons must register as a company but a variety of partnerships are exempt, eg partnerships of certain accountants, of solicitors, of estate agents and of actuaries⁵. Where a company is a member of a partnership neither the firm nor any individual partners are protected by the Policyholders Protection Act 1975, which authorises compensation for 'private policyholders' in insurance companies which become insolvent⁶.

1   Although the wisdom of an individual entering into a partnership with a limited company is doubtful.
2   *Goode v Harrison* (1821) 5 B & Ald 147.
3   If an existing partner becomes subject to mental impairment a petition to dissolve the partnership can be sought; see para 24.29, below.
4   See para 25.21, below.
5   Section 716.
6   *Scher v Policyholders Protection Board (No 2)* [1994] 2 AC 57, [1993] 4 All ER 840, HL.

Carrying on

24.8   Section 1 requires the persons to be 'carrying on' a business. Carrying on seems to imply a degree of continuity, although it is possible for an association of persons to be carrying on a business even when it was formed to carry out only one transaction[1].

However, no partnership arises where persons are merely preparing to carry on business in the future. Whether persons are carrying on a business and can thus be a partnership, or whether they are merely preparing to carry on a business (be it a partnership or not) is a question of the intention of the parties. For example, in *Keith Spicer Ltd v Mansell*[2], M and B decided to form a company to operate B's existing restaurant business. Prior to incorporation, B ordered goods from the plaintiff for the company; the company used the goods but did not pay for them. The plaintiff sued M for the price alleging that, at the time the goods were ordered, M was in partnership with B. The Court of Appeal held that there was no partnership between M and B; M and B's actions were referable to their imminent incorporation and did not connote a partnership. In contrast, in *Singh v Suman*[3], where property from which a business was operated was purchased in joint names and with a joint mortgage, the parties were held to be partners from that moment. This was because these facts manifested an intention to form an immediate partnership, even though the plaintiff ran the business, and it had been agreed that the defendant was to take no active part in its operation for at least two years. The Court of Appeal held that this was not a case where the defendant had an option to become a partner in due course, nor was it a type of deferred partnership, since the financial arrangements indicated an intention for a partnership to come into existence immediately. Where a person, who is currently carrying business with X, has an option to become a partner with X, the intention of the parties will be crucial in determining whether they are already to be treated as partners[4].

1   *George Hall & Sons v Platt* [1954] TR 331.
2   [1970] 1 All ER 462, [1970] 1 WLR 333, CA.
3   (1993) unreported.
4   *Re Young, ex p Jones* [1896] 2 QB 484.

A business

24.9   The persons must be carrying on a 'business'. Section 45 states that business includes every trade, occupation or profession. This definition is very wide but not everything which produces monetary gain is construed as a business for the purposes of defining a partnership; custom provides that barristers are not in partnership.

In common

24.10   The persons must be carrying on the business 'in common' for it to be a partnership. The mere fact that a business is carried on jointly with a view to making a profit is not in itself enough to make it a partnership. Factors which are relevant, in determining whether a business is being carried on by persons 'in common' and is thus a partnership, are that the concern is being carried on by or on behalf of all of them and that any profits earned or losses incurred will accrue to those persons. Thus, executors carrying on the business of a testator in accordance with his will are not partners because any benefits pass to the testator's estate[1]. A person may be carrying on business in common despite taking no active role in running the company, ie where he is a sleeping partner[2].

While all cases turn on their own facts, *Saywell v Pope*[3] is instructive. In this case S and P were partners in a business which in 1973 obtained a valuable contract. An agreement was drawn up for the formation of a new partnership between S, P, Mrs S and Mrs P (both wives did some work for the business) but it was not signed until 1975. The court held that Mrs S and Mrs P did not become partners until 1975 since they had no management role between 1973 and 1975 and they were not carrying on business in common with S and P; they were simply working for S and P.

1   *Re Fisher & Sons* [1912] 2 KB 491.
2   See para 24.14, below.
3   [1979] STC 824.

With a view to profit

24.11   Finally, the persons must be carrying on the business 'with a view to profit' if it is to be a partnership. Profit means primarily 'net profit' and s 2 provides that the sharing of gross returns does not automatically create a partnership. An example is *Cox v Coulson*[1], in which C, a theatre manager, agreed with M, a play promoter, to supply a theatre, lighting and publicity, for a play which M would provide; M was also to provide the cast and scenery. C was to receive 60% of the box-office takings and M 40%. During a performance, the plaintiff was accidentally shot by one of the actors. The court held that C was not M's partner and was thus not liable to pay damages to the plaintiff.

Section 2 further provides that co-ownership of property does not necessarily create a partnership, even if *net* profits from the property are shared[2]. Whether co-ownership gives rise to a partnership is a question of fact and the apparent intention of the parties may be a crucial determinant. Factors which have been held to negate the existence of a partnership between co-owners are: the absence of either a consensual relationship or a common aim of profit, that one co-owner may be able to transfer his share without the consent of the other co-owners, and that one co-owner generally has no power to enter into transactions on behalf of the other co-owners. In *Davis v Davis*[3], two sons inherited from their father a business and three houses. The sons continued to operate the business and each drew a weekly sum from it. They let one of the houses and used the rent to enlarge the workshops, attached to the other two houses, which were used by the business. It was held that there was a partnership in respect of the business but not as to the houses.

1   [1916] 2 KB 177, CA.
2   *French v Styring* (1857) 2 CBNS 357; joint owners of a racehorse who shared winnings and expenses were not partners.
3   [1894] 1 Ch 393.

24.12   Greater difficulty arises in determining whether persons who share net profits are partners. It is, as usual, a question of the apparent intention of the relevant parties. In *Cox v Hickman*[1], a debtor had assigned his business to trustees for the benefit of his creditors. The trustees carried on the business to try and generate profits to discharge those debts. The House of Lords held that the creditors were not partners in the business. Liability arises, it was held, not merely when there is a participation in profits but when there is such a participation in profits as to constitute the relation of principal and agent between the person taking the profits and those actually carrying on the business. Whether there is such a relationship is dependent on the intention of the parties. For example, in *Saywell v Pope*[2], which was outlined in para 24.10, above, the wives of the partners were credited with a share of the partnership profits before the partnership agreement was signed but this was not sufficient to render them partners since there was no evidence that they actually received these profits.

Section 2(3) provides that the receipt by a person of a share of the profits of a business carried on in common is prima facie, but not conclusive, evidence of partnership. The Act specifies five cases in which receiving a share of the net profits of a business does *not*, by itself, render the recipient a partner. These cases are:

a. payment of a debt to a creditor out of the profits of the debtor's business;
b. payment of a share of the profits of a business to an employee or agent of a person engaged in that business;
c. a payment by way of an annuity out of profits to the widow or child of a deceased partner;
d. a loan to a person carrying on business under a written contract which provides that the borrower will pay the lender a rate of interest varying with the profits or an actual share of the profits[3]; and
e. the payment out of the profits of an annuity or other consideration for the sale of the goodwill of the business[3].

1 (1860) 8 HL Cas 268.
2 [1979] STC 824.
3 Section 3 provides that in these cases if the recipient of the profit-share becomes insolvent the claims of the lender or annuitant rank after other creditors of the recipient. Where the lender has rights over and above those normally conferred on a creditor he may find that he is in law a partner; *Pooley v Driver* (1876) 5 Ch D 458.

Types of partnership

General partners
24.13 A partner who does not fall into any other category – and few do – can be called simply a partner or a general partner. The rights of such partners are such as may be agreed between the partners and, in the absence of any agreement, their rights are those set out in s 24[1]. Such a partner is not required by the Act to put any capital into the firm but the law holds every general partner liable to the full extent of his assets for the debts and other liabilities of the firm. No liability is imposed upon a partner for obligations which arose before he became a partner[2] unless he chooses to accept responsibility for them.

A person who is not a partner, but who has to his knowledge been held out as a partner, may incur liability to a third party as if he was a partner. Where a person has incurred liability to a third party by being deemed to be a partner (by virtue of being held out as such[3]) he is not a partner in any other respect. Thus, in *Re C & M Ashberg*[4], the court refused to treat a business run by a brother and sister as a partnership for the purposes of winding up, even though the sister was liable to third-party creditors of the business as if she had been a partner, since she had been held out as such.

1 Paras 24.56–24.63, below.
2 Section 17.
3 We discuss this further in para 24.47, below.
4 (1990) Times, 17 July.

Sleeping partners

24.14 The term 'sleeping partner' is not a term of law but it may be used to describe a partner who takes no part in the operation of the firm. A sleeping partner is treated as a general partner in respect of the firm's liabilities.

Limited partners

24.15 Limited partnerships were introduced by the Limited Partnerships Act 1907. Very little use has been made of this Act. However, the spate of litigation against, allegedly, negligent firms of accountants has led to renewed interest in the possibility of an amended type of limited partnership and it may be that the 1907 Act will be re-enacted in a more useful form than at present.

The Act of 1907 provides that a partnership may have one or more partners who have limited liability for the debts of the firm provided that there is always at least one partner (a general partner) whose liability is unlimited[1]. Limited partnerships must be registered with the Registrar of Companies[2]. A limited partner (who may be a company) is a person who contributes, on joining the firm, a specified amount of capital (in cash or in property) and whose liability for the firm's debts is limited to that capital contribution.

1 Limited Partnerships Act 1907, s 4.
2 Ibid, s 5.

24.16 Section 6 of the Limited Partnerships Act 1907 provides that a limited partner cannot, on penalty of ceasing to be such a partner, take part in the management of the firm. This means that he cannot vote on matters arising out of the normal running of the firm, nor has he the power to bind the firm, and he cannot terminate the partnership by giving notice. The death or bankruptcy of a limited partner does not automatically dissolve the firm[1].

Section 6 of the 1907 Act provides that a limited partner can give general advice on the running of the firm without incurring liability and he can demand to inspect the firm's books and may, with the consent of the general partners, assign his share in the partnership. If a limited partner assigns his share, the assignee is a limited partner with all his assignor's rights. A limited partner should be cautious as to the extent of any advice he gives lest it be construed as participation in management.

Apart from the modifications set out in the Act of 1907 and any express agreement between the partners, a limited partnership operates in the same way as a general partnership[2].

1 As it would if he was a general partner; see paras 24.26 and 24.27, below.
2 Limited Partnerships Act 1907, s 7.

Salaried partners

24.17 As we have seen in para 24.6, above, a 'salaried partner' may not be a partner at all. Where such a person is in law a partner, his rights and duties are not entirely certain. Each case probably turns on its own facts, although it seems clear that he is responsible for the debts of the firm[1]. A salaried partner may find he has the worst of both worlds – he is a mere employee internally while incurring liability to third parties to whom he is held out as a 'partner'[2].

1 *Stekel v Ellice* [1973] 1 All ER 465, [1973] 1 WLR 191.
2 See para 24.47, below on the liability of a person held out as a partner.

Ending a partnership

24.18 A partnership does not necessarily last for ever. A partnership may split up completely or continue to operate with different partners. Every change of partners, for example where a partner retires or a new partner is admitted, results in the ending of the old partnership and the inception of a new one even if the business continues to trade throughout. We discuss termination by the partners in paras 24.20–24.23, below, and dissolution (which may be automatic, or provided for in the partnership agreement or ordered by a court), in paras 24.24–24.33, below. Where the partnership ceases to exist the business must be wound up. Where a partner leaves the partnership his share must be valued. The effects of ending a partnership are considered in paras 24.66–24.72, below.

24.19 In addition to grounds for dissolution, a partner may have grounds to rescind the partnership agreement, eg for fraud or misrepresentation (which can include innocent misrepresentation) by a prospective partner, which would also have the effect of terminating the partnership[1]. The defrauded or misled partner has a right, in addition to any claim for damages[2], to invoke s 41 which entitles him:

a.   to a lien[3] on any surplus assets of the firm for any money paid by him for his share or for capital contributed by him, plus interest and costs;
b.   to a personal order for payment of such sum;
c.   to stand in place of the firm's creditors in respect of payments made by him on account of the firm's liabilities; and
d.   to be indemnified by the person guilty of the fraud or misrepresentation against all the debts and liabilities of the firm.

1 Rescission is discussed in Chap 14.

2 For deceit or under the Misrepresentation Act 1967, s 2, both of which are discussed in Chap 14, or, perhaps, for the tort of negligence which we discuss in Chap 18.
3 Liens are discussed in para 2.32, above.

Termination by the partners
24.20 A partnership can be terminated by the partners in a number of ways:

a. on the expiry of any fixed term agreed by the partners[1]; or
b. in the case of a partnership formed to carry out one single venture, for example to renovate a particular office block, on the termination of that venture unless there is an express agreement to the contrary. A partnership of this type may be called a syndicate; or
c. in the case of a partnership at will, on any one partner giving notice of termination. Section 26 provides that, unless a definite duration is specified, a partnership is a partnership at will.

A partnership is also presumed to be a partnership at will when an agreed, fixed term partnership has expired and the partnership has continued to operate without any express new agreement having been made[2].

A provision in a partnership agreement that it is to be terminated 'by mutual arrangement only' displaces the assumption that it is a partnership at will and hence precludes termination by a single partner[3]. However, the fact that the partners jointly acquire a fixed-term lease of property to be used by the partnership does not raise an inference that the partnership is intended to last for the duration of the lease or can only be terminated by reasonable notice[4].

1 Section 32.
2 Section 26.
3 *Moss v Elphick* [1910] 1 KB 846, CA.
4 *Popat v Shonchhatra* [1995] 4 All ER 646, [1995] 1 WLR 908.

24.21 Partners may also choose to include in their agreement a clause setting out other circumstances whose occurrence will either automatically dissolve the firm or require the retirement of a partner, or both. Examples are physical incapacity, or a partner's conviction for a serious criminal offence[1], or other conduct which is injurious to the partnership. In a recent case[2], the partnership agreement provided for the compulsory retirement of a partner (at the request of the other partners) for breach of the obligations, 'to be just and faithful to the other partners' and 'to act in the best interests of the partnership', which were set out in the partnership agreement. One partner, B, had disclosed to the Commissisoners of Customs and Excise that the firm had probably underpaid VAT and in the firm's accounts alleged fraud on the part of his partners; they had requested his retirement. The Court of Appeal held that he was not in breach of the partnership agreement in that his conduct, voluntary disclosure of underpayment, would be likely to influence the Commissioners not to prosecute the firm or its partners. Consequently B's conduct did not display any want of faith towards his fellow partners, nor was it detrimental to the firm, rather he had saved them from themselves and his retirement could not be required. If there is any doubt as to whether the partnership has been dissolved, it may be wise to seek a court order either confirming or granting a dissolution.

Additionally, the partnership agreement may provide that the partners can require the firm to be dissolved on the giving of reasonable notice. To avoid the inconvenience which would arise from a sudden and unprepared dissolution, a partnership agreement may well prescribe a lengthy period of notice or even provide that dissolution can only be by mutual consent.

1   *Essell v Hayward* (1860) 30 Beav 158.
2   *DB Rare Books Ltd v Antiqbooks* [1995] 2 BCLC 306, CA.

24.22   A partner who allows his partnership share to be charged gives the other partners an option to wind up the firm[1], even if the partnership agreement does not so provide.

1   Section 33.

24.23   A notice to terminate a partnership must be clear and communicated to all the partners[1]. A notice, once given, cannot be withdrawn unless all the partners agree[2] but a notice to terminate which is expressed to be operative only 'if the partners agree' does not take effect unless they do so[3].

A partnership at will is also terminated if the conduct of the parties makes such intention manifest even if no formal notice is given[4]. For example, in *Popat v Shonchhatra*[5], P, a partner who occupied the partnership premises as a residence as well as for the purpose of operating the business of the partnership (a newsagents), left the premises with his wife and belongings and handed the keys back to his partner. P then sought employment. The judge ruled that he his conduct was plainly inconsistent with an intention to return to the business and was a clear termination of the partnership.

1   Section 27.
2   *Jones v Lloyd* (1874) LR 18 Eq 265.
3   *Hall v Hall* (1855) 20 Beav 139.
4   *Pearce v Lindsay* (1860) 3 De GJ & Sm 139.
5   [1995] 4 All ER 646, [1995] 1 WLR 908.

Automatic dissolution[1]
24.24   A partnership is automatically dissolved by operation of law, in three cases: where the firm becomes tainted by illegality; on the death of a partner; and on the bankruptcy of a partner.

1   The partners may be able to override the dissolution by agreement; see paras 24.26 and 24.27, below.

24.25   *Illegal purpose*   A firm, which at the outset was untainted by illegality, may become so tainted. If this occurs the partnership is dissolved[1]. For example, the business of the firm may be declared illegal or a firm may consist of partners one or all of whom become an enemy alien on the outbreak of a war involving the United Kingdom[2]. In *Hudgell Yeates & Co v Watson*[3], one partner in a three-partner firm of solicitors forgot to renew his practising certificate, without which no solicitor can practise. The Court of Appeal held that since a solicitor cannot practise in partnership with a person not qualified to be a solicitor, the partnership was automatically dissolved despite the fact that all three partners were unaware of any problem and had been carrying on in practice.

1 Section 34.
2 *The Anglo-Mexican* [1918] AC 422, PC.
3 [1978] QB 451, [1978] 2 All ER 363, CA.

24.26 *Death* The death of a partner dissolves the firm unless there is an agreement to the contrary[1]. The dissolution of a corporate partner is treated as a death. A partnership agreement which provides that the partnership is to last for a specified number of years is not an agreement to the contrary[2]. However, since the winding up of a partnership (which may have many partners) on the death of any partner would be highly inconvenient, the partnership deed often provides that on the death of a partner the business may be continued by the survivors, either by themselves or in partnership with the deceased's personal representatives[3].

1 Section 33.
2 *Gillespie v Hamilton* (1818) 3 Madd 251.
3 This is technically a new partnership.

24.27 *Bankruptcy* The bankruptcy of a partner dissolves the firm unless there is an agreement to the contrary[1]. The effect of the winding up of a corporate partner is uncertain but, if it does not dissolve the partnership, it is probably a ground for dissolution by the court.

1 Section 33.

Dissolution by court order
24.28 Section 35 lists five grounds (which overlap) on which a partner may petition for the dissolution of the partnership. These grounds are:

a. if a partner becomes the subject of mental or other incapacity;
b. where a partner engages in injurious conduct;
c. where there is breach of agreement and destruction of confidence;
d. if the business can only be carried on at a loss; and
e. if it is just and equitable so to do.

The jurisdiction to dissolve a partnership is discretionary but a court is likely to be influenced by previous decisions. An application for dissolution by the court may indicate that there is conflict between the partners. The is because the all or some of the above grounds on which the court can dissolve a partnership may have been included in the partnership agreement, thereby allowing the partners to terminate their partnership by agreement on one of those grounds, ie consensual termination. The fact that consensual termination has proved impracticable suggests some degree of tension or conflict between the partners.

Many partnership agreements provide for arbitration in the case of dispute. It is a moot point whether such a provision precludes an application to the court to dissolve the partnership. The courts seem to treat each case on its merits and may hear a petition for dissolution, even when the ground for dissolution should, according to the partnership agreement, have been submitted to arbitration and this has not occurred[1].

1   *Olver v Hillier* [1959] 2 All ER 220, [1959] 1 WLR 551.

24.29   *Mental or other incapacity*   If a partner who was of sound mind becomes of unsound mind, the firm is not automatically dissolved[1]. However, the onset of mental incapacity in a partner is a ground for asking a court for a decree of dissolution[2]. Before the issue of dissolution is determined the court may grant an injunction to prevent the partner concerned from interfering in the firm's management.

The jurisdiction of the court to dissolve a firm is not limited to mental incapacity. Instead, it extends to other incapacity[3] which renders a partner permanently incapable of performing his partnership duties.

Any partner can seek dissolution on the grounds of the incapacity of another partner and, in the case of physical incapacity, the incapacitated partner can also petition.

1   *Jones v Noy* (1833) 2 My & K 125.
2   Mental Health Act 1983, s 96.
3   Section 35(b).

24.30   *Injurious conduct*   Conduct by a partner which has the effect of adversely affecting the carrying on of the partnership business is also a ground for dissolution[1]. The conduct need not be connected with the partnership business; it is enough that it is harmful to it. For example, in *Carmichael v Evans*[2], C, a partner in a firm of drapers, was convicted of travelling on the railway (more than once) with intent to avoid paying his fare. The partnership was dissolved; such conduct, involving as it did dishonesty, was contrary to the interests of any firm.

Any innocent partner can petition for dissolution on this ground.

1   Section 35(c).
2   [1904] 1 Ch 486.

24.31   *Breach of agreement and destruction of confidence*   A court may order the dissolution of a partnership if one partner deliberately or persistently breaks the terms of the partnership agreement or so conducts himself in matters relating to the partnership business that it is not reasonably practicable for the other partners to continue in business with him[1]. The wrongdoer cannot petition on this ground. To permit him to do so would allow a person deliberately to destroy a partnership by misconducting himself and then seeking dissolution citing his own misconduct.

The court will not exercise its discretion to dissolve a partnership simply because the partners disagree or sometimes quarrel; the essence of this ground is the destruction of mutual confidence which is the hallmark of partnership and without which partners cannot operate the business in accordance with the partnership agreement.

It is always a question of degree as to whether the misconduct effectively destroys the mutual confidence of the partners; constant quarrelling which manifests an underlying mistrust may suffice[2] as may refusal to meet or consult[3]. Even misconduct not directly related to the business of the firm may suffice if it destroys the trust of the malefactor's partners[4].

1   Section 35(d).
2   *Leary v Shout* (1864) 33 Beav 582.
3   *Re Yenidje Tobacco Co Ltd* [1916] 2 Ch 426, CA.
4   *Harrison v Tennant* (1856) 21 Beav 482; fraud of a partner in respect of a prior partnership sufficient to destroy the confidence of his current partners in the case of a solicitors' practice.

24.32   *Business can only be carried on at a loss*   The definition of a partnership provides that it is an association for profit. It follows that, if the partnership business is inherently loss-making, eg because the business has been destroyed, it can be dissolved[1].

1   Section 35(e).

24.33   *Just and equitable*   Finally, s 35(f) leaves it to the court 'to consider in the widest possible terms what justice and equity require'[1]. Justice and equity in this context mean what is just and equitable from the point of view of the partnership and not of anyone else, such as a creditor or employee. What is required for this ground to apply is for a partner to satisfy a court that it is impossible for the partners to place that confidence in each other which each has a right to expect, and that such impossibility has not been caused by the person seeking to take advantage of it.

1   This provision also applies to companies as a ground for compulsory winding up: Insolvency Act 1986, s 122(1)(g). For the winding up of companies see paras 25.65 and 26.53, below.

Process of dissolution
24.34   The process of dissolution of a firm is usually a matter for the partners but the court may, on the application of any partner, appoint a receiver if the partners are in serious dispute as to the conduct of the dissolution, or if special grounds for such an appointment are shown by the personal representatives of a deceased partner[1]. In an extreme case a receiver and manager may be appointed to conduct the entire winding up but the court is not usually willing to take control out of the hands of the partners in this way[2].

1   Section 44.
2   *Sobell v Boston* [1975] 2 All ER 282, [1975] 1 WLR 1587; *Toker v Akgul* (1996) unreported, CA.

Partnerships and Third Parties
24.35   Partnerships remain relatively free from judicial and non-excludable statutory intervention in their operation[1] – in contrast to companies. However, in regulating the relationship between a partnership and third parties, the courts and Parliament have provided a number of non-excludable obligations. It should be noted that both the firm and the individual partners may be liable in respect

of a transaction. In other words, the liability of a firm and the individual partners can co-exist.

The principal source of law for determining the relationship of a partnership and third parties is agency[2]. Partners are agents; each and every partner is prima facie an agent both of the firm and of each of his partners for the purposes of the partnership business. Consequently, all the partners can be collectively liable for the acts and omissions of each partner and each partner can have the authority to bind the firm and his partners; they are mutual agents.

It is this mutual agency which we discuss first. We then consider aspects of the liability of individual partners; which arise principally in contract and tort. Finally, the liability, if any, of a former partner for acts and omissions occurring after he has left the partnership is discussed.

1   Partnerships are, of course, subject to the general law on contracts, employment law etc.
2   Chap 24.

Liability of the partnership and co-partners

24.36   Section 5 (which is largely at one with the position at common law) provides that a partner is the agent of the firm and of all his co-partners. Thus, a partner acting on behalf of the partnership binds the firm and his co-partners[1]. Note that while this section provides that a partner is an agent of the firm, it does not provide that a partner can bind his firm or his partners to *any* transaction into which he purports to enter on the firm's behalf. Section 5 is not limited in its application to contracts entered into by one partner but can also extend to tortious acts and other wrondoing but in respect of such acts there is also a specific provision, s 10, which we discuss in para 24.42, below. Like any other agent, a partner can only bind his principal (the firm) to the extent of his authority. The interrelation of normal agency principles and specific rules under the Act is not always entirely clear.

A partner, since he is an agent, may have actual authority, usual authority or ostensible authority in accordance with the principles discussed in paras 24.40–24.44, above. Where a partner has such authority, a term in the partnership agreement purporting to limit the ambit of that authority partner does not affect a third party unless he has notice of that restriction[2].

In addition, s 5 states that:

> 'the acts of every partner who does any act for carrying on in the usual way business of the kind carried on by the firm of which he is a member bind the firm and his partners, unless the partner so acting has in fact no authority to bind the firm in the particular manner, and the person with whom he is dealing either knows that he has no authority, or does not know or believe him to be a partner.'

The effect of the common law and s 5 is to provide that a partner can bind the firm and his co-partners to a transaction if he has either actual, usual[3] or ostensible authority to enter into it or if his actions are 'carrying on in the usual way' the type of business in which the firm engages. The concept of a person who is 'carrying on in the usual way' having authority is a specific partnership provision. The name by which to call the novel authority conferred by s 5 is difficult to determine in that it overlaps with actual authority of the customary or usual type and with ostensible authority. We shall call it statutory ostensible authority.

Where a partner has actual authority which is either more extensive than, or co-extensive with, that provided by s 5, there is no difficulty in holding the firm and his co-partners liable. They are bound by the acts of the partner since he is an agent with actual authority. If the firm holds a partner out as having authority which is wider than that which he actually possesses it clothes him with ostensible authority, under the normal rules of agency, and his acts bind the firm and his partners. When does s 5 operate and what is the effect of this to statutory ostensible authority?

1 For a specific discussion of the liability of co-partners see also para 24.41, below.
2 Section 8.
3 See 23.40, above for an explanation of usual authority.

Statutory ostensible authority

24.37 Where a partner enters into a transaction, or undertakes an act, without actual authority or ostensible authority to do so, the firm and his co-partners will still be bound by his actions if they fall within the statutory ostensible authority set out in s 5.

Section 5 applies when:

a. the act was done in the firm's name by a person purporting to act as a partner; and
b. the act related to the kind of business carried on by the firm. Section 7 provides a gloss on this in that it says that a partner who pledges his firm's credit for a purpose not connected with its business is personally liable but the firm is not; and
c. it was an act for carrying on business in the usual way.

The scope of the latter two requirements is discussed in para 24.38, below.

An act which appears to satisfy these requirements prima facie binds the firm. However, s 5 provides that an act of a partner which satisfies these requirements does not bind the firm if the third party either knew that the partner lacked authority[1] or did not know or believe that the person with whom he was dealing was a partner at all. In the latter case the actions of the partner seem unlikely to satisfy the three requirements listed above.

An illustration of the operation of s 5 is provided by *Mercantile Credit Co v Garrod*[2]. P and G were partners in a firm carrying on a garage business which, in practice, was mainly concerned with letting lock-up garages and repairing cars: P ran the business and G was a sleeping partner. The partnership deed precluded the buying and selling of cars. However, P sold a car to which he had no title to the plaintiff finance company[3] which thereby lost money and the finance company successfully sued G. The court held that the sale of the car was an act 'for carrying on in the usual way business of the kind' carried on by the firm, in other words the buying and selling of cars fell within the usual way of conducting a garage business. It was irrelevant that this particular garage business did not usually deal in cars.

1   Section 8 specifically provides that a restriction in a partnership agreement does not affect a third party unless he knows of it. A third party who knows of a restriction on the power of a partner will not be able to rely on ostensible or usual authority either.
2   [1962] 3 All ER 1103.
3   In order to effect a sale of the vehicle on hire purchase to a customer.

24.38   Whether a transaction 'is an act for carrying on in the usual way business of the kind carried on by the firm. . .' raises two questions. First, is it an act for 'carrying on in the usual way' and, second, what is 'business of the kind carried on by the firm'? These provisions raise issues of fact which are assessed objectively. The courts must decide whether the act would have appeared to a reasonable third party to be designed to carry on the relevant kind of business in the usual way.

Whether a transaction is usual for a firm is a question of fact which depends upon the type of business it undertakes. What is a normal activity for a particular type of business is also a question of fact but since trade practice varies with the years so does what is normal or usual. The courts have held a number of transactions either to fall, or not to fall, within s 5 but these findings of fact are always open to challenge on the basis that the scope of a particular type of business, or what is usual for such a business, has changed[1]. Never forget that a transaction not binding by virtue of s 5 may still bind the firm or co-partners under normal agency principles.

1   See, eg, *United Bank of Kuwait v Hammoud* [1988] 3 All ER 418, [1988] 1 WLR 1051, CA, where the court doubted the applicability of several earlier cases on the scope of a solicitor's business.

24.39   In determining whether a transaction arose in the usual way, the courts have distinguished between trading and non-trading partnerships. A trading partnership is one whose business involves the buying and selling of goods[1].

Partners in trading partnerships have authority, ie it is usual and thus within s 5, to sell or pledge partnership goods, or buy goods necessary for the firm's business. They can also borrow money, pay debts, issue receipts and draw, accept or indorse negotiable instruments. Partners in a trading firm can also employ staff for the firm's business. Early cases held that where the business is not that of a trading firm (eg a firm of accountants or solicitors), it is not regarded as usual (and s 5 is thus inapplicable) for a partner to have power to draw, accept or indorse negotiable instruments, other than ordinary cheques, or to borrow money but the courts might be prepared to regard practice in such professions as having changed in more recent years[2].

Partners in trading partnerships do not have the power to give a guarantee in the firm's name (unless it is the custom of the trade) or submit a dispute to arbitration. Since the existence of a partnership confers authority on a partner to bind his co-partners (and render them liable for his acts) it is not surprising that a partner cannot put his partners into partnership with other persons in another business[3]. There may be difficulty in deciding whether a partner has purported to put his partners into partnership with another (no authority) or whether he has sought to carry on the business of a partnership by entering into a joint venture with others (which may be authorised if usual in the trade). In *Mann v D'Arcy*[3], D was the only active partner in a three-partner produce business. D made an agreement with M in respect of the purchase and re-sale of 350 tons of potatoes. The venture made a profit but D did not pay M his share of the profit. M sued D's partners, who claimed that D had no authority to put them into partnership with M, a person unknown to them. The judge, in upholding M's claim, ruled that D had not put the partnership into business with another. He had merely, on the facts, carried out the partnership's business (produce dealing) in a new way, ie by entering into a joint venture with M.

1   *Wheatley v Smithers* [1906] 2 KB 321, where an auctioneers was held not to be a trading partnership since auctioneers do not buy goods.
2   See, eg, *United Bank of Kuwait v Hammoud* [1988] 3 All ER 418, [1988] 1 WLR 1051, CA.
3   [1968] 2 All ER 172, [1968] 1 WLR 893.

24.40   It should also be noted, when considering the liability of partners on the basis of agency or agency-related grounds, that s 14 provides that a partner who holds himself out (or who is to his knowledge held out) as being a partner incurs *personal* liability to a person who 'extends credit' to the firm on the faith of that representation. Section 14 does not impose liability upon a firm but it does allow a third party to bring an action against the individual partner who falls within its ambit. We discuss this section in para 24.47, below.

Contractual liability of partners
24.41   We have seen in paras 24.36–24.39, above, how an individual partner can bind the firm. Section 9 then states the obvious and rules that every partner is liable, jointly with his co-partners, for all debts and obligations of his firm which are incurred while he is a partner. Thus, a partner is jointly liable on an authorised contract because he is a partner in a firm on behalf of which a contract has been negotiated by a partner. Partners, however, differ from other joint debtors in that the estate of a deceased partner is severally liable for any of the firm's debts incurred while the deceased was a partner[1].

Section 9 and the common law have been supplemented by the Civil Liability (Contribution) Act 1978, which provides that the mere fact that one partner has been sued (successfully or not) on a contract does not preclude an action on that contract against another partner[2]. A partner successfully sued on a contract can seek contribution from his co-partners[3].

1   Section 9.
2   Civil Liability (Contribution) Act 1978, s 3. See also paras 17.13 and 17.14, above.
3   Ibid, s 1.

Liability of the firm and partners in tort and for other wrongdoing
24.42   As we have said, the rules of agency are wide enough to impose liability on a firm and co-partners for tortious acts and other wrongs committed by a partner. However, in addition, the Act has a specific provision dealing with wrongful acts and omissions by a partner – s 10. Section 10 provides that, when any loss or injury is caused to a non-partner[1] by a wrongful act or omission[2] of any partner acting, either in the ordinary course of the business of the firm or with the authority of his co-partners, the firm and his co-partners are liable to the same extent as the individual partner responsible for that loss or injury.

Section 10 renders the firm, and each partner, liable for the wrongful acts or omissions of a partner if he was *authorised* (actually, usually, ostensibly or by virtue of s 5) to commit the act of wrongdoing (or if the act was subsequently ratified) or it was done in the ordinary course of the business of the firm. For example, liability can be imposed on a firm of solicitors or accountants for the negligent acts or omissions of a partner and even for deliberate acts of wrongdoing designed to benefit the wrongdoer (or the firm). The critical issue is whether the malefaction was performed in the ordinary course of carrying on the business of the firm. In *Hamlyn v John Houston & Co*[3], a partner bribed a clerk in a rival firm to disclose to him confidential information. The disclosure caused financial loss to that firm, who then successfully sued the partnership for damages. Since it was in the ordinary course of business for the partner to obtain information about a rival firm, the method by which it was obtained was immaterial.

As is usual, neither the firm nor the co-partners are liable for wrongdoing which is completely outside the scope of the authority of the relevant partner since in such a case he is not acting as the agent of either the firm or the individual partners. For example, if a partner libels his next door neighbour, with whom he is in dispute as to the situation of the property boundary, the partnership is not liable. There is also a statutory exception to the liability of a firm for the wrongdoing of its partners; a firm is not liable for a false and fraudulent misrepresentation as to the character or solvency of any person, unless the representation is in writing signed by all the partners[4]. This exemption does not extend to negligent declarations of solvency.

1   A partner may be liable to another partner under normal tortious principles.
2   The section extends to crimes so that a partner may incur criminal liability for the actions of his partner, for example where one partner neglects to submit the firm's VAT returns.
3   [1903] 1 KB 81, CA.
4   Statute of Frauds Amendment Act 1828, s 6.

24.43   The Act goes on to deal with certain specific acts of wrongdoing despite the fact that s 10 is wide enough to apply to these situations.

Section 11 provides that, if money or other property is misapplied by a partner, the firm and co-partners are liable[1] in two cases:

a.   When money or property is received by a firm from a third party which money etc, while it is in the custody of the firm, is misapplied by one or more of the partners. In this case the only issue is whether the money or property has been improperly applied by one or more of the partners (not necessarily the partner who received the money or property).
b.   When a partner, acting within the scope of his authority (be it conferred by s 5 or ostensibly), receives the money or property of a third person and that partner then misapplies it. The issue which usually arises in this case is determining whether the acceptance of the money or property by the defaulting partner was or was not within the scope of his authority. For example, it is within the ordinary course of business for a solicitor to receive money for investment in a specific security, and his firm is liable if he misappropriates the money[2]. In contrast, the receipt of money for general investment purposes is not within the ordinary course of a solicitor's practice[3].

Section 13, which deals with the improper employment of trust property for partnership purposes, says that a partner who is a trustee and who, without the knowledge of his co-partners, improperly brings trust money into the business of the firm does not by so doing render any other partner liable for his impropriety, unless that other partner had notice of the particular breach of trust. While s 13 will usually exempt from liability partners who did not know of, or participate in, the breach of trust, it does not prevent such trust money from being recovered from the partnership if it is still in its possession or under its control.

1 A partnership, and the partners, can also incur liability as constructive trustees, independent of s 11, if they knowingly received, or assisted in the dispersal of, misapplied trust property. Indeed, it may be that a firm and its partners can be vicariously liable for the acts of a partner who knowingly assists in the wrongful dispersal of trust property; *Agip (Africa) Ltd v Jackson* [1991] Ch 547, [1992] 4 All ER 451, CA.
2 *Rhodes v Moules* [1895] 1 Ch 236, CA.
3 *Harman v Johnson* (1853) 2 E & B 61.

Liability of partners for torts and other wrongdoing
24.44 If liability on the part of a firm can be established under s 10 and/or s 11, the liability of the partners is both joint and several. Consequently, a plaintiff can issue separate writs against each partner, either simultaneously or successively[1]. Partners may also be liable where they knowingly received, or assisted in the disposal of, property which was subject to a trust, and it may be that partners may also be vicariously liable for such receipt or assistance on the part of one of their number provided he was authorised to be involved in the transaction.

1 Section 12; see also paras 17.13 and 17.14, above.

Liability of former partners

Liabilities existing on retirement
24.45 The law holds every general partner liable to the full extent of his assets for the debts and other liabilities of the firm incurred while he is a partner. This is sometimes difficult to apply. For example, suppose a firm entered into a contract for the supply of goods in 12 monthly instalments, each of which was to be paid for on delivery, and the relevant partner retired after one delivery, is he liable for one delivery or all 12? The courts have ruled that the nature of the obligation must be determined – is it a series of individual contracts or one continuous contract? If the latter, the partner remains liable for all obligations due under the contract. A partner is not liable for obligations which arose before he became a partner[1] unless he chooses to accept responsibility for them.

On retirement, a retiring partner *prima facie* remains liable on transactions entered into while he was a partner[2]. However, the partnership agreement may provide (it often does) that such liabilities are to be borne by the remaining partners alone. This does not by itself release the retiring partner from any liabilities to third parties but allows him to claim from the remaining partners any moneys payable to a third party in respect of such liabilities. Clearly a retiring partner would be wise to ensure that the partnership agreement has this effect.

In addition, s 17 permits the release of the retiring partner from liability to third parties by an agreement to that effect with the third party. Such an agreement takes the form of a novation[3] between himself, his former partners and the relevant third parties. This novation substitutes a new agreement with a third party for the existing agreement which created the liability. The agreement may merely release a retiring partner from liability (ie leaving the remaining partners liable) or it may also make a new partner, if any, liable for pre-existing debts. The agreement can be express or implied from a course of dealing between the creditor and the newly constituted firm[4], although the courts will not infer such an agreement without clear evidence that such was the intention of all the parties. In particular, the mere fact that a creditor treats the newly constituted firm as the debtor , eg by sending a bill to the newly constituted firm, is not by itself sufficient to release from liability a retiring partner[5].

1 Section 17.
2 *Court v Berlin* [1897] 2 QB 396, CA.
3 Paras 22.20 and 22.21, above.
4 Section 17(3). Dealing with the newly constituted firm over a period of time without making a claim against a retired partner might suffice to constitute a novation.
5 *Thompson v Percival* (1834) 5 B & Ad 925.

Liabilities incurred after retirement

24.46 A former partner incurs liability on transactions entered into even after he has left the firm until the firm and his co-partners cease to be his agents.

A deceased partner's former partners cease to be his agents at the moment of death under the normal rules of agency[1]. Prima facie, a retired partner's former partners cease to be his agents on his retirement from a firm which is continued by other partners, or, if the firm is dissolved on his retirement, when the winding up of the firm is completed[2]. However, this apparent cessation of liability for post-retirement transactions must be considered in the light of the general rules of agency and ss 14 and 36.

1 Para 24.27, above.
2 Section 38.

24.47 Section 14, which overlaps with s 5 and with the normal agency rules on ostensible authority[1], provides that any person who by words or conduct represents himself, or knowingly suffers[2] himself to be represented, as a partner in a firm is liable as if he was a partner to any third party who has 'given credit' (ie incurred any liability) to the firm on the faith of that representation. Section 14 applies to a person who is not, and has never been, a partner in a firm but it can equally well apply to a former partner. The effect of s 14 is that the person held out as being a partner cannot deny that he was a partner if that was the impression created, by a representation to that effect, in the mind of the person who relied on that representation in his dealing with the firm[2]. Thus, a third party to whom it was represented that a retired partner remained a partner, can sue the retired partner on a contract entered into with the firm after the retirement of the partner if he relied on that representation.

Section 14 can be relied on by a person who can establish that:

a.   a representation was made that X was a partner, either by X or, to X's knowledge, by others who were authorised to hold people out as partners; and
b.   the representation was made to him directly or indirectly; and
c.   he acted on the faith of the representation in providing credit to the firm.

Section 14 is relevant to the possible liability of a retiring partner for future debts of the firm in that, unless he ensures that adequate notice of his retirement is given to the firm's creditors, actual and potential, he may be deemed to be held out as still a partner. Section 14 also interrelates with s 36 to which we now turn.

1   Paras 24.35–24.38, above.
2   What constitutes 'knowingly suffers' is uncertain but it connotes some degree of approval of the holding out.

24.48   It is a general rule of agency that the authority of an agent may continue until its revocation is known to a third party. This is reiterated by s 36, which states that, 'where a person deals with a firm after a change in its constitution he is entitled to treat all apparent members of the old firm as still being members of the firm until he has notice of the change'. 'Apparent' means appearing to be such to the person dealing with the firm. It must be stressed that s 36 does not confer authority on partners to enter into a particular transaction and thereby bind a retired partner: it simply provides that any authority to bind a partner which his partners had before he retired may continue after he has retired.

Consequently, s 36 means that a third party who has had dealings with a firm can treat all apparent partners (including a person falling within s 14) as a partner, for the purpose of imposing liability, until he has adequate notice of that person's retirement. Thus, it is crucial for a retiring partner to give adequate notice of his retirement to those who deal with the firm after his retirement. Particular difficulty arises in respect of those who had dealings with the firm prior to the retirement of the partner.

24.49   *Adequate notice*   What constitutes adequate notice of retirement depends upon the prior relationship of the third party, if any, with the firm from which the partner has retired.

a.   In the case of a third party who had previous dealings with the firm and who knew of its previous composition, it is necessary to show that he received actual notice (however it occurred) of the retirement.
b.   In the case of a third party who had no previous dealings with the firm but who can show that he became aware of the previous composition of the firm, the retiring member is free of liability for post-retirement transactions

if it can be shown that the third party received either actual notice of the retirement or notice of the retirement was published in the London Gazette (whether this was seen by the third party or not)[1].

c. A third party with no previous dealings with the firm and no knowledge of its previous constitution cannot hold the retired partner liable for post-retirement transactions. To this there is probably an exception: a retired partner who represented himself or knowingly suffered himself to be represented as a continuing member of the firm may, by virtue of s 14 (para 24.47, above), incur personal liability to the third party.

The operation of these principles is illustrated by *Tower Cabinet Co Ltd v Ingram*[1]. C and I had carried on the business of household furnishers as a partnership under the name Merry's. The partnership was dissolved in 1947, and C continued the business alone under the same name. In 1948, the plaintiff company, which had not previously dealt with Merry's, received an order to supply goods which order was accidentally confirmed on some old headed notepaper bearing the names of C and I. The goods were not paid for and the plaintiff obtained judgment against Merry's. The plaintiff was unsuccessful in its attempt to enforce this judgment against I. The court held that, prior to his retirement, I was not known to the plaintiff as a partner in the firm. Accordingly, he was under no obligation to give any notice of retirement to the plaintiff company or any other potential creditor. Furthermore, the court held, I had not knowingly allowed C to hold him (I) out as a partner. Consequently, he had not activated s 14 simply by failing to ensure that old notepaper was not used by C.

1   [1949] 2 KB 397, [1949] 1 All ER 1033.

The Relationship of the Partners

24.50   The relationship of partners one to another is based on two principles: that the association of partners is one of the utmost good faith, and that partners can determine their own mutual rights and duties by agreement between themselves. Where the partners have not reached an agreement on all or some of their rights and duties certain terms set out in the Act will be implied. Both contractual terms agreed by the partners and terms implied by the Act can be varied with the consent of the partners[1].

In paras 24.51–24.63, below, we discuss the duty of utmost good faith and these implied terms. We then consider the nature of partnership property and the consequences of a dissolution of a partnership.

1   Which consent may be express or inferred from the dealings of the partners; s 19.

Utmost good faith[1]

24.51   The obligation to display the utmost good faith one to another is a fundamental principle of partnership which applies to all partnerships whether specified in a partnership agreement or not[2]. The requirement of good faith applies not only to those who are partners but also to those who are negotiating the terms of a future partnership agreement[3]. This obligation continues while a partnership is being wound up but ceases when the partnership has been dissolved. However, a partner who has repudiated the partnership agreement is no longer owed this duty[4].

Illustrations of the principle are numerous. For example, it is a breach of good faith for a majority of partners to impose a decision on a firm without allowing the minority to be heard or without considering the issue impartially[5]. It is also breach of good faith to exercise a strict legal right, eg to expel a partner, for an improper motive[6]. Another example is the requirement that a sale of a share in the partnership business by one partner to another must be preceded by a full disclosure by the seller of any relevant information he has as to the accounts and circumstances of the firm. Failure so to do entitles the purchaser to rescind the agreement[7]. Other illustrations are provided in paras 24.52–24.55, below.

1 See also para 14.42, above.
2 Despite not being enunciated in the Act.
3 *United Dominions Corpn Ltd v Brian Pty Ltd* (1985) 60 ALR 741 (Aust HC).
4 *M'Lure v Ripley* (1850) 2 Mac & G 274.
5 *Const v Harris* (1824) Turn & R 496.
6 *Blisset v Daniel* (1853) 10 Hare 493.
7 *Law v Law* [1905] 1 Ch 140, CA. Rescission may become barred, see para 14.16, above.

Full disclosure

24.52 An application of the principle has been embodied in s 28, which requires every partner to render true accounts and provide full information concerning all things affecting the partnership to any partner or his legal representatives[1]. Failure to do so is a breach of duty even if the omission was neither fraudulent nor negligent[2]. Thus, if one partner persuades another partner to sell him partnership property for £X, when the buyer was privy to information which would have revealed that its true value was £2X, the contract of sale is voidable even if the purchaser made no untrue statements to the vendor.

1 Other than to a partner who has repudiated the partnership agreement.
2 *Law v Law* [1905] 1 Ch 140, CA.

Partners not to make undisclosed private profits

24.53 This application of the requirement that a partner must manifest the utmost good faith towards his co-partners precludes a partner from keeping any benefit (direct or indirect) obtained as a result of being a partner unless all the partners have consented to the arrangement. Thus, a partner who negotiates a deal on behalf of the partnership cannot keep any secret commission paid to him by the other contracting party. Similarly, a partner cannot keep any undisclosed profit obtained from use of a partnership asset. Assets include intangible assets such as the benefit of an existing contract and may extend to a contract which the partnership is about to enter into.

The duty not to make undisclosed profits is now enshrined in s 29. This section requires every partner to account to the firm for any benefit derived by him without the consent of the other partners from any transaction concerning the firm, or from any use by him of the partnership name or business connection. Transactions falling within s 29 include the obtaining by a partner of a lease of partnership property, either while the firm is still operational, or while it is in the course of dissolution but not yet wound up[1]. Undisclosed profits from the sale to, or purchase from, the firm of property are also recoverable[2].

Both the statutory and the non-statutory rule appear to apply even if the benefit to the partner was not at the expense of the firm[3].

1 *Featherstonhaugh v Fenwick* (1810) 17 Ves 298.
2 *Bentley v Craven* (1853) 18 Beav 75.
3 This seems to be the case with directors, who stand in a fiduciary position vis-à-vis their companies; see para 25.57, below.

24.54 Section 29 precludes a partner from making a profit from use of the business connections of the partnership. The scope of this provision is uncertain since it is not clear whether, if a partner uses information obtained by virtue of his being a partner to make a profit, the profit is recoverable by his co-partners even though they did not suffer from his actions. In cases concerning other fiduciaries – for example solicitors and company directors – it has been held that the fiduciary must account for any profit obtained by use of information obtained as a fiduciary, even if the person to whom the fiduciary duty was owed did not suffer from the actions of the fiduciary[1]. However, in *Aas v Benham*[2], a partner used information and experience obtained by virtue of being a partner in a ship-broking (hiring) business to assist a company set up to build ships. The company paid him and made him a director at a salary. His partners were unsuccessful in claiming any share of these profits. The Court of Appeal held that information used in a way which did not compete with the partnership did not fall within s 29. The position is unclear but it seems unduly onerous to require a partner to account for a profit which was not made at the expense of the partnership[3].

1 *Boardman v Phipps* [1967] 2 AC 46, [1966] 3 All ER 721, HL.
2 [1891] 2 Ch 244, CA, discussed but not disapproved in *Boardman v Phipps*.
3 See also para 25.57, below, where the position of company directors is discussed.

Partners not to compete with the firm
24.55 We saw in the previous paragraph that a partner may be unable to benefit from use of partnership *property* even where the partnership suffers no loss. Where the action of the partner involves *competition* with the partnership then s 30 applies. Section 30 states that a partner who, without the consent of his colleagues, carries on any business of the same nature as his firm so as to compete with his firm, must account to the firm for all profits made by him in that business. To permit a partner to compete with his own firm would be an abuse of his position as a partner. Section 30 does not apply to profits deriving from a non-competing business[1].

Cases on s 30 (duty not to compete) may well also involve an alleged breach of s 29 (duty not use partnership connections). For example, in *Trimble v Goldberg*[2], G, T and B entered into partnership to buy and then resell certain assets belonging to H, namely shares in a company and building plots. The principal assets of the company were building plots adjacent to those purchased by the partnership. T and B bought some plots of land from the company; G's claim to a portion of the land purchased by them failed. The Privy Council held that the purchase of the particular plots was neither within the scope of the partnership, in that there was no misuse of partnership property (information about the plots garnered while acting for the partnership[3]), nor made in competition with the firm.

1   Although s 29 would do so if there was any use of partnership assets, but see *Aas v Benham* [1891] 2 Ch 244, CA, discussed in para 24.54, above.
2   [1906] AC 494, PC.
3   It might be argued that the decision would now be different in the light of *Boardman v Phipps* [1967] 2 AC 46, [1966] 3 All ER 721, HL.

Implied terms

24.56   Most partnerships adopt the wise policy of having a self-contained partnership agreement before operating the partnership business. Such an agreement, which need not be in writing, governs the rights and duties of the partners, but in the absence of an agreement the Act lays down certain presumptions which are impliedly applicable to a partnership. Even when there is an agreement, these statutory implied terms, contained in ss 24 and 25, operate except in so far as they are inconsistent with the agreement.

The implied terms fall into three broad categories: financial affairs, management of the partnership and changes in the personnel or interests of partners.

Financial affairs

24.57   *Partnership capital*   Partnership capital is the total amount contributed by the partners for the purpose of starting up or carrying on the business. It is a fixed sum determined by the partners, who may well make unequal contributions, and it is not the same as the partnership assets which are a variable class comprising everything belonging to the firm. In the absence of an agreement to the contrary, s 24 provides that, even when the partners have provided unequal capital contributions, they are to be treated equally in respect of certain issues relating to capital. Thus, s 24 provides that:

a.   all partners bear an equal liability in respect of capital losses;
b.   no interest is to be credited to partners in respect of their capital in calculating the firm's profits; and
c.   a partner is entitled to interest at 5% on any money made available to the firm beyond the amount of capital he agreed to contribute to it.

In practice, unequal capital contributions are usually accompanied by a provision in the partnership agreement that capital losses are to be divided in proportion to the percentage of capital invested and for the payment of interest. Indeed, it is common for a partnership agreement to state that interest is to be paid on partnership capital before any division of profits.

Section 24 also provides that all partners are entitled to share equally in the capital of the business, but the word 'capital' is misleading in this context because it means not the capital contributed by the partners but the assets of the firm. Thus, if three partners, A, B and C, have contributed partnership capital of £5,000, £10,000 and £15,000, respectively, A's entitlement to any partnership capital is one-sixth, B's is one-third and C's is one-half whereas they are each entitled to one-third of the partnership assets. This provision does not, it seems, apply to partnership assets liquidated after the dissolution of the partnership but before the final settlement of the firm's accounts[1].

1   See *Popat v Shonchhatra* [1995] 4 All ER 646, [1995] 1 WLR 908, para 24.69, below.

24.58   *Profits and losses*   In the absence of any agreement to the contrary, s 24 provides that all partners are entitled to share equally in the profits of the business. Hence, there is no necessary correlation between the proportion of partnership capital provided by a partner and his share of the profits (or losses). For example, one of three partners who has contributed no capital is entitled to one-third of profits and must bear one-third of non-capital losses. Not surprisingly, this presumption is frequently displaced by an agreement which specifies the proportion of profits (or losses) attributable to each partner.

24.59   *Indemnity*   All partners are jointly and severally liable for the firm's debts. If one partner has paid one of the firm's debts the firm must indemnify him in the circumstances specified in s 24. Section 24 applies where the payment was made by the partner in the ordinary and proper conduct of the business of the firm provided that his actions were necessary and not merely ones which the partner who undertakes them thinks may be beneficial to the firm.

Management of the partnership
24.60   In the absence of an agreement to the contrary, s 24 provides that every partner may (and, by implication, should) take part in the management of the firm's business, which carries with it the right to have access to the firm's books of account.

The right to participate in management does not entitle a partner to a salary if he does take part in managing the firm. On the other hand, should a partner fail to undertake his management responsibilities the court may order him to compensate his co-partners[1]. Furthermore, partners who have extra burdens of management cast upon them by the death of a partner can, unless they are the executor of the deceased, be compensated for their extra efforts out of profits[2]. A partnership agreement may well provide that partners who run the business be paid a salary, in which case that sum is deductible from gross profits before determining the profit available to the partners.

1   *Airey v Borham* (1861) 29 Beav 620.
2   *Featherstonhaugh v Turner* (1858) 25 Beav 382.

24.61   *Decision-making*   Section 24 provides that any difference of opinion arising between partners in the course of their management of the firm can be determined by simple majority if it is in respect of ordinary matters connected with the partnership business. Each partner has one vote regardless of his capital contribution to the firm unless the partnership agreement provides otherwise.

In respect of more fundamental matters relating to partnership business, unanimity is required by the Act. Fundamental matters include:

a.   an alteration in the partnership constitution, eg changing the firm's business;
b.   the introduction of a new partner, or the substitution of a new partner for an outgoing one;
c.   the expulsion of a partner, although a majority vote to expel a partner is sufficient if there is an express agreement to that effect[1].

1   Section 25.

Change of partners and assignment of partnership interests
24.62   A new partner, unlike a new shareholder, can incur financial liabilities which are shared by his co-partners. Thus, it is not surprising that the introduction of a new partner is a matter in respect of which the unanimous agreement of the existing partners is required. However, a new partner may be admitted without unanimous consent if the partnership agreement provides that one or more of the partners may, at their option, introduce a new partner, whether as a successor or otherwise. Unanimous consent is deemed to have been given in advance in the agreement.

24.63   *Assignment*   In contrast to the rules relating to the admission of a new partner, the Act does allow a partner to assign[1] his share in the assets and profits of the firm. If this is done the assignee stands in the shoes of the assignor only in respect of a right to profits; he has no right to engage in the management of the firm. An assignor retains liability to the outside creditors for the debts of the firm but he may be entitled to an indemnity from the assignee.

An involuntary assignment of a partner's financial rights in the firm may be ordered by a court on the application of a judgment creditor of the partner. Section 23 provides that the other partners have the option to redeem the share which is subject to a charge or to seek a dissolution of the partnership.

1   This includes using the share as security.

Partnership property
24.64   It is important to distinguish between assets which are the property of the firm and assets which are the property of the individual partners. This is because:

a.   partnership property does not belong to any individual partner; it must be applied exclusively for partnership purposes and in accordance with the partnership agreement;
b.   any increase in the value of partnership property belongs to the firm and not to individual partners;
c.   partnership property is available for the firm's creditors in the event of the firm becoming insolvent, whereas a creditor of an individual partner can claim only the assets of that partner;

d. on dissolution every partner can insist that partnership property is sold and the proceeds divided between them; and

e. unless the partners agree otherwise, partnership property which consists of land is, in equity, deemed to be personal property[1] and is subject to rules on such property. Thus, partnership land can be the subject of an action for conversion[2].

1   Para 2.19, above.
2   Para 20.18, above.

24.65   It is frequently difficult to differentiate between partnership property and a partner's property. For example, where a partner's property is used for the purposes of the partnership, is it a partner's property or partnership property? Suppose a firm rents premises in a building which belongs to a partner, are those premises partnership property? Whether an item of property belongs to a firm or to a partner is a question of fact which has to be determined by reference to any express agreements between the partners relating to it and, in the absence of an agreement, the partners' intention is inferred from their dealings and the Act.

In the absence of an agreement guidance is provided by the Act, which states that:

a. All property and rights and interests in property originally brought into the partnership stock, or acquired on the firm's behalf for the purposes of (and in the course of) the partnership business, are partnership property and must be held and applied by the partners exclusively for the purposes of the partnership and in accordance with the partnership agreement[1].

b. Unless the contrary intention appears, property bought with money belonging to the firm is deemed to have been bought for the firm[2].

The combined effect of these sections and of the decided cases is that property bought with partnership money, or brought into common stock and credited in the books as part of the capital of one of the partners, or otherwise treated by the partners as part of the firm's property, is inferred to be partnership property. This is so even if the asset happens to have been conveyed to only one of the partners, or was originally transferred to the partners as co-owners[3]. However, a mere agreement that the private property of a partner is to be used for the firm's business does not make it partnership property unless the business would not be viable if the asset was not the firm's property[4].

The courts do not strain to treat property as belonging to the firm rather than the individual partner unless the circumstances plainly warrant such a conclusion. For example, where the partnership is described as the owner of the assets of the business, the courts will construe the word 'asset' narrowly and may find that an asset cannot be treated as partnership property if there is evidence that it was not treated as such by the partners[5].

1   Section 20.
2   Section 21.
3   *Waterer v Waterer* (1873) LR 15 Eq 402.
4   *Miles v Clarke* [1953] 1 All ER 779, [1953] 1 WLR 537.
5   *Gian Singh & Co v Nahar* [1965] 1 All ER 768, [1965] 1 WLR 412.

Consequences of dissolution

24.66 Circumstances, for example the retirement of a partner, which affect the firm may lead it to choose to terminate its business and be totally wound up or to carry on despite the change of circumstances. In the first case, the firm's assets must be collected in and duly distributed first to creditors and then, if there is anything remaining, among the partners in accordance with their agreement or in accordance with the implied terms set out in s 24. Where the firm continues, questions of account between the partners must be settled, which will generally require a valuation of the firm's assets, and the appropriate sums must be paid to the departing partner. Valuation of a departing partner's interest is a matter for a specialist.

After consideration of these issues we will consider some less important consequences of dissolution.

Realisation of assets

24.67 The assets of the firm are generally sold on dissolution. However, where the dissolution arises by virtue of the death or retirement of a partner, the partnership agreement will normally provide that the deceased or retiring partner's share is to be transferred to his surviving colleagues at a price to be ascertained by reference to the last set of accounts.

The sale of tangible property is straightforward but there can be difficulties over the sale of the firm's goodwill. Goodwill is an amalgam of trading reputation and trade connections built up over the lifetime of the firm's existence. It has been described as 'the element which enables a business to earn profits in excess of those expected from the capital and resources employed in that particular business'. Goodwill may attach to the firm or to an individual partner and in the latter case goodwill may not be a partnership asset.

24.68 *Sale of goodwill* The valuation of goodwill is a highly specialised matter. The consequences of the sale can, subject to any agreement to the contrary, be summarised as follows:

a.   only the buyer can represent himself as continuing or succeeding to the seller's business[1]; and

b.   the buyer has the exclusive right to use the former firm's name although the seller can carry on a similar business in competition with the buyer[2], even though this decreases the value of the goodwill which has been purchased, provided that he does not suggest that he is the successor to the previous firm; and

c.   the seller can advertise his business generally but cannot canvass the customers of the former firm.

When goodwill is sold covenants are usually entered into which set out the rights of seller and buyer after the sale[3] and this is much the wisest policy.

1 *Churton v Douglas* (1859) 28 LJ Ch 841.
2 *Trego v Hunt* [1896] AC 7, HL.
3 See para 15.14, above

Final accounts

24.69   The dissolution of the firm and the realisation of its assets are followed by the final account which must occur before the assets can be distributed.

Where there is total dissolution a general account is necessary. A general account can be requested not only by each of the outgoing partners but also by the executors of a deceased partner or by the assignee of a partner. A general account comprises a record of transactions from the date of the last settled balance sheet down to the conclusion of transactions in the actual winding up. In drafting such an account the standard practice of the firm with regard to previous accounts must, so far as is possible, be followed.

If a partner retires or dies, the firm may continue without any general account being taken for some time after this event. If this happens the rights of the deceased or retiring partner are either those prescribed in the partnership agreement or, in their absence, those provided for in the Act[1].

A firm may also continue to trade after it has been terminated by the partners. The issue can then arise as to how the revenue profits or any profits realised on a scale of an asset should be distributed. In *Popat v Shonchhatra*[2], the plaintiff, who had entered into a partnership with the defendant, left the partnership which S continued to operate for some two years. Applying s 42, P was held to be entitled to a share of the revenue profits proportionate to his partnership assets at the date the partnership ended less an allowance payable to the remaining partner for his trouble in carrying on the business. The judge then considered the appropriate division of the profit made on the sale on a capital asset during this two-year period. He took the view that any surplus capital (assuming the matter was not determined by the partnership agreement) should be divided between the partners in proportion to their entitlement to post-dissolution profits. However, it seems that this view does not prevail when a partner has died or been wrongfully expelled from the partnership – in such cases an equal splitting of the capital profit has been approved[3], albeit in cases where the entitlement of the partners to post-dissolution profits was equal anyway. The matter of the distribution of surplus capital profits cannot be said to be entirely settled.

1   Section 42.
2   [1995] 4 All ER 646, [1995] 1 WLR 908.
3   *Barclays Bank Trust Co Ltd v Bluff* [1982] Ch 172, [1981] 3 All ER 232 (deceased partner); *Chandroutie v Gajadhar* [1987] AC 147, PC (wrongfully ousted partner).

Distribution of assets

24.70   Where a firm is ceasing to trade, the assets, once realised, are distributed in accordance with the partnership agreement and the Act. Broadly, each partner is entitled to have the proceeds of the sale of the firm's property applied in payment of the debts and liabilities of the firm, and to have any surplus assets paid to him in accordance with his entitlement[1].

Detailed rules are provided by s 44, which states that, in the absence of an agreement to the contrary, the following rules are to apply:

a.   The firm's losses are to be paid, first, out of the firm's profits and, second, out of capital. If there is still a shortfall, the partners must make it up in the ratio in which they were entitled to share profits. If a partner is unable to pay his contribution to the firm's losses his partners must pay his share between them in the same proportions as profits were divided[2].

b. The assets of the firm (including any contributions by partners to make up losses or deficiencies of capital) are used:

   i.   first, in paying the firm's debts to outside creditors;

   ii. second, in repaying, to each partner rateably, any sums advanced to the firm by way of loan[3];

   iii. third, in repaying to each partner their capital contributions to the firm; and

   iv. finally, in dividing anything that is left between the partners in appropriate proportions (determined by reference to the partnership agreement of in default the profit-sharing ratios).

1 Section 39.
2 *Garner v Murray* [1904] 1 Ch 57.
3 If, after paying these first two debts, there is insufficient money to repay the partners their capital in full, deficiencies must be shared in the same manner as profits.

Return of premiums
24.71 A partner may pay a premium (a sum not referable to the purchase of partnership assets and not a contribution to partnership capital), in cash or kind, in order to join a partnership. Where the partnership is subsequently dissolved the premium may be at least partially recoverable but only if it is a fixed term partnership which has been prematurely dissolved for reasons other than the death of a partner[1] or the misconduct of the partner seeking to recover back his premium. This is stated by s 40, which provides that a partner can be awarded by the court such payment by way of return of premium as it thinks just. Any order usually apportions the premium by reference to the unexpired period of the partnership[2]. Section 40 does not operate when the partnership has been dissolved by agreement and that agreement for dissolution contains no provision for the return of premium.

1 Section 40; dissolution by death can be regarded as a chance which the potential partner must take. Apportionment may also be denied when dissolution is due to the bankruptcy of a partner.
2 *Atwood v Maude* (1868) 3 Ch App 369.

Other consequences
24.72 The other consequences of dissolution are that:

a. Any partner can give public notice of the fact, and require the other partners to join with him in so doing[1].

b. The authority of the individual partners to bind the firm continues only in so far as is necessary to complete unfinished transactions and then to wind up the affairs of the partnership[2]. For example, in *Re Bourne*[3], a firm was dissolved by the death of a partner. In carrying on the business, the surviving partner deposited with a bank, as collateral security for an overdraft, the title deeds to some land owned by the firm. The claim of the bank to that security was held to have priority over that of the deceased partner's executors because the deposit had been effected in order to wind up the affairs of the partnership.

c.   All the partners are under a duty to gather in the assets of the partnership so that they can be distributed appropriately. This obligation may be exercised by one partner in the name of the firm and he can require the assistance of his partners in this task.

1   Section 37.
2   Section 38.
3   [1906] 2 Ch 427, CA.

Chapter 25

Company Law: The Structure of Companies

25.1 As we said in Chapter 24, a person engaged in business may at the outset, or subsequently, decide to incorporate it[1]. The legal regime applicable specifically to companies is derived predominantly from statute, particularly the Companies Act 1985; all statutory references in this and the next chapter are to this Act unless otherwise indicated. Additionally, as we explained in para 2.6, above, a company, as a legal person, is generally subject to the same laws as any other person.

In this chapter we consider the incorporation of companies (including the consequences of incorporation and the process of formation) and the relationship between the company and both outsiders and insiders (the shareholders). In considering the company and its dealings with insiders and outsiders, it is necessary to consider not merely the laws applicable to a company but also those which govern the activities of organs of the company, in particular the directors.

In the next chapter we consider the financial structure of companies, the administration of companies and conclude with a brief outline of procedures relevant to companies in decline.

1 A company can be formed to pursue any legal objective; incorporation is not restricted to businesses.

25.2 Under British law, a company may be formed in any one of three ways:

a. by registration under the Companies Act 1985 (registered companies); or
b. by Private Act of Parliament (statutory companies); or
c. by Royal Charter (chartered companies).

All three types of company are associations of people who have amalgamated their ideas or resources to pursue some common lawful purpose. In practice all but a tiny handful of companies are registered companies. There are much greater practical difficulties in forming non-registered companies and the costs of so doing are very much higher.

536

Statutory companies are often specialised trading bodies, for example, building societies, friendly societies and insurance companies. Chartered companies are typically charitable or quasi-charitable associations or non-trading bodies, for example, the Institute of Chartered Accountants in England and Wales. However, in the past some famous trading companies have been incorporated by Royal Charter, for example, the East India Co and the Hudson's Bay Co.

In this chapter we discuss the rules applicable to registered companies.

25.3   Incorporation of an existing or projected enterprise can be achieved either by forming a company from scratch in compliance with the procedures laid down in the Companies Act 1985 or by buying a pre-existing company and merging the enterprise into the existing company. The majority of companies into which an existing or projected business is inserted are purchased 'off-the-shelf'. 'Off-the-shelf' companies are companies formed by specialists in company formation, which those forming the company do not intend to operate themselves, but which can be sold to a purchaser for him to operate, by selling him the company's shares.

To create a company by registration is reasonably quick and very cheap. The people concerned with its formation (the promoters) must submit certain documents, including a memorandum of association signed by at least two people who have agreed to take shares in the company (the subscribers), to the Registrar of Companies (a government appointed official) and pay a registration fee. The advantage of purchasing an 'off-the-shelf' company is that the company already exists and there is no delay between deciding to form a company and the company coming into existence through the registration process. This obviates the problem of pre-incorporation contracts[1] and the possibility of having stationery printed bearing a name which, by the time the company is registered, has been taken by another company. However, an off-the-shelf company will not have been formed with the specific requirements of the promoters in mind and alterations of the memorandum or articles may be required.

For most people interested in forming (or buying) a company the appropriate form of company will be a private company limited by shares[2].

1   Discussed in para 25.19, below.
2   Approximately 98% of registrations are of this type of company.

Incorporation

The effects of incorporation
25.4   A company is a legal person separate and distinct from its shareholders (often called members), directors and employees: this principle is long established[1]. A classic illustration of the separate legal identity of a company and its shareholders is provided by *Lee v Lee's Air Farming Ltd*[2], where Lee, who was founder, principal shareholder, managing director and chief pilot of a company, had been killed while engaged on the business of the company.

The Privy Council held that Lee and the company were distinct legal persons. Consequently, Lee could enter into a contract of employment with the company and his widow could therefore claim compensation under a government scheme which was limited to widows of employees[3].

1   See *Salomon & Co Ltd v Salomon* [1897] AC 22, HL; para 2.6, above.
2   [1961] AC 12, [1960] 3 All ER 420, PC.
3   But see *Buchan and Ivey v Secretary of State for Employment* [1997] IRLR 80 in which the Court of Appeal interpreted the Act as not giving employment rights to a director employed by a company of which he was the principal shareholder.

25.5   The consequences of the recognition that a company is a legal person separate and distinct from its members and employees are many. Some advantageous to the shareholders, others not. Examples of the benefits of incorporation include the following:

a.   A company can sue and be sued in its own name.
b.   A company has perpetual succession. A company does not die simply because all its shareholders are dead, although it can be wound up or struck off the register by the Registrar of Companies if it appears to be moribund, for example when no accounts or annual returns have been filed for some period of time. Because a company exists unless and until it is wound up or de-registered, property once transferred to the company remains the property of the company and there is no need to transfer legal title to the property on a change of shareholder or director.
c.   The shareholders, directors and employees are not liable for criminal or tortious acts committed by the company although they may incur personal liability concurrent with that of the company[1]. For example, a company might, through the combined acts or omissions of several employees, establish and operate an unsafe system of work which causes the death of an employee. The company would be liable but an individual employee would not be liable unless he or she was personally negligent.
d.   The shareholders, directors and employees are not liable on (nor can they enforce) contracts entered into by the company[2]. As with criminal and tortious liability, an individual may incur personal liability concurrent with that of the company if he is also a party to the contract. Furthermore, when the company acts as the agent of a shareholder or director that individual is liable under the normal rules of agency.
e.   A company may be formed with limited liability[3]. Limited liability does not allow a company to limit its liability for its debts but it permits the shareholders of a company to limit their responsibility for a company's debts. The company is a separate person, so there is no reason why its shareholders should incur liability for its debts unless they have agreed to do so. Liability may be limited to a predetermined sum payable on winding up (company limited by guarantee) or, more commonly, to the nominal value of the shares held unless this sum has been paid by the current or a former shareholder (company limited by shares). Since most shares in limited companies are issued fully paid, shareholders have, effectively, no liability for the company's debts.

f. Where a company has transferable shares, ownership of the company can be split or transferred without affecting the company itself. In practice the transferability of shares in many companies is so restricted that realistically they either cannot be sold or have a minimal sale value.

g. Formation of a company may bring financial benefits. For example, a company can create floating charges to raise money and incorporation may minimise the tax liability of shareholders.

1   See for example *Williams v Natural Life Health Foods Ltd* [1997] 1 BCLC 131, CA, para 25.11, below.
2   This is merely an application of the general law (and common sense) that a person cannot enforce or be liable on another person's contracts; for some exceptions see para 25.8, below.
3   Section 2(3). See further, para 25.19, below.

25.6   There are drawbacks to the recognition of the separate legal identity of a company. For example:

a. Members have no direct rights in respect of a company's property. We have seen that a company can own property in its own right; consequently, its members have no direct interest in the property of the company. Because the members of a company do not own its property, but only shares in it, they cannot pledge or insure such property. In *Macaura v Northern Assurance Co Ltd*[1], the plaintiff, who was the principal shareholder in a company which he had formed to take over his timber estate, sought to recover on an insurance policy (which he had taken out on the timber prior to the incorporation of the company) when the timber was destroyed by fire. The House of Lords held that, since the plaintiff no longer owned the property, he could not have a valid policy of insurance thereon, nor could the company claim the benefit of the policy because it was not a party to the contract of insurance[2].

b. The extensive requirements of disclosure, resulting in a loss of privacy for the affairs of a company, can be seen as the price to be paid for the benefits of incorporation. Disclosure is ordained in four different ways: first, information must be delivered to the Registrar of Companies; second, information may be published in the London Gazette (an official publication); third, a company must keep certain registers and information at its registered office; and fourth, certain information must be published in business documents. In addition, public, listed companies must comply with any additional disclosure requirements imposed by the Stock Exchange.

Information which has to be provided to the Registrar[3] is available for public inspection and any person can require a copy of such information. The most important aspect of publication in the London Gazette is the requirement that the Registrar publishes a notice of the receipt (or issue by him) of certain documents specified in s 711. Publication in this case constitutes 'official notification'. Section 42 provides that without official notification of certain events, for example, alteration of the constitution of the company or a change of directors, the company cannot rely on that change against any other person. Registers and information kept at the registered office of a company are not necessarily open to public inspection; the statutory provision requiring maintenence of the register etc will specify who has access to it and this is often limited to members of the company. Information which must be contained in business documents, for example, the name of the company[4], is obviously revealed to anyone who sees the relevant document.

c.   In addition, incorporation brings with it administrative burdens which do not apply to sole traders or partnerships[5]. Obviously sole traders and partners have to comply with an administrative regime imposed by Parliament but these are light compared to the provisions relating to companies. These burdens are outlined in the next paragraph.

1   [1925] AC 619, HL.
2   An application of the doctrine of privity; paras 6.24–6.34, above.
3   For example the annual return which all companies must provide, s 363.
4   Section 349 provides that the name of a company must be mentioned in all its business letters.
5   See, for example, *Neptune (Vehicle Washing Equipment) Ltd v Fitzgerald* [1996] Ch 274, [1995] 3 All ER 811, discussed in para 25.54, below.

25.7   While incorporation is cheap and easy, the registration of a company (or acquisition of an 'off-the-shelf' company) is not the end of the bureaucratic process. In return for the advantages of incorporation Parliament requires the observation of mandatory rules on the operation of a company. These rules are lengthy and complex. There can be no doubt that in most companies many administrative rules, for example, on the conduct of meetings, are largely ignored. Perhaps in recognition of the widespread lack of use of some of the rules, Parliament has recently sought to reduce the administrative burden on companies, especially smaller companies, by the insertion of new sections into the 1985 Act[1]. Such reforms are small measures and there remains an immense amount of law imposing obligations upon companies, shareholders and directors, which would not apply to a sole trader or to a partnership. These obligations fall into four broad groups:

a.   *Administration*   Much of company administration is governed by statute, for example, there are rules as to the qualification of directors and the company secretary[2]. The conduct of meetings of shareholders or directors is subject to statutory control[3].

b.   *Directors' powers*   The powers of the directors, who in smaller companies will almost certainly be majority shareholders, are limited in that certain things can be done only with the agreement of the shareholders. Many of these constraints on directorial power relate to the ability of the directors to benefit themselves[4].

c.   *Share structure*   The ability of the directors or shareholders to do as they wish with the shares of the company is restricted[5]. For instance, the share capital of the company cannot be reduced without the approval of the court[6] and a company cannot buy its own shares[7].

d.   *Accounts*   The major statutory requirement which imposes a continuing burden relates to company accounts. The financial results of the company must be presented to the shareholders in a balance sheet and profit and loss account[8]. The length and technicality of the accounting rules mean that company accounts must, in effect, be prepared by a qualified accountant. Since the accounts are largely the work of management it has become standard practice to have the accounts of a company checked (audited) by an independent, qualified accountant and auditing of accounts is mandatory for all companies other than those who have been made wholly or partly exempt[9]. Small companies are exempt from the requirment to have an annual audit but such a company may choose to have an audit if it wishes. These provisions are discussed further in para 26.13, below.

A summary of the audited accounts must be sent to the Registrar of Companies where it is open to public inspection (full accounts for larger companies). The obligation of a company to produce audited accounts in compliance with the Act imposes an annual financial burden on a company which is much resented by many smaller companies.

1   See para 26.5, below.
2   Sections 282-310.
3   Sections 366-384.
4   Sections 311-348.
5   Sections 80-181.
6   Section 135; see para 26.32, below.
7   Section 143; there are numerous exceptions; see further para 26.24, below.
8   Sections 221-262A.
9   Sections 249A to 249E (introduced in 1994).

Lifting the veil
25.8   There are some circumstances in which a court will ignore the separate legal personality of a company and find a member (or members) or a director (or directors), or both, legally responsible for its actions. This is called lifting or piercing the veil – the veil being the veil of incorporation which usually hides the members and directors from view. This disregard of corporate legal status may be required by statute or, in exceptional cases, be decreed by the courts. The cases where the court has lifted the veil are not easy to classify but most cases where legal personality has been disregarded involve either the interpretation of the words of a statute, or some element of fraud or bad faith, or public policy.

In addition, where the facts justify such a finding, a company can be regarded as the agent of its shareholders. In such cases the principal, the shareholders, are liable for the acts of the company under the normal principles of agency. Directors too, who purport to act for the company when not authorised so to do may incur liability under the normal principles or agency[1].

1   See Chap 24.

25.9   *Statutory provisions*   Two examples of statutory provisions which lead to the disregard of corporate status and imposition of liability on the members are as follows:

a.   When, on winding up, it appears that the business of the company has been carried on with intent to defraud creditors, shareholders (and anyone else) who are party to the fraud are personally liable for the debts of the company[1].

b.   Companies which are part of a group or are subsidiaries of another company may be required to produce not merely their own accounts but also group accounts, so that the financial position of the individual companies can be seen in context[2].

1   Insolvency Act 1986, s 213.
2   Section 630.

25.10   *Judicial 'lifting'*   The following are examples of cases where a court has disregarded corporate personality and imposed liability on members:

a.   If a company has been formed to promote a fraudulent design or avoid an existing legal obligation, the courts may treat the company as the alter ego of (ie as being synonymous with) the shareholders, in which case a court order will be made against the company and shareholders[1]. In *Jones v Lipman*[2], for example, where a vendor of property sought to avoid performance of a binding contract of sale by conveying it to a company which he had formed, both the vendor and the company were ordered to perform the contract of sale. The veil was also lifted in *Re H*[3], in which the issue was whether the property of the company should be regarded as belonging to the shareholders. The company had been formed for a lawful purpose but had been used by its shareholder-directors to evade VAT. The court accepted that where the main activity of a company is fraud its shareholders cannot object if the assets of the company are treated as their property.

b.   If a case involves an element of public policy, the courts may be more prepared to cast aside the corporate veil. In *Daimler Co Ltd v Continental Tyre and Rubber Co (Great Britain) Ltd*[4], the question before the House of Lords turned on whether a company registered in Great Britain was an alien enemy. Looking behind the corporate veil revealed that the shareholders and controllers of the company were German and therefore the company was held to be an alien enemy, since Britain was at war with Germany.

c.   Where a company, while acting in compliance with its own internal rules, ignores the legitimate expectations of the shareholders to participate in running the company, the company may be ordered to reflect those expectations or may even be compulsorily wound up[5].

d.   Where the wording of a statute so permits, the court will disregard a company's corporate personality. An example is provided by statutes which permit compensation for persons whose real property is subject to a compulsory purchase order. These statutes allow a court to disregard the separate legal personality of individual companies within a group and require the court to consider the effect of the order on the business of the group as a whole[6].

1 Sections 227-230.
2 [1962] 1 All ER 442, [1962] 1 WLR 832.
3 [1996] 2 All ER 391, CA.
4 [1916] 2 AC 307, HL.
5 Section 459; Insolvency Act 1986, s 122(1)(g); see paras 25.62-25.65, below.
6 *DHN Food Distributors Ltd v Tower Hamlets Borough Council* [1976] 3 All ER 462, [1976] 1 WLR 852, CA.

Imposing liability on the directors
25.11 Whether the corporate veil is lifted to reveal the shareholders or not, liability may sometimes be imposed upon the directors in respect of corporate activities. A director can incur liability for the company's debts in cases of fraudulent or wrongful trading, or for torts[1] or crimes committed by the company which he authorised, directed or procured applying normal tortious or criminal law principles. In *Williams v Natural Life Health Food Ltd*[2], M, the principal shareholder and managing director of the company, was held liable to the purchaser of a franchise who had relied on inaccurate profit projections provided by the company[3]. M was found to have undertaken personal responsibility for the accuracy of the profit projections, in that they were based on M's experience in a business which he personally owned and which had nothing to do with his position as a director of the company, and he had affirmed the validity of the figures when challenged as to their accuracy by another director of the company and the plaintiff's advisers.

A director who was knowingly a party to a company's fraudulent trading is liable to contribute to the assets of the company on winding up[4]. Fraudulent trading occurs when a director allows his company to continue trading, knowing that it cannot pay its debts at present and that there is no reasonable prospect that it will be able to pay them. Since fraud must be proved beyond reasonable doubt, actions for fraudulent trading are rarely successful.

A director who signs a company cheque, which the company does not honour, is not usually liable on that cheque, but he will incur liability if the name of the company does not appear on it in full[5].

It is wrongful trading, introduced by s 214 of the Insolvency Act 1986, which is most likely to be the basis for the imposition of personal liability for the debts of a company on its directors.

1 *Evans & Sons Ltd v Spritebrand Ltd* [1985] 2 All ER 415, [1985] 1 WLR 317, CA.
2 [1997] 1 BCLC 131, CA.
3 The company was also liable but insolvent.
4 Insolvency Act 1986, s 213. Such a director may also be disqualified from acting as a company director.
5 Section 349(4); even the omission of '&' has led to the imposition of liability.

25.12 *Wrongful trading* If, in the course of the winding up of a company, it appears that a director (or ex-director) is guilty of 'wrongful trading', the courts, on the application of the liquidator, may declare him liable to make a contribution to the company's assets of such an amount as it thinks proper. This is provided by s 214(1) of the Insolvency Act 1986. Section 214 does not authorise an order requiring a director to contribute towards the costs of liquidation or post-liquidation debts nor does it empower the court to order that a particular creditor be paid. It is limited to an order to contribute to the company's assets.

The power to make a declaration under s 214(1) applies in relation to a director (or ex-director) if:

a.   the company has gone into insolvent liquidation;
b.   at some time before the winding up of the company, that person knew or ought to have concluded that there was no reasonable prospect of the company avoiding insolvent liquidation; and
c.   he was a director at that time.

However, the court must not make a declaration if, after the person concerned first knew or ought to have concluded that there was no reasonable prospect of the company avoiding insolvent liquidation, he took every step to minimise the potential loss to the company's creditors that he ought to have taken.

Section 214(4) provides that, for the above purposes, the facts which a person ought to have known, the conclusions he ought to reach and the steps which he ought to take are those which would be known, reached or taken by a reasonably diligent person with the 'general knowledge, skill and experience that may reasonably be expected of a person carrying out the same functions as are carried out by that director' (ie the director potentially subject to an order) and with the 'general knowledge, skill and experience' of the director whom it is sought to make liable. This somewhat obscure provision seems to mean that what a director should have known or done is to be judged by reference to a theoretical director who possesses those skills that may 'reasonably be expected' of a director, unless the director is better qualified than this theoretical director when he is to be judged by reference to his own qualifications. The Act is silent as to what qualifications one can reasonably expect a director to possess and the courts have been reluctant to detail what can be expected[1].

The most important case on the operation of s 214 is *Re Produce Marketing Consortium Ltd (No 2)*[2]. In this case the company was engaged in the import of fruit; it traded successfully for some nine to ten years and remained profitable until 1980. Thereafter, between 1980 and 1984, the company built up an overdraft, and in 1984 had an excess of liabilities over assets and a trading loss. Between 1984 and 1987, when insolvent liquidation ensued, the trading loss continued as did the excess of liabilities over assets but the overdraft halved due to an increase in indebtedness to the company's principal supplier. By February 1987 one of the directors realised that liquidation was inevitable but the company was allowed to trade until October. This decision was justified by the directors as allowing disposal of the company's supplies of perishable goods which were held in cold-store. The judge found that the directors should have concluded by July 1986 that liquidation was inevitable because, although accounts were not available until January 1987, their knowledge of the business was such that they must have realised that turnover was down and that the gap between assets and liabilities must have increased. Since the Act provides that the directors are to be judged by reference to what they know and what they ought to know it was held that they ought to have known the financial results for the year ending 1985 in July 1986 at the latest so that the fact that these results were not known until 1987 was no excuse. Moreover, the directors had failed to take all steps to minimise loss; the directors had not limited their dealings to running down the company's stocks in cold-store, action which might have been justified as an attempt to minimise liability to creditors. The judge ordered both directors to contribute £75,000 to the assets of the company, this being the loss which could have been averted by speedy liquidation.

The most appropriate step to take on realising impending liquidation is probably to call in a qualified insolvency practitioner.

1   Cases suggest one cannot reasonably expect much; in *Re Elgindata Ltd* [1991] BCLC 959, the judge concluded that poor management was one of the risks which an investor had to bear. But see para 25.47, below.
2   [1989] BCLC 520.

The process of incorporation
25.13   To form a new registered company a set of documents must be prepared and submitted to the Registrar of companies. There are different types of registered company but certain documents and information are required whatever type is chosen.

All registered companies require a memorandum of association. The founders of the company (the promoters) will generally also submit to the Registrar articles of association for the company[1]. The memorandum of association can be described as the constitution of the company and the articles of association as the rulebook governing the relations of the participants in the company. The memorandum and the articles, once registered, are public documents. In other words, they are open to public inspection. A declaration that all the requirements of the Companies Acts have been complied with and a fee are also required.

Once the appropriate documentation has been checked by the Registrar of companies he issues a certificate of incorporation (a 'birth certificate') which is conclusive evidence that the procedures for incorporation have been complied with[2]. The date on the certificate marks the beginning of the legal life of the company (even if it is incorrect). Provided the documentation is in order, the Registrar has no discretion in the matter of registration. If the documentation is in order he must register a company even if the directors are hopelessly inexperienced and the company lacks capital.

1   Articles of association must be registered for unlimited companies and companies limited by guarantee; s 7.
2   *R v Registrar of Companies, ex p Central Bank of India* [1986] QB 1114, [1986] 1 All ER 105, CA. The Attorney General may seek judicial review of a registration.

The promoters
25.14   The person or people who seek to implement the setting up of a company are the promoters[1]; they are in a very powerful position at the beginning of the company's life. They decide what the company will do, what it will buy and who the first directors will be (usually themselves). Because the promoters occupy this pre-eminent role they are regarded by the law as being

in a fiduciary position[2] in their dealings with the company. For example, a promoter owes a duty of good faith in all dealings with the incipient corporation. In consequence, the law provides that they cannot make an undisclosed profit from their position.

A promoter will often sell his own property (perhaps an existing business) to the company he is forming either for cash or in exchange for shares[3] in the newly incorporated business. Subsequent shareholders may allege that the asset sold by the promoter was either not suitable for the company or was over-valued. The courts have held that a promoter can keep a profit made by selling property to the company he is forming, if he discloses that he is making it. Disclosure must be either to an independent board or the first shareholders[4]. A promoter who fails to make such disclosure is in breach of duty and the transaction is voidable by the company[5], but if the transaction cannot be rescinded[6] the company is bound by the contract. The rules on disclosure apply to profits made directly from the sale or in an indirect manner.

Where the promoter has either authorised the purchase of unsuitable property and made disclosure of his interest or failed to disclose and rescission is barred, an action for negligent misstatement or deceit might be possible.

The growth of specialist firms providing 'off-the-shelf' companies has greatly diminished the importance of the rules on both promoters and pre-incorporation contracts (which we discuss in the following paragraph).

1   Except those acting in a purely professional capacity.
2   *Foss v Harbottle* (1843) 2 Hare 461.
3   The allotment of shares for non-cash consideration of lesser value than the nominal value of the shares allotted, is not issue at a discount contrary to s 100 and its attendant provisions; see para 26.20, below.
4   *Gluckstein v Barnes* [1900] AC 240, HL.
5   *Erlanger v New Sombrero Phosphate Co* (1878) 3 App Cas 1218, HL.
6   The bars to rescission are discussed in para 14.16, above.

Pre-incorporation contracts

25.15   The promoters of a company may seek to make contracts on the company's behalf prior to its incorporation. In making such contracts they may or may not reveal that they act for an unformed company. Section 36C (which reiterates the common law decision of *Kelner v Baxter*[1]) provides that in neither case is the company bound since, at the time the contract was entered into, it had no capacity to contract. In *Kelner* the promoters ordered wines and spirits on behalf of a hotel company they were forming; the goods were not paid for by the company nor could they be recovered since they had been consumed; the company was held not liable on the contract. Pre-incorporation contracts cannot be ratified by a company although a company may choose to discharge a pre-incorporation contract and enter into a post-incorporation contract with the other contracting party[2]. This termination and re-creation can occur expressly or by implication but they do not arise merely by virtue of the company acting on the pre-incorporation contract[3].

Section 36C provides that a person purporting to enter into a transaction on behalf of, or as agent for, an unformed company is, subject to any agreement to the contrary, personally liable on it. This is so even if he believed he was acting for the company and the other party knew the company had not yet been formed[4].

If an 'off-the-shelf' company is purchased, the problem of pre-incorporation contracts does not arise because the purchasers of the company are never acting on behalf of an unformed company.

1 (1866) LR 2 CP 174.
2 *Howard v Patent Ivory Manufacturing Co* (1888) 38 Ch D 156. For ratification see paras 23.9-23.13, above.
3 *Re Northumberland Avenue Hotel Co Ltd* (1886) 33 Ch D 16, CA.
4 *Phonogram Ltd v Lane* [1982] QB 938, [1981] 3 All ER 182, CA.

The memorandum

25.16 We have said that the memorandum of association is one of the documents which must be submitted to the Registrar of Companies in order to obtain registration. Sections 1 and 2 provide that the memorandum of association must list:

a. the name of the company; and
b. whether the registered office of the company is in England and Wales or in Scotland; and
c. whether the company is limited or unlimited and, if limited, whether by shares or by guarantee and, if limited by shares, the amount of the company's share capital; and
d. the objects of the company.

The Act provides draft forms of memoranda[1] for various types of company. The clauses of a memorandum, once registered, can be altered by the shareholders in compliance with procedures laid down in the Act[2].

1 Section 3.
2 Sections 4-6, 28 and 121; a special resolution is usually required.

25.17 *The name*   A company can be registered with any name the promoters choose unless it is illegal, prohibited by statute (for example, Red Cross), or too similar to the name of an existing registered company. Certain words can be used in the name of a company only with the permission of an appropriate government minister, for example, bank, chartered, hospital and British[1].

Even if the Registrar registers a name, it does not preclude an action by an existing, similarly named, business for the tort of passing off, that is, creating confusion in the minds of the public as to which company is which and thereby effectively stealing the original company's goodwill[2]. Indeed, a name which has been registered may, within twelve months of registration, be directed to be changed by the Secretary of State if it is too like the name of an existing company. It is possible to change the name of the company at a later date if need be[3].

The final words of a limited company's name must either be 'public limited company' (which may be abbreviated to plc) if it is a public limited company, or, if it is a private limited company, 'limited' (which may be abbreviated to Ltd)[4].

Since the name of the company must appear on the company's seal, business letters, cheques etc and be affixed outside all places of business, brevity reduces printing costs.

1   Section 26.
2   See, eg, *Exxon Corpn v Exxon Insurance Consultants International Ltd* [1982] Ch 119, [1981] 3 All ER 241, CA.
3   Section 28; a special resolution is required.
4   Section 25 permits companies which have a registered office in Wales to use Welsh equivalents.

25.18   *Registered Office*   The registered office of a company is a place where documents can be served on the company. Hence, a document sent (or hand-delivered) to the registered office would be regarded as served on the company[1].

1   Section 725.

25.19   *Limited or unlimited*   The founders of a company have to decide whether the shareholders of the company will have limited or unlimited liability for the company's debts. The company itself always has unlimited liability.

On the winding up of an unlimited company, the shareholders are required to pay any of the company's debts which the company is unable to meet.

On the other hand, on the winding up of an insolvent limited company, the shareholders are required to pay only a limited sum to meet those of the company's debts which it lacks funds to discharge. The maximum amount which a shareholder can be required to contribute towards the undischarged debts of a limited company varies. It may be:

a.   a pre-determined, usually modest, sum (the guarantee) if the company is limited by guarantee; or
b.   the nominal value of his shares in so far as it has not already been paid by him or a previous shareholder, if the company is limited by shares.

It must be stressed that a shareholder in a company limited by shares does not have to pay the nominal value of his shares if the company goes into insolvent liquidation, but only the amount of the nominal value, if any, which has not already been paid by him or by a previous holder of those shares. Since shares generally have a relatively modest nominal value and are issued fully paid, the amount payable by shareholders on winding up is frequently nothing.

It will cause no surprise to learn that most companies are formed with the liability of the shareholders being limited.

25.20   *Share capital*   Section 2 provides that a company registered with liability limited by shares must specify the number of shares it is creating and the nominal value of each share. The total nominal value of a company's shares is the share capital of the company. Thus, if a company is formed with 100 shares, each with a nominal value of £1, the company has a share capital of £100.

The nominal value of a share is an arbitrary figure picked by the company and it does not necessarily bear any relation to the market value of the share, or the asset value or earning capacity of the company. In practice most private limited companies have a share capital of less than £5,000 and the nominal value of individual shares is fixed at one penny, ten pence or one pound.

A private limited company has no statutory minimum share capital so that, since a company need have no more than two shareholders at formation, it need not have share capital exceeding two pence[1]. Indeed, one common complaint against British company law is that it permits the all too easy formation of grossly undercapitalised companies. A private company may, if successful, wish to become a quoted company and it is possible to re-register as a public company[2] provided the company amends its share capital requirements.

A public limited company must have a minimum share capital of £50,000 on its formation and at least £12,500 must have been subscribed in cash as consideration for shares in the company[3]. A public company may re-register as a private company[4].

1 Whatever the nominal value of a private company's share capital, it is not required to allot more than two shares.
2 There are other requirements set out in ss 43-48; see also para 25.22, below.
3 Section 118.
4 Sections 53-55; see also para 25.22, below.

25.21 *Objects clause*   The memorandum of association must state the objects of the company, that is the purposes for which the company was formed and the aims and business it intends to pursue. This does not mean that the company must list everything it may need to do in order to operate its business. It is sufficient for a company to specify the business which the company intends to pursue since it will have implied power to do anything necessary to achieve its specified aims. Hence a company formed to run an estate agency business need not state it has the power to place advertisements in newspapers or provide staff with cars. However, a company can only exercise an implied power to do an act which is reasonably incidental to the attainment or pursuit of an express object and only in so far as that act is not expressly prohibited by the memorandum[1].

The objects clause defines the contractual capacity of the company[2]. As a result, companies have tended to register very long objects clauses specifying any business the company might wish to pursue at any time in its life. The need to register such monumental objects clauses has been ameliorated by s 3A, which permits a company to register as its object 'to carry on business as a general commercial company'. Hence, a company which has such an object is authorised to do practically anything. Section 3A also provides such a company 'has power to do all such things as are incidental or conducive to the carrying on of any trade or business by it'. Section 3A appears to be couched in objective terms. Consequently, companies using s 3A may wish to register an additional object which authorises the pursuit of activities which the *directors* believe to be incidental to the carrying on of trade or business. The memorandum of a company not intending to carry on a commercial business, for example, a charity, must be more specific in its objects clause.

If, unusually, a company was registered with a very specific objects clause, for example, to develop a particular building site, the situation is that on cessation of that object a shareholder can petition for the winding up of the company[3], even if the company is pursuing some other profitable business[4].

Section 4 permits a registered company to alter its objects clause if it so wishes. Such an alteration must be approved by special resolution[5]. The court may, on an application made by holders of at least 15% of the shares or any class of shares, in proceedings brought within 21 days of the alteration, cancel or affirm or amend the alteration[6]. Many companies have amended their memorandum to insert the new objects clause authorised in s 3A.

1   *Rolled Steel Products (Holdings) Ltd v British Steel Corpn* [1986] Ch 246, [1995] 3 All ER 52, CA.
2   Para 25.29, below.
3   On the grounds that it is just and equitable so to do: Insolvency Act 1986, s 122(1)(g); para 25.65, below.
4   *Re German Date Coffee Co* (1882) 20 Ch D 169, CA.
5   See para 25.7, above.
6   Section 5; no successful actions to block a change of objects have been reported for over 50 years.

Public or private

25.22   Registered companies can be public or private companies. Section 1 provides that a company which has a share capital (which must comply with the capital requirement already discussed) may state in its memorandum that it is a public company. A company which does not state itself to be a public company is a private company. Public companies must be limited and have a share capital. Private companies can be limited or unlimited and, if limited, be limited by shares or by guarantee. All types of company are subject to the same basic legal regime although with significant differences in certain areas[1]. However, only public companies can seek a Stock Exchange listing[2] or seek to raise money from the sale of shares (or other securities) to the public. The costs of a public flotation on the Stock Exchange are considerable.

A company formed as a public company may re-register as a private company. To do so the shareholders must approve the change by special resolution, alter its name by deleting 'plc' and substituting 'Ltd' and amend its memorandum of association to omit any features which identify it as a public company. The company must then apply to the Registrar for re-registration[3] and, subject to any application by a shareholder who objects to the re-registration, the Registrar issues a certificate of re-registration. A shareholder who did not vote in favour of the change who holds at least 5% of any class of share, or 50 members acting in concert, whatever the size of their shareholding, can petition the court to cancel the re-registration provided the application is lodged within 28 days of the passing of the special resolution[4]. Minority shareholders are given this right because the conversion of a company from public to private may result in diminished marketability of their shares. Instead of striking down the re-registration, a court can postpone a hearing to allow the other shareholders in the company, or the company itself, to buy out the dissenting shareholder or holders.

A private company can re-register as a public company provided it has a share capital. To effect the change the memorandum and articles must be altered to comply with the requirements imposed on a public company, and the name of the company must be changed by substituting 'plc' for 'Ltd'; these matters require a special resolution to be passed[5]. In addition, the requirements relating to the share capital of a public company must be satisfied[6]. Following this, the directors must deliver to the Registrar a declaration of compliance with the procedures and a relevant balance sheet together with an unqualified auditor's report[7]. Thereafter, the Registrar issues a new certificate of incorporation.

1　For example in respect of the rules on the content of accounts and the minimum share capital.
2　A public company seeking listing must also comply with the Stock Exchange requirements for listing which are extensive.
3　Section 53.
4　Section 54.
5　Section 43.
6　Section 45.
7　Section 43.

The articles

25.23　Generally all new companies register articles of association. However, this is not an absolute requirement for companies limited by shares since, if articles are not registered by such a limited company, the company is deemed to incorporate as its articles a model form of articles set out by statutory instrument: Table A[1]. Even if articles are registered by a company limited by shares, the articles include Table A, except to the extent that it is excluded or modified[1]. Most companies adopt the provisions of Table A either wholly or with modifications even if separate, self-contained articles are registered.

Among the matters provided for in the articles are the method of election of the directors, the rights attached to shares and how meetings are to be conducted and votes recorded. For example, they will provide whether proxies can vote, whether a vote is decided by show of hands or by poll and what the necessary majority is on particular issues. In construing the articles the courts will seek to interpret them in such a way as to validate them but a provision which is clearly inconsistent with the law or the memorandum is invalid and does not bind the shareholders[2]. Consequently, where the articles of a company provide that something can be achieved by a simple majority vote or by a particular majority, but the Act provides otherwise, the provision in the articles is ineffective[3].

The types of resolution which the Act (or the articles) may require are discussed in the next paragraph.

1　Section 8. The Table A which applies is the one that was in force at the time the company was registered. Consequently, most companies have either the 1929, 1948 or 1985 version.
2　*Welton v Saffery* [1897] AC 299, HL.
3　For example s 303 permits a director to be sacked by ordinary resolution whatever the articles provide.

25.24 *Resolutions*   The management of companies is in the hands of the directors particularly the executive directors. However, certain matters, predominantly constitutional issues such as amendments to the memorandum and articles, can be implemented only with the agreement of the shareholders, which is usually procured by passing a resolution at a company meeting. A resolution passed at a general meeting binds all shareholders, whether they attended or not and whether they voted for or against the resolution, and the company.

The Companies Acts may provide that a particular issue can be determined only if it is approved by the shareholders by the majority specified in the Acts, and such provisions generally prevail over the articles. The Act provides for the following types of resolution:

a.   an *ordinary resolution*, which requires an issue to be approved by at least a majority by value of those present and voting (including proxy votes[1]);

b.   a *special resolution*, which requires the approval of at least 75% by value of those present and voting (including proxy votes[1]);

c.   s 381A provides that, with limited exceptions[2], a private company can substitute a *written resolution* for a special or ordinary resolution. A written resolution requires unanimous shareholder approval which is evidenced by all shareholders having signed a document approving the measure. The signatures need not be contemporaneous, nor need any meeting be held.

d.   s 366A permits private companies to use an *elective resolution* to dispense with the holding of certain meetings or the laying of accounts and reports before a general meeting of the company[3]. An elective resolution is a resolution which must be approved by all the shareholders, in person or by proxy, at a meeting (21 days' notice of resolution required, s 399) and the resolution must be registered within 15 days (s 380). An elective resolution can be revoked by ordinary resolution.

1   In limited circumstances, proxy votes are not counted.
2   Dismissal of the directors or auditors cannot be done by written resolution: Sch 15A.
3   An elective resolution can also be used for other limited purposes the most important of which concerns the authority of the directors to allot shares.

25.25 *Changing the articles*   The articles can be changed by the shareholders by passing a special resolution[1]. Moreover, a provision in the memorandum which was not required by law to be in the memorandum can be changed as if it had been placed in the articles[2]. There is one exception to this[3]; a provision relating to the rights attached to a class of shares which has been placed voluntarily in the memorandum, can be altered only by using the procedures, if any, set out in the memorandum. Thus, it is possible to create a class of shares with inalienable rights, a procedure which has occurred with some government flotations of what had been state-owned industries, by specifying class-rights in the memorandum and declaring those rights to be incapable of change without the consent of the holders of that class of shares.

If a company changes its articles by special resolution, a shareholder who objects to the change may try to challenge it in court on the basis that such change is not 'bona fide for the benefit of the company'[4]. The courts, which invented this ground of challenge[5], have been extremely reluctant to strike down changes of articles on this ground and will be unlikely to do so unless the amendment discriminates unfairly against a shareholder or group of shareholders[6]; for example, by expropriating their shares[7]. A vivid illustration of the courts' reluctance to intervene in the shareholders' decision to change a company's articles is provided by *Greenhalgh v Arderne Cinemas Ltd*[8]. In this case the majority had amended the articles of the company to authorise any shareholder to offer to sell his shares to an outsider without first offering them to existing shareholders, provided that the offer was first approved by ordinary resolution. The court approved the alteration; it applied in theory to all shareholders equally (ie it was non-discriminatory) although in practice only one shareholder (not Greenhalgh) could obtain the necessary ordinary resolution.

A change of articles may also be challenged, and probably to more effect, as being unfairly prejudicial to a shareholder; this wide-ranging action is discussed in para 25.62, below.

1 Section 9.
2 Section 17.
3 Ibid.
4 *Allen v Gold Reefs of West Africa Ltd* [1900] 1 Ch 656, CA.
5 Ibid.
6 In *Dafen Tinplate Co Ltd v Llanelly Steel Co (1907) Ltd* [1920] 2 Ch 124 the court rejected the alteration of articles which expressly excluded one shareholder from its ambit.
7 *Brown v British Abrasive Wheel Co* [1919] 1 Ch 290.
8 [1951] Ch 286, [1950] 2 All ER 1120, CA.

The effect of the memorandum and articles

25.26 Section 14 says that the memorandum and articles are to be regarded as creating a contract between the company and each shareholder and also between shareholder and shareholder. This statutory contract (as it is called) is a rather odd one.

First, in that it can be altered by one party, the company, by passing a special resolution to amend the memorandum or articles[1], without the consent of the other contracting party, a shareholder. This can have a deleterious effect where an employee-shareholder (or any employee) has a contract of employment based on the articles since a change of articles changes the contract of employment. For example, if the articles provide that the managing director shall be paid a salary of £100,000 a year and his contract provides that he shall be paid such sum as the articles provide, he will only be entitled to £1 a year if the articles are changed to reduce the managing director's salary to that amount. Clearly, directors and others employed by companies should have self-contained service contracts, not ones based on the articles.

Second, in the interpretation placed on it by the courts. The courts have held that a shareholder can enforce the contract created by the memorandum and articles only in so far as the relevant provision creates a 'membership' right, that is a right attaching to each and every share and which relates to the holding of shares[2]. This precludes the enforcement of a right which, while vested in all shareholders (and others), does not relate to the ownership of shares. What constitutes a membership right is far from clear but it seems clear that the reimbursement of promotion expenses does not fall into this category[3] nor does the right of a member, set out in the articles, to occupy an executive post within the company[4]. For example, the Court of Appeal in *Beattie v E & F Beattie Ltd*[5], did not permit a director, who was also a shareholder, to enforce a term in the articles requiring disputes between the company and a member to be referred to arbitration. The court held that, although he was a member and was in dispute with the company he was in dispute over his rights as a director and had no contractual right to enforce the arbitration provision.

1   Section 9.
2   This view derives from the first instance decision of Astbury J in *Hickman v Kent or Romney Marsh Sheepbreeders' Association* [1915] 1 Ch 881.
3   *Melhado v Porto Alegre Rly Co* (1874) LR 9 CP 503.
4   A non-member who seeks to enforce a right conferred by the memorandum and articles is defeated by the doctrine of privity; *Eley v Positive Government Security Life Assurance Co Ltd* (1876) 1 Ex D 88, CA.
5   [1938] Ch 708, [1938] 3 All ER 214, CA.

25.27   *Shareholder agreements*   It is not uncommon for shareholders to seek to entrench their rights and interests within the company but as we have seen in paras 25.25 and 25.26, above, attempts to do so by putting provisions in the articles are unlikely to be successful. First, the articles may be changed (although a shareholder with 25% of the votes should be able to block this). Second, the articles are not an enforceable contract in respect of rights given to some shareholders but not others. Thus, shareholders have sought other ways of entrenching their rights. One is by the use of a shareholder agreement.

Generally, a shareholder agreement is an agreement between all or some of the shareholders whereby they agree to act in a particular manner, usually an agreement to vote as directed by X (who may or may not be a shareholder). A shareholder agreement may also purport to bind the company itself. It is plain that, even if the agreement seeks to bind the company, it cannot restrict or amend a power conferred by statute. Thus, an agreement not to alter the memorandum of a company is of no effect because the right to alter the memorandum is conferred by the Companies Act[1].

A shareholder agreement made between all or some of the shareholders is perfectly valid even if the effect is to circumvent a right which the Companies Act confers upon shareholders. Obviously it can only bind those who agree to it, and not subsequent shareholders in the company. Even if the agreement pre-determines how a shareholder will vote, there is no legal objection. A shareholder can sell his vote if he so chooses[2]. This allows a minority shareholder to ensure that any rights he has been given in the memorandum or articles cannot be changed despite the statutory right to change them conferred by statute. Any attempt to change his rights would be a breach of the shareholder agreement and could be restrained by injunction.

The effect of a shareholder agreeement is a matter of construction and in some cases an agreement conferring rights on a shareholder may have created what are known as class rights (see para 26.33, below). The significance of so doing is that a statutory regime relating to the variation of such rights may then apply, in addition to the normal contractual rights deriving from the agreeement itself.

1 *Russell v Northern Bank Development Corpn Ltd* [1992] 3 All ER 161, [1992] 1 WLR 588, HL.
2 *Welton v Saffery* [1897] AC 299, HL.

The Company and Outsiders

25.28 We have seen that a company is a separate entity distinct from its members and directors. Since a company must have dealings with other persons, natural or legal, it is necessary to determine to what extent a company can enter into contracts or commit torts or crimes. Moreover, in its dealings with outsiders a company must act through human intermediaries and the extent to which an intermediary can bind the company is relevant.

It is to these issues, liability in contract, tort and crime, and the ability of an intermediary to bind a company, that we now turn.

Liability of the company in contract

25.29 While a company is a legal person, its contractual capacity is not that of a natural legal person who, unless he is a minor, a mental patient or a drunkard[1], has the capacity to make any contract he chooses.

It is the objects clause of the company (which may now be drafted in broad terms[2]) which defines the contractual capacity of a company. If a company enters into a contract which has not been authorised, expressly or impliedly, by the objects clause, the contract is ultra vires (beyond the powers of the company). Traditionally an ultra vires contract was void and unenforceable. For example, in *Ashbury Railway Carriage and Iron Co Ltd v Riche*[3], Riche, who had been employed by a company to supervise the building of a railway, was not paid for the work and sued the company. The objects of the company permitted the building of railway rolling stock. The House of Lords held it was not thereby authorised to build railways; consequently, any contract designed to implement that unauthorised activity was void and Riche was not entitled to his money. Interestingly enough, this decision was no more popular with companies than it was with Riche and means were soon adopted to try and evade the effect of the decision (usually by adopting very long and wide-ranging objects[4]). This unpopularity stemmed from the fact that a company might expand into new areas without realising the need to amend its objects so that the company, or others who had financed the change of direction, would find that they had entered into a series of unenforceable transactions. However, while a company's contractual capacity is still determined by reference to its objects clause, statutory reform, contained in s 35, may render an ultra vires contract enforceable.

If a company has entered into a transaction which is beyond its powers (as defined by the objects clause), the shareholders can ratify it by special resolution, thereby rendering the transaction valid[5]. Even if the shareholders do not ratify a transaction entered into by the company, s 35(1) may still protect the person dealing with the company. Section 35 provides that transactions beyond the powers of the company (ie ultra vires transactions) are enforceable by the outsider and the company in most circumstances.

It is s 35 which we must now consider.

1 Chap 16. Chartered companies do have the capacity of natural legal persons; see *Sutton's Hospital Case* (1612) 10 Co Rep 1a, 23a.
2 Section 3A; para 25.21, above.
3 (1875) LR 7 HL 653.
4 This self-help approach was accepted, with reluctance, as effective in *Cotman v Brougham* [1918] AC 514, HL.
5 Section 35(3).

25.30 Section 35(1) states that: 'The validity of an act done by a company shall not be called into question on the ground of lack of capacity by reason of anything in the company's memorandum.' Hence, if a company enters into a contract with another person (X), which is not authorised by its objects clause, the contract binds the company and X. This provision, if it stood alone, would have given companies full legal capacity; unfortunately it does not stand alone. Section 35(2) allows a member of a company to restrain the company from doing an act which, but for s 35(1), would be beyond the company's capacity. Section 35(2) is itself limited in its effect in that a shareholder cannot restrain an act which would be in fulfilment of an existing legal obligation of the company. Consequently, a shareholder can stop a contract which it is proposed shall be entered into, but cannot stop the carrying out of a contract which has been entered into by the company.

Where a transaction is entered into by a company which is beyond its powers, the directors are in breach of their duty to the shareholders. However, s 35(3) provides that the shareholders may, by special resolution, absolve the directors from liability for this breach of duty[1]. Whether the directors are absolved or not, the transaction can be enforced by virtue of s 35(1).

1 A vote to ratify the transaction does not absolve the directors, a second special resolution is required.

Liability of the company for torts
25.31 There is no doubt that a company can commit a tort either where the actions of a human intermediary can be construed as the acts of the company, for example a publishing company would be liable for defamatory remarks contained in a book which it published, or where a non-delegable duty cast upon the company is broken[1]. Additionally, a company can incur vicarious liability for the actions of its agents and employees[2]. This vicarious liability can extend to acts by employees which cause the company to be in contempt of court[3].

1 See para 17.31, above.
2 See paras 17.15-17.25, above.
3 *Director General of Fair Trading v Pioneer Concrete (UK) Ltd* [1995] 1 AC 456, [1995] 1 All ER 135, HL.

Liability of the company for crimes
25.32 There is no doubt that companies are found guilty of crimes even though the objects clause of a company will not include the commission of crimes as an aim or object. The precise basis on which companies are liable for

criminal acts is not entirely clear. It seems certain that a company can be guilty of a crime which can be committed simply by the doing of a prohibited act in prescribed circumstances[1]. Additionally, a company can, if the wording of an offence supports this, incur vicarious liability for the criminal actions of its agents and employees[2].

Particular problems arise in respect of crimes the definition of which require a person to have done the prohibited deed with the requisite degree of *intention or fault* (which can vary from crime to crime). After some hesitation, it was accepted that a company can be guilty of a crime requiring intention or fault. What is required for guilt is some human being who had the necessary intention or had acted with the necessary fault and who can be identified with the company. This has been construed as meaning is there a director or other relevant person who can be treated as the directing mind and will of the company. The courts have refused to aggregate the state of mind of a number of directors, each of whom knows only part of the picture, to form a composite state of intention or fault. Hence, in larger companies it is difficult to find a person or small group of persons who can be said to have sufficient knowledge of the overall risks the company is running who can, thus, be treated as the directing mind of the company.

An example of where a company was found to have the necessary fault is provided by the case concerning the death of a number of persons engaged on an adventure holiday run by OLL Ltd. The company was found guilty of manslaughter after it was proved that the company had shown an almost total lack of regard for safety, in that there was inadequate planning and preparation for the trip, supervision of which was by staff who were barely competent canoeists, and a lack of safety equipment, and that these risks were known to the managing director of the company who was plainly the directing mind and will of the company.

An alternative approach to the idea of a controlling mind is to find that the knowledge of an individual can be treated as the knowledge of the company so that where the question of liability turns on whether a company 'knew' something, the company can be liable where an employee employed to deal with a relevant issue had the requisite knowledge. Thus, in *Meridian Global Funds Management Asia Ltd v Securities Commission*[3], the company was criminally liable for failing to give notice that it had acquired a substantial holding in a public company as soon as it knew, or ought to have known, it had acquired such a holding. The knowledge of the person authorised to acquire the shares was attributed to the company so that as soon as he knew of the acquisition the company was also treated as 'knowing'.

1 *Alphacell Ltd v Woodward* [1972] AC 824, [1972] 2 All ER 475, HL; unless the definition of the crime provides that it can only be committed by a person performing some physical act; see *Richmond upon Thames London Borough Council v Pinn & Wheeler Ltd* [1989] RTR 354, DC.
2 *National Rivers Authority v Alfred McAlpine Homes (East) Ltd* [1994] 4 All ER 286, the company was held criminally liable in respect of acts by junior employees who had released pollutants into a river. Compare *Seaboard Offshore Ltd v Secretary of State for Transport* [1994] 2 All ER 99, [1994] 1 WLR 541, HL.
3 [1995] 2 AC 500, [1995] 3 All ER 918, PC.

Liability for acts negotiated by intermediaries

25.33   A company, while in law a person, cannot go out into the world and negotiate contracts or enter into deals; it must act through agents or intermediaries. An agent of a company is subject to the usual rules of agency discussed in Chapter 23. Hence, an agent acting for a company must have actual, implied or ostensible authority to enter into a particular transaction if he is to bind the company.

In most companies, the board of directors has actual authority to make the decisions as to how the company is to operate[1] and the company is bound by transactions authorised by the board. If the board has negotiated a contract or other transaction on behalf of a company and it has actual authority the company is bound. If the powers of the board have been restricted by a decision of the shareholders, a transaction beyond the board's powers will still bind the company unless the person dealing with the board had notice of the restriction. A third party may have actual notice of a restriction but it is more likely that a third party will have constructive notice in that the memorandum and articles of a company, once notified to the Registrar, are deemed to be known to everyone[2]. However, even where the third party does have notice s 35A, (discussed in para 25.36, below) may allow the third party to enforce the transaction.

Further, where the board are given a power to enter into a transaction if approved in advance by the shareholders, a third party is entitled to assume that such permission has been given unless he has actual or constructive notice to the contrary[3]. Third parties do not have constructive notice of decisions taken by the company by ordinary resolution. Thus, if the articles of a company state that the board may do X if approved in advance by ordinary resolution, the third party is entitled to assume that approval has been given. Even if the third party has actual or constructive notice that no approval has been given, s 35A may render the transaction enforceable.

1   For example, by virtue of Table A, art 70; see para 25.39, below.
1   Section 711.
2   *Royal British Bank v Turquand* (1856) 6 E & B 327.

25.34   Merely because the board can enter into contracts or other transactions, it does not mean that the board has the exclusive jurisdiction to enter into contracts etc on behalf of the company. In practice the board's power to act for the company may well be delegated to other intermediaries (directors or others). Those intermediaries may also be capable of binding a company. It is a question of whether the intermediary had actual, usual or ostensible authority.

Obviously, when an intermediary with actual authority enters into a transaction on behalf of the company, the company is bound.

Where a person has been appointed to a particular office he has the authority which the holder of that type of office would usually possess[1]. The usual authority of any type of intermediary, for example a managing director or company secretary, is determined by the courts. The usual authority of a director or other intermediary may be restricted by the articles or by an instruction by those with actual authority within the company. In such a case a third party with notice of that restriction cannot rely on usual authority to hold the company bound by its intermediary's acts unless the restriction can, by virtue of s 35A, discussed in para 25.36, below, be ignored.

In addition, a properly appointed office-holder may be held out as having wider powers than that which his office would normally confer. For example, a tea-boy has by virtue of his office extremely modest usual authority but he could be held out as having more extensive powers - this is a form of ostensible authority. Ostensible authority may also arise when an intermediary who does not have any usual authority has been held out as having the power to bind the company. Thus, for example, a person acting as managing director who has not been appointed to that post will be regarded as being held out as having the authority to bind the company. It is the operation of ostensible authority to which we now turn.

1   *Armagas Ltd v Mundogas SA* [1986] AC 717, [1986] 2 All ER 385, HL.

25.35   *Ostensible authority*   Ostensible (sometimes called apparent) authority arises when the company, or an appropriate person within the company, makes a representation of fact, often by conduct, to a third party that a person is authorised to act on behalf of the company and the third party relies upon that representation. For ostensible authority to be created in respect of a transaction, the following conditions must be satisfied.

a.   There must be a *representation* or holding out[1]. The holding out could be in respect of a particular type of transaction, for example, a relatively junior employee might have been allowed without specific authority to order, on a regular basis, supplies of paper or other low-value office equipment, the company has invested the employee with ostensible authority for transactions of a similar type with the same supplier(s). Alternatively, a company may permit a person not appointed to a post, for example that of managing director, to act as if he had been validly appointed to that post. In such a case the person so held out has ostensible authority. A person held out as a valid office-holder has ostensible authority to do anything which would have been within his usual authority had he been properly appointed to the post he is, in fact, occupying.

b.   The representation must be one of fact and it must be made by the company (or an authorised agent acting on its behalf) to the third party. The alleged agent cannot hold himself out as having authority to act for the company[2].

c.   The third party must *rely* upon the representation. It might be said that when the company has made a representation to a third party who knows, either in fact or, more probably, as a matter of constructive notice, that the agent is not in fact authorised, the third party could not claim to have relied upon the representation. Such a conclusion might be seen as logical but it would be very hard on a third party who has constructive notice of all the public documents of the company. Consequently, it is sufficient for the third party to show reliance in fact for this condition to be satisfied.

There remains one major difficulty with ostensible authority. Where the third party knows (actually or constructively) of a restriction on the powers of the company's agent he is bound by that restriction even if the intermediary has been held out by the company as having wider powers; s 35A, discussed in para 25.36 below, may provide a solution in such a case.

A neat example of usual and ostensible authority is provided by *IRC v Ufitec Group Ltd*[3]. In this case, the Inland Revenue had denied tax-relief to the company because it had sold an asset sooner than it should have done to obtain the relief. The company was seeking to claim that the contract of sale was invalid in that it had been negotiated by one director, Z, and that the usual authority of a single director did not extend to the sale of corporate assets. The court accepted that even if Z did not have usual authority[4], the remainder of the board, by allowing him, with their knowledge, to negotiate the sale (a process which took several months) had held him out as having ostensible authority to sell the property on behalf of the company.

1 These conditions are based on the judgment of the Court of Appeal in *Freeman and Lockyer (a firm) v Buckhurst Park Properties (Mangal) Ltd* [1964] 2 QB 480, [1964] 1 All ER 630.
2 *Armagas Ltd v Mundogas SA* [1986] AC 717, [1986] 2 All ER 385, HL, in which the alleged agent made his own representation that he had authority to conclude a charterparty and the third party was unable to rely on ostensible authority. But see *First Energy (UK) Ltd v Hungarian International Bank* [1993] 2 Lloyd's Rep 194, [1993] BCLC 1409, CA, in which an agent who did not have authority in respect of the relevant transaction was held to have ostensible authority to say that his head office had approved the transaction.
3 [1977] 3 All ER 924.
4 It is generally accepted that the usual authority of a single director is extremely limited; see, for example *Kreditbank Cassel GmbH v Schenkers Ltd* [1927] 1 KB 826, CA.

25.36 *Section 35A* The authority which the board or any other agent of a company appears to possess may be restricted either by the constitution of the company or by those with actual authority to run the company but, unless that limitation is discoverable by a party who deals with the company, it can have no effect; the company is bound by the acts of its agents even when the agent over-steps the limitation. But as we have indicated, the fact that the public documents of a company are deemed to be known to everyone means that a restriction in, for example, the articles is 'known' to a third party dealing with a company. Thus, a company could hold out a person as having authority to enter into a contract but then escape from it by pointing to the articles which state that the person held out could not have authority to enter into such a contract. This was unsatisfactory and has been amended by s 35A.

Section 35A provides that:

a. in favour of a person dealing with a company[1];
b. the power of the board to bind the company (or authorise others so to do) is deemed to be free of any limitations contained in the company's memorandum or articles;
c. provided that the person dealt with the company in good faith.

This means that a company cannot enforce a transaction which it entered into by means of an unauthorised agent but the third party may be able to do so if he acted in good faith *and* the agent in question would have had authority but for the restriction. It must be stressed that s 35A does not confer authority on those who have never had any; it negates restrictions on the powers which an agent would otherwise possess.

A person does not manifest bad faith simply by knowing that there is a restriction on the powers of the directors or by failing to inquire if their powers are limited or by failing to realise that something is wrong. Cases on earlier versions of s 35A, which would probably remain applicable, have treated good faith as a subjective issue[2].

If the directors ignore a limitation on their powers the shareholders can sue them, even if the transaction is enforceable, and have the choice whether or not to ratify the unauthorised act.

1 The ability of a director to rely on s 35A is limited by s 322A.
2 In *Barclays Bank Ltd v TOSG Trust Fund Ltd* [1984] BCLC 1, it was said (the point did not arise on appeal) that: 'A person acts in good faith if he acts genuinely and honestly in the circumstances of the case.'

25.37 *Section 285*   The issue of whether an intermediary has bound the company is generally determined by reference to principles of agency, supplemented by s 35A, outlined above. However, company law developed alternative approaches to this issue which remain good law. One of these is now embodied in s 285.

Section 285 states that it validates the acts of a person appointed as a director whose appointment is defective. However, the section is of limited scope. First, it does not apply to a person who has not been appointed a director at all[1]; for example, a person held out as occupying a post to which no appointment has been made. Second, because the section has been construed as validating only those acts which a properly appointed director would have had the authority to undertake, it does not confer authority. Rather, it merely validates the acts of a person which, if that person had been properly appointed, would have bound the company anyway. Again, ostensible authority does the job of s 285.

1 *Morris v Kanssen* [1946] AC 459, [1946] 1 All ER 586, HL.

The Company and Insiders[1]

25.38   As we have seen, a company is a separate legal person distinct in law from its shareholders, who own it, and the directors who run it[2].

The relationship between the shareholders and the directors, the appointment and dismissal of directors and the obligations imposed on directors are of fundamental importance. In many companies, particularly those that are family owned, the majority shareholders and the directors will be one and the same. Thus, as well as considering the obligations of directors, we must consider the enforcement of those obligations by a minority shareholder. A majority shareholder, even if he is not a director, has no difficulty enforcing his rights; he can sack the directors or instruct them how to conduct the affairs of the company.

1 The employees, who may also be regarded as insiders, are rarely the concern of company law; their rights are protected by employment law.

2   This embraces the relationship between the majority shareholders and the minority shareholders, a matter which was also touched on in considering the alteration of the articles of a company; see para 25.25, above.

The division of power within a company

25.39   A company, while a legal person, can only operate and be operated through human intermediaries. This raises the issue of who has the power to run the company. The power to run the company is initially vested in the shareholders of the company: they own the company and they can run it as they choose. However, in all but the smallest companies, it is impractical for the shareholders to exercise day-to-day control over the company's affairs and their powers are delegated to surrogates. Since all companies must have at least one director[1], the directors are usually the shareholders' appointees. The issue then arises as to who has the right to determine what the company will do: the shareholders or the directors?

The directors have only such power as is delegated to them by the shareholders. Most companies have in their articles a provision vesting day-to-day control in the directors as a body or in a managing director. Where power has been vested in the directors, the shareholders have no right to interfere in management, unless that power has been reserved to the shareholders[2] in the articles or by statute. If the shareholders are unhappy with the actions of the directors they must change the articles[3] to restrict their powers or sack the directors[4]. Many companies have adopted Table A, article 70, which provides that the power to run the company is vested in the board. However, article 70 also provides that the exercise of the power to manage the company is subject to any instructions given by the shareholders by special resolution. Where directions are given by special resolution, they cannot invalidate any prior act of the directors but they can instruct the directors not to implement that prior act if it is still executory. The wording of article 70 seems also to allow the shareholders to instruct the directors to undertake a course of action which the board had already resolved not to pursue.

From the above discussion it could be concluded that the board always runs the company. However, where the board cannot or will not exercise the power vested in it, the general meeting regains, at least temporarily, the power to run the company. For example, in *Barron v Potter*[5], the two directors of the company were not on speaking terms and board meetings could not be held. It was held that, consequently, the power to conduct the company's affairs vested in the shareholders until an effective board was in place. It should be noted that the default powers of the general meeting operate only where the board is completely incapable of making decisions and not when a minority of directors use any power they may have been given by the articles to block the implementation of a decision by the majority of the board. In the latter case the board is precluded from acting by the operation of the articles not by any incapacity to act. Moreover, in a very limited number of cases[6] a shareholder can commence legal proceedings on behalf of the company even if such is not the wish of the board[7].

1   Section 282. A public company must have at least two directors.
2   *Automatic Self-Cleansing Filter Syndicate Co Ltd v Cunninghame* [1906] 2 Ch 34, CA, first

established the point. Powers vested exclusively in the shareholders by the Companies Acts include: the power to alter the objects or articles; to approve compensation to directors for loss of office; and to to alter or reduce share capital.

3 A special resolution would be required; s 9.
4 The directors can be dismissed by ordinary resolution in accordance with s 303.
5 [1914] 1 Ch 895.
6 As in *Breckland Group Holdings Ltd v London & Suffolk Properties Ltd* [1989] BCLC 100.
7 Where there is 'fraud on the minority'; see para 25.60, below.

Appointment and dismissal of directors

Appointment

25.40 The first directors of a company must be nominated at the outset[1], thereafter the articles will provide when and how the initial and subsequent directors can be replaced. There are few restriction upon who can be appointed a director of a company. Neither extreme youth not extreme age[2] are bars nor is there any restriction on a company being a director of another company. However, an undischarged bankrupt, the auditor of the company[3] and a person disqualified[4] from being concerned in company management cannot be appointed as a director and must, if already a director, vacate office if they acquire any one of these bars. There are no qualifications needed to be a director, although a company secretary cannot be the sole director of his company[5]. The law generally does not distinguish between directors who are actively engaged in running the company (executive directors) and those who are not so engaged (non-executive directors).

Some companies retain the rather outmoded requirement that the directors acquire shares to be eligible to be a director (qualification shares). In such cases, s 291 provides that if such shares are not acquired within two months of appointment the errant director has to quit his office and is not eligible for reappointment until the shares are acquired.

1 Section 10.
2 A director of a public company must be under 70 unless the articles provide otherwise or the shareholders approve such an appointment by ordinary resolution following special notice; s 293.
3 Section 27.
4 Disqualification is discussed in para 25.44, below.
5 Section 283.

25.41 *Shadow directors* A person who has neither been appointed a director (a *de jure* director) nor acted as director (*de facto* director)[1] may, for certain purposes, be treated as a director if he is 'a person in accordance with whose directions or instructions the directors of the company are accustomed to act' other than where that advice is given in a professional capacity[2]. Such a person is termed a 'shadow director'.

A person is not a shadow director simply because *some* of the directors are accustomed to act as he directs[3] nor is a person a shadow director if the directors sometimes do as he says. What is required to classify a person as a shadow director is in a consistent policy of that person's advice being followed by the directors[4]. Hence, in *Re PFTZM Ltd*[5], the landlord of the company's premises, who was entitled, because the company was unable to pay its rent, to attend weekly meetings with the directors of the company and indicate which creditors were to be paid by the company, but was not otherwise engaged in management of the company, was not regarded as a shadow director. The judge ruled that the landlord was simply trying to rescue what he could out of the company using his rights as a creditor of the company.

1   *Re Hydrodam (Corby) Ltd* [1994] 2 BCLC 180.
2   Section 741.
3   *Kuwait Asia Bank EC v National Mutual Life Nominees Ltd* [1991] 1 AC 187, [1990] 3 All ER 404, PC.
4   *Re Unisoft Group Ltd (No 3)* [1994] 1 BCLC 609
5   [1995] 2 BCLC 354; see also *Secretary of State for Trade and Industry v Laing* [1996] 2 BCLC 324.

Service contracts

25.42   A person who is an executive director, ie a person involved in the day-to-day running of the company, will almost certainly have a contract with the company: a service contract. Such a service contract could:

a.   derive entirely from any conditions of service set out in the articles of the company; or
b.   be a separate contract which, expressly or impliedly, incorporates any conditions of service set out in the articles; or
c.   be a self-contained contract.

The third type offers the greatest protection to an executive director (or other executive officer). This is because a contract which derives from the articles, or which incorporates the articles, may be changed by the company in accordance with the usual rules for the alteration of a company's articles[1]. Consequently, as the articles change, the service contract changes[2] although a change in the articles cannot deprive a director of rights which had accrued before the change[3]. A further drawback to a contract which derives entirely from the articles is that a contract based on the articles is only enforceable in so far as it confers 'membership rights' and would not allow a person to enforce a right as a director[4]. Where a director has a self-contained service contract, any amendment of the articles cannot affect that contract and such a contract gives the director rights, for example to be paid, enforceable under normal contractual principles.

As we shall see in para 25.43, the self-contained service contract also has advantages for a director if the shareholders seek to dismiss a director.

Section 319 provides that any term in a service contact (whatever its source) whereby a director is to be employed for a period exceeding five years, without the contract being terminable, is void to the extent that it exceeds five years unless the term has first been approved by the shareholders in general meeting. One consequence of s 319 is that directors now tend to have contracts for less than five years, but which contain a provision for re-appointment for a similar period to the intial period of appointment on the same terms; if the contract so specifies, the reappointment may arise automatically. These so-called rolling contracts have been the subject of unfavourable comment but remain popular with directors.

1 Table A, articles 85 to 94 provide guidelines as to the type of disclosure requirements companies might adopt and limit the ability of an interested director to vote on his own contracts. A company may choose to adopt a different set of disclosure requirements.
2 *Read v Astoria Garage (Streatham) Ltd* [1952] Ch 637, [1952] 2 All ER 292, CA.
3 *Swabey v Port Darwin Gold Mining Co Ltd* (1889) 1 Meg 385, CA; hence if a director's entitlement to be paid derives from the articles, he could have his salary for the future reduced but could not be deprived of sums already earned.
4 See para 25.26, above.

Dismissal

25.43 A director may be dismissed in accordance with either a provision in his service contract or the articles of the company Dismissal on a ground specified in the articles may constitute a breach of a separate service contract, thus entitling the dismissed director to claim damages. Whether or not the articles or any service contract provide a method of dismissal, s 303 allows the shareholders to dismiss a director by ordinary resolution passed at a general meeting of the company[1]. This section operates notwithstanding anything in the articles of a company, so that, for example, a provision in the articles that a director could only be dismissed by special resolution would not prevail over s 303. The director under threat is allowed to address the meeting and circulate a written protest. The effectiveness of s 303 is diminished by two things.

First, a director's shares (if any) may benefit from a weighted voting clause. This is a provision in the articles which provides that on a vote to dismiss a director his shares will carry sufficient votes to block an ordinary resolution[2]. Such a clause effectively entrenches a director.

Second, an executive director who has a service contract and is then dismissed in breach of that contract will be entitled to compensation[3]. Where the dismissed director commanded a high salary, the damages awarded to compensate him for the breach will be commensurately large.

1 Those seeking to dismiss a director must give the company 28 days' notice of a resolution to this effect and the company must give all shareholders at least 21 days' notice of the motion.
2 Such a device was approved by the House of Lords, at least in respect of private companies, in *Bushell v Faith* [1970] AC 1099, [1970] 1 All ER 53, HL.
3 *Southern Foundries (1926) Ltd v Shirlaw* [1940] AC 701, [1940] 2 All ER 445, HL. This case also established that a director cannot restrain the company from changing its articles even if the change effects a breach of his contract.

Disqualification

25.44 The shareholders can decide to dismiss a director, but a court has the power, contained in the Company Directors Disqualification Act 1986 (hereafter the CDDA), to disqualify a person from acting as a director.

Section 1 of the Act, permits a court to disqualify a person from being a director, or being directly or indirectly concerned in the management of a company, in a number of prescribed circumstances. Sections 2 to 6, 8 and 10 CDDA set out the grounds for disqualification; sections 2 to 5, 8 and 10 give specific grounds, for example, conviction of indictable offence in connection with the management of a company, but the majority of reported cases involve the more general provision, s 6. Section 6 provides that a person shall be disqualified (for a minimum of two years) from corporate management where he is or has been a director (or shadow director) of a company which has become insolvent *and* his conduct as a director (or shadow director) of that, or any other company, makes him unfit to be concerned in company management[1]. Acting as a director etc while disqualified is a criminal offence punishable, on indictment, by a fine and/or imprisonment for up to two years.

A leading case on s 6 is *Re Sevenoaks Stationers (Retail) Ltd*[2], in which the Court of Appeal held that the words 'unfit to be concerned in the management of a company' should be treated as ordinary English words and that each case turned on its own facts. The court held that a director need not display total incompetence to be unfit but that simple commercial misjudgment should not merit disqualification; what was needed was some lack of commercial probity and an appropriate degree of incompetence. There are many reported cases on disqualification, most of which turn on their own facts but factors which are particularly relevant in deciding whether to disqualify include: breach of fiduciary or other duties, misuse of company property or money and failure to comply with the accounting and publicity requirements imposed by the Companies Acts.

The appropriate period for disqualification was discussed in *Re Sevenoaks Stationers*. Dillon LJ suggested that ten to fifteen years' disqualification should be reserved for particularly serious cases (such as where this was a second disqualification) and two to five years for not very serious cases, leaving six to ten years for serious cases which do not merit the top bracket. Where a disqualification order is made, the court can give the disqualifed director leave to be involved in corporate manaement[3]. Leave will only be granted where a company has need of the disqualified person's services and there is adequate protection for the public[4].

1   Other grounds include persistent breaches of company law and fraud in connection with the running of a company.
2   [1991] Ch 164, [1991] 3 All ER 578, CA.
3   Section 17. A director can also apply for leave during the period of his disqualification.
4   Generally there is a requirement that a solicitor or chartered accountant is also involved in the management of the company.

Directors' duties

25.45   A director, in so far as he is acting as an agent or employee of the company, owes the usual obligations imposed upon an agent[1] or employee to his principal or employer, the company. Additionally, a director, as a director, has imposed upon him obligations which are an amalgam of common law, equity and statute.

Breach of some of the duties imposed upon directors is unratifiable; others can be ratified by a resolution of the shareholders in general meeting[2]. A director-shareholder who is in breach of his duty can vote on whether or not to ratify a ratifiable breach and hence may be able to absolve himself from liability[3].

1   Paras 23.16-23.21, above.
2   *North-West Transportation Co Ltd and Beatty v Beatty* (1887) 12 App Cas 589, PC.

3 Even if the breach is not ratifiable by the shareholders, the court has power to absolve a director from liability for such, or any other, breach of duty, s 727.

To whom are the duties owed?

25.46 It is vital to determine to whom a director owes a duty because it is that person alone who can sue for breach of the duty[1]. The cases establish that a director owes his duty to the company and not, generally, to the shareholders or to the employees or to the creditors of the company. A director must act in the best interests of the company.

The leading case on this point is *Percival v Wright*[2]. In this case, the directors of a company were privy to confidential information which, once released, was likely to increase the value of the company's shares. P, a shareholder, offered to sell his shares to the directors, who accepted the offer. When the confidential information was released, P sought to have the contract of sale set aside and to recover the shares on the ground that the lack of disclosure was a breach of fiduciary duty by the directors. Swinfen-Eady J, in rejecting P's claim, held that a director did not, simply by being a director, owe a fiduciary duty (or any other type of duty) to an individual shareholder; a director's duty was to have regard to the interests of the company. This case does not preclude a director choosing to undertake some responsibility to a shareholder (fiduciary or contractual) but the duty does not arise from the fact that he is a director[3]. In most cases there is no question of the directors undertaking such a responsibility.

The interests of the company are generally concurrent with the economic interests of current and future shareholders but not with the interests of any particular shareholder. However, when the company is the subject of a take-over bid, the interests of the company have been treated as concurrent with the interests of current shareholders; hence, directors have a duty to give them honest advice about the merits of the bid[4].

It is generally thought that the interests of the company do not include the interests of creditors of the company[5]. The interests of the company might seem to extend to the interests of the employees of the company. Certainly s 309 provides that the directors must have regard to the interests of the employees. However, it does not require the directors to do anything for the employees. It is sufficient to acknowledge that they have interests[6]!

Since a director owes his duties to the company, it is obvious that the power to sue a director for breach of duty is vested in the company even where the breach also (or only) harms a shareholder. Further, the company can sue only for the harm which it has suffered[7]; it cannot recover on behalf of a shareholder for any loss suffered by him.

1 In accordance with the usual rule that a person cannot litigate another's cause of action.
2 [1902] 2 Ch 421.
3 *Allen v Hyatt* (1914) 30 TLR 444, PC.
4 *Heron International Ltd v Lord Grade* [1983] BCLC 244, CA.
5 In *Kuwait Asia Bank EC v National Mutual Life Nominees Ltd* [1991] 1 AC 187, [1990] 3 All ER 404, the Privy Council rejected the view that the directors owed a duty to creditors, thus reversing the dicta in a number of earlier cases.
6 In *Re Saul Harrison* plc [1995] 1 BCLC 14, CA, the court, in rejecting an application under s 459, regarded the fact that the directors considered the adverse impact liquidating the company would have on the employees as a valid reason, in conjunction with others, to refuse

to liquidate the company and release its assets to the shareholders; see further para 25.62, below
7   *Foss v Harbottle* (1843) 2 Hare 461; see further para 25.59, below.

Common law duties

25.47   A director may incur liability for negligence in accordance with the general principles of the law of tort and a negligent director will be liable to the company for any damage resulting from his want of care. The critical issue is usually what standard of care should a director display in order avoid liability for negligence[1]. The traditional formulation of the nature and extent of this duty is that given by Romer J in *Re City Equitable Fire Insurance Co Ltd*[2], in which he held that a director:

a.   need display only such skill as may reasonably be expected from a person of his knowledge and experience;

b.   need not give the affairs of the company continuous attention; and

c.   is entitled to leave the day-to-day running of the company to the officials of the company and is entitled to assume, in the absence of suspicious circumstances, that such officials are performing their duties honestly[3].

These propositions remain good law with regard to non-executive directors but executive directors will generally be constrained by their service contracts to devote a set percentage of their time to the affairs of the company.

A director who does his honest best may be held to have exercised sufficient care and skill to evade liability for negligence and there is no requirement that a person appointed a director must have any special knowledge or skill relevant to the business of the company he is joining. The question then is did the relevant director, given his qualities, display adequate care and skill? Since the test is subjective, a professionally qualified person will be expected to display more skill than a non-qualified person.

Liability was imposed for a want of care in *Dorchester Finance Co Ltd v Stebbing*[4]. In this case, the company had three directors: S, who ran the company, P and H. S and P were chartered accountants and H had considerable accounting experience. P and H did little more than call in periodically and sign blank cheques for S to use; no board meetings were held. The judge, in determining the appropriate degree of care and skill to be expected from S, P and H, took into account their experience of accountancy and business and held that the complete failure by P and H to do anything in respect of the running of the company was, even for non-executive directors, negligent. In a recent case[5], the judge held, obiter, that the duty of care and skill at common law was co-extensive with that imposed by s 214 of the Insolvency Act 1986 (wrongful trading)[6], namely that a director should display such care when carrying out functions in relation to the company as could reasonably be expected from a person carrying out those functions. This seems to have a more objective ring about it than Romer J's view in *Re City Equitable Fire Insurance* which assessed a director's conduct by reference to the relevant director's abilities and not by reference to those of *a* person carrying out directorial functions. Breach of the duty of care and skill is ratifiable by the shareholders either by ordinary resolution[7] or by implication provided all the shareholders have had a chance to consider the question of releasing the director from liability[8]; a director who is also a shareholder can vote on the decision[8].

1 Directors are exempt from the requirement to exercise their calling with reasonable care and skill normally imposed upon the provider of services by the Supply of Goods and Services (Implied Terms) Act 1982.
2 [1925] Ch 407, CA.
3 In *Re Cardiff Savings Bank, Marquis of Bute's Case* [1892] 2 Ch 100, a director who had been appointed at the age of six months and who had attended one board meeting in 38 years (he was, said the judge, a busy man), was held not liable to compensate the company (a bank) for failing to notice that officials of the bank were milking it of funds.
4 [1989] BCLC 498.
5 *Norman v Theodore Goddard* [1991] BCLC 1028; see also *Re Macro (Ipswich) Ltd* [1994] 2 BCLC 354, para 25.63, below.
6 Discussed in para 25.12, above.
7 It is not possible to ratify a breach which also constitutes fraud on the minority; see further para 25.60, below.
8 *Re D'Jan of London Ltd* [1994] 1 BCLC 561.

Statutory duties
25.48 The statutory duties imposed upon directors are detailed and complicated and breach of them may give rise to a criminal penalty as well as a civil remedy for the company. Examples include a prima facie prohibition on the granting of loans to directors[1], provisions requiring the disclosure by a director of any interest he has in any contract entered into by the company[2], and the requirement that substantial property transactions between a director and the company must be approved by the shareholders[3]. Certain of these statutory duties are discussed in connection with related fiduciary duties.

These provisions are of limited value in that these duties are owed to the company and, thus, generally, it is the company which can sue a director who has broken a statutory duty. Consequently, a shareholder-director who controls a majority of the votes in general meeting appears to be free of the risk of litigation[4].

One statutory duty which does not carry a civil penalty but only a criminal sanction is insider dealing. Information about a company is an important factor in determining the value of the company's shares. Such information is available to those closely connected with the company, giving them the opportunity to deal in the shares of the company before that information is generally known. Use of inside information (insider dealing) is generally regarded as reprehensible. First, in that it lowers investor confidence in the Stock Exchange (although not everyone condemns insider dealing on this ground). Second, because insider dealing may constitute fraud on the shareholders; for example if they are persuaded to sell their shares to the directors at an undervalue relative to the value of the shares once the information, already known to the directors, is widely known. Where fraud is provable, which is difficult, directors who defraud shareholders can be prosecuted. More importantly, the Criminal Justice Act 1993 (which replaces earlier legislation) makes insider dealing a criminal offence. The 1993 Act does not apply to unlisted securities, that is shares in private companies and shares in unquoted public companies, nor to face-to-face, as opposed to market, dealings[5].

1   Sections 330-346; there are a number of exceptions.
2   Discussed in para 25.54, below.
3   Section 320. See para 25.55, below.
4   The limited circumstances in which a shareholder can sue in respect of wrongs done to the company are discussed in paras 25.60 and 25.61, below.
5   In addition, the Stock Exchange Code for Securities Transactions, which forms part of the Listing Agreement, limits the right of a director of a company to deal in its shares and requires disclosure of all authorised dealings.

Fiduciary duties

25.49   As Lord Porter said in *Regal (Hastings) Ltd v Gulliver*[1]: 'Directors, no doubt, are not trustees, but they occupy a fiduciary position towards the company whose board they form.' As a fiduciary each director is individually subject to fiduciary (equitable) duties; these duties require him to exercise his powers in a way which has regard to the interests of the person to whom the duties are owed and not to abuse his position of trust and influence within the company. Indeed, in respect to corporate property, which we discuss in para 25.52, below, the director's fiduciary duty goes further.

Fiduciary or equitable duties can be sub-divided into the general duty, that is the obligation to act bona fide in exercising his powers and the requirement that certain powers are used only for 'proper purposes', discussed in paras 25.50 and 25.51 below, and the applied, discussed in paras 25.52–25.54, below.

1   [1967] 2 AC 134n, [1942] 1 All ER 378, HL.

25.50   *Bona fide for the benefit of the company*   The obligation to act bona fide for the benefit of the company is subjective. Consequently, provided that a director honestly believes he is acting for the benefit of the company he is not in breach of this duty[1].

Since a director must make decisions on the basis of his own honest belief of what is best for the company, it is a breach of fiduciary duty for a director to fetter his freedom to exercise his power to make decisions on the running of the company[2]. Thus, an agreement by a director that he would always vote for proposals put forward by X would be a breach of fiduciary duty. However, it is not a breach of this duty for the directors to enter into a binding agreement that they will act in a particular way in respect of a transaction, provided that they bona fide believe it to be in the interests of the company to make such an agreement. Thus, in *Fulham Football Club Ltd v Cabra Estates plc*[3], the directors of the football club, who had entered into a series of binding agreements with a developer in connection with the exploitation of the club's ground, were not permitted to object to the developer's application for planning permission. The directors genuinely believed that the agreements, when made, were for the benefit of the club and that the club would receive substantial sums from the developers. Consequently the directors were bound by an agreement not to oppose planning permission.

Breach of this aspect of the general equitable duty is unratifiable.

1   *Re Smith & Fawcett Ltd* [1942] Ch 304, [1942] 1 All ER 542, CA; affirmed by the Privy Council in *Howard Smith Ltd v Ampol Petroleum Ltd* [1974] AC 821, [1974] 1 All ER 1126.
2   *Bishopgate Investment Management Ltd v Maxwell* [1993] Ch 1, [1992] 2 All ER 856, CA.
3   [1994] 1 BCLC 363, CA.

25.51 *Proper purposes* A director must exercise certain of his powers (called fiduciary powers) not only honestly but also for a purpose consistent with that for which the powers were conferred on him[1]. This is known as the proper purpose test. When a use of power is challenged, the court should first consider the nature of the power – that is, the court must decide why this power was conferred on the directors whose exercise thereof is in question? – and then examine the substantial purpose for which it was exercised. If the power was not exercised for the proper purpose the exercise of the power is improper. An example of the operation of the proper purpose test is provided by *Hogg v Cramphorn Ltd*[2]. In this case, the directors genuinely believed that a potential take-over of the company was not in its best interests. To ensure the defeat of the bid, they allotted shares to the employees. The court accepted that the directors had acted bona fide and in what they believed to be the best interests of the company. However, the court ruled that the directors are given the power to allot shares in order to raise capital for the company and that, since the purpose of this allotment was to defeat the take-over bid, the allotment must be set aside[3].

Whether a power has been exercised principally for proper purposes or not is assessed objectively. Breach of the duty to act for proper purposes is ratifiable by the shareholders by ordinary resolution[4]. In *Hogg v Cramphorn*, the shareholders in general meeting subsequently approved the disputed allotment which was thus validated.

It is uncertain which of the powers conferred on directors must be exercised for proper purposes but the following powers have been held to be subject to this requirement: to borrow and give security; to forfeit shares; to refuse to register a transfer of shares; to make calls on shares; and, most recently, to enter into contracts which will continue to bind the company after the current directors have vacated office and will limit the ability of the new directors to run the company[5].

1 *Howard Smith Ltd v Ampol Petroleum Ltd* [1974] AC 821, [1974] 1 All ER 1126, PC.
2 [1967] Ch 254, [1966] 3 All ER 420.
3 The facts of this case could now also fall within ss 80–96.
4 *Bamford v Bamford* [1970] Ch 212, [1969] 1 All ER 969, CA.
5 *Lee Panavision Ltd v Lee Lighting* Ltd [1992] BCLC 22, CA.

25.52 *Trusteeship* A director cannot, without the unanimous approval of the shareholders, misuse (even innocently) corporate property. Hence, if a director appropriates the company's tangible property he will be liable to return the property to the company. The same is true of misuse of intangible corporate assets, for example the benefit of a contract possessed by the company[1].

Commercial opportunities which are within the company's grasp may also be classified as intangible corporate assets. For example, in *Cook v Deeks*[2], a company, X, was about to sign a contract to build a railway for company Y. Y was persuaded by some of the directors of X to award the contract to a new company which they had formed. The directors (and their new company) were held liable to hold the benefit of the contract on behalf of X.

Misuse of corporate assets is a breach of a director's duty which can only be ratified by a unanimous vote by the shareholders. The company or, in some cases, a shareholder acting for the company can sue a director[3] who has misused a corporate asset. A director in breach of this duty is a constructive trustee of the asset, in other words he holds the asset and any profits deriving from it on behalf of the company. A person who receives corporate assets knowing that the transfer is a breach of duty or knowingly facilitates a breach of fiduciary duty in respect of those assets (whether he receives them or not) is also a constructive trustee[4]. Where it is sought to impose liability on a non-director for knowingly facilitating a breach of trust, it is not necessary to prove that the director was dishonest, provided the director was in breach of his fiduciary duty. What is critical is dishonesty on the part of the third party.

In other respects, for example, profiting from his office, a director is not to be equated with a trustee.

1   *Menier v Hooper's Telegraph Works* (1874) 9 Ch App 350, CA.
2   [1916] 1 AC 554, PC.
3   This is one of the exceptional cases where a shareholder may be able to sue a director for a wrong done to the company; see further para 25.60, below.
4   *Royal Brunei Airlines v Tan* [1995] 2 AC 378, 1995] 3 All ER 97, PC.

25.53   *Benefiting from contracts made with the company*   A director has an equitable duty to ensure that there is no conflict between his personal interests and his obligation to advance the interests of the company. This gives rise to difficulties in respect of corporate contracts: a director who enters into a contract with his company, a service contract perhaps, wishes to advance his own interests but is supposed to give priority to the interests of the company.

The basic rule is that a director cannot make a profit from a contract made between himself and his company[1] or from a contract made by the company with a third party[2], if the contract gives rise to a conflict between his duty and interest. An early case in point is the House of Lords' decision in *Aberdeen Rly Co v Blaikie Bros*[3]. In *Blaikie*, the company wished to purchase iron chairs for use on railway stations; the contract was awarded to Blaikie Bros, a partnership in which a director of the company was a partner. The company repudiated the contract and its repudiation was upheld. The House of Lords held that, if a director enters into a contract in circumstances where there is a conflict of interest, or there is a sensible risk of such a conflict, the contract is voidable at the company's option even if the contract is entirely fair and reasonable. Thus, a company can rescind a contract from which a director benefits, directly or indirectly, if he has entered into it in breach of fiduciary duty even if the contract terms are fair and are no less favourable to the company than those obtainable from non-directors.

This onerous obligation soon became the subject of modification.

1   *Aberdeen Rly Co v Blaikie Bros* (1854) 2 Eq Rep 1281, HL.
2   *Imperial Mercantile Credit Association v Coleman* (1873) LR 6 HL 189; an example of an indirect benefit would be where a director is paid a commission by X for ensuring a company contract was placed with X.
3   (1854) 2 Eq Rep 1281, HL.

25.54 Subsequent to *Blaikie Bros*, it was decided that a director *can* benefit from a contract between himself (or a third party) and his company provided that he makes adequate disclosure of his own interest before the contract is entered into by the company. Originally, disclosure to the shareholders was required to remove any issue of conflict but companies soon began to adopt articles which provided that disclosure to the directors would suffice[1]. It remains the law that disclosure must be to the shareholders unless the articles provide otherwise: Table A, article 85, permits disclosure to the board and most companies have adopted this provison (or one similar). As with failure to make adequate disclosure to the shareholders (ie in those cases where there is no article 85 or equivalent), failure to make disclosure in accordance with any lesser requirements set out in the articles allows the company to rescind any contract. The relationship between article 85 and s 310 has caused some difficulty. Section 310 provides that a director cannot be exempted from liability for breach of duty and it could be argued that to allow disclosure to the board exempts the director from a liability he would otherwise incur. While the position cannot be regarded as settled, the case law suggests that article 85 will be treated as a provison which defines the obligation owed by a director at a lower level than that imposed by the common law rather than as a provision which allows him to break his duty and then be let off[2].

On a vote to adopt or reject a contract entered into without adequate disclosure, an errant director who is also a shareholder is permitted to vote unless the articles provide otherwise[3].

Since disclosure to the board is not as onerous as disclosure to the shareholders, Parliament has intervened in a number of ways to try and ensure adequate disclosure to shareholders and fair dealing by directors. There is a general provision, s 317, and provisions dealing with particular types of contract. The most important provisions are contained in ss 320 (substantial property transactions) and 330 (loans to directors); these sections are discussed in paras 25.55 and 25.66, below).

Section 317 provides rules for the nature and degree of disclosure where disclosure to the board is sanctioned by the articles of the company. Failure to comply with s 317 is a criminal offence[4] but it is less clear whether a company can set aside a contract with a director who has complied with the articles of the company but not with s 317. Since most companies exempt directors from liability when they have disclosed an interest to the board, the shareholders have little control over directors' contracts, even though shareholders must be informed of contracts which benefit a director in the annual accounts. This exlains the importance of the more specific provisions.

1 See *Movitex Ltd v Bulfield* [1988] BCLC 104.
2 *North-West Transportation Co Ltd and Beatty v Beatty* (1887) 12 App Cas 589, PC. Article 85 provides that a director cannot vote except in the cases specified in article 94.
3 In *Guinness plc v Saunders* [1990] 2 AC 663, [1990] 1 All ER 652, HL, members of the House were split upon whether simple breach of s 317 would render a contract voidable; in an earlier Court of Appeal decision, a majority of the court took the view that breach of s 317 would render the contract voidable. The views on s 317 were obiter in both cases.
4 Disclosure by a director is required even if he is the only director and is disclosing to himself; such a director should ensure that the minutes of the company reveal his disclosure, *Neptune (Vehicle Washing Equipment) Ltd v Fitzgerald* [1996] Ch 274, [1995] 3 All ER 811.

25.55 *Section 320*   Section 320 provides that, if a transaction between a director[1] and a company is a 'substantial property transaction, it is voidable unless approved in *advance* by the shareholders in general meeting. A director-shareholder can vote on a resolution to approve such a transaction. Approval of such a transaction need not be at a general meeting but may be informal[2] provided all the shareholders are aware of the transaction. A transaction is a 'substantial property transaction' if a director acquires from, or transfers to, the company an interest in a non-cash asset and the value of the asset exceeds £100,000 or 10% of the asset value of the company (provided its value exceeds £2,000). Section 322 provides that an unapproved substantial property transaction is voidable at the instance of the *company*. Hence, a shareholder has no legal right to challenge an unapproved transaction. A transaction entered into in breach of these sections ceases to be voidable, even by the company, if restitution is no longer possible and the company has been indemnified against any losses, or avoidance would affect the rights of a third party who, bona fide, purchased the property for value and without notice, or the company in general meeting has affirmed it.

A director who enters into a transaction in breach of this section is liable to account to the company for any gain he has made, directly or indirectly, from the transaction and to indemnify the company for any losses it may have suffered from the transaction. In addition, a director who authorised the transaction which was not approved in advance is also liable to account for any gains which the transaction conferred on him or, which is more probable, indemnify the company. A director who authorised a transaction (not the director with whom it was made) is exempted from liability if he shows he was not aware of the circumstances which constitute breach of s 320.

In a recent case on s 320[3], it was held that a solicitor who failed to advise a company that a transaction between the director of a subsidiary company and the holding company required prior shareholder approval, was negligent. Since the company was unable to rescind the transaction (because restitution was impossible), and had to pay to unscramble the deal, the solicitor ended up with a bill for £2.1 million.

1   The obligation to disclose also applies where the transaction is between a director and the holding company or a subsidiary of his company. The section also applies to persons connected to a director (defined in s 346), for example a spouse and minor children.
2   *Niltan Carson Ltd v Hawthorne* [1988] BCLC 298. In this there was knowledge of, and acquiescence in, the activities of a director by the majority shareholders and this was held to constitute approval.
3   *British Racing Drivers' Club v Hextall Erskine & Co* [1996] 3 All ER 667.

25.56 *Sections 330 to 346*   These sections provide a highly elaborate set of provisions affecting the ability of a company to make loans to, or enter into related transactions with, directors. These provisions provide both civil remedies and, where the company is a relevant company, that is, a public company or a company which is part of a group containing a public company, criminal penalties.

Section 330 provides that a company may not make loans (or guarantee a loan) to a director of the company, or a director of a holding company, or to a shadow director. Further, where the company is a relevant company the prohibition is extended to credit transactions (or guarantees thereof) and quasi-loans[1] to the same people. In addition, a relevant company may not make quasi-loans or enter into credit transactions for the benefit of a person 'connected' to such a director. A connected person[2] includes a spouse and children (under the age of 18) of a director of a company, a company with which the director is associated[3], trustees of a settlement the beneficiaries of which include the director or his spouse or children or a company with which he is associated and partners of the director or any person connected to him.

Sections 332 to 338 provide a number of exceptions to the basic prohibition, some of which operate only with the approval of the shareholders in general meeting. Section 334 permits the making of small loans, that is loans which do not exceed £5,000 in total. Section 335 allows a company to lend up to a total of £10,000 if it is in the ordinary course of business and is on normal business terms. Section 337 allows a company to provide a director with funds (up to a maximum of £20,000 for a relevant company) to carry out his duties on behalf of the company provided that the provision of funds is disclosed to and approved by the shareholders in advance, or at, or before the next AGM of the company. Failure to obtain the necessary approval or inadequate disclosure will result in the director having to repay the sums provided within six months of the AGM. Section 338 allows a money-lending company to lend up to a total of £100,000 (unless the company is a banking company, when there is no limit) to a director. provided that it is on normal business terms. Further, s 338 permits a money-lending company to lend money up to a total of £100,000 to a director for the purchase or improvement of a house if loans for such purchases are made to employees. The terms of a house loan must not be more favourable than those applicable to employees. Sections 333 and 336 provide that intra-group loans etc are not prohibited by s 330.

All loans etc to directors must be disclosed in the accounts of the company[4].

Section 341 sets out the consequences of breach of section 330. A transaction entered into in breach of s 330 is voidable at the instance of the company unless restitution is impossible, or the company has been indemnified, or avoidance would affect the rights of a person who had acquired those rights bona fide for value and without actual notice of the contravention. The beneficiary of a prohibited loan etc, and any other director who authorised it, is required to account for any gain emanating from the loan or indemnify the company against any loss it has made. A director who authorised a prohibited loan to a connected person escapes liability if he took all reasonable steps to ensure compliance with the Act. A director who authorised a prohibited loan, and a connected person who was the recipient of the loan are not liable if it can be shown that they were unaware of the breach of the Act at the time the loan etc was made[5].

1 Defined in s 331(3); essentially a quasi-loan is when someone other than the director pays, or agrees to pay, or reimburses a sum paid for the benefit of a director and he agrees to repay that person.
2 Section 346.
3 A director is associated with a company when he has an interest in shares of a nominal value of at least one-fifth of that company's share capital or controls more than one-fifth of the voting power of a company in general meeting.

4   Section 343, there are minor exceptions for loans to individuals not exceeding £2,000 and for loans within a group of companies.
5   This does not apply to the director to whom the connected person is connected

25.57   *Benefiting from the position of director*   This aspect of the equitable duty imposed on directors provides that a director should not benefit from his position as director at the expense of the company. This prohibition does not prohibit a director from profiting from his position but prevents him so doing where acquiring such a benefit would conflict with his duty to the company. If there is no real conflict of interest with his duty to promote the interests of his company he is not in breach of duty.

Two case can be contrasted. In *Island Export Finance Ltd v Umunna*[1], a former director, who successfully tendered for a contract with the Cameroon postal authorities, was held not in breach of his fiduciary duty even though he had gained useful contacts with the authority while negotiating a contract with it on the company's behalf some two years previously. The company had failed to pursue the contacts the director had made or to seek further contracts, and had effectively washed its hands of the Cameroons. Hutchinson J saw no reason why the company should benefit from a contract which was not obtained at its expense. However, in *Industrial Development Consultants Ltd v Cooley*[2], C, the former managing director of the company was held to be in breach of duty. In this case, C was party to negotiations by the company for the design and construction of a gas terminal. It became clear that the company was unlikely to obtain the contract and C feigned illness, resigned his directorship and successfully tendered for the contract on his own account. The judge held C liable to account for the profits he had made on the contract since, even though the company was unlikely to get the contract, C was not entitled to use for his own benefit information concerning it obtained in corporate service while there was any chance that the company might get the contract. In the latter case there was a clear conflict between the director's duty to further the interests of the company and his own interests whereas in *Umunna* the company had no interest in the contract.

A difficulty can arise when a company has been forced by circumstances to reject an opportunity. It is uncertain whether a director can then exploit the opportunity without incurring liability to the company. In *Regal (Hastings) Ltd v Gulliver*[3], a company was forced to reject an opportunity to buy shares in a subsidiary company (through lack of funds); the directors then bought the shares which they later resold (with their shares in Regal (Hastings) Ltd). The directors' actions were known to the majority of the shareholders but the directors were held to be in breach of duty and were required to hand the profit to Regal (Hastings) Ltd. This seems a particularly harsh decision in that the profit was effectively handed over to the very people who had bought the shares from the directors. The House of Lords suggested, obiter, that the shareholders could probably have ratified the directors' actions by ordinary resolution but by the time of the case the shares had been sold and the new owners were not going to ratify the directors' acts.

While a breach of this duty can, it seems, be ratified[4], it is uncertain whether a company can relieve a director of liability in advance by declaring itself to be uninterested in a particular contract or project and authorising him, after full disclosure, to pursue the project. Dicta in *Regal (Hastings)* suggest that even where a company has rejected a project or contract, a director cannot be authorised to take the benefit of it. However, Commonwealth authority has rejected this view[5].

1   [1986] BCLC 460.
2   [1972] 2 All ER 162, [1972] 1 WLR 443.
3   [1967] 2 AC 134n, [1942] 1 All ER 378, HL.
4   *North-West Transportation Co Ltd and Beatty v Beatty* (1887) 12 App Cas 589, PC.
5   In *Queensland Mines v Hudson* (1978) 52 ALJR 399, PC, the Australian courts allowed advance absolution.

Shareholders and their rights

25.58   We have seen that the shareholders generally confer the power to run the company on the directors. This does not allow the directors unfettered powers since they are subject to direction by special resolution, or their powers could be curtailed by a change in the articles (special resolution), or they could be sacked (ordinary resolution) and they are subject to the provisions of the Companies Acts, but what other rights do the shareholders as a body or as individuals have? Every shareholder has certain rights conferred upon him by statute and by the memorandum and articles (contractual rights). The ability of a shareholder to enforce a statutory right depends upon the wording of the statutory provision. As we have seen[1], a shareholder can enforce the contractual rights which derive from the memorandum and articles provided the right in issue is classifed as a membership right. If a shareholder has a contract with a company distinct from the memorandum and articles that contract is enforceable on normal contractual principles. Moreover, the shareholders as a body (to the extent that they are the company) are owed duties by the directors of the company[2]. These duties are usually enforceable only by the company.

We must now consider the ability of an individual shareholder to enforce the duties owed by the directors to the company, that is the shareholders as a body, at common law. We then turn to two important general statutory remedies available to shareholders unhappy with the conduct of the company's affairs: s 459 of the Companies Act 1985 and s 122(1)(g) of the Insolvency Act 1986.

1   Para 25.46, above.
2   Since a director owes his duty to the company and not an individual shareholder, breach of director's duty is not, in itself a wrong done to a shareholder and a shareholder has no cause of action against a director.

Enforcing a duty owed to or by the company

25.59   *The rule in Foss v Harbottle*   The famous case of *Foss v Harbottle*[1] established that where a wrong is done to a company, be it by an outsider or a director, the right to initiate proceedings is vested in the company because it is the company to whom the duty is owed (the proper plaintiff rule). However, since a company can only act through human intermediaries it is important to determine who can initiate litigation in respect of such wrongs. The right to pursue legal claims on behalf of a company is usually vested in the board of directors[2]. Hence, directors may be faced with a decision as to whether to sue themselves or one of their number – they may be reluctant to do so. Is it possible for a shareholder to enforce the rights of the company where the board is unable or unwilling so to do?

In addition, the rule in *Foss v Harbottle* has been extended to cover certain cases of internal irregularity. Where a shareholder is aggrieved by some failure by the company to follow internal procedures but the wrong is regarded either a matter solely for the company or where it is ratifiable by a simple majority of the shareholders who show no inclination to complain, the shareholder is denied the right to bring an action against the company (the internal irregularity rule).

1   (1843) 2 Hare 461. The rule also prohibits a shareholder suing the company when the company has failed to comply with the rules for the internal management of the company but the breach is ratifiable.
2   Because the board have the power to operate the company; para 25.39, above.

25.60   *An exception to Foss v Harbottle*   In respect of the first situation to which *Foss* applies, wrongs done to the company, there is an exceptional case when a shareholder may, if justice so requires, bring an action to enforce the company's rights. Such an action is called a derivative action in that the shareholder derives his right to sue from the rights of the company[1].

A derivative action can be brought when the actions complained of are a 'fraud on the minority' by those who control the company. This arises when there has been a fraudulent act committed by a person who commands a majority of the votes within a company. Fraud embraces not only fraud in the strict sense, for example breach of the Theft Act 1968, but also other conduct which can be characterised as equitable fraud, that is, conduct tainted with impropriety. For example, in *Daniels v Daniels*[2], the judge refused to hold that negligence, however gross, was fraudulent. However, he was prepared to hold that negligence by a director, in this case the sale of a company asset for a tiny fraction of its value, which directly benefited the directors (who had purchased the asset sold), was a 'fraud on the minority'.

A court will, however, deny a shareholder a right to sue on behalf of the company, even though there is fraud on the minority and wrongdoer control, if it would not serve the interests of justice. Examples of where a shareholder has been denied the chance to bring a derivative action include, where the conduct of the shareholder seeking to sue is itself tainted by impropriety[3], or where the independent shareholders (ie not the wrongdoer or the applicant) have already indicated that they do not wish there to be litigation on behalf of the company[4]. In a recent case[5], the court denied locus to a shareholder, B, who sought to bring an action on behalf of the company against a director, her ex-son-in-law, when it became clear that she was really pursuing a personal vendetta against the director for deserting her daughter rather than displaying concern for the interests of the company.

The benefits deriving from a successful derivative action accrue to the company since it is the company's rights which have been vindicated.

1   The company may be required to fund the action; see *Wallersteiner v Moir (No 2)* [1975] QB 373, [1975] 1 All ER 849, CA.
2   [1978] Ch 406, [1978] 2 All ER 89.

3   *Nurcombe v Nurcombe* [1985] 1 All ER 65, [1985] 1 WLR 370, CA, where a shareholder, who
    had, to her knowledge, benefited from the fraud of the director who controlled the company,
    was denied the right to sue on the company's behalf.
4   *Smith v Croft (No 2)* [1988] Ch 114, [1987] 3 All ER 909.
5   *Barrett v Duckett* [1995] 1 BCLC 243, CA.

25.61   *A further exception to Foss v Harbottle*   In respect of the second situation
to which *Foss* applies, the internal irregularity cases, there are a number of
cases where shareholders have been entitled to litigate in respect of the actions
of the company. Such actions are permitted when the shareholder is seeking to
enforce some personal right. Since it is the shareholder's right which has been
ignored he is the proper plaintiff and the benefits of any action accrue to him.

There are many examples of a breach of a personal right. For example,
where a company decided to pay dividends in bonds rather than cash, although
the right to receive cash dividends was enshrined in the articles[1], the shareholder
could require payment in cash. A shareholder has a right to challenge a decision
to enter into an illegal or *ultra vires* transaction[2]. A shareholder can object
where a decision which should be taken in a particular manner, for example
by something other than a simple majority, has been taken in some other way[3].

1   *Wood v Odessa Waterworks Co* (1889) 42 Ch D 636.
2   Section 35 may permit the ratification of an *ultra vires* act, see para 25.30, above.
3   *Quin & Axtens Ltd v Salmon* [1909] AC 442, HL.

Statutory remedies open to shareholders
25.62   *Section 459*   As we have seen, the remedies open to unhappy
shareholders who are unable to pass a special or ordinary resolution are limited.
For example, breach of the articles not involving a membership right leaves a
shareholder with no remedy and dealings in shares by the company (for example
reduction or capital or an amendment of class rights[1]) may be contrary to the
wishes of a minority of shareholders.

Section 459 may provide a remedy for disgruntled shareholders (the
Secretary of State can also petition). The section provides that when the acts
or omissions, current, past or proposed, of the company, the directors, or the
majority shareholders are unfairly prejudicial to all or some of the shareholders,
a shareholder can bring an action to complain. What constitutes unfair prejudice
is a question of fact in each case but it is plain that in order to obtain a remedy,
a member must be unfairly prejudiced in his capacity as a member. Thus,
failure to buy goods from a shareholder would not affect a member in a
shareholder capacity and could not found an action under s 459.

Useful guidance on the operation of s 459 has been provided by the Court
of Appeal in *Re Saul Harrison & Sons plc*[2]. In this case the holder of non-voting
shares claimed that the directors of the company were keeping the company
running purely to earn substantial salaries when a reasonable board would,
given the company's prospects, have liquidated the company and distributed
its assets. In support of her claim for unfair prejudice, the petitioner claimed
that, when the company had negotiated a sale of its premises, it was the ideal
time to wind up the company and distribute its assets rather than, as had
happened, to acquire new premises, and that the directors had failed to wind
up the company simply to continue to receive large salaries as directors. The

court refused to find unfair prejudice. It ruled that construction of the words 'unfair prejudice' was a matter for the court. Further, in deciding what is fair or unfair for the purposes of s 459, it was said that that it was important to bear in mind that fairness was being used in the context of a commercial relationship. Consequently, the relationship of shareholders is primarily governed by the memorandum and articles of the company, and commercial fairness can be seen as predominantly a question of complying with them. Even if conduct is not in accordance with the memorandum or articles and the powers thereby conferred it is not necessarily unfair. For example, trivial and technical infringements of the articles will not attract the statutory remedy. However, the court accepted that there are cases where the memorandum and articles do not represent the understandings upon which the shareholders are associated, and that in such cases, it may be unfair to a shareholder for those who control a company to exercise the powers set out in the memorandum and articles if to do so denies the legitimate expectations of that shareholder. Such expectations may derive from a contract independent of the memorandum and articles but is not restricted to such cases; there is also a question of whether equitable considerations require express or implied promises not contained in the memorandum and articles to be honoured. The court suggested, for example, that the widow of a joint venturer might have legitimate expectations about the benefits she should receive from the company founded by her deceased husband. Where there is no reason to look beyond the memorandum and articles to determine the relationship of the shareholders, compliance with them cannot be unfair. In this case the petitioner had no legitimate expectations beyond the general expectation that the memorandum and articles would be complied with and the directors' powers exercised properly. This has happened and there was no unfair prejudice.

Other general points are that conduct can be unfairly prejudicial even if it was not intended to have that effect[3] by the person whose conduct is allegedly unfairly prejudicial, and that misconduct on the part of the petitioner does not preclude him obtaining a remedy for unfair prejudice[3]. In the next paragraph we discuss a number of cases where s 459 was pleaded.

1   See paras 26.32 and 26.34, below.
2   [1995] 1 BCLC 14, CA.
3   *Re R A Noble & Sons (Clothing) Ltd* [1983] BCLC 273.

25.63   An action alleging unfair prejudice has been successful where there has been a misappropriation corporate assets[1], or where there has been a dilution of the voting strength of a shareholder by the allotment of further shares where the allotment was designed to 'freeze out' a person who had a legitimate expectation that he would be involved with the company[2].

Exclusion of a shareholder from managment may be unfairly prejudicial[3], provided that he had a *legitimate* expectation that he would so participate; such an expectation may be based on an agreement not contained in the articles (it may even be contrary to the articles). However, where the company is a public company, or the articles were the product of considerable legal scrutiny before adoption[4], it is unlikely that the court will find a shareholder is entitled to expect to participate in management if this is not provided for in the articles[5].

Many cases concern lack of confidence in the policy adopted by management. Loss of confidence in itself does not render the policies adopted by the company unfairly prejudicial[6]. Indeed the court has rejected the idea that, simply because the board is proposing some new, legitimate business venture, the court should intervene at the behest of a shareholder. However, in some cases the loss of confidence may be justified and then the court may award a remedy. For example, failing to increase dividends when the company's profits increase, while at the same time increasing the salaries of the directors[7], may be unfairly prejudicial.

The courts have been ambivalent about whether incompetence on the part of the directors could found a s 459 action. Certainly, mismanagement allied to attempts to do down a shareholder has been held to be unfairly prejudicial[8], as has mismanagement linked to breaches of company law[9]. In *Re Macro (Ipswich) Ltd*[10], mismanagement was found to justify a s 459 petition. In this case, the judge found that the serious shortcomings in the conduct of management were prejudicial to the company's financial interests and thus prejudicial to the members of the company. Whether, she ruled, such prejudice can be called unfair requires the court to perform a balancing of the interests within the company. The judge held that the court would not interfere in questions of commercial judgment but where the alleged mismanagement was so serious as to cause considerable loss to the company it could be unfairly prejudicial conduct. The mismanagement in this case, failure by the principal director, T, to supervise employees and consequent failure to realise they were taking bribes and inadequate supervision of work done on the company's properties, was so serious as to be unfairly prejudicial. The personality of T and his dominant role within the companies also meant that the interests of the minority shareholders (the petitioners) were inadequately protected.

1   *Re London School of Electronics Ltd* [1986] Ch 211.
2   *Re Bird Precision Bellows Ltd* [1984] Ch 419, [1984] 3 All ER 444.
3   *Re OC (Transport) Services Ltd* [1984] BCLC 251
4   *Re a Company, (No 005685 of 1988), ex p Schwarcz* [1989] BCLC 424.
5   *Re Blue Arrow plc* [1987] BCLC 585. Approved in *Re Tottenham Hotspur plc* [1994] 1 BCLC 655.
6   *Re a Company (No 004475 of 1982)* [1983] Ch 178, [1983] 2 All ER 36.
7   *Re Sam Weller & Sons Ltd* [1990] Ch 682, [1989] 3 WLR 923.
8   *Scottish Co-operative Wholesale Society Ltd v Meyer* [1959] AC 324, [1958] 3 All ER 66, HL.
9   *Re a Company (No 00789 of 1987), ex p Shooter* [1990] BCLC 384.
10 [1994] 2 BCLC 354.

25.64   Section 461 provides that the remedies available for breach of the section are at the discretion of the court. For example, in *Re H R Harmer Ltd*[1], the Court of Appeal allowed an elderly director who snooped on staff, ignored board decisions and insulted customers, to remain as chairman of the company but deprived him of any executive role.

The remedy most commonly awarded is an order to purchase the shares of the disgruntled shareholder at a fair price. If such an order is made the question arises as to how the shares should be valued. If the articles contain a price-fixing formula the court will use it unless there is a risk that that method of valuation will depreciate the value of the interest to be acquired. In one case[2], the judge found that such a risk arose in that the auditor/valuer was not required to explain how he reached his valuation, leaving the petitioner, H, no basis to attack it. In addition, there was no machinery for H to put relevant matters to the valuer, particularly those relating to any other legal claims against the company (the effect of which might considerably affect the value of shares), and the potential capital gains tax liability the company's valuation procedure would impose on H. Other situations where a court has rejected the valuation machinery in the articles have included: where the conduct of those prejudicing the petitioner has depressed the value of the shares[3] or where the valuation machinery is arbitrary and unfair on its face[4].

Generally an order under s 461 will require the majority shareholders or the company to buy the shares of the petitioner. However, it is perfectly possible for the court to order the majority to sell its shares to the petitioner. For example, in *Re Brenfield Squash Racquets Club Ltd*[5], a company which had been formed to acquire and run a squash club was owned by FMR (86% of the shares) and S (14%), one of the founders of Brenfield. The judge found found that the FMR nominees failed to recognise the proper distinction between the affairs of Brenfield and FMR and treated Brenfield's assets as "freely available" for FMR's benefit. Indeed at one point the assets of Brenfield were used by FMR as security for a loan to FMR without even consulting S. Relations between S and the other directors broke down and S was replaced as managing director and eventually removed from the board. There was little doubt that s 459 was made out. The judge ordered the majority to sell its shares to the minority.

Where a court substitutes its own valuation machinery for shares, it can also fix its own valuation date. Dates chosen have included the date of the judgment, the date of the petition alleging unfair prejudice, and a date preceding the unfairly prejudicial conduct.

Once unfair prejudice is found to exist a remedy may be granted against a third party who was not party to the wrongful acts if it appropriate to do so. In *Re Little Olympian Each-Ways Ltd (No 3)*[6], an asset had allegedly been transferred by the company at a gross undervalue to X who transferred it to Y who then transferred it to OAG (who were not alleged to be wrongdoers). The judge accepted that it could be possible for OAG to be subject to an order under s 461 but, on the facts, declined to hold it liable. The reason was that OAG was not party to any wrongdoing and had paid a fair price for the asset.

1 [1958] 3 All ER 689, [1959] 1 WLR 62, CA.
2 *Re a Company (No 00330 of 1991), ex p Holden* [1991] BCLC 597.
3 *Re a Company (No 006834 of 1988), ex p Kremer* [1989] BCLC 365.
4 *Re a Company (No 004377 of 1986)* [1987] 1 WLR 102.
5 [1996] 2 BCLC 184.
6 [1995] 1 BCLC 636.

25.65   *Section 122(1)(g) of the Insolvency Act 1986*   Section 122(1)(g) of the Insolvency Act 1986 gives a court the power to wind up a company when it 'is of the opinion that it is just and equitable that the company should be wound up'. The courts have always held that the exercise of this provision is not restricted to particular circumstances or categories. However, there are certain factual situations where a case for just and equitable winding up is likely to be in issue. One area is where the company has been formed or is being run to advance a fraudulent purpose[1]. Another is where members of a company cannot agree on how the company should be run so that it is effectively inoperable or that a company, while operable and operating, is not being run in a manner which reflects the objectives upon which the shareholders agreed when the company was formed[2]. This section is less used now that s 459, which we discussed in paras 25.62–25.64, above, which provides an alternative, more flexible, remedy for disgruntled shareholders[3]. Indeed, the court can refuse to allow just and equitable winding up[4] where there is an alternative remedy open to the petitioning members and it is unreasonable to pursue winding up rather than that alternative remedy (most probably a s 459 remedy).

A petition for just and equitable winding up can be presented by a contributor. A contributory is either the sole remaining shareholder in a company, or a member who has been registered as a shareholder for at least six months during the previous eighteen prior to the winding up or who has inherited shares, or a person who may be required to contribute to the assets of the company if it is wound up[5].

1   See, for example, *Re Walter Jacob Ltd* [1989] BCLC 345, CA, in which a company which built up a database of relatively unsophisticated investors by selling privatisation stocks at a low rate and then sought to sell their clients illiquid shares in two unquoted US companies of poor quality, was wound up on the application of the Secretary of State.
2   *Loch v John Blackwood Ltd* [1924] AC 783, PC.
3   The effect of s 122(1)(g) is to destroy the company, which is why s 459 is likely to prove a more popular remedy both for those shareholders who are unhappy, since they are likely to be bought out, and for those causing the unhappiness, since they still have a viable company.
4   Insolvency Act 1986, s 125.
5   Ibid, s 124. A member may be denied the right to petition if there is no realistic prospect of there being any distribution of assets to shareholders if winding-up was authorised.

25.66   The leading case on s 122(1)(g) is *Ebrahimi v Westbourne Galleries Ltd*[1]. In *Ebrahimi*, E and N had traded in partnership as sellers of fine carpets from about 1945. In 1958 they incorporated the business, becoming the sole directors and shareholders. Shortly afterwards, N persuaded E to admit his son, G, into the business and G became a director and was given shares by both N and E; N and G held the majority of the shares. The company traded profitably and all profits were paid out as directors' fees. In 1969 disputes arose and N and G combined to vote E off the board using what is now s 303. Since no other remedy was then available, E sought just and equitable winding up. In ordering the winding up of the company, Lord Wilberforce laid down general principles for the operation of the section. He stated that the words 'just and equitable' allowed a court to look behind the strict legalities and consider the rights and expectations of the shareholders. Justice and equity would not, he held, allow one party to disregard the obligations which he undertook on joining a company; the section allowed a court to subject the exercise of legal rights to equitable considerations. In other words, Lord Wilberforce accepted that, where people had combined to form a company, consideration must be given to their legal rights tempered by reference to their agreements and expectations in entering into the company. He accepted that this equitable overlay could not apply to all companies but only those which displayed specified characteristics.

Traditionally, such companies are called quasi-partnerships. Lord Wilberforce held that the circumstances which permit the application of equitable considerations cannot be laid down conclusively. The fact that the company was small or private was not enough, but typically a company would display all or some of the following characteristics:

a.   it will be an association formed or continued on the basis of a personal relationship involving mutual confidence;
b.   in which it was agreed that all, or some, of the shareholders would participate in management;
c.   the shares of the company will not be freely marketable, thus locking a disappointed shareholder into the company.

When, as in this case, the company is of the appropriate type the conduct of the majority should not be judged purely by reference to their legal rights but by reference to the hopes and expectations of the parties. Plainly, E had anticipated remaining part of the company he had founded and since his hopes had been dashed it was just and equitable to wind the company up.

1   [1973] AC 360, [1972] 2 All ER 492, HL.

Chapter 26

Company Law: Administration and Finance

26.1 In the previous chapter we considered the structure of a company and the relationship between the company, its directors and its members. We now turn to the administration of a company, the financial structure of companies and conclude with a brief outline of procedures relevant to companies in decline.

Administration of Companies

26.2 The administration of a company is primarily a matter for the board; the role of the directors has been considered in the previous chapter. However, the way in which decisions are reached by the board has not been discussed and there has been only passing reference to the types of meeting which the shareholders can attend and the use of resolutions as a means of decision making[1]. There are also a number of reports and registers which are significant and which reinforce a fundamental idea which underpins company law – that of disclosure of information.

In addition, there is also an administrative officer within a company whose role requires some elucidation: the company secretary.

1 Resolutions were touched on in para 25.24, above.

Meetings

Board meetings
26.3 The appropriate procedure to adopt at meetings of directors[1] is determined by the articles of a company. As we said[2] in the previous chapter, many companies adopt, wholly or in part, the draft articles set out by statutory instrument: Table A. Table A, article 88 provides a model which permits decisions to be taken by majority vote and for the chairman of the board to have a casting vote. A director has a right to attend meetings of the board. The quorum for a board meeting is determined by the articles but Table A, article

89 provides for a quorum of two unless some other figure is specified. Section 382 requires the keeping of minutes of directors' meetings.

1   It is not mandatory to have meetings of directors, and decisions taken by the directors other than in a meeting bind them; *Charterhouse Investment Trust Ltd v Tempest Diesels Ltd* [1986] BCLC 1.
2   See para 25.23, above.

Shareholders' meetings
26.4   Shareholders' meetings provide an opportunity for the interchange of information and opinion between the shareholders and directors of a company and a number of statutory provisions require the holding of meetings to determine certain issues by shareholder vote. While decisions of shareholders may be obtained other than by the holding of a meeting it will often be more convenient to have a meeting rather than trying to consult all the shareholders informally. A meeting which all members can attend is a general meeting. A meeting limited to members holding a particular class of shares is a class meeting. The quorum of a meeting is determined by the articles; Table A, article 40 provides for a quorum of two voting members.

The holding of an annual general meeting (AGM) is a statutory requirement[1] and a new company must hold its first meeting within 18 months of incorporation and not more than 15 months can elapse between one AGM and the next. The members of a private company can elect to dispense with the holding of an AGM[2]. Such a decision must be taken by elective resolution[3]. The directors will present their annual report to the AGM which will also be the meeting at which the auditors are appointed.

The directors may also call other general meetings of the company and these are called extraordinary general meetings (EGM). This power is a fiduciary power and it must be exercised for a proper purpose[4]. In addition, s 368 allows shareholders who between them hold at least ten per cent of the company's voting shares to demand the calling of an EGM. Once such a requisition has been received, the directors must, within 21 days, call a meeting which must take place within 28 days of the issue of the notice calling the meeting.

Section 371 gives the court power to call a meeting if it is 'impracticable' to convene a meeting in any other way.

1   Section 366.
2   Section 366A.
3   Section 379A; discussed in para 26.5, below.
4   See para 25.51, above for the proper purpose doctrine.

Resolutions
26.5   Decisions of shareholders' meetings are embodied in resolutions. Unless the articles or the Companies Acts provide otherwise, a resolution is passed by simple majority (where the votes are equal the resolution is lost); such a resolution is an ordinary resolution.

The Companies Acts (or the articles) often specify that a decision must be taken by a special resolution or by an extraordinary resolution. The only significant difference between them is that there must be at least 21 days' notice of an intention to propose a special resolution[1]. In order for a special or extraordinary resolution to be passed, three-quarters of the votes cast[2] must support the resolution. A shareholder who has sufficient votes to block such a resolution may be described as having negative voting control.

Section 381A provides that, with limited exceptions[3], a *private* company can substitute a written resolution for anything which may be done by resolution at a general meeting. A written resolution requires unanimous shareholder approval which is evidenced by all shareholders having signed a document (or identical documents) approving the measure. The signatures need not be contemporaneous, nor need any meeting be held. Both s 381A and s 366A (referred to below) are designed to minimise the amount of meetings which a company must hold; it is recognised that, particularly in a small company, the idea of having formal meetings of shareholders (perhaps between husband and wife) is unrealistic.

Section 366A permits *private* companies to use an elective resolution to dispense with the holding of certain meetings or the laying of accounts and reports before a general meeting of the company[4]. An elective resolution is a resolution which must be approved by all the shareholders, either in writing or in person (or by proxy), at a meeting of which the shareholder has had at least 21 days' notice[5]. An elective resolution must be registered within 15 days of it having been passed[6]. An elective resolution can be revoked by ordinary resolution.

Section 382 requires minutes to be kept of all proceedings at shareholders' meetings. Section 380 requires copies of some resolutions to be sent to the Registrar of companies; the list includes special, extraordinary and elective resolutions.

1 Section 378; this section provides an extensive set of provisions applicable to such resolutions.
2 Voting is discussed in para 26.6, below. Abstentions do not count as votes against the resolution.
3 Dismissal of the directors or auditors cannot be done by written resolution: Sch 15A.
4 An elective resolution can also be used for other limited purposes the most important of which concerns the authority of the directors to allot shares; see para 26.18, below.
5 Section 399.
6 Section 380.

26.6 *Voting* Unless some other system is adopted, every voting member who attends a shareholders' meeting is entitled to one vote which is exercised on a show of hands. However, most companies provide that voting may be by poll. On a poll a member has a number of votes proportional to the number of shares held[1]. Where a vote is taken on a show of hands, only a member can vote (unless the articles provide otherwise[2]) but on a poll a person appointed to exercise the voting rights of a member (a proxy) can vote[3].

Table A, article 46 states that a vote is to be taken on a show of hands unless a poll is demanded. Section 373 provides who can demand a poll[4] but the company may extend (but not narrow) the group of those eligible to demand a poll. Article 46 is wider than s 373[5] in that it empowers the chairman of the meeting to call a poll.

1 A share may carry more than one vote.

2   Table A, does not give proxies the right to vote on a show of hands.
3   Section 373 provides that a company cannot refuse to allow proxy voting.
4   Essentially a group of five voting members or a group which represents not less than one-tenth of the voting rights of members entitled to vote at the meeting. A proxy counts as a member for these purposes.
5   It allows two members to call a poll.

26.7   *Unanimous agreement* There are many cases where shareholders agree on a proposal unanimously but no formal meeting to pass a resolution is held. If the agreement is by written resolution it is, of course, validly passed. But what of the cases where there is agreement but neither a meeting nor a written resolution? The attitude of the courts has been to uphold the decision of the members if they can do so[1]. However, an informal agreement is not effective to overcome a requirement of company law (or of the memorandum) which is stated to be incapable of amendment[2]. If company law provides that something can be done by the passing of a resolution (that is it simply lays down a *procedure*) then an informal, unanimous agreement is as effective as far as the company is concerned as a resolution. An informal agreement cannot, however, bind future shareholders. Moreover, where a decision, if taken by resolution, would have to be notified to the Registrar and would be subject to the process of official notification[3], the informal agreement can not be relied upon by the company against any other person. Thus, if the shareholders unanimously, but informally, agreed to change the articles of the company, perhaps to restrict the powers of a managing director, this change would not bind third parties and a person who dealt with the managing director would be entitled to assume he had the normal powers of a managing director.

It is difficult to discern a pattern in the cases which would allow one to predict when an informal unanimous agreement will suffice[4].

A court will distinguish between informal agreement (which may be upheld) and informal acquiescence (which is usually completely ineffective).

1   See for example, *Re Duomatic Ltd* [1969] 2 Ch 365, [1969] 1 All ER 161, where directors (who owned all the shares of the company) had drawn salaries without the formal approval of a general meeting, the salaries were held, on liquidation, to have been validly approved by the shareholders.
2   Such an agreement might take effect as a shareholder agreement, see para 25.27, above.
3   Section 42, see para 25.6, above.
4   Compare *Cane v Jones* [1981] 1 All ER 533, [1980] 1 WLR 1451, informal agreement to alter articles valid when statute provides a company *may* alter by special resolution with, *Re Barry Artists Ltd* [1985] BCLC 283, informal agreement to seek to reduce capital invalid when statute provides a company *may* reduce share capital.

Reports and registers

Registers
26.8   All companies are required to keep a number of registers. For example s 352 requires a company to keep a register of members and to record the number of shares a member owns and the amount paid or agreed to be paid on those shares. Section 325 requires a register of directors' interests and s 288 a register of directors and the company secretary. There is no requirement

to keep a register of creditors though many companies will have a register of debentures. Generally, registers are open to inspection by members (no fee can be charged) and others (from whom a fee may be levied).

There is one register which requires further consideration: the register of substantial shareholdings.

26.9 *Register of substantial shareholdings* This register must be kept by *public* companies[1]. It contains valuable information in that it lists the beneficial owners of shares whose holding exceeds a statutory minimum. This information could reveal to a searcher (and the company) a possible take-over bid; it is open to inspection by members and the public.

The regulations relating to substantial shareholdings require notification and registration of the ownership of voting shares in excess of the prescribed minimum. The minimum is currently 3% of aggregate nominal value of the company's issued voting shares (the notifiable percentage[2]). Where there are classes of voting share, interest in 3% of any class must be notified. Notification is to the company. In addition, a shareholder is required to make further disclosure when, having reached the 3% barrier, there is a known increase or decrease of more than 1% in the interest. The requirement to notify the company that one's shareholding exceeds the notifiable percentage is cast upon the share owner and disclosure must occur within two days of the share owner becoming aware of the change. If the company is listed, it must notify the Stock Exchange of any notifications it has received on the day on receipt. In addition, the company must record the details of the notification on the register within three days of receiving the notification. Failure to notify is a criminal offence.

1   Section 211.
2   Sections 198-200.

Reports
26.10 Certain documents have to be delivered to the Registrar of companies shortly after the occurrence of the events which they record; for example, changes to the memorandum or articles or to the directors. In addition, s 363 provides that every company is required to make an Annual Return to the Registrar. The Annual Return serves two purposes. First, it provides a convenient summary of information relating to the company (which is available for public inspection). Second, it acts as a means of alerting the Registrar that the company may have effectively, even if not legally, ceased to exist. If a company fails to make an Annual Return, the Registrar, after due notice, can take steps to remove the company from the register. Many more companies are removed from the register than are ever wound up since winding up is appropriate only where the company has assets to gather in and then distribute.

The Annual Return must be in the prescribed form and must be delivered to the Registrar, made up to its return date (which is usually the anniversary of its incorporation) within 28 days of that date. Failure to make the return renders the company, the directors and the company secretary liable to a fine and a daily default fine. However, many companies fail to make returns at the appropriate time and until recently it seemed probable that over half the registered companies were in arrears. Of late the Registrar has adopted a tougher policy on late return and this figure is falling. Section 713 permits any member or creditor to serve notice on the company requiring it to file an Annual Return and, if the company fails to do so, to seek a court order instructing the company to make the return.

The content of the return falls into two categories. First, general information such as the address of the registered office, details of the directors and the company secretary, whether the company has elected to dispense with an annual general meeting etc. Second, if the company has a share capital, particulars of share capital and shareholders must be listed. This information is as at the return date and is necessarily out-of-date so that the Annual Return must also give the location of the company's membership register to allow anyone interested to obtain up-to-date information on the current membership of the company. In practice the Registrar issues a 'shuttle document', that is a pre-printed form containing all the information relevant to the annual return and the company merely has to confirm or amend the form before sending it back to the Registrar.

Other reports which are highly significant include the annual accounts, the auditor's report and the directors' report.

26.11 *Accounts*   Section 221 requires all companies to keep accounting records; failure to comply is a criminal offence. Companies are required to circulate members with the annual accounts of the company and with a copy of the profit and loss account. One principle underlying the requirements relating to reports and accounts is that those who have invested in the company should be kept informed of the state of the company and, thus, of their investment. These rules on disclosure are immensely detailed but assume that if the directors have to tell the shareholders certain things this will, even if shareholder approval is not required, constrain the behaviour of the directors to avoid shareholder disapproval. A small company may be able to avoid some of the more onerous reporting requirements which may be justified in that the shareholders and directors of such companies may be co-extensive or overlap to a significant degree. However, the reports and accounts required are also designed to provide information for interested third parties, for example, employees and creditors, so that their publication could be justified even for a company where there are few shareholders and the directors control the company. Reports and accounts are presented not just to the shareholders but must also be available, via submission to the Registrar of Companies[1], to the wider public (listed companies also have to disclose information to the Stock Exchange). Small and medium sized companies can deliver abbreviated accounts.

There are strict time limits for the preparation of accounts and their delivery to the Registrar. Late submission renders the company and its directors liable to a fine[2].

Since the purpose of these accounts is to inform the shareholders of the state of financial health of the company and provide an account of the directors' stewardship in the previous year, the accounts must present a true and fair view of the company's financial position and must comply with Schedule 4 of the Act[3]. Section 241 requires the directors to lay the accounts before a general meeting of the company. However, a private company can elect to dispense with the laying of accounts before a general meeting if such election is in compliance with s 252 (an elective resolution is required). The election to dispense with the laying of accounts lasts indefinitely (it can be revoked by ordinary resolution) but an auditor or shareholder can require the company to hold a general meeting for the purpose of laying accounts[4]. If no meeting is held the members must be circulated with the relevant accounts[5].

The Act requires four documents to be presented to the shareholders and the Registrar annually. These are, the balance sheet (as at the last day of the financial year), the profit and loss account (for the financial year), the directors' report and the auditor's report (we discuss the latter two in para 26.12 and 26.13, below). Generally the accounts presented to shareholders will also include a statement of the source and application of corporate funds in accordance with SSAP (Statement of Standard Accounting Practice) 10 unless the turnover of gross income is less than £25,000. Directors may also choose to issue other reports, eg a chairman's report, but are not required so to do. The profit and loss account, which shows such things as the company's trading record and other income and expenditure, is a temperature chart of the company's financial health throughout the year. The balance sheet is a snapshot of the company's financial position on a particular date. Both documents must give a 'true and fair view' of the company's profit and loss for the year and the position at the end of the year.

The Act specifies the content, format and valuation rules to apply to the balance sheet and profit and loss account (there are various format prescribed depending upon the size of the company). There is no legal requirement that the company comply with SSAPs in preparing these documents but compliance with SSAPs gives rise to a presumption that the accounts give a 'true and fair view' and deviation therefrom gives rise to a presumption that they do not. The Act also lists various disparate items which must be included as notes to the accounts.

Failure to comply with the statutory requirements relating to accounts has civil and criminal consequences. Section 245 allows, but does not require, the directors to issue revised accounts (or a directors' report) if the original accounts did not comply with the Act – the absence of compulsion is designed to encourage openness and compliance rather than relying on punishment which may induce concealment. The whole system is aimed at providing the best possible information to shareholders and others. However, the Secretary of State can require the directors to explain any deviation from the statutory provisions and he can instruct the directors to revise the accounts and if the directors fail so to do, he (or others authorised to act on his behalf, for example the Financial Reporting Review Panel) can seek a court order instructing the directors to issue revised accounts. In addition it is a criminal offence for directors to approve annual accounts which they know do not comply with the Act or are reckless as to whether they comply or not[6].

Failure to produce proper accounts is a matter which would also be of concern to a court if the company went into insolvent liquidation and it was considering a disqualification order against the directors. The courts have stressed that failings in this area are serious matters and that the directors must be punctilious in observing the safeguards laid down by Parliament for the benefit of others who have dealings with their companies. This is part of the price to be paid for the benefits of incorporation.

1   Section 242.
2   Sections 242 and 242A.
3   Section 226.
4   Section 253.
5   Section 238 requires the sending of reports to all debenture-holders whether a meeting is held or not.
6   Section 233.

26.12   *Auditor's report*   Traditionally, all companies were required to appoint an auditor in accordance with s 385 (or s 385A). However, the Companies Act (Audit Exemption) Regulations 1994 amended the Companies Act 1985 to exempt small companies from the requirement to hold an annual audit. A company will qualify as a small company if it is not part of a group, has a balance sheet total of less than £1.4 million, and a turnover of not more than £90,000. If its turnover is between £90,000 and £350,000 it will be exempt if the directors send a special report to the shareholders (in compliance with s 249C). Section 249B provides that an exempt company must hold an audit if a member or members holding at least 10% of any class of shares demands one.

If an audit is required, s 385 provides that the members must appoint an auditor at each general meeting at which accounts are laid. If the company has elected not to hold such a meeting the auditor must be appointed at another meeting of the company. However, since the company has up to ten months before it need hold a meeting at which accounts are laid, the section also provides that the first directors, can appoint an auditor who will remain in office until the conclusion of the first relevant general meeting.

To appoint an auditor at every general meeting may be thought cumbersome, even if the same auditor is just nodded through, and the company may wish to use s 386 to dispense with the need for an annual appointment. Section 386 permits a private company to dispense with the annual appointment of an auditor and provides that the auditor, once appointed, continues in office until a resolution is passed to terminate the appointment[1] (s 393) or the company becomes dormant. To take advantage of this section, the company must pass an elective resolution in accordance with s 379A, the auditor must be a member of a recognised supervisory body and be qualified under that body's rules for appointment as an auditor, be independent of the company and hold appropriate qualifications[2] To remove an auditor requires an ordinary resolution but special notice of any such resolution is required[3].

The function of the auditor is to report to the members on the financial statements made by the directors particularly as to whether they comply with the Companies Act and give a true and fair view of the state of the company's affairs and its results for the period under consideration[4]. In preparing his report, the auditor must satisfy himself that proper accounting records have been kept and that the annual accounts agree with the underlying accounting record. If the auditor is not satisfied that records etc are accurate he must so state in his report. In order to prepare his report, the auditor has a right of access at all times to the books and accounts of the company and can require the company, its subsidiaries and its directors to provide any information required for the performance of his duties. Any failure to provide information must be reported in the auditor's report and it is a criminal offence for an officer of the company to make, knowingly or recklessly, a false statement to an auditor. Where information is not provided, the auditor has a duty to try and remedy the omission. In addition to the statutory duties, the accountancy bodies have laid down a number of guidelines relating to the auditor's report (SSAPs) which should be complied with unless the company can justify departure from them.

1   Section 393.
2   Companies Act 1989, Sch 11.
3   Sections 391 and 391A.
4   Section 235.

26.13   *Directors' report*   The minimum content of the directors' report is set out in s 234. It must include such items as information both about the directors, for example the size of their shareholding, and information about the company's business, for example the principal activities of the company, any significant changes from the previous year and any likely future developments. The directors' report must also include information about employment and any charitable or political donations. No approval is required for such donations but the company must have the power to make such donations and the power to make them must be exercised bona fide[1]. The directors' report, unlike the accounts, is not audited.

1   Where the company has an express power to make such donations there is no need to show that it is beneficial to the company to make such a payment, see *Re Horsley & Weight Ltd* [1982] Ch 442, [1982] 3 All ER 1045, CA.

The company secretary
26.14   All companies are required to have a company secretary[1] who may be a natural legal person or a company. A company secretary may also be a director of the company, although a company secretary cannot also be the sole director of a company. The directors generally appoint the secretary, determine the terms of his appointment and have the power of dismissal – although dismissal in breach of contract gives rise to a claim for damages in accordance with normal contractual principles. Public companies are encouraged to appoint as company secretary a person of appropriate qualification and experience[2] but private companies can pick anyone they like.

The company secretary is likely to carry out many of the administrative tasks imposed on companies by the Companies Act and to supervise the general administration of the company, including the maintenance of the company's registers, for example, the register of members which must be kept at the company's registered office[3]. Certain statutory duties are imposed directly on the secretary by the Companies Act. These duties include the submission of statutory declarations, for example, a declaration of compliance when a private company re-registers as a public company, and the submission of the Annual Return.

The company secretary, in common with the directors, owes a fiduciary duty to the company; he cannot, for example, take bribes or make a secret profit from his office. The status of the company secretary has increased since the position was first recognised and he is no longer seen as a humble minion but as master of his field, that is the administration of the company.

A company secretary has the power to bind the company to contracts (in common with other agents of the company) and his enhanced status means that his usual authority is now quite extensive in his area of competence[4]. It must be stressed that his authority does not extend to commercial matters (unless expressly authorised) so that a secretary cannot, for example, negotiate loans on behalf of the company.

1   Section 283.
2   Section 286.
3   Section 353.
4   See for example, *Panorama Developments Ltd v Fidelis Furnishing Fabrics Ltd* [1971] 2 QB 711, [1971] 3 All ER 16, CA.

The Financial Structure of Companies

26.15   The overwhelming majority of registered companies are limited by shares[1]. Hence, most companies have shares and shareholders. Shares may be divided into classes with differing rights which rights may be varied by the company. A company may seek to reduce share capital by abolishing some shares or extend its share capital by creating new shares. A company may also wish to re-structure its share capital.

Many companies need to borrow money to finance their operations; these loans may be secured or unsecured. Loans (or loan capital, as it is sometimes called) can be divided into two categories:

a.   sums owed by the company as a debt, such as a loan by X or, more probably, the company's overdraft; and
b.   marketable loans.

Marketable loans are in essence documents creating a potential indebtedness containing the terms and conditions of the loan which may be issued (sold) to investors. A company could create one million pounds of marketable debt divided into £1 units bearing interest at x%[2] which it can sell as and when required. Marketable loans are more relevant for larger companies. Any document which states the terms on which a company has borrowed money may be called a debenture[3] whether or not it carries security but in the business world an unsecured loan is likely to be called an unsecured loan note rather than a debenture.

The law relating to shares and charges is detailed and complex. Both shares and loans provide a means of raising money but a share also creates rights of ownership. We now consider some of the issues relating to shares and loans.

1   Companies limited by guarantee are generally non-trading companies.
2   Marketable debt need not carry interest and 'zeroes', debts carrying no interest are a recognised category of marketable loan.
3   Section 744.

26.16   Some significant differences between being a shareholder and being a creditor (particularly a secured creditor) of a company are as follows:

a.   A company is not required to pay a dividend on its shares whereas loans are likely to be interest bearing. Where interest is payable it must be paid even if the company has not made a profit. However, interest on a loan is an allowable expense for tax purposes thereby reducing the corporation tax liability, if any, of the company. Dividends are paid out of net profits and are not tax-deductible.
b.   Shares can be offered for sale at a premium, that is, a price in excess of their face value, but cannot be offered for sale at a discount[1]. Loans can be issued at a premium or a discount (unless they are convertible into shares in which case they cannot be issued at a discount). Shares are rarely redeemable so that if the company wishes to reduce share capital it must comply with the statutory procedures for reduction including court confirmation[2]. Loan stock can be irredeemable but is generally redeemable and redemption is not a reduction of capital. Hence use of redeemable loans allows the company more flexibility in its financing.
c.   Should a company fail to pay dividends the shareholders have no immediate remedy, whereas a lender with a secured loan may be able to seize the charged asset if his interest remains unpaid or if he regards the security as in jeopardy.
d.   Shares are not secured on any assets of the company and ownership of a share does not make a shareholder an owner of any portion of the company's assets[3]. A secured loan, on the other hand, gives an investor rights in respect of the asset charged as security. On winding up, shareholders receive the nominal value (or more) of their shares only if there are surplus assets available after the payment of all creditors. Even creditors may find themselves ranked behind certain statutory debts (preferential debts) on winding up, but a secured creditor, provided that he has checked the value of his security, is likely to receive his money back.
e.   Shareholders, at least ordinary shareholders, are likely to have votes (non-voting shares can be issued but the Stock Exchange is not enthusiastic about such shares) and must be consulted to some degree about the running of the company. Creditors, in theory, play no part in the running of the company. The Act gives no such formal role to creditors. However, substantial creditors, for example, a company's banks, wield considerable influence over the running of a company, particularly if a company needs to reschedule a loan or otherwise extend its indebtedness.

1   Section 100.
2   Section 135.
3   *Short v Treasury Comrs* [1948] AC 534, [1948] 2 All ER 509, HL.

Share capital
26.17 A share is evidence of a contract between the shareholder and the company which contract confers rights and duties on both parties[1]. A share can be transferred from person to person; the process of transfer is subject to the rules specified in the company's articles which may, in the case of a private company, restrict transferability. A share does not give a shareholder a proprietary right over the assets of the company[1]. A shareholder may own 50% of the shares in a company but he is not entitled to 50% of the assets nor can he demand 50% of the profits. Shares in quoted public companies are used principally as an investment; the investor is looking for income or capital growth and may not expect to exercise any significant control over the actions of the directors. Shareholders in private companies, many of which are small and/or family run, may well be involved in management or otherwise work for the company, for such companies the shares are more significant as a measure of the degree of control an individual has over the company.

The provisions relating to the issue (or allotment) of shares by companies and their subsequent dealings with them are elaborate. However, the underlying theme is simple enough; it is that a company should receive, in cash or otherwise, the nominal value of its shares and should not use such the money received to discharge the liability to pay the nominal value of a share for unauthorised purposes. There are a number of provisions which are designed to ensure that these aims are achieved; we discuss them in paras 26.20 and 26.23, below.

1　*Borland's Trustee v Steel Bros & Co Ltd* [1901] 1 Ch 279.

Issuing shares
26.18 Section 80 provides that the power to issue or allot shares is vested in the general meeting unless it has specifically conferred this power on the board. In practice, the general meeting will have given the power of allotment to the directors[1]. An allotment made in breach of s 80 is still a valid allotment but the directors are in breach of their duty and are liable to a fine.

In exercising their power to allot shares, directors must comply with their fiduciary obligations[2]. The relevant fiduciary duty is that they must exercise the power of allotment bona fide for the benefit of the company and for a proper purpose. This requires the directors to exercise their power honestly and also for a purpose consistent with that for which the powers were conferred on them, that is, for a 'proper purpose'. The proper purpose of the power to allot shares is to raise funds for the company[3]. Where shares are allotted other than for a proper purpose, the allotment is void but it can be ratified by ordinary resolution[4].

If directors propose to allot shares wholly for cash they must first offer them to existing shareholders in proportion to their existing holdings (the right of pre-emption)[5] but private companies may (and most do) exclude this provision in their articles[6]. An allotment in breach of the right of pre-emption is not void but a shareholder who has suffered loss can sue the company to recover any sum lost[7].

1　The power to allot shares in a public company can be given to the directors for a maximum of five years which can be renewed; if the company is a private company the general meeting can, by elective resolution, choose to grant an unlimited power; s 80A.
2　Fiduciary duties are discussed in paras 25.49-25.54, above.

3   *Howard Smith Ltd v Ampol Petroleum Ltd* [1974] AC 821, [1974] 1 All ER 1126, PC.
4   *Bamford v Bamford* [1970] Ch 212, [1969] 1 All ER 969, CA.
5   Section 89.
6   Section 91.
7   Section 92.

26.19   Section 89 provides that if the directors propose to allot equity shares[1] wholly for cash they must first offer them to existing shareholders in proportion to their existing holdings (the right of pre-emption)[2]. This right does not apply unless payment for the shares is wholly for cash so that the provision is easily evaded by issuing shares for a consideration which is partly in non-cash form, perhaps transfer of an asset[3]. Private companies may (and most do) exclude the right of pre-emption in their articles[4]. Even if the articles do not disapply pre-emption rights in all cases, s 95 states that where the directors have a general power to allot shares conferred by s 80, they may be given the power, either in the articles or by special resolution, to allot shares without regard to rights of pre-emption. The power to disregard pre-emption rights by virtue of this section may be withdrawn or modified by the shareholders by special resolution in respect of a particular allotment of shares.

An allotment in breach of the right of pre-emption is not void but a shareholder who has suffered loss by a failure to comply with s 89 can sue the company and every officer who knowingly contravened the section to recover any loss incurred as a result[5].

1   Defined in s 94; it excludes bonus shares.
2   In addition, companies may have their own versions of pre-emption in the articles. For example it is not uncommon for the articles of a private company to state that when a shareholder wishes to sell shares they must first offer the shares to existing shareholders.
3   If the company is a public company the asset must be valued; see further para 26.21, below.
4   Section 91.
5   Section 92; A shareholder must bring an action within two years of the allotment in contravention of s 89.

Paying for shares
26.20   *Discounts*   In order to ensure that the company obtains from allotttees the appropriate share capital, that is, the full nominal value of the shares, a number of rules apply.

First, s 100 provides that a contract to issue or allot shares between the company and the initial shareholder must specify that the price of the shares is at least their nominal value set out in the memorandum (ie not at a discount)[1]. Provided the agreed price equals or exceeds the nominal value, the nominal value (or agreed higher price) of the shares need not be paid at once; payment of the agreed price can be requested as and when the company desires. If a company chooses to delay payment of the agreed price, it may call up all or part of the agreed price at a later date. The directors' power to make calls is a fiduciary power and it must be used for a proper purpose[2]. Most shares are issued fully paid or with payment over a relatively short and pre-determined period.

The allotment of shares at a discount does not invalidate the allotment but the shareholder to whom the shares are issued or allotted remains liable to make good that discount at any time when requested to do so by the company (or its liquidator)[3]. Subsequent owners of the shares are, while they own the shares, also jointly and severally liable to make good any discount unless that owner is a purchaser for value without actual notice of breach of s 100 or derives title to those shares from such an owner[4].

Subsequent sales of shares by a shareholder can be at whatever price he can get, there is no requirement to achieve a particular figure.

1   Commission can be paid to underwriters even if they buy the shares.
2   *Anglo-Universal Bank v Baragnon* (1881) 45 LT 362, CA. Section 119 allows different calls to be made on different shares if the articles so authorise, Table A, art 17 gives authorisation.
3   Section 112; the directors would be liable to a fine, s 114.
4   Section 112(3); the original allottee of the shares is not protected even if he sells his shares and re-acquires them from a purchaser for value without notice.

26.21   *Non-cash consideration*   The rules on discounts are easy to apply when shares are paid for in cash. However, the courts have accepted that non-cash consideration is an acceptable means of payment for shares, and it might be thought that such an allotment, unless the consideration was subject to professional valuation, would form an easy means of evading the discount rule and be prohibited. However, it is not uncommon for a businessman to incorporate his existing business and seek to transfer (sell) the business and its assets to the company in return for shares in the company. Common law and statute provide a system for dealing with non-cash consideration.

Section 99 allows shares to be paid for in money or money's worth and money's worth includes goodwill and know-how. A private company can accept as consideration for shares an undertaking to work or perform services for the company[1]. Unless the value of such non-cash consideration is 'wholly illusory', a court will not challenge the validity of the allotment even if the assets transferred (and the services rendered) prove to be less valuable than the nominal value of the shares allotted[2].

If shares in public companies are to be paid for other than in cash, s 103 provides that the consideration must be valued by a qualified person[3]. If there is no such valuation, the allottee is liable to pay the full price of the shares[4] and so is any subsequent owner of the shares if asked to do so during his period of ownership. An allottee who is not the original purchaser is not liable if he is a purchaser for value without actual notice of the contravention of the valuation requirement or derives his title from such a person[5].

Section 113 allows a court to relieve, wholly or in part, a person who is liable to pay the price of the shares because of a breach of s 99 or s 103 if it is just and equitable so to do[6].

1   Where a public company allots shares in return for such an agreement, the allottee is required to pay the full agreed price of the shares, s 99.
2   *Re Wragg Ltd* [1897] 1 Ch 796, CA.
3   Section 108 specifies the qualification s of the valuer.
4   Section 112.
5   Section 112(3).
6   In *Re Ossory Estates plc* [1988] BCLC 213, the court granted exemption when the part of the asset received by the company as payment for the shares, without compliance with s 103, had been resold by the company for a price exceeding the value of the shares transferred: for example, ss 159-164 (redeemable shares), s 137 (reduction of capital), ss 153-155 (financial assistance).

26.22 *Share premiums* When a company issues or allots shares for a price (however payable) which exceeds its nominal value the excess is called the share premium. A share premium must be paid at the time of allotment if the company is a public company[1]. Share premium is recorded under a separate sub-heading in the company's balance sheet.

Share premium may be used to pay preliminary expenses or the expenses of an issue of shares or a redemption premium on the redemption of certain loans. Share premium used for such purposes may be written off the share premium account in the balance sheet.

1 Section 101. Breach of this provision leaves the allottee and subsequent holders liable to pay the premium (and interest). A purchaser for value without actual notice will as usual be exempt (s 112) and the court can relieve a party from liability (s 113).

Capital maintenance

26.23 Having obtained the appropriate sum from the initial shareholders, the company must 'maintain' its share capital. This does not mean the money so raised cannot be spent, but it cannot be spent in certain unauthorised ways.

One important provision is the requirement that dividends (or other distributions) paid to shareholders are payable only if the company has made an operating profit calculated in compliance with the accounting provisions of the Acts[1]. Dividends not paid out of profits (ie out of capital) are recoverable from the recipients[2] and any shortfall in recovery is chargeable to the directors who authorised the payment[3].

The basic principle as to what may be paid to shareholders as a distribution is set out in section 263(3) thus:

' its accumulated, realised profits, so far as not previously utilised by distribution of capitalisation, less its accumulated, realised losses, so far as not previously written off in a reduction or reorganisation of capital duly made.'

In addition, s 264 provides that a distribution by a public company cannot exceed its net assets minus the total of its called-up share capital and its undistributable reserves.

While dividends must not be paid out of capital, there is nothing to stop a company paying director-shareholders large salaries as directors whether the company has distributable profits or not.

In addition to the rules on distributions a company cannot buy its own shares or provide financial assistance to another so that he can buy them. However, there are numerous exceptions to these prohibitions. These provisions are discussed further in paras 26.24–26.28, below.

1 Section 263.
2 Section 277.
3 *Re Exchange Banking Co, Flitcroft's Case* (1882) 21 Ch D 519, CA, a director who takes reasonable care to ensure that the accounts are properly prepared and who exercised proper commercial judgment as to whether a dividend was properly payable may be relieved of liability if, it transpires, the dividend was wrongly paid other than out of profits, see *Dovey v Cory* [1901] AC 477, HL.

26.24 *Share acquisition* As indicated in the previous paragraph, s 143 prohibits a company from buying its own shares. Section 143 re-states the common law decision in *Trevor v Whitworth*[1], in which the House of Lords showed the courts' concern for the interests of creditors and held that since a creditor effectively 'lent' money to the company (by allowing credit) he has a right to expect that the company will retain its capital and not use it improperly (including not returning it to the shareholders). The share capital (plus undistributable reserves) can be called the creditors' buffer. Breach of s 143 renders the acquisition of shares void and the company and the company and its directors incur criminal liability.

Section 151 prohibits a company (or its subsidiary) from providing financial assistance, either directly or indirectly, to another person to purchase shares in the company. Breach of s 151 renders the company and its directors criminally liable. The civil consequences of breach are not set out in the Act but the majority of cases have concluded that where the unlawful financial assistance is crucial to the acquisition of shares, the acquisition is void[2]. Where it is possible to sever the illegal part of an agreement to buy shares, the contract may be upheld[3].

There are exceptions to both ss 143 and 151. Underpinning the exceptions are certain general principles. There must be adequate publicity for the purchase or assistance and shareholder approval. Further, where the funds used by the company are not distributable profits (which could have been paid to the shareholders anyway), but payments out of capital (this is only open to private companies), the protection of creditors is also required.

1 (1887) 12 App Cas 409, HL.
2 *Heald v O'Connor* [1971] 2 All ER 1105, [1971] 1 WLR 497.
3 *Carney v Herbert* [1985] AC 301, [1985] 1 All ER 438, PC.

26.25 *Exceptions to section 143* Section 143(3) provides that a company can acquire its own shares when:

a. the redemption or purchase of shares is made in accordance with ss 159 to 181 (the statutory exemption discussed in the next paragraph); or
b. the acquisition is part of an authorised reduction of capital; or
c. the acquisition of shares is ordered by the court pursuant to its powers under s 5 (alteration of objects), or s 54 (re-registration of public company as private), or s 461 (remedy for unfair prejudice); or
d. the shares are forfeited by the company because the acquirer has not paid for them.

26.26 The statutory exemption is of recent origin and its use and operation are controversial. When a company wishes either to redeem redeemable shares or to purchase its own shares, there are onerous procedural requirements designed to ensure that only certain funds are used for such a purpose and that an appropriate amount of publicity is provided. However, a court order is not required.

For a company to acquire (or redeem) it must first have authority to purchase its own shares; Table A, article 35 provides authority. Second, the purchase must be appropriately funded. Section 162 sets out conditions for payments made out of 'income'. The conditions are that the contract to purchase was approved in advance by special resolution[1] and that the purchase so authorised was paid for out of the company's distributable profits[2]. Further, s 170 requires a transfer of a sum representing the share-purchase price from distributable profits to the capital redemption reserve.

Section 171, which applies only to private companies, allows companies to purchase their own shares out of capital; such a payment (which may represent all or part of the purchase price) is a 'permissible capital payment', a PCP. Needless to say, there are strict rules for the use of a PCP. Section 173 provides that the payment must have been approved by special resolution (at a meeting or unanimously by written resolution) obtained after the directors had made a statutory declaration. This statutory declaration by the directors must have specified:

a. the amount of the PCP;
b. that the directors, having made full inquiries into the affairs and prospects of the company, are of the opinion that the company will be able to met its debts immediately after the PCP; and
c.   it will continue as a going concern for the next 12 months after the PCP and be able to pay its debts as they fall due.

The auditor must approve the statutory declaration and state that, having inquired into the company's affairs, he was not aware of anything which would render the directors' opinion unreasonable[3]. After the special resolution approving the PCP has been passed the decision must be duly publicised[4]. Section 76 of the Insolvency Act 1986 provides that if a company goes into insolvent liquidation within twelve months of the payment out of capital being made, the directors who signed the statutory declaration are liable to contribute to the company's assets. The directors can escape liability if they can establish they had reasonable grounds for their opinions; it seems probable that the auditors' approval would be a 'reasonable ground'. Section 76 also renders the recipient of the PCP liable to contribute to the assets of the company to the extent of the PCP.

1   Section 164; a written resolution would suffice.
2   Section 168; or a fresh issue of shares made for the purpose, ss 160, 162.
3   Section 173.
4   Section 175. The publicity must mention the power of members and creditors to object.

26.27   *Exceptions to section 151*   Sections 153 to 158 provide exceptions to the prohibition in s 151, described in para 26.24, above. These include where:

a. the company lends money in the ordinary course of business, for example where a bank customer borrows money to buy shares in the bank; or
b. the financial assistance is authorised by some other provision of company law; or

c.   s 153(1) applies. Section 153(1) states that a company can give financial
assistance for the purchase of its shares if its principal purpose in so doing
is to facilitate the acquisition, or to reduce or discharge any liability incurred
by a person for the purpose of the acquisition of the shares, if the assistance
is an *incidental* part of some larger purpose of the company *and* it is given
in good faith in the interests of the company. We discuss this section further
in para 26.28, below; or

d.   s 155 applies. This section, which applies only to private companies permits
a company to make financial assistance for the purchase of its shares, if
approved by special resolution, provided there is no reduction of net assets
or it is made out of distributable profits. It is necessary that the directors
give a statutory declaration (affirmed by the auditors) that, after the
assistance, the company can pay its debts and will continue to be able so
to do for a further 12 months. In effect a company can make a loan etc if
it gets its money back (no reduction of net assets) or if the loan comes out
of money payable to shareholders (net profits) so that the creditors of the
company are not affected by the self-dealing. A director who makes a
statutory declaration without reasonable grounds for his opinion is
criminally liable to a fine or imprisonment, but is not liable in civil law.
There are onerous publicity requirements.

26.28   Section 153(1) appears to be of wide scope but has been given a narrow
interpretation by the courts. In *Brady v Brady*[1], the facts of which have been
characterised as 'labyrinthine', two brothers, who had fallen out, sought to
split a family business, which operated through a series of interlinked companies
in two main spheres. A plan was evolved which was designed to leave one
brother with the haulage-based business and the other brother with the soft
drinks-based business. The plan (in simplified form) required M to purchase
all the shares in Brady Ltd (the holding company) from O leaving M with a
debt due to O. This debt was partly paid by the transfer to O of assets belonging
to Brady Ltd. Clearly, Brady Ltd was contributing financial assistance to the
purchase of its own shares.

The House of Lords expressed the view that s 153(1) would exempt this
scheme from the prohibition in s 151 if two conditions were satisfied. First,
those responsible for authorising the financial assistance must have acted in the
genuine belief that it was being done in the company's interests. This was satisfied
here since the only alternative to the deadlock within the company was to wind
it up. Second, the financial assistance must be simply incidental to a larger
purpose. It was argued that the reorganisation of the family business was the
larger purpose. However, the House of Lords found no larger purpose to which
the financial assistance was merely incidental. The House accepted that the
financial assistance in this case was driven by a more important *reason* than the
provision of the assistance, that is, the reorganisation plan, but held that purpose
and reason were different. Simply because there was an important reason
underpinning the scheme did not make the scheme incidental to a larger purpose.
On the facts, the scheme was designed to facilitate the purchase of shares in
Brady, even if the reason was to split the family businesses. It should be noted
that s 155 could anyway have been used to effect the scheme in *Brady*.

1   [1989] AC 755, [1988] 2 All ER 617, HL.

Transfer of shares

26.29   Shares in a company are freely transferable[1] except to the extent, if any, that transfer is restricted by the articles. Most private companies restrict the transferability of shares.

Even when a transfer is effected, a transferee does not become a member of a company until he is registered as such by the company. Table A, article 24 entitles the directors to refuse to register partly paid shares but this right does not extend to fully paid shares. Hence, the directors have no discretion to refuse to register fully paid shares unless the articles so provide. In respect of a quoted public company, the Stock Exchange listing requirements (which require shares in such a company generally to be freely transferable) preclude the articles empowering its directors to refuse transfers.

Where the articles of a private company give the directors a discretion to refuse to register the transfer of fully paid up shares, the courts will construe the power to refuse to register narrowly since the shareholder has a prima facie right to be registered. If the directors are given an absolute discretion to refuse to register, they need not give reasons for their refusal even if legal proceedings are brought[2]. A refusal to register can be challenged if the directors were not acting bona fide for the benefit of the company in the interests of the company. The burden of proving a lack of bona fides falls on the person challenging the refusal to register. Given that no reason may have been given, this is a heavy burden. When directors decline to register a shareholder they must notify him within two months; failure so to do renders the company liable to a fine and the directors liable to a fine and/or imprisonment[3]. Further, the courts have determined that a refusal to register must be taken within a reasonable time and treat the two-month period as the reasonable period[4]. However, the period can be extended if there are special circumstances.

The traditional method of transferring shares is for the registered holder of certificated shares to complete and sign an instrument of transfer and deliver it with his share certificate to the transferee who completes the transfer, has it stamped, and then delivers it with the share certificate to the company. It has been anticipated for some time that a paperless system of share transfer would be introduced and the day has at last dawned. The CREST settlement system allows the transfer of shares electronically and obviates the need for share certificates. Not all companies are members of CREST and members of companies using CREST can still opt to hold their shares in certificated form.

1   Section 182.
2   *Berry and Stewart v Tottenham Hotspur Football and Athletic Co Ltd* [1935] Ch 718.
3   Section 183.
4   *Re Swaledale Cleaners Ltd* [1968] 3 All ER 619, [1968] 1 WLR 1710, CA.

26.30   *Share certificates*   A share certificate is prima facie evidence of title[1]. Despite the advent of paperless share-dealing, share certificates are likely to exist for some considerable time.

The presumption raised by the share certificate, that the person named has title to those shares, can be rebutted. Thus, a company can produce evidence to show that the person named is not a shareholder, although there are cases where the company is estopped from relying on that evidence. For example, the company might seek to disclaim all liability for a share certificate on the basis that the person who had issued it on behalf of the company, X, was not authorised so to do[2] or that the share certificate was forged.

Where there is a genuine share certificate, an instrument purporting to transfer those shares may be forged but a new share certificate is issued before the forgery is discovered. For example, a company might issue a share certificate to a person, X, on the basis that the previous owner of the shares, Y, has transferred them to X only for it to transpire that the instrument of transfer was forged. In such a case, the company is estopped from denying the genuineness of X's share certificate, provided the issue of a certificate to him was effected by an authorised agent of the company[3] and X was not the forger. Even if the company is estopped from denying X's right to be a member it has to re-instate Y as a shareholder: the company can seek compensation from X even if he was not party to the fraud[4]. If X has to compensate the company he can seek a contribution from the company if it was negligent in registering the transfer.

Public companies generally insure themselves against the consequences of acting on a forged transfer.

1   Section 186.
2   *Ruben v Great Fingall Consolidated* [1906] AC 439, HL.
3   *Re Bahia and San Francisco Rly Co Ltd* (1868) LR 3 QB 584.
4   *Sheffield Corpn v Barclay* [1905] AC 392, HL.

Restructuring share capital
26.31   In addition to allotting shares, a company may seek to sub-divide shares, increase share capital or re-arrange share capital. All these things are, subject to the existence of authority in the articles[1], permitted by s 121. Section 121 requires the restructuring to be approved by ordinary resolution.

The directors may also seek to reduce share capital. This is subject to special rules.

1   Table A, article 32 provides authority.

26.32   *Reduction of capital*   Section 135 permits a company to reduce its share capital provided that:

a.   the articles of the company permit a reduction; and
b.   a reduction has been authorised by special resolution; and
c.   the court has approved the reduction.

Section 135 does not limit the circumstances in which a company may seek to reduce capital but it does specify three possible grounds for so doing. Where one of these three grounds is the basis of an application, a court is likely to approve the reduction, provided that the position of the company's creditors is secured. Section 135 lists as possible grounds for reduction:

a. the extinction or reduction of unpaid share capital; or
b. cancellation of paid-up share capital which is lost or unrepresented by available assets; and
c. payment off of any paid-up share capital in excess of the company's wants.

Cancellation of paid-up share capital is designed to reflect reality. There is little point in a company having a high nominal capital when trading losses have reduced its net assets to a lower figure. Reduction of capital in such a case would allow a company to resume dividend payments. Paying off unneeded share capital involves returning money to the shareholders and is most often encountered when a company is scaling down its trading activities (commonly encountered in the past following nationalisation).

There are no specific provisions in the Act dealing with shareholders' rights on reduction but the House of Lords has held that the courts have a discretion to confirm or reject a proposed reduction of capital[1]. However, despite the existence of a broad jurisdiction to reject an application to reduce, the courts have exercised that power very infrequently. In *Re Ratners Group plc*[2], Harman J ruled that, assuming the reduction was not a 'hollow and pointless act', the court would confirm a reduction where three principles have been satisfied. First, all shareholders should be treated equitably (which generally means 'equally' unless some shareholders have agreed to being treated differently). Second, the proposals should have been properly explained to the shareholders so that they could exercise an informed judgment on them. Third, creditors must be adequately protected.

Where a reduction of capital involves a variation of the class rights of the relevant shareholders the court will not treat the proposal as fair and equitable unless the relevant class have consented to the proposal[3].

1 *Scottish Insurance Corpn Ltd v Wilsons and Clyde Coal Co Ltd* [1949] AC 462, [1949] 1 All ER 1068, HL, in which it was held that the jurisdiction of the courts was not limited to ensuring the technical accuracy of a petition to reduce but extended to ensuring that the reduction was fair and reasonable.
2 [1988] BCLC 685.
3 Para 26.34, below.

Classes of shares
26.33 A company may choose to have only one class of shares: ordinary shares. Alternatively, a company may have a more complex share structure with more classes of shares; for example, ordinary shares, non-voting ordinary shares or preference shares. Preference shares are shares which have either preferential claims on any surplus assets on winding up and/or which pay a pre-determined percentage dividend before anything is payable to the ordinary shareholders.

Preference shares have the following characteristics which may make them attractive to a company. First, the preference dividend (in common with dividends on ordinary shares) must be paid only if the company has made a distributable profit and the directors have declared a dividend. Second, the directors know from year to year the amount which must be paid in preference dividend (if a dividend is declared).

On the other hand, preference shares have the following characteristics which may make them unattractive to a company. First, the shares may be issued at a time of high interest rates thus requiring the company to issue them with a relatively high fixed dividend which remains a continuing commitment even when interest rates fall. This problem can be obviated by the use of redeemable shares. Second, extra classes of shares complicate the share structure of the company and can give rise to problems if the company wishes to vary class rights.

Rights attaching to a particular class of share are called class rights. Any attempt to *vary* class rights without the consent of the relevant class is limited by statute[1]. However, many *amendments* of class rights are not in law variations. In such cases the shareholders may have no right to be consulted on the amendment, although they may be able to claim that they have been unfairly prejudiced by the amendment[2].

1   Sections 125-127.
2   Para 25.62, above.

26.34   *Variation of class rights*   If a company proposes to vary the rights attaching to a class of shares it must comply with its own internal procedures for varying such rights and also the provisions of ss 125 to 127. This raises two issues: what is a class right and what is a variation?

In *Cumbrian Newspapers Group Ltd v Cumberland and Westmorland Herald Newspaper and Printing Co Ltd*[1], Scott J postulated two situations which would create class rights. First, where there are rights attaching to a particular group of shares, and second, where rights were conferred on a shareholder in his capacity as a shareholder (as in the *Cumbrian* case itself). In this case, rival newspaper companies came to an arrangement whereby one of the companies (W) would publish a local paper for the Cumberland and Westmoreland area and would issue 10% of its ordinary shares to the other (C). C was concerned to ensure that the paper remained locally owned and so the agreement also led W to amend its articles to give C a right of pre-emption if the company issued new shares or existing shareholders sold their shares. This right was not attached to a share or shares but was given to C by name. C was also given the right (while it retained at least 10% of the W shares) to nominate a director of W. W then sought to amend the articles by special resolution and delete the articles conferring special rights on C. C challenged this as a variation of class rights and thus subject to special procedures. Scott J found that the rights conferred on C were 'rights that, although not attached to any particular shares were nonetheless conferred upon the beneficiary in the capacity of member or shareholder of the company' and were, thus, class rights.

Even where there is a class right, alteration of such a right is not always a variation. For example, a diminution in voting strength is unlikely to be seen as a variation of class rights. In *Greenhalgh v Arderne Cinemas Ltd*[2], G's ordinary shares had been sub-divided into five shares thereby quintupling his votes. The company then proposed similarly to sub-divide the rest of the ordinary shares, thereby affecting the efficacy of G's votes and depriving him of negative voting control. The Court of Appeal held that, since the rights attaching to G's shares remained the same (because he was not losing votes), there was no variation of his class rights notwithstanding the fact that the result was to alter the voting equilibrium of the shareholders. In *Re Mackenzie & Co Ltd*[3], the company had £20 nominal value preference shares paying 4% dividend so that they paid a dividend of 80p per share. The company amended its articles to reduce the nominal value of the preference shares to £12 thus reducing the preference dividend to 48p per share. The court held that, since the preference shareholders had the same right both before and after the amendment (ie a 4% dividend), their class rights had not been varied.

1   [1987] Ch 1, [1986] 2 All ER 816.
2   [1951] Ch 286, [1950] 2 All ER 1120, CA.
3   [1916] 2 Ch 450.

26.35   In those rare cases where the proposed alteration is a variation of class rights a company must comply with its own procedures for the variation of such rights as well as any statutory provisions.

The Act provides that class rights contained in the articles can be varied if the company has a class rights variation clause and complies with it. There is no such clause in Table A but s 125(2) provides that in such a case variation can be effected if three-quarters of the relevant class (not merely three-quarters of those voting) consent. However, if the proposed variation is in connection with the power to allot shares in compliance with s 80 or is in connection with a reduction of capital under s 135, it is not sufficient for the company to approve the variation in compliance with its own procedure. In these two cases, at least three-quarters (by value) of the relevant class the class to be varied must approve the variation.

If the relevant shareholders approve the variation, s 127 allows a shareholder(s) who holds 15% of the relevant class of shares and who did not vote for the variation to apply to the court to have the variation set aside. The application must be within 21 days of the vote and until the court confirms the variation it has no effect. The court will refuse to confirm a variation if it would unfairly prejudice the shareholders of the class represented by the applicant. There are very few cases on this provision. Consequently, it is difficult to determine what constitutes unfair prejudice in this context.

Section 125(4) deals with the case where the class rights are contained in the memorandum. It provides that they can be varied if the company has a class rights variation clause in the memorandum or in the articles with which the company has complied. If the variation clause is in the articles, it can be used only if the clause was included in the articles at the time of incorporation. If the variation clause did not form part of the original articles, or if there is no variation clause, s 125(5) applies. It provides that in such a case class rights can be varied only if *all* the shareholders in the company agree to it. If a variation is approved, a shareholder can apply to have the variation struck down under s 127 as outlined previously.

Loan capital
26.36   In addition to share capital, a company may (and generally will) have loan capital, that is borrowings. Borrowing is an important means by which a company can finance its activities and that the overwhelming majority of

companies have the power, express or implied, to borrow money[1]. Any document by which a company creates or acknowledges a debt may be called a debenture although this term is rarely applied to short term debts[2]. Marketable loans are more relevant for larger companies whereas the overdraft is a fact of life for companies large and small.

A person lending money to a company has such rights as are given by the contract creating the loan. Typically, the contract will include provisions for repayment of the loan, the payment of interest (if any), and the ability (generally none) of the creditor to attend company meetings or otherwise influence company policy. A debenture-holder should be sent a copy of the company's annual accounts and reports submitted to members[3] and is entitled to ask for the company's accounts. A debenture is transferable (unless the contract creating it prohibits transfer). A transfer may be by simple delivery from the current holder to the new holder (a bearer debenture) or by delivery and the completion of a transfer document.

It is not a legal requirement but a prudent lender may insist on having some claim upon the assets of the company so that if the company goes into insolvent liquidation he will have some security which he can sell to repay his debt. In the business world an unsecured loan is likely to be called an unsecured loan note rather than a debenture. Where the contract of loan, or a linked contract, provides that if the company fails to meet its obligations the lender can have recourse to the company's assets and can obtain the sums outstanding by selling the assets or receiving income generated by those assets the lender has a direct security. The assets of the company covered by this security are said to be charged and the lender may be called a chargee; the person (the company) whose assets are secured can be called a surety or chargor[4].

In addition to (or instead of) a contract of direct security, a lender may have some claim upon a third party if the company does not meet its obligations under the contract of loan. Such a claim may be by way of indemnity or be a contract of guarantee. A guarantor may also charge his assets to the lender as security for meeting his obligations under the guarantee. This is a contract of collateral or indirect security. Thus, a company might charge its assets to secure its overdraft with its bank and one of its directors might guarantee that if the company failed to repay the debt he would do so and charge his property (perhaps the matrimonial home) as security should he be called upon to meet his guarantee.

1   *General Auction Estate and Monetary Co v Smith* [1891] 3 Ch 432.
2   Section 744 defines a debenture as including 'debenture stock, bonds and any other securities of the company whether constituting a charge on the assets of the company or not'.
3   Section 238.
4   A company may have an express power to give security but any company with the power to borrow money has an implied power to give security for its repayment, see *Re Patent File Co* (1870) 6 Ch App 83. Any of the assets of a company, for example real property, machinery, goods in the course of production or book debts, can be charged to provide security for a loan but its uncalled capital can be used as security only if this is expressly authorised by the memorandum.

The contract for security
26.37   The contract for security must comply with the usual contractual rules if it is to be legally enforceable. In practice, most contracts to provide security

are made by deed. The contract can only be enforced in accordance with its terms. Thus, the security (or charge) can only be enforced if the obligation it secures has not been met. It must be noted that an overdraft is generally repayable on demand so that a bank can recall an overdraft at any time and failure to repay will result in the obligation secured by the charge being broken which would allow the bank to enforce its security. Obviously, if the loan is repaid or terminated by agreement in some other way the security contract be it direct or collateral also terminates and the security is discharged.

Any charge created by a company over an asset may be a legal charge or an equitable charge. A legal charge will, potentially, bind any person who acquires a charged asset from the company even if that person knows nothing of the charge (but note the position is different where the charge is registrable; see further below). In contrast, an equitable charge does not bind a person who subsequently acquires an interest in the charged asset bona fide, for value and without notice of the existence of the charge. However, since most charges created by companies have to be registered in compliance with s 395, and registration gives constructive notice of the existence of the charge, a person acquiring an interest in a charged asset will generally have notice of its existence. Note that charges over some corporate assets may have to be registered in two registers. For example, a charge on land owned by a company must be registered in the company charges register and the appropriate district land registry (if the land is registered land) or the Land Charges Registry (if the land is unregistered). Registers of charged property are open to public inspection. Consequently, there can be no question of a person pretending he has an uncharged asset when such is not the case since a potential lender can search the register and discover the existence of any prior charge.

Where a charge, legal or equitable, is required to be registered, and registration has not taken place, the contract for security is valid as between the person charging the asset and the chargee, but any subsequent buyer or chargee of the asset is not bound by the prior charge even if he had notice of its existence.

A legal charge will be created when the company transfers to the chargee a legal interest in the charged property. It is common to find a company creating a legal charge over its real property or choses in action, for example company shares. A legal charge of this type will generally be called a mortgage, the person mortgaging the property may be called the mortgagor and the chargee in such a case is a mortgagee. There is no precise definition of an equitable charge but in *Re Charge Card Services Ltd* [1], the judge said that '... the essence of an equitable charge is that, without any conveyance or assignment to the chargee, specific property of the chargor is expressly or constructively appropriated to or made answerable for the payment of a debt, and the chargee is given the right to resort to the property for the purpose of having it realised and applied in or towards payment of the debt'.

1   [1987] Ch 150, [1986] 3 All ER 289; affd on appeal [1989] Ch 497, [1988] 3 All ER 702, CA.

Fixed and floating charges
26.38   A security interest in property created by a company may be fixed (legal or equitable) or floating (equitable only). The security known as a floating

charge is a means by which a company can create a charge over a type of asset rather than a specified asset. One merit of a floating charge is that it can attach to a nominated class rather than an individual asset within that class. However, floating charges are subject to at least two drawbacks compared to fixed charges: a floating charge may be declared void by the courts in compliance with s 245 of the Insolvency Act 1986[1], and it has no priority over a preferential debt[2]. Whether a charge has been created as a fixed charge or as a floating charge is not always clear.

If there are fixed and floating charges over the same asset, the fixed charge (being fixed and legal) will generally have priority over the floating charge, even if created later than the floating charge. To protect themselves, floating charge-holders may include in their charge notification that they take priority over later charge-holders (even if fixed). Such a provision, a 'negative pledge clause', is effective only if the later charge-holder has *actual* notice of the clause.

Floating chargees are also experimenting with automatic crystallisation clauses (see, para 26.39, below). Such clauses seek to provide that, if a company attempts further to charge an asset already subject to a floating charge, the floating charge automatically crystallises (ie without any intervention on the part of the charge-holder) and becomes fixed, thus retaining its priority over the new charge; the efficacy of such clauses is not yet settled.

1   See below para 26.40, below.
2   Insolvency Act 1986, s 40, see para 26.40, below.

26.39 *Automatic crystallisation* The essence of a floating charge is that it leaves the company free to deal with the charged asset in the ordinary course of business without consulting the charge-holder (although the security contract may restrict this freedom). Since a floating charge is over a class of assets, the chargee is uncertain as to the value of his security at any moment before the charge 'crystallises'. Crystallisation, when a floating charge becomes a fixed charge over the assets currently comprising the relevant class, occurs automatically on the happening of certain events, namely:

a.   if a receiver is appointed by the court or any chargee; or
b.   when winding up commences; or
c.   when the company ceases to carry on its business as a going concern[1].

While the onset of receivership and winding up is a determinable fixed point it is more difficult to determine when a company has ceased to carry on business. The English cases reject the view that crystallisation (other than by the appointment of a receiver which itself crystallises all floating charges) necessarily means the company has ceased to carry on business[2].

A charge also crystallises when the security contract provides that the chargee is entitled to give notice of crystallisation and such notice is given. Typically, the security contract will allow notice on the happening of certain specified events, such as interest falling into arrears, the levying of execution on the assets of the company, or the company being unable to pay its debts. In cases where the chargee seeks to crystallise the charge by notice, strict compliance with the security contract is necessary for crystallisation to occur[3].

It is also generally accepted (although not yet entirely free from doubt) that a chargee can put a provision in the security contract providing for the charge to crystallise automatically on the happening of specified events (ie without notice being given). If this is so, a chargee can provide that a floating charge is to crystallise automatically if the company attempts to create a further charge over an asset to which his floating charge attaches or the assets of the company fall below a specified figure[4]. It can be argued that to allow a chargee to rely on his contractual rights is unfair to a third party (a second charge-holder) who has no means of knowing about the automatic crystallisation clause. It is true that a prudent third party would inquire of the company whether his charge would crystallise any prior floating charges but the company might provide an inaccurate answer. It is open to the Secretary of State to make regulations relating to such clauses, for example, it could be required that such a provision is registered. What is certain, is that an automatic crystallisation clause, will be construed strictly against the party who seeks to rely on it.

On crystallisation the charge becomes fixed from that moment but it is not retrospectively transformed into a fixed charge from its inception. This has important consequences on winding up. If there are two charges attaching to the same asset a floating charge being, until crystallisation, an equitable charge, is ranked in the order of priorities after a fixed legal charge over the same asset. The fixed charge has priority even if it was created after the floating charge and that charge had been registered. It is this problem which automatic crystallisation is designed to address

1   The first two grounds are well established, the third is more controversial but, it is submitted, is justified by the decisions in *William Gaskell Group Ltd v Highley (Nos 1, 2, 3)* [1994] 1 BCLC 197 and *Bank of Credit and Commerce International SA v BRS Kumar Bros Ltd* [1994] 1 BCLC 211.
2   *Re Woodroffes (Musical Instruments) Ltd* [1986] Ch 366, [1985] 2 All ER 908.
3   *Re Brightlife Ltd* [1987] Ch 200, [1986] 3 All ER 673.
4   The courts have indicated, obiter, see *Re Woodroffes (Musical Instruments) Ltd* [1986] Ch 366, [1985] 2 All ER 908 and ; *Re Brightlife Ltd* [1987] Ch 200, [1986] 3 All ER 673 that such clauses are effective. The validity of such clauses has been accepted in New Zealand and Australia but rejected in Canada.

26.40   *Distinguishing fixed and floating charges*   A fixed charge is a charge over a specific, identifiable asset of a company. There is no statutory definition of a floating charge and what the parties call the charge is not conclusive evidence of its status[1]. Judicial pronouncements have isolated certain factors which are likely to be present if a charge is to classified as floating. These factors, derived from *Re Yorkshire Woolcombers' Association Ltd*[2] are:

a.   that the charge is over a class of assets both present and future;
b.   which assets are constantly changing, eg book debts; and
c.   that the charge leaves the company free to use and deal with those assets.

While it is tempting to see fixed charges as relating to permanent assets and floating charges as affixing to changing assets this is not the case. In the important decision of *Siebe Gorman & Co Ltd v Barclays Bank Ltd*[3], where the issue was whether the company had created a fixed charge over book debts, the courts have stressed that the courts will not regard any single factor as crucial in seeking to classify a charge as fixed or floating. However, freedom to deal with the assets without consulting the chargee has generally been regarded as close to conclusive evidence that the charge is floating[4].

1   *Re New Bullas Trading Ltd* [1994] 1 BCLC 485, CA.
2   [1903] 2 Ch 284, CA (approved on appeal by the House of Lords under the name *Illingworth v Houldsworth* [1904] AC 355.
3   [1979] 2 Lloyd's Rep 142.
4   See *Re Cimex Tissues* [1995] 1 BCLC 409 and more recently *Royal Trust Bank v National Westminster Bank plc* [1996] 2 BCLC 682, CA.

26.41   *Drawbacks to floating charges*   As we have said, there are drawbacks to floating charges.

First, a floating charge ranks behind preferential debts on winding up. Preferential debts are certain debts specified in the Insolvency Act 1986; they include taxes collected from a company's employees but not yet paid over to the Revenue (PAYE) and unpaid wages (up to a maximum of £800 per employee).

Second, a floating charge attaches only to assets of the relevant class which belong to the company. Consequently, where a floating chargee has a charge over raw materials to be used in production he may find that the supplier of the goods has retained title to them until he is paid (a retention of title clause). Such a clause allows the supplier, if unpaid, to remove the goods from the company's premises and out of the grasp of the floating charge. Similarly, goods are not company assets susceptible to the clutch of a floating charge if they are subject to a lien or a trust or have been leased.

Third, s 245 of the Insolvency Act 1986 provides that a floating charge created within 12 months of winding up (or two years if the charge-holder is a connected person, eg a director of the company) is invalid unless the company was solvent at the time the charge was granted. A charge which appears to be invalidated by s 245 will remain valid to the extent of any consideration provided to the company for the charge. The working of the section can be illustrated by *Re Yeovil Glove Co Ltd*[1]. In this case, the company had an overdraft of around £66,000. The company's bank sought security which the company granted by creating a floating charge over its assets. Within a year the company went into insolvent liquidation having at that time an overdraft of around £66,000. The issue for the court was whether the overdraft at liquidation and the overdraft at the time the charge was created should be treated as the same overdraft; if they were the same then no consideration had been provided. The Court of Appeal held that since the company had been allowed to operate its bank account during the period between the granting of the charge and the liquidation (some £110,000 had been paid in and drawn out), the liquidation overdraft was not to be regarded as the same debt as the overdraft in existence at the granting of the charge. The money paid in after the charge was granted paid off the original overdraft even if the company then drew out an equal amount of money from its account; those drawings created a new debt. Hence, the liquidation overdraft was a post-charge debt which provided new money to the company and was, in consequence, secured.

1   [1965] Ch 148, [1964] 2 All ER 849, CA.

Priorities between charges

26.42   A floating chargee has no right to possession of the charged asset and may find that his claims upon the charged asset rank after a subsequent fixed chargee even if the fixed charge was created later than his charge; of course, the floating charge retains priority if the fixed charge was expressly stated in its security contract to rank behind the floating charge. Thus, if the asset is of insufficient value to satisfy both charge-holders in full, the floating charge-holder is paid only what remains after the fixed charge-holders claims have been satisfied in full.

Logically the argument which permits subsequent fixed charges to obtain priority over prior floating charges - that a floating charge gives the company freedom to deal with charged assets which may include creating further charges - also applies where the subsequent charge is itself floating. However, in *Re Benjamin Cope Ltd*[1] it was held that a company's freedom to deal with charged assets did not extend to permitting a company to create a second floating charge over assets which ranked in priority or equally with the first charge even if the second charge purported to have such priority. Of course the first charge could specifically permit the creation of subsequent floating charges with priority which would allow the second charge to take priority over the first. This view was modified in *Re Automatic Bottle Makers Ltd*[2], in which the Court of Appeal held that a floating charge (even if over all the assets of a company) did not prevent the company creating a second floating charge with priority over the first in respect of *part* of the charged assets (perhaps book debts).

Hence, a subsequent floating charge may, and a subsequent fixed charge will generally, obtain priority over a floating charge.

1   [1914] 1 Ch 800.
2   [1926] Ch 412.

26.43   *Negative pledge clauses*   Since there is the risk of a later charge obtaining priority, prudent floating chargees commonly insert negative pledge clauses into the security contract.

A negative pledge clause is a clause specifically precluding the creation of a second charge with priority. Such a clause restricts the company's freedom to deal with the charged asset, but since the restriction does not prevent all dealings, but merely one, it is not thought to render the first clause fixed. However, the efficacy and status of the clause as between the company and the floating chargee does not necessarily mean it affects the rights of third parties. It can be argued that for the company to ignore such a clause and grant a further charge would be a case of equitable fraud and thus the second charge would be void and the floating charge is unaffected by it, however, the prevalent view is that the second charge is not void. The first charge will, thus, retain its priority only if the second charge-holder has notice both of the existence of the first charge (which is provided by registration) *and* of the restriction on the freedom of the company to further charge the relevant asset.

It seems that registration does not provide constructive notice of a restriction since a restriction need not be registered. Despite the frequency of negative pledge clauses, the cases support the view that, even if a later chargee has actual knowledge of the existence of a prior floating charge (which he will have at least constructively through registration), this is neither notice of a restriction nor to require the potential charge-holder to make inquiries as to the nature and extent of the registered charge.

Where, however, a potential charge-holder searches the Register of Charges, and thereby obtains actual knowledge of the existence of the charge he will also obtain actual knowledge of any restriction registered with the charge so that the restriction will be effective in retaining the priority of the floating charge over the subsequent charge.

Registration

26.44   The position on registration is currently something of a mess in that the registration of company charges is subject to the 1985 Act but it has been announced that its provisions are to be replaced by a new system. Until some change is executed the 1985 Act prevails. Section 395 provides that failure to register within the statutory period renders a charge void against the liquidator, an administrator and any other creditor of the company even if that person actually knew of the existence of the charge. If a registrable charge is not registered, s 395 provides that the money secured by it is repayable immediately.

Section 398 provides that specified details of most charges on the assets of a company must be delivered to the Registrar of Companies for entry into the charges register within 21 days of the charge's creation Failure so to do results in the security, but not the debt secured by the charge, being void against specified persons. Late delivery of the details may result in the charge being void against the liquidator if the company goes into insolvent liquidation within a specified time after the delivery of the details. Section 401 provides that the register of charges is open to public inspection but the possible 21-day gap between creation and registration means that a person searching the register may not receive accurate information on the state of a company's registrable charges.

Registration of a charge gives constructive notice to the whole world of the existence of the charge but it does not provide notice of the terms of the registered charge. Hence, as we have seen, the registration of a negative pledge clause in a floating charge does not provide constructive notice of the clause (it does give actual notice to anyone who searches the register).

26.45   *What is registrable?*   Section 396 provides a list of what is required to be registered. It includes:

a.   a charge to secure an issue of debentures;
b.   a charge on uncalled share capital;
c.   a charge which, if created by an individual, would require registration as a bill of sale;
d.   a charge on land (wherever situate);
e.   a charge on book debts;
f.   a floating charge; and
g.   a charge on certain assets such as goodwill or any intellectual property.

It should be noted that liabilities created by a company such as hire-purchase transactions and conditional sale agreements which might well have an adverse affect on the company's financial stability are not registrable, and thus are not capable of discovery by searching the register. The interpretation of s 395 is that any transaction for value which gives a third party the benefit of a corporate asset creates a charge whatever its wording. However, where the third party becomes entitled to an asset and not merely the benefit of it that is not a charge. Hence debt factoring agreements are not charges nor are sale and leaseback agreements even, it seems, if the company has the right to regain the asset in the future[1].

Section 401 specifies the details of what should be registered. This includes, the date of creation, the sum secured, the names of the chargees and short details of the property subject to the charge.

If the details submitted for registration are incomplete the Registrar will return the particulars for amendment but the obligation to register within 21 days of creation remains in force. Consequently, the lender will have to move swiftly to comply with the Act. Once a charge is registered the Registrar gives a certificate which is conclusive evidence that the registration requirements have been complied with even if this is not in fact the case[2].

1 *Welsh Development Agency v Export Finance Ltd* [1992] BCLC 148, CA. Rights arising by operation of law are not registrable since they have not been created by the company.
2 Section 401(2) and see *Re CL Nye Ltd* [1971] Ch 442, in which a charge was overlooked and when discovered the date was amended then registered within 21 days of amended date - charge validly registered. The benefits of correction fluid are all-pervasive.

26.46 *Rectification of the register* Section 404 permits rectification of the register of charges to supply an omission or correct a misstatement. An application for rectification must be made to the court and it is permitted only if the court is satisfied that the error sought to be corrected arose through inadvertence or other sufficient cause and will not prejudice the creditors or shareholders of the company.

26.47 *Late registration* Where a charge has not been registered within 21 days of creation all is not lost for the lender. He can use s 404 and apply for late registration. However, he must do so as soon as he discovers the omission to register. Late registration, when permitted, will normally be subject to the term that the charge now being registered can not obtain priority over any charge created and registered between the time when the original charge should have been registered and its actual date of registration.

Other than in exceptional circumstances, late registration is not permitted once a winding-up order has been made. To allow late registration is such a case would give priority to the holders of the charge over the unsecured creditors whose rights might be said to vest on the commencement of winding up. In *Re Braemar Investments Ltd*[1], late registration was permitted, despite the imminence of winding-up when it was clear that the failure to register was not attributable to the chargee, but his solicitor, and that the chargee had acted promptly on discovering the situation.

1 [1989] Ch 54, [1988] BCLC 556.

Companies in Decline

26.48   If a company is unsuccessful, or its members no longer wish it to continue, a number of different procedures may be relevant. They are:

a.   receivership;
b.   administration;
c.   liquidation (winding up); and
d.   deregistration.

It should be noted that the majority of companies which cease to exist do so as a result of being deregistered rather than subject to any formal process of winding up. Where a company becomes moribund and does not submit an Annual Return or accounts the Registrar will ultimately strike it off the register[1].

We now consider the other procedures.

1   Section 652.

Receivership

26.49   Receivership is a procedure which is not implemented by the company but by a secured debenture-holder (or the courts) in accordance with the terms of the debenture. While the procedure cannot be implemented by the company (despite reports in the press which often speak of a company 'calling in the receiver') it may be initiated by the company, in conjunction with a creditor, when the company recognises that it cannot continue to trade in its current format. However, a company cannot veto the appointment of a receiver if a creditor seeks to appoint one. Receivers may be appointed by a fixed charge-holder or by a floating charge-holder. In the latter case the receiver is called an administrative receiver and must be a licensed insolvency practitioner[1] (generally a solicitor or accountant). The function of a receiver is to receive income or realise property to which the charge attaches in order to pay off the charge-holder (subject to the claims of preferential creditors if the charge was created as a floating charge).

Receivership does not preclude a creditors' or members' petition to wind up the company. Where a liquidator is also appointed, the receiver remains in office and continues to manage and realise the assets to which the charge attaches but his actions are monitored by the liquidator on behalf of the creditors. After the receiver has satisfied his client (the charge-holder), the liquidator disposes of surplus assets, if any, in compliance with the order of priority for the payment of creditors.

It must be stressed that a receiver's principal duty is to his client and he is not obliged to consider, other than as a secondary matter, the interests of other creditors. Thus, a receiver appointed by a bank could choose to sell a company's assets to pay the bank at a time which suits him and he is not obliged to wait for a rise in the market which might increase the amount of surplus, after the bank is paid, available for other creditors. Receivership does not inevitably lead to liquidation but it is obviously not a very promising sign.

1   Insolvency Act 1986, s 230.

26.50 A receiver appointed by a fixed charge-holder is concerned only with the asset to which his client's charge attaches and he has no general power to run the company. However, a receiver appointed by a floating charge-holder has the enhanced powers of an administrative receiver[1]. An administrative receiver has considerable powers designed to enable him to keep potentially successful companies afloat, perhaps by selling the enterprise to another company or by restructuring the company and jettisoning loss-making portions of the business. The enhanced powers of administrative receivers include some of the powers given to liquidators and administrators. However, administrative receivers do not have the power to reopen transactions, or to set aside floating charges, or to initiate proceedings for fraudulent or wrongful trading.

1 Insolvency Act 1986, s 29.

Administration[1]

26.51 Administration is a relatively recent innovation designed to permit restructuring of a debt-ridden business; it is comparable with Chapter XI of the American Federal Bankruptcy Code. Administration was introduced to provide a company with a 'breathing space' to enable it to continue as a going concern or at least result in a better realisation of the company's assets than a sale on liquidation. Administration may be preferable for the company and the creditors to liquidation in that it:

a. is likely to be cheaper;
b. may allow the sale of a going concern rather than a 'fire-sale' on liquidation where the assets are sold off for whatever price the liquidator can get;
c. allows a company currently trading profitably, but burdened by debt from past unsuccessful enterprises, to trade on with some form of debt moratorium or restructuring operating; and
d. means that creditors (including directors and employees) may have better prospects of payment than in a liquidation.

An administration order, which can be sought by the company, its directors or a creditor, is a court order that, for the duration of the order, the company's affairs are to be managed by an administrator who must be a licensed insolvency practitioner. An administrator becomes in effect the board and runs the company on behalf of everyone (unlike an administrative receiver who acts for his client). If the court is petitioned by the company to grant an administration order any floating charge-holder must be informed and can veto the order by appointing an administrative receiver.

1 Insolvency Act 1986, ss 8-27.

26.52 An administrator can be appointed if the company is unable to pay its debts or likely to reach this position but not if the company is already in liquidation. A court will grant the order only if there is a reasonable prospect of it achieving one of four aims[1]:

a.   the survival of all or part of the business as a going concern; or
b.   the approval of a voluntary arrangement under the Insolvency Act; or
c.   a scheme of arrangement under the Companies Act; or
d.   a more advantageous realisation of assets on winding up.

If an order is made, an administrative receiver can no longer be appointed, the company cannot be put into liquidation and creditors cannot enforce any security against, or seize goods from, the company. The administrator has three months from appointment to come up with a scheme to achieve the purpose for which the order was made and the creditors then vote on the scheme. If the scheme is approved by a majority in value of creditors, it proceeds; if not it lapses. If the scheme is approved the administrator continues in office until discharged by the court when his task is complete, or it is clear it cannot be completed, or a voluntary arrangement is agreed by members and creditors.

1   *Re Harris Simons Construction Ltd* [1989] 1 WLR 368.

Liquidation
26.53   Liquidation or winding up is the final step before the death of a company. It is the process by which the assets of the company are collected and realised, its debts are paid and any surplus is returned to the members. Liquidation can take one of three forms:

a.   a members' voluntary liquidation; or
b.   a creditors' voluntary liquidation; or
c.   a compulsory liquidation.

26.54   A members' voluntary liquidation is apposite if the members of a solvent company – ie one which can pay its debts – decide that they no longer wish the company to exist. If, within five weeks of the directors having made a statutory declaration of solvency (there are rules for determining solvency in this context), the shareholders pass a special resolution to wind up the company, the winding up is a members' voluntary liquidation[1]. If no declaration has been made, it is a creditors' voluntary liquidation[2]. When it is a creditors' voluntary winding up, a meeting of creditors must be summoned[3] and without such a meeting, the liquidator has no power to deal with the assets of the company. A list of the company's debts must be submitted to that meeting.

Whether it is a members' or a creditors' liquidation, the members nominate a liquidator. However, the members' nominee can be vetoed by creditors[4]. A creditors' voluntary winding up is supervised by a liquidation committee consisting of five members and five creditors. A creditors' voluntary liquidation is the cheapest way to wind up an insolvent company.

1   Insolvency Act 1986, s 89.
2   Ibid, s 90.
3   Ibid, s 166.
4   Ibid, s 100.

26.55 Section 122 of the Insolvency Act 1986 sets out the grounds on which a petition for compulsory winding up may be made to the court. The commonest ground of application is the inability of the company to pay its debts and the Act specifies how this can be proved[1]. Another ground, which we discussed in para 25.65, above, is that it is 'just and equitable' to wind the company up.

Section 124 of the Insolvency Act 1986 provides that a petition for winding up under s 122 can be presented by any one of the following: the company; the directors; a creditor (the usual petitioner); the Secretary of State (in some cases); or a contributory, ie a person liable to contribute to the assets of a company on winding up.

Compulsory liquidation is both more lengthy and more expensive than a creditors' voluntary winding up. It is possible to petition for a compulsory winding up order even if the company is in voluntary liquidation.

1 In s 123. One method is by a creditor making a written demand for a sum in excess of £750. If the sum remains unpaid after 21 days, the company is deemed to be unable to pay its debts.

26.56 The Insolvency Act 1986 sets out in detail the supervision of a voluntary or compulsory winding up.

Winding up is supervised by a liquidator, who must be a licensed insolvency practitioner. His function is to collect in and realise the assets of the company, swelling those assets, where appropriate, by pursuing any claims on behalf of the company (perhaps against an errant director) or by an action for wrongful trading[1]. The liquidator must represent the interests of all those interested in the assets of the company[2] but must seek to deny any claims brought by creditors whose claims are invalid[3]. In fulfilling this task, a liquidator can continue the company's business but only in so far as it is beneficial to the creditors[4]. Not all creditors rank equally and one of the responsibilities of the liquidator is to ensure that they are paid (in so far as there are assets) in the correct order. In practice, there is frequently nothing left for the unsecured creditors after payment has been made to secured and preferential creditors. If there are surplus assets after the creditors have been paid, they are returned to the shareholders.

The appointment of a liquidator, who is a type of fiduciary and who has a duty of care and skill imposed on him, has several consequences. The most important are that:

a. it terminates the appointment of the directors; and
b. the company's assets fall under the control of the liquidator; and
c. if the liquidation is compulsory, the company's employees are dismissed[5]; and
d. any subsequent disposition of corporate property, or transfer of shares or alteration of the status of shareholders, is void, unless the court orders otherwise[6].

1 Para 25.12, above.
2 Which will include the shareholders where the company is solvent.

3   Perhaps because the charge is invalidated by Insolvency Act 1986, s 245, see para 26.41, above, or has not been registered, see para 26.44, above.
4   Ibid, Sch 4.
5   *Re General Rolling Stock Co* (1866) LR 1 Eq 346.
6   Insolvency Act 1986, s 127.

Index

Index

Index